12 95

ART

AND VISUAL
PERCEPTION
The New Version

RUDOLF ARNHEIM

ART
AND VISUAL
PERCEPTION

A Psychology of the Creative Eye

The New Version

UNIVERSITY OF CALIFORNIA PRESS

Berkeley, Los Angeles, London

University of California Press
Berkeley and Los Angeles, California

University of California Press, Ltd.
London, England

This is an expanded and revised edition,
with some new illustrations,
of the original publication of 1954.

ISBN: 0–520–02327–7 (clothbound)
ISBN: 0–520–02613–6 (paperbound)
Library of Congress Catalog Card Number: 73–87587
Printed in the United States of America

7 8 9 0

CONTENTS

PREFACE TO THE
NEW VERSION

This book has been entirely rewritten. Such a revision may come more naturally to a teacher than to other authors, for a teacher is accustomed to being given another chance every year: to formulate his ideas more clearly, to drop dead weight and add new facts and insights, to improve the arrangement of his material, and in general to profit from the reception his presentation has received.

About twenty years ago, the first version of this book was written at a headlong pace. I had to do it in fifteen months if I wanted to do it at all. I wrote it essentially in one long sitting, looking up only rarely to consult resources beyond those stored in my head, and I let the demonstrations and arguments follow one another as they presented themselves to my mind. It was an exhilarating effort and a very personal one. The friendly reception the book has received may be due in part to this reckless verve of a lightly shod man, uncommon in a systematic work of theoretical exposition.

However, some drawbacks of the procedure became apparent, as I continued to teach the subject of the book and observed reactions to my presentation. Much of what I had described derived from a few basic principles, but this derivation was not always made explicit in the text, nor were the principles themselves spelled out with sufficient emphasis. This style was not averse to the mentality of artists and art students who fastened on the visual specifics and caught the general sense pervading the whole. But even they, I came to feel, would be better served by a more unified organization. And certainly I could do better by the scientists and thinkers who preferred something more systematic.

Moreover, the underlying principles were not outlined in my mind two decades ago as sharply as they are now. In the new version I endeavor to show that the tendency toward the simplest structure, the development by stages of differentiation, the dynamic character of percepts, and other fundamentals apply to each and every visual phenomenon. These principles do not seem to me to have been superseded by more recent developments. On the contrary, my impression is that they are slowly coming into their own, and I hope that a more explicit insistence on their ubiquitous presence will let the reader see the many aspects of shape, color, space, and movement more compellingly as manifestations of one coherent medium.

In every chapter some passages have stood the test of time, and if the judgment of my readers agrees at all with mine, they are likely not to miss too many of the formulations to which, as faithful users, they may have become accustomed and perhaps attached. They may find them, however, at a different point in the chapter or even in a different chapter, and I can only hope that these translocations have made for more logical context.

While a sentence here, a whole page there, has been clipped or torn from the first edition, most of the text is new, not only in the wording but in substance as well. Twenty years of active concern with a subject will leave their traces. Predictably also, the book has gone the way of all flesh toward increased girth. New thoughts have accumulated, new examples have come my way, and many pertinent studies have been published. Even so, the new version makes no more claim than did the old to being an exhaustive survey of the professional literature. I have continued to look for striking demonstrations and confirmations of visual phenomena relevant to the arts. At the same time, I have trimmed the book of certain intricacies and digressions, some of which have been given separate treatment in essays now collected in my *Toward a Psychology of Art*. If readers notice that the language of this book seems to have been dusted, lubricated, and tightened, I would like them to know that these improvements are due to the efforts of an excellent editor, Muriel Bell. I owe many thanks also to my wife, Mary, who deciphered and typed the entire manuscript.

Most of the illustrations used in the first edition have been retained, although some have been replaced with more attractive ones. All in all, I can only hope that the blue book with Arp's black eye on the cover will continue to lie dog-eared, annotated, and stained with pigment and plaster on the tables and desks of those actively concerned with the theory and practice of the arts, and that even in its tidier garb it will continue to be admitted to the kind of shoptalk the visual arts need in order to do their silent work.

R. A.

Department of Visual and Environmental Studies
Harvard University
Cambridge, Mass. 02138

INTRODUCTION

Art may seem to be in danger of being drowned by talk. Rarely are we presented with a new specimen of what we are willing to accept as genuine art, yet we are overwhelmed by a flood of books, articles, dissertations, speeches, lectures, guides—all ready to tell us what is art and what is not, what was done by whom and when and why and because of whom and what. We are haunted by the vision of a small, delicate body dissected by crowds of eager lay surgeons and lay analysts. And we feel tempted to assume that art is unsure in our time because we think and talk too much about it.

Probably such a diagnosis is superficial. True, the state of affairs seems unsatisfactory to almost everyone; but if we seek its causes with some care, we find we are heirs to a cultural situation that is both unsuited to the creation of art and likely to encourage the wrong kind of thinking about it. Our experiences and ideas tend to be common but not deep, or deep but not common. We have neglected the gift of comprehending things through our senses. Concept is divorced from percept, and thought moves among abstractions. Our eyes have been reduced to instruments with which to identify and to measure; hence we suffer a paucity of ideas that can be expressed in images and an incapacity to discover meaning in what we see. Naturally we feel lost in the presence of objects that make sense only to undiluted vision, and we seek refuge in the more familiar medium of words.

The mere exposure to masterworks does not suffice. Too many persons visit museums and collect picture books without gaining access to art. The inborn capacity to understand through the eyes has been put to sleep and must be reawakened. This is best accomplished by handling pencils, brushes, chisels, and perhaps cameras. But here again, bad habits and misconceptions will block the path of the unassisted. Often he is helped most effectively by visual evidence: by being shown weak spots or presented with good examples. But such assistance rarely takes the form of silent pantomime. Human beings have excellent reasons for talking to one another. I believe this is true also in the field of the arts.

Here, however, we must heed the warnings of artists and art teachers against the use of speech in the studio and art room, even though they themselves may use many words to express their warning. They may assert, first of all, that visual things cannot be conveyed by verbal language. There is a core of truth in this. The particular qualities of the experience created by a Rembrandt painting are only partly reducible to description and explanation. This limitation, however, applies not only to art, but to any object of experience. No description or explanation—whether a secretary's verbal portrait of her employer or a physician's account of a patient's glandular system—can do more than present a few general categories in a particular configuration. The scientist builds conceptual models, which, if he is fortunate, will reflect the essentials of what he wants to understand about a given phenomenon. But he knows that there is no such thing as the full representation of an individual instance. He also knows that there is no need to duplicate what already exists.

The artist, too, uses his categories of shape and color to capture something universally significant in the particular. He is neither intent on matching the unique nor able to do so. To be sure, the outcome of his effort is a uniquely particular object or performance. The world we approach when we look at a picture by Rembrandt has never been presented by anybody else; and to enter this world means to receive the particular mood and character of its lights and shadows, the faces and gestures of its human beings, and the attitude toward life conveyed by it all—to receive it through the immediacy of our senses and feelings. Words can wait and must wait until our mind distills, from the uniqueness of the experience, generalities that can be grasped by our senses, conceptualized, and labeled. To derive such generalities from a work of art is laborious, but not different in principle from trying to describe the nature of other complex things, such as the physical or mental make-up of living creatures. Art is the product of organisms and therefore probably neither more nor less complex than these organisms themselves.

It often happens that we see and feel certain qualities in a work of art but cannot express them in words. The reason for our failure is not that we use language, but that we have not yet succeeded in casting those perceived qualities into suitable categories. Language cannot do the job directly because it is no direct avenue for sensory contact with reality; it serves only to name what we have seen or heard or thought. By no means is it an alien medium, unsuitable for perceptual things; on the contrary, it refers to nothing but perceptual experiences. These experiences, however, must be coded by perceptual analysis before they can be named. Fortunately, perceptual analysis is very subtle and can go far. It sharpens our vision for the task of penetrating a work of art to the limits of the ultimately impenetrable.

Another prejudice has it that verbal analysis paralyzes intuitive creation and comprehension. Again there is a core of truth here. The history of the past and the experience of the present provide many examples of the destruction wrought by formulas and recipes. But are we to conclude that in the arts one power of the mind must be suspended so another may function? Is it not true that disturbances occur precisely when any one mental faculty operates at the expense of another? The delicate balance of all a person's powers—which alone permits him to live fully and to work well—is upset not only when the intellect interferes with intuition, but equally when sensation dislodges reasoning. Groping in vagueness is no more productive than blind adherence to rules. Unchecked self-analysis can be harmful, but so can the artificial primitivism of the person who refuses to understand how and why he works. Modern man can, and therefore must, live with unprecedented self-awareness. Perhaps the task of living has become more difficult—but there is no way around it.

It is the purpose of this book to discuss some of the virtues of vision and thereby to help refresh and direct them. As long as I can remember I have been involved with art, studied its nature and history, tried my eyes and hands at it, and sought the company of artists, art theorists, art educators. This interest has been strengthened by my psychological studies. All seeing is in the realm of the psychologist, and no one has ever discussed the processes of creating or experiencing art without talking psychology. Some art theorists use the findings of psychologists to advantage. Others apply them one-sidedly or without admitting what they are doing; but inevitably they all use psychology, some of it up-to-date, some of it homegrown or left over from theories of the past.

On the other side, some psychologists have taken a professional interest in the arts. But it seems fair to say that for the most part they have contributed only marginally to our understanding of what matters. This is so, first of all, because psychologists are often interested in artistic activity mainly as an instrument for exploration of the human personality, as though art were little different from a Rorschach inkblot or the answers to a questionnaire. Or they limit their approaches to what can be measured and counted, and to concepts they have derived from experimental, clinical, or psychiatric practice. Perhaps this caution is well advised because the arts, like any other object of study, require the kind of intimate knowledge that springs only from long love and patient devotion. Good art theory must smell of the studio, although its language should differ from the household talk of painters and sculptors.

My own undertaking here is limited in many ways. It refers only to the visual media, and among them mostly to painting, drawing, and sculpture. This emphasis, to be sure, is not altogether arbitrary. The traditional arts have accumulated innumerable examples of the greatest variety and highest quality. And they illustrate aspects of form with a precision obtainable only from the handiwork of the mind. These demonstrations, however, point to similar, though often less sharply manifest, phenomena in the photographic and performing arts. In fact, the present study developed from a psychological and aesthetic analysis of the film conducted in the twenties and thirties.

A further limitation of my work is psychological. All aspects of the mind bear on art, be they cognitive, social, or motivational. The artist's place in the community, the effect of his occupation on his relations with other human beings, the function of creative activity in the mind's striving for fulfillment and wisdom—none of these are the central focus of this book. Nor am I concerned with the psychology of the consumer. But I hope the reader will feel compensated by the rich imagery of shapes, colors, and movements that will meet him here. To establish some order in this lush overgrowth, to lay out a morphology, and to derive some principles gives us plenty to do.

This will be the first task: a description of what sorts of things we see and what perceptual mechanisms account for the visual facts. To stop at the surface level, however, would leave the whole enterprise truncated and meaningless. There is no point to visual shapes apart from what they tell us. This is why we shall constantly proceed from the perceived patterns to the meaning they convey; and once we endeavor to look that far, we may hope to recapture in depth what we lost in scope by deliberately narrowing our horizon.

The principles of my psychological thinking and many of the experiments I shall cite below derive from gestalt theory—a psychological discipline, I should probably add, which has no relation to the various forms of psychotherapy that have adopted the name. The word *gestalt*, the common German noun for shape or form, has been applied since the beginning of our century to a body of scientific principles that were derived mainly from experiments in sensory perception. It is generally admitted that the foundations of our present knowledge of visual perception were laid in the laboratories of the gestalt psychologists, and my own development has been shaped by the theoretical and practical work of this school.

More specifically, from its beginnings gestalt psychology had a kinship to art. Art pervades the writings of Max Wertheimer, Wolfgang Köhler, and Kurt Koffka. Here and there the arts are explicitly mentioned, but what counts more is that the spirit underlying the reasoning of these men makes the artist feel at home. Indeed, something like an artistic vision of reality was needed to remind scientists that most natural phenomena are not described adequately if they are analyzed piece by piece. That a whole cannot be attained by the accretion of isolated parts was not something the artist had to be told. For centuries scientists had been able to say valuable things about reality by describing networks of mechanical relations; but at no time could a work of art have been made or understood by a mind unable to conceive the integrated structure of a whole.

In the essay that gave gestalt theory its name, Christian von Ehrenfels pointed out that if each of twelve observers listened to one of the twelve tones of a melody, the sum of their experiences would not correspond to the experience of someone listening to the whole melody. Much of the later experimentation of the gestalt theorists was designed to show that the appearance of any element depends on its place and function in an overall pattern. A thoughtful person cannot read these studies without admiring the active striving for unity and order manifest in the simple act of looking at a simple pattern of lines. Far from being a mechanical recording of sensory elements, vision proved to be a truly creative apprehension of reality—imaginative, inventive, shrewd, and beautiful. It became apparent that the qualities that dignify the thinker and the artist distinguish all performances of the mind. Psychologists also began to see that this fact was no coincidence: the same principles apply to all the various mental capacities because the mind always functions as a whole. All perceiving is also thinking, all reasoning is also intuition, all observation is also invention.

The relevance of these views to the theory and practice of the arts is evident. No longer can we consider what the artist does to be a self-contained activity, mysteriously inspired from above, unrelated and unrelatable to other human activities. Instead, we recognize the exalted kind of seeing that leads to the creation of great art as an outgrowth of the humbler and more common activity of the eyes in everyday life. Just as the prosaic search for information is "artistic" because it involves giving and finding shape and meaning, so the artist's conceiving is an instrument of life, a refined way of understanding who and where we are.

As long as the raw material of experience was considered an amorphous agglomeration of stimuli, the observer seemed free to handle it according to his arbitrary pleasure. Seeing was an entirely subjective imposition of shape and meaning upon reality; and in fact, no student of the arts would deny that individual artists or cultures form the world after their own image. The gestalt studies, however, made it clear that more often than not the situations we face have their own characteristics, which demand that we perceive them appropriately. Looking at the world proved to require an interplay between properties supplied by the object and the nature of the observing subject. This objective element in experience justifies attempts to distinguish between adequate and inadequate conceptions of reality. Further, all adequate conceptions could be expected to contain a common core of truth, which would make the art of all times and places potentially relevant to all men. If it could be shown in the laboratory that a well-organized line figure imposes itself upon all observers as basically the same shape, regardless of the associations and fantasies it stirs up in some of them because of their cultural background and individual disposition, one could expect the same, at least in principle, with respect to people looking at works of art. This trust in the objective validity of the artistic statement supplied a badly needed antidote to the nightmare of unbounded subjectivism and relativism.

Finally, there was a wholesome lesson in the discovery that vision is not a mechanical recording of elements but rather the apprehension of significant structural patterns. If this was true for the simple act of perceiving an object, it was all the more likely to hold also for the artistic approach to reality. Obviously the artist was no more a mechanical recording device than his instrument of sight. The artistic representation of an object could no longer be thought of as a tedious transcription of its accidental appearance, detail by detail. In other words, here was a scientific analogy to the fact that images of reality can be valid even though far removed from "realistic" semblance.

It was encouraging for me to discover that similar conclusions had been reached independently in the field of art education. In particular Gustaf Britsch, with whose work I had become acquainted through Henry Schaefer-Simmern, asserted that the mind in its struggle for an orderly conception of reality proceeds in a lawful and logical way from the perceptually simplest patterns to patterns of increasing complexity. There was evidence, then, that the principles revealed in the gestalt experiments were also active genetically. The psychological interpretation of the growth process advanced in Chapter IV of the present book relies heavily on Schaefer-Simmern's theoretical formulations and lifelong experience as an educator. His work, *The Unfolding of Artistic Activity*, has demonstrated that the capacity to deal with life artistically is not the privilege of a few gifted specialists, but is available to every sane person whom nature has favored with a pair of eyes. To the psychologist this means that the study of art is an indispensable part of the study of man.

At the risk of giving my fellow scientists good reason for displeasure, I am applying the principles in which I believe with a somewhat reckless one-sidedness, partly because the cautious installation of dialectic fire escapes, side entrances, emergency closets, and waiting rooms would have made the structure impractically large and orientation difficult, partly because in certain cases it is useful to state a point of view with crude simplicity and leave the refinements to the ensuing play of thrust and counterthrust. I must also apologize to the art historians for using their material less competently than might have been desirable. At the present time it is probably beyond the power of any one person to give a fully satisfactory survey of the relations between the theory of the visual arts and the pertinent work in psychology. If we try to match two things which, although related, have not been made for each other, many adjustments are necessary and many gaps have to be closed provisionally. I had to speculate where I could not prove, and to use my own eyes where I could not rely on those of others. I have taken pains to indicate problems that await systematic research. But after all is said and done, I feel like exclaiming with Herman Melville: "This whole book is but a draught—nay, but the draught of a draught. Oh, Time, Strength, Cash, and Patience!"

The book deals with what can be seen by everybody. I rely on the literature of art criticism and aesthetics only insofar as it has helped me and my students to see better. I have tried to spare the reader a hangover caused by reading many things that serve no good purpose. One of my reasons for writing this book is that I believe many people to be tired of the dazzling obscurity of arty talk, the juggling with catchwords and dehydrated aesthetic concepts, the pseudoscientific window dressing, the impertinent hunt for clinical symptoms, the elaborate measurement of trifles, and the charming epigrams. Art is the most concrete thing in the world, and there is no justification for confusing the mind of anybody who wants to know more about it.

To some readers the approach may seem inappropriately sober and pedestrian. They might be answered by what Goethe once wrote to a friend, Christian Gottlob Heyne, professor of rhetoric in Göttingen: "As you can see, my starting point is very down-to-earth, and it may seem to some that I have treated the most spiritual matter in too terrestrial a fashion; but I may be permitted to observe that the gods of the Greeks were not enthroned in the seventh or tenth heaven but on Olympus, taking a giant-sized stride not from sun to sun but, at most, from mountain to mountain." And yet, some caution on how to use this book may be in order. Recently, a young instructor at Dartmouth College exhibited an assemblage which, I am pleased to report, was called *Homage to Arnheim*. It consisted of ten identical mousetraps, arranged in a row. At the spot where the bait was to be affixed, he had written the titles of this book's ten chapters, one on each contraption. If this artist's work was fair warning, what was he warning against?

This book may indeed act as a trap if it is used as a manual on approaching works of art. Anyone who has watched teachers guiding groups of children through a museum knows that to respond to the works of the masters is difficult at best. In the past, visitors could concentrate on the subject matter and thereby avoid facing the art. Then a generation of influential critics taught that even to consider the subject matter was a sure sign of ignorance. From then on, interpreters of art began to preach formal relations. But since they considered shapes and colors in a vacuum, theirs was nothing but a new way of avoiding art. For, as I suggested earlier, there is no point to visual shapes apart from what they tell us. Imagine now that a teacher used the method of this book superficially as a guide to approaching a work of art. "Now, children, let us see how many spots of red we can find in this painting by Matisse!" We proceed systematically, establishing an inventory of all the round shapes and all the angular ones. We hunt for parallel lines and for examples of superposition and of figure and ground. In the higher grades we seek out systems of gradients. When all the items are strung in order, we have done justice to the whole work. It can be done, and it has been done, but it is the last approach an adherent of gestalt psychology would want laid at his door.

If one wishes to be admitted to the presence of a work of art, one must, first of all, face it as a whole. What is it that comes across? What is the mood of the colors, the dynamics of the shapes? Before we identify any one element, the total composition makes a statement that we must not lose. We look for a theme, a key to which everything relates. If there is a subject matter, we learn as much about it as we can, for nothing an artist puts in his work can be neglected by the viewer with impunity. Safely guided by the structure of the whole, we then try to recognize the principal features and explore their dominion over dependent details. Gradually, the entire wealth of the work reveals itself and falls into place, and as we perceive it correctly, it begins to engage all the powers of the mind with its message.

This is what the artist works for. But it is also in the nature of man that he wishes to define what he sees and to understand why he sees what he does. Here the present book may be helpful. By making visual categories explicit, by extracting underlying principles, and by showing structural relations at work, this survey of formal mechanisms aims not to replace spontaneous intuition but to sharpen it, to shore it up, and to make its elements communicable. If the tools provided here kill the experience rather than enrich it, something has gone wrong. The trap must be avoided.

My first attempt to write this book dates back to the years 1941–1943, when I received a grant from the John Simon Guggenheim Memorial Foundation for the purpose. In the course of my work I was driven to the conclusion that the tools then available in the psychology of perception were inadequate for dealing with some of the more important visual problems in the arts. Instead of writing the book I had planned, I therefore undertook a number of specific studies, mainly in the areas of space, expression, and movement, designed to fill some of the gaps. The material was tested and expanded by my courses in the psychology of art at Sarah Lawrence College and the New School for Social Research in New York. When, in the summer of 1951, a fellowship from the Rockefeller Foundation made it possible for me to take a year's leave of absence, I felt ready to give a reasonably coherent account of the field. Whatever the worth of this book, I am greatly indebted to the officers of the Foundation's Humanities Division for enabling me to satisfy my need to put my findings on paper. It should be understood that the Foundation assumed no control over the project and has no responsibility for the result.

In 1968 I moved to Harvard University. The Department of Visual and Environmental Studies, housed in a beautiful building by Le Corbusier, became a new inspiration. In the company of painters, sculptors, architects, photographers, and film-makers I was able, for the first time, to devote all my teaching to the psychology of art and to test my suppositions against what I saw around me in the studios. The alert comments of my students continued to act as a stream of water, polishing the pebbles that make up this book.

I wish to express my gratitude to three friends, Henry Schaefer-Simmern, the art educator, Meyer Schapiro, the art historian, and Hans Wallach, the psychologist, for reading chapters of the first edition in manuscript and making valuable suggestions and corrections. My thanks are due also to Alice B. Sheldon for alerting me to a large number of technical flaws after the book came out in 1954. Acknowledgments to the institutions and individual proprietors that permitted me to reproduce their works of art or to quote from their publications appear in the captions and in the notes at the end of the volume. I wish explicitly to thank the children, most of them unknown to me, whose drawings I have used. In particular, I am happy that my book preserves some of the drawings of Allmuth Laporte, whose young life of beauty and talent was destroyed by illness at the age of thirteen years.

I BALANCE

Cut a disk out of dark cardboard and place it on a white square in the position indicated by Figure 1.

The location of the disk could be determined and described by measurement. A yardstick would tell in inches the distances from the disk to the edges of the square. Thus it could be inferred that the disk lies off-center.

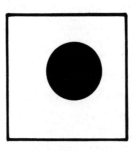

Figure 1

This result would come as no surprise. We do not have to measure—we saw at a glance that the disk lies off-center. How is such "seeing" done? Did we behave like a yardstick by first looking at the space between the disk and the left edge and then carrying our image of that distance across to the other side to compare the two distances? Probably not. It would not be the most efficient procedure.

Looking at Figure 1 as a whole, we probably noticed the asymmetrical position of the disk as a visual property of the pattern. We did not see disk and square separately. Their spatial relation within the whole is part of what we see. Such relational observations are an indispensable aspect of common experience in many sensory areas. "My right hand is larger than the left." "This flagpole is not straight." "That piano is out of tune." "This cocoa is sweeter than the kind we had before."

Objects are perceived immediately as having a certain size, that is, as lying somewhere between a grain of salt and a mountain. On the scale of brightness values, our white square lies high, our black disk low. Similarly, every object is seen as having a location. The book you are reading appears at a particular spot, which is defined by the room about you and the objects in it—among them notably you yourself. The square of Figure 1 appears somewhere on the book page, and the disk is off-center in the square. No object is perceived as unique or isolated. Seeing something involves assigning it a place in the whole: a location in space, a score on the scale of size or brightness or distance.

One difference between measurement with a yardstick and our visual judgments has already been mentioned. We do not establish sizes, distances, directions, singly and then compare them piece by piece. Typically we see these characteristics as properties of the total visual field. There is, however, another, equally important difference. The various qualities of the images produced by the sense of sight are not static. The disk in Figure 1 is not simply displaced with regard to the center of the square. There is something restless about it. It looks as though it had been at the center and wished to return, or as though it wants to move away even farther. And the disk's relations to the edges of the square are a similar play of attraction and repulsion.

Visual experience is dynamic. This theme will recur throughout the present book. What a person or animal perceives is not only an arrangement of objects, of colors and shapes, of movements and sizes. It is, perhaps first of all, an interplay of directed tensions. These tensions are not something the observer adds, for reasons of his own, to static images. Rather, these tensions are as inherent in any percept as size, shape, location, or color. Because they have magnitude and direction, these tensions can be described as psychological "forces."

Notice further that if the disk is seen as striving toward the center of the square, it is being attracted by something not physically present in the picture. The center point is not identified by any marking in Figure 1; as invisible as the North Pole or the Equator, it is nonetheless a part of the perceived pattern, an invisible focus of power, established at a considerable distance by the outline of the square. It is "induced," as one electric current can be induced by another. There are, then, more things in the field of vision than those that strike the retina of the eye. Examples of "induced structure" abound. An incompletely drawn circle looks like a complete circle with a gap. In a picture done in central perspective the vanishing point may be established by the convergent lines even though no actual point of meeting can be seen. In a melody one may "hear" by induction the regular beat from which a syncopated tone deviates, as our disk deviates from the center.

Such perceptual inductions differ from logical inferences. Inferences are thought operations that add something to the given visual facts by interpreting them. Perceptual inductions are sometimes interpolations based on previously acquired knowledge. More typically, however, they are completions deriving spontaneously during perception from the given configuration of the pattern.

A visual figure such as the square in Figure 1 is empty and not empty at the same time. Its center is part of a complex hidden structure, which we can explore by means of the disk, much as we can use iron filings to explore the lines of force in a magnetic field. If the disk is placed at various locations within the square, it looks solidly at rest at some points; at others it exhibits a pull in a definite direction; and in others its situation seems unclear and wavering.

The disk is most stably settled when its center coincides with the center of the square. In Figure 2 the disk may be seen as drawn toward the contour

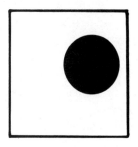

Figure 2

to the right. If we alter the distance, this effect is weakened or even reversed. We can find a distance at which the disk looks "too close," possessed by the urge to withdraw from the boundary. In that case the empty interval between the boundary and the disk will appear compressed, as though more breathing room were needed. For any spatial relation between objects there is a "correct" distance, established by the eye intuitively. Artists are sensitive to this requirement when they arrange the pictorial objects in a painting or the elements in a piece of sculpture. Designers and architects constantly seek the proper distance between buildings, windows, and pieces of furniture. It would be most desirable to examine the conditions for these visual judgments more systematically.

Informal explorations show that the disk is influenced not only by the boundaries and the center of the square, but also by the cross-shaped framework of the central vertical and horizontal axes and by the diagonals (Fig. 3). The center, the principal locus of attraction and repulsion, establishes itself through the crossing of these four main structural lines. Other points on the lines are less powerful than the center, but the effect of attraction can be established for them as well. The pattern sketched in Figure 3 will be referred to as the

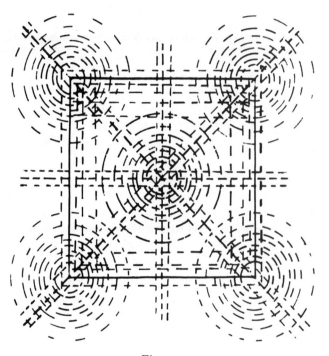

Figure 3

structural skeleton of the square. It will be shown later that these skeletons vary from figure to figure.

Wherever the disk is located, it will be affected by the forces of all the hidden structural factors. The relative strength and distance of these factors will determine their effect in the total configuration. At the center all the forces balance one another, and therefore the central position makes for rest. Another comparatively restful position can be found, for example, by moving the disk along a diagonal. The point of balance seems to lie somewhat closer to the corner of the square than to the center, which may mean that the center is stronger than the corner and that this preponderance has to be offset by greater distance, as though corner and center were two magnets of unequal power. In general, any location that coincides with a feature of the structural skeleton introduces an element of stability, which of course may be counteracted by other factors.

If influence from a particular direction predominates, there results a pull in that direction. When the disk is put at the exact midpoint between center and corner, it tends to strive toward the center.

An unpleasant effect is produced by locations at which pulls are so equivocal and ambiguous that the eye cannot decide whether the disk is pressing in any particular direction. Such wavering makes the visual statement unclear and interferes with the observer's perceptual judgment. In ambiguous situations the visual pattern ceases to determine what is seen, and subjective factors in the observer, such as his focus of attention or his preference for a particular direction, come into play. Unless an artist welcomes ambiguities of this sort, they will induce him to search for more stable arrangements.

Our observations have been checked experimentally by Gunnar Goude and Inga Hjortzberg at the Psychological Laboratory of the University of Stockholm. A black disk of 4 cm. diameter was attached magnetically to a white square of 46 x 46 cm. As the disk was moved to various locations, subjects were asked to indicate whether it exhibited a tendency to strive in any direction, and if so, how strong this tendency was with regard to the eight principal directions of space. Figure 4 illustrates the results. The eight vectors at each location summarize the movement tendencies observed by the subjects. Obviously the experiment does not prove that visual dynamics is experienced spontaneously; it shows only that when a directional tendency is suggested to subjects, their responses do not distribute randomly but cluster along the principal axes of our structural skeleton. Noticeable also is a striving toward the edges of the square. No clear attraction toward the center was evident, but rather an area of relative stability around it.

When conditions are such that the eyes cannot clearly establish the actual location of the disk, the visual forces discussed here may possibly produce genuine displacement in the direction of the dynamic pull. If Figure 1 is seen for only a split second, is the disk seen as closer to the center than it is on leisurely inspection? We shall have many occasions to observe that physical and psychological systems exhibit a very general tendency to change in the

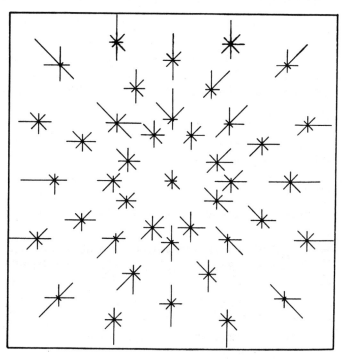

Figure 4
From Gunnar Goude and Inga Hjortzberg, *En Experimentell Prövning*, etc. Stockholm University, 1967.

direction of the lowest attainable tension level. Such a reduction of tension is obtained when elements of visual patterns can give in to the directed perceptual forces inherent in them. Max Wertheimer has pointed out that an angle of ninety-three degrees is seen not as what it is, but as a somehow inadequate right angle. When the angle is presented tachistoscopically, i.e., at short exposure, observers frequently report seeing a right angle, afflicted perhaps with some undefinable imperfection.

The roving disk, then, reveals that a visual pattern consists of more than the shapes recorded by the retina. As far as retinal input is concerned, the black lines and the disk are all there is to our figure. In perceptual experience, this stimulus pattern creates a structural skeleton, a skeleton that helps determine the role of each pictorial element within the balance system of the whole; it serves as a frame of reference, just as a musical scale defines the pitch value of each tone in a composition.

In still another way we must go beyond the black-and-white picture drawn on paper. The picture plus the hidden structure induced by it is more than a lattice of lines. As indicated in Figure 3, the percept is really a continuous field of forces. It is a dynamic landscape, in which lines are actually ridges sloping off in both directions. These ridges are centers of attractive and repulsive forces, whose influence extends through their surroundings, inside and outside the boundaries of the figure.

No point in the figure is free from this influence. Granted there are "restful" spots, but their restfulness does not signify the absence of active forces. "Dead center" is not dead. No pull in any one direction is felt when pulls from all directions balance one another. To the sensitive eye, the balance of such a point is alive with tension. Think of a rope that is motionless while two men of equal strength are pulling it in opposite directions. It is still, but loaded with energy.

In short, just as a living organism cannot be described by an account of its anatomy, so the nature of a visual experience cannot be described in terms of inches of size and distance, degrees of angle, or wave lengths of hue. These static measurements define only the "stimulus," that is, the message sent to the eye by the physical world. But the life of a percept—its expression and meaning—derives entirely from the activity of the perceptual forces. Any line drawn on a sheet of paper, the simplest form modeled from a piece of clay, is like a rock thrown into a pond. It upsets repose, it mobilizes space. Seeing is the perception of action.

What Are Perceptual Forces?

The reader may have noted with apprehension the use of the term "forces." Are these forces merely figures of speech, or are they real? And if they are real, where do they exist?

They are assumed to be real in both realms of existence—that is, as both psychological and physical forces. Psychologically, the pulls in the disk exist in the experience of any person who looks at it. Since these pulls have a point of attack, a direction, and an intensity, they meet the conditions established by physicists for physical forces. For this reason, psychologists speak of psychological forces, even though to date not many of them have applied the term, as I do here, to perception.

In what sense can it be said that these forces exist not only in experience, but also in the physical world? Surely they are not contained in the objects we are looking at, such as the white paper on which the square is drawn or the dark cardboard disk. Of course, molecular and gravitational forces are active in these objects, holding their microparticles together and preventing them from flying away. But there are no known physical forces that would tend to push an eccentrically placed patch of printer's ink in the direction of the center of a square. Nor will lines drawn in ink exert any magnetic power on the surrounding paper surface. Where, then, are these forces?

In order to answer this question we must recall how an observer obtains his knowledge of the square and the disk. Light rays, emanating from the sun or some other source, hit the object and are partly absorbed and partly reflected by it. Some of the reflected rays reach the lenses of the eye and are projected on its sensitive background, the retina. Many of the small receptor organs situated in the retina combine in groups by means of ganglion cells. Through these groupings a first, elementary organization of visual shape is obtained very close to the level of retinal stimulation. As the electrochemical messages travel toward their final destination in the brain, they are subjected to further shaping at other way stations until the pattern is completed at the various levels of the visual cortex.

At which stages of this complex process the physiological counterpart of our perceptual forces originates, and by what particular mechanisms it comes about, is beyond our present knowledge. If, however, we make the reasonable assumption that every aspect of a visual experience has its physiological counterpart in the nervous system, we can anticipate, in a general way, the nature of these brain processes. We can assert, for instance, that they must be field processes. This means that whatever happens at any one place is determined by the interaction between the parts and the whole. If it were otherwise, the various inductions, attractions, and repulsions could not occur in the field of visual experience.

An observer sees the pushes and pulls in visual patterns as genuine properties of the perceived objects themselves. By mere inspection he can no more distinguish the restlessness of the eccentric disk from what occurs physically on the page of the book than he can tell the reality of a dream or hallucination from the reality of physically existing things.

Whether or not we choose to call these perceptual forces "illusions" matters little so long as we acknowledge them as genuine components of everything seen. The artist, for example, need not worry about the fact that these forces are not contained in the pigments on the canvas. What he creates with physical materials are experiences. The perceived image, not the paint, is the work of art. If a wall looks vertical in a picture, it is vertical; and if walkable space is seen in a mirror, there is no reason why images of men should not walk right into it, as happens in some movies. The forces that pull our disk are "illusory" only to the man who decides to use their energy to run an engine. Perceptually and artistically, they are quite real.

Two Disks in a Square

To move a bit closer to the complexity of the work of art, we now introduce a second disk into the square (Figure 5). What is the result? First of all,

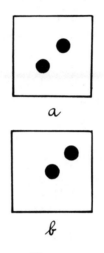

Figure 5

some of the previously observed relations between disk and square recur. When the two disks lie close together, they attract each other and may look almost like one indivisible thing. At a certain distance they repel each other because they are too close together. The distance at which these effects occur depends on the size of the disks and the square, as well as on the location of the disks within the square.

The locations of the disks may balance each other. Either of the two locations in Figure 5a might look unbalanced by itself. Together they create a symmetrically located pair at rest. The same pair, however, may look badly unbalanced when moved to another location (Figure 5b). Our earlier analysis of the structural map helps explain why. The two disks form a pair because of their closeness and their similarity in size and shape, and also because they are the only "content" of the square. As members of a pair they tend to be seen as symmetrical; that is, they are given equal value and function in the whole. This perceptual judgment, however, conflicts with another, deriving from the location of the pair. The lower disk lies in the prominent and stable position of the center. The upper one is at a less stable location. Thus location creates a distinction between the two that conflicts with their symmetrical pairness. This dilemma is insoluble. The spectator finds himself shifting between two incompatible conceptions. The example shows that even a very simple visual pattern is fundamentally affected by the structure of its spatial surroundings, and that balance can be disturbingly ambiguous when shape and spatial location contradict each other.

Psychological and Physical Balance

It is time to state more explicitly what we mean by balance or equilibrium. If we demand that in a work of art all elements be distributed in such a way that a state of balance results, we need to know how balance can be attained. Moreover, some readers may believe the call for balance to be nothing but a particular stylistic, psychological, or social preference. Some people like equilibrium, some don't. Why, then, should balance be a necessary quality of visual patterns?

To the physicist, balance is the state in which the forces acting upon a body compensate one another. In its simplest form, balance is achieved by two forces of equal strength that pull in opposite directions. The definition is applicable to visual balance. Like a physical body, every finite visual pattern has a fulcrum or center of gravity. And just as the physical fulcrum of even the most irregularly shaped flat object can be determined by locating the point at which it will balance on the tip of a finger, so the center of a visual pattern can be determined by trial and error. According to Denman W. Ross, the simplest way to do this is to move a frame around the pattern until the frame and pattern balance; then the center of the frame coincides with the weight center of the pattern.

Except for the most regular shapes, no known method of rational calculation can replace the eye's intuitive sense of balance. From our previous assumption it follows that the sense of sight experiences balance when the corresponding physiological forces in the nervous system are distributed in such a way that they compensate one another.

If, however, one hangs an empty canvas on a wall, the pattern's visual center of gravity coincides only roughly with the physical center ascertained by balancing the canvas on a finger. As we shall see, the canvas's vertical position on the wall influences the distribution of visual weight, and so do colors, shapes, and pictorial space when the canvas has a picture painted on it. Similarly, the visual center of a piece of sculpture cannot be determined simply by suspending it on a string. Here again, vertical orientation will matter. It also makes a difference whether the sculpture hangs in midair or rests on a base, stands in empty space or reposes in a niche.

There are other differences between physical and perceptual equilibrium. On the one hand, the photograph of a dancer may look unbalanced even though his body was in a comfortable position when the photograph was taken. On the other, a model may find it impossible to hold a pose that appears perfectly poised in a drawing. A sculpture may need an internal armature to hold it upright despite its being well balanced visually. A duck can sleep peacefully standing on one oblique leg. These discrepancies occur because factors such as size, color, or direction contribute to visual balance in ways not necessarily paralleled physically. A clown's costume—red on the left side, blue on the right—may be asymmetrical to the eye as a color scheme, even though the two halves of the costume, and indeed of the clown, are equal in physical weight. In a painting, a physically unrelated object, such as a curtain in the background, may counterbalance the asymmetrical position of a human figure.

An amusing example is found in a fifteenth-century painting that represents St. Michael weighing souls (Figure 6). By the mere strength of prayer, one frail little nude outweighs four big devils plus two millstones. Unfortunately prayer carries only spiritual weight and provides no visual pull. As a remedy, the painter has used a large dark patch on the angel's robe just below the scale holding the saintly soul. By visual attraction, nonexistent in the physical object, the patch creates the weight that adapts the appearance of the scene to its meaning.

Why Balance?

Why is pictorial balance indispensable? It must be remembered that visually as well as physically, balance is the state of distribution in which all action has come to a standstill. Potential energy in the system, says the physicist, has reached the minimum. In a balanced composition all such factors as shape, direction, and location are mutually determined in such a way that no change seems possible, and the whole assumes the character of "necessity" in all its parts. An unbalanced composition looks accidental, transitory, and therefore invalid. Its elements show a tendency to change place or shape in order to reach a state that better accords with the total structure.

Under conditions of imbalance, the artistic statement becomes incomprehensible. The ambiguous pattern allows no decision on which of the possible configurations is meant. We have the sense that the process of creation has been accidentally frozen somewhere along the way. Since the configuration

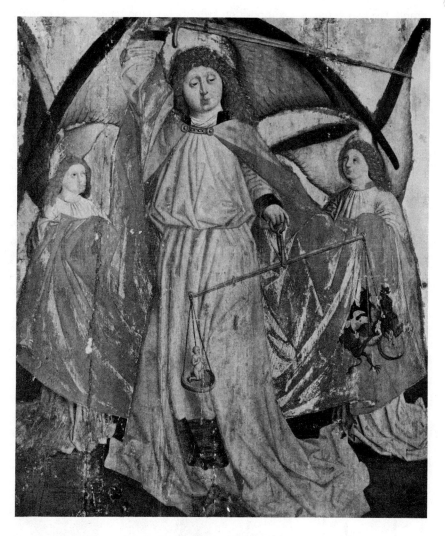

Figure 6
St. Michael Weighing Souls. Austrian, c. 1470. Allen Memorial Museum, Oberlin College.

calls for change, the stillness of the work becomes a handicap. Timelessness gives way to the frustrating sensation of arrested time. Except for the rare instances in which this is precisely the effect the artist intends, he will strive for balance in order to avoid such instability.

Of course balance does not require symmetry. Symmetry in which, for example, the two wings of a composition are equal is a most elementary manner of creating equilibrium. More often the artist works with some kind of inequality. In one of El Greco's paintings of the Annunciation, the angel is much larger than the Virgin. But this symbolic disproportion is compelling only because it is fixated by counterbalancing factors; otherwise, the unequal size of the two figures would lack finality and, therefore, meaning. It is only seemingly paradoxical to assert that disequilibrium can be expressed only by equilibrium, just as disorder can be shown only by order or separateness by connection.

The following examples are adapted from a test designed by Maitland Graves to determine the artistic sensitivity of students. Compare *a* and *b* in Figure 7. The left figure is well balanced. There is enough life in this combination of squares and rectangles of various sizes, proportions, and directions, but they hold one another in such a way that every element stays in its place, everything is necessary, nothing is seeking to change. Compare the clearly established internal vertical of *a* with its pathetically wavering counterpart in *b*. In *b*, proportions are based on differences so small that they leave the eye uncertain whether it is contemplating equality or inequality, symmetry or asymmetry, square or rectangle. We cannot tell what the pattern is trying to say.

Somewhat more complex, but no less irritatingly ambiguous, is Figure 8a. Relations are neither clearly rightangular nor clearly oblique. The four lines are not sufficiently different in length to assure the eye that they are unequal. The pattern, adrift in space, approaches on the one hand the symmetry of a crosslike figure of vertical-horizontal orientation, and on the other the shape of a kind of kite with a diagonal symmetry axis. Neither interpreta-

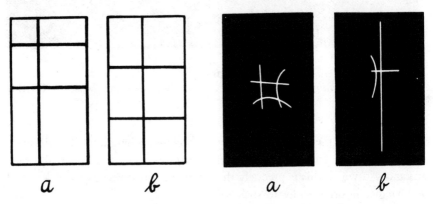

a   *b*   *a*   *b*

Figure 7   Figure 8

tion, however, is conclusive; neither admits of the reassuring clarity conveyed by Figure 8*b*.

Disequilibrium does not always make the whole configuration fluid. In Figure 9 the symmetry of the Latin cross is so firmly established that the deviating curve may be perceived as a flaw. Here, then, a balanced pattern is so strongly established that it attempts to preserve its integrity by segregating any departure as an intruder. Under such conditions, disequilibrium causes a local interference with the unity of the whole. It would be worth studying in this respect the small deviations from symmetry in frontally oriented portraits or in traditional representations of the crucifixion, in which the inclination of Christ's head is often balanced by slight modulations of the otherwise frontal body.

Weight

Two properties of visual objects have a particular influence on equilibrium: weight and direction.

In the world of our bodies we call weight the strength of the gravitational force pulling objects downward. A similar downward pull can be observed in pictorial and sculptural objects, but visual weight exerts itself in other directions as well. For example, as we look at objects within a painting their weight seems to produce tension along the axis connecting them with the eye of the observer, and it is not easy to tell whether they pull away from or push toward the person looking at them. All we can say is that weight is always a dynamic effect, but the tension is not necessarily oriented along a direction within the picture plane.

Weight is influenced by *location*. A "strong" position on the structural framework (Figure 3) can support more weight than one lying off-center or

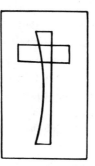

Figure 9

away from the central vertical or horizontal. This means, e.g., that a pictorial object in the center can be counterbalanced by smaller ones placed off-center. The central group in paintings is often quite heavy, with weights petering out toward the borders, and yet the whole picture looks balanced. Furthermore, according to the lever principle, which can be applied to visual composition, the weight of an element increases in relation to its distance from the center. In any particular example, of course, all the factors determining weight must be considered together.

Another factor influencing weight is *spatial depth*. Ethel Puffer has observed that "vistas," leading the glance to distant space, have great counterbalancing power. This rule can probably be generalized as follows: the greater the depth an area of the visual field reaches, the greater the weight it carries. We can only speculate why this should be so. In perception, distance and size correlate so that a more distant object is seen as larger and perhaps as more substantial than it would be if located near the picture's frontal plane. In Manet's *Déjeuner sur l'herbe*, the figure of a girl picking flowers at a distance has considerable weight in relation to the group of three large figures in the foreground. How much of the girl's weight derives from the increased size that the distant perspective gives her? It is also possible that the volume of empty space in front of a distant part of the scene carries weight. The phenomenon might be observable even in three-dimensional objects. Which factors, for example, balance the weight of the protruding wings in some Renaissance buildings, such as the Palazzo Barberini or the Casino Borghese in Rome, against the weight of the recessed central part and the cubic volume of the enclosed court space created by such a plan?

Weight depends also on *size*. Other factors being equal, the larger object will be the heavier. As to *color*, red is heavier than blue, and bright colors are heavier than dark ones. The patch of a bright red bedcover in Van Gogh's painting of his bedroom creates a strong off-center weight. A black area must be larger than a white one to counterbalance it; this is due in part to irradiation, which makes a bright surface look relatively larger.

Puffer has also found that compositional weight is affected by *intrinsic interest*. An area of a painting may hold the observer's attention either because of the subject matter—for example, the spot around the Christ child in an Adoration—or because of its formal complexity, intricacy, or other peculiarity. (Note in this connection the multicolored bouquet of flowers in Manet's *Olympia*.) The very tininess of an object may exert a fascination that compensates the slight weight it would otherwise have. Recent experiments have suggested that perception may also be influenced by the observer's wishes and fears. One could try to ascertain whether pictorial balance is changed by the introduction of a highly desirable object or a frightening one.

Isolation makes for weight. The sun or moon in an empty sky is heavier than an object of similar appearance surrounded by other things. On the stage, isolation for emphasis is an established technique. For this reason the star often insists that others in the cast keep their distance during important scenes.

Shape seems to influence weight. The regular shape of simple geometrical figures makes them look heavier. This effect can be observed in abstract paintings, notably some of Kandinsky's works, in which circles or squares provide remarkably strong accents within compositions of less definable shapes. Compactness—that is, the degree to which mass is concentrated around its center—also seems to produce weight. Figure 10, taken from the Graves test, shows

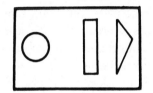

Figure 10

a relatively small circle counterweighing a larger rectangle and triangle. Vertically oriented forms seem to be heavier than oblique ones. Most of these rules, however, await verification by exact experiment.

What about the influence of *knowledge*? In a picture, no knowledge on the part of the observer will make a bundle of cotton look lighter than a lump of lead of similar appearance. The problem has come up in architecture. According to Mock and Richards: "We know from repeated experiences how strong wood or stone is, for we frequently handled them in other contexts, and when we look at a piece of wood or masonry construction we are immediately satisfied that it is able to do the job it has to do. But reinforced concrete construction is different; so is a building of steel and glass. We cannot see the steel bars inside the concrete and reassure ourselves that it can safely span several times the distance of the stone lintel it so much resembles, nor can we see the steel columns behind a cantilevered store window, so that a building may appear to stand unsafely on a base of glass. It should be realized, however, that the expectation that we shall be able to understand at a glance why a building stands up is a survival of the handicraft age that had disappeared even in the days of William Morris."

This kind of reasoning is common nowadays, but seems open to doubt. Two things must be distinguished. On the one hand there is the technical understanding of the craftsman, who deals with such factors as methods of construction and strength of materials. Such information cannot ordinarily be obtained by looking at the finished building, and there is no artistic reason why it should be. Quite another matter is the visual relation between, say, the perceived strength of columns and the weight of the roof they appear to support. Technical information or misinformation has little influence on visual evaluation. What perhaps does count is certain stylistic conventions—relating, for example, to the width of the span. Such conventions oppose change everywhere in the arts, and may help explain the resistance to the visual statics of modern architecture. But the main point is that the visual discrepancy between a large mass and a thin supporting pole is in no way alleviated by the architect's assurance that the structure will not collapse. In some early buildings of Le Corbusier, solid cubes or walls, whose appearance is a carry-over from abandoned construction methods, appear to rest precariously on slender pilotis. Frank Lloyd Wright called such buildings "big boxes on sticks." When later the architects revealed the skeleton of girders and thus drastically reduced the building's visual weight, style caught up with technology and the eye ceased to be troubled.

Direction

Equilibrium, we noted, is attained when the forces constituting a system compensate one another. Such compensation depends on all three properties of forces: the location of their point of attack, their strength, and their direction. The direction of visual forces is determined by several factors, among them the attraction exerted by the weight of neighboring elements. In Figure 11 the horse is drawn backward because of the attraction exerted by the figure of the rider, whereas in Figure 12 it is pulled forward by the other horse. In the composition of Toulouse-Lautrec from which this sketch was made, the two factors balance each other. Weight by attraction was demonstrated earlier, in Figure 6.

The shape of objects also generates direction along the axes of their structural skeletons. The triangular group of El Greco's *Pietà* (Figure 13) is perceived dynamically as an arrow or wedge, rooted at its broad base and

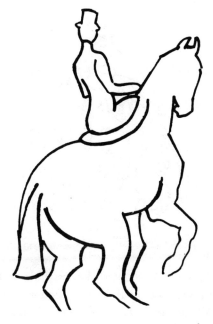

Figure 11

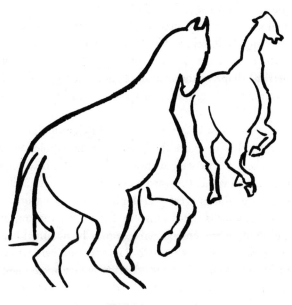

Figure 12

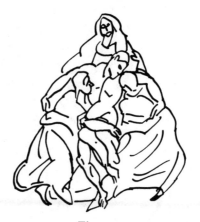

Figure 13

pointing upward. This vector counterbalances the gravitational downward pull. In European art, the traditional standing figure of classical Greek sculpture or Botticelli's Venus owes its compositional variety to an asymmetrical distribution of body weight. This allows a variety of directions at the various levels of the body (see, for example, Figure 115), thus producing a complex equilibrium of visual forces.

Subject matter also creates direction. It can define a human figure as advancing or retreating. In Rembrandt's *Portrait of a Young Girl*, at the Chicago Art Institute, the eyes of the girl are turned to the left, thus providing the almost symmetrical shape of the front-face figure with a strong lateral force. Spatial directions created by the actor's glance are known on the stage as "visual lines."

In any particular work of art, the factors just enumerated may act with and against one another to create the balance of the whole. Weight through color may be counteracted by weight through location. The direction of shape may be balanced by movement toward a center of attraction. The complexity of these relations contributes greatly to the liveliness of a work.

When actual motion is used, as in the dance, the theater, and the film, direction is indicated by movement. Balance may be obtained between events that occur simultaneously—as when two dancers walk symmetrically toward each other—or in succession. Film cutters often have a movement toward the right followed, or preceded, by one toward the left. The elementary need for such balancing compensation was shown clearly by experiments in which observers, after fixating a line bent at the middle into an obtuse angle, saw an objectively straight line as bent in the opposite direction. In another experiment when observers inspected a straight line that was moderately tilted away from the vertical or the horizontal, the objective vertical or horizontal later appeared bent in the opposite direction.

Speech creates visual weight at the place from which it issues. For example, in a duet between a dancer who speaks poetry and another who is silent the asymmetry may be compensated for by the more active movement of the silent dancer.

Patterns of Balance

Visual balance can be obtained in infinitely different ways. The mere number of elements may vary from a single figure—say, a black square holding the center of an otherwise empty surface—to a screen of innumerable particles covering the entire field. The distribution of weights may be dominated by one strong accent to which everything else is subservient, or by a duet of figures, such as Adam and Eve, the angel of the Annunciation and the Virgin, or the combination of red ball and feathery black mass that appears in a series of paintings by Adolph Gottlieb. In works consisting of only one or two units on a plain ground, the "hierarchic gradient" can be said to be very steep. More often, an assembly of many units leads in steps from the strongest to the weakest. A single human figure may be organized around secondary balance centers in the face, the lap, the hands. The same may hold for the total composition.

The hierarchic gradient approaches zero when a pattern is composed of many units of equal weight. The repetitive patterns of wallpaper or the windows of high-rise buildings obtain balance by homogeneity. In some works by Pieter Brueghel, the rectangular space of the picture is filled with small episodic groups, fairly equal in weight, which represent children's games or Flemish proverbs. This approach is better suited to interpreting the overall character of a mood or mode of existence than to describing life as controlled by central powers. Extreme examples of homogeneity can be found in Louise Nevelson's sculptural reliefs, which are shelves of coordinated compartments, or in Jackson Pollock's late paintings, evenly filled with a homogeneous texture. Such works present a world in which one finds oneself in the same place wherever one goes. They may also be termed atonal, in that any relation to an underlying structural key is abandoned and replaced by a network of connections among the elements of the composition.

Top and Bottom

The force of gravity dominating our world makes us live in anisotropic space, that is, space in which dynamics varies with direction. To rise upward means to overcome resistance—it is always a victory. To descend or fall is to surrender to the pull from below, and therefore is experienced as passive compliance. It follows from this unevenness of space that different locations are dynamically unequal. Here again, physics can help us, by pointing out that because moving away from the center of gravity requires work, the potential energy in a mass high up is greater than that in one low down. Visually an object of a certain size, shape, or color will carry more weight when placed higher up. Therefore, balance in the vertical direction cannot be obtained by placing equal objects at different heights. The higher one must be lighter. An experimental demonstration with regard to size is mentioned by Langfeld: "If one is asked to bisect a perpendicular line without measuring it, one almost invariably places the mark too high. If a line is actually bisected, it is with difficulty that one can convince oneself that the upper half is not longer than the lower half." This means that if one wants the two halves to look alike, one must make the upper half shorter.

If we conclude that weight counts more in the upper part of perceived space than in the lower, we must remember, however, that in the physical world uprightness is defined unambiguously while in perceptual space it is not. When we deal with a totem pole as a physical object we know what is meant by top and bottom; but applied to what we see when we *look* at an object, the meaning of the term is not obvious. To the sense of sight, uprightness means more than one thing. When we stand upright or lie in bed or tilt our heads we are at least approximately aware of the objective, physical vertical direction. This is "environmental orientation." However, we also speak of the top and bottom of a bookpage or picture lying flat on the table. As our head bends over the table, the "top" of the page is in fact at the top of our visual field. This is "retinal orientation." It is not yet known whether the distribution of visual weight differs depending on whether we see a picture on the wall or on the table.

Although weight counts more in the upper part of visual space, we observe in the world around us that many more things are generally assembled near the ground than high up. Therefore we are accustomed to experiencing the normal visual situation as bottom-heavy. Modern painting, sculpture, and even some architecture have tried to emancipate themselves from earthly gravity by distributing visual weight evenly throughout the pattern. To this end, the weight at the top must be slightly increased. Seen in the intended upright position, a late Mondrian painting displays no more weight at the bottom than at the top. But turn it upside down, and the picture will look top-heavy.

The stylistic preference for overcoming the downward pull is in keeping with the artist's desire to liberate himself from the imitation of reality. Certain particularly modern experiences may have contributed to this attitude, e.g., the experience of flying through the air and the upsetting of visual conventions in photographs taken from above. The motion picture camera does not keep its sight line invariably parallel to the ground, and thus presents views in which the gravitational axis is freely displaced and the lower part of the picture is not necessarily more crowded than the upper. Modern dance has run into an interesting inner conflict by stressing the weight of the human body, which classical ballet tried to deny, and at the same time following the general trend in moving from realistic pantomime to abstraction.

A powerful tradition, however, still tends to make the bottom part of a visual object look heavier. Horatio Greenough observed: "That buildings, in rising from the earth, be broad and simple at their bases, that they grow lighter not only in fact but in expression as they ascend, is a principle established. The laws of gravitation are at the root of this axiom. The spire obeys it. The obelisk is its simplest expression." Here the architect confirms for his viewers what they know from the muscle sensations in their bodies, namely, that things on our planet are pulled downward. Enough weight at the bottom makes the object look solidly rooted, reliable, and stable.

In realistic landscapes of the seventeenth and eighteenth centuries, the bottom part tends to be clearly heavier. The center of gravity is placed below the geometrical center. But the rule is observed even by typographers and layout designers. The number 3 in Figure 14 looks comfortably poised. Turn it upside down, and it becomes macrocephalic. The same holds for letters like

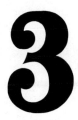

Figure 14

S or *B*; and book designers and picture framers leave customarily more space at the bottom than at the top.

The strictly spherical building at the New York World's Fair in 1939 created the unpleasant impression of wanting to rise from the ground but being tied to it. Whereas a securely balanced building points freely upward, the contradiction between the symmetrical sphere and asymmetrical space made for frustrated locomotion in this particular structure. The use of a completely symmetrical form in an asymmetrical context is a delicate undertaking. One successful solution is the positioning of the rose window in the façade of Notre Dame in Paris (Figure 15). Relatively small enough to avoid the

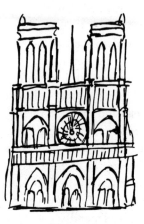

Figure 15

danger of drifting, it "personifies" the balance of vertical and horizontal elements obtained around it. The window finds its place of rest somewhat above the center of the square-shaped surface that represents the main mass of the façade.

As I mentioned earlier, there can be a discrepancy between orientation in physical space and in the visual field, i.e., between environmental and retinal orientation. A Roman floor mosaic may depict a realistic scene, the top and bottom of which both lie in the horizontal plane, but which is surrounded by a square or circular ornamental border devoid of such asymmetry. Jackson Pollock felt most at ease working on the floor: "I feel nearer, more a part of the painting, since this way I can walk around it, work from the four sides, and literally be *in* the painting." This, he said, was akin to the method of the Indian sand painters of the western United States. A similar tradition prevailed among Chinese and Japanese artists. Pollock's paintings were intended to be viewed on the wall, but the difference in orientation seems not to have disturbed his sense of balance.

In ceiling paintings, artists have adopted varying principles. When Andrea Mantegna painted on the ceiling of the Camera degli Sposi in the Ducal Palace at Mantua a realistic "oculus" with a view of the open sky and with ladies and winged children peeping downward over a railing, he treated pictorial space as a direct extension of the room's physical space. He relied on "environmental orientation." But when, some thirty-five years later, Michelangelo depicted the story of the Creation on the ceiling of the Sistine Chapel, the spaces of his scenes were totally independent of that of the chapel. The viewer has to rely on "retinal orientation"; he has to match top and bottom with the dimensions of his own visual field by facing in the proper direction as he looks upward. Ceilings were pierced visually once again in the Baroque churches; but whereas the painters of the fifteenth century extended physical space to include that of the painting, those of the seventeenth can be said, on the contrary, to have dematerialized the physical presence of the building by making it a part of the pictorial vision.

Right and Left

The anisotropy of physical space makes us distinguish between top and bottom but less so between left and right. A violin standing upright looks more symmetrical than one lying on its side. Man and animal are sufficiently bilateral creatures to have trouble in telling left from right, *b* from *d*. Corballis and Beale have argued that such a symmetrical response is biologically advantageous so long as nervous systems are focused on movement and orientation in a world in which attack or reward are equally likely from either side.

However, as soon as man learned to use tools that are better operated by one hand than by two, asymmetrical-handedness became an asset; and when sequential thought began to be recorded in linear writing, one lateral direction came to dominate the other. In the words of Goethe: "The more perfect the creature, the more dissimilar its parts get to be."

Visually, lateral asymmetry manifests itself in an uneven distribution of weight and in a dynamic vector leading from the left to the right of the visual field. The phenomenon is unlikely to be noticeable in strictly symmetrical patterns, e.g., the façade of a building, but it is quite effective in paintings. The art historian Heinrich Wölfflin has pointed out that pictures change appearance and lose meaning when turned into their mirror images. He realized that this happens because pictures are "read" from left to right, and naturally the sequence changes when the picture is inverted. Wölfflin noted that the diagonal that runs from bottom left to top right is seen as ascending, the other as descending. Any pictorial object looks heavier at the right side of the picture. For example, when the figure of Sixtus in Raphael's *Sistine Madonna* is moved to the right by inverting the painting, he becomes so heavy that the whole composition seems to topple (Figure 16). This agrees with the experimental

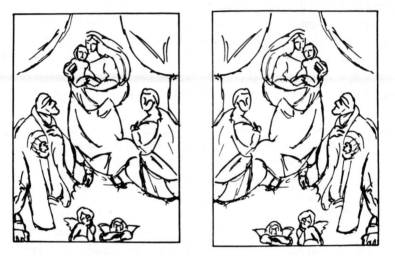

Figure 16

observation that when two equal objects are shown in the left and right halves of the visual field, the one on the right looks larger. For them to appear equal, the one on the left has to be increased in size.

The investigation was carried further by Mercedes Gaffron, notably in a book which attempted to demonstrate that Rembrandt's etchings reveal their true meaning only when we see them as the artist drew them on the plate, and not in the inverted prints, to which we are accustomed. According to Gaffron, the observer experiences a picture as though he were facing its left side. He subjectively identifies with the left, and whatever appears there assumes greatest importance. When one compares photographs with their mirror images, a foreground object in an asymmetrical scene looks closer on the left side than it does on the right. And when the curtain rises in the theater, the audience is inclined to look to its left first and to identify with the characters appearing on that side. Therefore, according to Alexander Dean, among the so-called stage areas the left side (from the audience's viewpoint) is considered the stronger. In a group of actors, the one farthest left dominates the scene. The audience identifies with him and sees the others, from his position, as opponents.

Gaffron relates the phenomenon to the dominance of the left cerebral cortex, which contains the higher brain centers for speech, writing, and reading. If this dominance applies equally to the left visual center, then "there exists a difference in our awareness of visual data in favor of those which are perceived within the right visual field." Vision to the right would be more articulate, which would explain why objects appearing there are more conspicuous. Heightened attentiveness to what goes on at the left would compensate for that asymmetry, and the eye would move spontaneously from the place of first attention to the area of most articulate vision. If this analysis is correct, the right side is distinguished for being the more conspicuous and for increasing an object's visual weight—perhaps because when the center of attention is on the left side of the visual field, the "lever effect" adds to the weight of objects on the right. The left side, in turn, is distinguished for being the more central, the more important, and the more emphasized by the viewer's identification with it. In Grünewald's Crucifixion of the Isenheim altar, the group of Mary and the Evangelist to the left assumes greatest importance next to Christ, who holds the center, whereas John the Baptist to the right is the conspicuous herald, pointing to the scene. If an actor comes on stage from the viewers' right, he is noticed immediately, but the focus of the action remains at the left if it does not lie at the center. In traditional English pantomime the Fairy Queen, with whom the audience is supposed to identify, always appears from the left, whereas the Demon King enters on the prompt side, on the audience's right.

Since a picture is "read" from left to right, pictorial movement toward the right is perceived as being easier, requiring less effort. If, on the contrary, we see a rider traverse the picture from right to left, he seems to be overcoming more resistance, to be investing more effort, and therefore to be going more slowly. Artists prefer sometimes the one effect, sometimes the other. The phenomenon, readily observed when one compares pictures to their mirror images, may be related to findings by the psychologist H. C. van der Meer that "spontaneous movements of the head are executed more quickly from left to right than in the opposite direction," and that when subjects are asked to compare the speeds of two locomotions, one going from left to right, the other from right to left, the movement to the left is seen as faster. One may speculate that the movement to the left is seen as overcoming stronger resistance; it pushes against the current instead of drifting with it.

It should be noted that the directional vector, which makes compositions asymmetrical, has little to do with eye movements. From tracings of eye movements we know that viewers explore a visual scene by roaming about irregularly and concentrating on the centers of major interest. The left-right vector results from this exploration, but it does not derive from the direction of eye movements themselves. Nor is there any hard evidence that lateral bias is related to handedness or eye dominance. Van der Meer claims that scholastic training may have some influence: she found that persons of limited education are less inclined than university students to perceive directed tension toward the right in pictorial objects. She also reports, however, that sensitivity to the left-right vectors appears rather suddenly at the age of fifteen—strangely late if training in reading and writing is decisive.

Balance and the Human Mind

We have noted that weight is distributed unevenly in visual patterns and that these patterns are pervaded by an arrow pointing to "movement" from left to right. This introduces an element of imbalance, which must be compensated if balance is to prevail.

Why should artists strive for balance? Our answer thus far has been that by stabilizing the interrelations between the various forces in a visual system, the artist makes his statement unambiguous. Going a step further, we realize that man strives for equilibrium in all phases of his physical and mental existence, and that this same tendency can be observed not only in all organic life, but also in physical systems.

In physics the principle of entropy, also known as the Second Law of Thermodynamics, asserts that in any isolated system, each successive state represents an irreversible decrease of active energy. The universe tends toward a state of equilibrium in which all existing asymmetries of distribution will be eliminated, and the same holds true for narrower systems if they are sufficiently independent of external influences. According to the physicist L. L. Whyte's "unitary principle," which he believes to underlie all natural activity, "asymmetry decreases in isolable systems." Along the same lines, psychologists have defined motivation as "the disequilibrium of the organism which leads to action for the restoration of stability." Freud, in particular, interpreted his "pleasure principle" to mean that mental events are activated by unpleasant tension, and follow a course that leads to reduction of tension. Artistic activity can be said to be a component of the motivational process in both artist and consumer, and as such participates in the striving for equilibrium. Equilibrium achieved in the visual appearance not only of paintings and sculpture, but also of buildings, furniture, and pottery is enjoyed by man as an image of his broader aspirations.

The quest for balance, however, is not sufficient to describe the controlling tendencies in human motivation generally or in art particularly. We end up with a one-sided, intolerably static conception of the human organism if we picture it as resembling a stagnant pool, stimulated to activity only when a pebble disturbs the balanced peace of its surface and limiting its activity to the reëstablishment of that peace. Freud came closest to accepting the radical consequences of this view. He described man's basic instincts as an expression of the conservatism of all living matter, as an inherent tendency to return to a former state. He assigned a fundamental role to the "death instinct," the striving for a return to inorganic existence. According to Freud's economy principle, man constantly tries to expend as little energy as possible. Man is lazy by nature.

But is he? A human being in good physical and mental health finds himself fulfilled not in inactivity, but in doing, moving, changing, growing, forging ahead, producing, creating, exploring. There is no justification for the strange notion that life consists of attempts to put an end to itself as rapidly as possible. Indeed, the chief characteristic of the live organism may well be that it represents an anomaly of nature in waging an uphill fight against the universal law of entropy by constantly drawing new energy from its environment.

This is not to deny the importance of balance. Balance remains the final goal of any wish to be fulfilled, any task to be accomplished, any problem to be solved. But the race is not run only for the moment of victory. In a later chapter, on *Dynamics*, I shall have occasion to spell out the active counter-principle. Only by looking at the interaction between the energetic life force and the tendency toward balance can we reach a fuller conception of the dynamics activating the human mind and reflected in the mind's products.

Madame Cézanne in a Yellow Chair

It follows from the foregoing discussion that an artist would interpret human experience quite one-sidedly if he allowed balance and harmony to monopolize his work. He can only enlist their help in his effort to give form to a significant theme. *The meaning of the work emerges from the interplay of activating and balancing forces.*

Cézanne's portrait of his wife in a yellow chair (Figure 17) was painted in 1888–1890. What soon strikes the observer is the combination of external tranquillity and strong potential activity. The reposing figure is charged with

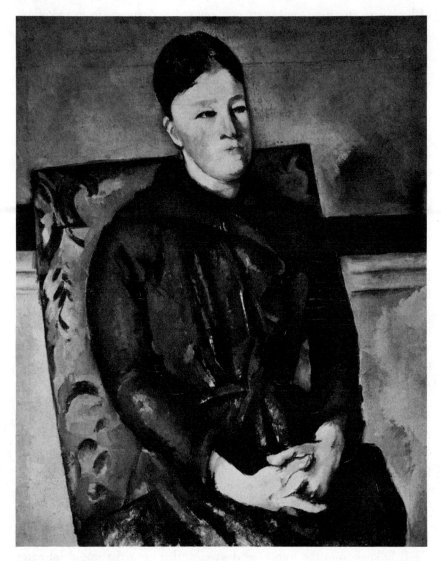

Figure 17
Paul Cézanne. *Mme. Cézanne in a Yellow Chair*, 1888–90. Art Institute, Chicago.

energy, which presses in the direction of her glance. The figure is stable and rooted, but at the same time as light as though it were suspended in space. It rises, yet it rests in itself. This subtle blend of serenity and vigor, of firmness and disembodied freedom, may be described as the particular configuration of forces representing the theme of the work. How is the effect achieved?

The picture has an upright format, the proportion being approximately 5:4. This stretches the whole portrait in the direction of the vertical and reinforces the upright character of the figure, the chair, the head. The chair is somewhat slimmer than the frame, and the figure slimmer than the chair. This creates a scale of increasing slimness, which leads forward from the background over the chair to the foreground figure. Correspondingly, a scale of increasing brightness leads from the dark band on the wall by way of chair and figure to the light face and hands, the two focal points of the composition. At the same time the shoulders and arms form an oval around the middle section of the picture, a centric core of stability that counteracts the pattern of rectangles and is repeated on a smaller scale by the head (Figure 18).

The dark band on the wall divides the background into two horizontal rectangles. Both are more elongated than the whole frame, the lower rectangle being 3:2 and the upper 2:1. This means that these rectangles are stressing the horizontal more vigorously than the frame stresses the vertical. Although the rectangles furnish a counterpoint to the vertical, they also enhance the upward movement of the whole by the fact that vertically the lower rectangle is taller than the upper. According to Denman Ross, the eye moves in the direction of diminishing intervals—that is, in this picture, upward.

The three main planes of the picture—wall, chair, figure—overlap in a movement going from far left to near right. This lateral movement toward the right is counteracted by the location of the chair, which lies mainly in the left half of the picture and thus establishes a retarding countermovement. On the other hand, the dominant rightward movement is enhanced by the asymmetrical placement of the figure in relation to the chair: the figure presses forward by occupying mainly the right half of the chair. Moreover, the figure itself is not quite symmetrical, the left side being slightly larger and thus again emphasizing the sweep toward the right.

Figure and chair are tilted at about the same angle relative to the frame. The chair, however, has its pivot at the bottom of the picture and therefore tilts to the left, whereas the pivot of the figure is its head, which tilts it to the right. The head is firmly anchored on the central vertical. The other focus of the composition, the pair of hands, is thrust slightly forward in an attitude of potential activity. An additional secondary counterpoint further enriches the theme: the head, although at rest, contains clearly directed activity in the watchful eyes and the dynamic asymmetry of the quarter profile. The hands, although moved forward, neutralize each other's action by interlocking.

The free rising of the head is checked not only by its central location but also by its nearness to the upper border of the frame. It rises so much that it is

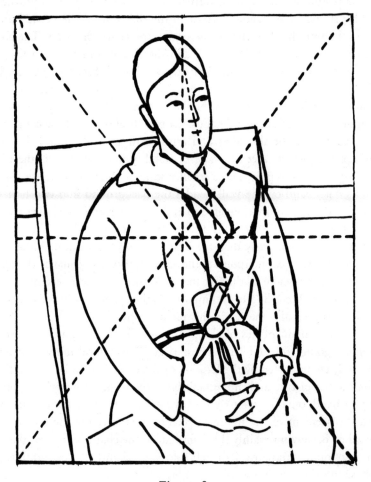

Figure 18

caught by a new base. Just as the musical scale rises from the base of the key tone only to return to a new base at the octave, so the figure rises from the bottom base of the frame to find new repose at the upper edge. (There is, then, a similarity between the structure of the musical scale and the framed composition. They both combine two structural principles: a gradual heightening of intensity with the ascension from bottom to top; and the symmetry of bottom and top that finally transforms ascension from the base into an upward fall toward a new base. Withdrawal from a state of rest turns out to be the mirror image of the return to a state of rest.)

If the foregoing analysis of Cézanne's painting is correct, it will not only hint at the wealth of dynamic relations in the work, it will also suggest how these relations establish the particular balance of rest and activity that impressed us as the theme or content of the picture. To realize how this pattern of visual forces reflects the content is helpful in trying to appraise the artistic excellence of the painting.

Two general remarks should be added. First, the subject matter of the picture is an integral part of the structural conception. Only because shapes are recognized as head, body, hands, chair, do they play their particular compositional role. The fact that the head harbors the mind is at least as important as its shape, color, or location. As an abstract pattern, the formal elements of the picture would have to be quite different to convey similar meaning. The observer's knowledge of what is signified by a seated, middle-aged woman contributes strongly to the deeper sense of the work.

Second, it will have been noticed that the composition rests on point and counterpoint—that is, on many counterbalancing elements. But these antagonistic forces are not contradictory or conflicting. They do not create ambiguity. Ambiguity confuses the artistic statement because it leaves the observer hovering between two or more assertions that do not add up to a whole. As a rule, pictorial counterpoint is hierarchic—that is, it sets a dominant force against a subservient one. Each relation is unbalanced in itself; together they all balance one another in the structure of the whole work.

II   SHAPE

I see an object. I see the world around me. What do these statements imply? For the purposes of everyday life, seeing is essentially a means of practical orientation, of determining with one's eyes that a certain thing is present at a certain place and that it is doing a certain thing. This is identification at its bare minimum. A man entering his bedroom at night may perceive a dark patch on the white pillow and thus "see" that his wife is in the familiar place. Under better lighting conditions he will see more, but in principle orientation in a familiar setting requires only a minimum of cues. A person suffering from visual agnosia because of brain damage may lose the ability to recognize at a glance even such basic shapes as a circle or a triangle. He may nonetheless hold a job and get along in daily life. How does he manage in the street? "On the sidewalk all things are slim—those are people; in the middle of the street, everything is very noisy, bulky, tall—that can be busses, cars." Many people use their unimpaired sense of sight to no better advantage during much of the day.

Vision as Active Exploration

Obviously, seeing can mean more than that. What does it involve? The physicists' description of the optical process is well known. Light is emitted or reflected by objects in the environment. The lenses of the eye project images of these objects onto the retinas, which transmit the message to the brain. But what about the corresponding psychological experience? One is tempted to rely on analogies to the physiological events. The optical image on the retina stimulates some 130 million microscopically small receptors, each of which responds to the wavelength and intensity of the light it receives. Many of these receptors do not do their work independently. Teams of receptors are established by neural wiring. In fact, it is known at least from the eyes of certain animals that such teams of retinal receptors cooperate in reacting to certain movements, edges, kinds of objects. Even so, some ordering principles are needed to transform the infinity of individual stimuli into the objects we see.

From this description of the physiological mechanisms one may be tempted to infer that the correlated processes of shape perception are almost wholly passive and proceed in linear fashion from the registering of the smallest elements to the compounding of larger units. Both these assumptions are misleading. First, the world of images does not simply imprint itself upon a faithfully sensitive organ. Rather, in looking at an object, we reach out for it. With an invisible finger we move through the space around us, go out to the distant places where things are found, touch them, catch them, scan their surfaces, trace their borders, explore their texture. Perceiving shapes is an eminently active occupation.

Impressed by this experience, early thinkers described the physical process of vision accordingly. For example, Plato asserts in his *Timaeus* that the gentle fire that warms the human body flows out through the eyes in a smooth, dense stream of light. Thus a tangible bridge is established between the observer and the thing observed, and over this bridge the impulses of light emanating from the object travel to the eyes and thereby to the soul. Primitive optics has had its day, but the experience from which it sprang remains alive and may still become explicit in poetical description. T. S. Eliot, for example, wrote: "And the unseen eyebeam crossed, for the roses had the look of flowers that are looked at."

Grasping the Essentials

If vision is an active grasp, what does it take hold of? All the innumerable elements of information? Or some of them? If an observer intently examines an object, he finds his eyes well equipped to see minute detail. And yet, visual perception does not operate with the mechanical faithfulness of a camera, which records everything impartially: the whole set of tiny bits of shape and color constituting the eyes and mouth of the person posing for the photograph as well as the corner of the telephone protruding accidentally behind his or her head. What do we see when we see?

Seeing means grasping some outstanding features of objects—the blueness of the sky, the curve of the swan's neck, the rectangularity of the book, the sheen of a piece of metal, the straightness of the cigarette. A few simple lines and dots are readily accepted as "a face," not only by civilized Westerners, who may be suspected of having agreed among one another on such "sign language," but also by babies, savages, and animals. Köhler terrified his chimpanzees by showing them "most primitive stuffed toys" with black buttons for eyes. A clever caricaturist can create the speaking likeness of a person through a few well-chosen lines. We identify an acquaintance at long distance by nothing more than the most elementary proportions or motions.

A few outstanding features not only determine the identity of a perceived object, but also make it appear as a complete, integrated pattern. This applies not only to our image of the object as a whole, but also to any particular part on which our attention is focused. A human face, just like the whole body, is grasped as an overall pattern of essential components—eyes, nose, mouth—into which further detail can be fitted. And if we decide to concentrate on a person's eye, that eye, too, will be perceived as a whole pattern: the circular iris with its central dark pupil, surrounded by the boat-shaped, flagellate frame of the lids.

By no means am I saying that the sense of sight neglects detail. On the contrary, even young children notice slight changes in the appearance of things they know. The minute modifications of muscle tension or skin color that make a face look tired or alarmed are quickly observed. The viewer may, however, be unable to pinpoint what has caused the change in overall appearance because the telltale signs fit smoothly into an integrated framework. When the thing observed lacks this integrity, i.e., when it is seen as an agglomeration of pieces, the details lose their meaning and the whole becomes unrecognizable. This is often true of snapshots in which no pattern of salient shapes organizes the mass of vague and complex nuances. Anthropologists have been surprised to find that in groups unfamiliar with photography people have trouble identifying human figures in the kind of picture that looks so "realistic" to us because we have learned to decipher their devious shapes.

Perceptual Concepts

There is good evidence that in organic development, perception starts with the grasping of outstanding structural features. For example, when two-year-old children and chimpanzees had learned that of two boxes presented to them the one with a triangle of a particular size and shape always contained attractive food, they had no difficulty applying their training to triangles of very different appearance. The triangle was made smaller or larger or turned upside down. A black triangle on white ground was replaced by a white triangle on black ground, or an outlined triangle by a solid one. These changes seemed not to inhibit recognition. Similar results were obtained with rats. Lashley has asserted that simple transpositions of this type "are universal from the insects to primates."

The perceptual process revealed by this kind of behavior is still referred to as "generalization" by psychologists. The term is a vestige of a theoretical approach refuted by the very experiments to which it was applied. It was assumed that perception starts with the recording of individual cases, whose common properties could be realized only by creatures capable of forming concepts intellectually. Thus the similarity of triangles different in size, orientation, and color was thought to be discoverable only by observers whose brain was refined enough to have drawn the general concept of triangularity from a variety of individual observations. That young children and animals, untrained in logical abstraction, performed such tasks without difficulty came as a puzzling surprise.

The experimental findings demanded a complete turnabout in the theory of perception. It seemed no longer possible to think of vision as proceeding from the particular to the general. On the contrary, it became evident that overall structural features are the primary data of perception, so that triangularity is not a late product of intellectual abstraction, but a direct and more elementary experience than the recording of individual detail. The young child sees "doggishness" before he is able to distinguish one dog from another. I shall presently show that this psychological discovery is of decisive importance for the understanding of artistic form.

The new theory poses a peculiar problem. The overall structural features of which the percept is thought to consist are obviously not furnished explicitly by any particular stimulus pattern. If, for example, a human head—or a number of heads—is seen as round, that roundness is not a part of the stimulus. Every head has its particular complex outline, which approaches roundness. If that roundness is not just distilled out intellectually but actually seen, how does it get into the percept? One plausible answer is that the stimulus configuration enters the perceptual process only in the sense that it awakens in the brain a specific pattern of general sensory categories. This pattern "stands for" the stimulation, much as, in a scientific description, a network of general concepts "stands for" an observed phenomenon. Just as the very nature of scientific concepts excludes the possibility of their ever seizing the phenomenon "itself," percepts cannot contain the stimulus material "itself," either totally or partially. The nearest a scientist can get to an apple is to measure its weight, size, shape, location, taste. The nearest a percept can get to the stimulus "apple" is to represent it through a specific pattern of such general sensory qualities as roundness, heaviness, fruity taste, greenness.

As long as we look at a simple, regular shape—a square, say—this formative activity of perception does not become apparent. The squareness seems literally given in the stimulus. But if we leave the world of well-defined, man-made shapes and look around a real landscape, what do we see? Perhaps a rather chaotic mass of trees and brushwood. Some of the tree trunks and branches may show definite directions, to which the eyes can cling, and the whole of a tree or bush often presents a fairly comprehensible sphere or cone shape. We may also take in an overall texture of leafiness and greenness, but there is much in the landscape that the eyes are simply unable to grasp. And it is only to the extent that the confused panorama can be seen as a configuration of clear-cut directions, sizes, geometric shapes, colors, or textures that it can be said to be truly perceived.

If this description is valid, we are compelled to say that perceiving consists in the formation of "perceptual concepts." By usual standards this is uncomfortable terminology, because the senses are supposed to be limited to the concrete whereas concepts deal with the abstract. The process of vision as it was described above, however, seems to meet the conditions of concept formation. Vision deals with the raw material of experience by creating a corresponding pattern of general forms, which are applicable not only to the individual case at hand but to an indeterminate number of other, similar cases as well.

In no way is the use of the word "concept" intended to suggest that perceiving is an intellectual operation. The processes in question must be thought of as occurring within the visual sector of the nervous system. But the term concept is intended to suggest a striking similarity between the elementary activities of the senses and the higher ones of thinking or reasoning. So great is this similarity that many psychologists attributed the achievements of the senses to secret aid supposedly rendered them by the intellect. Those psychologists spoke of unconscious conclusions or computations because they assumed that perception itself could do no more than mechanically register the impingements of the outer world. It seems now that the same mechanisms operate on both the perceptual and the intellectual level, so that terms like concept, judgment, logic, abstraction, conclusion, computation, are needed in describing the work of the senses.

Recent psychological thinking, then, encourages us to call vision a creative activity of the human mind. Perceiving accomplishes at the sensory level what in the realm of reasoning is known as understanding. Every man's eyesight anticipates in a modest way the justly admired capacity of the artist to produce patterns that validly interpret experience by means of organized form. Eyesight is insight.

What Is Shape?

The physical shape of an object is determined by its boundaries—the rectangular edge of a piece of paper, the two surfaces delimiting the sides and the bottom of a cone. Other spatial aspects are not generally considered properties of physical shape: whether the object is placed right-side-up or upside-down, or whether other objects are present nearby. Perceptual shape, by contrast, may change considerably when its spatial orientation or its environment changes. Visual shapes influence one another. In addition, we shall see later (Figure 72) that the shape of an object is determined not only by its boundaries; the skeleton of visual forces created by the boundaries may, in turn, influence the way the boundaries are seen.

Perceptual shape is the outcome of an interplay between the physical object, the medium of light acting as the transmitter of information, and the conditions prevailing in the nervous system of the viewer. Light does not traverse objects, except for those we call translucent or transparent. This means that the eyes receive information only about outer, not inner, shapes. Moreover, light travels in straight lines, and therefore the projections formed on the retinas correspond only to those parts of the outer surface that are linked to the eyes by straight lines. A ship looks different from the front than from the side.

The shape of an object we see does not, however, depend only on its retinal projection at a given moment. Strictly speaking, the image is determined by the totality of visual experiences we have had with that object, or with that kind of object, during our lifetime. If, for example, we are shown a melon that we know to be a mere hollow leftover, a half shell whose missing part is not visible, it may look quite different from a complete melon that on the surface presents us with the identical sight. A car known to contain no motor may actually look different from one known to contain one.

Correspondingly, if someone makes an image of something he has experienced, he can choose how much of the shape he wishes to include. The Western style of painting, created by the Renaissance, restricted shape to what can be seen from a fixed point of observation. The Egyptians, the American Indians, and the cubists ignore this restriction. Children draw the baby in the mother's belly, bushmen include inner organs and intestines in depicting a kangaroo, and a blind sculptor may hollow out the ocular cavities in a clay head and then place round eyeballs in them. It also follows from what I said that one may omit the boundaries of an object and yet draw a recognizable picture of it (Figure 19). When a person who has been asked what a winding staircase looks like describes with his finger a rising spiral, he is not giving the outline but the characteristic main axis, actually nonexistent in the object. Thus the shape of an object is depicted by the spatial features that are considered essential.

The Influence of the Past

Every visual experience is embedded in a context of space and time. Just as the appearance of objects is influenced by that of neighboring objects in space, so also is it influenced by sights that preceded it in time. But to acknowledge these influences is not to say that everything surrounding an object automatically modifies its shape and color or, to pursue the argument to its extreme, that the appearance of an object is merely the product of all the influences exerted upon it. Such a view applied to spatial relations would be patently absurd, and yet it has frequently been applied to relations in time. What a person sees now, we are told, is simply the outcome of what he has seen in the past. If I perceive the four dots of Figure 26 as a square now, it is because I have seen many squares in the past.

The shape relations between present and former times must be considered in a less naive way. First, we cannot go on passing the buck to bygone days without admitting that there must have been a beginning at some point. Gaetano Kanizsa puts it this way: "We have been able to become familiar with the things of our environment precisely because they have constituted themselves for us through forces of perceptual organization acting prior to, and independent of, experience, thereby allowing us to experience them." Second, the interaction between the shape of the present object and that of things seen in the past is not automatic and ubiquitous, but depends on whether a relation is perceived between them. For example, Figure 20*d*, taken by itself, looks like a triangle attached to a vertical line. But in the company of Figures

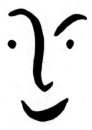

Figure 19

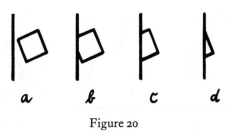

a   *b*   *c*   *d*

Figure 20

20*a*, *b*, and *c*, it will probably be seen as a corner of a square about to disappear behind a wall. This effect is brought about by spatial context, as in Figure 20, or even more compellingly by temporal context, e.g., if *a*, *b*, *c*, *d* follow one another as phases of an animated film. The effect comes about because a sufficiently strong structural resemblance ties the figures together. Similarly, Figure 21 may change its shape abruptly when we are told that it represents a

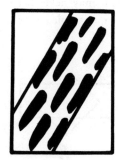

Figure 21

giraffe passing behind a window. Here the verbal description stirs up a visual memory trace that resembles the drawing sufficiently to establish contact with it.

In an experiment familiar to all students of psychology, the perception and reproduction of ambiguous shapes was shown to be influenced by verbal instruction. For example, Figure 22*a* was reproduced as 22*b* when the subject had been told an hourglass would appear briefly on the screen, whereas *c* resulted when the subject expected a table. Such experiments do not prove that what we see is determined entirely by what we have seen before, let alone that such a determination is brought about by language. They do show that memory traces of familiar objects may influence the shape we perceive, and that they may make it appear to us in quite different ways if its structure

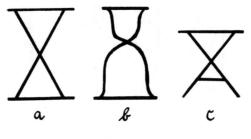

Figure 22

permits. Most stimulus patterns are ambiguous in some way. Figure 22*a* can be read in different ways because it offers a range of freedom within which past experience and expectation can determine whether an hourglass or a table is seen. But no power of the past will make us see Figure 22*a* as a giraffe.

Other experiments have shown that even if a given figure is shown to observers hundreds of times, it may nevertheless remain invisible when presented in a new context. For example, after Figure 23*a* has been learned

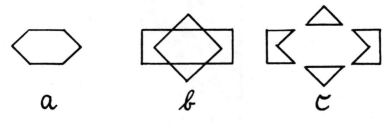

Figure 23

thoroughly, *b* still appears spontaneously as a rectangle and a square, and not as the familiar hexagon surrounded by other shapes, as shown in *c*. The observer is also unlikely to see the well-known number 4 in Figure 24 spontaneously. In such cases camouflage is obtained by putting old connections out of action and introducing new ones, by changing angles into crossings, and by manipulating correspondences, structural axes, and symmetries. Even an overdose of past experience cannot counteract such tricks. To be sure, squares and rectangles are just as familiar as hexagons and fours. What matters is which structures are favored by the given configuration.

The influence of memory is heightened when a strong personal need makes the observer want to see objects of given perceptual properties. Gom-

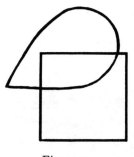

Figure 24

brich says: "The greater the biological relevance an object has to us, the more will we be attuned to its recognition—and the more tolerant will therefore be our standards of formal correspondence." A man waiting at a street corner for his girl friend will see her in almost every approaching woman, and this tyranny of the memory trace will get stronger as the minutes pass on the clock. A psychoanalyst will discover genitals and wombs in every work of art. The stress that needs exert on perception is exploited by psychologists in the Rorschach test. The structural ambiguity of the ink blots used in this test allows a great variety of interpretations, so that the individual observer is likely to spontaneously choose one that points to his own mental state.

Seeing Shape

How can the spatial features that represent shape be described? The most accurate way might seem to be to determine the locations of all the points that make up these features. In his treatise *Della Statua*, Leon Battista Alberti highly recommended to the sculptors of the Renaissance the procedure illustrated in Figure 25. By means of ruler, protractor, and plumb line, any point of the statue can be described in terms of angles and distances. With a sufficient number of such measurements, one could make a duplicate of the statue. Or, says Alberti, half the figure can be made on the island of Paros and the other in the Carrara Mountains, and still the parts will fit together. It is characteristic of this method that it allows reproduction of an individual object, but that the result comes as a surprise. In no way can the nature of the statue's shape be gleaned from the measurements, which must be applied before the result is known.

The procedure is very similar to what happens in analytic geometry when, in order to determine the shape of a figure, the points of which the figure consists are defined spatially by their distances from a vertical (y) and a hori-

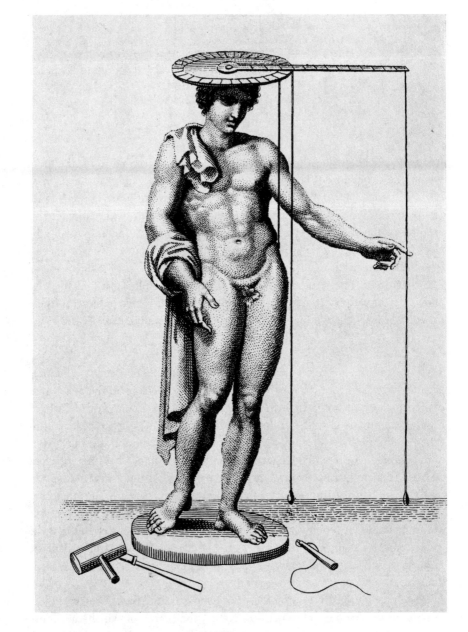

Figure 25

zontal (x) Cartesian coordinate. Here, too, a sufficient number of measurements will permit construction of the figure. Whenever possible, however, the geometrician will go beyond the mere accumulation of unrelated data. He will try to find a formula that indicates the location of any and every point of the figure—that is, he looks for an overall law of construction. For example, the equation for a circle with the radius r is:

$$(x - a)^2 + (y - b)^2 = r^2$$

if the center of the circle lies at the distance a from the y-axis and at the distance b from the x-axis. Even a formula of this kind, however, does little more than summarize the locations of an infinite number of points, which happen to add up to a circle. It does not tell us much about the nature of the resulting figure.

How does the sense of sight take hold of shape? No person blessed with a healthy nervous system apprehends shape by patching it together through the tracing of its parts. Visual agnosia, to which I referred earlier, is a pathological incapacity to grasp a pattern as a whole. Someone suffering from this condition can follow an outline with head or finger motions and then conclude from the sum of his explorations that the whole must be, say, a triangle. But he is unable to see a triangle. He can do no better than the tourist who, by reconstructing his meandering path through the maze of an unfamiliar town, concludes that he has walked in a kind of circle.

The normal sense of sight does nothing of the sort. Most of the time it grasps shape immediately. It seizes an overall pattern. But how is this pattern determined? At the meeting of the stimulus projected on the retinas and the nervous system processing that projection, what makes for the shape that appears in consciousness? When we look at a simple outline figure, there seems to be no problem, not much of a choice. And yet, why do we tend to see the four dots of Figure 26 as a square like Figure 27a, but hardly as a leaning diamond or a profile face (Figures 27b, c), even though the latter shapes contain the four points as well?

If four more dots are added to Figure 26, the square disappears from the now octagonal or even circular pattern (Figure 28). White circles or—for some observers—squares appear in the centers of the crosses shown in Figure 29, even though there is no trace of a circular or square-shaped contour. Why circles and squares rather than any other shape?

Phenomena of this kind find their explanation in what gestalt psychologists describe as the basic law of visual perception: *Any stimulus pattern tends to be seen in such a way that the resulting structure is as simple as the given conditions permit.*

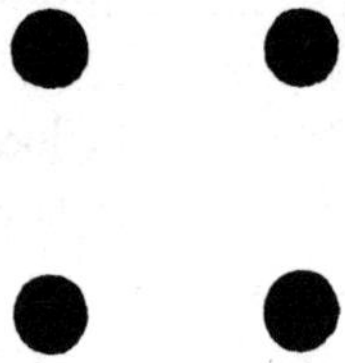

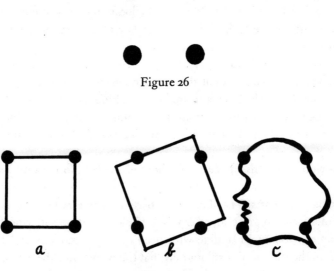

Figure 26

Figure 27

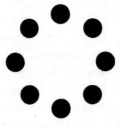

Figure 28

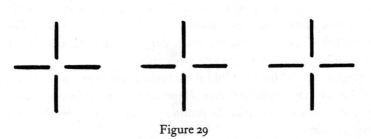

Figure 29

Simplicity

What do we mean by simplicity? First, it may be described as the subjective experience and judgment of an observer who feels no difficulty in understanding what is presented to him. What Spinoza said about order can be applied to simplicity. According to a passage in the *Ethics*, we firmly believe that there is order in things themselves even though we know nothing about these things or their nature. "For, when things are arranged in such a way that when they are represented to us by the senses we can easily imagine and, in consequence, easily remember them, we call them well ordered and, in the opposite case, call them badly ordered or confused." An experimenter can use objective criteria to determine how easy or hard certain patterns are on observers. Christopher Alexander and Susan Carey asked the following questions: In a collection of patterns, which pattern can be recognized most quickly? How do the patterns rank in order of seeming simplicity? Which patterns are the easiest to remember? Which are the most likely to be confused with others? Which are the easiest to describe in words?

The subjective reactions explored in such experiments are only one aspect of our problem. We must also determine the objective simplicity of visual objects by analyzing their formal properties. Objective and subjective simplicity do not always run parallel. A listener may find a sculpture simple because he is unaware of its intricacy; or he may find it confusingly complex because he has little acquaintance with even moderately elaborate structures. Or he may be puzzled only because he is not accustomed to a new, "modern" style of shaping things, simple though that style may be in itself. Regardless of how particular viewers react, we may ask: How can simplicity be determined by analysis of the shapes constituting a pattern? A temptingly elementary and exact approach would be that of merely counting the number of elements: Of how many lines or colors does this picture consist? Such a criterion, however, is misleading. Granted, the number of elements has an influence on the simplicity of the whole, but as the musical examples of Figure 30 show, the longer sequence may be simpler than the shorter. The seven elements of the full-tone scale (*a*) are combined in a pattern that grows in a consistent direction and by equal steps. If we consider this sequence by itself —not, for example, in relation to the diatonic mode—it is surely simpler than the four-tone theme of Figure 30*b*, which consists of a descending fourth, an ascending sixth, and an ascending third. The theme uses two different directions and three different intervals. Its structure is more complex.

An elementary visual example can be found in the above-mentioned ex-

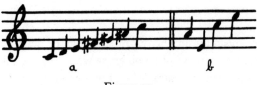

Figure 30

periment by Alexander and Carey, for which a horizontal row of three black and four white squares was used. The smallest number of parts obtainable is two: a bar of three black squares adjacent to a bar of four white ones (Figure 31). Actually, the subjects judged this arrangement the second simplest

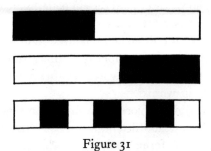

Figure 31

among the 35 possible combinations if the black bar was on the left, and the fourth simplest when the white bar was on the left. Regarded as simpler than both was the arrangement that contained the largest possible number of units: the regular alternation of black and white squares was considered the simplest possible structure.

If we proceed from a linear sequence to the second dimension we find, for example, that the regular square, with its four edges and four angles, is simpler than the irregular triangle (Figure 32). In the square all four edges are equal

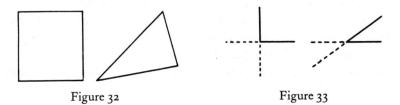

Figure 32   Figure 33

in length and lie at the same distance from the center. Only two directions are used, the vertical and the horizontal, and all angles are the same. The whole pattern is highly symmetrical around four axes. The triangle has fewer elements, but they vary in size and location, and there is no symmetry.

A straight line is simple because it uses one unchangeable direction. Parallel lines are simpler than lines meeting at an angle because their relation is defined by one constant distance. A right angle is simpler than other angles because it produces a subdivision of space based on the repetition of one and the same angle (Figure 33). Figures 34*a* and *b* are made up of identical parts,

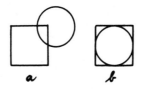

Figure 34

but *b* is the simpler pattern because the parts have a common center. An additional simplifying factor is conformity to the spatial framework of vertical and horizontal orientation. In Figure 32 the square conforms to this framework with all its edges, the triangle with none.

These examples suggest that we may arrive at a good approximate definition of simplicity by counting not the elements, but the structural features. Such features, as far as shape is concerned, can be described by distance and angle. If I increase the number of equally spaced radii drawn in a circle from ten to twenty, the number of elements has increased but the number of structural features is unchanged; for whatever the number of radii, one distance and one angle are sufficient to describe the build of the whole.

Structural features must be determined for the total pattern. Fewer features in a limited area will often make for more features in the whole, which is another way of saying that what makes a part simpler may make the whole more complex. In Figure 35 the straight line is the simplest connection between points *a* and *b* only as long as we overlook the fact that a curve will make for a simpler total pattern.

Julian Hochberg has attempted to define simplicity (he preferred the value-laden term "figural goodness") by means of information theory: "The smaller the amount of information needed to define a given organization as compared to the other alternatives, the more likely that the figure will be so perceived." Later he specified the needed information by three quantitative features: the number of angles enclosed within the figure, the number of different angles divided by the total number of angles, and the number of con-

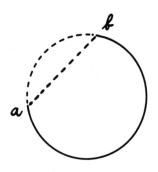

Figure 35

tinuous lines. It should be noted that the features in question are not those actually drawn on paper, but those perceived in the drawing. For example, a wire cube drawn in central perspective contains only one size of angle and one size of edge when perceived as a regular cube, but at least nine sizes of angle and ten sizes of edge in the actual drawing. For precisely this reason, the three-dimensional cube is considered simpler than its two-dimensional projection.

If some such method of counting structural features correlates sufficiently with the simplicity level of perceived patterns, it will suffice for scientific measurement. However, both the psychologist and the artist must come to realize that the perceptual experience of looking at a figure cannot be described as the sum of the perceived components. The character of a sphere, for example, resides in its concentric symmetry and the constant curvature of its surface, even though a sphere can be constructed, identified, and commissioned over the telephone by the length of its radius alone. Moreover, simple geometrical figures are obviously a far cry from the intricate kind of pattern we commonly meet in art and nature. But then, theoretical constructs never do pretend to more than approximate the complexities of reality.

So far I have discussed absolute simplicity. In an absolute sense, a folk song is simpler than a symphony and a child's drawing is simpler than a painting by Tiepolo. But we must also consider relative simplicity, which applies to every complexity level. When someone wishes to make a statement or needs to fulfill a function he must concern himself with two questions: What is the simplest structure that will serve the purpose (parsimony), and what is the simplest way of organizing this structure (orderliness)?

Compositions by adults are rarely as simple as the conceptions of children; when they are we tend to doubt the maturity of the maker. This is so because the human brain is the most complex mechanism in nature, and when a person fashions a statement that is to be worthy of him, he must make it rich enough to reflect the richness of his mind. Simple objects may please and satisfy us by serving limited functions appropriately, but all true works of art are quite complex even when they look "simple." If we examine the surfaces of a good Egyptian statue, the shapes that make up a Greek temple, or the formal relations in a good piece of African sculpture, we find that they are anything but elementary. The same holds true for the bisons of the prehistoric caves, the Byzantine saints, or the paintings of Henri Rousseau and Mondrian. The reason why we may hesitate to describe the average child's drawings or an Egyptian pyramid or some high-rise office buildings as "works of art" is precisely that a minimum of complexity, or richness, seems to be indispensable. Some time ago, the architect Peter Blake wrote: "In another year or so there will be only one type of industrial product in the U.S.—a shiny, smoothly finished lozenge. The small lozenges will be vitamin capsules; the bigger ones will be television sets or typewriters; and the big ones will be automobiles, planes or trains." Blake was not suggesting that in his opinion we were moving toward a peak of artistic culture.

Relative simplicity, I have said, implies parsimony and orderliness whatever the level of complexity. Charlie Chaplin once said to Jean Cocteau that after completing a film, one must "shake the tree" and keep only what holds fast to the branches. The *principle of parsimony*, adopted by scientists, demands that when several hypotheses fit the facts, the simplest one should be accepted. According to Cohen and Nagel, "one hypothesis is said to be simpler than another if the number of independent types of elements in the first is smaller than in the second." The chosen hypothesis must permit the scientist to explain all aspects of the phenomenon under investigation with the minimum number of assumptions, and if possible should explain not only a particular set of things or events, but the whole range of phenomena in the same category.

The principle of parsimony is valid aesthetically in that the artist must not go beyond what is needed for his purpose. He follows the example of nature, which, in the words of Isaac Newton, "does nothing in vain, and more is in vain when less will serve; for Nature is pleased with simplicity, and affects not the pomp of superfluous causes." To say too much is as bad as to say too little, and to make one's point too complicatedly is as bad as to make it too simply. The writings of Martin Heidegger and the poems of Wallace Stevens are no more intricate than they need to be.

The great works of art are complex, but we also praise them for "having simplicity," by which we mean that they organize a wealth of meaning and form in an overall structure that clearly defines the place and function of every detail in the whole. This way of organizing a needed structure in the simplest possible way may be called its *orderliness*. It may seem paradoxical for Kurt Badt to say that Rubens is one of the simplest of all artists. He explains, "It is true that in order to grasp his simplicity, one must be able to understand an order that dominates an enormous world of active forces." Badt defines artistic simplicity as "the wisest ordering of means based on insight into the essentials, to which everything else must be subservient." As examples of artistic simplicity he mentions Titian's method of creating a painting from a tissue of short brushstrokes. "The double system of surfaces and outlines is abandoned. A new degree of simplicity is achieved. The entire picture is accomplished by one procedure only. Until then, line was determined by the objects; it was used only for boundaries or shadows or, perhaps, highlights. Now line also represents brightness, space, and air, thus fulfilling a demand for greater simplicity, which requires that the lasting stability of form be identified with the ever-changing process of life." Similarly, at a certain point in his development, Rembrandt for simplicity's sake renounced the use of the color blue, because it did not fit his chords of golden brown, red, ocher, and olive green. Badt also cites the graphic technique of Dürer and his contemporaries, who represented shadow and volume by the same curved strokes they used to outline their figures, thus again achieving simplicity by a unification of means.

In a mature work of art all things seem to resemble one another. Sky, sea, ground, trees, and human figures begin to look as though they were made of the same substance, which falsifies the nature of nothing but recreates everything by subjecting it to the unifying power of the great artist. Every great artist gives birth to a new universe, in which familiar things look as they have never before looked to anyone. This new appearance, rather than being distortion or betrayal, reinterprets the ancient truth in a grippingly fresh, enlightening way. The unity of the artist's conception leads to a simplicity that, far from being incompatible with complexity, shows its virtue only in mastering the abundance of human experience rather than escaping to the poverty of abstinence.

Subtle complexity can be obtained by combining geometrically simple shapes; and the combinations, in turn, may be held together by a simplifying orderliness. Figure 36 shows the compositional scheme of a relief by Ben Nicholson. Its elements are as simple as can be found anywhere in a work of art. The composition consists of one regular and complete circle plus a number of rectangular figures, which lie parallel to one another and to the frame.

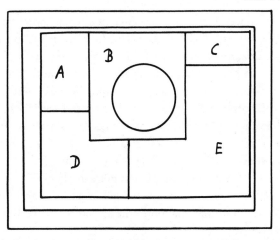

Figure 36

Yet even without the differences in depth that in the original relief play the various planes against one another, the total effect is not elementary. Most of the form units do not interfere with one another, but rectangle B overlaps D and E (Figure 37). The three outermost rectangles, which frame the composition, are roughly but not exactly of the same proportion, and their centers, though close, do not coincide. The close approximation of proportion and location produces considerable tension by compelling the observer to make subtle distinctions. This holds true for the entire composition. Two of the

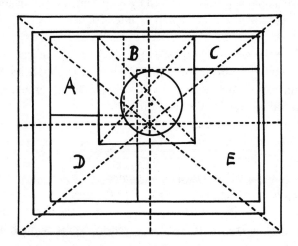

Figure 37

inner units, A and C, are clearly rectangular; D, when completed, is perceived as a square (since it is a little broader than high, which compensates for the familiar overestimation of the vertical); B and the completed E look marginally rectangular, but their proportions flirt with squareness. The center of the whole pattern does not coincide with any point in the composition, nor does the central horizontal touch any corner. The central vertical axis comes close enough to the center of B to create an element of simplicity in the relation between that rectangle and the total area of the work. The same is true for the circle, and yet both B and the circle deviate enough from the central vertical to look clearly asymmetrical in relation to each other. The circle lies neither in the center of B nor in the center of the whole pattern; and the overlapping corners of B have no simple relation to the structures of the rectangles D and E, into which they intrude.

Why does the whole pattern hold together nevertheless? Some of the simplifying factors have already been mentioned. In addition, the prolongation of the bottom edge of C would touch the circle; and if A were enlarged to a square, the corner of that square would touch the circle also. These coincidences help to keep the circle in place. And, of course, there is the overall balance of proportions, distances, and directions, less easily analyzed but equally important for the unity of the whole.

Every painting or sculpture carries meaning. Whether representational or "abstract," it is "about something"; it is a statement about the nature of our existence. Similarly, a useful object, such as a building or a teapot, interprets its function to the eyes. The simplicity of such objects, therefore, involves not only their visual appearance in and by itself, but also the relation between the image seen and the statement it is intended to convey. In language, a sentence whose intricate verbal structure exactly corresponds to the intricate structure of the thought to be expressed has a welcome simplicity; whereas any discrepancy between form and meaning interferes with simplicity. Short words in short sentences do not necessarily make for a simple statement—popular prejudice to the contrary notwithstanding.

In the arts, a shaped mass of clay or an arrangement of lines may be meant to represent a human figure. An abstract painting may be called *Victory Boogie-Woogie*. The meaning or content can be relatively simple (*Reclining Nude*), or quite complex (*Rebellion Tamed by Wise Government*). The character of the meaning and its relation to the visible form intended to express it help to determine the degree of simplicity of the whole work. If a percept that is quite simple in itself is employed to express something complex, the result is not simple. If a deaf mute who wants to tell a story utters a groan, the structure of the sound is simple enough; but the total result involves as much tension between the audible form and what it is meant to convey as the squeezing of a human body into a cylindrical corset.

The discrepancy between complex meaning and simple form may produce something quite complicated. Suppose a painter represented Cain and Abel by two figures that looked exactly alike and faced each other symmetrically in the identical attitude. Here the meaning would involve the differences between good and evil, murderer and victim, acceptance and rejection, whereas the picture would convey the similarity of the two men. The effect of the pictorial statement would not be simple.

These examples show that simplicity requires a correspondence in structure between meaning and tangible pattern. Gestalt psychologists call such structural correspondence "isomorphism." It is a requirement for design in the applied arts as well. To return to an example I used earlier: if a television set and a typewriter looked exactly alike, we would be deprived of a desirably simple correspondence between form and function. The simplification of form would diminish communication—not to mention the impoverishment of our visual world.

Simplification Demonstrated

According to the basic law of visual perception, any stimulus pattern tends to be seen in such a way that the resulting structure is as simple as the given conditions permit. This tendency will be less apparent when the stimulus is so strong that it exerts a compelling control. Under such conditions the receptor mechanism is free only to arrange the given elements in the simplest possible way. When the stimulus is weak, the organizing power of perception can assert itself more fully. According to Lucretius, "when far off we see the foursquare towers of a city, they often appear to be round," and Leonardo da Vinci observes that when the figure of a man is seen from afar, "he will seem a very small round dark body. He will appear round because distance diminishes the various parts so much as to leave nothing visible except the greater mass." Why does the reduction make the beholder see a round shape? The answer is that distance weakens the stimulus to such an extent that the perceptual mechanism is left free to impose upon it the simplest possible shape—namely, the circle. Such weakening of the stimulus also occurs under other conditions, for example, when the perceived pattern is dimly illuminated or exposed for only a split second. Distance in time has much the same effect as distance in space; when the actual stimulus has disappeared, the remaining memory trace weakens.

Experimenters have investigated the effects of weakened stimuli on perception. The results of these experiments may look confusing and even contradictory. In the first place, percepts and memory traces are not directly accessible to the experimenter. They must be communicated to him by the observer in some indirect way. The observer gives a verbal description, or makes a drawing, or chooses from a number of patterns the one most resembling the figure he saw. None of these methods is very satisfactory, since there is no telling how much of the result is due to the primary experience itself and how much to the medium of communication. For our purposes, however, this distinction is not essential.

In considering drawings made by the observers, one must take into account their technical ability as well as their personal standards of exactness. A person may consider a rather irregular scrawl a sufficiently exact image of the remembered form, in which case the details of his drawings cannot be taken literally. Unless some leeway between the actual drawing and the intended image is provided for, the interpretation of results will lead to confusion. Furthermore, the perceiving and remembering of a pattern is not an isolated process. It is subject to the influence of the innumerable potentially active memory traces in the observer's mind. Under these conditions we cannot expect the underlying tendencies clearly to manifest themselves in all cases. It is best, therefore, to base an interpretation on examples that illustrate some clear-cut effect.

Traditionally it was assumed that with the passing of time memory traces slowly fade out. They dissolve, become less distinct, and drop their individual characteristics, thus looking more and more like everything and nothing. This amounts to a gradual loss of articulate structure. Later investigators raised the question whether this process did not involve more tangible modifications from one structural form to another, changes that could be described in concrete terms. Indeed such changes have been identified. As a simple demonstration, Figure 38 is exposed for a split second to a group of persons who were asked beforehand to keep paper and pencil ready, and to draw without much

Figure 38

reflection but as accurately as possible what they have seen. The examples in Figure 39 schematically illustrate the kind of result that is typically obtained.

The samples give an idea of the impressive variety of reactions, which is due partly to individual differences and partly to such factors as differences in

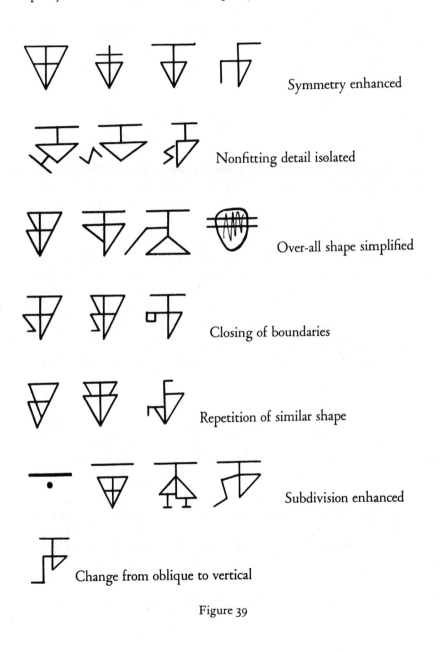

Symmetry enhanced

Nonfitting detail isolated

Over-all shape simplified

Closing of boundaries

Repetition of similar shape

Subdivision enhanced

Change from oblique to vertical

Figure 39

exposure time and the distance of the observer. All the samples represent simplifications of the stimulus pattern. One admires the ingenuity of the solutions, the imaginative power of vision, which reveals itself even though the drawings are done quickly, spontaneously, and with no other pretense than faithfully to record what has been seen. Some aspects of the figures may be graphic interpretations of the percept rather than properties of the percept itself. Nevertheless, such an experiment gives sufficient evidence that seeing and remembering involves the creation of organized wholes.

Leveling and Sharpening

Although the observers reveal in their drawings (Figure 39) a tendency to reduce the number of structural features and thereby to simplify the pattern, other tendencies are active as well. For example, the fourth drawing in the row "Subdivision enhanced" is more complex than the model in that it breaks the central horizontal line and thereby intensifies rather than reduces the dynamics of the model. This countertendency manifested itself more clearly in experiments first performed by Friedrich Wulf. He used figures containing slight ambiguities, such as Figure 40*a* and *d*. The two wings of *a* are almost but not quite symmetrical, and the small rectangle in *d* is slightly off-center. When such figures are presented under conditions that keep the stimulus control weak enough to leave observers with a margin of freedom, two principal types of reaction follow. In making drawings of what they have seen, some subjects perfect the symmetry of the model (*b*, *e*) and thereby increase its simplicity; they reduce the number of structural features. Others exaggerate the asymmetry (*c*, *f*). They, too, simplify the model, but in the

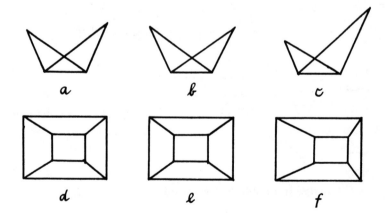

Figure 40

opposite way. Instead of reducing the number of structural features, they discriminate the given ones more clearly from one another. By eliminating the ambiguities, they certainly make the task of the viewer simpler.

Both tendencies, the one toward "leveling" and the one toward "sharpening," are applications of one superordinate tendency, namely, the tendency to make perceptual structure as clear-cut as possible. Gestalt psychologists have called this tendency "the law of prägnanz," and unfortunately have not distinguished it sufficiently from the tendency toward simplest structure. (To compound the confusion, translators have rendered the German *Prägnanz* with the English *pregnance*, which means very nearly the opposite.)

Leveling is characterized by such devices as unification, enhancement of symmetry, reduction of structural features, repetition, dropping of nonfitting detail, elimination of obliqueness. Sharpening enhances differences, stresses obliqueness. Leveling and sharpening frequently occur in the same drawing, just as in a person's memory large things may be recalled as larger, small ones as smaller, than they actually were, but at the same time the total situation may survive in a simpler, more orderly form.

It will have become evident that leveling and sharpening differ not only in the shapes they create, but in their effect on dynamics. Leveling involves also a reduction of the tension inherent in the visual pattern. Sharpening increases that tension. This will be evident from the examples in Figure 40. Art historians will be reminded here of the difference between classicistic and expressionistic styles. Classicism tends toward simplicity, symmetry, normality, and the reduction of tension. Expressionism heightens the irregular, the asymmetrical, the unusual, and the complex, and strives for the increase of tension. The two types of style epitomize two tendencies whose interplay, in varying ratio, constitutes the structure of any work of visual art and indeed of any visual pattern. More will be said about this later.

A Whole Maintains Itself

It appears that the things we see behave as wholes. On the one hand, what is seen in a particular area of the visual field depends strongly on its place and function in the total context. On the other hand, the structure of the whole may be modified by local changes. This interplay between whole and part is not automatic and universal. A part may or may not be influenced noticeably by a change in the total structure; and a change in shape or color may have little effect on the whole when the change lies, as it were, off the structural track. All these are aspects of the fact that any visual field behaves as a gestalt.

This is not necessarily true for the physical objects that serve as stimuli to the sense of sight. A body of water is a gestalt since what happens in one place has an effect on the whole. But a rock is not, and in a countryside trees and clouds and water interact only within the limits of severe constraints. Moreover, whatever physical interaction occurs in the world we see does not necessarily have a visual counterpart. An electric radiator has a strong but unseen effect on a nearby violin, whereas a pale human face made to look green by contrast with an adjacent red dress suffers from a perceptual effect that has no physical counterpart.

It did not matter to the marble torso of Michelangelo's Madonna that a deranged man broke one of her arms with a hammer; nor does the pigment on a canvas undergo any physical change when half the picture is cut off. The interactions we observe visually must be due to processes in our nervous system. The architect Eduardo Torroja observes: "The total vision of a straight line, a curve, or a volume is influenced by the other surrounding lines and planes. So, for example, the straight line of the tie member of a flattened arch may appear as a curve, whose convexity is opposite to that of the arch. A rectangle placed within an ogive has a deformed shape."

Earlier I suggested that interactions within the visual field are controlled by the law of simplicity, which asserts that the perceptual forces constituting such a field will organize themselves in the simplest, most regular, most symmetrical pattern available under the circumstances. The extent to which this law can impose itself depends in each case on the constraints prevailing in the system. As long as an articulate stimulus pattern is projected upon the retinas of the eyes, perceptual organization must accept this given shape; it must limit itself to grouping or subdividing the existing shape in such a way that the simplest possible structure results. As Figures 38 and 39 have shown, further simplification becomes possible when the effect of the stimulus input is weakened by short exposure, dim light, or some similar condition.

In visual experience we observe only the results of this organizing process. Its causes must be sought in the nervous system. Of the exact nature of such physiological organization, next to nothing is known. By inference from what occurs in vision one can tell that the organization must involve field processes. Wolfgang Köhler has pointed out that field processes are frequently observed in physics and therefore can occur in the brain as well, since the nervous system belongs to the physical world. "As a familiar example," Köhler wrote, "take the stationary distribution of water current in a network of pipes. By mutual influence throughout the system, the extended process maintains itself as a whole."

Three examples will suffice to illustrate the strength and ubiquity of the tendency in a visual whole to maintain or re-establish its simplest state. The psychologist Ivo Kohler has been working with distorting goggles. His curiosity was aroused by the fact that, considering the defects of man's visual apparatus, "the image is better than it should be." For example, the lens of the eye is not corrected for spherical aberration, and yet straight lines do not look curved. Kohler used prismatic lenses, which create a "rubber world": when the head is turned right or left, objects become broader or narrower; when the head is moved up or down, objects seem to slant first one way, then the other. After the goggles have been worn for several weeks, however, the distortions disappear and the usual stable simplicity of visual shapes re-establishes itself.

Other observations show that when brain injuries cause blind areas in the visual field, incomplete figures are seen as complete, provided their shape is sufficiently simple and enough of it appears in the sighted area. An extensive injury to one of the cortical lobes in the back of the brain may black out either the right or left half of the visual field completely, a condition known as hemianopia. If the patient is made to fixate the center of a circle for one tenth of a second, even though only half of it actually stimulates the visual centers in his brain, he reports seeing a complete circle. On being shown a smaller portion of the circle he will report seeing "a kind of bow," and the same is true for half an ellipse. The patient is not merely guessing by inference from past experience, but actually sees either the complete or the incomplete figure. In fact, even the afterimages of completed figures are perceived as complete. Apparently, when enough of the projected figure is received by the visual cortex, the electrochemical process caused by the projection can complete itself in the brain and thereupon produces the percept of a complete whole in consciousness.

Finally, the psychologist Fabio Metelli has contributed a particularly elegant reference to an elementary phenomenon, one likely to be taken for granted. If one rotates a black disk around its center, no locomotion will be perceived although every spot of the entire surface is actually moving. If, however, one rotates a black square around its center, the entire surface is seen as rotating, including any circular surface (Figure 41), which by itself would show no locomotion at all. Whether a moving spot is perceived as being in motion or at rest depends on the simplest visual situation available for the total pattern: for the square it is rotation, for the disk it is repose.

Subdivision

Even though well-organized figures cling to their integrity and complete themselves when mutilated or distorted, we should not assume that such fig-

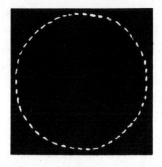

Figure 41

ures are always perceived as undivided, compact masses. To be sure, a black disk is seen as one unbroken thing rather than, say, as two halves. This is so because undivided unity is the simplest way of perceiving the disk. But what about Figure 42? Although on paper it is a continuous mass, an observer has

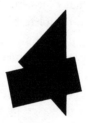

Figure 42

great difficulty seeing it that way. At first glance, the figure may look awkward, strained, not in its final shape. As soon as it appears as a combination of rectangle and triangle, tension ceases, the figure settles down and looks comfortable and definitive. It has assumed the simplest possible structure compatible with the given stimulus.

The rule is readily derived from Figure 43. When the square (*a*) is divided into two halves, the whole pattern prevails over its parts because the 1:1 symmetry of the square is simpler than the shapes of the two 1:2 rectangles. Even so, we can manage at the same time to single out the two halves without much effort. If now we divide a 1:2 rectangle (*b*) in the same manner, the figure breaks apart quite readily because the simplicity of the two squares imposes itself against the less compact shape of the whole. If, on the other hand, we wish to obtain a particularly coherent rectangle, we may apply

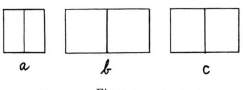

Figure 43

our subdivision to the rectangle of the golden section (*c*), in which the longer, horizontal side is related to the shorter, vertical side as the sum of both is to the longer. Traditionally and psychologically, this proportion of 1: .618 . . . has been considered particularly satisfying because of its combination of unity and dynamic variety. Whole and parts are nicely adjusted in strength so that the whole prevails without being threatened by a split, but at the same time the parts retain some self-sufficiency.

If subdivision depends on the simplicity of the whole as compared to that of the parts, we can study the relation between the two factors by leaving the shapes of the parts constant while varying their configuration. In Figure 44

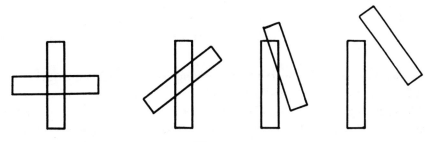

Figure 44

we move from the maximum coherence of the cross shape to the virtual disappearance of any integrated pattern at all. We also notice in the two central examples a distinct visual tension: greater simplicity and a corresponding relaxation of tension would be obtained if the two bars came apart, either in the depth dimension—and in fact the two bars seem to lie in slightly different planes—or sideways. This tension is absent in the two outer figures, in which the two components either fit in a tightly symmetrical whole or are removed from interfering with each other.

What holds true for subdivision in isolated figures must be applied to the entire visual field. In complete darkness or when we watch a cloudless sky, we are presented with unbroken unity. Most of the time, however, the visual world is made up of more or less distinct units. A given area of the field stands out amidst its surroundings insofar as its shape is both clear and simple in itself and independent of the structure of the surrounding area. Conversely, an area of the field is hard to isolate when its own shape is quite irregular or when, in part or as a whole, it fits snugly into a larger context. (Figure 23*a* disappears in the context *b*, whereas it retains much of its identity in Figure 45.)

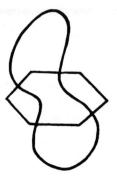

Figure 45

Shape is not the only factor determining subdivision. Similarities and differences in brightness and color can be even more decisive, and so can differences between motion and repose. An example involving the perception of movement can be taken from Metelli's experiments. Figure 46 is perceived spontaneously as a combination of a white bar and a complete or incomplete

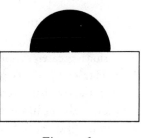

Figure 46

disk or circle. If subsequently the figure is rotated slowly around the center of the circle, it subdivides even more radically. The black disk seizes the possibility of remaining still, whereas the white bar circles around it, uncovering different portions of the immobile disk.

Why the Eyes Often Tell the Truth

Subdivision of shape is of the greatest biological value because it is a principal condition for discerning objects. Goethe has observed that "Erscheinung und Entzweien sind synonym," meaning that appearance and segregation are one and the same. But to see shapes is not enough. If visual shapes are to be useful, they must correspond to the objects out there in the physical world. What is it that enables us to see an automobile as one thing and the person in it as another, rather than paradoxically unifying part of the automobile and part of the person into one misleading monster? Sometimes our eyes fool us. Wertheimer has cited the example of a bridge that forms a compelling whole with its own mirror image in the water (Figure 47). Con-

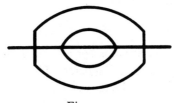

Figure 47

stellations are seen in the sky that do not correspond to the actual locations of the stars in physical space. In military camouflage the unity of objects is broken up into parts that fuse with the environment, a technique used also by nature for the protection of animals. The eyes of frogs, fishes, birds, and mammals tend to betray the presence of an otherwise well-protected animal by the striking simplicity and independence of their round shape, and are therefore frequently concealed by dark stripes crossing the head. Modern artists have experimented with reorganizing objects in ways that contradict everyday experience. Gertrude Stein reports that when, during the First World War, Picasso saw the camouflage paint of guns he exclaimed in surprise: "We are the ones who made this—it's cubism!"

Why, then, do our eyes serve us well most of the time? It is more than a lucky coincidence. For one thing, the man-made part of the world is fitted to human needs. Only the secret doors in old castles and modern automobiles blend with the walls. The letter boxes in London are painted a bright red to make them stand out from their surroundings. However, not only the mind of man but physical nature as well must obey the law of simplicity. The outer shape of natural things is as simple as conditions permit; and this simplicity of shape favors visual segregation. The redness and roundness of apples, as distinct from the different colors and shapes of leaves and branches, exist not as a convenience to pickers, but are external manifestations of the fact that apples grow differently and separately from leaves and branches. Separate internal processes and different materials create, as a by-product, segregated appearance.

A third factor favoring perceptual subdivision is not independent of the other two, but is worth explicit mention. Simple shape, notably symmetry, contributes to physical equilibrium. It keeps walls and trees and bottles from falling, and is therefore favored in construction work by nature as well as by man. In the last analysis, then, the useful correspondence between the way we see things and the way they actually are comes about because vision, as a re-flection of physical processes in the brain, is subject to the same basic law of organization as the things of nature.

Subdivision in the Arts

In the work of painters, sculptors, or architects, the subdivision of visual shape is particularly necessary and apparent. Here again, most of all in the case of architecture, it may facilitate practical orientation. Principally, how-ever, subdivision conveys visual statements for their own sake. In his sculpture *The Lovers* (Figure 48), Constantin Brancusi has fitted the two embracing figures into a regularly shaped square block so tightly that the unity of the whole dominates the subdivision, the two human beings. The obvious sym-bolism of this conception contrasts strikingly with, for instance, Auguste Rodin's well-known representation of the same subject, in which the futile struggle for union is conveyed by the indomitable independence of the two figures. Here the parts are made to jeopardize the unity of the whole.

For the artist's purposes, subdivision tends to be much more complex than it is in the schematic figures I have used to demonstrate basic principles. In the arts, subdivision is rarely limited to one level as it is in a checkerboard, but proceeds at hierarchic levels, subordinated to one another.

A primary segregation establishes the main features of the work. The larger parts are again subdivided into smaller ones, and it is the task of the artist to adapt the degree and kind of the segregations and connections to his

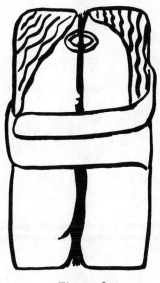

Figure 48

intended meaning. In Manet's painting *The Guitarist* (Figure 49) the primary subdivision distinguishes the entire foreground scene from the neutral backdrop. Within the frontal scene the musician, the bench, and the small still life with the jug amount to a secondary division. The separation of man and bench is partly compensated by a countergrouping, which unites the bench and the similarly colored trousers and sets them off against the dark top part of the man. This halving of the man by means of brightness and color gives added weight to the guitar, which is placed between the upper and lower sections of his body. At the same time the endangered unity of the figure is reinforced by several devices, notably the all-around distribution of the white areas, knitting together the shoes, the sleeves, the kerchief, and the shirt; of the shirt a tiny but important bit appears below the left elbow.

Each of the painting's major parts is in turn subdivided, and on each level one or several local concentrations of more densely organized form appear in relatively empty surroundings. Thus the strongly articulated figure stands against the empty ground, and, similarly, the face and the shirt, the hands and the fingerboard, the shoes and the still life, are islands of heightened activity on a secondary level of the hierarchy. The various focuses tend to be seen together as a kind of constellation; they represent the significant high spots and carry much of the meaning.

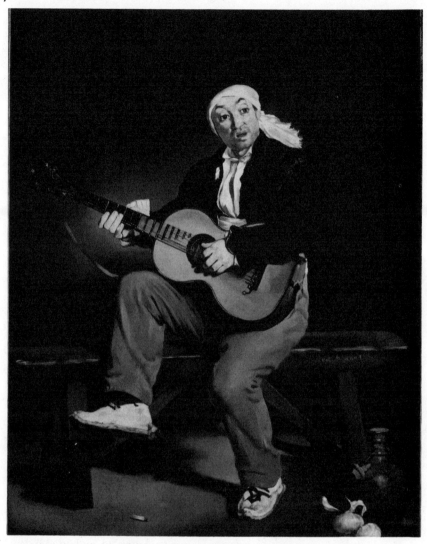

Figure 49
Edouard Manet. *The Guitarist*, 1961, Metropolitan Museum of Art, New York.

What Is a Part?

Chuang Tzu tells of a master cook whose cleaver remained sharp for nineteen years because when he carved an ox, he did not cut arbitrarily but respected the natural subdivision of the animal's bones, muscles, and organs;

in response to the barest tap at the right interstices, the parts seemed almost to detach themselves. The Chinese prince, listening to his cook's explanation, said it had taught him how to proceed successfully in life.

To know how to distinguish between pieces and parts is indeed a key to success in most human occupations. In a purely quantitative sense, any section of a whole can be called a part. Sectioning may be imposed on an object from the outside, by the whim of the carver or the mechanical force of a slicing machine. To partition by mere amount or number is to ignore structure. No other procedure is available, of course, when structure is absent. Any section of the blue sky is as good as any other. But the subdivision of a sculpture is not arbitrary, even though as a physical object it may be dismantled into any kind of section for shipping purposes.

The parts of most simple shapes are easily determined. A square is seen as consisting of four straight lines with divisions at the corners. But when shapes are less clear-cut and more complex, the structural components are not so obvious. Mistakes in the comprehension of an artistic structure are easily made when a viewer judges by relations within narrow limits rather than taking into account the overall structure. The same mistake may also lead to faulty phrasing in the performance of a musical passage, or to an actor's misinterpretation of a scene. The local situation suggests one conception, the total context prescribes another. Max Wertheimer used Figure 50 to show

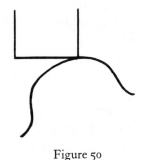

Figure 50

that in restricted local terms the horizontal base slides as an undivided whole into the right wing of the curve, although the total structure breaks the same line into two sections, belonging to different subwholes. Is the swastika of Figure 51a a part of Figure 51b? Obviously not, because the local connections and segregations that form the swastika are overruled by others in the context

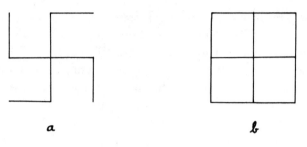

Figure 51

of the square. It is necessary therefore to distinguish between "genuine parts" —that is, sections representing a segregated subwhole within the total context— and mere portions or pieces—that is, sections segregated only in relation to a limited local context or to no inherent breaks in the figure at all.

When in this book I speak of parts, I always mean genuine parts. The statement "the whole is greater than the sum of its parts" refers to them. The statement is, however, misleading because it suggests that in a particular context the parts remain what they are, but are joined by a mysterious additional quality, which makes the difference. Instead, the appearance of any part depends, to a greater or lesser extent, on the structure of the whole, and the whole, in turn, is influenced by the nature of its parts. No portion of a work of art is ever quite self-sufficient. The broken-off heads of statues often look disappointingly empty. If they carried too much expression of their own, they would have marred the unity of the whole work. This is why dancers, who speak through their bodies, often wear deliberately blank facial expressions; and it is why Picasso, after experimenting with sketches of rather complex hands and figures for his mural *Guernica*, made them much simpler in the final work.

The same is true for completeness. A truly self-contained subwhole is very hard to accommodate, as I have mentioned in reference to circular windows (Figure 15). Good fragments are neither surprisingly complete nor distressingly incomplete; they have the particular charm of revealing unexpected merits of parts while at the same time pointing to a lost entity beyond themselves. A similar coherence of the total structure exists in organic shape. The geneticist Waddington says that although whole skeletons have a "quality of completeness," which resists additions or omissions, the single bones have only "a certain degree of completeness." Their shape carries implications about the other parts to which they are attached, and when isolated they are "like a tune which breaks off in the middle."

Similarity and Difference

Once it is understood that relations between parts depend on the structure of the whole, we may safely and profitably isolate and describe some of these piecemeal relations. In his pioneering study of 1923, Wertheimer described several of the properties that tie visual items together. A few years later, Cesare L. Musatti showed that Wertheimer's rules could be reduced to one, the rule of homogeneity or similarity.

Similarity and subdivision are opposite poles. Whereas subdivision is one of the prerequisites of sight, similarity can make things invisible like a pearl on a white forehead—"perla in bianca fronte"—to use Dante's image. Homogeneity is the limiting case, in which, as some modern painters have demonstrated, vision approaches or attains the absence of structure. Similarity acts as a structural principle only in conjunction with separation, namely, as a force of attraction among segregated things.

Grouping by similarity occurs in time as well as in space. Aristotle thought of similarity as one of the qualities creating mental associations, a condition of memory linking the past with the present. To demonstrate similarity independently of other factors, one must select patterns in which the influence of the total structure is weak, or at least does not directly affect the particular rule of grouping to be demonstrated.

Any aspect of percepts—shape, brightness, color, spatial location, movement, etc.—can cause grouping by similarity. A general principle to be kept in mind is that although all things are different in some respects and similar in others, comparisons make sense only when they proceed from a common base. Under most circumstances there is no point in comparing Michelangelo's David with the Mare Tranquillitatis on the moon, although the logician will let us say that the statue is smaller and looks larger than the Mare. Western adults can be coaxed into senseless comparisons, young children cannot. In an experiment with preschool children, Giuseppe Mosconi showed six pictures, of which five represented large mammals, one a warship. The subjects were asked to tell which of these pictures was "most different" from a seventh, representing sheep. Although adults and older children pointed to the warship without hesitation, only four out of 51 preschoolers did the same. If asked why they did not pick the ship, they responded: "Because it is not an animal!"

The same sensible attitude prevails in perception. Comparisons, connections, and separations will not be made between unrelated things, but only when the setup as a whole suggests a sufficient basis. Similarity is a prerequisite for the noticing of differences.

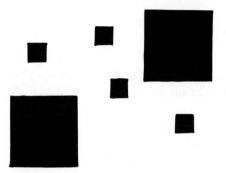

Figure 52

In Figure 52, shape, spatial orientation, and brightness are kept constant. These similarities knit all the squares together and at the same time forcefully point to their difference in size. The size difference, in turn, results in a subdivision, by which the two large squares, as against the four small ones, are connected at a secondary level. This is an example of *grouping by similarity of size*.

Groupings and separations are produced by other perceptual features in Figures 53 to 56. Grouping by difference of *shape* is seen in Figure 53. Difference of *brightness* collects the black disks as against the white ones in Figure 54. We observe that similarities of size, shape, or color will unite items distant in space from one another. But spatial location by itself is also a grouping factor; Figure 55 illustrates "proximity" or "nearness," in Wertheimer's terminology; we prefer to speak, with Musatti, of grouping by the similarity and difference of *spatial location*, which produces visual clusters. Finally, Figure 56 shows the effect of *spatial orientation*.

Movement introduces the additional factors of *direction* and *speed*. If in a group of five dancers three move in one direction, two in another, they will segregate, much more strikingly than the immobile Figure 57 can show. The same holds true for differences in speed (Figure 58). If in a film an excited man plows his way through a crowd he attracts attention; in a still photograph he might not stand out at all. Subjective speed differences intensify depth perception when a landscape is observed from a train or automobile or photographed by a traveling camera. This is so because the apparent speed of things rushing by the moving vehicle depends on their distance from the viewer. The telegraph poles along the tracks are moving faster than the houses and trees seen a few hundred feet away. Thus similarity and difference in speed help define distance.

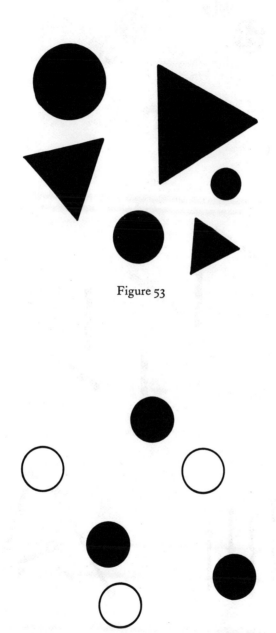

Figure 53

Figure 54

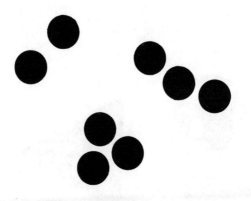

Figure 55

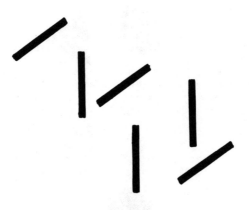

Figure 56

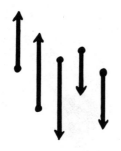

Figure 57

Figure 58

Admittedly, the effects of grouping and separation in our examples are not particularly strong. This is so because in order to show what similarity and difference can do by themselves, I kept the various elements from forming patterns as much as possible. Actually, the similarity factors are most effective when they support patterns. The approach "from below," one senses, is quite limited, and must be supplemented by the approach "from above." Wertheimer used these terms to describe the difference between starting the analysis of a pattern with its components and proceeding to their combinations—the method I just used with the rules of grouping—and beginning with the overall structure of the whole and descending from there to more and more subordinated parts.

Grouping from below and subdivision from above are reciprocal concepts. An important difference between the two procedures is that in starting from below we can apply the principle of simplicity only to the similarity that obtains between unit and unit, whereas when we apply it from above, the same principle accounts for overall organization as well. The Vienna Kunsthistorisches Museum owns a group of paintings by the sixteenth-century painter Giuseppe Arcimboldo, in which Summer, Winter, Fire, and Water are represented symbolically by profile portraits. Each figure is composed of objects, e.g., Summer of fruits, Fire of burning logs, candles, lamp, flintstone, etc. When the viewer proceeds from the components of one of these paintings, he recognizes the objects and appreciates how artfully they are fitted together. But he will never arrive in this way at the profile figure, constituted by the structure as a whole.

One step beyond the mere similarity of separate units is the grouping principle of *consistent shape*. This principle relies on the intrinsic similarity of the elements constituting a line, surface, or volume. Figure 59 is a rough tracing from a painting by Picasso. Why do we see the right leg of the woman as a continuous shape, despite its interruption by the left leg? Even though we know what a woman is expected to look like, the two shapes representing the leg would not unite into one if the contour lines were not related by similarity of direction and location.

What makes us combine the seven stars of the Big Dipper in the particular continuous sequence to which we are accustomed? We could see them as separate luminous dots or connect them in some other fashion. Figure 60 shows the result of an experiment in which the biologist Paul Weiss used seven drops of silver salt on a gelatin plate that had been soaked in a chromate solution. As the drops slowly diffuse, periodic concentric rings of insoluble silver chromate connect the seven dots in the same order spontaneously pro-

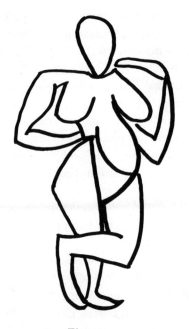

Figure 59

duced in the perception of star gazers. Asks Weiss, does not this unequivocal correspondence suggest that "a similar dynamic interaction pattern in man's brain has guided his interpretation" of the constellation?

In this last example, consistent shape was not produced by lines but by a mere sequence of dots. There are other ways of creating compelling consistency. In a drawing by the Italian artist Pio Semproni (Figure 61), the outlines of the white figure, so clearly visible, are rendered indirectly by the

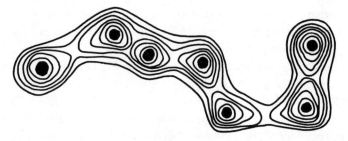

Figure 60

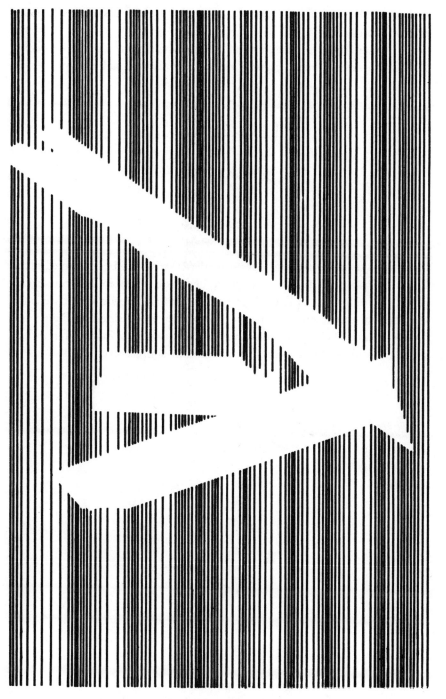

Figure 61
Pio Semproni. *Analisi dello Spazio*, 1971.

endings of the vertical background lines, each of which contributes a point-sized element to the virtual boundary.

The more consistent the shape of the unit, the more readily will it detach itself from its environment. Figure 62 shows that the straight line is more easily

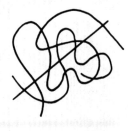

Figure 62

identifiable than the irregular ones—an effect that would be intensified if the lines were tracks of actual movements. When there is a choice between several possible continuations of lines (Figures 63), the spontaneous preference is for the one that carries on the intrinsic structure most consistently. Figure 63*a* will be seen more easily as a combination of the two parts indicated in *b* than of the two indicated in *c*, because *b* provides the simpler structure.

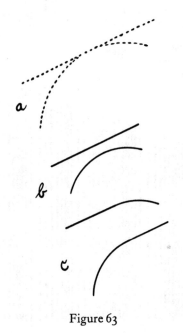

Figure 63

The principle of consistent shape finds interesting applications in what is known as harmonic progression in music. Here the problem consists in maintaining the "horizontal" unity of the melodic lines against the "vertical" harmonic coherence of the chords. This is achieved by keeping the melodic lines as simple and consistent as the musical task permits. For the progression from one chord to the next this means, for example, the use of grouping by "similarity of location." Walter Piston writes: "If two triads have one or more notes in common, these are repeated in the same voice, the remaining voice or voices moving to the nearest available condition" (Figure 64).

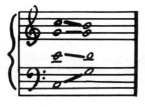

Figure 64

By going beyond the relations between parts one arrives at similarities definable only in reference to the whole pattern. Similarity of location can be extended to apply not only to units lying together, but also to similar position within the whole. Symmetry is such a similarity (Figure 65). In the same way, similarity of direction can go beyond mere parallelism—for instance, when dancers move along symmetrical paths (Figure 66).

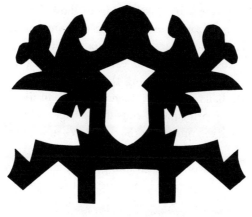

Figure 65

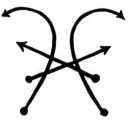

Figure 66

The limiting case of similarity of location is contiguity. When there are no intervals between units, a compact visual object results. It may seem artificial to think of a line or area as an agglomeration of units, and the need for explaining why a red cherry is seen as one coherent object may not be immediately apparent. The problem is more readily appreciated if one thinks of the halftone screen by which the printer succeeds in representing continuous shades of varying brightness and color as well as readable outlines even when the dots composing the picture are quite coarse. It must also be remembered that the images formed by the lenses of the eyes are picked up point by point by millions of tiny retinal receptors, whose messages, although bunched to some extent before they reach the brain centers, must be grouped into objects for the purpose of perception. Object formation is accomplished through the principle of simplicity, of which the rules of similarity are a particular application. A visual object is the more unitary the more strictly similar its elements are in such factors as color, brightness, and speed and direction of movement.

Examples from Art

All works of art have to be looked at "from above," that is, with a primary grasp of the total organization. At the same time, however, relations among the parts often play an important compositional role. Similarity and dissimilarity shape the principal theme, for example, of Pieter Brueghel's famous *Parable of the Blind Men*, illustrating the biblical saying that "if the blind lead the blind, both shall fall into the ditch." A group of six coordinated figures is tied together by the principle of consistent shape (Figure 67). The heads form a descending curve, connecting the six figures into a row of bodies, which slopes downward and finally falls rapidly. The painting represents successive stages of one process: unconcerned walking, hesitation, alarm, stumbling, falling. The similarity of the figures is not one of strict repetition but of gradual change, and the eye of the observer is made to follow the course of the action. The principle of the motion picture is applied here to a sequence of simul-

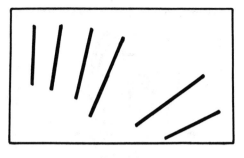

Figure 67

taneous phases in space. It will be shown later that the illusory film motion is based on the application of the rules of similarity to the time dimension.

In other works, a group of dispersed items is held together by similarity. In Grünewald's Crucifixion of the Isenheim altar, the figures of John the Baptist and John the Evangelist, placed at opposite sides of the panel, are both clad in bright red; white is reserved for the coat of the Virgin, the lamb, the Bible, the loincloth of Christ, and the inscription on the top of the cross. In this way the various symbolic carriers of spiritual values—virginity, sacrifice, revelation, chastity, and kingship—which are distributed over the entire panel, are not only united compositionally but also interpreted to the eye as having a common meaning. In contrast, the symbol of the flesh is suggested in the pink dress of Mary Magdalene, the sinner, who in this way is associated with the naked limbs of the men. Gombrich has pointed out that there is also in this picture an unrealistic but symbolically significant scale of sizes, leading from the gigantic figure of Christ down to the undersized Mary Magdalene.

The unifying power of consistent form is used symbolically in Cézanne's *Uncle Dominic* (Figure 68). The crossed arms seem chained in their position as though they could never come apart. This effect is achieved partly by fastening the border of the sleeve to the central vertical established by the symmetry of the face and the cross. Thus the powerful connection between a man's mind and the symbol of the faith to which his thought is dedicated constrains the physical activity of his body and creates the stillness of collected energy.

By connecting two or more spots through similarity, a painter may establish a significant visual movement. El Greco's *Expulsion from the Temple* (Figure 69) is painted in drab yellowish and brownish shades. A bright red is reserved for the clothes of Christ and those of one of the money changers, who bends down in the lower left corner of the picture. As the beholder's attention is caught by the central figure of Christ, similarity of color makes his glance

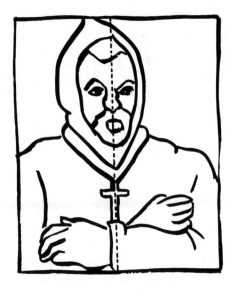

Figure 68

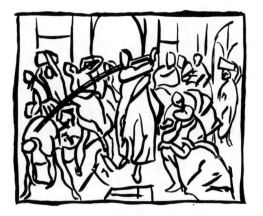

Figure 69

sweep to the left and downward to the second red spot. This movement duplicates the stroke of Christ's whip, the path of which is emphasized further by
the raised arms of the two interposed figures. Thus the eye truly performs
the action that represents the main subject of the picture.

Perceptual comparison requires, as we saw earlier, some kind of similarity
as a base. Just as the size differences in Figure 52 showed up clearly because

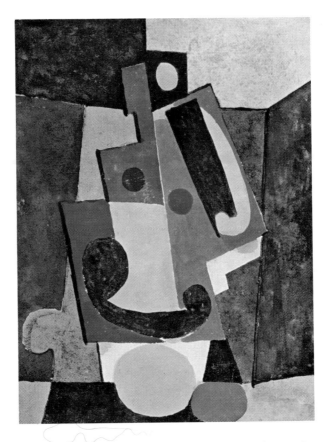

Plate I. Pablo Picasso. *Seated Woman*. Gouache, 1918.
Museum of Modern Art, New York.

shape and spatial orientation were kept constant, so the size difference between the two chairs in Van Gogh's painting *The Bedroom* (Figure 70) is emphasized by the same means. The difference in size, which helps create depth, is underlined by the striking similarity of color, shape, and spatial orientation.

The similarity and difference of parts contribute conspicuously to the composition of Picasso's small gouache *Seated Woman* (Plate 1). The similarity of the geometric shapes throughout the picture emphasizes the unity of the whole and understates, in the cubist manner, the distinction between the woman and the screen-like background. The distinction, however, is made clear by other means. Essentially a left slant is used for the figure, a right slant for the ground; the factor of orientation, that is, serves to subdivide the picture into its two main subjects. As to shape, the circular units are limited to the figure of the woman, and are distributed in such a way that they emphasize the figure's pyramidal structure. The one curved form outside the woman's body is the elbow rest of the green chair—an intermediary between the angular setting and the organic body.

Color supports the subdivision produced by orientation and shape, but at the same time adds variety to the composition by counteracting these structural tendencies to some extent. With the exception of the dark brown shades, used outside as well as inside the figure, every color belongs either to the figure or to the background. The vertical chain of the yellows gives unity and distinction to the woman. The step-like head-shoulder-body progression at the left is unified by the light browns, and orange holds the right side together

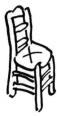
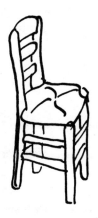

Figure 70

and connects it with the egg-shaped patch at the bottom. The continuity of the background, interrupted by the figure, is re-established by similarity of color. The greens "mend" the split-up chair, and on the right side a darkish brown connects two parts of the background that are separated by the woman's protruding arm. The interplay of similarities and corresponding dissimilarities in this picture creates a tight-knit relational network.

Two general points are well illustrated by the Picasso example. First, similarity and difference are relative judgments. Whether objects look alike depends on how different they are from their environment. Thus the round shapes resemble each other compellingly despite their differences because they are surrounded by angular, straight-lined shapes. Second, in the complexity of artistic composition the factors of grouping are often set against one another. Broken shapes are mended across spatial distance by similarity of color. Difference of color is counteracted by similarity of shape. This counterpoint of connection and segregation enhances the richness of the artist's conception.

The Structural Skeleton

Although the visual shape of an object is largely determined by its outer boundaries, the boundaries cannot be said to *be* the shape. When a man in the street is asked to take the route indicated in Figure 71*a*: "Walk two blocks, turn left, walk two more blocks, turn right, walk one block. . . ." he will end up back where he started. This will probably surprise him. Although he has moved along the entire contour, his experience is unlikely to have contained the essentials of the image he will suddenly form in his mind when he grasps the cross shape he covered on his walk (Figure 71*b*). The pair of axes, although not coincident with the actual physical boundaries, determines the character and identity of the shape. Similarly, in Figure 67 it was possible to present the basic compositional theme of Brueghel's painting by means of straight lines,

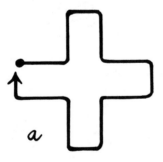
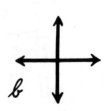

Figure 71

which in no way resembled the actual outlines of the figures. We conclude that in speaking of "shape" we refer to two quite different properties of visual objects: (1) the actual boundaries produced by the artist: the lines, masses, volumes, and (2) the structural skeleton created in perception by these material shapes, but rarely coinciding with them.

Delacroix said that in drawing an object, the first thing to grasp about it is the contrast of its principal lines: "one must be well aware of this before one sets pencil to paper." All through a piece of work, the artist must bear in mind the structural skeleton he is shaping while at the same time paying attention to the quite different contours, surfaces, volumes, he is actually making. By necessity, human handiwork proceeds in sequence; what shall be seen as a whole in the final work is created piece by piece. The guiding image in the artist's mind is not so much a faithful preview of what the completed painting or sculpture will look like, but mainly the structural skeleton, the configuration of visual forces that determines the character of the visual object. Whenever that guiding image is lost sight of, the hand goes astray.

A similar discrepancy between physical action and physical shape on the one side, and the image obtained on the other, exists in what the viewer does when he looks at an object. In recent years, exact recordings of eye movements have shown which parts of a picture observers look at, how often and how long they fixate each place, and in what time sequence. Not surprisingly, fixations are found to cluster in the areas of greatest interest to the viewer. Otherwise, however, there is little relation between the tracks and directions of eye movements and the perceptual structure of the final image that emerges from the scanning. The structural skeleton is no more due to the movements of the viewer's eyes than it is to those of the artist's hands.

Different triangles have distinctly different visual characters, which cannot be inferred from their actual shape, but only from the structural skeleton their shape creates by induction. The five triangles in Figure 72 are obtained by vertically displacing one corner point while leaving the other two constant.

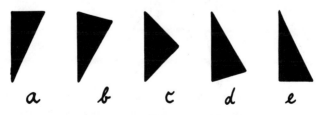

Figure 72

Wertheimer noted that as the moving point continuously slides downward, chances occur in the triangle that are not continuous. Rather, there is a series of transformations culminating in the five shapes shown. Although caused by changes in the contour, the structural differences between the triangles cannot be described in terms of their contour.

Triangle *a* (Figure 73) is characterized by a main vertical and a secondary

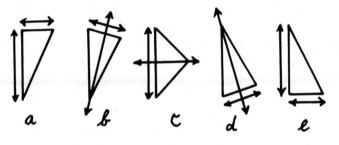

Figure 73

horizontal axis, which meet at right angles. In *b* the main axis is slanted to the right and divides the whole into two symmetrical halves. The edge to the left, although objectively still a vertical, now looks hardly vertical at all. It has become an oblique deviation from the main axis of the pattern. In *c* the obliqueness of the whole has disappeared, but now the shorter, horizontal axis has become dominant because it is the center of a new symmetrical division. Triangle *d* reverts to obliqueness, and so on.

The structural skeleton of each triangle derives from its contours through the law of simplicity: the resulting skeleton is the simplest structure obtainable with the given shape. It takes a distinct effort to visualize less simple structures—for example, *c* as an irregular oblique triangle or *d* as a deviation from the right-angled type *e* (Figure 74). Symmetry is used wherever it is available

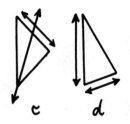

Figure 74

(*b, c, d*) : in *a* and *e* rightangularity provides the simplest available pattern.

The structural skeleton consists primarily of the framework of axes, and the axes create characteristic correspondences. For instance, in the three isosceles triangles of Figure 72, the two equal edges correspond to each other; they become the "legs," whereas the third is seen as the base. In the other two triangles the right angle makes for a correspondence between the two sides that oppose the hypotenuse.

From what has been said it follows, first, that the same structural skeleton can be embodied by a great variety of shapes. Looking ahead to Figure 95, we see three of the innumerable versions of the human figure produced by artists of different cultures. One is surprisingly ready to recognize the human body in the most primitive stick figure or the most elaborate paraphrase—if only the basic axes and correspondences are respected.

It follows second that if a given visual pattern can yield two different structural skeletons, it may be perceived as two totally different objects. Ludwig Wittgenstein's discussion of the famous duck-rabbit, a drawing that can be seen as the head of a duck looking to the left or as that of a rabbit looking to the right, shows what puzzles one must face if one assumes that the actual outlines on paper contain everything there is to the percept. This particular drawing allows for two contradictory, but equally applicable structural skeletons, pointing in opposite directions. Wittgenstein, an acute observer, realized that this was not a matter of two different interpretations applied to one percept, but of two percepts. That two percepts could derive from one stimulus struck him as a cause of wonder.

III   FORM

"Form is the visible shape of content," wrote the painter Ben Shahn, and this is as good a formula as any to describe the distinction between shape and form I am observing in these chapters. Under the heading "Shape" I discussed some of the principles by which visual material, received by the eyes, organizes itself so it can be grasped by the human mind. Only for the sake of extrinsic analysis, however, can shape be separated from what it stands for. Whenever we perceive shape, consciously or unconsciously we take it to represent something, and thereby to be the form of a content.

Most practically, shape serves, first of all, to inform us about the nature of things through their external appearance. What we see of the shape, color, and external behavior of a rabbit tells us much about the nature of a rabbit, and the difference in appearance between a teacup and a knife indicates which object is suited to containing a liquid and which to cutting a cake. Furthermore, while the rabbit, the cup, and the knife tell us about their individual selves, each of them teaches us automatically about whole categories of things —rabbits in general, cups, and knives—and, by extension, about animals, containers, cutting tools. Thus, a shape is never perceived as the form of just one particular thing, but always as that of a kind of thing. Shape is a concept in two different ways: first, because we see every shape as a *kind* of shape (compare what was said about perceptual concepts on p. 44); second, because each kind of shape is seen as the form of whole kinds of objects. To use an example of Wittgenstein's: the line drawing of a triangle can be seen as a triangular hole, a solid, a geometrical figure; as standing on its base or hanging by its top corner; as a mountain, a wedge, an arrow, a pointer, etc.

Not all objects concentrate on telling by their shape about their own physical nature. A painted landscape has little reference to a flat piece of canvas covered with traces of pigment. A figure carved in stone reports about living creatures, creatures that differ so much from inert pieces of marble. Such objects are made for vision only. But they, too, serve as form for whole categories of things: the painted view of the Grand Canyon reports about landscapes, the bust of Lincoln speaks of thoughtful men.

In addition, form always goes beyond the practical function of things by finding in their shape the visual qualities of roundness or sharpness, strength or frailty, harmony or discord. It thereby reads them symbolically as images of the human condition. In fact, these purely visual qualities of appearance are the most powerful of all. It is they that reach us most directly and deeply. All this will come up repeatedly in this book. But one further point needs to be made before we proceed to details. All shape, I implied, is semantic; that is, merely by being seen it makes statements about kinds of subjects. In doing so, however, it does not simply present replicas of its subjects. Not all the shapes recognized as rabbits are identical, and Dürer's picture of a rabbit is not strictly identical with any rabbit anybody has ever seen.

This fundamental condition of all imagery would not have had to be pointed out to a peasant living in the Maya's Classic age—at least, not as far as pictorial and sculptural likenesses are concerned, because the woven and ceramic images of his time differed all too obviously from the subjects they represented. The fact is less evident in our own tradition, based on centuries of more or less realistic art. Dürer's rabbit looks in fact so strikingly like a real animal that it takes enlightened inspection to discover the fundamental difference. "He was a very skillful artist," says Goethe of a painter friend of his, "and he was among the few who know how to transform artifice entirely into nature and nature entirely into art. They are exactly the ones whose misunderstood merits keep giving rise to the doctrine of false naturalness."

The doctrine to which Goethe referred long ago held, and still holds, that art aims at a deceitful illusion, and that any deviation from this mechanical ideal needs to be explained, excused, justified. It is an approach developed from some of the principles underlying Renaissance art from the fifteenth century on. If a style of picture-making fails to fit this standard—and all styles of art, modern or ancient, in practice fail more or less conspicuously to do so—the discrepancy is explained in one of the following ways. The draftsman lacks the skill to accomplish what he wants to do; he depicts what he knows rather than what he sees; he blindly adopts the pictorial conventions of his peers; he perceives wrongly because of defects in his eyes or his nervous system; he applies the correct principle from an abnormal point of view; he deliberately violates the rules of correct representation.

This illusionistic doctrine, as I would call it, continues to produce a great deal of misleading interpretation. Therefore it cannot be said strongly enough, or often enough, that *image-making, artistic or otherwise, does not simply derive from the optical projection of the object represented, but is an equivalent, rendered with the properties of a particular medium, of what is observed in the object.*

The illusionistic doctrine springs from a double application of what is known in philosophy as "naive realism." According to this view, there is no difference between the physical object and the image of it perceived by the mind; the mind sees the object itself. Similarly, the work of a painter or sculptor is considered simply a replica of the percept. Just as the table seen by the eye is supposed to be identical with the table as a physical object, so the picture of the table on the canvas simply replicates the table the artist saw. At best, the artist is able to "improve" reality or enrich it with creatures of fantasy, by omitting or adding details, selecting suitable examples, rearranging the given order of things. As an example, we may cite Pliny's famous anecdote, so widely quoted in Renaissance treatises. The Greek painter Zeuxis, unable to find any one woman beautiful enough to serve as a model for his painting of Helen of Troy, "inspected the maidens of the city naked and chose out five, whose peculiar beauties he proposed to reproduce in his picture."

The manipulations ascribed to the artist by this theory might be called "cosmetic," because in principle they could be performed just as well on the model object itself. The procedure reduces art to a kind of plastic surgery. Illusionists are oblivious to the fundamental difference between the world of physical reality and its image in paint or stone.

Orientation in Space

What I have just said about the form of images refers specifically to representation in particular media, whether two-dimensional or three-dimensional. However, there are characteristics of form that come into play even in ordinary perception when we recognize or fail to recognize an object as itself or as one of its kind. The appearance of a particular object does not remain always the same, and an individual specimen does not look exactly like all other members of the same species. We therefore have to ask: what conditions must visual form meet for an image to be recognizable?

To start with a relatively simple factor, how important is spatial orientation? What happens when we see an object not right-side-up, but in an unfamiliar position?

The identity of a visual object depends, as was previously shown, not so much on its shape as such as on the structural skeleton created by the shape.

A lateral tilt may not interfere with such a skeleton, but then again it may. When a triangle or rectangle is tilted (Figure 75a), it does not become a different object. One sees it merely as deflected from its more normal position. This was strikingly demonstrated many years ago in experiments by Louis Gellermann, in which young children and chimpanzees were confronted with variations of a familiar triangle. When the triangle was turned sixty degrees, the children as well as the animals turned their heads by the same angle to re-establish the "normal" orientation of the figure.

If, however, one tilts a square by a similar angle it changes into a completely different figure, so different that it acquires a name of its own—diamond or rhombus (Figure 75b). This is so because the structural framework has not shifted with the figure. A new symmetry lets the vertical and horizontal axes pass through the corners, thereby placing the accents of the figure on the four points and transforming the edges into oblique roof shapes. Visually we are dealing with a new figure, a pointed, more dynamic, less stably rooted thing.

This may lead to misunderstandings when an experimenter unquestioningly bases his evaluations on a materialistic definition of sameness. He may cut a square from a piece of cardboard and show it to children in different positions, asking: Is this the same square? Until about age seven, children deny that the tilted figure is the same square. The rash experimenter may conclude that the child, misled by mere appearance, has failed to acknowledge the correct state of affairs. But was the child referring to the piece of cardboard or to the visual object? And who has decreed that sameness is to be based on material rather than visual criteria? Certainly any artist would protest.

Spatial orientation presupposes a frame of reference. In empty space, pervaded by no forces of attraction, there would be no up and down, no straightness or tilt. Our visual field provides such a framework—"retinal orien-

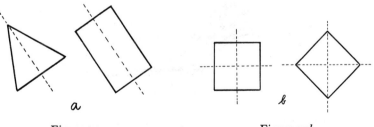

Figure 75a   Figure 75b

tation," I called it earlier. When the children and chimpanzees cocked their heads, they eliminated the tilt of the figure in relation to their visual field. But there is also "environmental orientation." When a painting on the wall hangs crookedly, we see the tilt even though we may tilt our heads correspondingly, as long as we refer the picture to the framework of the walls. Within the narrower world of the painting itself, however, the verticals and horizontals of the frame determine the two basic axes. In Figure 76, taken from an investi-

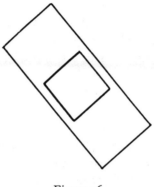

Figure 76

gation of space perception by Hertha Kopfermann, the inner figure, under the influence of the tilted frame, tends to look like a tilted square, although by itself or within a vertical or horizontal frame, it looks like an upright diamond. In Figure 77, which comes from the ornamentation of a tablecloth in a Picasso still life, the diamonds have a tendency to look parallel to one another although objectively they differ in orientation. Children often draw the chimney perpendicular to the inclined edge of the roof even though this adherence to the more specific framework puts the chimney in an oblique position. As a rule, then, the spatial orientation of units in a picture is determined by a number of

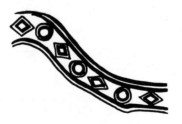

Figure 77

different influences. If a face is turned sideways, the nose will be perceived as upright in relation to the face but as tilted relative to the entire picture. The artist must see to it not only that the desired effect prevails, but also that the strength of the various local frames of reference is clearly proportioned; they must either compensate one another or be subordinated to one another hierarchically. Otherwise the viewer will be confronted with a confusing crossfire. Note the disturbingly indeterminate orientation of the central line in Figure 78.

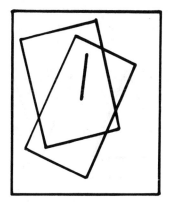

Figure 78

In addition to the coordinates of the retinal field and those of the visual environment, a third framework of spatial orientation is provided kinesthetically, by the muscular sensations in the body and the organ of equilibrium in the inner ear. In whatever position our body or head or eyes may be, we sense the direction of gravitational pull. In daily life these kinesthetic sensations are usually in harmony with those derived from the visual framework of the environment. But when one looks up at a tall building, even the awareness of the tilted head may not be quite sufficient to compensate for the apparent backward tilt of the facade; and when the same view appears on a movie screen, the observer's upright posture together with the upright picture frame make the photographed world look tilted.

Experiments by Herman Witkin have shown that people vary markedly in how much their spatial orientation relies on the visual sense and how much on the kinesthetic. The more visually responsive persons, taking their cues from the outside world, were found to be more generally outer-directed, more dependent on standards of the environment, whereas the more kinesthetically responsive persons, listening to the signals from within their bodies, seemed to be more inner-directed, following their own judgment rather than the tenets of the world.

So far I have referred to examples of moderate tilt, which often leaves the structural skeleton essentially unaltered. A turn of ninety degrees tends to interfere with the character of visual shapes more drastically by causing the vertical and the horizontal to exchange places. When a violin or sculpted figure is seen lying on its side, the symmetry axis loses much of its compelling strength, and the shape points in a lateral direction like a boat or arrow. Even more radical is the change when the object is turned upside down. The two figures in Figure 79 are both triangular but their shapes differ. Version *a* rises

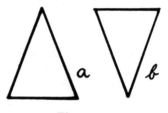

Figure 79

from a stable basis to a sharp peak; in version *b* a broad top balances heavily and precariously on a pointed foot.

These are dynamic changes, due to the direction of gravitational pull. The effect is greatest in objects for which dynamic expression determines visual identity most strongly, notably the human face. In surrealist films, faces are sometimes shown upside-down. The effect is frightening: even though we know better, visual evidence insists that we are seeing a new kind of face, a monstrous variation dominated by the blind opening of the mouth, thrusting forward with the raised prow of the nose, and displaying at the base two rolling eyes, cradled in baggy lids, which close upward.

To be able to recognize objects regardless of their spatial position is, of course, advantageous. Young children seem to handle picture books with little consideration of whether the illustrations are right-side-up or upside-down; and it used to be assumed that quite generally the spatial orientation of objects did not matter either to children or to primitive tribesmen. Recent experiments have indicated, however, that under certain conditions pictures projected on the wall are more easily recognized by the young child when they are right-side-up, and that this difference tends to become irrelevant when the child reaches school age. At this point we cannot be certain just how much the recognition of visual objects is influenced by the modifications of perceptual appearance accompanying change of spatial orientation.

In any case, to observe the spatial orientation of objects in the physical world is one thing; to draw pictures of them is quite another. This is particularly true for young children. In the physical world they observe buildings, trees, and cars rooted to the ground, and they would be surprised to see people or animals standing on their heads. The empty space of the drawing paper, however, imposes no such constraints, and in the beginning one spatial orientation seems to be as good as any other, e.g., for the depicting of human figures. Spatial orientation is not yet differentiated. Only gradually does the "correct" upright position impose itself, for reasons yet to be explored. One of them must surely be that under normal conditions, the retinal projection obtained from the upright picture corresponds to the one received when the child looks at the physical model. Furthermore, it is true even for the simple pictures produced by children that the one-sidedness of the gravitational pull introduces the distinction between up and down, which enriches our visual world both physically and symbolically. When modern painters or sculptors create works that can be looked at validly in any spatial position, they pay for this freedom by settling for a relatively undifferentiated homogeneity.

Projections

In the examples of spatial orientation thus far discussed one might have expected no change of visual identity since geometric shape had remained unaltered. Instead we noted that under certain conditions a new orientation will bring to the fore a new structural skeleton, which gives the object a different character. Turning now to deviations that involve a modification of geometric shape we find that "non-rigid" change may or may not interfere with the identity of the pattern, depending on what it does to the structural skeleton.

Cut a fairly large rectangle of cardboard and observe its shadow cast by a candle or other small light source. Innumerable projections of the rectangle can be produced, some of them looking like the examples of Figure 80. Figure 80*a*, obtained by placing the rectangle exactly at right angles to the direction of the light source, resembles the object very closely. All other angles of projection lead to more or less drastic deviations of appearance. Figure 80*b*, though devoid of symmetry and right angles, is readily seen as an undistorted rectangle, tilted in space. Here again the principle of simplicity is at work. Whenever a three-dimensional version of a figure is sufficiently stabler and

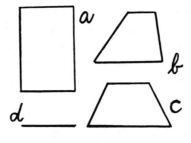

Figure 80

more symmetrical than the flat projection, the observer will tend to see the simpler shape, extended in depth. Figure 80*c* is much less likely to be seen as the projection of the rectangle which in fact it is. As a flat upright, it has a vertical symmetry of its own. It is a rather simply shaped regular trapezoid, and the tension created by the unequal angles is compensated within the plane. Its structural skeleton does not point to a rectangle.

Figure 80*d*, finally, is no longer a projection of the rectangle at all, but rather one of the thickness of the piece of cardboard. One can understand intellectually that this view, too, is derived from our object, but the deviation can no longer be *seen*. This problem, specific to the perception of three-dimensional objects, will be taken up again shortly.

Looking at projections has confronted us with the phenomenon known as the *constancy of shape and size*. More often than not, perceptual constancy is interpreted by textbooks of psychology in a misleadingly simplified fashion. It is pointed out, correctly, that if we saw physical objects the way they are projected on the retinas of the eyes, they would undergo dreadful amoebic transformations of shape and size every time the objects changed their position toward us or we changed our position toward them. Fortunately this does not happen. The percept produced by the brain from the retinal projection is such that we see the object as it *is* physically. Asked what he sees when shown the shadow of our tilted cardboard rectangle, a person will tell us that he *sees* a rectangle of constant, stable shape. Asked to draw a picture of it, he may well draw a rectangle.

All this is true enough, but the impression often given is that this particular "correction" of the stimulus pattern occurs automatically and universally, although not quite completely, and that it is due either to an inborn mechanism, which requires no further explanation, or to accumulated experience, which corrects the faulty retinal input on the basis of better knowledge. Experiments such as those by T. G. R. Bower have shown that infants between two and twenty weeks of age discriminate among test objects, e.g., cubes, according to their objective size, and see tilted rectangles as rectangles and not according to the shape of their retinal projection. This shows that at least the elements of shape and size constancy are already present at an early age. However, this is not really the main point of interest.

Another glance at Figure 80 reminds us that by no means all projections are perceived according to objective shape, and the same is true for size. All depends on the particular nature of the projection and the other conditions prevailing in the given situation. Depending on these conditions, there may be compelling constancy, or none at all, or some intermediate effect. No matter whether constancy processing is inherent in the nervous system or acquired by experience, there must be in either case an intricate mechanism equipped to deal with the input data appropriately. We need to know two things: (1) what kind of projection leads to what kind of percept, and (2) by what principles operate the mechanisms that do the processing?

What matters to the artist in particular is to know which shapes will produce which effect. He can acquire this knowledge by studying the principles at work in shape perception. To be sure, the visual conditions prevailing in daily life are by no means identical to those prevailing in a drawing or painting. Instead of the isolated projections picked out in Figure 80, for example, in the physical environment one more commonly experiences whole sequences of continuously changing projections, and this increases the constancy effect considerably. When the cardboard square shifts gradually from position to position, momentary projections support and interpret one another. In this respect, immobile media such as drawing, painting, or photography are quite different from the mobile ones. A projection that, frozen in its momentary aspect, looks compelling, mysterious, absurd, or unrecognizable passes by unnoticed as a mere phase in a sequence of changes when an actor moves on the stage or in a film, or when the camera or a human observer moves around a piece of sculpture. In experiments on the shape and depth perception of infants, a most influential factor proved to be the motion parallax, i.e., the changes of spatial appearance caused by the movements of the viewer's head.

Figure 80*a* indicated that as long as we deal with a flat object, such as a cardboard rectangle, there exists one projection that does such complete justice to the visual concept of the object that the two can be considered identical— namely, the orthogonal projection, obtained when the plane of the object is hit by the line of sight at a right angle. Under this condition, the object and its retinal projection have roughly the same shape.

The situation is much more complicated with truly three-dimensional things, because their shapes cannot be reproduced by any two-dimensional projection. It will be recalled that the projection on the retina is created by light rays that travel from the object to the eye along straight lines, and that consequently, the projection renders only those areas of the object whose straight-line connection with the eyes is unobstructed. Figure 81 shows how the selection and relative position of these areas change in the example of a cube (*b, c, d*), depending on the angle at which the observer (*a*) sees it. The corresponding projections are indicated approximately in *b', c', d'*.

Here again, as the projection changes, the observer should be expected to see the shape of the object change accordingly. The sickening sensation produced by a distorting mirror should be the normal visual reaction to most objects most of the time. This would interfere with the practical business of life since the immutable physical object would be represented by a constantly changing image. Once more, "constancy of shape" comes to the rescue. We must ask, however, what is it that remains constant since a three-dimensional solid cannot be truly represented by any flat projection?

Which Aspect is Best?

The visual concept of the object derived from perceptual experiences has three important properties. It conceives of the object as being three-

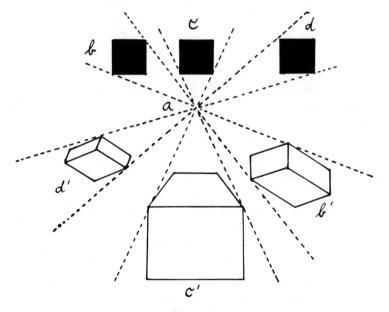

Figure 81

dimensional, of constant shape, and not limited to any particular projective aspect. Examples can be found in Francis Galton's investigations of visual imagery. He asserts that "a few persons can, by what they often describe as a kind of touch-sight, visualize at the same moment all round the image of a solid body. Many can do so nearly, but not altogether round that of a terrestrial globe. An eminent mineralogist assures me that he is able to imagine simultaneously all the sides of a crystal with which he is familiar." Galton's examples serve to show what is meant by a three-dimensional concept, which is not bound to any one aspect. If a person has an all-around concept of a crystal or a globe, no one point of observation predominates. This is so because a person's visual concept of an object is generally based on the totality of observations from any number of angles. Yet it is a visual concept, and not a verbal definition obtained by intellectual abstraction. Intellectual knowledge sometimes helps form a visual concept, but only to the extent that it is translatable into visual attributes.

Visual concepts must be distinguished also from so-called eidetic memory images, which make it possible for some persons to project upon an empty surface an exact replica of a scene they have perceived before, e.g., to read details on a geographic map as though the map were still in front of their eyes. Eidetic images can be described as physiological vestiges of direct stimulation. In that sense one can compare them with afterimages, although they can be scanned by eye movements, which is not true for afterimages. Eidetic images are substitute percepts and as such mere raw material for active vision; they are not constructs of the formative mind like visual concepts.

Strictly speaking, the visual concept of anything that has volume can be represented only in a three-dimensional medium, such as sculpture or architecture. If we wish to make pictures on a plane surface, all we can hope to do is to produce a translation—that is, to present some structural essentials of the visual concept by two-dimensional means. The pictures achieved in this way may look flat like a child's drawing or have depth like those obtained with a stereoscope or holograph, but in both the problem remains that the all-aroundness of the visual conception cannot be reproduced directly in a single plane.

If we look at a human head from some particular angle we realize that any aspect, however well-selected, is arbitrary in two ways: it creates contours where none exist in the object, and it excludes some parts of the surface while displaying others. An art student, drawing from the model, grapples with the problem of how to convey the continuity of roundness. He is tempted to take the arbitrary contour literally and to produce the image of a shield rather than a volume. William Hogarth, in his *Analysis of Beauty*, describes the dilemma eloquently: "But in the common way of taking the view of any opaque object, that part of its surface which fronts the eye is apt to occupy the mind alone, and the opposite, nay even every other part of it whatever is left unthought of at that time; and the least motion we make to reconnoiter any other side of the object confounds our first idea, for want of the connexion of the two ideas, which the complete knowledge of the whole would naturally have given us, if we had considered it in the other way before."

How arbitrarily any view selects the portions visible in the projective image becomes most evident when we learn how much trouble the "hidden-surface problem" gives the practitioners of computer graphics. The image of a wire frame model of a solid can be rotated and distorted by the computer with relative ease. If the solid's transparent body is given in a certain position, the computer can show it from the back or from the top, thus saving today's architects much labor. But when it comes to simulating the actual look of the opaque solid from a given viewpoint, it is no longer sufficient to manipulate the properties of the solid itself. Arbitrary effects are always hard to calculate. The computer must determine the interaction between the spatial system of the object and the projective system imposed upon it—an expensive, time-consuming operation.

Once we put up with reducing a volume to one of its aspects, we must decide which view to select for any particular purpose. For some objects all aspects are equal or equally good—for example, a sphere or an irregularly shaped piece of rock. Usually, however, there are definite distinctions. In a cube the orthogonal projection of any surface dominates. In fact, oblique aspects of the surface are seen as mere deviations from the square-shaped one. This distinction is based on the law of simplicity. The dominant projections are those which produce patterns of the simplest shape.

Are these simplest and perceptually preferred aspects best suited to convey the visual concept of the three-dimensional object? Some of them are. Our visual concepts of many objects are characterized by structural symmetries, which are brought out most directly by certain aspects of the object. Thus a straight front view of a human figure displays this striking feature. But an undistorted sideface of a cube can be shown only at the price of hiding all the others. Or consider Figure 82. It is surely the simplest possible representation of a Mexican wearing a large sombrero. Yet such a view would be used only as a joke, which results precisely from the contradiction between the representation's indisputable correctness and its patent inadequacy. The picture is certainly faithful—a similar view can be obtained photographically from a third-floor hotel window—but it is inadequate for most purposes because it does not distinguish a Mexican from a millstone or a doughnut. The structural skeleton of Figure 82 is too slightly related to the structure of the visual concept to be conveyed; instead it creates other, misleading associations.

The example reminds us that for some special purpose, the draftsman may deliberately choose a view that misleads and hides rather than informs. Early stages of pictorial representation avoid any such concealment. They aim for the clearest and most direct sight, and so do all illustrations aimed at straight instruction. At levels of higher sophistication, back views, tilted heads, and the like are admitted for the enrichment they bring to the spatial conception.

The elementary task of depicting on a surface the main properties of an object's shape is a difficult one. Should the portrait of a given person show the front-face view or the profile? G. K. Chesterton speaks of "one of those women whom one always thinks of in profile, as of the clean-cut edge of some weapon." Police records require both views, as do anthropometric studies, because important characteristics often show up in one view and not in the other. Alberto Giacometti once said jokingly to a man whose portrait he was painting: "Full face you go to jail, and in profile you go to the asylum." A further complication is introduced when some parts of an object show best from one angle whereas others do so from another. The typical shape of a bull is conveyed by a side view, which, however, hides the characteristic lyre pattern of the horns. The wingspread of a flying duck does not show in profile. The angle that must be chosen to identify the goblet and stem of a wineglass destroys the circularity of the mouth and foot. The problems multiply with combinations of objects: how can a pond, whose undistorted outline is revealed

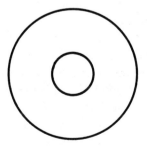

Figure 82

only through a birdseye view, and trees, which display their typical shape in profile, be shown in the same picture?

Take an apparently simple object—a chair (Figure 83). The top view (*a*) does justice to the shape of the seat. The front view (*b*) shows the shape of the

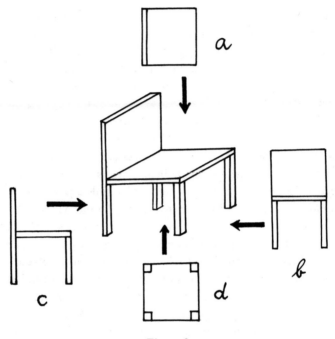

Figure 83

chair's back and its symmetrical relation to the front legs. The side view (*c*) hides almost everything, but gives the important rectangular arrangement of back, seat, and legs more clearly than any other view. Finally, the bottom view (*d*) is the only one to reveal the symmetrical arrangement of the four legs attached to the corners of the square seat. All this information is indispensable and feeds into the normal visual conception of the object. How can it be conveyed in one picture? No more eloquent demonstration of the difficulty can be given than the drawings of Figure 84, derived from findings by Georg Kerschensteiner. These drawings schematically present types of solutions worked out by school children who had been asked to reproduce from memory "a three-dimensional picture of a chair drawn in correct perspective."

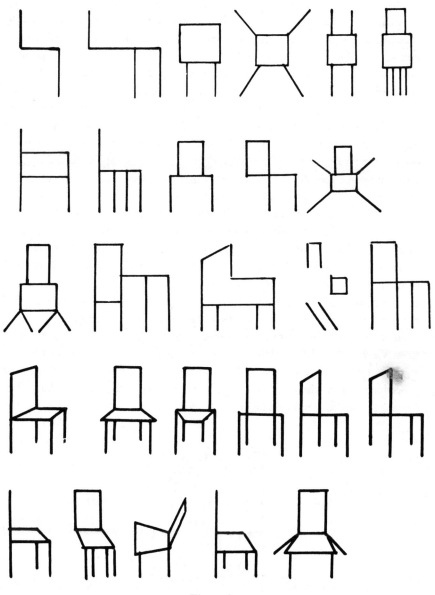

Figure 84

The Egyptian Method

One solution of the problem is best exemplified in the wall paintings and reliefs of the Egyptians and in the drawings of children. It consists in choosing for each part of an object or combination of objects the aspect that best suits the pictorial purpose. The pictures obtained by this procedure were formerly condemned, or at best tolerated, as the inferior creations of people who were incapable of doing better or who drew what they knew rather than what they saw. In 1867, Ernst Mach in a popular lecture on "Why Has Man Two Eyes?" observed that the principle employed by the Egyptians might best be described by saying that their figures are pressed in the plane of the drawing like plants in a herbarium. Only when similar methods were adopted by artists of our own century did theorists begin hesitantly to realize that deviations from correct projection are not due to such operations as twisting or squashing the faithfully perceived object, but are freely invented equivalents of the observed shape in the two-dimensional medium.

The Egyptians—as well as the Babylonians, early Greeks, and Etruscans, who used a similar style of representation—were commonly thought to have avoided foreshortening because it was too difficult. This argument was disposed of by Heinrich Schäfer, who showed that the side view of the human shoulder occurs in a few examples as early as the Sixth Dynasty, although it continued to remain an exception throughout the history of Egyptian art. He cites two examples of reliefs that represent workmen chiseling or towing a stone statue; the shoulders of the living men are given in the conventional front view, but the statue has the perspectively "correct" side view (Figure 85). Thus, in order to express lifeless rigidity the Egyptians had recourse to a procedure that, in the opinion of the average nineteenth-century art teacher, created the much more lifelike effect. Schäfer further points out that, for the

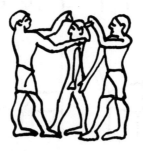

Figure 85

purpose of carving a sphinx, elevations were drawn on the sides of the rectangular block at least as early as 1500 B.C. and probably earlier. Naturally, projective drawing was required for these elevations.

It is evident, therefore, that the Egyptians used the method of orthogonal projection not because they had no choice, but because they preferred it. This method permitted them to preserve the characteristic symmetry of chest and shoulders and the front view of the eye in the profile face.

Pictorial representation is based on the visual concept of the total three-dimensional object. The method of copying an object or arrangement of objects from one fixed point of observation—roughly the procedure of the photographic camera—is not truer to that concept than the method of the Egyptians. Drawing or painting directly from the model is quite rare in the history of art. Even in the epoch of Western art that began with the Italian Renaissance, work from the model is often limited to preparatory sketches and does not necessarily result in mechanically faithful projection. When the figures in Egyptian art look "unnatural" to a modern observer, it is not because the Egyptians fail to present the human body the way it "really is," but because the observer judges their work by the standards of a different procedure. Once freed of this distorting prejudice, one finds it quite difficult to perceive the products of the "Egyptian method" as wrong.

What is required of the viewer is much more than enlightened tolerance for a method that has been "superseded by the discovery of correct perspective." Rather he must realize that there are different solutions to the problem of representing three-dimensional objects in a two-dimensional plane. Each method has its virtues and its drawbacks, and which is preferable depends on the visual and philosophical requirements of a particular time and place. It is a matter of style. Compare Figures 86 and 87. Figure 87 is a tracing after a painting of Oskar Schlemmer. Drawn in rough accordance with the rules of central perspective, it corresponds in that respect to what a camera would set down if such a scene were taken from a particular station point. In this sense the picture is quite realistic.

An advocate of the traditional realistic method would object to Figure 86, which indicates schematically how a similar scene would be represented in children's drawings and early forms of art. He would point out that the table is upright rather than horizontal, that foreground and background figures are the same size, and that one figure is lying sideways and another is upside-down. However, a partisan of this early method would object to Figure 87, deploring the representation of a rectangular table as a crooked trapezoid. He would point out that the three figures, objectively of equal size, vary in the

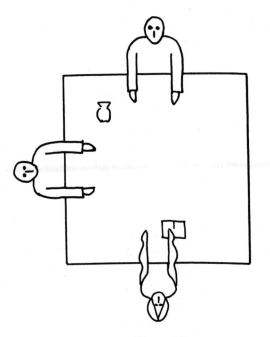

Figure 86

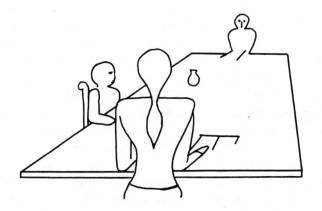

Figure 87

picture from giant to dwarf. Although all three should be in the same relation to the table, one is shown frontally, the second in profile, the third from the back; two figures are intersected by the table, whereas the third covers much of the table top with his own body and rubs shoulders with his neighbor, supposed to be seated at some distance. Nothing could be less realistic than such a crazily distorted picture.

Our *naïf* will show little appreciation for the fact that the distortion of size and shape makes possible a strong depth effect, or that the projection offers an interpretation of the scene from the viewpoint of one particular spatial location. Nor will he acknowledge that the alteration of sizes, angles, and shapes creates a witty and fascinating variation of the objective situation. Instead, he will tell the practitioner of perspective distortion that deplorably he has lost all the natural sensitivity to the requirements of the two-dimensional medium he had possessed as a child.

The apparently modest request that a picture reproduce the structural skeleton of a visual conception apparently has disturbing consequences. The *naïf* fulfills this demand to the letter by matching squareness with squareness, symmetry with symmetry, location with location.

Now it is true that the perspectively distorted drawing of the square looks like a square not only to the grown-up Westerner, but also to his child and to a "primitive" if he is able to look at the perspective drawing not as a surface decoration but as the real object. Schäfer reports the experience of an artist who was sketching the house of a German peasant while the owner watched him. As he was drawing the oblique lines required by perspective, the peasant protested: "Why are you making my roof so crooked—my house is quite straight!" But when he later saw the picture finished, he admitted with surprise: "Painting is a strange business! Now it is my house, just the way it is!"

The puzzle of perspective representation is that it makes things look right by doing them wrong. There is an important difference between the two procedures discussed here. The primitive or child accounts for the squareness he sees in reality with an actual square in the picture, a method that greatly strengthens the direct impact of the shape. He actually makes it be what it suggests it is. Perspective distortion, to be sure, is compensated in perception by the "constancy" of size and shape, but there is a weakening indirectness about this method. The distorted stimulus pattern, which gives rise to the experience, influences the percept even though the viewer may not be aware of it and be unable to realize or copy it. This is particularly true for flat pictures —even the most "lifelike" ones—because the depth effect is diminished and therefore constancy of shape is quite incomplete.

The power of all visual representation derives primarily from the properties inherent in the medium and only secondarily from what these properties suggest by indirection. Thus the truest and most effective solution is to represent squareness by a square. There is no question that in relinquishing this directness, Western art has suffered a serious loss. It has done so in favor of new virtues of realism and expression, which were more important to the men who developed perspective art than the qualities they had to relinquish.

Foreshortening

Both methods, Egyptian and Western, make particular two-dimensional aspects represent complete solids. Whether perspectively distorted or rectangular, the table top stands for a whole table. In order to fulfill this function an aspect should meet two conditions. It should indicate that in itself it is not the complete thing but only a part of something larger; and the structure of the whole it suggests should be the correct one. When we look at a cube head on, there is nothing in the perceived square to show that it is part of a cubic body. This may make it unsatisfactory as a projection, although it may be acceptable as a pictorial equivalent.

According to a rule in perception—again an application of the principle of simplicity—the shape of the perceived aspect (i.e. the projection) is taken spontaneously to embody the structure of the whole object. If we are shown a flat square, we see it as one aspect of a flat board. The same is true for a disk, which we see as part of a disk-shaped board. If the circular object is rounded, however—for example, by means of shading—we see it as part of a sphere. This may very well be misleading. The rounded object may be the bottom of a light bulb. Even so, perception automatically completes the whole body according to the simplest shape compatible with the perceived projection.

This perceptual tendency often produces satisfactory results. A sphere is in fact what any of its aspects promise it to be. To some extent this is true also for the human body. The whole volume roughly bears out what the front view suggests. No basic surprises emerge when the body is turned; nothing essential is hidden. Within obvious limits, the shape of the projection embodies the law of the whole.

This was not true for the drawing of the Mexican (Figure 82), where the law of completion suggested a disk-shaped object. Nor is it true in a straight front view of a horse, like the one in Figure 88, taken from a Greek vase. Knowledge may tell us that this is a horse, but contrary perceptual evidence overrules—and should always overrule in the arts—such knowledge, and tells us that this is a penguin-shaped creature, a monstrous horse-man. Atypical

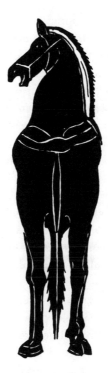

Figure 88

front views of this kind are artistically risky, though they are sought out sometimes precisely for this reason.

The term "foreshortening" can be used in three different ways: (1) It may mean that the projection of the object is not orthogonal—that is, its visible part does not appear in its full extension but projectively contracted. In this sense, a head-on front view of the human body would not be considered foreshortened. (2) Even though the visible part of the object is given in its full extension, an image can be described as foreshortened when it does not provide a characteristic view of the whole. In this sense, the bird's-eye-view of both the Mexican and the Greek horse are foreshortenings, but not in a truly perceptual and pictorial sense. It is only our knowledge of what the model object looks like that makes us regard these orthogonal views as deviations from a differently shaped object. The eye does not see it. (3) Geometrically, every projection involves foreshortening, because all parts of the body that do not run parallel to the projection plane are changed in their proportions or disappear partly or completely. Delacroix notes in his journals that there is always foreshortening, even in an upright figure with its arms hanging downward. "The arts of foreshortening and of perspective are one and the same thing. Some schools of painting have avoided foreshortenings, truly believing that they did not use any because they were using no violent ones. In a profile head, the eye, the forehead, etc., are foreshortened, and so it goes everywhere."

Projective contraction always involves an oblique position in space. What Max Wertheimer used to call the *Dingfront*, or "façade," of the object is seen as turned, and the given projection appears as a deviation from that "façade." Obliqueness provides visual evidence that different parts of the object lie at different distances from the observer. At the same time it preserves direct perception of the structural pattern from which the projection deviates. The foreshortening of a face, brought about by a turn to an oblique position, is not perceived as a pattern in its own right but as a mere variation of the frontal symmetry. No trace of that symmetry is left in a straight profile view, which is why the profile is not generally thought of as a foreshortening. The profile has a structure of its own.

It seems best, then, to call a pattern foreshortened when it is perceived as a deviation from a structurally simpler pattern, from which it is derived by a change of orientation in the depth dimension. Not all projective contractions succeed in making clear the structural pattern from which they deviate. A number of perceptual problems are involved here, of which I shall mention only a few. If, for example, the projective pattern has a simple shape, this simplicity will tend to interfere with its function because the simpler the shape of a two-dimensional pattern, the more it resists being perceived three-dimensionally—it tends to look flat. It is difficult to see a circle as a foreshortened ellipse or a square as a foreshortened rectangle. In Figure 89 the top view of a sitting man is foreshortened into a square-shaped projection. Owing to its squareness, the figure displays great stability in the plane and resists

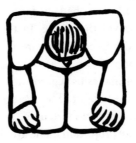

Figure 89

decomposition into a three-dimensional object. The conditions for subdivision in plane figures apply also to the third dimension.

Contractions along symmetry axes must be handled with caution. A face seen from below (Figure 90) produces a much more compelling distortion than an oblique view from the side. This is so because the symmetrical view looks "frozen," much more stable in itself. The asymmetrical side view clearly implies the "normal" front view from which it deviates, whereas the fore-shortened front view has a dangerous tendency to look like a squashed creature in its own right. The same holds true for symmetrical bird's-eye and worm's-eye views of whole figures. Such "abnormal" views are rare in the arts, and in the most famous of them—Mantegna's picture of the dead Christ—the fossilizing effect of the symmetry is mitigated by the sideward leaning of head and feet.

Another problem comes up frequently in the foreshortening of inward-bent forms, when the continuity of the body is replaced in the projection by discontinuous, overlapping units. The dropping out of the hidden parts,

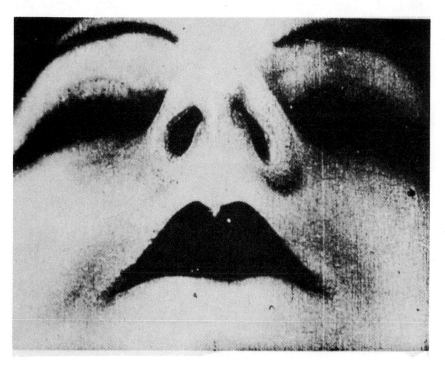

Figure 90
Fernand Léger. From *Ballet Mécanique*, 1924.

together with the change from continuity to discontinuity, produces a strong interference with the underlying visual concept. In Figure 91*b*, one of two figures roughly traced from Picasso drawings, a contour line leads without interruption from the left buttock to the foot. This same outline is interrupted in Figure 91*a*. More like a fugue than a linear melody, the drawing presents a sequence of overlaps, held together by the artist's skill in such a way that despite local leaps, the eye fuses the steps into a coherent whole. In bad drawing, it is precisely at these seams that the unity of the figure breaks down. Extreme examples of such risky discontinuity are found in fists that reach out of the picture toward the observer and often look quite detached from their arms, and in the back views of horses that show their buttocks cutting across their necks. Here visual comprehensibility approaches its limits. A sculptor, used to the continuity of his three-dimensional surfaces, may dislike such projective disruptions. Ernst Barlach writes: "I do not represent what I for my part see, or how I see it from here or there, but what *is*, the real and the truthful, which I have to extract from what I see in front of me. I prefer this kind of representation to drawing because it eliminates all artificiality. Sculpture, I would say, is a healthy art, a free art, not afflicted by such necessary evils as perspective, expansion, foreshortening, and other artificialities."

Overlapping

In spite of the visual acrobatics it entails, overlapping cannot be avoided since objects and parts of objects block one another's access to sight everywhere; and indeed, once the relations of shapes in pictorial compositions are carried beyond the simple array of coordinated units, there is great visual de-

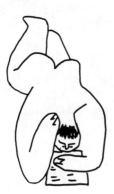

Figure 91*a*

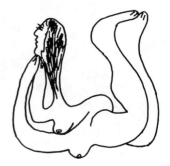

Figure 91*b*

light in the interferences and paradoxical juxtapositions produced by the stacking of things in space.

A requirement for the adequate perception of overlap—or superposition— is that the units which, because of projection, touch each other in the same plane must be seen as: (a) separate from each other and (b) belonging to different planes. The two drawings of Figure 92, again derived from Picasso,

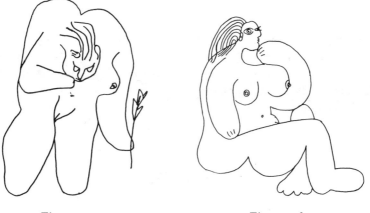

Figure 92*a*   Figure 92*b*

show that overlapping is perceived when the frontal shape—in this case, the breast—renders the other, the arm, clearly incomplete (*a*). In *b*, by contrast, both elements, arm and breast, are undisturbedly complete and therefore are seen as placed ambiguously side by side rather than behind each other. I shall discuss the more specific problems of "figure and ground" in Chapter V.

When the overlapping units together form a particularly simple shape, they tend to be seen as one and the same thing. Thus in Figure 93 the shoulder and arm of the woman may be taken to belong to the man—a misinterpretation strengthened by the fact that the resulting simple symmetry also fits the basic visual concept of a human body.

Since in every example of overlapping one unit is partly covered by another, the curtailed unit must not only be made to look incomplete, it must also evoke the right kind of completion. When frames or other impediments cut across limbs at the joints (shoulders, elbows, knees), visual amputation rather

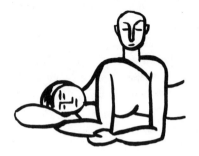

Figure 93

than overlapping is the result, because the stump looks complete in itself. Again, when the direction of the cut is in a simple relation to the structure of the visible unit, the fragment is more likely to show an inorganic completeness. See, for example, in Michelangelo's *Last Judgment*, the famous figure of the damned man (Figure 94) whose face is divided along the sagittal axis by

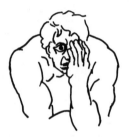

Figure 94

the hand shielding one of his eyes from the horrors before him, while the other eye dominates the visible half of the face like a monstrous thing with a shape of its own. Oblique cuts tend to prevent such effects. When the border of a picture cuts across a figure, the painter or photographer generally avoids the effect of amputated stumps or torsos by placing the cut so that the shape is seen as continued beyond the border.

These rules are by no means limited to the images of objects known from nature, such as animals or humans. The segment of a disk will or will not appear as a part of a circular shape depending on whether the curvature, at the points of interruption, suggests continued extension or an inward turn toward closure. It is not our anatomical knowledge but the nature of the shapes in which the body is cast that determines whether an organic object is perceived as complete, transformed, or mutilated.

What Good Does Overlapping Do?

The simplest kind of visual representation, as it is found, for example, in the drawings of young children and Mesolithic draftsmen, and in the Chinese ideogram for *man* (Figure 95), closely resembles in its structure the norm

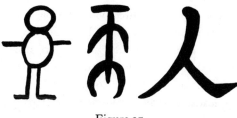

Figure 95

images we create in our minds. These norm images serve as "key tones" for overlappings, which deviate from the base in two ways. First, the norm arrangement, which presents a surveyable deployment of all limbs in their typical interrelation, gives way to intricate crossings as soon as the artist undertakes to depict the actions of working, gesticulating, sitting, climbing, falling. This transformation is inevitable wherever the artist wishes to present more than mere unmodified existence. Second, the body is subjected to alterations resulting from projection. It is this sort of transformation that requires a more detailed justification.

If one compares Figure 96*a* with a drawing of two ducks walking in single file without overlapping (Figure 96*b*), one realizes that the parallelism of the two birds, which conveys their togetherness to the eye, is brought out more compellingly when it occurs within one visual unit. Similarly, in Figure

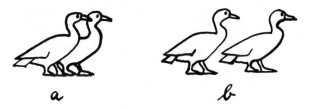

Figure 96

97 the contrast between the vertical body and the oblique arm imposes itself more forcefully when the two directions cross within one unit (*a*), rather than unfold in the looser lateral succession of *b*. In music the effect of harmony or disharmony is similarly more compelling when several tones are combined in one chord rather than played in succession. Overlapping intensifies the formal relation by concentrating it within a more tightly integrated pattern. The connection is not only closer but also more dynamic. It represents togetherness as interference through mutual modification of shape.

Strictly speaking, the interference caused by overlapping is not mutual. One unit always lies on top, unimpaired, violating the wholeness of the other. In Figure 98 the effect is rather one-sided. King Sethos is in front and complete, whereas Isis, who gives his majesty the support of her godship, endures all the inconveniences that befall a seat. Thus, overlapping establishes a hierarchy by creating a distinction between dominating and subservient units. A scale of importance leads, by way of two or more steps, from foreground to background.

The relationship is one-sided, however, only in the specific instance. In a complex whole the dominance-subservience relation at one place may be counteracted by its reversal at another, so that each partner is shown as both active and passive. A comparison of Figure 98 with the compositional scheme of a Rubens painting (Figure 99) illustrates the difference between the simple, one-sided relations in the Egyptian composition and the baroque counterpoint of overlapping and overlapped elements in the Rubens, which adds up to a complex intertwining of the two lovers.

Overlapping shows hiding and being hidden in a particularly expressive way. Dress is seen as covering or exposing the body. When the motion picture camera shows a prisoner behind bars, it makes all the difference for the meaning of the scene whether the shot is taken from inside or outside the cell, even

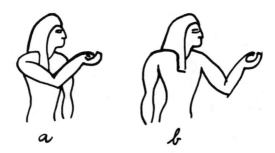

Figure 97

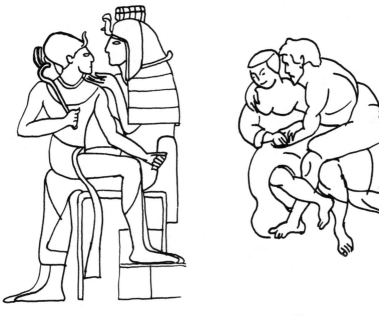

Figure 98   Figure 99

though the objective spatial situation is unchanged. If the scene is shot from inside the cell, we see the margin of freedom that remains to the man against the background of the prison; from outside, we see the bars shut him off visually by striking across his body. Alschuler and Hattwick found that young children who in their "abstract" easel paintings overlaid one patch of color on another tended to be "repressed" and (when cold colors were overlaid on warm ones) "of a passive nature," as distinguished from others who preferred side-by-side placement. Assuming that such a correspondence between personal attitude and pictorial expression in fact exists, it would be interesting to know to what extent the children were motivated by the physical act of hiding through overlay rather than the visual effect of the result.

Overlapping offers a convenient solution to the problem of how to represent symmetry in relation to a figure within the picture. Suppose a painter wants to depict the Judgment of Paris. The three goddesses are to be presented as having equal chances of being chosen, which means in visual terms that they should be placed symmetrically in relation to their judge. It is simple enough to show a symmetrical arrangement of the three women to the person who looks at the picture (Figure 100a), because his glance meets the plane perpendicularly. This, however, is not possible with the same means when

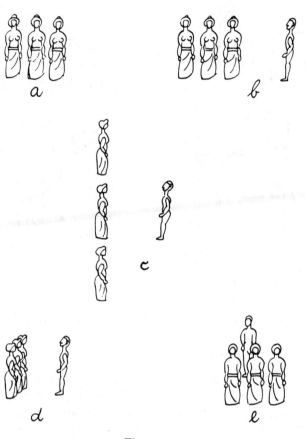

Figure 100

the beholder (Paris) is located in the picture plane (*b*). The three women do not face him symmetrically; one is closest to him, the second is farther away, and the third has the poorest chance. This arrangement undercuts the theme. The painter may show the situation in ground plan (*c*). This restores the symmetry but piles the goddesses awkwardly one on the other in totem-pole fashion. To display the pattern on the ground plane the picture space must be expanded into the third dimension by oblique arrangement, which often (though not necessarily) involves overlapping (*d*). The tilt may also be applied vertically (*e*).

The charioteer with his horses on the Greek vases and coins is another illustration of the same problem. The visual concept of the Horatii and the Curatii calls for two groups of three, set against each other symmetrically. The task is even more difficult when the group to be related to another party in the picture is not linear but, for example, circular. Figure 101 shows the compositional scheme of a twelfth-century calendar illustration. St. Ursula, surrounded by her maidens, is attacked by an archer. The group is symmetrical to the beholder but not to the archer. Only overlapping could overcome the spatial inconsistency.

The same dilemma arises from the spatial confrontation of individual objects. Medieval painters were plagued by the problem of how to make the evangelist write in his book. The spatial concept calls for the book to be facing the writer, whereas the picture requires that both writer and book be shown in revealing frontality.

Interplay of Plane and Depth

The third dimension enriches pictorial possibilities in somewhat the same way as the addition of more voices to the monophony of the simple melodic line created new opportunities in music. There are striking parallels in the development of the two arts. In music, the several voices are at first relatively independent of each other. With the passage of time, they become interrelated in an integrated composition; finally, the separate voices fuse in modern homophony (compare Figures 186 and 187). Rather similarly, pictorial depth is represented at early stages by separate horizontal strips, one on top of the other. At a later stage, overlapping is employed to obtain a three-dimensional stacking of foreground, middle ground, and background, more or less interrelated. Later still, the whole depth dimension fuses into one indivisible continuum, leading from front to back, from back to front.

When pictorial compositions are meant to occupy three-dimensional

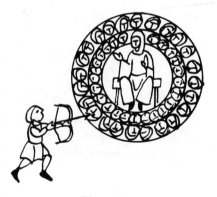

Figure 101

space, they are at a midpoint between two extreme spatial conceptions, to both of which they must be related. The two conceptions are those of zero percent constancy and one hundred percent constancy. At zero percent constancy, the picture is a total projection squashed in a flat frontal plane; at one hundred percent it occupies a fully three-dimensional stage. In practice, no picture occupies either of these extreme positions. Any picture has intermediate spatiality, tending to one or the other extreme in accordance with its style; it derives its meaning precisely from the interplay of both views.

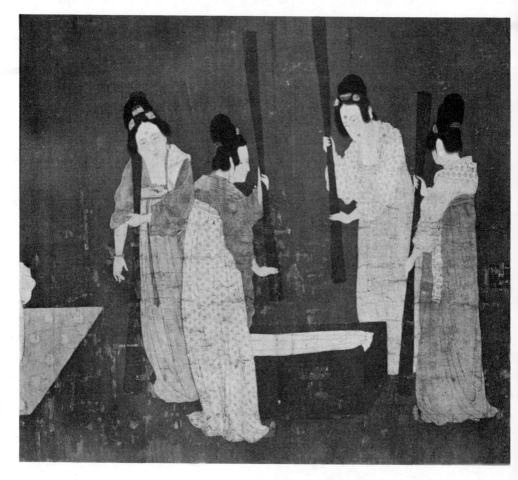

Figure 102
Hui Tsung. The Silk Beaters. Detail of a scroll, c. 1100. Boston Museum of Fine Arts.

The three-dimensional arrangement of the *Silk Beaters* (Figure 102) has four women standing around the table in a rectangular group, which is an oblique variation of the shape of the table itself (Figure 103). Three of the figures face one another symmetrically (II, III, IV); the fourth, getting herself ready to work, stands turned away. Thus the group of four is subdivided into a triangle and an outsider, woman IV being the connecting link between the two who are working already and the one who is not. The connections between the two dark robes and the two light robes correspond to the diagonals of the rectangular group. The two dark figures establish the lateral limits of the group. The light ones do the same for the depth dimension, woman II dominating in the foreground and III being removed to the greatest distance.

The arrangement in the projective pattern of the picture plane is quite different. The women are not located around the table. Two of them flank it, and of the other two one overlaps it and the other is overlapped by it. The group now subdivides more clearly into two pairs, each knitted together by overlapping and separated from the other by empty space. The triangular symmetry of II, III, IV has disappeared; the fourth figure is no longer separate. Instead there is something like a sequence of four lunar phases that leads in a decrescendo from the dominating full face of I over the obliqueness of III to the profile of II and finally the almost hidden face of IV. This establishes a linear zigzag connection, which does not exist in the three-dimensional composition. There are now two outer figures (dark) and two inner figures (light)—an approximate lateral symmetry around a central axis formed by the two sticks. The four heads are the corners of a flat parallelogram, in which women I and III dominate the other two by the higher position of their heads, but are overlapped by them if the whole figures are considered.

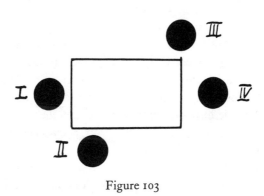

Figure 103

A wealth of form and meaning springs from the interaction of the two compositional structures, which partly support and partly oppose each other contrapuntally. It would be worthwhile to study the relative functions of the two patterns more precisely. Obviously, the three-dimensional grouping always describes more accurately the factual or "topographic" situation (for example, Christ surrounded by his disciples), whereas its expressive or symbolic function may well be weaker than that of the visually more direct projective pattern. Since the relative strength of the two depends on the strength of the depth effect in the particular picture, however, an investigation of their functions may lead to different results for different styles.

Competing Aspects

No more than one aspect of any three-dimensional object is visible at any place and time. In the course of his life and in fact during almost any particular episode of his daily experience, a person overcomes this limitation of visual projection by looking at things from all sides and thereby forming a comprehensive image from the totality of partial impressions. I have mentioned the difficulty arising when such all-around visual concepts are to be represented on a pictorial surface.

Inevitably, some aspects are selected, to the derogation of others. The tradition established by Renaissance art admitted of only one solution for this dilemma. The painter had to choose the one aspect best suited for his purpose and had to put up with whatever was hidden, foreshortened, or distorted from that particular point of view. We have noted that early forms of art are unaffected by this rule and freely combine the most informative aspects of each part of an object or spatial situation, disregarding the concomitant discrepancy of viewpoints. Such styles of representation are committed to the object or situation as such, not to any one of its views.

There is one rule, however, that these early styles tend to respect. In general, they do not use more than one aspect of an object or part of an object in the same picture. They would not, for example, show both a front view and a back view of the same object. However, occasional transgressions of the rule are found even at fairly primitive levels. In children's drawings the combination of a frontal nose with a profile nose in the same face may occur at stages of transition from one form of representation to another.

Genuine examples of such dual-aspect representation occur here and there as local inventions of limited range, often for playful, decorative purposes. The American Indians solved the problem of presenting the characteristic side view and the frontal symmetry of an animal at the same time by splitting the body into two side views. These were combined in a symmetrical whole and kept precarious contact with each other by sharing either the middle line of the back or the head or by cohering at the tip of the nose or the tail (Figure 104). Morin-Jean has shown that similar forms, which he misinterprets as "monsters

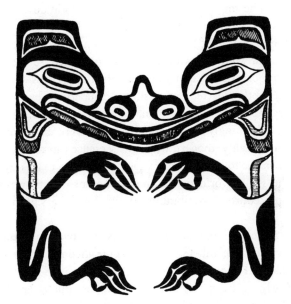

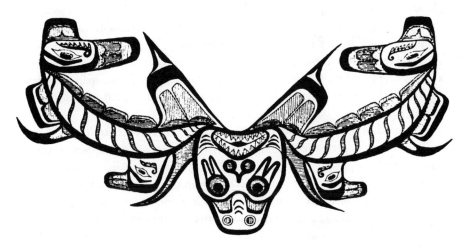

Figure 104

with a double body and single head," occur in Oriental decorative art, on Greek vases and coins, and again on Romanesque capitals. All these examples, however, are fanciful exceptions from the general rule.

Some modern art, especially cubism, also resorted to combining views from several angles in the same whole, but it did so in a characteristically different way. The modern artist was heir to a tradition that had come to identify an object with its pictorial projection. The correctness of the projection seemed to guarantee the validity of the image. Later, in the nineteenth century, such representation was found to be one-sided, subjective, accidental —which at first occasioned applause, and then apprehension. Although the fleeting images aptly reflected the passing and superficial experiences that had come to typify the life of Western man, the world represented by these images began to look alarmingly insubstantial. Artists were exposing the fact that in his relation to reality, modern man was sentenced to catching nothing but glimpses. When the following generations, in reaction to this trend, struggled to recover the stable world of the more innocent eye, they resorted to the "primitive" procedure of combining aspects, but in a significantly modern way.

At early stages of representation, aspects are always put together in such a manner that, despite inherent spatial contradictions, there results an organic and characteristic whole. Since the intention is to reproduce things as correctly, clearly, and completely as possible, the aspects are fitted together harmoniously, organically, and often symmetrically. The most characteristic aspects are chosen, especially front views and side views; head and neck are placed symmetrically between the shoulders; and a frontal eye can be located in a profile head because it represents a relatively independent entity. In a child's drawing of a glass of water (Figure 105*a*), the combination of side view and top view in a symmetrical pattern expresses the solid completeness of a trustworthy reality, whereas in Picasso's rendering of a saucepan (Figure 105*b*), front view and side view, roundness and angularity, left tilt and right tilt, all coincide in a clashing contradiction.

The cubist procedure has sometimes been interpreted as if the artist wanted simply to give a more complete view of an object by combining various aspects. To appreciate the result, the beholder is presumably to fly on the wings of his mind from one perspective view to the other, or to find himself at different locations simultaneously. By such mental acrobatics the viewer himself would perform the dynamics actually inherent in the work. In fact, of course, he is looking not at the three-dimensional object but at a flat picture of it, in which the aspects clash in deliberate contradiction. The tension

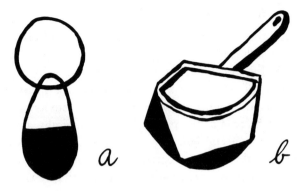

Figure 105

created by visual incompatibility is heightened when different, mutually exclusive views appear together, e.g., a profile view fitted into a frontal view.
The more intimately fused the two views, the stronger the tension, as for
example in Figure 106, a tracing after the head of a bull by Picasso. Even in
sculpture, where no need exists to collect incompatible aspects in the interest
of realistic completeness, the cubist artist practices the same violent interpene-
tration of units. He presents the image of a world in which interaction is
possible only as the mutual invasion of self-contained units, each intent on
its own purpose. The whole is kept in balance by no higher principle than
that of a multiplicity of pushes compensating one another by the variety of
their directions. The contradictions of which the Marxists speak are made
visual.

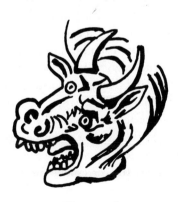

Figure 106

Realism and Reality

In dealing with the two-dimensional representation of three-dimensional space we have encountered a peculiar paradox. The example of three persons sitting at a table (Figures 86, 87) showed that when such a scene is presented as a mechanically correct projection, it leads to awkward distortions in the frontal plane. Conversely, when the scene is translated into its two-dimensional equivalent, it can be read as the projection of a physically absurd scene, in which the table top stands upright and the three persons are attached to it like flaps. It follows that there are appropriate and inappropriate ways of reading pictorial representations of space, and that the proper way is determined in each case by the style of a given period or developmental stage.

It is in keeping with this paradoxical situation that when the influence of scientific optics made pictorial representation move toward mechanical projection, the objective correctness of this procedure authorized an unheard-of freedom from the structural norm. It gave license to radical distortions of the simple visual skeletons by which people understood and continue to understand the build of a human body, an animal, a tree. Protected by the "correctness" of their foreshortenings, artists twisted the axes of objects, destroyed the symmetrical correspondence of parts, altered proportions, and rearranged the relative location of things. In a realistic painting, a human figure could reach above the trees into the sky, the feet could adjoin the face, and the outline of the body could assume almost any shape. Heinrich Wölfflin writes about the Slaves Michelangelo painted on the Sistine ceiling: "The deviation from the norm in the structure of the bodies is insignificant by comparison with the way Michelangelo arranges the limbs. In their relations he discovers entirely new effects. Here he brings an arm and the two lower legs tightly together as a set of three parallels; there he crosses the thigh with the downward-reaching arm so that they form almost a right angle; then again he comprehends the whole figure from head to heels in one unitary sweep of line. And these are not mathematical variations that he sets himself as an exercise. Even the most outlandish posture looks convincing." For a similar example see the figure of Abias in Figure 107.

Evidently, the Renaissance artists practiced the new skill of faithful projection not only in tribute to the ideal of scientifically authenticated realism, but because of the inexhaustible variety of appearances derivable from natural objects in this fashion and the corresponding wealth of individual interpretation. It is not surprising that this extreme exploitation of projective distortion eventually led to a radical countermovement, a return to ele-

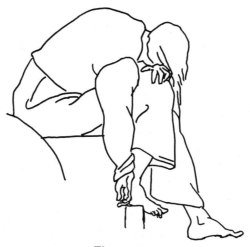

Figure 107

mentary shapes and the elementary schemata of permanent structural norms. The reaction became conspicuous in the geometrical simplifications of Seurat and Cézanne and the primitivism pervading much art of the early twentieth century.

At the same time, however, that art sought refuge from complexities of distortions that the human eye could no longer organize, an expressionist trend took advantage of the new freedom from the basic norm and adopted all the licenses of projective art without any longer bothering to justify them as the mechanically correct projections of physical objects. The realists had initiated the destruction of organic integrity. They had made objects incomplete or separated their parts with intervening foreign bodies. Modern artists did the same without the requirements of overlapping as an excuse. Obliqueness had been introduced to represent depth. Modern artists distorted the orientation of axes without that justification. The destruction of local color had been carried to its extreme by the impressionists, who had used reflections to apply the green of a meadow to the body of a cow or the blue of the sky to the stones of a cathedral. In consequence, modern artists became free not only to make a red object blue, but also to replace the unity of one local color with any combination of different colors. In the past, artists had learned to reorganize organic subdivisions with paradoxical results. They fused several human figures into one triangle, or detached an arm from the mass of the body and united it with the arm of another figure to make a new, continuous whole.

This enabled the modern artist, for example, to split up a face and fuse part of it with the background. By illuminating objects from a particular direction, artists had come to cast shadows across them, subdividing them in ways that had little organic justification. Carrying this device still further, Braque made one female figure consist of two—a black profile woman and a light front-face woman (see Figure 233).

What Looks Lifelike?

We have come a long way from the narrow belief that only mechanically faithful replication is true to nature. We realize that the whole range of infinitely different styles of representation is acceptable, not only to those who share the particular attitude that created it, but also to those of us who can adapt to it. However, mere tolerance for different approaches to the same goal is not good enough. We must go further and realize that just as persons of our own civilization and century may perceive a particular manner of representation as lifelike even though it may not look lifelike at all to the adherents of another approach, so do the adherents of those other approaches find their preferred manner of representation not only acceptable, but entirely lifelike.

This would be hard to believe had we not documents to prove it. Stories about paintings or statues so lifelike that they deceived man and beast have come to us from periods of Chinese and Greek art whose style would by no means deceive us into believing that we were facing reality rather than man-made images. We do not know exactly what the paintings of Zeuxis looked like, but we have reason to doubt that his painted grapes really made sparrows peck at them in the belief that they were real. More probably these stories express the visual experiences of contemporary viewers, to whom the pictures looked most lifelike.

Boccaccio tells in the *Decamerone* that the painter Giotto "was a genius of such excellence that there was no thing of nature . . . that he did not depict with the pencil or the pen or the brush in a manner so similar to the object that it seemed to be the thing itself rather than merely resembling it; so much so that many times the visual sense of men was misled by the things he made, believing to be true what was only painted." The highly stylized pictures of Giotto could have hardly deceived his contemporaries if they had judged lifelikeness by direct comparison with reality. Compared with the work of his immediate predecessors, however, Giotto's rendering of expressive gestures, depth, volume, and scenery could indeed be considered very lifelike, and it was this deviation from the prevailing norm level of pictorial representation that produced the astonishing effect on Giotto's contemporaries.

The principle of adaptation level, introduced into psychology by Harry Helson, indicates that a given stimulus is judged not according to its absolute qualities, but in relation to the norm level established in the person's mind. In the case of pictorial representation, this norm level seems to be derived not directly from perception of the physical world itself, but from the style of the pictures known to the observer.

Reactions to photography and film have shown that progress in pictorial lifelikeness creates the illusion of life itself. The first motion pictures, shown about 1890, were so crude technically that they give us little illusion of reality today, but the mere addition of movement to the black-and-white image sufficed to make the first spectators scream with fear when the train rushed headlong toward them. Curiously enough, the advent of color produced hardly any additional increment; but the spatial resonance of sound temporarily increased the visual depth and volume of the picture considerably. And the first life-size holographs, which added the powerful motion parallax to the still image, were so shockingly real that the absence of live motion made the portrayed person look like a corpse.

Actual illusions are, of course, rare; but they are the extreme and most tangible manifestation of the fact that, as a rule, in any given cultural context the familiar style of pictorial representation is not perceived as that at all—the image looks simply like a faithful reproduction of the object itself. In our civilization this is true for "realistic" works; they look "just like nature" to many persons who are unaware of their highly complicated and specific style. However, this "artistic reality level" may shift quite rapidly. Today we can hardly imagine that less than a century ago the paintings of Cézanne and Renoir were rejected not only because of their unusual style, but because they in fact looked offensively unreal. It was not merely a matter of different judgment or taste, but of different perception. Our forefathers saw on those canvases incoherent patches of paint that we are no longer able to see, and they based their judgment on what they saw.

Those of us who live with the art of our century find it increasingly difficult to see what "the man in the street" means when he takes exception to deviations from realistic rendition in the Picassos, the Braques, the Klees. In Picasso's portrait of a schoolgirl we see the elementary liveliness of the young creature, the girlish repose, the shyness of the face, the straightly combed hair, the burdensome tyranny of the big textbook. The strongly colored, wildly overlapping geometrical shapes do not detract from the subject but carry its expression with such mastery that we no longer see them as mere shapes: they are consumed in the task of representation. In fact, it seems safe to assert that every successful work of art, no matter how stylized and remote from mechanical correctness, conveys the full natural flavor of the object it represents. Picasso's painting not only depicts a schoolgirl; it *is* a schoolgirl. "I always aim at resemblance," said Picasso in 1966. And he exclaimed that an artist should observe nature, but never confuse it with painting. "It is only translatable into painting by signs."

If someone sees the shapes instead of the subject, something may be wrong with the picture. Or the observer may be perceiving from an inappropriate adaptation level. (In fact, the "man in the street" is often fixated at a style level established by the painters of the seventeenth century.) It is also true that for informational illustrations in anthropology textbooks or biology manuals, a different style, perhaps the linear classicism of the Ingres school, is taken for granted; a painting by Matisse, perceived as though it were intended as such a textbook illustration, will necessarily show its shapes rather than its subject.

As far as the artists themselves are concerned, there seems to be little doubt that they see in their work the embodiment of the intended object. The sculptor Jacques Lipchitz tells of admiring one of Juan Gris' pictures while it was still on the easel. It was the kind of cubistic work in which many a layman even today discovers little but an agglomeration of abstract shapes. Lipchitz exclaimed: "This is beautiful! Do not touch it any more! It is complete." At which Gris, flying into a rage, shouted in reply: "Complete? Don't you see that I have not finished the moustache?" To him the picture contained the image of a man so clearly that he expected everyone to see it immediately in all its detail.

The utterances of artists make it clear that they think of "style" simply as a means of giving reality to their image. "Originality" is the unsought and unnoticed product of a gifted artist's successful attempt to be honest and truthful, to penetrate to the origins, the roots, of what he sees. The deliberate search for a personal style inevitably interferes with the validity of the work, because it introduces an element of arbitrariness into a process that can be governed only by necessity. Picasso once said: "Always strive for perfection. For instance, try to draw a perfect circle; and since you can't draw a perfect circle, the involuntary flaw will reveal your personality. But if you want to reveal your personality by drawing an imperfect circle—*your* circle—you will bungle the whole thing."

One misunderstanding must be avoided. When I assert that in a successful work of art one perceives the subject rather than the shapes, I may seem to be suggesting that form does not matter. Nothing could be further from my intention. In fact, the same suggestion holds for "abstract" or nonmimetic art. It makes all the difference whether in an "abstract" painting we see an arrangement of mere shapes, i.e., visual objects that can be completely described by their area, outline, color, location, etc., or see instead the organized action of expressive visual forces. In the latter case, the shapes vanish in the dynamic play; and it is only this dynamic play that conveys the meaning of the work. The bulging, twisting columns, the swinging scrolls and roofs of a Baroque façade leave the geometry of their shapes and the material substance of the stone behind as the total architectural composition transfigures itself into a symphony of movement. Similarly, in a representational work of painting or sculpture, the shapes made by the artist and the pigment or metal or wood of the medium are transformed into visual action, which gives life to the subject matter. Good form does not show.

Form as Invention

Many of our examples will have helped to illustrate what I suggested early in this chapter, namely that image-making, artistic or otherwise, does not start from the optical projection of the object represented, but is an equivalent, rendered with the properties of a particular medium, of what is observed in the object. Visual form can be evoked by what is seen, but cannot be taken over directly from it. It is well known that the death masks and plaster casts of actual persons, which are mechanically lifelike, nevertheless often have a purely material presence and tend to let us down when we expect them to interpret character through visual appearance. They are essentially shapeless and therefore cannot serve as form. Any beginner, drawing from the model, discovers that the shapes he expects to find by looking carefully at a face, a shoulder, a leg, are not really there. The same problem, however, seems to have caused the tragic struggle that Alberto Giacometti never overcame. It started in 1921, when he wanted to portray a figure and found that *tout m'échappait, la tête du modèle devant moi devenait comme un nuage, vague et illimité*—"everything escaped me, the head of the model in front of me became like a cloud, vague and limitless." He tried to represent this unreachability of the model in the evasive surfaces of his sculpted and painted figures, while insisting at the same time upon the pursuit of the shapes he thought had to exist objectively in those human heads and bodies.

The attempt to find representational form in the model was doomed to failure because all form must be derived from the particular medium in which the image is executed. The elementary act of drawing the outline of an object in the air, in the sand, or on a surface of rock or paper means a reduction of the thing to its contour, which does not exist as a line in nature. This translation is a very elementary accomplishment of the mind—there are indications that young children and monkeys recognize the outline pictures of familiar objects almost spontaneously. But to grasp the structural similarity between a thing and any depiction of it is a tremendous feat of abstraction nevertheless.

Each medium prescribes the way in which the features of a model are best rendered. For example, a round object may be represented as a circular line by means of a pencil. A brush, which can make broad spots, may produce an equivalent of the same object by a disk-shaped patch of paint. In the medium of clay or stone, the best equivalent of roundness is a sphere. A dancer will create it by running a circular course, spinning around his own axis, or arranging a group of dancers in a circle. In a medium that does not yield curved shape, roundness may be expressed by straightness. Figure 108 shows a snake

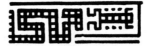

Figure 108

pursuing a frog as represented in a basketry pattern by the Indians of Guyana. A shape expressing roundness best in one medium may not do so in another. A circle or disk may be the perfect solution in the flat picture plane. In three-dimensional sculpture, however, circle and disk combine roundness with flatness and thus represent roundness imperfectly. A black-and-white apple becomes "colorless" when transferred from a monochromatic lithograph to an oil painting. In a painting by Degas a motionless dancer is a suitable representation of a moving dancer, but in a film or on the stage a motionless dancer would not be in motion but paralyzed.

Form is determined not only by the physical properties of the material, but also by the style of representation of a culture or an individual artist. A flat-looking patch of color may be a human head in the essentially two-dimensional world of Matisse; but the same patch would look flat instead of round in one of Caravaggio's strongly three-dimensional paintings. In a cubist statue by Lipchitz a cube may be a head, but the same cube would be a block of inorganic matter in a work of Rodin. Figure 109 shows Picasso's drawing *The End of a Monster*. The way in which the head of the monster is drawn serves in other works by the same artist to represent undistorted, non-monstrous shape (compare the bull of Figure 106). There is no paradox here.

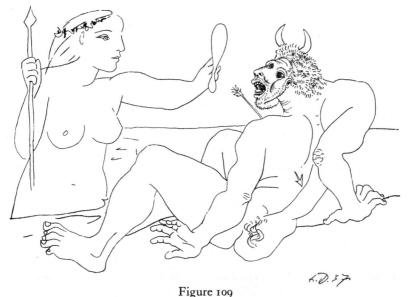

Figure 109
Pablo Picasso. *La Fin d'un Monstre*. Coll. Roland Penrose, London.

A pattern that produces a monster in a relatively realistic picture may stand for "straight" anatomy in a work that applies the same manner of distortion to everything.

Such translations of the appearance of physical objects into the form appropriate to particular media are not esoteric conventions thought up by artists. They are in common usage everywhere in life. Scale models, line drawings on blackboards, and road maps all deviate markedly from the objects they depict. We easily discover and accept the fact that a visual object on paper can stand for a quite different one in nature, provided it is presented to us in its structural equivalent for the given medium. In the next chapter I shall demonstrate the unerring logic and consistency of children in this matter.

The psychological reason for this striking phenomenon is, first, that in human perception and thinking, similarity is based not on piecemeal identity but on the correspondence of essential structural features; second, that an unspoiled mind spontaneously understands any given object according to the laws of its context.

It takes a great deal of "spoiling" before we come to think that representation is not only an imitation of the object but also of its medium, so that we expect a painting not to look like a painting but like physical space, and a statue not like a piece of stone but like a living body of flesh and blood. This unquestionably less intelligent concept of representation, far from being natural to man, is a late product of the particular civilization in which we happen to have lived for a while.

As one walks through a museum and looks at the shapes given by sculptors of different ages and cultures to the human head, one realizes that the same simple prototype can be reflected in an infinity of equally valid representations. The head may be fitted to a very few overall shapes or subdivided into many small ones; the shapes may be straight or curved, edged or voluminous, clearly separated or fused; they may derive from cubes or spheres, ellipsoids or paraboloids; they may employ deep cavities or slight depressions. Each has its validity, and each makes its point.

This capacity to invent a striking pattern, especially when applied to such familiar shapes as a head or a hand, is what is known as artistic imagination. Imagination is by no means first of all the invention of new subject matter, and not even the production of just any kind of new shape. Artistic imagination can be more nearly described as the finding of new form for old content, or—if the handy dichotomy of form and content is eschewed—as a fresh conception of an old subject. The invention of new things or situations is valuable only to the extent that they serve to interpret an old—that is, universal—topic of human experience. There is more imagination in the way Titian paints a hand than in hundreds of surrealist nightmares depicted in a dull, conventional manner.

Visual imagination is a universal gift of the human mind, a gift that in the average person demonstrates itself at an early age. When children start to experiment with shape and color, they are faced with the task of inventing a way to represent in a given medium the objects of their experience. Occasionally they are helped by watching others, but essentially they are on their own. The wealth of original solutions they produce is all the more remarkable because their subject matter is so elementary. Figure 110 shows representations of the human figure copied from drawings by children at early stages of development. Certainly these children were not trying to be original, and yet the attempt to put down on paper what he sees makes each of them discover a new visual formula for the old subject. Every one of these drawings, which could easily be multiplied by the hundreds, respects the basic visual concept of the human body—as witnessed by the fact that it is understood by the beholder—and at the same time offers an interpretation that distinguishes it from the other drawings.

It is evident that the object itself dictates only a bare minimum of structural features, thus calling for "imagination" in the literal sense of the word—

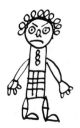
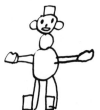
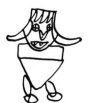
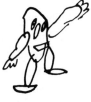
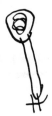
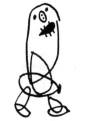
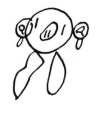
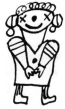
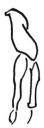
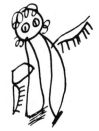
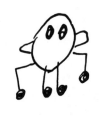
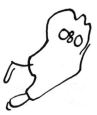
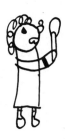
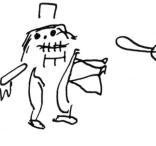
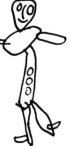
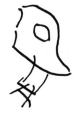

Figure 110

that is, the activity of making things into images. If we examine the drawings more closely, we find broad variations in many formal factors. The considerable differences in absolute size do not show in Figure 110. The relative size of parts, for example, that of the head in comparison with the rest of the body, varies considerably. Many different solutions are found for the subdivision of the body. Not only the number of parts but also the placing of boundary lines varies. There is much detail and differentiation in some, little in others. Round shapes and angular shapes, thin sticks and solid masses, juxtapositions and overlappings, all are used to represent the same object. What is more, the simple enumeration of geometric differences does not do justice to the individuality evident in the overall appearance of these drawings. Some of the figures look stable and rational, others are carried away in reckless action. There are sensitive ones and crude ones, simple ones and subtly complex ones, plump ones and frail ones. Every one of them expresses a way of living, of being a person. The differences are due partly to the stage of development, partly to the individual character of the child, partly to the purpose of the drawing. Together these pictures demonstrate the abundant resources of pictorial imagination that are found in the average child until lack of encouragement, unsuitable teaching, and an uncongenial environment suppress them in all but a fortunate few.

A successful artistic solution is so compelling that it looks like the only possible realization of the subject. Different renditions of the same theme must be compared before the role of imagination can be truly appreciated. Systematic accounts of the various ways in which a particular subject can be represented have been given much too rarely. A good example is Lucien Rudrauf's analysis of Annunciations as "variations of a plastic theme." He shows how differently the famous encounter has been interpreted, depending on which moment of the event the artist chose and how his imagination distributed active and passive function, dominance and submission, and so on. Historic surveys, which follow a given theme through the ages, are more frequent. Among other things they show how on occasion an artist comes upon an image that embodies some basic subject with a spellbinding validity. The same story, the same composition, or the same posture lives on for centuries as an indelible contribution to the way man visualizes his world.

Levels of Abstraction

One dimension in which the artist can exercise his freedom is the degree of abstraction he uses to render his subject. He can replicate the appearance of the physical world with the meticulous faithfulness of the *trompe l'oeil* painter, or, like Mondrian and Kandinsky, he can work with completely nonmimetic shapes, which reflect human experience by pure visual expression and spatial relations. Within the representational realm, many styles of picture-making limit themselves to portraying the things of nature with just a very few structural features. This highly abstract mode is prominent in early stages of art, i.e., in the work of children and "primitives," but also in certain aspects of the Byzantine style of Christian art, modern Western art, and the artwork of schizophrenics. These are strange bedfellows, but if we assume that similarity of form points to some corresponding similarity of mental state, we shall have to resort to bold generalization.

The patterns that result from limiting representation to just a few features of the object are often simple, regular, and symmetrical. Offhand there would seem to be no compelling reason for this. Shape may be made more complicated by omissions. The theorists of the last century, who were inclined to derive all properties of images from observed aspects of reality, tried to account for this tendency by pointing to regular shapes in nature that man was supposed to have imitated—the disk of the sun, the symmetrical build of plant, animal, and man himself. As an extreme example, Wilhelm Worringer cites an anthropologist who undertook to show by means of snapshots that the shape of the cross was derived from the pattern made by flying storks. Obviously, this approach does not take us very far, since it cannot explain why man should have picked the regularly shaped percepts among the immensely more frequent irregular ones. Occasionally the simple form of an image can be derived in part from the medium in which it was executed—for example, in basketry—but nothing like a generally valid principle can be obtained from such an observation.

More plausibly, we might observe that when by some circumstance the mind is freed from its usual allegiance to the complexities of nature, it will organize shapes in accordance with the tendencies that govern its own functioning. We have much evidence that the principal tendency at work here is that toward simplest structure, i.e., toward the most regular, symmetrical, geometrical shape attainable under the circumstances.

It should be noted that although in the instances under discussion the representational features derived from the physical world are few, the artist may nevertheless develop those few features into an elaborate play of shapes, which may be described variously as geometric, ornamental, formalistic, stylized, schematic, or symbolic.

As a first step toward the understanding of such highly abstract styles, we note that under certain cultural conditions more realistic art would not serve the artist's purpose better, but on the contrary interfere with it. Primitive images, for example, do spring neither from detached curiosity about the appearance of the world nor from the "creative" response for its own sake. They are not made to produce pleasurable illusions. Primitive art is a practical instrument for the important business of daily life; it gives body to super-human powers so that they may become partners in concrete undertakings. It replaces real objects, animals, or humans, and thus takes over their jobs of rendering all kinds of services. It records and transmits information. It makes it possible to exercise "magic influences" on creatures and things that are absent.

What counts in all these operations is not the material existence of things, but the effects they exert or submit to. Modern natural science has accustomed us to thinking of many of these effects as physical events that reflect the composition and behavior of matter. This view is of relatively recent origin, and is quite different from a simpler notion that finds its purest expression in primitive science. We think food is necessary because it contains certain physical substances that our bodies absorb and utilize. To the primitive, food is the carrier of immaterial powers or forces whose vitalizing virtue is trans-ferred to the eater. Disease is caused not by the physical action of germs, poisons, or temperature, but by a destructive "fluid" emitted by some hostile agency. For the primitive it follows that the specific appearance and behavior of natural things, from which we derive information about probable physical effects, are as irrelevant to their function as a book's shape and color are to the content we find in it. Thus, for example, in depicting animals the primi-tive limits himself to the enumeration of such features as limbs and organs, and uses geometrically clear-cut shape and pattern to identify their kind, func-tion, importance, and mutual relations as precisely as possible. He may use pictorial means also to express "physiognomic" qualities, such as the ferocity or friendliness of the animal. Realistic detail would obscure rather than clarify these relevant characteristics. (Similar principles of representation are found in our own civilization, in the illustrations for medical treatises written before the advent of modern natural science.)

Early stages of development produce highly abstract shapes because close contact with the complexities of the physical world is not, or not yet, pertinent to the task of picture making. It is not possible, however, to turn this statement around and assume that highly abstract shape is always the product of an early mental stage. People often create elementary images, not because they have so far to go, but because they have so far withdrawn. An example may be found in Byzantine art, which was a withdrawal from the most realistic style of representation the world had then seen. Art became the servant of a state of mind that, in its extreme manifestations, condemned the use of images altogether. Life on earth was considered a mere preparation for life in Heaven. The material body was the vessel of sin and suffering. Thus visual art, instead of proclaiming the beauty and importance of physical existence, used the body as a visual symbol of the spirit; by eliminating volume and depth, by simplifying color, posture, gesture, and expression, it succeeded in dematerializing man and world. The symmetry of the composition represented the stability of the hierarchic order created by the Church. By eliminating everything accidental and ephemeral, elementary posture and gesture emphasized lasting validity. And straight, simple shape expressed the strict discipline of an ascetic faith.

The art of our own century offers another striking example of high abstraction obtained through withdrawal. Like Byzantine art, it renounced the skillful illusionism of its forebears. Here, a specific psychological reason can be found in the changed position of the artist. The craftsman who had fulfilled an established need in the affairs of government and religion was gradually transformed into an outsider—the producer of surplus luxury goods to be stored in museums or used to demonstrate the wealth and refined taste of the rich and privileged. This exclusion from the economic mechanism of supply and demand tended to transform the artist into a self-centered observer.

Such a detachment from the give and take of civic existence has its pros and cons. On the positive side, a spectator can stand back, and thus see better and more independently. At a distance, personal commitments lose their power; accidental detail drops out and essence reveals its broad shape. The detached artist, like the scientist, withdraws from individual appearance to seize more directly upon fundamental qualities. An immediate grasp of the pure essentials, for which Schopenhauer praised music as the highest of the arts, is attempted through the abstractness of the best modern painting and sculpture. Pure form aims more directly at the hidden clockwork of nature, which more realistic styles represent indirectly by its manifestations in material things and events. The concentrated statement of these abstractions is valid as long as it retains the sensory appeal that distinguishes a work of art from a scientific diagram.

Negatively, high abstraction risks detaching itself from the wealth of actual existence. The great works of art and science have always avoided this limitation; they have encompassed the whole range of human experience by applying the most general forms or principles to the greatest variety of phenomena. We need only think of the teeming variety of creatures that a Giotto,

Rembrandt, or Picasso subordinates to the overall principles determining his view of life and thereby his style. When contact with a full range of human experience is lost, there results not art, but formalistic play with shapes or empty concepts.

Extreme instances of this danger can be studied in certain types of schizophrenic art, in which ornamental geometric patterns are elaborated with as much precision and care as the disorganization of the patient's mental state permits. Striking examples are the drawings made by the dancer Nijinsky during his years of confinement in a mental institution. If we inquire about the corresponding state of mind, we find a freezing of feeling and passion accompanied by a withdrawal from reality. A shell of glass seems to surround the schizophrenic. Life around him appears as an alien and often threatening spectacle on a stage, which can be watched, but which permits no give and take. The secluded intellect weaves fantastic cosmologies, systems of ideas, visions, grandiose missionary projects. Since the sensory sources of natural form and meaning are clogged and the vital passions dried up, formal organization remains, as it were, unmodulated. The tendency to simple shape operates unhampered in the void. The result is order as such, with little life to be ordered. Remnants of thoughts and experiences are organized not according to their meaningful interaction in the world or in reality, but by purely formal similarities and symmetries. Patterns are built around visual "punning"—the fusion of heterogeneous contents on the basis of external resemblance. In some of Van Gogh's last paintings, pure form overpowered the nature of the objects he depicted. The violence of his disturbed mind transformed the world into a tissue of flames, so that the trees ceased to be trees and the cottages and farmers became calligraphic brush strokes. Instead of being submerged in the content, form interposed itself between the viewer and the theme of the work.

An example of schizoid art is "Dance of the Swan Dolls" (Figure 111), one of many pictures executed in colored crayon by Friedrich Schröder, who called himself the "Sun Star." After spending much of his life in prisons and mental hospitals, this alcoholic vagrant, a faith healer and leader of a religious sect, began to paint systematically at the age of fifty-seven. All the traits of alienated art are strikingly present. A rigidly symmetrical, ornamental pattern is placed on a landscape of reduced depth. The shapes of nature, devoid of their organic complexity and imperfection, have the smooth regularity of an unmodulated carrier wave. Extricated from their natural context, the limbs and trunks of animal and man combine without restraint on the basis of purely formal affinities: arms are fitted with birds' heads instead of hands,

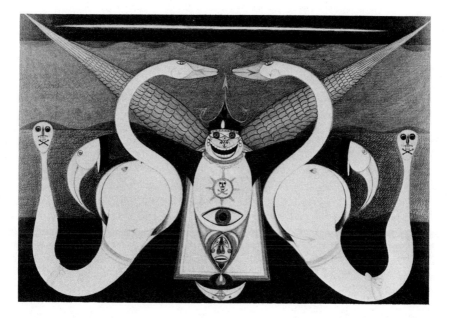

Figure 111
Friedrich Schröder-Sonnenstern. *The Swan-Doll's Dance of Death.* Color crayon.
Coll. Siegfried Poppe, Hamburg.

swans' necks lead into human buttocks.

Not by accident, similar formalistic characteristics are found in the "doodles" of persons whose minds are empty or concentrated on some other train of thought while their sense of visual organization, uncontrolled by guiding idea or experience, directs the eyes and hands. Geometric shapes generate one another, sometimes combining to form well-structured wholes, but more often just chance agglomerations of elements (Figure 112).

Finally, there is a significant relation between formalism and ornament. When we speak of ornament, we mean, first of all, visual form subordinated to a larger whole, which it completes, characterizes, or enriches. Thus scepter, crown, or wig serve as ornaments of king or judge, and wooden scrolls or lion's paws enrich the appearance of traditional furniture. Second, we call a pattern ornamental when it is organized by a simple formal principle. In works of art, such ornamental features are used with caution. Strict symmetry, for example, is as rare in painting and sculpture as it is frequent in decorations and the applied arts, such as ceramics or architecture. Figure 113

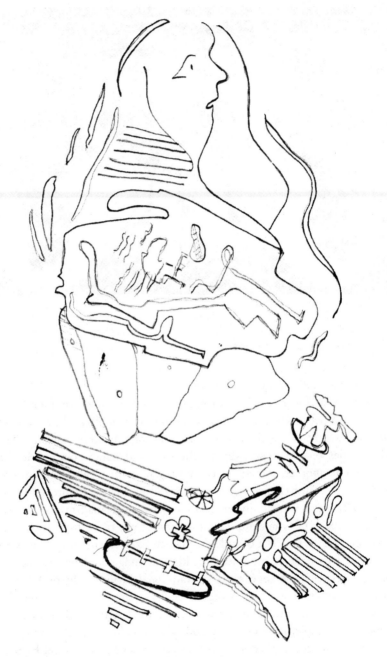

Figure 112

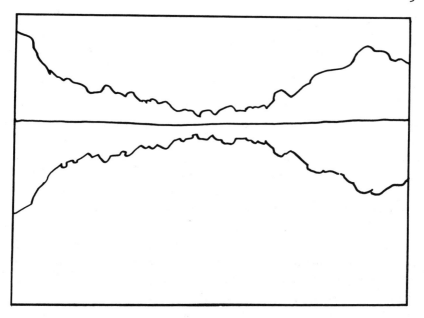

Figure 113

gives the main outlines of a landscape by Ferdinand Hodler depicting mountains reflected in a lake. The basic composition is completely symmetrical around a horizontal axis, and almost symmetrical around the central vertical. By turning nature into ornament, the artist has obtained a chilly preponderance of order. William Hogarth was aware of this danger when he wrote: "It may be imagined that the greatest part of the effects of beauty results from the symmetry of parts in the object, which is beautiful: but I am very well persuaded this prevailing notion will soon appear to have little or no foundation." He said it was a constant rule of composition in painting to avoid regularity. In fact, even in works in which an overall symmetry is appropriate to the subject, its severity is always mitigated by enlivening deviations.

Strict symmetry and repetition are frequently used to obtain a comic effect. Symmetrically arranged action occurs in comedy on the stage. As an example from literature, the humorous opening scene in Flaubert's novel *Bouvard et Pécuchet* may be cited. Two men of the same profession walk at the same moment to the same park bench from opposite directions and in sitting down discover that they both have the habit of inscribing their names in their hats. The use of twins, the repetition of situations, the persistent mannerisms in a person's behavior, are all favorite "ornamental" devices in comedy because they uncover mechanical order—that is, lifelessness—in life, which is precisely what Henri Bergson has described as the function of all humor.

If we look at an ornamental design as though it were a work of art, the one-sidedness of its content and form makes it look empty and silly. If, on the other hand, a work of art is used for decoration, it will overstep its function and disturb the unity of the whole it has been asked to serve. The late abstractions of Mondrian, although composed of a few elementary formal features, are by no means ornaments. An ornament, as we can now define it, presents an easy order, undisturbed by the vicissitudes of life. Such a view is quite justified when the pattern is not intended as an independent whole but as a mere component of a larger context, in which an easy harmony has a legitimate place. The patterns of wallpaper or dress material fulfill such a limited function. Architectural design has in all cultures so insistently relied on symmetry because buildings serve as an element of stability and order in the midst of human existence, which is pervaded by struggle, accident, discord, change, and irrationality. The same is true for jewelry, pottery, and furniture, but not for works of art in the more restricted sense of the term.

Paintings or sculpture are self-contained statements about the nature of human existence, and therefore they refer to this existence in all its essential aspects. An ornament presented as a work of art becomes a fool's paradise, in which tragedy and discord are ignored and an easy peace reigns. A work of art displays the interaction between underlying order and the irrational variety of clashes. *Nostra res agitur.*

La Source

In a work of art, an abstract pattern organizes the visual matter in such a way that the intended expression is directly conveyed to the eyes. This is perhaps most strikingly demonstrated by analyzing in some detail a work that at first glance seems to offer little more than pretty triteness displayed in a standard naturalistic manner.

La Source, painted by Ingres at the age of seventy-six in the year 1856, represents a girl standing upright in a frontal position and holding a water jug (Figure 114). At first sight it shows such qualities as lifelikeness, sensuousness, simplicity. Richard Muther notes that Ingres' nudes make the observer almost forget that he is looking at works of art. "An artist who was a god seems to have created naked human beings." We may well share this experience and at the same time ask: How lifelike is, for example, the posture of the figure? If we judge the girl as a person of flesh and blood, we find that she is holding the jug in a painfully artificial way. This discovery comes as a

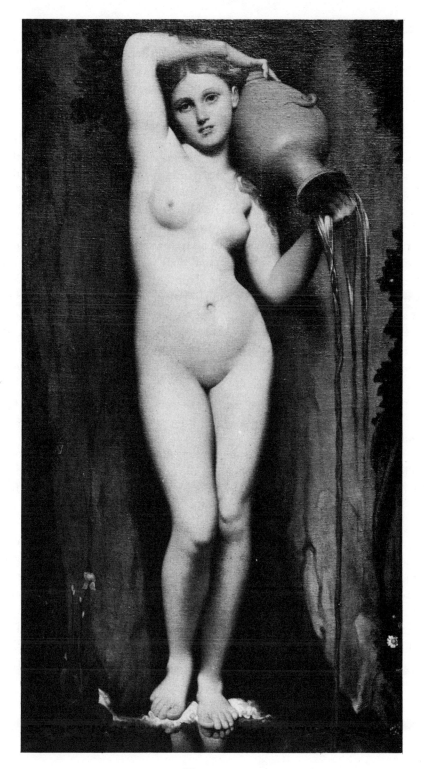

Figure 114
Jean Auguste Dominique Ingres. *La Source*, 1856. Louvre, Paris.

surprise because to the eye her attitude was and is rather natural and simple. Within the two-dimensional world of the picture plane it presents a clear and logical solution. The girl, the jug, and the act of pouring are shown completely. They are lined up side-by-side in the plane with a thoroughly "Egyptian" passion for clarity and neglect of realistic posture.

Thus the basic arrangement of the figure turns out to be anything but an obvious solution. To make the right arm take such a detour around the head and "get away with it" required imagination and mastery. Moreover, the location, shape, and function of the jug evoke significant associations. The body of the jug can be seen as an inverted likeness of its neighbor, the head of the girl. Not only are they similar in shape, but both have one free, unob-structed flank, which carries an ear (handle), and one flank that is slightly overlapped. Both are tilted to the left, and there is a correspondence between the flowing water and the flowing hair. This formal analogy serves to under-score the faultless geometry of the human shape, but by inviting comparison it also stresses the differences. In contrast to the empty "face" of the jug, the features of the girl establish a more conspicuous contact with the observer. At the same time, the jug openly permits the flow of the water, whereas the girl's mouth is all but closed. This contrast is not limited to the face. The jug with its uterine connotations rhymes also with the body, and again the resemblance serves to emphasize that whereas the vessel openly releases the stream, the pelvic area of the body is locked. In short, the picture plays on the theme of withheld but promised femininity.

Both aspects of this theme are developed in further formal inventions. The virginal refusal in the compression of the knees, the tight adherence of the arm to the head, and the grip of the hands are counteracted by the full exposure of the body. A similar antagonism can be found in the posture of the figure. Its overall shape indicates a straight vertical axis of symmetry; but the symmetry is nowhere strictly fulfilled, except in the face, which is a small model of completed perfection. The arms, the breasts, the hips, the knees, and the feet are merely swinging variations on a potential symmetry (Figure 115). Similarly, the vertical is not actually realized anywhere; it merely results from the obliquities of smaller axes, which compensate one another. The di-rection changes at least five times in the axes of the head, the chest, the pelvis, the calves, and the feet. The straightness of the whole is made up of oscillating parts. It offers us the serenity of life, not of death. There is in this undulating movement of the body something truly waterlike, which puts the straight flow from the jug to shame. The still girl is more alive than the running water. The potential is stronger than the actual.

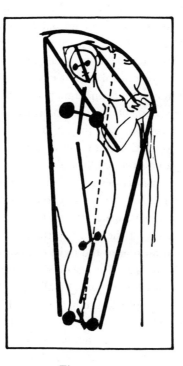

Figure 115

Looking further at the oblique central axes on which the body is built, we notice that these axes are short at the extremities and get larger toward the center. A crescendo of size leads from the head over the chest to the long expanse of belly and thighs, and the same is true for the approach from the feet over the calves to the center. This symmetry between top and bottom is enhanced by a decrescendo of pictorial "action" from the extremities toward the center. In both the top and the bottom areas there is an abundance of small units and angular breaks, a crowding of detail and forward and backward movement in the depth dimension. This action dies gradually as the units grow in size, until beyond the gateways of the breasts and knees all small motion is hushed, and in the center of the silent plane lies the closed sanctuary of sex.

In the left contour of the figure from the shoulder downward, there are small curves leading to the large arc of the hip, followed again by curves of decreasing size in the calf, the ankle, and the foot. This left contour strongly contrasts with the right, which is nearly a straight perpendicular. The vertical is lengthened and strengthened by the raised right arm. This combined trunk and arm contour is a good example of formal reinterpretation of a subject, because it is a discovery, a new line, not foreseen in the basic visual concept of the human body. The right contour spells out the vertical that is only implied in the zigzag of the central axis. It embodies rest and approximates geometry, and thus fulfills a function similar to that of the face. The body, then, lies between pure statements of the two principles it unites in itself: the perfect calm of its right contour, and the undulating action of the left.

The symmetry of top and bottom that the artist invented for his figure is not derived from organic structure. It is also checked by the overall outline of the figure. The figure is inscribed in a slim, tilted triangle, formed by the raised elbow, the left hand, and the feet as corners. The triangle establishes a secondary, oblique central axis, which teeters unstably on a narrow base. Its sway adds subtly to the life of the figure without disturbing its basic verticality. It relieves the plumb line of the right contour of some of its rigidity because the vertical contour is read as a slanted deviation from this secondary axis of the triangle (compare Figure 72b). Finally, the oblique symmetry of the two elbows should be observed because here is an element of angularity that is quite important in giving the "salt" of sharpness to a composition that otherwise might have suffered from the monotony of sweet curves.

A few of the features described above follow simply from the objective shape and construction of the human body, but a comparison of La Source with a Venus by Titian or Michelangelo's David will demonstrate how little the bodies artists create have in common. The remarkable fact about a painting like La Source is that in looking at it we sense the effect of the formal devices that make it represent life so fully, even though we may not be conscious of these devices at all. So smoothly are they blended into a whole of great overall simplicity, so organically is the compositional pattern derived from the subject and the pictorial medium, that we seem to see simple nature at the same time that we marvel at the intelligence of the interpretation it conveys.

Visual Information

What has been said against the mechanical replication of physical things and about the visual interpretation of meaning through organized abstract form may have seemed to apply only to art. When it comes to images intended to convey factual information for scientific texts, dictionaries, technical manuals, etc., mechanical exactness of representation would seem to be the one obvious requirement. And yet this is not so.

Recording by photography, the most faithful method of image-making, has not really superseded the human craftsman, and for good reasons. Photography is indeed more authentic in the rendering of a street scene, a natural habitat, a texture, a momentary expression. What counts in these situations is the accidental inventory and arrangement, the overall quality, and the complete detail rather than formal precision. When pictures are to serve technological or scientific purposes—for example, illustrations of machines, microscopic organisms, surgical operations—the preference is for drawings, or at least for photographs retouched by hand. The reason is that pictures give us the thing "itself" by telling us about some of its properties: the characteristic outline of a bird, the color of a chemical, the number of geological layers. A medical illustration is meant to distinguish between smooth and rough texture, to show the relative size and position of organs, the network of blood vessels, the mechanism of a joint. A technological picture must give exact proportions and angles, establish the concavity or convexity of a given part, and distinguish between units. Properties of this kind are all we need to know. This means not only that the better picture is one that omits unnecessary detail and chooses telling characteristics, but also that the relevant facts must be unambiguously conveyed to the eye. This is done by means of perceptual factors, some of which are discussed in this book: simplicity of shape, orderly grouping, clear overlapping, distinction of figure and ground, use of lighting and perspective to interpret spatial values. Precision of form is needed to communicate the visual characteristics of an object.

A draftsman charged with producing a faithful likeness of an electric clockwork or a frog's heart must invent a pattern that fits the object—exactly as the artist must do. And since producing a likeness means nothing but bringing out the relevant traits, it is not surprising that the draftsman must understand what these traits are. Biological, medical, technological training may be needed to make a usable reproduction of an object. Such knowledge will suggest to the artist an adequate perceptual pattern to be found in the object and applied to the picture. All reproduction is visual interpretation. The interpretations of the uninformed draftsman, based on nothing but what he can see at the moment, are likely to be misleading or too vague. Leonardo da Vinci's scientific drawings are remarkable because he thoroughly understood the structure and function of the things he was depicting and at the same time could organize complex perceptual patterns with the utmost clarity (Figure 116).

The relation between intellectual knowledge and visual representation is frequently misunderstood. Some theorists talk as though an abstract concept could be directly rendered in a picture; others deny that theoretical knowledge

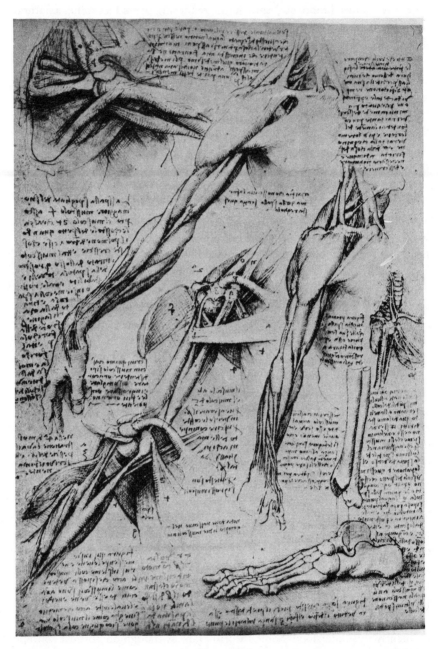

Figure 116

can do anything but disturb a pictorial conception. The truth would seem to be that any abstract proposition can be translated into some kind of visual form and as such become a genuine part of a visual concept. Leonardo's statement, "The neck has four movements, of which the first consists of raising, the second of lowering, the face, the third of turning right or left, the fourth of bending the head right or left" does not in itself dictate a particular image. But it is based on a visual conception, and anybody can use this bit of theory to look for the mechanisms of the four movements in the human body and articulate a visual idea of his own.

Although temporarily out of fashion, the study of anatomy is valuable to the artist because it permits him to acquire a visual concept of things that cannot be seen directly but that help shape what can be seen. The human body is like a Christmas stocking stuffed with objects whose shapes, though they produce conspicuous bulges, cannot be discerned clearly because the bag smooths over the contours and hides everything that does not emerge on the outside. Thus the shape of the bag is likely to look chaotic and elusive. A pattern of form must be imposed upon it, and, as I pointed out earlier, there are an infinite variety of ways to do it. Some of them can be derived from knowledge of how the muscles and tendons and bones beneath the skin are shaped and how they fit together. With the memory image of this internal structure in his mind, an artist can invent patterns that interpret the outside in ways that accord with the inside. Something very similar is true for the illustrator of anatomical, physiological, or biological material.

Since representing an object means showing some of its particular properties, one can often achieve the purpose best by deviating markedly from "photographic" appearance. This is most evident in diagrams. The pocket map of subway lines issued by the London Transport Corporation gives the needed information with utmost clarity, and at the same time delights the eye with the harmony of its design (Figure 117). This is achieved by renouncing all geographic detail except for the pertinent topological features— that is, the sequence of stops and interconnections. All roads are reduced to straight lines; all angles to the two simplest, ninety and forty-five degrees. The map omits and distorts a great deal, and because it does so is the best possible picture of what it wants to show. Still another example may be taken again from Leonardo, who suggests: "When you have represented the bones of the hand and you wish to represent above this the muscles which are joined with these bones, make threads in place of muscles. I say threads and not lines in order to make known what muscle passes below or above the other muscle, which thing cannot be shown with simple lines." Nothing but the points of

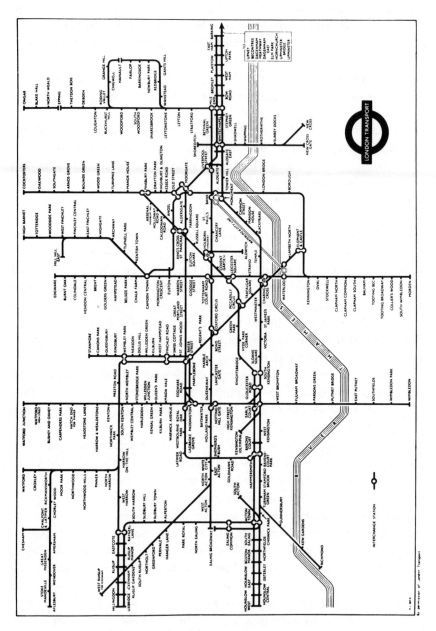

Figure 117

attack and the crossings in space is considered. Rendition of the size and shape of the muscles would distract and obstruct the view.

The expression conveyed by any visual form is only as clear-cut as the perceptual features that carry it. A clearly curved line expresses its swing or gentleness with corresponding clarity; but a line whose overall structure is confusing to the eye cannot carry any meaning. An artist may paint a picture in which a ferocious tiger is easily recognizable; but unless there is ferocity in the colors and lines, the tiger will look taxidermic, and there can be ferocity in the colors and lines only if the pertinent perceptual qualities are brought out with precision. Figure 118 is taken from a Dürer woodcut that shows Christ's head crowned with thorns. Direction, curvature, brightness, and spatial position are defined in such a way that each perceptual element helps to convey to the eyes a precise expression of anguish, which rests on such features as the heavy lid overhanging the staring pupil. Not often does visual form offer such a simple weave of simple elements; but however complex the pattern of color, mass, or contour, it can deliver its message only if in its own way it has the precision of Dürer's lines.

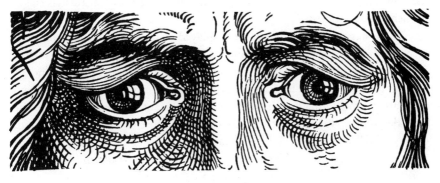

Figure 118

IV GROWTH

Much of what is said about visual perception and representation in this book applies to human behavior quite in general. The tendency toward simplest shape, for example, governs the activities of the organism at so basic a physiological and psychological level that the country or historical period from which we take our human examples makes little difference. However, even a survey of such generality cannot ignore certain characteristic differences in the handling of visual patterns, differences that reflect the successive stages of mental development.

These stages of development are displayed in their purest, most complete form in the artwork of children. But we find striking analogies to children's art in the early phases of so-called primitive art all over the world, and indeed in what happens when a beginner of whatever age or place first tries his hand at an artistic medium. Obviously, there are important differences between the attitudes and products of Western children and those of Eskimo children, of clever children and dull ones, well-cared-for and neglected ones, educated town dwellers and wild hunters, but here again it will be useful for our purpose to emphasize the similarities rather than the differences.

Early forms of visual representation invite our attention not only because they are of obvious educational interest, but also because all the fundamental features that operate in refined, complicated, and modified ways in mature art show up with elementary clarity in the pictures of a child or a bushman. This is true for the relations between observed and invented form, for space perception in relation to the two-dimensional and three-dimensional media, for the interaction of motor behavior and visual control, for the close connection between perception and knowledge, and so forth. There is, therefore, no more enlightening introduction to the art of the adult than a look at the early manifestations of the principles and tendencies that forever govern visual creation.

Why Do Children Draw That Way?

From the outset I have insisted that we cannot hope to understand the nature of visual representation if we try to derive it directly from optical projections of the physical objects that constitute our world. Pictures and sculptures of any style possess properties that cannot be explained as mere modifications of the perceptual raw material received through the senses.

This is true also for the sequence of stages in which representational form typically develops. If we assumed that the point of departure for visual experience was the optical projections supplied by the lenses of the eyes, we would expect that the earliest attempts at imagery would cleave most closely to these projections. To be sure, they would resemble their models no more faithfully than a limited power of observation and limited technical dexterity would permit, but the intended image, transpiring through those clumsy endeavors, should surely be that of the optical projection. Any deviation from that model, we would expect, would be a later development, reserved for the freedom of mature sophistication. But instead, the opposite is true.

The early drawings of children show neither the predicted conformity to realistic appearance nor the expected spatial projections. What is the explanation? Since it was assumed that for normal human beings, visual percepts could only be faithful projections, a reason for the deviation had to be found. It was suggested, for example, that children are technically unable to reproduce what they perceive. Just as they cannot hit the bull's-eye with a gun because they lack the concentrated glance and steady hand of an adult marksman, so their eyes and hands lack the skill to hit the right lines with a pencil or brush. Now it is quite true that the drawings of young children show incomplete motor control. Their lines sometimes steer an erratic zigzag course and do not meet exactly where they should. Much of the time, however, the lines are accurate enough to indicate what the drawing is supposed to be like, particularly to the observer who compares many drawings of the same kind. Moreover, at an early age the former imprecision of the stroke gives way to an exactness that is more than sufficient to show what the child is trying to do. Compare these early forms with the drawings of an unskilled amateur who tries to copy photographs or realistic pictures, and you will notice the fundamental difference. The reader is invited to put a pencil in his mouth or between his toes and copy a realistic picture of a human ear. The lines may turn out to be so crooked as to be totally unrecognizable; but if the drawing is at all successful, it will still differ fundamentally from the usual child's drawing of an ear as two concentric circles, one for the outer border and one for the hole inside. No lack of motor skill can explain this difference in principle.

Other theorists have maintained that children aim at making straight lines, circles, and ovals because these simple shapes are relatively easy to draw. This is perfectly true, but does not indicate what mental process induces children to identify complex objects with geometric patterns that we cannot interpret as simplified projective images.

Nor can lack of interest or carelessness of observation be adduced. Children observe with an acuteness that puts many adults to shame; and no one who has seen the expression of breathless fascination in their eyes or the intense concentration with which they draw or paint will accept an explanation based on negligence or indifference. It is true that up to a certain age if the child is asked to draw a picture of his father, he will make little use of the particular man standing before him as a model. This behavior, however, does not prove that the child is unwilling or unable to observe his environment; the child ignores the model simply because fresh information is neither needed nor usable for what he regards as a proper drawing of a man.

Then there are explanations that are little more than wordplay, such as the assertion that children's pictures look the way they do because they are not copies but "symbols" of real things. The term "symbol" is used so indiscriminately nowadays that it can be applied whenever one thing stands for another. For this reason it has no explanatory value and should be avoided. There is no way of telling whether such a statement is right, wrong, or no theory at all.

The Intellectualistic Theory

The oldest—and even now most widespread—explanation of children's drawings is that since children do not depict what one assumes they see, some mental activity other than perception must intervene. It is evident that children limit themselves to representing the overall qualities of objects, such as the straightness of legs, the roundness of the head, the symmetry of the human body. These are facts of generalized knowledge; hence the famous theory which holds that "the child draws what he knows rather than what he sees."

Now knowledge has more than one meaning. Much picture-making does not in fact rely on what the eyes happen to see at the moment the picture is produced. Instead the draftsman relies on a synthesis of his many previous observations of a certain kind of thing, whether horses, trees, or human figures.

This process can indeed be described as drawing from knowledge; but it is a knowledge that cannot be taken to be an alternative to seeing.

The intellectualistic theory asserts that the drawings of children as well as other art at early stages are derived from a non-visual source, namely from "abstract" concepts. The term *abstract* is meant to describe non-perceptual knowledge. But, we must ask, in what other realm of mental activity can a concept dwell if it is banned from the realm of images? Is the child relying on purely verbal concepts? Such concepts exist—for example the fiveness in the statement "a hand has five fingers." The child does in fact possess this knowledge verbally; and when he draws the picture of a hand, he counts the fingers to make sure he gets the right number.

This is what happens, that is, when a child has been alerted to the proper number of fingers. His usual procedure is precisely the opposite. Normally in his work the child indeed relies on concepts, but on visual concepts. The visual concept of a hand consists of a round base, i.e. the palm, from which fingers sprout as straight spikes in sunbeam fashion, their number being determined, as we shall see, by purely visual considerations.

The mental life of children is intimately bound up with their sensory experience. To the young mind, things are what they look like, sound like, move like, or smell like. If the child's mind contains any nonperceptual concepts at all, they must be very few, and their influence on pictorial representation can only be negligible. But even if the child had nonperceptual concepts of roundness, straightness, or symmetry—and who is willing to tell us the stuff such concepts might be made of?—how would they be translated into visual shape?

We must also ask: where would such concepts come from in the first place? If they are derived from visual experiences, are we expected to believe that the primarily visual raw material is processed into a nonvisual "abstraction," only to be translated back into visual shape for the purpose of picture-making? Or, if these concepts are transmitted to children by their elders, and to primitives by cultural convention, how can this be done nonvisually?

Psychological speculation has put a good deal of stock in the sense of touch. On the assumption that visual perception is based on optical projection, the sense of sight was deemed incapable of conveying a truthful image of what three-dimensional things really look like. Such knowledge therefore had to come from the sense of touch. One reasoned: Touch is not dependent on projections transmitted by light across empty space; touch relies on direct contact with the object; it applies from all sides. Touch can be trusted to provide objective information.

The hypothesis sounded good; and in fact there is no doubting the effective interaction of touch and sight at all stages of human development. But the priority of touch or "motor behavior" is another matter. It seems to be a mere assumption, unsupported by evidence. The child psychologist Arnold Gesell asserted years ago that "ocular prehension precedes manual." He wrote: "Nature has given top priority to the sense of sight. Six months before birth the eyes of the fetus move sketchily and independently beneath their sealed lids. In time the eyes move in unison, so the child is born with two eyes partly yoked in a single organ. . . . The infant takes hold of the world with his eyes long before he does so with his hands—an extremely significant fact. During the first eight weeks of life the hands remain predominantly fisted, while the eyes and brain are busy with looking, staring, seeking and, in a rudimentary manner, apprehending." Recently, T. G. R. Bower has suggested by ingenious experiments that infants come to know physical objects as solid and tangible through visual experience, and not through a primary reliance on touch.

This is not surprising once we realize that to apprehend the shape of an object by touch is in no way simpler or more direct than apprehension by vision. To be sure, there is a physical distance between the eyes and a box they see, whereas hands are in immediate contact with the box. But the mind does not partake in the directness of the contact out there. It depends entirely on the sensations aroused in the sense organs. As the hands explore the box, the so-called "touch spots," independent of one another, are stimulated in the skin. The touch image of a surface, a shape, or an angle must be composed by the brain, just as it must create the visual image from a multitude of retinal stimulations. Neither physical size nor distance are given directly to the sense of touch. All the brain receives are messages about the muscular extensions and contractions that occur when a hand reaches out or around a corner. As a person moves through space, his brain is notified of a series of successive leg motions. These sensations do not in themselves include space. To experience space kinesthetically, the brain must create that experience from sensory messages that are not spatial. That is, kinesthesia involves the same kind of task as vision, except that the way it is accomplished seems immensely more difficult to understand in the case of kinesthesia—so much so that, to my knowledge, no psychologist has attempted to describe the process. It cannot be doubted that the sensations deriving from the organs of touch, from muscles, joints, and tendons, contribute enormously to our awareness of shape and space. But anyone who tries to avoid the problems in visual perception by referring to kinesthesia is leaping from the frying pan into the fire.

The intellectualistic theory has been applied not only to children's drawings but to all kinds of highly formalized, "geometric" art, particularly that of primitive peoples. And since it could not very well be asserted that all art was derived from nonvisual concepts, the theory led to the contention that there existed two artistic procedures, different in principle from each other. Children, Neolithic painters, American Indians, and African tribesmen worked from intellectual abstractions; they practiced "conceptual art." Paleolithic cave dwellers, Pompeian muralists, and Europeans during and after the Renaissance represented what they saw with their eyes; they practiced "perceptual art." This absurd dichotomy was one of the main drawbacks of the theory, for it obscured the essential fact that the same kind of well-defined form so prominent in the work of many primitives is indispensable to any "realistic" representation that deserves the name of art. A child's figure is no more a "schema" than one by Rubens. It is only less differentiated. And, as I have pointed out, Albrecht Dürer's highly naturalistic studies of hands, faces, and birds' wings are works of art only because the innumerable strokes and shapes form well-organized, even though complex, patterns that interpret the subject.

On the other hand, the theory neglects the important contribution of perceptual observation even to highly stylized work. When a South Sea Islander paints the sea stirred by the wind as a rectangle striped with oblique parallel lines, essentials of the model's visual structure are rendered in a simplified but entirely un-"symbolic" manner.

They Draw What They See

A theory so palpably in conflict with the facts could never have been widely accepted had an alternative been available. None was, so long as it was believed that percepts can refer only to particular, individual instances: a particular person, a particular dog, a particular tree. Any general notion about persons, dogs, or trees as kinds of things had to derive necessarily from a nonperceptual source.

This artificial distinction between perception and conception has been superseded by evidence that perception does not start from particulars, secondarily processed into abstractions by the intellect, but from generalities. "Triangularity" is a primary percept, not a secondary concept. The distinction between individual triangles comes later, not earlier. Doggishness is perceived earlier than the particular character of any one dog. If this is true we can expect early artistic representations, based on naive observation, to be concerned with generalities—that is, with simple, overall structural features. Which is exactly what we find.

Children and primitives draw generalities and nonprojective shape precisely because they draw what they see. But this is not the whole answer. Unquestionably children see more than they draw. At an age when they easily tell one person from another and notice the smallest change in a familiar object, their pictures are still quite undifferentiated. The reasons must lie in the nature and function of pictorial representation.

Here again we have to get a superannuated but hardy prejudice out of the way. Just as it was assumed that all visual perception apprehended the totality of individual appearance, so pictures and other images were assumed to aim at the faithful replication of everything the draftsmen can see in his model. This is by no means true. What an acceptable image of an object looks like depends on the draftsman's standards and on the purpose of his picture. Even in adult practice, a mere circle or dot may suffice to depict a city, a human figure, a planet; in fact, it may serve a given function much better than a more detailed likeness. Therefore, when a child portrays himself as a simple pattern of circles, ovals, and straight lines, he may do so not because this is all he sees when he looks in a mirror, and not because he is incapable of producing a more faithful picture, but because his simple drawing fulfills all the conditions he expects a picture to meet.

Another fundamental difference between percept and picture must be considered here. If perception consists not in "photographically" faithful recording but in the grasping of global structural features, it seems evident that such visual concepts possess no explicit shape. For example, seeing the shape of a human head may involve seeing its roundness. But obviously this roundness is not a tangible perceptual thing. It is not materialized in any one head or in any number of heads. There are shapes that represent roundness to perfection, such as circles or spheres. However, even these shapes stand for roundness rather than being it, and a head is neither a circle nor a sphere. In other words, if I want to represent the roundness of an object such as the head, I cannot rely on any shape actually given in it but must find or invent a shape that will satisfactorily embody the visual generality "roundness" in the world of tangible things. If the child makes a circle stand for a head, that circle is not given to him in the object. It is a genuine invention, an impressive achievement, at which the child arrives only after laborious experimentation.

Something similar is true for color. The color of most objects is anything but uniform in space or time; nor is it identical in different specimens of the same group of things. The color the child gives to the trees in his pictures is hardly a specific shade of green selected from the hundreds of hues to be found in trees. It is a color that matches the overall impression given by trees. Again we are dealing not with an imitation but with an invention, the discovery of an equivalent that represents the relevant features of the model with the resources of a particular medium.

Representational Concepts

We can express the same fact more sharply by saying that image-making of any kind requires the use of representational concepts. Representational concepts furnish the equivalent, in a particular medium, of the visual concepts one wishes to depict, and they find their external manifestation in the work of the pencil, the brush, the chisel.

The formation of representational concepts, more than anything else, distinguishes the artist from the nonartist. Does the artist experience world and life differently from the ordinary man? There is no good reason to think so. To be sure, he must be deeply concerned with—and impressed by—his experiences. He also must have the wisdom to find significance in individual occurrences by understanding them as symbols of universal truths. These qualities are indispensable, but they are not limited to artists. The artist's privilege is the capacity to apprehend the nature and meaning of an experience in the terms of a given medium, and thus to make it tangible. The nonartist is left "speechless" by the fruits of his sensitive wisdom. He cannot give them adequate material form. He can express *himself*, more or less articulately, but not his experience. During the moments in which a human being is an artist, he finds shape for the bodiless structure of what he has felt. "For rhyme can beat a measure out of trouble."

Why do some landscapes, anecdotes, or gestures "ring the bell"? Because they suggest, in some particular medium, a significant form for a relevant truth. In search of such telling experiences, the artist will look around with the eyes of the painter, the sculptor, the dancer, or the poet, responding to what fits his form. On a walk through the fields a photographer may look at the world with camera eyes and react only to what will "come" photographically. But the artist is not always an artist. Matisse was once asked whether a tomato looked to him when he ate it as it did when he painted it. "No," he replied, "when I eat it I see it like everybody else." The ability to capture the "sense" of the tomato in pictorial form distinguishes the response of the painter from the frustrating, shapeless gasping by which the nonartist reacts to what may be a very similar experience.

Experiments with children have helped us realize the importance of representational concepts by pointing up the difference between recognizing and imitating. David Olson has done pioneering work on the problem of why, at a certain stage in their development, children can recognize a diagonal and distinguish it from a vertical or horizontal, but cannot imitate a model diagonal either by drawing one or by arranging checkers on a checkerboard. In one of his experiments, children were shown a diagonal array on the model board, except that the bottom right checker was moved over one space to the left. All the children immediately said the arrangement was not a "criss-cross," but none of them was able to say or show how they knew this, or to correct the deviation by moving the checker to the right place.

The only effective way of making the children succeed was by attracting their attention to the formal components involved in making a diagonal: Start at one bottom corner, go straight across, end up at the opposite top corner, do *not* move in the vertical or horizontal direction, etc. In other words, what the children had to learn was not just the visual concept of the diagonal but the formal features of which it is composed. "The difference," I have stated in this connection, "is not primarily between perception and representation, but between perception of effect and perception of form, the latter being needed for representation."

Whether taught or not, children eventually acquire the art of making diagonals. As we shall see, during the development of spontaneous drawing children first master the relation between horizontal and vertical and then proceed from there to oblique directions. That is, they attain the representational concepts needed to handle increasingly complex shapes and shape relations.

The kinds of shapes the novice can control are sometimes described as "schemata." Not much would be wrong with this term if, as I said earlier, it were applied to all art and did not carry negative connotations. Unfortunately, the term often implies that the child is bound by rigid conventions which bind his eyes and hands to primitive templates and which must be broken like eggshells if the fledgling is to acquire his freedom of expression. Such a view can only block understanding and lead to harmful educational practices. When someone climbs a staircase, he must overcome the first step in order to reach the second; however, the first step was not an obstacle to the second, but rather a prerequisite for reaching it. In the same way, early representational concepts are not strait-jackets but the indispensable forms of early conceptions. Their simplicity is appropriate to the level of organization at which the mind of the young draftsman operates. As the mind becomes more refined, the patterns it creates become more complex, and the two growth processes constantly reinforce each other. At levels of high complexity, representational concepts are no longer as easily detected as they are in early work, but, far from being overcome or cast aside by the mature artist, they remain—at a level appropriate to the richness of his thought—the indispensable forms that alone enable him to express what he has to say.

Credit is due to Gustaf Britsch for having been the first to demonstrate systematically that pictorial form grows organically according to definite rules, from the simplest to progressively more complex patterns, in a process of gradual differentiation. Britsch showed the inadequacy of the "realistic" approach, which found in children's drawings nothing but charming imperfection and which could deal with the phases of their development only in terms of increasing "correctness." An art educator, Britsch did not avail himself of the psychology of perception, but his findings support and are supported by the more recent trends in that field. Like many pioneers, in attacking the realistic approach Britsch seems to have carried his revolutionary ideas to the opposite extreme. As far as can be determined from the writings published under his name, his analysis leaves little room for the influence of the perceived object upon pictorial form. To him the development of form was a self-contained mental process, an unfolding similar to the growth of a plant. But this one-sidedness makes his presentation all the more impressive; and I acknowledge that as I try to describe some phases of formal development as an interplay of perceptual and representational concepts, I am proceeding from the base laid by Britsch.

Drawing as Motion

The eye and the hand are the father and mother of artistic activity. Drawing, painting, and modeling are kinds of human motor behavior, and they may be assumed to have developed from two older and more general kinds of such behavior—expressive and descriptive movement.

The first scribbles of a child are not intended as representation. They are a form of the enjoyable motor activity in which the child exercises his limbs, with the added pleasure of having visible traces produced by the vigorous back-and-forth action of the arms. It is an exciting experience to bring about something visible that was not there before. This interest in the product for its own sake can be observed even in chimpanzees whitewashing their cages with lumps of white clay or wielding a paint brush. It is a simple sensory pleasure, which remains undiminished even in the adult artist.

Children have a need for abundant movement, and thus drawing starts as gamboling on paper. The shape, range, and orientation of the strokes are determined by the mechanical construction of arm and hand as well as by the child's temperament and mood. Here are the beginnings of expressive movement, i.e., the manifestations of the draftsman's momentary state of mind as well as his more permanent personality traits. These mental qualities are constantly reflected in the speed, rhythm, regularity or irregularity, and shape of bodily movements, and thus leave their mark on the strokes of pencil or brush. The expressive characteristics of motor behavior have been studied systematically in handwriting by graphologists, but they also contribute importantly to the style of painters and sculptors, as will be discussed later.

In addition to being expressive, movement is also descriptive. The spontaneity of action is controlled by the intent to imitate properties of actions or objects. Descriptive gestures use the hands and arms, often supported by the entire body, to show how large or small, fast or slow, round or angular, far or close something is or was or could be. Such gestures may refer to concrete objects or events—such as mice or mountains or the encounter between two people—but also figuratively to the bigness of a task, the remoteness of a possibility, or a clash of opinions. Deliberate pictorial representation probably has its motor source in descriptive movement. The hand that traces the shape of an animal in the air during a conversation is not far from fixating this trace in the sand or on a wall.

We used to take it for granted that the motor behavior of the artist is merely a means to the end of producing painting or sculpture and that it counts no more in and by itself than the action of saw and plane in a cabinet-maker's work. In our own time, however, the so-called action painters have stressed the artistic quality of the motion performed while producing a work of art, and there probably has never been an artist for whom some of the expressive properties of stroke and body motion did not count as part of his "statement."

This representational aspect of motor behavior is quite apparent in young children. Jacqueline Goodnow reports that when kindergarten children are asked to match a series of sounds with a series of dots, they draw the dots in a line from left to right but do not leave blank spaces on the paper to match the intervals between groups of sounds. Instead they often use motor pauses: make two dots, pause, make another two dots, etc. For them, this does justice to the sound model even though the intervals do not show up on paper. Figure 119 is a four-year-old girl's drawing of a man mowing the lawn. The mower, on the right, is depicted by a whirl not only because the rotating lines render the characteristic motion of the machine visually, but also because the child's arm re-enacted the motion as a gesture during the drawing.

In the same way the sequence in which different parts of an object are drawn is significant for the child even though nothing of it may show in the completed picture. At early stages the figure is often drawn first and then

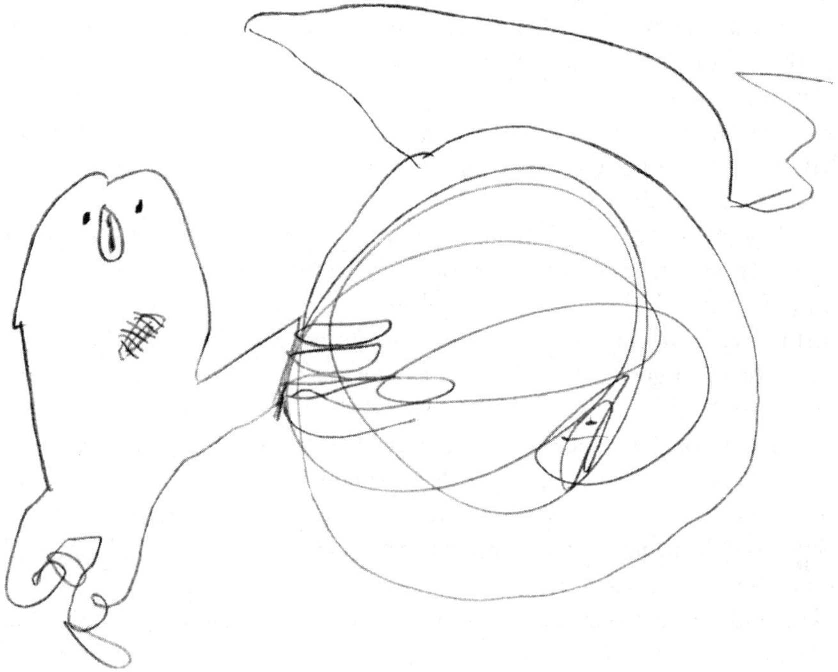

Figure 119

later dressed with suitable coat and pants. Feeble-minded and weak-sighted children in particular are sometimes satisfied with the mere time connection, in the act of drawing, of items that belong together. They do not bother to render this connection visually on paper, but spread the eyes, the ears, the mouth, and the nose of the face over the paper in almost random disorder. The order in which children produce the various parts of their drawings is most relevant to the psychological meaning of the work and should not be neglected in research.

This reminds us of one of the most fundamental features of visual art, namely, that all manual picture-making—as distinguished from photography —comes about sequentially, whereas the final product is to be seen all at once. At the most elementary level this shows in the difference between the experience of drawing a line, of seeing it wind its way across the paper, like a growing line in an animation film, and the static final product, from which much of this dynamics has vanished. The circular path of a line is very different in nature from the centric symmetry of the two-dimensional circle, which remains as the final product.

The artist's task is made harder not only by the fact that he cannot count on the live motion he felt while he drew or sculpted, but also by the difficulty of having to keep in mind a whole, partly present and partly to be completed as the work proceeds, while producing a small part. How is one to draw the left contour of a leg without being able to correlate it to the right contour, which is not yet there?

As a matter of general strategy, the sequence in which an artist produces a work is important and characteristic. For example, if the whole composition is to depend on the basic structural skeleton, this skeleton is preferably laid out first in its overall features and gradually perfected as a whole. Charles Baudelaire writes: "A good painting, faithful and equal to the dream that gave birth to it, must be created like a world. Just as the Creation we see is the result of several creations, of which the earlier ones were always made more complete by the next, so a painting, if handled harmoniously, consists of a series of superposed pictures, where each new layer gives more reality to the dream and makes it rise another step toward perfection. On the contrary, however, I remember having seen in the studios of Paul Delaroche and Horace Vernet huge paintings not sketched in but partly done, that is, absolutely finished in certain areas while others were indicated only by a black or white outline. One could compare this sort of work with a purely manual job that must cover a certain amount of space in a certain time or with a long route divided into many stages. When one section is done it is done, and when the whole route has been run through, the artist is delivered of his picture."

The Primordial Circle

To see organized form emerge in the scribbles of children is to watch one of the miracles of nature. Indeed the observer cannot help being reminded of that other process of creation, the shaping of cosmic whirls and spheres from amorphous matter in the universe. Circular shapes gradually appear in the clouds of zigzag strokes. At first they are rotations, traces of the corresponding arm movement. They show the smoothing or simplification of curves that always comes with motor training. Any manual operation arrives after a while at fluent motions of simple shape. Horses will turn the familiar corner of the barnyard gate in a perfect curve. The rounded paths of rats running angular mazes and the beautiful spirals described by a swarm of pigeons in the air are further examples of such motor skill. The history of writing shows that curves replace angles and continuity replaces discontinuity as the slow production of inscriptions gives way to rapid cursive. The lever construction of the human limbs favors curved motion. The arm pivots around the shoulder joint, and subtler rotation is provided by the elbow, the wrist, the fingers. Thus the first rotations indicate organization of motor behavior according to the principle of simplicity.

The same principle also favors the visual priority of circular shape. The circle, which with its centric symmetry does not single out any one direction, is the simplest visual pattern. It is common knowledge that objects too far away to reveal their particular outline are perceived as round rather than as any other shape. The perfection of circular shape attracts attention. I noted that the roundness of the pupil makes the animal's eye one of the most striking visual phenomena in nature. A dummy eye on the wing of a butterfly simulates the presence of a strong adversary, and in reptiles, fish, and birds elaborate camouflage devices hide the revealing disks of the pupils. Experiments by Charlotte Rice have shown that young children often pick the circles from a collection of different shapes even though they have been asked to look for diamonds, and Goodnow reports that when children draw human figures they begin with the circle of the head. In fact, as we shall see, the human figure develops genetically from the "primordial circle," which originally represents the whole figure.

The circle is the first organized shape to emerge from the more or less uncontrolled scribbles. Of course, we must not look for geometrical perfection in these drawings. Not only is the child's motor and eye control insufficient to produce exact shape, but more important, from the child's viewpoint there is no need for it. As Piaget and Inhelder put it, early shapes are topological rather than geometrical, i.e., they aim at such general, nonmetric properties as roundness, closedness, straightness, not at specific, ideal embodiments. Much of the time these shapes resemble circles or balls sufficiently to make us understand what is intended; and as one studies children's drawings in large numbers one learns to distinguish intended circles from aimless scribbles or other shapes, such as ovals or rectangles. In particular, one notices a clear difference between the mere motor product of rotation and the intentionally round and closed shape, controlled by the eye of the draftsman. We can also assume that quite soon in the child's experience the linear curve traced by pencil or brush transforms itself into a two-dimensional visual object, a disk that is perceived as a "figure" lying on a ground. More on the perceptual nature of figure and ground will be said in the chapter on "Space." Here it suffices to note that this phenomenon is responsible for the transformation of the one-dimensional pencil line into the perceived contour of a solid object.

This perceptual transformation favors another fundamental event in the genesis of picture-making: the recognition that shapes drawn on paper or made of clay can stand for other objects in the world, to which they are related as the signifier to the signified. This discovery of the young mind is so specifically human that the philosopher Hans Jonas has described picture-making as the most decisive and unique attribute of man. We have no way of telling with certainty at which point in a child's development he first takes his shapes to be representational. Probably this occurs before he confirms the fact for the adult observer by pointing to his scribble and saying "Doggie!" Even after the stage has demonstrably been reached, there is no reason to assume that *all* the shapes he makes from then on will be perceived by the child as representational.

It has been maintained that the child receives the inspiration for his earliest shapes from various round objects observed in the environment. The Freudian psychologist derives them from the mother's breasts, the Jungian from the mandala; others point to the sun and the moon. These speculations are based on the conviction that every form quality of pictures must somehow be derived from observations in the physical world. Actually the fundamental tendency toward simplest shape in motor and visual behavior is quite sufficient to explain the priority of circular shapes. The circle is the simplest shape available in the pictorial medium because it is centrically symmetrical in all directions.

However, once the circular shape emerges in pictorial work, it establishes contact with the similar shape of objects perceived in the environment. This similarity rests at first on a very broad, unspecific basis. In order to understand this early use of round shapes we must remember that even adults use circles or balls to represent any shape or all shapes or none in particular. Being the most unspecific, universal shape, spheres, disks, and rings figure prominently in early models of the earth and the universe, not so much on the basis of observation as because unknown shape or unknown spatial relations are represented in the simplest way possible. After a god had separated the heavens, the waters, and the dry land from one another, reports Ovid in the *Metamorphoses*, "his first care was to shape the earth into a great ball, so that it might be the same in all directions."

In the molecular models of the chemists, particles are represented as balls; and ball-shaped were the atoms of which, according to the Greek atomists, the world was made. Just as the adult uses this most general shape when no further specification is needed or available, a young child in his drawings uses circular shapes to represent almost any object at all: a human figure, a house, a car, a book, and even the teeth of a saw, as can be seen in Figure 120, a drawing by a five-year-old. It would be a mistake to say that the child neglects or mis-

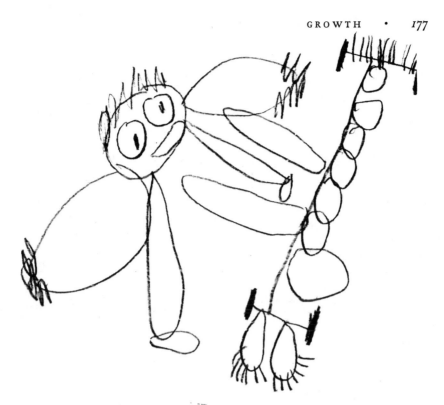

Figure 120

represents the shape of these objects. Only to adult eyes is he picturing them as round. Actually, intended roundness does not exist before other shapes, such as straightness or angularity, are available to the child. At the stage when he begins to draw circles, shape is not yet differentiated. The circle does not stand for roundness but for the more general quality of "thingness"—that is, for the compactness of a solid object as distinguished from the nondescript ground.

In the course of enriching the early shapes, sooner or later the child develops the primordial circle in two directions. One is the combination of several circles in a more complex pattern. Figure 121 is an example of how the child experiments with placing circles concentrically or a number of small ones into a larger one. "Containing" is probably the simplest spatial relation between pictorial units that the child learns to master. At the most elementary level, two concentric circles may be used to represent an ear with its hole or a head with its face. Later elaborations of the container theme serve to show people in a house or train, food on a plate, bodies surrounded by dress.

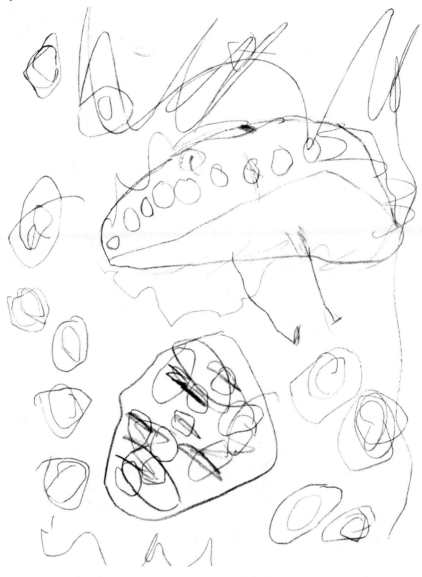

Figure 121

The other elaboration of the circle makes its radii explicit and leads to sunburst patterns, in which straight lines or oblongs radiate from a central circle or a combination of concentric circles. Whereas mere roundness indicates no spatial direction at all, every radius does; but since the family of radii covers all directions more or less evenly, the sunburst figure as a whole still operates at a stage prior to that of differentiated direction. The sunburst pattern may be used as a free design (Figure 122*a*); at various levels of differentiation it may recur as a flower (*b*), a tree with leaves (*c*), the headdress of an Indian (*d*), a pond surrounded by plants (*e*), a tree with branches (*f*), a head surrounded by hair (*g*), a hand with its fingers (*h*), the sun with a core of fire or a lamp with its bulb in the center (*i*), a running man (*k*).

Here is a good illustration of how a formal pattern, once it has been added to a child's repertory, will be used—in a more or less identical fashion— to describe different objects of corresponding structure. For example, Figure 122*i*, the inner circle painted red, the outer yellow, was used by one child to depict the sun as well as a lamp. Figures 122*g*, *h*, and *k* show that, to maintain the structurally simple all-around symmetry, considerable violence may be done to the model. Hair, fingers, and legs are made to sprout from all around the central base in order to preserve the centric symmetry of the whole. Such application of an acquired pattern to a great variety of subjects, often at the expense of verisimilitude, may be found even at the highest levels of human thinking—for example, in the shapes characteristic of an artist's style or in the key concepts of a scientific theory.

The Law of Differentiation

In dealing with the primordial circle I have already referred to differentiation. In its most elementary form this principle indicates that organic development always proceeds from the simple to the more complex. In the nineteenth century, which gave rise to the idea of biological evolution, this principle came to mean the splitting up of a unitary organization into more specific functions. Herbert Spencer presents this notion in his *First Principles* of 1862 and reports that he found it in Karl von Baer's treatise on the evolution of animals, published in 1828. In Spencer's view, differentiation involves also a development from the indefinite to the definite, from confusion to order. In our own time, the concept is used by Piaget to describe, for example, how the self and the external world, originally undifferentiated, become separate at a certain stage of mental development. Prior to this differentiation, explains Piaget, "impressions that are experienced and perceived are not attached to a personal consciousness sensed as a 'self' nor to objects conceived as external to the self. They simply exist in a dissociated block or are spread out on the same plane, which is neither internal nor external, but midway between these two poles."

For our particular purpose it will be useful to combine the principle of

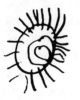

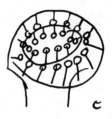

a

b

c

d

e

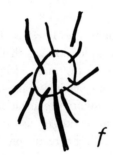

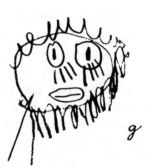

f

g

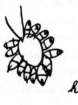

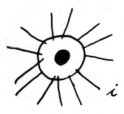

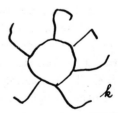

h

i

k

Figure 122

differentiation with the gestalt principle of simplicity. In keeping with our premise that perceiving and conceiving proceed from the general to the specific, we state first of all that *any shape will remain as undifferentiated as the draftsman's conception of his goal object permits.* If, for example, the purpose of a drawing is limited to describing the triangularity of a pyramid as distinguished from the roundness of a cloud, the drawing may show nothing more specific than triangularity vs. roundness.

Second, the law of differentiation states that *until a visual feature becomes differentiated, the total range of its possibilities will be represented by the structurally simplest among them.* For example, I mentioned that the circle, being the simplest of all possible shapes, stands for the totality of all shapes until shape becomes differentiated. It follows that at the stage preceding differentiation, the circle does not yet represent roundness—the saw teeth in Figure 120 are not intended as round—but merely includes roundness in the undifferentiated array of all possible shapes. Only when other shapes, e.g., straight lines or squares, have become articulated, do round shapes begin to stand for roundness: heads, the sun, palms of hands. We can also express this principle by saying, with E. H. Gombrich, that the meaning of a particular visual feature depends on the alternatives considered by the draftsman. A circle is a circle only when triangles are available as an alternative.

In this connection it is useful to refer to a distinction made by linguists between marked and unmarked units. As an example John Lyons uses the words "dog" and "bitch." He says that "dog" is semantically unmarked (or neutral) since it can be applied to either males or females ("that's a lovely dog you've got there: is it a he or a she?") But "bitch" is marked (or positive) since it is restricted to females. It may be used in contrast with the unmarked word to determine the sense of the latter as negative rather than neutral ("Is it a dog or a bitch?"). Lyons concludes that "the unmarked term has a more general sense, neutral with respect to a certain contrast; its more specific negative sense is derivative and secondary, being a consequence of its contextual opposition with the positive (non-neutral) term."

The parallel to the differentiation of visual shapes is very close. The circle is an unmarked or neutral shape, which stands for any shape at all until it is explicitly opposed to other, marked shapes, such as squares or triangles. In response to their opposition, the circle assumes the specific semantic function of designating roundness. Nevertheless, it still should be called "unmarked" because even amidst the other differentiated shapes, the circle retains a generality and simplicity not found in the others.

Only for the purpose of systematic theory can the development of form be presented as a standard sequence of neatly separated steps. It is possible and useful to isolate various phases and to arrange them in order of increasing complexity. However, this ideal sequence corresponds only roughly to what happens in any particular case. Different children will cling to different phases for different periods of time. They may skip some and combine others in individual ways. The personality of the child and the influences of the environment will account for these variations. The development of perceptual structure is only one factor, overlaid and modified by others, in the total process of mental growth. Furthermore, earlier stages remain in use when later ones have already been reached; and when confronted with a difficulty, the child may regress to a more primitive solution. Figure 121 shows experimentation with concentric circles; but at the same time a higher level is indicated by the singling out of the horizontal direction in the oblong figure that contains a row of circles. The simple sunburst patterns of Figure 122 occur in drawings that contain fairly advanced forms of human figures, trees, and houses.

It should also be mentioned that there is no fixed relation between the age of a child and the stage of his drawings. Just as children of the same chronological age vary in their so-called mental age, so their drawings reflect individual variations in their rate of artistic growth. An attempt to correlate intelligence and drawing ability has been initiated by Goodenough on the basis of fairly mechanical criteria of realism and completeness of detail. It would be worthwhile to follow up this lead, using structural criteria for the evaluation of drawings and some more adequate means than I.Q. tests for the determination of general cognitive maturity.

Vertical and Horizontal

The variety of shapes produced by young children in their drawings is of course limitless. An extensive morphology has been worked out by Rhoda Kellogg. I shall confine my description to the few most fundamental features, which are at the same time those found not only in the work of children but wherever shapes are handled at early stages of visual conception.

The visually simplest line is the straight line. If we think of the circle as the boundary of a surface rather than a line, the straight line is the earliest shape of a line conceived by the mind. This is somewhat obscured by the fact that for the arm and the hand, which must execute the lines in practice, the straight line is by no means the simplest. On the contrary, a complex muscular arrangement must be activated to produce straightness, the reason being that upper arms, lower arms, hands, and fingers are levers, which naturally pursue curved paths. Figure 123 schematically indicates the intricate changes of speed, angle, and direction that are necessary if a jointed lever (pivoting around point C) is to trace a straight line (L) at even speed. To produce a reasonably straight line is difficult, especially for a child. If nevertheless straight lines occur frequently in early art, this proves how highly they are valued.

The straight line is an invention of the human sense of sight under the mandate of the principle of simplicity. It is characteristic of man-made shapes but occurs rarely in nature, because nature is so complex a configuration of forces that straightness, the product of a single, undisturbed force, seldom has a chance to come about. Delacroix notes in his journal that the straight line, the regular serpentine, and parallels, straight or curved, "never occur in nature; they exist only in the brain of man. Where men do employ them, the elements gnaw them away."

Being the simplest, the straight line stands for all elongated shapes before differentiation of this feature takes place. It represents arms, legs, and tree trunks. The so-called stick men, however, seem to be an invention of adults. Kerschensteiner, who examined large numbers of children's drawings, claims never to have found a stick man whose trunk consisted of a mere line. Apparently a drawing must preserve the solidity of "thingness" at least in one two-dimensional unit in order to satisfy the child. Oval oblongs are used early to combine solidity with "directedness"—for example, in representations of the human or animal body.

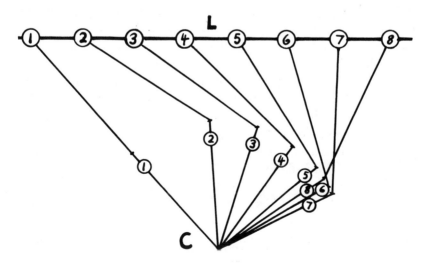

Figure 123

Straight lines look stiff in comparison with curved ones. For this reason adults, who view straightness as one line shape among many, sometimes misread the straight legs, arms, or fingers of early drawings as "rigid" and proceed to use them diagnostically as symptoms of a rigid personality or a means of expressing a momentary sensation of "freezing up," for example, in fear. Such misinterpretations show how indispensable it is to keep the law of differentiation in mind and to avoid taking straightness as a specific shape before it has abandoned its function of representing all elongated shapes. In the history of art, Heinrich Wölfflin has warned that the "rigidity" of archaic representations must not be judged as though later *"Formmöglichkeiten"* (possibilities of form) were already known. "All effects are relative. The same form does not mean the same thing at all times. The meaning of the vertical in Renaissance portraits differs from that in the portraits of the primitives. Here it is the only form of representation; there it is set off from other possibilities and thus acquires its particular expression."

The straight line introduces linear extension in space and thereby the notion of direction. In keeping with the law of differentiation, the first relation between directions to be acquired is the simplest one, that of the right angle. The rightangular crossing stands for all angular relations until obliqueness is explicitly mastered and differentiated from rightangularity. The right angle is the simplest because it creates a symmetrical pattern, and it is the basis for the framework of vertical and horizontal, on which rests our entire conception of space.

In fact, when spatial relations are first practiced they are limited to the rightangular one between horizontal and vertical. I mentioned earlier that a square tilted at 45 degrees completely changes its character. The objectively right angle at the corners is perceived as a roof-shaped, peaked pattern, whose two legs deviate obliquely from a central symmetry axis. Visually, this angle is not identical with the right angle; and because of its more complex relation to the vertical and horizontal framework, it is mastered only later, together with obliqueness of direction quite in general. The Stanford-Binet Intelligence Test indicates that the average five-year-old can copy a square, whereas only the average seven-year-old can successfully cope with the diamond.

The fundamental difference between horizontal and vertical is introduced by gravitational pull. This does not mean, however, that kinesthetic sensations alone account for the dominant role of these spatial directions in vision. It is now known that in the visual cortex of the cat, special teams of cells respond only to vertical stimuli, others only to horizontal ones, and still others again to oblique ones. More cells are concerned with the horizontal and vertical directions than with the oblique ones. If the same situation prevails in the human brain, it would mean that under the influence of gravity, evolution has built the dominance of the two fundamental directions into the human nervous system.

The perceptual preference for the vertical and the horizontal exists even at a very elementary level. Fred Attneave reports that when four lights are arranged in a square and the diagonal ones are flashed on together, the observer sees lights move back and forth either horizontally or vertically; he does not see switching diagonals.

The introduction of the basic framework goes a long way toward establishing a solid spatial trellis. Figure 124 shows this newly acquired order, imposed on a pattern of circles, oblong, and straight lines in the drawing of a four-year-old. The simple "dog" of Figure 125 is built entirely in this spatial system. Figure 126, *Mother and Daughter*, illustrates the consistency with which an intricate theme is subjected to a given law of form. The overall construction of the two figures clings strictly to the two main directions, and the design of dress, socks, and shoes, as well as the teeth and the dignified wrinkles that distinguish the forehead of the mother from that of the daughter, obey the law with equally strict visual logic. Many an artist might justly envy the incorruptible discipline imposed by the child upon reality and the clarity with which he interprets an involved subject. The drawing can also serve to show how earlier stages survive when higher ones are already attained. To represent the hair the child has fallen back on the disorganized motions of the scribble stage, using half-controlled zigzag and spiral forms. Circles and sunbursts appear in cheeks, eyes, and the mother's right hand, and the right arm seems to indicate the transition from rightangularity to the higher level of bent shapes, which is not yet attained otherwise. Finally, Figure 127, copied from a more complex drawing in colored crayon, demonstrates how a single formal device—the vertical-horizontal T pattern—is used ingeniously to render two very different things: the body and skirt of the girl, and the traffic-light pole. Only a large number of examples could indicate the inexhaustible wealth of formal inventions that children derive from the simple vertical-horizontal relation, every one of them surprisingly new and at the same time faithful to the basic concept of the object.

Like all pictorial devices, the vertical-horizontal relation is at first worked out within isolated units and then applied at a later stage to the total picture space. In early drawings an internally well-organized figure may float in space, totally unrelated to other figures or the picture plane; whereas in Figure 127 the entire picture, including the rectangular boundaries of the sheet of drawing

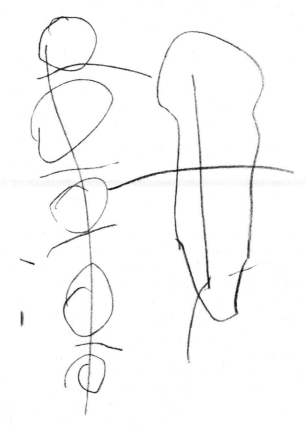

Figure 124

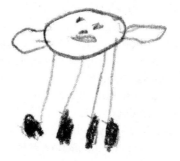

Figure 125

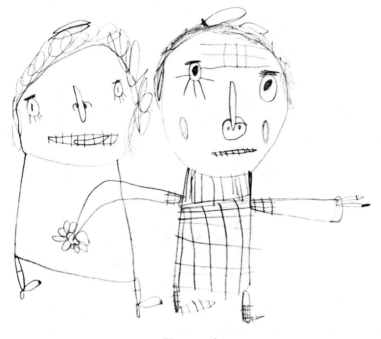

Figure 126

paper, is spatially integrated. The uprights of figures, plants, and poles are seen in relation to the horizontal ground. The picture has become a unified visual entity, in which every detail occupies a clearly defined place in the whole.

The vertical-horizontal framework remains inherent in visual composition, just as the measured beat does in music. Even when no one shape embodies either direction explicitly, all the shapes that are present in a picture are perceived as deviations from them. Piet Mondrian in his late paintings reduced his conception of the world to the dynamic relation between the vertical as the dimension of aspiration and the horizontal as the stable base.

Obliqueness

The deliberate use of obliqueness must be carefully distinguished from the random distribution of spatial directions in the earliest work. We are now concerned with a controlled enrichment of the vertical-horizontal framework. This framework must have been mastered first, and it remains the base of reference that alone makes obliqueness possible. Obliqueness is always perceived as a deviation, hence its strongly dynamic character. It introduces into the visual medium the vital difference between static and dynamic shapes,

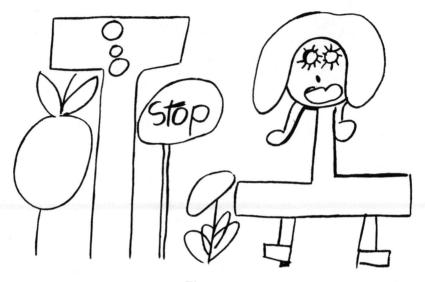

Figure 127

still undifferentiated in the earlier phase. As we look back from this new standpoint at Figure 126, we may be tempted to perceive the outstretched arms of the mother as a gesture of despair, a declaration of bankruptcy. This would be a misinterpretation because at the earlier level the rightangular relation, the maximal directional difference, serves to clarify the functional distinction between body and arms. Only when the divergence of limbs and torso has been understood through its greatest contrast can it be handled in subtler deviations.

In thinking about why artwork proceeds from the simpler to the more complex level, we realize that internal as well as external factors must be considered. Internally, the organism matures, and as it becomes capable of more differentiated functioning, it develops an urge to apply this capacity. This development, however, is not conceivable without the external world, which offers the whole variety of directional relations and which is better understood especially through the distinction between things at rest and things in motion. Motion is of such vital importance to the child that he derives great pleasure from making things visibly move in his pictures.

Oblique relations are applied gradually to everything the child draws. They help to make his representation richer, more alive, more lifelike, and more specific. This can be seen by a comparison of Figures 128 and 129. They are traced from two drawings made by the same child—one about a year earlier than the other. Figure 128 shows two separate details of the earlier drawing; Figure 129, a part of the later. The earlier tree and flower are done with the limited means of vertical-horizontal angularity, clearly and consistently. But the later tree is more interesting to the eye; it looks more like a tree, and the constant application of oblique angles conveys the impression of a live, growing thing. In the earlier giraffe the main relations between head, neck, and body are rendered by right angles. There is the beginning of obliqueness, in the legs, but it looks as though this refinement is due not so much to the girl's observation of the animal as it is to lack of space. (As often happens, her spatial planning had been insufficient, so that by the time she came to the legs she found that she had to squeeze them in sideways if they were not to cross the base line of the ground.) A year later the animal walks freely, in a more lively, more specifically giraffe-like attitude. Differentiation serves not only to distinguish between separate parts but also makes for a more subtle rendering of shape. Undulating ground has replaced the straight base line.

In all these respects the later drawing makes the earlier look stiff and schematic; but the later stage could not have been truly mastered if the earlier had not preceded it. For this reason it is inadvisable to teach the child how to

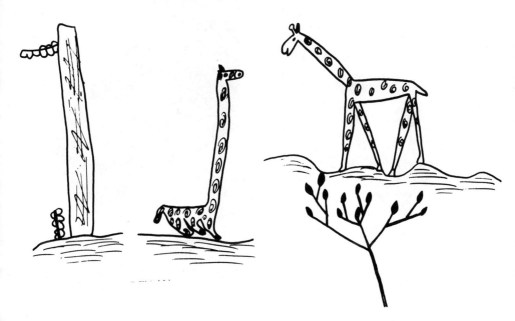

Figure 128   Figure 129

make more complex shapes—which can easily be done and flatters the social ambitions of the child, even though it disturbs his cognitive development. Once the earlier stage has been sufficiently explored, the urge to attain higher complexity leads to progress in its own good time without outside help.

If we adults find it hard to imagine that so simple a matter as the angular relation between shapes could offer so much difficulty, we may be sobered by the perceptual puzzles created by a piece of furniture, a table that has angles of 120° in addition to the usual ones, which we call the right ones (Figure 130). These tables are designed to be more versatile in seating people and relating them to their work and to each other. Combined in clusters, they produce surprising new shapes. To predict how they will look in a certain position or even simply to remember their shape requires considerable visual skill. In practical matters, such as furniture, we tend to cling to the elementary right-angular shapes and relations.

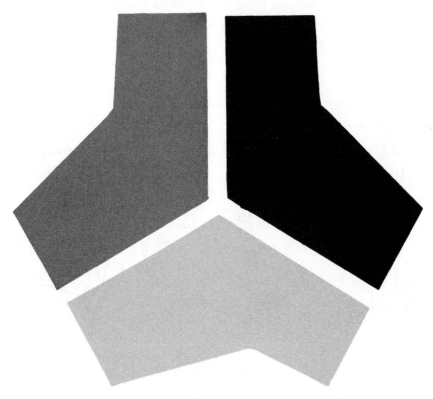

Figure 130

The Fusion of Parts

Throughout the early stages differentiation of shape is accomplished mainly by the adding up of self-contained elements. For example, the child proceeds from the earliest representation of the human figure as a mere circle by adding straight lines, oblongs, or other units. Each of these units is a geometrically simple, well-defined form. They are connected by equally simple directional relations, at first vertical-horizontal, later oblique. The construction of relatively complex whole patterns is made possible by the combination of several simple ones.

This does not mean that, at the earlier stage, the child has no integrated concept of the total object. The symmetry and unity of the whole and the planning of proportions show that—within limits—the child shapes the parts with a view to their final place in the total pattern. But the analytic method makes it possible for him to deal at every particular moment with a simple shape or direction. Some children extend this procedure to highly intricate combinations, building the whole on a hierarchy of detail, which reveals careful observation. The result is anything but poor.

In time, however, the child begins to fuse several units by a common, more differentiated contour. Both the eye and the hand contribute to this development. The eye familiarizes itself with the complex form that results from the combination of elements until it is able to conceive of the compound whole as a unit. When this is achieved, the eye safely guides the continuously moving pencil around the uninterrupted outline of an entire human figure, including arms and legs. The more differentiated the concept, the greater the skill required to work in this fashion. At the highest levels, masters of the "linear style," such as Picasso or Matisse, move with unswerving precision along a contour that captures all the subtleties of muscle and bone. But considering the basis on which the child operates, even the earliest applications of the method require courage, virtuosity, and a differentiated sense of shape.

Contour fusion also accords with the motor act of drawing. At the scribble stage, the child's hand often pendulates rhythmically for some time without lifting the pencil from the paper. As he develops visually controlled form, he begins to make neatly separate units. Visually, the subdivision of the whole into clearly defined parts makes for simplicity; but to the moving hand, any interruption is an obstacle. In the history of writing, there was a change from the detached capital letters of monumental inscriptions to the fluently connected curves of cursive script, in which the hand took precedence over the eye for the sake of speed. Similarly the child, with increasing facility, favors the continuous flow of line. Figure 131, a horse drawn by a five-year-old boy, has the elegance of a businessman's signature. The extent to which the individual draftsman permits the motor factor to influence shape depends considerably on the relation between spontaneously expressed temperament and rational control in his personality. (This can be shown convincingly in graphological analyses of handwriting.)

The two fishes (Figure 132 and 133) are taken from drawings made by one child at different times. In the earlier picture only a first hint of fusion can be observed in the jagged fins. Otherwise the body is constructed from geometrically simple elements in vertical-horizontal relation. Later the entire outline is given in one bold, uninterrupted sweep. It will be seen that this procedure enhances the effect of unified movement, favors oblique direction, and smoothes corners—for example, in the tail of the fish. It also tends to produce shapes more complex than those the eye can truly control and understand at this stage; thus the earlier fish, although relatively less interesting and sprightly, is the more successfully organized.

The snowball fight of Figure 134, drawn even later by the same child, shows how in time the experimentation with more differentiated shape enables him to modify the basic static shape of individual body units. Movement is no longer limited to the relative spatial orientation of different parts, but the trunk itself is bent. At this stage, the child copes more convincingly with figures sitting on chairs, riding horseback, or climbing trees. Beyond bending lies the deformation of shape that is employed in foreshortening. This final differentiation, however, is so sophisticated that it is rarely accomplished spontaneously, except in the simple cases of circles, squares, or rectangles.

The difference between the combination of basic elements and the shaping of more complexly structured units has parallels in other activities of the mind.

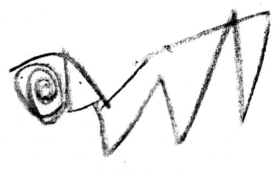

Figure 131

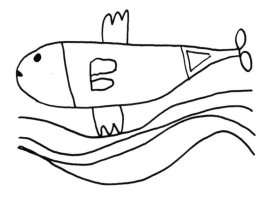

Figure 132

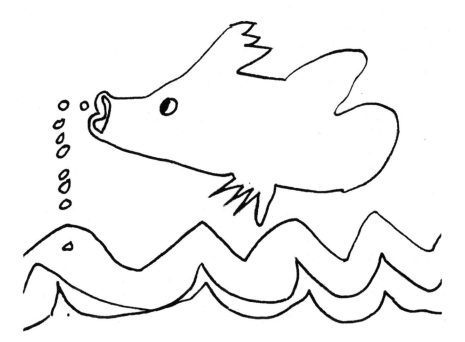

Figure 133

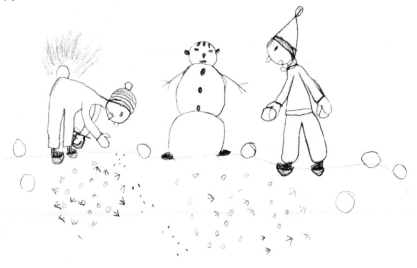

Figure 134

In language, for example, it marks the difference between the English system of declension, which adds prepositions to unchangeable nouns, and the more complex Latin system of inflecting the noun within its own body, even though in language the former does not necessarily precede the latter. Or, to cite an example from the psychology of concept-formation, primitive thinking conceives of soul, passion, or disease as separate entities added to, or subtracted from, the unchangeable unit of the body or mind; whereas more highly differentiated reasoning describes them as fused with or produced by the internal functioning of the body or mind itself. In our own science and philosophy we are witnessing the transition from more primitive "atomistic thinking," which interprets natural phenomena through interrelations between constant elements, to the gestalt conception of integrated field processes. The musician might be reminded of the development from constant tones, which change only in pitch as they move along the melodic line, to integrated chords, which modify their internal structure during harmonic progression.

In a broader sense, the development here described must probably be viewed as a phase of an ongoing process in which subdivision and fusion alternate dialectically. An early global shape is differentiated by subdivision, e.g., when an oval figure breaks down into separate head and torso. This new combination of simple units calls for a more thorough integration at a higher level, which, in turn, will be in need of subdivision for further refinement at a later stage; and so on.

Size

The "illusionistic" approach to visual representation leads us to expect that any picture will represent the sizes of objects the way they look or the way they are or the way the draftsman chooses them to be. Lack of skill or carelessness in observation are cited to account for deviations from the "true" size. Reproachful terms such as "incorrect size" or "exaggerated size" are typical of such evaluations.

From the developmental point of view, we recognize that as a general rule the sizes of pictorial objects are likely to be equal before they are differentiated. We expect that sizes will not be differentiated unless there are good reasons for it. Thus our question should not be, "Why do the size relations in some pictures or sculptures not correspond to reality?" but rather, "What makes children and other image-makers give different sizes to the objects in their pictures?"

Hierarchy based on importance is certainly a factor. In Egyptian reliefs, kings and gods are often more than twice as large as their inferiors. Child psychologists and educators assert that children draw things large when they are important to them. However, this leads to doubtful interpretations; e.g., when Viktor Löwenfeld asserts that in a drawing of a horse bothered by flies, the fly is given roughly the size of the horse's head because of its importance for the child. Such explanations come easy, but often hide the more decisive cognitive factors.

Consider Figure 135, an illustration from a Venetian edition of the *Fables of Aesop*, published in 1491. The hungry fox tries to induce the crow to drop the desirable morsel by flattering him. The visual logic of the story calls for two coordinated principals, fox and crow, comparable to horse and fly in Löwenfeld's example. Because the two are of equal importance in the story, there is no reason to give them different sizes in the world of the picture. In fact, any such difference would make it difficult to read the story as a dialogue between equals. We have reason to admire the appropriateness of the form chosen by the draftsman, who is not deflected from his task by a mechanical, visually unjustified imitation of sizes in nature.

Similarity of size ties items together. It is almost impossible to establish a direct visual relation between, say, a human figure and a tall building if both are drawn to scale. Where such great size differences are desirable, artists generally bridge the gap between the large and small units of their compositions by others of intermediate size.

In medieval painting, not committed to mechanical naturalism, a man

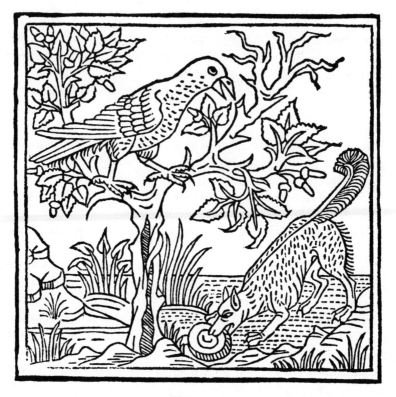

Figure 135

may be the size of a building. At the same time, a bishop may carry in his hand the church he built. It is not the "model" of a church but the church itself; just as the small tower always depicted next to St. Barbara *is* not a "symbol" but a tower, even though it has symbolic meaning. These examples show how size differences arise in response to considerations of meaning, e.g., when the relation between creator and creature or saint and emblem is to be expressed. More technically: if a man is to stand in a doorway or look out of a window, his size must be reduced appropriately. If, in a child's drawing, a face is to accommodate explicit eyes, a mouth with teeth, and a nose with nostrils, it must be made large—just as Marc Chagall enlarges a cow's head to make room inside it for another cow and a milkmaid. If, on the other hand, size is not yet differentiated, the various parts of the body—head, trunk, and limbs—are given roughly the same order of magnitude (Figure 136).

What is true for the size of objects holds also for the intervals between

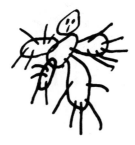

Figure 136

them. The need for clear presentation makes the child leave sufficient empty space between objects—a sort of standard distance which, from the realistic point of view, looks sometimes too large and sometimes too small, depending on the subject matter. An overlong arm may be required to connect a human figure with an apple on a tree, from which the figure is kept at suitable distance. Realistic closeness between items remains visually uncomfortable for some time.

Realistic size is only marginally relevant to the size of things in pictures because perceptual identity does not rely much on size. The shape and the spatial orientation of an object remain unimpaired by a change in size, just as in music a moderate augmentation or diminution of temporal size through a change of speed does not interfere with the recognition of a theme. The basic irrelevance of visual size is shown most strikingly by our habitual obliviousness to the constant change in size of the objects in our environment brought about by changes in distance. As far as images are concerned, nobody protests against an inch-high photograph of a human being or against a gigantic statue. A television screen looks small in the living room, but we need only concentrate on it for a short time and it becomes an acceptable frame for "real" persons and buildings.

The Misnamed Tadpoles

Perhaps the most striking case of misinterpretation due to illusionistic bias is that of the "tadpole" figures, called *hommes têtards* by the French and *Kopffüssler* by the Germans. The popular view is that in these very common drawings the child leaves out the trunk entirely, and that he erroneously attaches the arms to the head or the legs. Figures 137 and 138, drawn by four-year-olds, show some of these mysterious creatures. Various theories have been offered. The child was believed to overlook or forget the body or even to

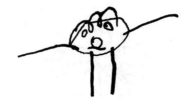

Figure 137

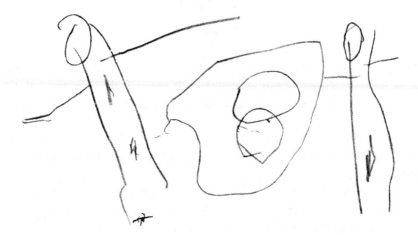

Figure 138

"repress" it for reasons of modesty. If we look at the developmental process, we discover that no such explanation is pertinent, since in these drawings the trunk actually is not left out.

At the earliest stage the circle stands for the total human figure, just as it stands for so many other complete objects. Later, its shape is differentiated through the addition of appendages. For example, in Figure 139, an eight-

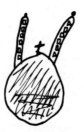

Figure 139

year-old boy's drawing of a church, the original circle is still clearly discernible. In the human figure the original meaning of the circle is gradually limited by the additions. There are essentially two types. In Figure 137 the circle functions as an undifferentiated representation of head and trunk. Therefore the child is entirely consistent in attaching legs and arms to it. Only to adults does the picture look as though something is left out. The circle is often extended to an egg-shaped oblong, which may contain the features of a face in its upper part or indications of clothing in the lower. Figure 138 illustrates the other type. In the center is a house with two fish in it, at the right a cowboy, and at the left a cow. The cowboy has one stomach in his body, and the cow has two. These stomachs are useful for our purpose, because they show that here the two parallel vertical lines are an undifferentiated representation of trunk and legs, whereas the circle is now limited to being a head. The arms are attached where they belong—to the verticals. The double function of the line as self-contained unit and as contour is not yet clearly differentiated; the two verticals are contours (trunk) and object lines (legs) at the same time. It may be added that a similar lack of differentiation is often evident in the way other parts of the body are represented. The features of the face may be drawn as a single circle, contained in the larger circle of the head, before they split up into eyes, nose, and mouth; and in Figure 136 the limbs are not yet articulated, so that to the adult observer the fingers may seem to be attached to the arms, and the toes to the legs.

Translation into Two Dimensions

The law of differentiation leads us to expect that the distinction between two-dimensional and three-dimensional views in pictures does not exist from the beginning. Instead, the two-dimensional view, as the simpler one, is "unmarked" and serves indiscriminately for both. Nothing distinguishes at first between depthlessness and depth, or between a flat object and a voluminous one. The spatial qualities of a dinner plate are treated no differently from those of a football, and all things lie at the same distance from the observer.

A good way of coming to understand how children represent space is to read E. A. Abbott's fantastic novel *Flatland*. Flatland is a two-dimensional country in which, as compared with our own world, everything is reduced by one dimension. The walls of houses are mere outlines of plane figures; but they serve their purpose, because in a flat world there is no way of penetrating a closed outline. The inhabitants are planimetric shapes. Their bodies, too, are satisfactorily bounded by a line. A visitor from three-dimensional Spaceland makes a nuisance of himself by telling them that their houses are open: he can see them inside and outside at the same time. He also proves that he can touch a Flatlander's intestines, producing a shooting pain in the Square's stomach. To the Flatlanders their houses are neither closed nor open at the top since they have no such dimension; and their intestines are kept properly invisible and untouchable by the surrounding contour line.

Those who assert that children draw open houses and X-rayed stomachs resemble the inopportune Spacelander. They are unaware of the admirable logic by which the child adapts his pictures to the conditions of the two-dimensional medium. It is not enough to say that children draw the insides of things because they are interested in them. With all their interest they would be horrified by the picture of a man with an open stomach. An Australian bark painting comes to mind in which the outline of a kangaroo's body is visibly filled with the anatomy of bones, organs, and intestines. The picture does not represent a "section" through the animal's body, as a zoology textbook might. It also shows the figure of a hunter, who shoots his prey with bow and arrow; and obviously one does not hunt a section, but a whole, live animal. This proves that the kangaroo's body is not meant to be open or "transparent." Similarly, a child's drawing of a gorilla that has eaten his dinner (Figure 140) is neither a section nor an X-ray view.

The same point is made in the schematic diagram of Figure 141. The drawing of the house is neither a transparent front view nor a section. It is

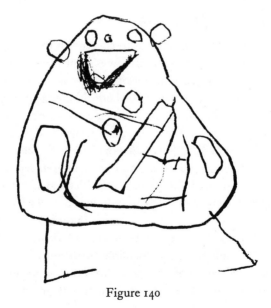

Figure 140

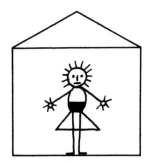

Figure 141

the two-dimensional equivalent of a house. The rectangle stands for cubic space, and its outline for the six boundary surfaces. The figure stands inside, completely surrounded by walls. Only a gap in the contour could provide an opening. The child's invention lingers on through the ages, so that even in the highly realistic art of a Dürer or Altdorfer the Holy Family is housed in a building without front wall, camouflaged unconvincingly as a broken-down ruin. And of course in our modern theater, the stage is accepted without hesitation by the same people who accuse the child of "X-ray pictures."

As indicated in Figure 141, pictures of this kind present hair as a single row of lines, all touching the contour of the head. This is quite correct in that the circular head line stands for the complete surface of the head, which is thus shown as being covered with hair all over. Yet there is in this method an ambiguity deriving from the fact that inevitably the child is using it for two different and incompatible purposes at the same time. Obviously the face is not meant to lie inside the head, but on its outer surface; and the two oblique lines represent arms, and not an open cape hanging down from the shoulders and surrounding the entire body. That is, the two-dimensional units of the drawings are equivalents of solids, of two-dimensional aspects of the outside of solids, or both, depending on what is needed. The relation between flatness and depth is undifferentiated, so that by purely visual means there is no way of telling whether a circular line stands for a ring, a disk, or a ball. It is because of this ambiguity that the method is used mostly at primitive levels and is quickly abandoned by the Western child.

The process was well documented in an experiment by Arthur B. Clark, in which children of different ages were asked to draw an apple with a hatpin stuck horizontally through it and turned at an angle to the observer. Figure 142*d* illustrates the position in which the children saw the model. Figure 142*a*

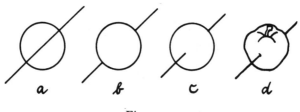

Figure 142

shows the earliest solution of the problem. It is logical in that the pin goes uninterruptedly through the inside of the circle, which stands for the inside of the apple. But it is ambiguous in that the straight line inevitably depicts a one-dimensional object (pin) and not a surface. At the next stage, *b*, the child makes a first concession to projective representation by showing the center part of the pin hidden inside the apple. (To the younger child this would look like a picture of two pins touching the apple at the outside.) But the contour of the circle still stands for the entire surface of the apple, as shown by the way the pin stops at the contour. At *c* the contour has become the horizon line, and the area of the circle represents the front face of the apple. With some refinement of shape, this leads to the realistic solution, *d*. This final picture is spatially consistent, but it sacrifices the striking visual clarity with which the essentials of the three-dimensional conception were rendered in the two-dimensional medium at stage *a*. The differentiation between two-dimensional and three-dimensional form has been achieved, but only through the suspect trick of making the picture plane appear as an image of three-dimensional space.

As long as the two-dimensional view is not differentiated from the projective view, the flat pictorial plane serves to represent them both. This can be done in two ways. The child can use the vertical dimension of his picture plane to distinguish between top and bottom and the horizontal for right and left and thus obtain "vertical space" (elevation). Or he can use his two dimensions to show the directions of the compass in a ground plan, which produces "horizontal space" (Figure 143). Upright objects, such as human beings, trees, walls, table legs, appear clearly and characteristically in vertical space, whereas gardens, streets, table tops, dishes, or carpets ask for horizontal space. To further complicate matters, in vertical space only one among the innumerable vertical planes can be represented directly, so that the picture can take care of the front face of a house but not, at the same time, of the side faces without recourse to some trick of indirect representation. Similarly, horizontal

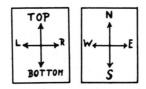

Figure 143

space can show the dishes on the table top but not, in the same picture, the dog lying under the table.

In dealing with the "Egyptian method" we showed how at an early level of spatial representation the artist chooses for each object, or part of an object, the aspect presenting it most characteristically. It may be mentioned here that the highly sophisticated and realistic technique of the motion picture has re-captured some of the striking effects of elementary representation. By decom-posing the visual world into a succession of partial views, the film has been able, for example, to return to the principle that the units of a visual statement are basically of equal size. If a person is shown watching a butterfly, a close-up may make the insect as large as the person. Similarly, a change in camera angle will make the screen picture switch from vertical to horizontal space, so that the spectator may see a side view of people sitting at the dinner table and, a second later, a top view of the food. This procedure is "justified" realistically through the succession of the shots in time, which sanctions a change in dis-tance or angle. In the actual experience of the spectator, however, these changes in observation point are not clearly perceived as such. Essentially, he accepts things as being presented at a size and angle that fits them best without worry-ing whether or not such visual correctness is "true-to-life." In much modern art, of course, all realistic pretense has been frankly dropped: objects are clearly given whatever size and angle accords with the visual purpose.

Educational Consequences

In discussing some of the earliest features of visual form, I have tried to show, in their pristine clarity, some of the elements on which image-making is forever built. But an understanding of this early development should also help the educator evaluate and assist in the work of his students. The principal message is, of course, that the work of children, "primitives," etc., is not to be regarded negatively as something below standard, something to be overcome, the sooner the better, on the road to "competent" art. The preceding sections of this chapter will have suggested that visual form, when permitted to grow undisturbed, moves from stage to stage lawfully, and that each stage has its own justification, its own capacities for expression, its own beauty. Since these early stages depend on one another and lay the foundation for any mature achievement, they must be worked through unhurriedly. This is true not only for children but for any developing artist. "An artist does not skip steps," said Jean Cocteau; "if he does, it is a waste of time because he has to climb them later."

In our discussion it will have become evident also that deviations from lifelike representation are not due to deficiencies, but to a remarkable, spontaneous sensitivity for the requirements of the medium. As the teacher watches the manifestation of this enviable native endowment, the sureness of intuitive decision, the logical progression from the simple to the complex, he will ask himself whether the best thing to do is not to leave his pupils alone, entrusted to their own guidance. Is art not one of those skills that one can and should learn by oneself? To some extent this is surely so. Every untoward intervention on the part of the teacher may disorient the student's own visual judgment or cheat him out of a discovery he would more profitably have made himself. In this respect, the old-fashioned teacher who hands out the tricks of central perspective is no more guilty than his progressive colleague who makes the child fill the accidental loops of his scribbles with paint, or the new-styled primitivist who admonishes him: "This is a nice picture, but in second grade we do not make noses yet!" To insist on a child's doing "abstractions" is as harmful as forcing him to draw lifelike representations.

This is true at any level of education. The art student who copies the manner of an impressive teacher is in danger of losing his intuitive sense of right and wrong in the struggle with a form of representation that he can imitate but not master. His work, instead of being convincing and congenial, is puzzling to him. He has lost the honesty of the child, which every successful artist preserves and which gives the simplest possible shape to any statement, complicated as the result may be objectively. Arnold Schönberg, the composer of some of the most intricate music ever written, told his students that their pieces should be as natural to them as their hands and feet. The simpler they seemed to them, the better they would be. "If something you have written looks very complicated to you, you do well to doubt its genuineness right away!"

And yet there is much the art teacher can do. Like his colleagues in other areas, he must steer a course somewhere between the two easy escape routes: to teach everything and to teach nothing. The most helpful suggestion deriving from the study of the developmental stages is that all teaching should be based on an awareness that the student's visual conception is growing in accordance with principles of its own, and that the teacher's interventions should be guided by what the individual process of growth calls for at any given time.

The best example I can find comes from the history of art. The discovery of the geometrical formula for central perspective came in the fifteenth century, after many painters had attempted intuitively to unify pictorial space by making depth lines converge. It is fascinating to observe how in the paintings and woodcuts of the time those perspective lines reach for a common center, attain it approximately, or create separate foci for different sections of the picture. The geometrical formula, which prescribes a common vanishing point, merely codified the solution to a problem that had been thoroughly researched by intuition. The time was ripe for it.

At any earlier historical period, the teaching of the geometrical trick might have been disruptive or useless. Something very similar holds for the development of the individual. The teacher feels tempted to communicate his knowledge in order to satisfy his own aspirations along with those of the student, who begs his instructor to show him how one makes things "go back" into space. However, these are merely social urges, not deriving from the demands of the work itself. Out of ambition the student wishes to equal the standards of some prestigious accomplishment, and would as soon reach that pleasant goal with a minimum of effort. Such social motives must be distinguished from the cognitive motives that arise from the state of the student's visual development. The former must not be gratified at the expense of the latter.

In recent years, art teachers have legitimately striven to go beyond the traditional drawing and modeling and acquaint their students with many materials and techniques. Not only does this accord with the practices of our modern artists, it also keeps the attention of students alive and makes legitimate use of their love of gadgetry. Adolescents in particular grant more prestige to technology than to art. It is essential, however, that materials be selected and employed in such a way that they challenge the student to work on tasks of visual organization at his own level of conception and make it possible for him to do so. Techniques inviting visual confusion or creating excessive difficulty or complexity are destructive; so is the practice of changing tasks so often that the student cannot explore the visual characteristics of a particular medium thoroughly. There is enough unproductive distraction outside the schoolroom.

It is natural for the artist and art educator to think of his field as self-contained, governed by its own rules and dedicated to its own purpose. However, one cannot hope to cultivate the sense of visual form in one area of the curriculum if this sense is neglected or even abused elsewhere. In another book I have made the point as follows: "At a level of development at which the free art work of the child still employs relatively simple geometrical shapes, the art teacher may respect his pupils' early stage of visual conception, but in geography class the same children may be compelled, perhaps by the same teacher, to trace the coastlines of the American continent or the irrational windings of rivers—shapes that can be neither perceived nor understood nor remembered. When a college student is asked to copy what he sees under the microscope, he cannot aim, mechanically, for mere accuracy and neatness. He must decide what matters and what types of relevant shapes are represented in the accidental specimen. Therefore, his drawing cannot possibly be a reproduction; it will be an image of what he sees and understands, more or less actively and intelligently. The discipline of intelligent vision cannot be confined to the art studio; it can succeed only if the visual sense is not blunted and confused in other areas of the curriculum. To try to establish an island of visual literacy in an ocean of blindness is ultimately self-defeating. Visual thinking is indivisible."

Finally, it is necessary to point to a limitation of the present book. It discusses visual organization and invention as deriving from the cognitive functions of the mind: the sensory perception of the outer world, the elaboration of experience in visual and intellectual thinking, the conservation of experience and thought in memory. From this standpoint, pictorial work is a tool for the task of identifying, understanding, and defining things, for investigating relations, and creating order of increasing complexity. We must not forget, however, that the cognitive functions are at the service of the whole personality. They reflect attitudes and fulfill desires, as psychologists have emphasized in using visual experiences for diagnostic or therapeutic purposes. Some art educators have followed suit, interpreting as "emotional" many features that are derived from the conditions of visual perception and representation.

Examples abound in the literature; I will limit myself to one. In his book on art education Herbert Read comments on a drawing done by a girl just under five years old. A tiger is represented very simply by a horizontal stroke for the body and two verticals for the legs. The lines are crossed with short stripes, meant to depict the tiger's skin. Read speaks of the "wholly introvert, inorganic" basis of the picture. The child, he says, has shown no regard for whatever image of a tiger she may have had; she has created "an expressive symbol which [does not] correspond . . . to her perceptual awareness or conceptual knowledge of the tiger." Actually, the picture is a typical example of the horizontal-vertical stage, at which the average child will represent an animal in just this way. Very often no differentiation between organic and inorganic shape is possible at this stage; straight lines stand for both. Such pictures are meager in content not because the child is unable or unwilling to observe and to use his observations, but because the elementary stage of representation does not permit him to use much of what he has seen. Whether or not this particular child is a withdrawn introvert cannot be determined on the basis of her drawing and age alone. Introversion may retard differentiation of form, but undifferentiated form in itself does not suggest introversion. The same drawing could come from a bubbling extrovert, passionately interested in the way animals look and behave.

Here, then, a one-sided emphasis on personality factors leads to a misinterpretation of traits that in fact arise from the stage of the child's cognitive development and the properties of the pictorial medium. Conversely, however, an equally one-sided concentration on the cognitive aspects may create the impression that the young organism is occupied with nothing but perceptual and intellectual growth, and that the mind is merely a kind of processing mechanism tackling the shapes of the outer world at a continuously more complex level. The present book, by trying to fill some of the gaps left by others, means to contribute to a broader conception. The educator of tomorrow should be able to view the thinking and perceiving mind in interaction with the aspirations, passions, and fears of the total human being.

The emphasis on personality factors has induced some art educators to regard techniques that favor precision of form with suspicion. They have replaced the old-fashioned pencil with materials that foster the spontaneous stroke, the impulsive flash, the raw effect of amorphous color. Spontaneous expression is certainly desirable, but expression becomes chaotic when it interferes with visual organization. Broad brushes and dripping easel paints compel the child to create a one-sided picture of his state of mind, and the possibility cannot be excluded that the kind of picture he is permitted to make may, in turn, influence the state of mind he is in. Unquestionably, modern methods have given an outlet to aspects of the child's mind that were hobbled by the traditional procedure of having him copy models with a sharpened pencil. But there is equal danger in preventing the child from using his pictorial work for clarifying his observation of reality and for learning to concentrate and to create order. Shapeless emotion is not the desirable end result of education and therefore cannot be used as its means. The equipment of the art room and the mind of the art teacher should be comprehensive and variable enough to let each child act as a whole person at any time.

The Birth of Form in Sculpture

The principles of visual development described in this chapter are so fundamental that they do not apply only to shapes in drawing and painting. Probably they control the use of color as well. Early art does best with a few simple colors, especially the three fundamental primaries, which serve to separate shapes from one another but do not connect them. Mixed colors introduce the more complex interrelations. Similarly, the homogeneous coloring of objects and areas belongs to an earlier stage than do composites of variously colored parts or deliberate color modulation within a shape. More precise knowledge in this field awaits further research.

More directly, our principles can be applied to the visual arts of the theater, choreography, film, and architecture. In the history of styles as well as in the development of the individual stage director or choreographer, are there early compositional forms, distinguished perhaps by symmetrical arrangements and a preference for frontal and rectangular spatial orientations, or groupings according to simple geometric figures? Can differentiation be shown to proceed step by step from these to more and more complex conceptions? In architecture it would be possible to show the changes from simple circular and rectangular plans to more intricate ones, the gradual breaking up of the unified block and wall, the deviation from the symmetrical façade, the introduction of oblique orientation and curves of an increasingly high order.

Sculpture certainly lends itself to the same kind of description, although three-dimensionality makes for more complex relations. For technical reasons it is difficult to document the early stages of children's sculptural work. The mechanical problems involved in handling clay and similar materials and in keeping constructions from collapsing make it harder for the child to produce the shapes he has in mind; and the rough surfaces of children's work photograph badly. The following analyses are therefore illustrated with the early sculptural work of adults.

It might be supposed that the three-dimensional objects of nature are more easily represented in sculpture than on paper or canvas, because the sculptor works in volumes and therefore is not faced with the problem of rendering three dimensions in a two-dimensional medium. Actually this is true only to a limited degree, because the lump of clay or piece of stone presents the sculptor with three dimensions only materially. He still has to acquire the conception of three-dimensional organization step by step, and it might well be maintained that the task of mastering space is more difficult in sculpture than in the pictorial arts for the same reason that playing three-dimensional tick-tacktoe requires a higher level of visual intelligence than the two-dimensional version.

When the child draws his first circle, he has not mastered two-dimensional space but merely annexed a bit of territory on paper. We have seen that he must go through the slow process of differentiating the various angular relations before he can be said to be truly in command of the medium's formal possibilities. Similarly, modeling a first ball of clay does not mean the conquest of three-dimensional organization. It merely reflects the most elementary kind of form concept, which differentiates neither shape nor direction. If we may judge by analogy with what happens in drawing, the "primordial ball" will represent any compact object—a human figure, an animal, a house. I cannot tell whether this stage exists in the work of children, nor have I found any example in the history of art. The examples that come closest seem to be the small Paleolithic stone figures of fat women, the best-known of which is the "Venus of Willendorf." These figures, with their round heads, bellies, breasts, and thighs, indeed look as though they had been conceived as combinations of spheres modified to fit the human shape. One may wonder whether their obesity is to be explained only by the subject matter—symbols of motherhood and fertility, a preference on the part of prehistoric man for fat women—or also as a manifestation of early form conception at the spherical stage.

Sticks and Slabs

The simplest way of representing one direction in sculpture, corresponding to the straight line in drawing, is by means of a stick. A stick is of course always a three-dimensional object physically; but just as the breadth of a brush stroke does not "count" in early drawing and painting, so the stick in sculpture is the product of one-dimensional conception, counting mainly in its direction and length. Good examples can be found among the terra-cotta figures made on Cyprus and at Mycenae during the second millennium B.C. (Figure 144). The bodies of men and animals—legs, arms, snouts, tails, and horns—are made of stick-like units of roughly identical diameter. Stick elements are found also in the small bronzes of the Geometric period in Greece, around the eighth century B.C. Children make sausage-like sticks for their clay and plasticine figures. Probably this stage exists universally at the beginnings of modeling. It has also produced very refined constructions of modern sculpture, in which metal rods are combined in spatially intricate arrangements.

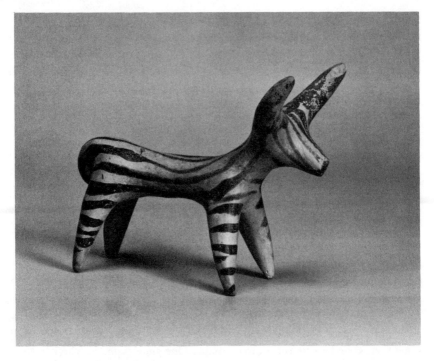

Figure 144
Mycenaean terra cotta figure of an ox. 1400–1100 B.C. Metropolitan Museum of Art,
New York.

To describe further differentiation in a three-dimensional medium we
need two terms. The spatial dimensions of an object refer to its own shape
(*object dimensions*) and to the pattern it creates in space (*spatial dimensions*).
Thus a wire ring is stick-like or one-dimensional as an object, but two-
dimensional as a pattern in space.

The simplest combination of sticks leads to patterns of two spatial dimensions—that is, an arrangement within one plane, limited at first to the
rightangular relation (Figure 145*a*). Later the third dimension is added in
patterns that occupy more than one plane (*b*). Here again the earliest relation
is the right angle. Further differentiation of orientation yields oblique connections between units in two or three dimensions (*d*) and bending and
twisting (*c*). The length of the units is probably at first undifferentiated, just
as we have found it to be in drawing (compare Figure 136). Distinctions of
length are worked out only gradually.

In the foregoing examples, the object dimension was kept constant while

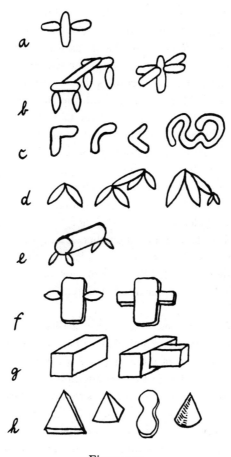

Figure 145

only the spatial dimensions were modified. In Figure 145*e* the shape of the object itself has been changed in the simplest possible way by introducing a difference in girth: the trunk is thicker than the legs. Figure 145*f* introduces slabs, a two-dimensional shape, and in the cubic forms of *g* the third object dimension becomes an active part of the visual conception rather than just being physically present. Finally, in *h* there is a differentiation of shape within the two-dimensional or three-dimensional unit. It will be understood that the variations in spatial orientation and size indicated for the undifferentiated objects in *a–e* can also be applied to these more complex objects, which leads to compositions of considerable intricacy.

Object dimensions offer some difficult, specifically sculptural problems.

A ball looks the same from all sides because it is symmetrical in relation to one central point. A stick, a cylinder, or a cone is symmetrical in relation to a central axis, and therefore does not change aspect when rotated around the axis. But such simple shapes do not satisfy the sculptor's need for long. The human figure in particular soon requires the representation of patterns that are symmetrical in two dimensions and are therefore most simply rendered on a flat surface. Consider the example of the face. If the head is rendered by a sphere, features of the face may be scratched on its surface. This solution, however, can look quite unsatisfactory. In the first place, one aspect is singled out on the surface of the sphere, whose shape makes such a distinction quite arbitrary; also, the two-dimensional symmetry of the face is rendered on a curved surface rather than on the simpler flat one. The same is true for the human body as a whole. What can be done? With regard to the face, the simplest solution is to leave it out altogether. Examples can be found among the Paleolithic "Venus" figures. For example, the Willendorf woman has a head symmetrically surrounded by plaits of hair, but no face. Again we may speculate that this was done, partly or wholly, to avoid interfering with the logic of visual simplicity.

There are other solutions. One can cut a slice off the sphere and place the face on the resulting segmental plane. Flat, mask-like faces of this kind are frequent in early styles of sculpture, in African figures and the Japanese *haniwa* terra-cotta, as well as in the first attempts at sculptural portraiture by Western art students. Picasso has sometimes rendered a head as a combination of two pieces: a spherical volume attached to a flat vertical shield bearing the face. The problem can be solved more radically by reducing the whole head or figure to flatness. Figure 146 illustrates an Indian figurine in which the frontal symmetry of the body is given the simplest, two-dimensional form. The most primitive variety of the small stone idols found in Troy and on the Cycladic Islands were made from rectangular slates of marble and shaped like a violin. Even where the front and the back views have developed some relief, there is not yet a side view that can be considered an active part of a three-dimensional concept. In the same culture are combinations of two- and one-dimensional form; for example, the trunk of the body is a flat, frontal shield, whereas head and legs have the vaselike, undifferentiated roundness of an earlier stage.

Some parts of the body do not fit into the frontal plane: noses, breasts, penises, feet. One radical solution of this problem can be found in the head of the baby, held by the figure to the left in Figure 147. The head is wedged

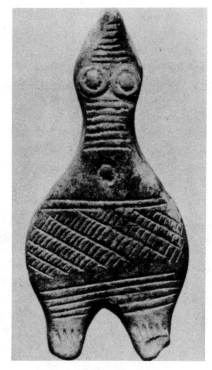

Figure 146
Indian figurine. Boston Museum of Fine Arts.

like the blade of an ax—nothing but nose, so to speak, with the eyes scratched in laterally.

At the stage of rectangular connections, noses and breasts stick out perpendicularly from the frontal plane. Figure 148*a* shows the section of a flat head with a nose protruding at a right angle. When, in the course of further differentiation, this pattern is smoothed to more organic shape (*b*), we arrive quite logically at the curious bird-like heads of the Cyprian statuettes in Figure 147—a solution found also, perhaps quite independently, in the early sculpture of other cultures.

The strict frontal symmetry of primitive sculpture is abandoned gradually. Even in Egyptian and early Greek art, however, symmetry is still evident to such an extent that Julius Lange described it as the basic law of sculptural composition in these archaic styles.

As in drawing, the differentiation of the figure comes about not only by

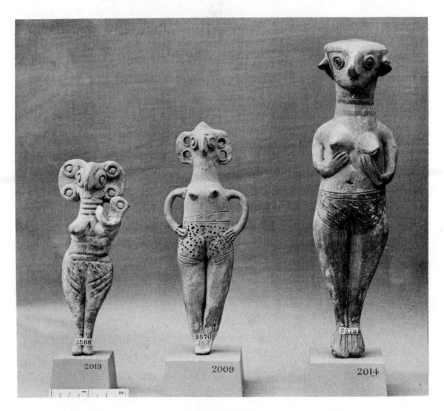

Figure 147
Statuettes from Cyprus. Metropolitan Museum of Art, New York.

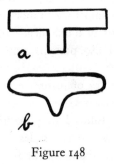

Figure 148

the addition of units to the main base but also through internal subdivision. In Figures 146 and 147 clothing is represented by scratched-in lines. At the same time these early figures show how subdivision develops from scratching to a more sculptural, three-dimensional procedure. The scratched-in lines, remnants of the technique of drawing, are replaced with moldings. Ribbons are applied to the surface to outline the eyes. In the archaic Greek statues of young men (sixth century B.C.), such ribbons are used, for example, to mark the dividing line between the belly and the thigh. Angular steps, rather than mere dividing lines, distinguish the protruding chest from the stomach. These moldings become gradually smoother and fuse with the ground plane; the scratched-in lines develop into cavities representing such things as the mouth or the hollow of the eye. From a combination of separate units a continuous relief gradually evolves. Figure 149 illustrates this development by two schematic sections.

The Cube and the Round

The flat figure, of which the Cycladic marble idols served as examples, conceives the human body in two object dimensions. Further differentiation adds the third object dimension. The simplest realization of this shape is the three-dimensional cube, in which the three directions of space meet at right angles. In addition to the front and back planes, there are now two side views. The visual construction of the figure out of four main views that lie at right angles to one another was first formulated by Emanuel Löwy as a law for archaic Greek sculpture. It can be applied more generally, however, to all sculpture at this particular stage of early development. The continuous roundness of the human body or animal is broken down into independent and relatively self-contained partial views, i.e., front face, profiles, back—the perceptually simplest aspects. This makes it possible for the sculptor to concentrate at any particular moment upon a relatively closed partial composition, which he can survey without changing his point of observation. He may work

Figure 149

first on the front view, later on the side view, and so forth. The combining of the views is left to a secondary phase of the process.

The independence of the four views is most strikingly illustrated by the winged bulls and the lions serving as gatekeepers of Assyrian palaces (Figure 150). Viewed from the front, such an animal shows two symmetrical front legs standing still. The side view has four legs walking. This means that from an oblique angle of vision we count five legs. But to add up unrelated elements this way is to violate the intended concept. The important thing for the Assyrians was the completeness of each view in itself.

Every beginner in the art of sculpture finds that the simplicity of the cubic concept imposes itself upon his work. When he tries to abandon it in favor of the kind of roundness that was achieved during the Renaissance, he has to overcome the "Egyptian" in himself. Furthermore, he will be tempted constantly to finish one aspect of the work as it appears from a given observation point, only to discover that when he turns his figure the horizon of his previous view is no longer valid as a boundary. In consequence he will find himself with unexpected breaks and ridges and with incomplete planes that shoot into outer space instead of turning around the figure. The ability to think of the total volume as a continuous whole marks a late mastery of three-dimensional space. It would be a mistake to assume that this had been accomplished already in the shaping of the primordial ball. Rather, it took the gradual development from the one-dimensional stick and the step-by-step differentiation by way of flat and cubic bodies to arrive at the genuine roundness of Michelangelo's or Bernini's figures.

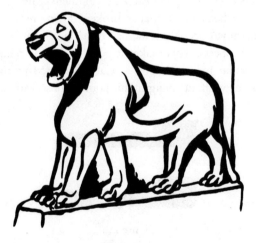

Figure 150

In baroque sculpture the subdivision into well-defined aspects is abandoned, and sometimes it is impossible to find one main view. Every aspect is an inseparable part of constantly changing form. Emphasis on oblique foreshortening prevents the glance from stopping. From any point of observation, planes lead beyond the given view and demand an endless change of position. The screw is the underlying structural pattern, which is applied most simply in the bands of pictorial reliefs spiraling around the Roman columns of Trajan or Marcus Aurelius. A characteristic example is Michelangelo's Christ in the Church of Santa Maria Sopra Minerva in Rome. Every segment of the figure is set obliquely against the next, so that at any given aspect the frontality of one of the segments is counteracted by the obliqueness of others. This adds up to a screw-like rotation of the whole body. According to Lomazzo, Michelangelo advised his students to make their figures "serpent-like."

Needless to say, the style of such figures is not of higher artistic quality than the simpler cubes of the Egyptian or African carver. It is merely more complex; and although the richness of the unending symphonic flow may enchant the educated eye, the artist who strives for it risks losing control and ending up with visually incomprehensible multiformity or amorphous imitations of nature. The danger diminishes when the artist has gradually arrived at complex form through the organic sequence of stages, never going beyond what his eye has learned to organize, and being accustomed to accepting nothing he cannot master. The danger is greatest when a highly differentiated style, whether realism or cubism, is sprung prematurely on the unprepared student. There are no short cuts on the road to the refined manifestations of a late culture.

Of other late stages of complexity, I shall mention only one. Throughout the history of sculpture there is a clear distinction between the solid block and surrounding empty space. The figure is bounded by straight or convex planes, and the holes that detach arms from the body or legs from each other do not impair the compactness of the main volume. In the next chapter I will have occasion to show how the introduction of concave form draws space into the realm of the figure and thereby overcomes the elementary distinction between figure and empty space. The block begins to disintegrate, until in our century we find sculpture that surrounds empty space in addition to being surrounded by it.

V   SPACE

Geometry tells us that three dimensions suffice to describe the shape of any solid and the locations of objects relative to one another at any given moment. If changes in shape and location are also to be considered, the dimension of time must be added to the three dimensions of space. Psychologically we can say that although we move freely in space and time from the beginning of consciousness, the artist's active grasp of these dimensions develops step by step, in accordance with the law of differentiation.

At the stage of the first dimension, spatial conception is limited to a linear track. There is no specification of shape. Disembodied entities, defined only by their relative location, can be conceived in terms of their distance, their relative speeds, and the difference between two directions, coming and going. A mind limited to this elementary conception of space would be primitive indeed. It would apprehend no more than what we can perceive going on behind a narrow slot.

A two-dimensional conception brings two great enrichments. First, it offers extension in space and therefore the varieties of size and shape: small things and large things, round and angular and most irregular ones. Second, it adds to mere distance the differences in direction and orientation. Shapes can be distinguished according to the many possible directions they point in, and their placement in relation to one another can be endlessly varied. Motion in the whole range of directions can now be conceived, as can the curves an imaginative skater might execute.

Three-dimensional space, finally, offers complete freedom: shape extending in any perceivable direction, unlimited arrangements of objects, and the total mobility of a swallow. Beyond these three spatial dimensions visual imagery cannot reach; the range can be extended only by intellectual construction.

If for our particular purpose we apply these facts to visual representation, we find, first of all, that a purely one-dimensional performance seems not to be realizable for the normal human mind. Even a mere spot of light moving back and forth in the dark, or a single animated dot moving on an empty screen, is perceived as acting in full space and in relation to that space. In the same way, a single line drawn on a piece of paper cannot be seen simply as itself. First of all, it is always related to the two-dimensional extent around it. Depending on the range and also the shape of this empty environment, the appearance of the line changes. Furthermore, there also seems to be no way of seeing the line strictly in a flat plane. Instead, it is seen as lying in front of (or within) an uninterrupted ground. Figure 151 shows an assortment of dots and lines active in front of empty space.

Our first, surprising discovery, then, is that there is no such thing as a strictly flat, two-dimensional image. We are reminded here of the struggles of the painter Piet Mondrian, who during the last years of his life renounced all references to physical subject matter, even to any shape, except for undifferentiated straight bands. But there was one remnant of the visual world he could not overcome: the distinction between objects and surrounding empty space. However he tried, this basic trait of physical reality remained.

Line and Contour

Line presents itself in three basically different ways: as *object line, hatch line,* and *contour line.* In the painting by Klee (Figure 151) the lines are perceived as one-dimensional *objects,* as though they were wrought in iron or made of some other solid material. If they cross one another, they either remain independent objects like sticks piled up for a wood fire or fuse into more complex objects, whose branchings resemble the limbs of animals or trees.

The visual combination of lines is controlled by the law of simplicity. When the combination produces a simpler figure than the mere sum of sep-

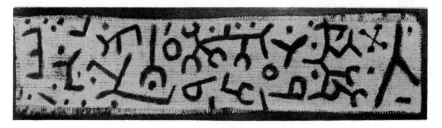

Figure 151
Paul Klee. *The Script,* 1940. Courtesy Curt Valentin.

arate lines would, it is seen as one integrated whole. One extreme case of such simplicity is obtained by what is called shading: a group of closely packed parallel lines create so simple an overall pattern that they combine to form a coherent surface. The lines cease to be individual objects and act as *hatch lines*. This way of creating surfaces in a linear medium is used in drawing, engraving, and woodcuts. The detail of the Dürer woodcut in Figure 118 shows how the curvature of parallel hatch lines is used to represent the bending of a surface in depth. Several families of parallels can be made to cross one another in order to show bending in more than one direction, e.g., in a saddle shape.

Hatch lines can also be used in sculpture. Naum Gabo and Antoine Pevsner have created transparent shells from surfaces composed of parallel strings, and Picasso and Henry Moore have occasionally done the same. In the eighteenth century, William Hogarth, in his *Analysis of Beauty*, recommended the interpretation of volumes through systems of lines: "Hollow forms, composed of such lines, are extremely beautiful and pleasing to the eye; in many cases more so than those of solid bodies." Moholy-Nagy has pointed in this connection to the skeletons of certain technological constructions, for example, zeppelins and radio towers. The natural grain of wood helps the eye interpret sculptural shapes. In the physical environment, alleys of trees or telegraph poles, fences, venetian blinds and their shadows, as well as various architectural grids, combine linear units in similar patterns.

Now to the third kind of line—the *contour line*. If we draw a closed loop, e.g. a circle, the result will be variously perceived, but especially in one of the following two ways. The shape may look like a piece of wire, lying on a ground; i.e., we see it as an object line. As our Klee example shows, such empty loops will be perceived fairly readily when they are seen in company with other object lines. Even under such favorable conditions, however, this view tends to be uncomfortable and hard to hold. This is so because the empty loop requires us to see the surface of the paper as a continuous background, or, to put it differently, to see the spaces on both sides of the line as related to it symmetrically. This works well as long as we are dealing with a straight line, but the symmetry is not supported by the shape of the loop, which creates a distinct difference between the small, closed, surrounded space inside (Figure 152*a*), and the unbounded, large, surrounding space outside. The total visual experience gains in simplicity when this difference in shape is logically supported by a difference in spatial quality. This is accomplished when the surrounded shape is perceived as a substantial object and its surroundings as empty ground. In the process, the line changes function: from an independent

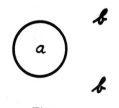

Figure 152

one-dimensional object it is transformed into the *contour* of a two-dimensional object. It becomes a part of a whole.

The area surrounded by the loop line gives the impression of greater density than the area outside it, it is more solid-looking; whereas the ground is looser, less limited to a given stable plane. This impression may seem to be nothing but a carry-over from our experience with physical objects, which are seen against the empty space of their surroundings. Experiments suggest, however, that it probably derives from physiological factors underlying the perceptual process itself, quite independently of previous experience. Some of these studies have shown that in comparison to the outer ground, the area within the contour offers greater resistance to the appearance of a visual object projected upon it with gradually increasing strength—that is, it takes stronger light to make the object barely visible inside the contour. Other experiments have proved that visual objects shrink in size when their image falls on an area of the retina upon which an outline figure had been projected earlier. Thus the perceived density or cohesiveness of the surrounded area does not seem to be due to mere assumptions based on past experience.

When the loop line functions as a contour, it is seen as the boundary of a circular or spherical object. If we wish to relate drawings to situations in the physical world we can say that contour lines (to use a formulation of John M. Kennedy) stand for spatial discontinuities, either of depth or direction of slant, or of texture, brightness, or color. Even taken simply by itself, the outline drawing produces, as we just noted, such discontinuities—a spatial leap from foreground to background, a difference in the density of the surfaces— to which a painter can add differences of color, brightness, or texture and thereby strengthen the action of the line.

A line embracing an area creates a visual object; e.g., a circular line creates a flat disk. We tend to take this perceptual phenomenon for granted until we ask ourselves why the contour induces a flat surface (see the section in Figure 153*a*) instead of any of the myriad other surfaces of which the draw-

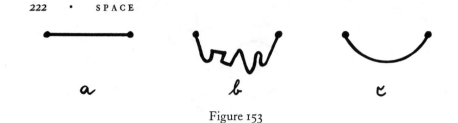

Figure 153

ing could serve as a projection, such as *b* or *c*. The straightness of a drumhead is only one of the innumerable shapes we could obtain if, instead of the taut skin, we draped a tablecloth over the drum. Here again the law of simplicity is at work. Since the surface comes about by indirection only, perceptual organization takes advantage of the freedom from stimulation and produces the simplest available surface. The straight plane is the simplest surface by which the circle can be filled. With any change of the contour the inner surface changes accordingly, always assuming the simplest available shape. We are reminded of experiments in physics designed to solve Plateau's problem: how to find the surface of smallest area bounded by a given closed contour in space. If we dip wire contours into a soap solution, the resulting soap film will show the smallest possible surface—which, however, is by no means always the perceptually simplest.

The influence of the contour on the induced inner surface varies with the distance. The larger the enclosed area, the weaker the influence of the boundary line, and the effect decreases toward the center with increasing distance from the outline. Also relevant is the size of the area in comparison to other nearby shapes. If one looks at the line drawings of Rembrandt alongside those by Matisse or Picasso, one will notice that the older master obtains solidity by keeping the outlined units relatively small. Rembrandt further reinforces the enclosed surfaces by inner design, such as folds of clothing. In the modern drawings, by contrast, the units are often so large that the contour all but loses its capacity to modulate space. The borderline character of the Matisse contours is weak; they have much of the quality of self-contained object lines. The bodies look loose, and tend to reveal that they are nothing but pieces of empty paper surface. The drawing lies like a transparent web of lines on the ground. The three-dimensional effect is reduced to a minimum. Of course, this is done deliberately. Whereas the older artists wished to stress solid volume and clearly discernible depth, the moderns wanted to dematerialize objects and minimize space. The modern drawings are meant as light-weight products, obvious creations of man, figments of the imagination, rather than illusions of physical reality. They are meant to stress the surface from which they spring.

To some extent this is true not only for outline drawings but also for painted surfaces. They, too, are determined largely by the shape of their boundaries. A large, unmodulated stretch of color tends to look loose and empty. In the older paintings this effect is reserved for the representation of empty space, as in the gold ground of Byzantine mosaics or the blue ground of Holbein's portraits or the skies of landscapes; in modern paintings it is often applied to solid objects also.

Contour Rivalry

One structural problem created by the one-sidedness of contours has not yet been discussed. If the contour is monopolized by one of the surfaces bordering on it, in our example the circular disk, what happens to the other? The surrounding ground is left in a predicament; it reaches the border, which prevents it from expanding farther, but it has no demarcation since the border belongs to the internal shape. The situation is visually paradoxical. A way out is suggested by what we observe even for the single object line: the ground is not seen as divided by the line but continues uninterrupted underneath it. This is indicated in Figure 154a, where the dot represents a section of the line. Similarly the ground continues also beneath the outlined surface (Figure 154b). In this way the structural problem obtains a stable solution.

A further question arises. What happens when two similarly qualified competing surfaces both claim the contour? In Figure 155 we observe what is known as contour rivalry. Perceived as a whole, the figure looks stable enough, but when we concentrate on the common central vertical we notice a tug-of-war. The sharing of borders is uncomfortable, and the two hexagons exhibit an urge to pull apart, since each figure has a simple, independent shape of its own.

Under special conditions the separation can actually be seen to happen.

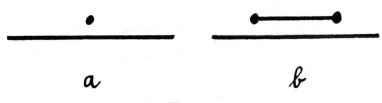

a   *b*

Figure 154

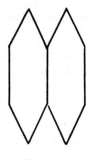

Figure 155

When the control of the stimulus over the organizing forces in the brain is weakened—for example, by the exposure of dim figures for a split second—it is sometimes found that a pattern like Figure 156a is rendered by the observer as one like *b*, showing a tendency to give each unit its own contour. When young children were asked by Piaget to copy geometric designs in which circles or triangles touched each other, they often eliminated the contact in their reproductions. In an ability test developed by Rupp, people were asked to draw a honeycomb pattern (Figure 157a). They often made the hexagons independent of one another by leaving space between them (*b*), and even emphasized the interstices by shading the figures (*d*); or they introduced overlapping, which interfered with the shape of one figure in order to free its neighbor (*c*).

The ambiguity of the common contour is aggravated by the fact that, although physically unchangeable, its shape often looks different, depending on which of the two adjoining surfaces it is seen as belonging to. This has been shown strikingly by Edgar Rubin, the author of the first and fundamental book on the phenomenon of figure and ground. He gives examples in which the figure-ground situation is ambiguous and therefore reversible. Everyone

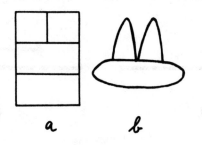

a   b

Figure 156

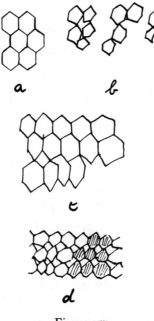

Figure 157

is familiar with the goblet whose outlines can be seen alternatively as two profile faces confronting each other. When one sees the goblet, the outlines look so completely different from those of the faces that the identity can only be understood intellectually, not acknowledged visually. Nor can the two versions be seen at the same time.

The shared contour is perceptually ambiguous because the dynamics, which determines the visual identity of shapes, is reversed. Recognition is always based on dynamics, not on the dead shapes as such, which are perceptually nonexistent. For example, the circular line in Figure 152 is convex in relation to the inner surface, concave with regard to the outer. Convexity and concavity are not only mutually exclusive, they are also opposites dynamically, the one actively expanding, the other passively withdrawing. Consider Figure 158a. Characterized by several protrusions, it is vaguely reminiscent perhaps of the prehistoric "Venus" figures. In Figure 158b, which is adapted from a detail of Picasso's painting *La Vie*, the same pattern—now a part of a larger whole—has lost most of its identity. The unity of the outline has been torn asunder, its left side now belonging to the woman, its right side to the man. What is more, the left side has become an overlap; it no longer confines

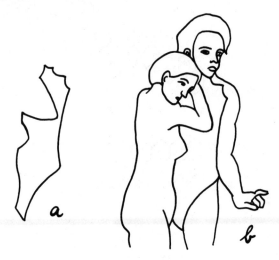

Figure 158

the surface, which continues underneath instead. Most decisively, however, the dynamics of the shapes has been reversed. For example, the concave interval between the two most active protrusions in *a* becomes the actively protrusive elbow of the woman in *b*.

Perhaps the example of Figure 159, derived from a painting by Braque,

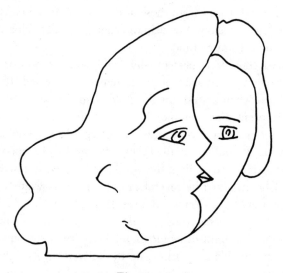

Figure 159

is even more instructive. The shape of the profile line changes entirely, depending on which face it is seen to belong to. What was empty becomes full; what was active, passive. Some surrealist artists, such as Dali, Tchelitcheff, and particularly Maurice Escher, have used the phenomenon to play hide-and-seek with the beholder, producing ambiguous pictures, susceptible to different, mutually exclusive views. This technique, which originated historically with some painters of the Mannerist school, is designed to shock the observer out of his complacent trust of reality. Painted in the *trompe l'oeil* manner, the objects create the illusion of being materially present, only to change without notice into something completely different but equally convincing.

Aubrey Beardsley's drawing *Madame Réjane* (Figure 160) may be used as an exercise in the study of figure-ground factors. Beardsley manipulates them in a way that tends to make the spatial relations ambiguous almost everywhere in the picture.

Figure and Ground

As I said earlier, there is no such thing as a truly flat two-dimensional picture. There are many examples, however, in which two-dimensionality prevails in the sense that the image consists of two or more planes or shallow

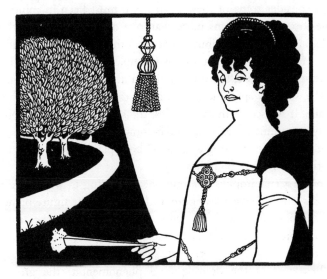

Figure 160

spaces extending parallel to the frontal plane and appearing at different distances from the observer.

Two-dimensionality as a system of frontal planes is represented in its most elementary form by the figure-ground relation. No more than two planes are considered. One of them has to occupy more space than the other and in fact has to be boundless; the directly visible part of the other has to be smaller and confined by a rim. One of them lies in front of the other. One is the figure, the other the ground.

The numerous investigations of the figure-ground phenomenon have mostly been designed to explore the conditions determining which of the two shapes lies in front. The situation is more often ambiguous than one might suspect. In the old cosmologies the stars were sometimes seen as pinholes in the curtain of the night sky, through which glimpses of a brighter, heavenly world are received; thus, according to Kant, the French scientist Maupertuis interpreted the nebulae as openings in the firmament, through which the empyrean is seen. I have already referred to the goblet that can be perceived as empty space between two profiles—a trick that recently found a new application when someone discovered that the red maple leaf of the new Canadian flag could be seen as the empty ground between two white angry profiles, Liberal and Conservative, yakking at each other. Such ambiguous patterns approach a state of "multistability," as Fred Attneave has called it, in which various figure-ground factors balance one another in opposite directions.

As we consider some of these factors, we must keep in mind that even the simplest example contains more than one of them, and that the percept derives from the pooled contributions of all of them. Edgar Rubin identified a number of such factors. He found, for example, that the surrounded surface tends to be seen as figure, the surrounding, unbounded one as ground. If we perceive the stars as sparkling in front of the dark sky, they conform to Rubin's rule. If we see them as pinholes, the sky becomes the figure and the bright heavens assumed to exist beyond become the ground. We note that when the surrounded shapes are seen as ground, both planes involved in the figure-ground situation become boundless.

Rubin's first rule implies a second one, according to which the relatively smaller areas tend to be seen as figure. In Figure 161 the figure plane is represented by the narrower bands or sectors. This presupposes the "rule of similarity of location" (page 80), which holds that the more closely located lines are grouped together. Note here that, strictly speaking, these examples fall beyond the range of the figure-ground phenomenon: the ground is not boundless but outlined like the figure, and it lies on a third plane, the surface of the book page.

If we try to reverse the spatial situation in Figure 161 by making the larger bands or sectors come forward, we experience a strong resistance and succeed only for brief moments. The two patterns remind us that in a figure-ground situation, all shapes belonging to the ground plane tend to be seen as parts of a continuous backdrop. In the present examples, this backdrop takes the shape of a large rectangle or disk lying in front of the ground plane. In Figure 162 the situation is reversed. The larger units lie in front because the small squares and sectors are perceived as the visible portions of a strongly coherent horizontal bar or small disk.

It will be remembered that even in a simple line drawing, the surrounded figure possesses greater density than the looser ground. We may say that the two areas have different textures. Following this lead, we find that when the density of texture is increased by graphic means, the figure-ground situation created by the contour can be either strengthened (Figure 163a) or reversed (b). Texture makes for figure. In the Matisse woodcut (Figure 164) the factors of enclosed shape and texture are pitted against each other. The relatively empty body of the woman looks almost like a hole torn in the tissue of the environment. The artist deliberately dematerializes the body—a specifically modern effect, to which I referred earlier.

In his chapter on "Rules for the probability that a surface will be perceived as figure," Rubin reports that if the field consists of two horizontally divided areas (see, e.g., Figure 165) the lower one tends to be seen as figure. He relates this to the typical situation in the physical world, where "trees, tower, persons, vases, lamps are often perceived under circumstances in which the ground, e.g., the sky or the wall, occupies more or less the upper part of the

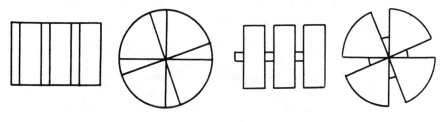

Figure 161   Figure 162

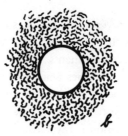

Figure 163

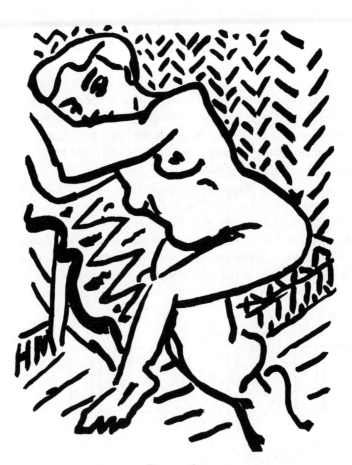

Figure 164
Henri Matisse. *Reclining Nude*. Woodcut, 1906.

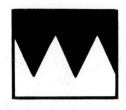

Figure 165

field." This goes with our earlier observation that the lower part of the picture carries more weight.

Note also that Rubin's rule holds for Figure 165 even when it is turned upside-down and the black part appears at the bottom. This is the case even though in general, brighter areas seemingly tend to be figure when other factors are kept equal. As far as colors are concerned we are not surprised to find that a saturated red makes for figure more strongly than a saturated blue; this corresponds to the general tendency of red to advance and of blue to recede.

Simplicity of shape, especially symmetry, predisposes an area to function as figure. The simpler figure will prevail. In the magic banisters of Figure 166, the contradiction between the right and left sides of each of the drawings makes it impossible to obtain a stable image. But in this fluctuation we rather vividly experience the effect of the various perceptual factors. In *a*, both versions yield symmetrical patterns. For most people the convex columns are more often seen as figure, because, as one of Rubin's rules maintains, convexity tends to win out over concavity. But in *b*, the concave units clearly prevail, because they give the picture more symmetry.

Simplicity affects not only the shape of a pattern, but also its spatial orientation. The two Maltese crosses in Figure 167 are identical except for their

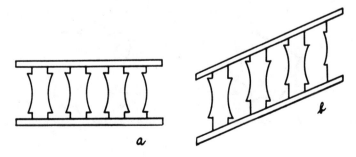

Figure 166

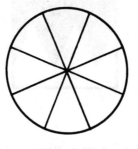

Figure 167

orientation to the framework of the visual field. Under these conditions the cross whose main axes coincide with the vertical and horizontal coordinates of the visual field tends to become the figure, whereas the other more often vanishes into the ground.

Of particular interest for the artist is the fact that convexity makes for figure, concavity for ground. Figure 168a tends to look like a hole in the plane, although both a and b are enclosed areas and are thus more likely to be seen as figure. The phenomenon varies somewhat, depending on which part of the pattern holds the observer's attention. If he looks at the bulges, a will be more clearly a hole, and b a solid patch on top of the ground. The opposite effect is usual when he fixates the pointed angles between the bulges because their narrowness makes for figure character. The examples of Figure 168 also show strikingly that figure-ground is not just a matter of static spatial location but involves a difference of dynamics. Bulges and pointed angles are like wedges pushing forward. Thus the "figure" has the character of active advance. In a, the surrounding figure closes in actively on the central hole from all sides; in b the central rosette expands vigorously across the ground. Since the ground has no shape, it lacks a dynamics of its own.

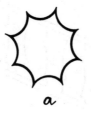

a

b

Figure 168

Finally, relative movement can strongly enhance the figure-ground effect. In accord with what I said earlier about motion as a factor of grouping (p. 80), a barely noticeable figure may become conspicuous when it moves across the ground. What is more, James J. Gibson has pointed out that relative motion also helps to clarify which area is figure and which ground. As motion occurs in the field, the figure maintains its integrity whereas the ground undergoes deletion on the one side, accretion on the other, thereby revealing itself as the area that is submitting to interference. Stereoscopy also will make a figure-ground effect visible even when it is not seen in the two images singly and when, as Bela Julesz has shown, no contour but merely a slight displacement of texture distinguishes the two areas.

Depth Levels

The terms "figure" and "ground" are suitable only as long as we are dealing with an enclosed, homogeneous pattern in an equally homogeneous, endless environment. But conditions are rarely so simple. Even in most of our elementary examples, more than two levels were involved. For example, in Figure 167 the cross appears on a ground that is not endless but circular, and in turn lies like a disk on top of the surrounding empty plane. The disk is ground for the cross but figure for the surrounding surface. This is awkward terminology. Also, some of the more interesting organizational factors do not come into play as long as we are dealing with only two planes, one of which must be boundless and therefore shapeless. It seems more adequate to speak of patterns distributed over a number of depth levels, the basic figure-ground pattern being a special case, namely an organization of only two levels.

If we consult the principles so far described, Figure 169 should be seen as a disk on top of a square base, which in turn rests on the ground. Instead the figure is perceived more stably, as a square with a circular opening in it. This is seemingly due to a tendency to simplification by economy, which means that the number of depth levels in a given pattern is as small as conditions

Figure 169

permit. If the circle produces a disk that lies on top of the square, the result is a three-level distribution, whereas the perforated square makes for a total of only two levels. This leaves us with a smaller number of planes—that is, with a spatially simpler pattern. We conclude that when the perforation (interruption) of the square is weighed against the three-level arrangement, the former represents the simpler solution. The physiological reasons for this preference are not known.

A somewhat more complex example may further illustrate the point. Figure 170 is a woodcut by Hans Arp. The artist has balanced the perceptual factors against one another in such a way that several spatial conceptions are equally possible. We may see a four-plane arrangement (Figure 171a): a pyramid, consisting of a small black patch on top, a larger white one underneath, this resting in turn on a black patch, and the whole lying on an endless white ground. Figure 171 b illustrates a three-plane solution, in which a white ring lies on a black patch. Two two-plane solutions are given in c and d: a large black ring with a black patch in the center lies on a white ground; or everything white lies in front, and a black background is seen through the cutouts. The principle of economy would of course favor a one-plane solution as the simplest (e); but this would involve a series of interruptions, which is avoided by a three-dimensional conception. The only solution that has the advantage of avoiding all interruptions is the pyramid (a), which is also favored by the rule of enclosedness. The pyramid, however, requires the largest number of planes. If brightness makes for figure character, d will be favored; this version is also enhanced by the two narrow bridges in the white ring. Finally, similarity of brightness tends to group all whites as against all blacks in two separate planes (c and d).

Application to Painting

There are, then, definite rules according to which perceptual factors determine the depth location of frontally oriented planes in pictorial space. Artists apply these rules intuitively or consciously to make depth relations visible. In looking at photographs or representational paintings, the viewer is helped somewhat by what he knows about physical space from his own experience. He knows that a large human figure is meant to be closer by than a small house. The artist, however, cannot rely much on mere knowledge. If he wants a figure to stand out against the background, he must use the direct visual effect of perceptual factors such as the ones we have just discussed. He may also choose to reverse the way these same factors are usually employed to obtain a paradoxical effect, as exemplified in the works of Matisse and

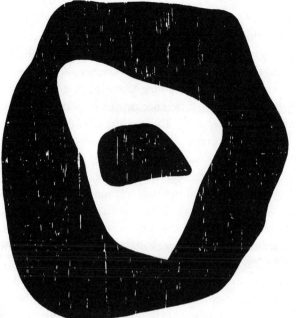

Figure 170
Jean Arp. From *Eleven Configurations*. Woodcut. Courtesy of the artist.

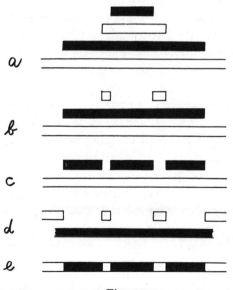

Figure 171

Lipchitz reproduced here (Figures 164 and 172). Lipchitz's drawing contains white areas bounded mostly by concavities. The contradiction between the solidity of the organic bodies suggested by the subject matter and the perceptual emptiness of the white spaces due to the cavities and the absence of texture intensifies the conflict that the drawing is meant to express.

Actually there is a basic difference in this respect between the vision of the artist and everyday behavior. In practical orientation we concentrate on identifying objects. How prone we are to overlook the background is known to every amateur photographer who, to his chagrin, discovers in looking at his prints that some unnoticed branches or street signs distract attention from the figure of the lady portrayed in the foreground. A. R. Luria showed by an experiment in which children aged three to five had to discriminate between differently colored patterns that the children reacted to the colors of the foreground figures, but ignored changes of color in the back. Similarly, when adults were asked to copy the pattern of Figure 173 as accurately as possible, many of them reproduced the shape and size of the crosses and squares quite well, but entirely neglected the fact that the inner edges of the squares lie on the same lines as the outer edges of the crosses. This relationship was not seen as part of the pattern. Even in the Rorschach ink blots, in which figure-ground reversal is facilitated by structural ambiguity, positive use of the interstices is said to suggest a diagnosis of negativism, stubbornness, doubt, suspiciousness, or even incipient paranoia. Such a clinical criterion, however, is hardly applicable to artists, who are trained to perform perceptual reversals routinely.

A painter cannot treat the interstices between figures as nondescript because the relations between the figures can be understood only if the spaces separating them are as carefully defined as the figures themselves. If, for example, the distance between the two women on the Attic red-figured cup by Douris (Figure 174) were not precisely controlled, the subtle relations between the richly modulated figures would lose the quality of a musical chord. This means that the negative spaces, as many painters call them, must be given sufficient figure quality to be perceivable in their own right. If ambiguity is to be avoided they remain subdominant; but the narrow, enclosed, and partially convex black spaces on the Greek cup are strong enough to fit into a continuous surface of playfully alternating red and black shapes, which constantly define each other. A similar effect is obtained in Jacques Lipchitz's drawing (Figure 172). Here the areas of the bodies of man and vulture are held back by strong concavities in the contours, which make the dark background intrude actively into the figures.

Pictorial space, therefore, is best described as a continuous relief in which

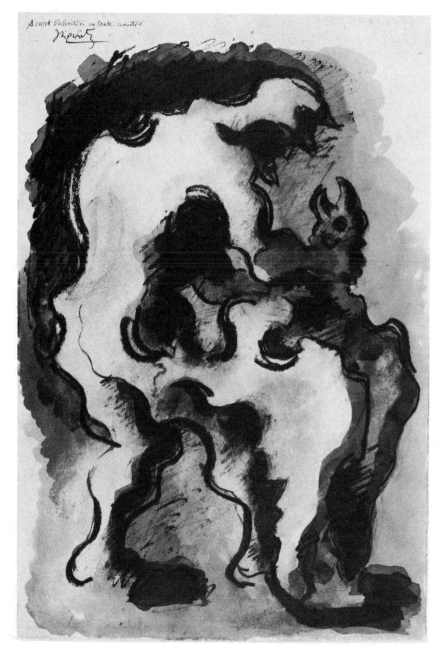

Figure 172
Jacques Lipchitz. *Prometheus Strangling the Vulture*, 1936. Courtesy Curt Valentin.

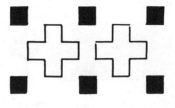

Figure 173

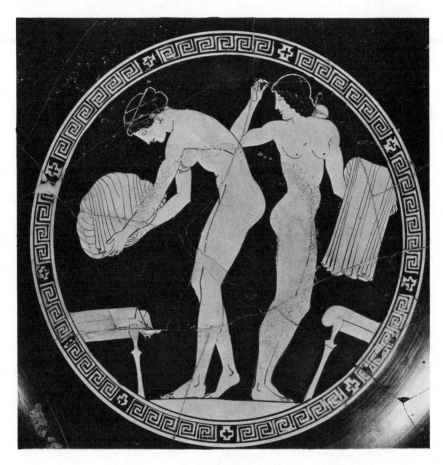

Figure 174
Douris. Red-figured cup, c. 470 B.C. Metropolitan Museum of Art, New York.

areas at different distances border upon one another. In a relatively simple case, such as that of the Greek decoration, the content of the picture is accommodated essentially in two frontal planes. In more differentiated works the pictorial relief may give little emphasis to frontality. It may be shaped like a concave funnel, with the objects in the center lying at the greatest distance; or, on the contrary, a convex protrusion may come forward in the center. The relief may be deep or shallow, it may work with very few distance values or with many, with steep intervals, e.g., between foreground and background, or with "chromatic" scales of very small steps. Such an analysis of depth relief could be applied to sculpture and architecture as well, and could serve as a means of describing differences between styles.

Concerning the more specific problem of the negative spaces, it may be added that the delicate task of determining the proper distances between pictorial objects probably requires a sensitive attention to physiologically determined attractions and repulsions in the visual field. The biologist Paul Weiss has pointed to a similarly subtle balancing of objects and interstices under physical or physiological field conditions, e.g., in the branching networks of electrostatic discharges, the blood capillaries in organic tissue, and the venation of leaves. The interaction between the separate elements creates a systemic order that keeps the distances between the branches all nearly constant, even though the individual details of ramification are totally unpredictable.

Frames and Windows

The function of picture frames is also related to the psychology of figure and ground. The frame as we know it today developed during the Renaissance from the façade-like construction of lintels and pilasters that surrounded the altarpieces. As pictorial space emancipated itself from the wall and created deep vistas, a clear visual distinction became necessary between the physical space of the room and the world of the picture. This world came to be conceived as boundless—not only in depth, but also laterally—so that the edges of the picture designated the end of the composition, but not the end of represented space. The frame was thought of as a window, through which the observer peeped into an outer world, confined by the opening of the peephole but unbounded in itself. In our present discussion this means that the frame was used as figure, with the picture space supplying an underlying borderless ground. This trend was brought to a climax in the nineteenth century, when (for example, in the work of Degas) the frame was made to cut across human bodies and objects much more ostentatiously than ever before. This emphasized the accidental character of the boundary and therefore the figure character of the frame.

At the same time, however, painters began to reduce the depth of pictorial space and to stress flatness. Instead of representing a pictorial world, quite detached from the physical space of canvas and beholder, they began to think of the picture as an elaboration of the surface of the canvas. Pictorial space was no longer boundless but tended to end at the edges of the composition. This meant that the boundary line between frame and canvas was no longer the inner contour of the frame, but the outer contour of the picture. The picture was no longer ground behind the frame, but figure. Under these conditions the figure character of the traditional heavy frame and the spatial interval between the window in front and the pictorial world in back became unsuitable. The frame adapted itself to its new function by either narrowing to a thin strip, a mere contour, or even slanting backward ("reverse section") and thus establishing the picture as a bounded surface—a "figure," lying well in front of the wall.

A somewhat similar problem exists in architecture in the perceptual appearance of windows. Originally the window is a hole in the wall—a relatively small area of simple outline within the large surface of the wall. This involves a peculiar visual paradox, in that a small enclosed area on a ground plane is destined to be "figure." At the same time it is physically a hole in the wall and is meant to look like one.

Perhaps this is why there is something perceptually disturbing about modern windows that are mere cutouts. The naked edges of the wall around the window look unconvincing. This is not surprising if we remember that because perceptually the contour belongs to the figure, the ground is borderless and tends to continue beneath the figure without interruption. This solution is not feasible, however, when the figure is a deep hole, which bars the continuation of the ground. Thus the wall must stop but has no boundary. There are various means of dealing with this dilemma. One is the traditional cornice. The cornice is not just decoration; it is a way of framing the window. It confirms the figure character of the opening and provides a protrusion beneath which the ground surface of the wall can end. Another solution consists in enlarging the area of the windows so that the wall is reduced to narrow ribbons or strips, both vertical and horizontal. In Gothic architecture, where the remnants of the wall are often further disguised by relief work, the typical effect is an alternation of open and solid units, neither of which is clearly figure or ground. An even more radical transformation is found in modern architecture, where by an actual reversal of the perceptual situation, the walls become grids of horizontal and vertical bars through which the inside of the building can be seen as an empty cube. The network of crossing bars, a visible counterpart of steel construction, has become the dominant figure, in possession of the contours, whereas the windows are parts of the underlying continuous and empty ground, Figure 175 schematically illustrates the three principles.

Concavity in Sculpture

The rules governing the relation of figure and ground can be applied to three-dimensional volume, notably to sculpture. This will be attempted here only for convexity and concavity.

Even in painting and drawing, convexity and concavity are found not only in the linear contours of surfaces, but also in the surface boundaries of volumes. The human body is represented mainly through shapes that bulge forward, whereas a cave is rendered, appropriately, as concave. What I called the depth relief of a picture may be concave, as in the hollow box space of a Dutch interior, or convex, as in some cubist pictures that build up from the sides toward a protrusion in the center.

Obviously, figure-ground relations between volumes can be perceived visually only when the outer volume is transparent or empty. We cannot see

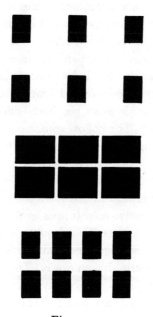

Figure 175

the hollow of the cavity that harbors the eyeball in a human head, although as mentioned earlier blind sculptors, not bound to the surface perception of vision, have been known to model the ocular cavity first and then insert a ball of clay to represent the eye. Visually, a statue and the surrounding space can be considered as two adjoining volumes—if indeed we are willing to think of the environment as a volume rather than mere vacancy, since the statue seems to monopolize all the figure qualities. The statue is the enclosed, smaller volume, and it has texture, density, solidity. To these perceptual qualities practically all sculpture throughout the history of art has added convexity. The statue is conceived as an agglomeration of spherical or cylindrical shapes that bulge outward. Intrusions into the block, and even perforations, are treated as interstices, that is, as empty space between solids that monopolize the outer surface. It is true that like the painter, the sculptor has kept an eye on these negative spaces, but traditionally they play a lesser role in sculpture than they do in painting, where even the ground is part of a substantial and bounded surface.

Concavities occur now and then, particularly in Hellenistic, medieval, baroque, and African sculpture. In Bernini's horseback-riding Louis XIV, the sweeping locks and folds collect air in hollow pockets. In these examples, however, the concavities are so thoroughly subordinated to the convexity of larger units that at most they contribute a minor enrichment. It was only after 1910 that sculptors like Archipenko and Lipchitz, and later particularly Henry Moore, introduced concave boundaries and volumes to rival the traditional convexities. The effect can be predicted from what is found in patterns like Figure 168a. The cavities and holes assume the character of positive— though empty—bulges, cylinders, cones. In fact it seems not even correct to call them empty. Their inside looks peculiarly substantial, as though space had acquired quasi-solidity. The hollow containers seem filled with air puddles, an observation that agrees with the rule that figure character makes for increased density.

As a result the sculpture reaches beyond the limits of its material body. The surrounding space, instead of passively consenting to being displaced by the statue, assumes an active role. It invades the body and seizes the contour surfaces of the concave units. This description indicates that, just as we observed in two-dimensional figure-ground relations, space and sculpture interact here in an eminently dynamic way. The aggressiveness of convex shape and the passive compression in concavity are symbolized by arrows in Figure 176. What could be the section of a piece of modern sculpture is repre-

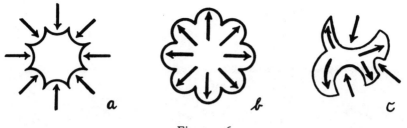

Figure 176

sented schematically in *c*, showing how the protruding bulges push outward whereas the surrounding space invades the concavities.

It is tempting to speculate that this daring extension of the sculptural universe may have been made possible by the advent of the passenger plane. We live at a time when vivid kinesthetic experience has taught us that air is a material substance like earth or wood or stone, a medium that not only carries heavy bodies but pushes them hard and can be bumped into like a rock.

Traditionally, the statue was the image of a self-contained entity, isolated in a nonexistent environment and in sole possession of all activity. A comparison of Maillol's and Moore's treatment of a similar subject (Figure 177) shows that the convexity of all form in the Maillol preserves an active element in spite of the essentially passive subject matter. The figure seems to expand and to rise. In Moore's work a passive and receptive quality is obtained not only through the attitude of the woman, but even more compellingly through the hollowness of shape. In this way the figure comes to embody the effect of an outer force, which intrudes and compresses material substance. A feminine element has been added to the traditional masculinity of the sculptural form— a particular aspect of the more universal theme of activity and passivity.

It was noted that convexity renders a statue essentially self-contained and independent. This creates a problem for any combination of a piece of sculpture with others of its kind or with architecture. Sculptural groups of human figures, except for those fused in one block, have never gone much beyond rows of isolated units or the kind of loose grouping achieved by dancers or actors. Similarly, in order to fit sculpture to buildings at all intimately, the buildings had to provide the concavity of niches.

The use of concavity in modern sculpture seems to permit a more complete fitting of one unit to another. A family group by Henry Moore shows a man and a woman sitting beside each other, holding an infant. Hollow ab-

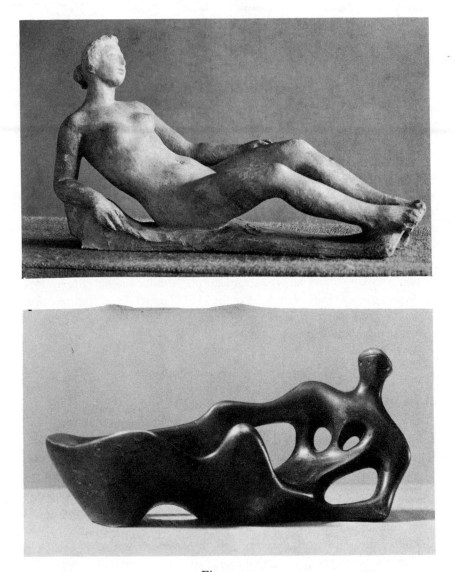

Figure 177
Aristide Maillol. *Resting Nude*, 1912. Henry Moore. *Reclining Figure*. 1945. Courtesy Curt Valentin.

domens make the two seated figures into one large lap or pocket. In this shadowed cavity space seems tangible, stagnant, warmed by body heat. In its center the suspended infant rests safely, as though contained in a softly padded womb. The convexity of the child's body dovetails with the concavity of the container.

The empty volume as a legitimate element of sculpture has led to works in which the material block is reduced to a shell surrounding a central body of air. Moore's *Helmet*, an empty head, would offer a mouse-sized visitor the experience of being inside a work of sculpture. More recently, sculptors have experimented with providing such experiences for the full-grown viewer. Architecture, of course, has always been concerned with hollow interiors. The concavity of vaults and arches makes the internal space assume positive figure function as though it were a powerful extension of the human visitor, who then feels able to fill the room with a rising and expanding presence. The portals of medieval churches seem to draw in the parishioners by their con-verging shape. Figure 178 shows how the baroque architect Borromini used the counterpoint of convexity and concavity to animate architectural form. Above the hollow round of the courtyard wall rises the cupola, whose pro-truding bulges are in turn compensated on a smaller scale by the receding niches in the lantern. Outer space seems to react to the vigorous expansion of the building by nipping playfully into the compact solid here and there.

Why Do We See Depth?

As we proceed from the limited figure-ground relation between two planes to the stacking of frontal visual objects more generally, we realize that we are dealing with a special case of subdivision. In the organization of plane figures, it was found that subdivision occurs when a combination of self-contained parts yields a structurally simpler pattern than the undivided whole. This rule holds true not only for the second dimension but also for the third. Areas physically located in the same picture plane split apart in depth and assume a figure-ground configuration because simplicity increases when the one-sidedness of the contour is uncontested and when the ground can be seen as continuing beneath the figure without interruption.

In Figure 179, *a* looks like a circle fitted into a square although the pattern could be the projection of two figures, one located at some distance from the other. The pattern clings to the second dimension because it is strongly unified: the centers of circle and square coincide, and the diameter of the circle is equal to the side of the square. The situation is quite different in *b* and *d*, where the

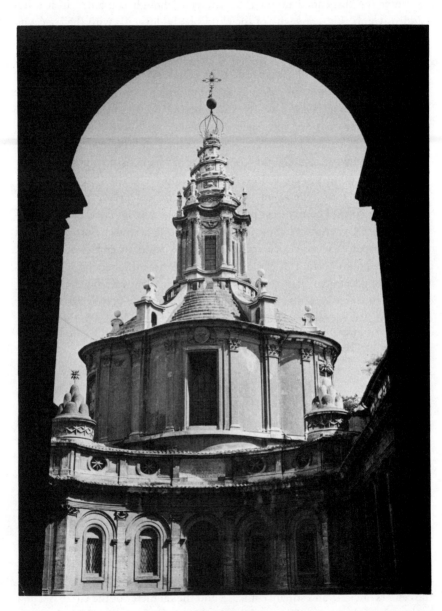

Figure 178
Francesco Borromini. St. Ivo's Chapel, Rome, c. 1650. Photo Ernest Nash.

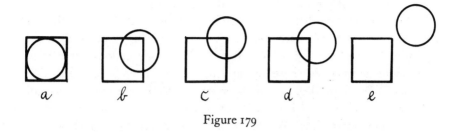

Figure 179

two components are much more independent of each other. In fact, they tend
to detach themselves from each other in depth because this divorce frees them
from the stressful combination that exists in the flat projection. The tendency
is weaker in *c*, where the projective structure has some simplicity: the center
of the circle lies on one of the corners of the square and thereby produces symmetry around a diagonal of the square. In *e* the divorce has become complete:
both shapes display their simplicity without interference from the other. With
the diminution of tension, the urge to separate in depth is no longer observable.
If anything, the relative location in depth of square and circle is now undefined.

As long as the eye looks at these figures, their location within the frontal
plane is unchangeable; it is controlled by the stimulus pattern on the retina.
This pattern does not, however, prescribe location in the depth dimension. As
a projection it may represent figures or parts of figures at any apparent distance
from the eye. The third dimension is therefore an "avenue of freedom," which
allows for changes in the interest of simplification of structure. If detachment
increases simplicity, the segregation in depth can be accomplished without any
modification of the projective pattern.

We are now ready for an answer to the question *Why do we see depth?*
The answer may seem strange. As long as we look at the physical world, the
three-dimensionality of vision seems to offer no problem—until we recall that
the optical input for all our visual experience consists in the two-dimensional
projection on the retina. This does not mean that visual experience is primarily two-dimensional. It is not, but why it is not requires explanation.

The usefulness of three-dimensional perception is obvious for humans
and animals that need to find their way around in the physical world. However, the final cause is one thing, the efficient cause another. Our question is:
How does depth perception come about? The answer is particularly relevant
for the artist who is concerned with visual representation on a flat plane; because in his case all physically derived cues, of whose efficiency we shall have

occasion to speak, proclaim that the eyes are faced with a surface. Therefore, the experience of depth must be provided by the picture itself.

The artist realizes that he cannot simply rely on what the viewer knows about the physical world. Such knowledge must always be restated with visual means in order to be artistically effective, and it is easily undercut by perceptual counterevidence. When we look at a map of the United States we see that a corner of Wyoming lies on top of a corner of Utah, and that a corner of Colorado lies on top of Nebraska. No knowledge that this is not so prevents us from seeing what we see. Which are the visual factors that promote depth?

The basic principle of depth perception derives from the law of simplicity and indicates that *a pattern will appear three-dimensional when it can be seen as the projection of a three-dimensional situation that is structurally simpler than the two-dimensional one.* In Figure 179 we watched this principle in action.

Depth by Overlapping

As long as the contours touch or cross but do not interrupt one another the spatial effect is absent or weak. However, when one of the components actually cuts off a part of the other, as in Figure 180a, the perceptual urge to see a superposition becomes compelling because it serves to complete the incomplete shape.

This statement implies an important assumption. It presupposes that in Figure 180a the upper shape is seen as an incomplete rectangle. But why should this be so? By itself, it would be seen as an L-shape; and a could be the projection of a physical situation in which an L-shape lies next to a rectangle or in front or in back of one. Instead, we have trouble seeing anything but an interrupted rectangle. In order to explain this we must understand under what conditions a shape looks incomplete.

If one of two contiguous visual objects is as simply shaped as is possible under the given circumstances while the other can be made simpler by completion, the first will annex the boundary line between them. In Figure 180a, the rectangle cannot become simpler, but the L-shape can. When the rectangle annexes the boundary, the other shape is left borderless. It is forced to continue beneath its neighbor. Therefore it is seen as partially occluded, i.e., as incomplete. The occlusion provides the incomplete figure with a range of freedom: a cover behind which it can complete itself.

It is tempting to seek the criterion for superposition in the local conditions under which the visual objects meet. The two contours of Figure 180a meet at two points, at which one line continues while the other stops. Is this differ-

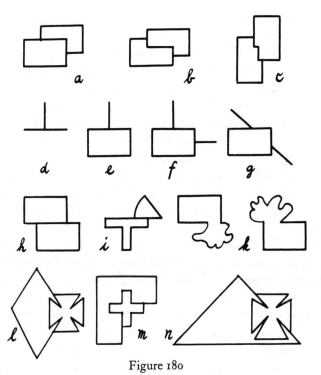

Figure 180

ence alone not sufficient grounds for designating the latter as occluded, the former as superposed? Helmholtz thought so. In 1866 he wrote: "The mere fact that the contour line of the covering object does not change its direction where it joins the contour of the one behind it, will generally enable us to decide which is which." More recently Philburn Ratoosh formulated this condition in mathematical terms, asserting that it is decisive in all cases. "Interposition can provide a cue only at the points where the outlines of two objects meet." The object with the continuous contour will be seen as lying in front. Ratoosh also said, "What happens at one point of intersection is independent of what happens at the other."

We are dealing here with what is in fact an influential structural feature. The rule predicts correctly that the unit whose contour is interrupted will take the back position in Figure 180*a*, whereas in *b* conflicting conditions will produce a correspondingly ambiguous situation, each unit overlapping the other at one place and being overlapped by it at the other. An instructive example (*c*) has been contributed by James J. Gibson. Here both spatial versions could produce a complete rectangle in the back and a broken one in front; yet the unit whose contours continue uninterrupted at the point of intersection is seen in front.

It is quite true that the factor of "consistent shape" is the decisive one in most cases, but it seems unlikely that what happens at two independent points should alone determine the spatial situation of the whole pattern. In the somewhat related Figures 180d-g we notice that what happens at the points of intersection depends on the context. In d and e the interrupted line shows no spontaneous desire to continue underneath the obstacle. In f there is a weak tendency to three-dimensionality, directly related to the fact that the two interrupted lines are not independent of each other but can be seen as parts of an angular whole. In g, where the rule of consistent shape strengthens the connection between the two lines, they clearly fuse into one line that continues beneath the rectangle.

Of course Figures 180d-g do not meet Ratoosh's condition, but h and i do. According to the rule, the contradictory situation at the points of intersection should create spatial ambiguity, as in b. Instead there is no trace of three-dimensionality. If someone asserted that these examples have no bearing on the problem at hand because they show no superposition, he would be begging the question because the problem consists precisely in defining the conditions under which superposition is perceived to occur. Figure 180h could very well be brought about by two interlocking cutouts of the shape k.

Figures l, m, and n show that it is possible to construct patterns in which the unit whose contours are interrupted tends to lie on top. Significantly, the effect is least convincing when one concentrates on the common contour and strongest when one looks at the pattern as a whole, thereby giving the total structure a chance to exert its influence. The Helmholtz-Ratoosh effect is strongly counteracted by the complete, simple shape of the unit theoretically destined for occlusion by the interruption of its contours. The point of this demonstration is that the structure of the whole may reverse the effect of a local configuration.

In general, however, the rule of intersecting contours is quite useful in predicting the perceptual effect, especially if, as in the tracing after Paul Klee's *The Vigilant Angel* (Figure 181), it is strengthened by other figure-ground factors acting in the same direction. We notice, however, that the convexity of a opposes occlusion by d. Other ambiguities can be studied in b and c.

Overlapping is particularly useful in creating a sequence of visual objects in the depth dimension when the spatial construction of the picture does not rely on other means of perspective. This was observed even in antiquity. The Greek sophist Philostratus notes in the description of a painting: "The clever artifice

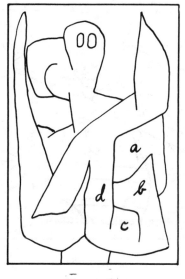

Figure 181

of the painter is delightful. Encompassing the walls with armed men, he depicts them so that some are seen in full figure, others with the legs hidden, others from the waist up, then only the busts of some, heads only, helmets only, and finally just spear-points. This, my boy, can be accomplished by *analogy*, since the problem is to deceive the eyes as they travel back along with the proper receding planes of the picture." (By *analogy* the author apparently means the art of completing the hidden parts of an object through their similarity to what is visible.) The guidance of the eyes on their path from the front to the back is evident in Figure 182, where judicious overlaps assign each object its place in the scale of spatial locations, from the man and his arm with the oar to the child, the mother, the stern of the boat, the water, and the coastline. The space-building role of superposition in Chinese landscape painting is well known. The relative location of mountain peaks or clouds is established visually by overlaps, and the volume of a mountain is often conceived as a skeleton of echelons or slices in staggered formation. The complex curvature of the solid is thus obtained through a kind of "integral" based on the summation of frontal planes.

The perceptual effect of overlapping is strong enough to overrule actual physical differences in distance. Hertha Kopfermann drew the components of a pattern on different glass plates and arranged them in front of each other

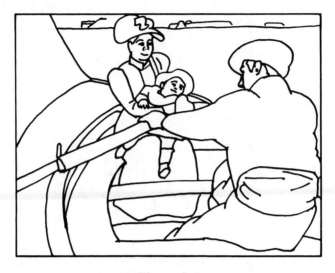

Figure 182

so that observers saw the total pattern through a peephole. If plate *a* (Figure 183), about 5 inches high, is viewed from a distance of about 80 inches and *b* lies one inch in front of *a*, the combination one sees does not correspond to the physical facts; instead, the larger triangle is seen as overlapping the smaller (*c*). This happens even though the observer readily perceives the correct physical situation when the two items are shown separately on the two plates.

Finally, it should be mentioned that occlusion always creates visual tension. We sense the occluded figure's striving to free itself from the interference with its integrity. It is one of the devices used by the artist to give his work the intended dynamics. When tension is undesirable, occlusions are avoided; and since every superposition produces structural complication, in early levels of visual conception objects typically are lined up in the plane without mutual interference. Similarly, when in experiments observers are asked to copy from

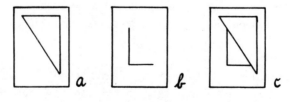

Figure 183

memory a picture they have been shown, they tend to eliminate the overlaps and thereby to simplify the pattern.

Transparency

A special case of superposition is transparency. Here the occlusion is only partial in that visual objects are seen as overlapping each other, yet the occluded object remains visible behind the occluding one. It is necessary, first of all, to distinguish between physical and perceptual transparency. Physically, transparency is obtained when a covering surface lets sufficient light pass through to keep the pattern underneath visible. Veils, filters, vapors, are physically transparent. However, physical transparency is by no means a guarantee of perceptual transparency. If we put on tinted eyeglasses, which cover the entire visual field, we do not see a transparent surface in front of a normally colored world, but a pink or green world. Nor do we see a transparent layer covering a painting when a coat of varnish has been evenly applied. In women's wear, transparent nylon hose is not seen as such, but its color and texture merge with those of the leg.

We conclude that if the shape of a physically transparent surface coincides with the shape of the ground, no transparency is seen. Nor is transparency visible when a piece of transparent material is laid on a homogeneous ground. It takes three planes to create transparency. On the other hand, perceptual transparency effects such as those in Figure 184 can be obtained without any physically transparent materials. Art students learn to obtain compelling transparency by means of opaque colored papers or opaque paint. Josef Albers in his *Interaction of Color* offers striking examples. Our question is therefore: under what conditions does perceptual transparency come about?

By means of three colored papers—red, blue, and purple—we construct the patterns of Figure 185 on a piece of white paper. We observe strong transparency in c, none in a, and perhaps some in b. It will be evident that the formal conditions are the same as those controlling superposition: c produces a strong separation of the two objects in depth, a produces none, b perhaps some. Therefore, superposition of shapes is a prerequisite of transparency—a necessary, though not a sufficient, perceptual condition.

In Figure 185c, the rule of simplicity predicts that we shall see two rectangles crossing each other instead of two quite irregular hexagons bordering on an equally irregular quadrilateral. Subdivision will here produce two, not three, components because the rectangles are the simplest, most regular figures available. So far we are on home territory. However, the presence of three different colors opposes this solution and will in fact prevent it, unless the

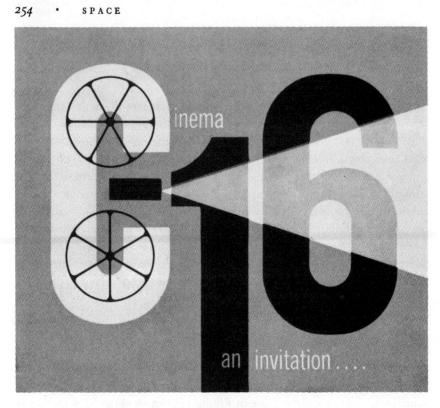

Figure 184

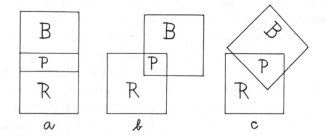

Figure 185

relationship between colors satisfies another condition. The color of the overlap must be seen as a combination of the other two, or at least as a fairly close approximation of such a combination. In fact, purple is a combination of red and blue. If this condition is met, the area of the overlap will split into the two components corresponding to the two other colors, thereby making possible a subdivision according to simplest shape.

When we look at the area of the overlap through a peephole that excludes the rest of the pattern, we see no transparency. Thus transparency is entirely induced by the context; it is the device by which color meets the exigencies created by a conflict of shapes. The structural mechanism at work here may become more evident if we cite a similar application in music. All the sounds reaching the ear at a given moment are processed by the eardrum into one complex vibration, which must be teased apart by the analyzing mechanism in the inner ear when this is necessary. In polyphonic music, such as the example from Adrian Willaert (Figure 186), the parts must be heard as separate melodic lines; therefore at every moment the unitary sound input is

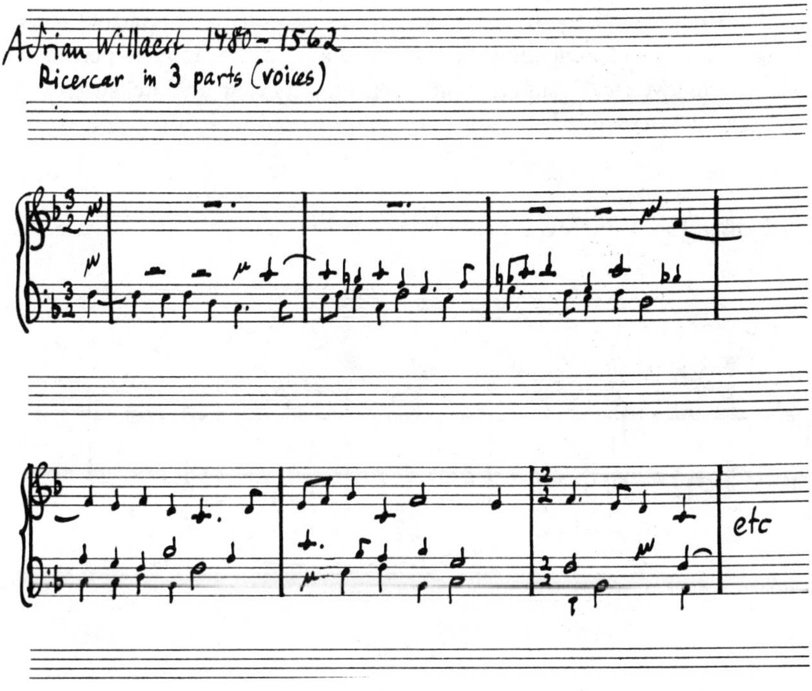

Figure 186

split into its components in order to satisfy the structural demands imposed by the horizontal context. In harmonic music, by contrast, e.g. the passage from Wagner (Figure 187), similar clusters of sounds are heard as a sequence of complex chords because no splitting up into single tones is required by the context. Thus, in music the structure of shape in the time dimension will determine whether sound emitted at a given point will be subdivided into its elements or not. The spatial context will do the same in the visual realm.

We noted that the color of the overlap must approximate a visual combination of the other two. However, there is some leeway to this rule. Modern artists have experimented with pitting shape against color to see how much deviation from the optimal color condition can be overcome by the shape demand for subdivision, and vice versa. This holds true not only for hue but also, notably, for brightness. Depending on the brightness of the transparency area, we obtain the effect of either an additive or a subtractive light mixture (cf. p. 341). If the area is rather bright we see something similar to two colored patches of light projected upon a screen and partially overlapping each other: the area of the overlap reflects roughly as much light as the other two added together. On the other hand, in the situation depicted by the designer in Figure 184, the black numerals subtract more whiteness from the projector beam than does the gray background.

The brightness of the transparency area is also one of the factors determining which of the competing shapes is seen as lying in front. Experiments by Oyama and Morinaga suggest that when subjects view a white bar crossed by a black one, the white bar tends to be seen in front when the transparency

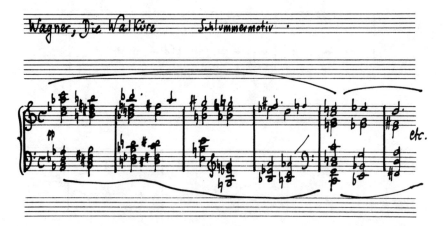

Figure 187

area is light gray, whereas the black bar appears in front when the central area is dark gray. This means that the smaller brightness step promotes an unbroken, frontal shape. It may be mentioned here that transparency is not necessarily limited to two shapes. In Figure 184, the transparency relation between black letters and white light beam creates, by induction, an additional transparency of the beam in relation to the gray ground.

Finally, a weak transparency effect can be obtained without any help from color or brightness by the sheer strength of the shapes. In the line drawing of a "wire cube" (Figure 188), for example, we perceive a distinct double representation of surfaces, a glassy front face lying in each case transparently in front of a back face. This can be studied in some of the outline drawings of Josef Albers.

Transparency based purely on shape relations is perceived also in painting and sculpture when the volumes of the human body are "seen through" the folds of a covering garment. Two systems of shapes, the relief of the limbs and the relief of the folds cross each other, and this interference pattern produces a subdivision of the unitary relief actually offered by the painter or sculptor. The two systems are sufficiently organized within themselves and sufficiently discordant with each other to bring about the split in depth as a resolution of the conflict of shapes. When one looks at the marble relief of some of the classical Greek sculpture, one can hardly believe that one sees one surface only, not a body covered by a pliable fabric of stone.

To avoid confusion, the term "transparency" should be applied only when the effect of "showing through" is intended by the artist. The notion of two things appearing in the same place is sophisticated and found only at refined stages of art, e.g. in the Renaissance. Modern artists, including the cubists and especially Lyonel Feininger and Paul Klee, have used the device to dematerialize physical substance and break up the continuity of space. Such a mentality is worlds away from that of paleolithic cave dwellers or Australian aborigines,

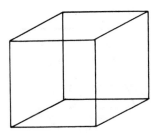

Figure 188

whose paintings have been compared with those of modern artists by Siegfried Giedion. He misinterpreted two features, the superposition of bodies or lines and the simultaneous portrayal of inside and outside—neither of which has anything to do with transparency.

Deformations Create Space

So far, the third dimension of space has been discussed essentially as a variable of distance for the location of visual objects. The objects lay behind or in front of one another, but by themselves they did not truly participate in the third dimension. Although some of them were reliefs rather than flat surfaces, they conformed to frontally oriented planes, perpendicular to the observer's line of sight.

Objects can partake of the third dimension in two ways: by tilting away from the frontal plane and by acquiring volume or roundness. This further differentiation of spatial conception can be observed in all the visual arts, in sculpture, in architecture, and in stage design and choreography, but it represents a particularly decisive step in the pictorial medium. In the flat plane, three-dimensionality can be represented only indirectly, and all indirection weakens the immediacy of the visual statement. When we compared two ways of representing persons sitting around a table (Figures 86 and 87), we noted that one of these procedures translated physical space into a two-dimensional array. Although this method means forgoing the third dimension entirely, it achieves great directness and immediacy. The other procedure must distort sizes, shapes, and spatial distances and angles in order to convey depth, thus doing considerable violence not only to the character of the two-dimensional medium but also to the objects in the picture. We understand why the film critic André Bazin has called perspective "the original sin of Western painting." In manipulating objects to foster the illusion of depth, picture-making relinquishes its innocence.

Figure 189 tends to lean backward, away from the observer. This inclina-

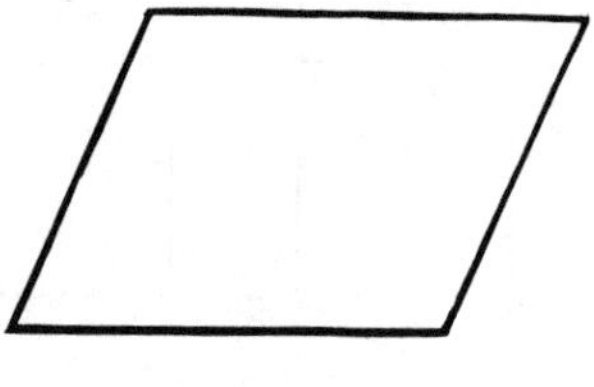

Figure 189

tion is weak in a drawing on paper, stronger when the outline figure is replaced with a colored surface; it is also stronger when a figure is projected on a screen, or when a luminous shape is viewed in a dark room. Freed from the texture of the paper surface, the figure may tilt forward as well as backward.

What makes the pattern deviate from the plane in which it is located physically? With some effort we can indeed force it into the frontal plane. When we do so we observe that the parallelogram is not perceived as a figure in its own right, but as a deviation from another, simpler, more regular figure: it is seen as a leaning rectangle or square. Instead of a parallelogram we see a deformed rectangular figure.

Deformation is the key factor in depth perception because it decreases simplicity and increases tension in the visual field and thereby creates an urge toward simplification and relaxation. This urge can be satisfied under certain conditions by transferring shapes into the third dimension.

But what exactly is deformation? Not just any alteration of shape. If I clip a corner from a square and add it at some other place in the outline, there results a change of shape but no deformation. If I enlarge the entire square, I get no deformation. But if I look at the square or at my own body in a curved mirror, deformation occurs. A deformation always conveys the impression that some mechanical push or pull has been applied to the object, as though it had been stretched or compressed, twisted or bent. In other words, the shape of the object (or of part of the object) as a whole has undergone a change in its spatial framework.

Deformation always involves a comparison of what *is* with what *ought* to be. The deformed object is seen as a digression from something else. How is this "something else" conveyed? At times only by previously acquired knowledge. Alice's long neck is perceived as a deformation, whereas the stem of a flower is not. When the peasant on his first visit to the zoo said of the giraffe, "There is no such animal!" he was comparing it to some vague norm of animal shape.

Alberto Giacometti relates that after he had spent a good deal of time with a Japanese friend, whom he also used as a model, he was appalled to find one day that his Caucasoid friends looked unhealthily pink and puffy. Here the deformation was not inherent in the given shape, but arose from the interaction between what was seen at a given moment and the norm image stored in the artist's memory. Such deformations are used, for example, in caricature. On the other hand, the effect of Figure 189 does not depend on past knowledge. For anybody used to seeing depth in a pictorial surface, the rectangle or square is directly visible as a projection of the leaning parallelogram, and under the pressure of the tendency toward simplest structure, the opportunity is spontaneously seized.

Not all deformations of simpler shape serve our purpose. Many of the so-called anamorphic images do not. The best-known example is the death's-head in Holbein's *Ambassadors*. It looks as though it had been painted on a rubber sheet and then stretched beyond recognition. To see this long streak of paint as a projection of a normal death's-head is beyond the power of human perception; furthermore, its spatial environment in the painting supports no such view. John Locke has said of such pictures that they are "not discernible in that state to belong more to the name man, or Caesar, than to the name baboon, or Pompey." A rectangle can be described technically as a distorted square, but it is not seen as such because it is a stable, symmetrical figure in its own right.

As long as the leaning parallelogram is recorded on the retinas of the eyes, it cannot be straightened out into a rectangle or square in the frontal plane. But, as I observed earlier, the depth dimension is an avenue of freedom since the same projection holds for the whole range of distances. We can think of the processing center in the brain as a kind of three-dimensional abacus (Figure 190), in which the various components of the stimulus can move freely back and forth like beads but are held to their rods by the configuration of the retinal projection. Thus the leaning parallelogram can be changed into a rectangular figure by being seen as tilted backward. It therefore obeys our principle that "a pattern will appear three-dimensional when it can be seen as the projection of a three-dimensional situation that is structurally simpler than the two-dimensional one" (p. 248).

Remember that any visual pattern can be the projection of an infinity of shapes. This is indicated by the abacus model. While our parallelogram is a projection of a tilted rectangle, a rectangle or square is, by the same token, a projection of an infinity of tilted parallelograms. (I am leaving aside for the

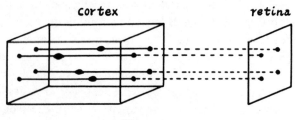

Figure 190

moment the additional modification due to the dependence of size on distance.) However, no one sees a frontal square as a tilted parallelogram or a frontal circle as a tilted ellipse. The frontal figure is seen as a projection only when the resulting three-dimensional shape is structurally simpler.

Note furthermore that by seeing a parallelogram as a tilted square or rectangle, we not only gain simplicity, we also lose some. For although the square is surely the simpler shape, frontality is a structurally simpler spatial orientation than an oblique tilt toward the back, which enlists the third dimension. What occurs here is actually a trade-off between the simplicity factors of the two versions. *When we call the three-dimensional version the simpler one, we mean that it wins the trade-off.* This is true for all applications of the simplicity principle. Much experimentation is still needed before we can establish the comparative weight of the various simplicity factors, and not without much greater knowledge of the physiology of vision shall we be able to understand why their powers compare in just this way. For the time being we must be content to state that when visual perception has the choice between simpler shape and simpler spatial orientation, it chooses the former.

Boxes in Three Dimensions

What has been said about tilted plane figures can be applied to geometric solids. Figure 191*a*, which we see as a cube, is a combination of three oblique parallelograms, each of which tends to straighten out into a rectangular figure receding in depth. The resulting solid is seen either as a cube or, if the three central edges withdraw into depth, as an open interior, composed of ceiling, back wall, and side face. The cube version, which lets the object rest on the ground, is the stabler one.

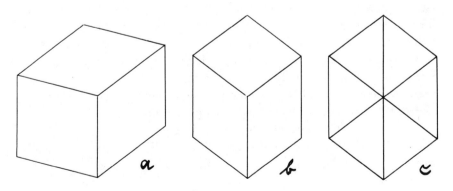

Figure 191

However, we cannot treat these more complex figures simply as a three-fold application of what we have learned from Figure 189. In Figure 191*b*, the depth effect is much reduced because the three planes combine to form a symmetrical figure, which enjoys considerable stability in the frontal orientation. Even so, it is difficult to see *b* as a flat hexagon, whereas *c* can hardly be seen as anything but a hexagon even though this figure is a more complete projection of a cube than the others. In *c*, all edges are present, but the symmetry of the figure not only serves to make its simplicity irresistibly stable, it also destroys the relations between elements necessary to a cube: the central corners of the square faces are dissolved into crossings, front edges and back edges fuse into continuous lines, etc. Here again three-dimensionality comes about only when the frontal figure is seen as the projection of a simpler shape in the third dimension.

It is rather remarkable that Figures 189 and 191 look reasonably convincing. If we take photographs of a rectangular board or a wooden cube tilted in space, no two edges will look strictly parallel. All surfaces will be trapezoids converging toward depth. The same is true for the projections received by the retina. Therefore our line drawings should look quite unnatural. To some extent they do. In Figure 191*a*, the back edges of the cube look somewhat longer than the front edges, so that the top and side faces seem to diverge toward distance. The effect is strong enough to have created the belief that in Japanese and Chinese paintings parallel edges diverge, although measurements show no such principle to be operative.

We can interpret this phenomenon to mean that our eyes expect parallelism to be represented by converging lines. However, it took the introduction of central perspective to supply such convergence in pictures, whereas the representation of parallels by parallels remains the more common and the more natural procedure. It is used spontaneously at early stages of art, wherever the representation of space goes beyond the flatness of the "Egyptian" procedure—in children's drawings, in the work of Sunday painters and other "primitives"—but it is also common in the highly refined art of the Far East. Furthermore, it is universally preferred by mathematicians, architects, engineers—wherever unambiguous representations of geometrical solids are required. What are the virtues of this "unnatural" procedure?

It is true that the converging lines in a photograph or in a drawing done in central perspective yield a more compelling depth effect. But it is equally true that the cube done with parallel lines looks more cube-like. This is so because parallelism preserves an essential objective property of the cube. The advantage is even more striking in technological applications. If a carpenter or builder were asked to construct an exact replica of the objects in Figure 192, he would be at a loss to know whether the irregular angles and oblique shapes were intended as properties of the objects themselves or only as perspective convergences. Both factors in any ratio could contribute to the effect.

The method of spatial representation we are considering now is known by several names; I prefer to call it *isometric perspective*. In order to evaluate it properly we need to keep in mind that pictorial form does not develop from the faithful imitation of nature. The objects of the physical world are not squashed in the picture like a honey bee on the windshield. Pictorial form derives instead from the conditions of the two-dimensional medium. The rule that controls the rendering of depth in the plane prescribes that *no aspect of visual structure will be deformed unless space perception requires it*—regardless of what a mechanically correct projection would call for.

A brief look at developmental stages will clarify matters. At an early level, a child represents a cubic object, e.g., the body of a house, as a simple square or rectangle (Figure 193*a*). This is not a front face but the two-dimensional "unmarked" equivalent of the cube as a whole. The next step toward differentiation derives from the need to subdivide the cube into several faces. The original square or rectangle now assumes the more particular function of the façade, to which side faces are added symmetrically, at first within the frontal plane (*b*). Next comes the need to differentiate between frontal dimension and depth dimension. This is achieved by the discovery that under certain conditions obliqueness is perceived as recession into depth—a most consequential invention.

Deformation, I said earlier, is the principal device by which depth is rep-

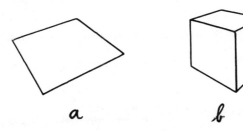

a   *b*

Figure 192

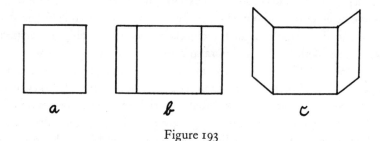

Figure 193

resented in the plane. Now obliqueness is the most elementary deformation of shape resulting in depth perception. To be sure, not all oblique shapes produce depth; only those do that can be read as deviations from the normal framework of the vertical and horizontal. When this condition is met, obliqueness vanishes in favor of a reversion to the simpler framework. This is what the child has discovered when he produces Figure 193c. In all applications of isometric perspective, obliqueness alone is deemed sufficient to represent depth.

If Figure 193c is not understood as a logical derivation from the conditions of the two-dimensional medium, it is easily misinterpreted as "inverted perspective." It then appears as the opposite of what the imitation of nature would suggest. Instead of converging toward distance, the shapes diverge. This sort of interpretation can only confound the issue. The divergent shapes do not come about as a deviation from an earlier adherence to convergent perspective, but are worked out as an elementary device of spatial representation, long before the sophisticated artifice of central perspective is conceived.

Figure 194 is an illustration to Vitruvius's treatise on architecture in the Cesariano edition, published at Como in 1521. To the modern eye, the woodcut may represent a prismatic building with side walls obliquely receding toward the back. But both the ground plan of the building and the text illustrated by the picture assure us that cubic shape was indeed intended. ("The Greeks lay out their forums in the form of a square surrounded by very spacious double colonnades . . ."). In fact, the illustration fulfills its purpose. The obliqueness of the side walls defines their spatial position sufficiently. These side walls would be invisible if the frontal view of the building were drawn in convergent perspective.

This makes us realize that divergent perspective is one of the devices employed by the draftsman to cope with a characteristic trait of the pictorial medium: Except for the special case of transparency, *no more than one thing at a time can ever be directly visible in any one spot of the surface.* Now, when

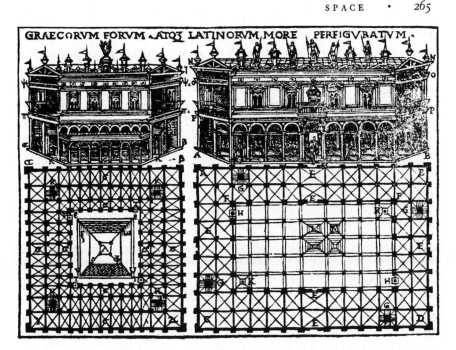

Figure 194
From Cesare Cesariano's edition of Vitruvius, *Ten Books of Architecture*, Como, 1521.

physical space is projected upon a surface, each location of the projective plane corresponds inevitably to more than one object or portion of an object. Foreground hides background; front side hides back side. Convergent perspective hides side faces; divergent perspective reveals them.

Consider Figure 195*a*, a detail from a Spanish altarpiece of the fourteenth century; *b* shows the same subject drawn in convergent perspective. We note that *a* clearly reveals the lateral wings of the cubic object and thereby gives it more volume. In addition, the obtuse angles of the front corners in *a* cause the top surface to broaden toward the back and embrace the Christ child with a

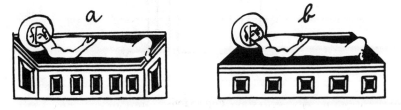

Figure 195

kind of semicircular enclosure, whereas the convergent base cuts into the child in *b*. The visual conveniences of the device are so obvious that not surprisingly it was used again by modern artists as soon as Western art had freed itself from the compulsion of "realistic" perspective. Examples can be found in the work of Picasso (Figure 196). In some architectural styles, a preference for hexagonal and semi-hexagonal shapes (of the bay window type) is also directly related to the fact that divergent side faces reveal the volume of the structure much more directly than those of rectangular cubes.

Since the pictorial representation of cubic solids derives from the primordial square (Figure 193*a*), there are good reasons for the universal use of shapes such as those in Figure 197. The original square is still visible, and in the course of differentiation it has now assumed the function of the front face. As such it need not be deformed because it represents no deviation from the frontal plane. Added to it are top face and side face, which express depth by obliqueness. All this is logical enough, and in fact most people will look at this sort of drawing for a lifetime without ever seeing it as anything but a correct and convincing picture of a cube. We have been accustomed from childhood to perceiving spatial representations in the terms of the two-dimensional medium. In the realm of that medium, the drawing is correct.

And yet it is violently wrong from the point of view of optical projection. When the front face of a cube is seen head-on, the side faces cannot possibly be seen at the same time. The drawing gives the projection of an asymmetrically bent hexahedron, which would contain oblique angles. Even so, the

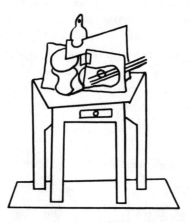

Figure 196

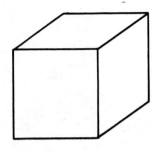

Figure 197

visual economy and logic of this combination of frontal view and isometric obliqueness makes us see a coherent, faithfully portrayed cube.

The undeformed frontal square has the advantage of offering the eye a stable base, a "tonic" in the musical sense of the term, from which everything else can be perceived as a clearly defined deviation. For this reason, the receding faces produce a more compelling depth effect than they would if they were not connected with a norm base from which to deviate. The frontal rightangular shape also helps attune the picture space to the framework of the observer by being oriented perpendicularly to his line of sight. And finally, if used as an architectual setting in a painting, the frontal façade provides a stabilizing backdrop for displays within the frontal plane, such as pageants or other figural scenes.

Figure 198 is a black-and-white reproduction of a painting by Horst Scheffler. It uses isometric perspective in combination with frontality to study the ambiguous interplay between flatness and depth. The short oblique edge in the center is seen as a part of the isometric tilt into depth when approached from the left, but as a leaning edge in the frontal plane when approached from below. The parallelism maintained in isometric perspective lends itself to being forced back into the frontal plane, at least for brief moments, and the instability of the balance between second and third dimensions produces a particularly modern, teasing dynamics.

At the same time, the anchoring to the frontal plane can be experienced as an obstacle to free movement in space. This is illustrated in Figure 199. Isometric perspective in two directions is used in *b*. Having abandoned every element of frontality, the pictorial object moves much more freely, and although it is anchored in the spatial framework of pictorial space, it seems to float in relation to the viewer, to whose orthogonal coordinates it is no longer

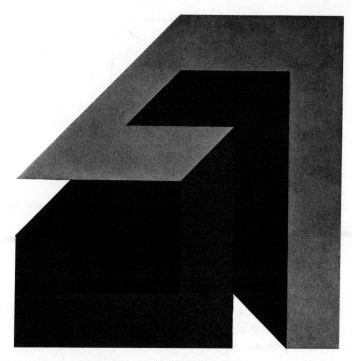

Figure 198
Horst Scheffler. *Gegenwinkel-Modulation*, 1971.

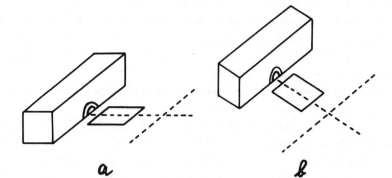

Figure 199

tied. This is the compositional pattern of traditional Japanese paintings, such as the ancient illustrations for the *Tale of Genji*, and also the Ukiyo-e wood-cuts of the eighteenth century. The observer, instead of being directly related to the pictorial world, peeps into it obliquely. He sees a world that would seem totally independent of him if the vertical dimension did not maintain its full frontality. This inconsistency comes out most clearly in the human figures, which are neither foreshortened nor seen from above as the spatial construction would require, but meet the observer's line of sight perpendicularly in their full extension.

Finally, I will mention a practice found in isometric drawings, e.g. by Theo van Doesburg. Since the angle between the two directions for represen-tations of the type of Figure 199*b* can be selected at will, it can be made ninety degrees. Such a right angle produces a new tie to the otherwise aban-doned frontal plane—a subtly paradoxical device, this being one of those hard-to-obtain instances in which the spatial setting asks us to read right angles as the projection of acute ones.

Help From Physical Space

It will have become clear that all depth effects in visual experience must be created by the nervous system and the mind. This is particularly evident when we are dealing with two-dimensional pictures, but it is equally true when we are looking at objects or images in physical space, e.g., works of archi-tecture or sculpture. To be sure, the depth effect produced by objects in physi-cal space or holograms is much more compelling than that created by pictures. This is so because the light input from these sources permits the use of addi-tional powerful criteria of depth and almost none that counteract depth.

These additional indicators are generally referred to as "physiological clues" in textbooks of psychology—an unfortunate term because it obscures the fact that all input of depth perception has a physiological basis. It also creates the misleading impression that these factors are somehow different in principle from those inherent in the shapes, brightnesses, and colors recorded on the retina. Actually, the indicators that may be called "depth-determined" are by no means purely physiological; they are based on visual perception just as much as the ones not so determined.

The most effective of these depth-determined indicators is binocular vi-sion, which produces stereoscopy. As Wittgenstein pointed out, it is by no means self-evident that the cooperation of the two eyes should lead to depth per-ception; it could also produce a blurred image. Figure 200 shows schematically that when the two eyes look at the same objects, e.g., two spots located at dif-

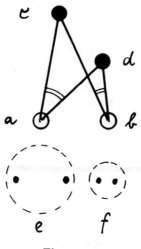

Figure 200

ferent distances, they will receive different images. In the present case the two spots will be farther apart for the left eye *a* than for the right eye *b*, the two images being indicated in *e* and *f*. Confronted by two different images, the sense of sight faces a dilemma. The stimulus pattern recorded by the retinas is invariable, but here again, just as in the case of figure and ground and superposition, the third dimension offers an avenue of freedom, which permits the fusion of the two flat images into one three-dimensional image. Thus once again, three-dimensionality is brought about by the tendency toward simplification and tension reduction.

In stereoscopy, the conflict between images derives from spatial parallax, i.e., from the difference between images due to the different locations of the two eyes. A similar mechanism is operative in time parallax, when different images result because the viewer changes location. When one moves one's head from side to side one receives different images, which again can be fused into a unitary three-dimensional image. Experiments, such as those by Eleanor J. Gibson on the "visual cliff," suggest that this depth indicator already functions in infants and young animals. In the arts it is employed when the eyes of the viewer or the motion picture camera move from one station point to another, thereby strongly increasing the depth effect of the solids perceived. A corresponding effect is brought about when a sculpture is made to rotate on a turntable.

Neither spatial nor temporal parallax can be employed to increase depth in flat pictures. On the contrary, it serves to reveal the flatness of the surface. The depth effect of a picture is increased when one eliminates parallax by looking with one eye from a strictly immobile position. In holography, however, parallax works exactly as it does in real space because this technique does not produce flat pictures; it reconstructs the light input of the original situation.

Finally, two depth indicators may be mentioned that derive information from kinesthetic perception. In order to record images of the same object, the two eyes must make the lines of sight converge. The angle formed by the eye axes is large when the object is close by and becomes smaller with increasing distance. The changing tension in the muscles that hold and move the eyeballs is correlated to distance by the nervous system. The convergence is activated, of course, by the tendency to make the two images coincide and thereby to simplify the perceptual situation.

Similarly, the kinesthetic sensations from the ciliary muscle that controls the curvature of the crystalline lens in the eye, are used by the nervous system as an indirect indicator of distance. This focusing device is steered by the gradient from blurred to sharp image in the visual field.

Simple Rather Than Truthful

When we abandon the parallelism of isometric perspective and add size variation as a further indicator of the third dimension, we obtain a correspondingly stronger depth effect (Figure 192). In this case the more distant edges of the figure are shorter than the closer ones. Even so, we may be able to perceive a more or less convincing rectangle or cube. This ability of the sense of sight to straighten out the deformed projection and to perceive it as an obliquely oriented, rightangular object is commonly ascribed to the "constancy of size and shape."

This term has some misleading connotations. It is often taken to mean that despite the projective deformations, visual objects are seen according to their objective physical shape. The objects are said to remain "constant." There is some truth to this observation, but it does not hold as universally as it pretends to, and it substitutes a secondary principle of explanation for the primary one. It is essential for the artist to realize that the constancy of size and shape depends on the tendency to simplest shape, which may or may not produce a "truthful" percept.

Suppose a luminous trapezoid is set up on the floor of a dark room at some distance from the observer in such a way that it produces a square-shaped projection in the observer's eyes (Figure 201). If the observer looks at the

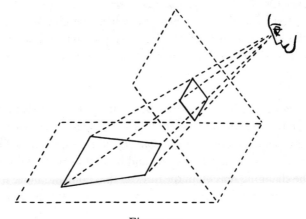

Figure 201

figure through a peephole (not indicated in the illustration) he will probably see a frontal square. This will happen not because the projection is square-shaped, but because the frontal square is the simplest percept the projection will yield. As far as the physical object on the floor is concerned, he sees the wrong thing, which means that in this case the constancy principle does not produce a truthful image. We conclude that *the percept will correspond to the shape of a foreshortened physical object when, and only when, this shape happens to be the simplest figure of which the projective pattern can be seen as a deformation.* Fortunately this occurs quite often. In the man-made world, parallels, rectangles, squares, cubes, and circles are frequent, and in nature also there is a tendency toward simple shape.

The kind of deception illustrated in Figure 202 is welcome in the world of visual illusion, e.g., on the stage and in certain styles of architecture. It is often desirable to create the impression of greater depth than is available physically. If a stage designer builds a regular room with level floor and right-angular walls (Figure 202a, ground plan), the spectator will receive the projective pattern *b* and consequently see the room approximately the way it is (*c*). If, however, the floor slants upward, the ceiling downward, and trapezoidal walls converge toward the back (*d*), the physical slant will combine with the perspective slant and projection *e* will result. Owing to the larger size difference between the frontal opening and the back wall, a much deeper cubic room will be seen (*f*).

This contradicts the principle of constancy, but corresponds exactly to what the principle of simplicity would lead us to expect. A striking example

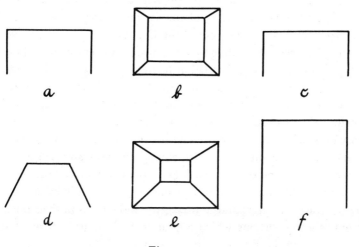

Figure 202

can be found in the Palazzo Spada in Rome. When Francesco Borromini rebuilt the Palazzo around 1635, it was his intention to have a deep architectural vista tapering off in a vaulted colonnade. As an observer stands in the courtyard and looks into the colonnade, he sees a long tunnel, flanked by columns and leading to an open space in which he notices the fairly large statue of a warrior. But as soon as he walks into the colonnade he experiences a strong sensation of seasickness, caused by a loss of spatial orientation. Borromini had only a limited site at his disposal, and the colonnade is actually short. It measures about twenty-eight feet from the frontmost arch to the back one. The front arch is almost nineteen feet high and ten feet wide. The back arch is reduced to a height of eight feet and a width of about three feet. The side walls converge, the floor rises, the ceiling slants downward, and the intervals between the columns diminish. As the observer reaches the statue of the warrior, he is surprised to find it quite small.

There are other examples. St. Mark's Square in Venice is ninety yards wide at the east end, but only sixty-one at the west. The lateral buildings, the Procuratie, diverge toward the church. Thus, standing in front of the church on the east side and looking at the 192-yard-long piazza, the observer finds the vista much deeper than from the west side. Medieval architects increased the depth effect in many churches by making the sides converge slightly toward the choir and gradually shortening the intervals between columns.

The opposite device maintains regular shape against the distorting influence of perspective and shortens apparent distance. This is true for the quadrangle formed by Bernini's colonnades on St. Peter's Square in Rome and Michelangelo's square in front of the Capitol. Both converge toward the approaching observer. According to Vitruvius, the Greeks increased the thickness of columns at the top in relation to that at the bottom in a ratio that increased with the height of the columns. "For the eye is always in search of beauty, and if we do not gratify its desire for pleasure by a proportionate enlargement in these measures and thus make compensation for ocular deception, a clumsy and awkward appearance will be presented to the beholder."

Plato mentions a similar practice among sculptors and painters. "For if artists were to give the true proportions of their fair works, the upper part, which is farther off, would appear to be out of proportion in comparison with the lower, which is nearer; and so they give up the truth in their images and make only the proportions which appear to be beautiful, disregarding the real ones." During the Renaissance, Vasari said: "When statues are to be in a high position, and there is not much space below to enable one to go far enough off to view them at a distance, but one is forced to stand almost under them, they must be made one head or two taller." If this is done, "that which is added in height comes to be consumed in the foreshortening, and they turn out when looked at to be really in proportion, correct and not dwarfed, nay rather full of grace."

Adalbert Ames has given striking examples of discrepancies between physical and psychological space. In the best known of these demonstrations (Figure 203), the observer looks through a peephole (o) into a room that seems to have normal rectangular shape (e-f-c-d). The actual plan of the room

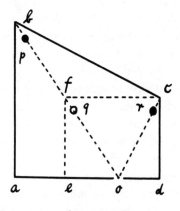

Figure 203

is *a-b-c-d*. The room is constructed in such a way that it gives the observer a retinal image identical to that of a regular cubic room. For this purpose walls, floor, and ceiling are appropriately slanted and deformed, and so is the furniture. Mysterious things happen in such a room. A person standing at *p* is perceived as being at *q*, and therefore looks like a midget in comparison to another person standing at *r*; a six-foot man at *p* looks smaller than his young son at *r*. There are two windows in the back wall. The face of a person looking through the window at the left appears much smaller than a face in the right window.

The phenomenon is puzzling only if we forget that, for an observer who looks with one eye through a peephole, vision depends mainly upon the projective pattern on his retina. Whether this pattern comes from a deformed or a rectangular room or from a photograph of either does not make any difference. If the deformed room is seen as rectangular, this needs no more and no less of an explanation than the fact that a physically rectangular room is seen as what it is; for the projection of such a room corresponds to an infinite number of more or less deformed cubic shapes, among which the simplest, most symmetrical and regular one is chosen. Ames himself used this demonstration to assert that we see what we expect to see: nobody expects to see a crooked room. This may be true, but who expects a father to be smaller than his child or a person to shrink to a fraction of his size as he walks from the right to the left? What the demonstration does show is that when vision has to choose between a deformed cubic room populated by normal-sized people and a regular rightangular room with people of weirdly unnatural size, it chooses the latter. "Past experience" would not seem to take kindly to either sight.

Gradients Create Depth

Obliqueness, we noted, creates depth when it is perceived as a deviation from the vertical-horizontal framework because tension can be reduced and simplicity increased when the frontal obliqueness straightens out in the third dimension. For our next step we must treat obliqueness as a special case of an even broader perceptual feature, by asserting that obliqueness creates depth because it is a gradient. When we relate an oblique visual object to the standard coordinates (Figure 204*a*) we observe that the distance from the vertical or horizontal increases or decreases gradually. If the principle of convergence is employed, e.g., in central perspective, an additional size gradient, a tapering from broader to narrower shape, obtains in the figure itself (Figure 204*b*).

A gradient is the gradual increase or decrease of some perceptual quality

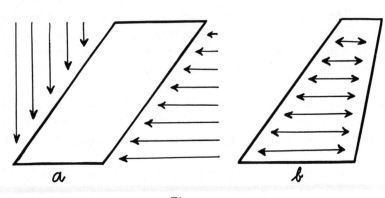

Figure 204

in space and time. James J. Gibson was the first to draw attention to the depth-creating power of gradients. He emphasized texture gradients, such as the gradually changing density of grain or shading, the coarser texture being correlated with nearness, the finer with distance. Although he realized that gradients create depth in line figures as well, he thought of these as "ghostly abstractions" of what is observed in daily experience. Since he assumed that gradients create depth in pictures because they do so in the perception of the physical world, he believed that the most realistic texture gradients, e.g., in the photograph of a pebbly beach, create depth most efficiently. Actually, the opposite is more nearly correct. Purely geometrical line drawings such as converging checkerboard floors or the highly abstract constructions of the painter Vasarely contain most powerful depth gradients. This is so because the effectiveness of a perceptual gradient depends on the visual articulation of the pattern. The more explicitly the gradient is presented in shape, color, or movement, the more compelling is the depth effect. Fidelity to the physical world is not a crucial variable.

When in an animated film a small disk expands, perception has to choose between keeping the distance constant and recording a change of size, or keeping the size constant and changing the distance. In weighing these simplicity factors against each other, perception opts for the latter alternative. It transforms the projective gradient of size into a gradient of distance. Any perceptual feature at all can serve to form gradients. Figure 205 schematically indicates a few of them: distance from the horizontal-vertical framework, size of objects, size of intervals. Since in this example they all act in the same direction, they reinforce one another. Such gradients are the principal cause of our seeing rows of telegraph poles, fences, trees, or columns recede into depth.

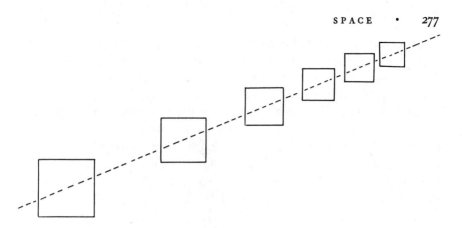

Figure 205

The more regular the gradient, the stronger its effect. A row of equal cardboard squares produces a convincing gradient, in the manner of Figure 205. If, however, the squares are made to vary in size irregularly, there will be confusion between size due to projection and size due to the physical measurements of the objects, and therefore the gradient will be impaired or even destroyed or reversed. (One can experiment with a row of squares whose physical size grows more quickly than their projective size diminishes.) A field strewn with rocks of varying size may produce this sort of partial gradient, whereas Van Gogh's two chairs in Figure 206 display a strong depth effect because they vary in nothing but size and location.

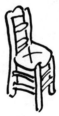

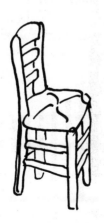

Figure 206

The size gradient is one of the early devices to represent depth in pictures. Children soon learn that when figures are made larger they look closer. This device, together with a height gradient that correlates depth with vertical distance from the base line of the picture, goes a long way toward satisfying spatial needs. Georges Seurat in his best-known painting, *An Afternoon on the Grande Jatte*, organizes the distance dimension by distributing figures of decreasing size over the entire field. These figures are not ordered in rows but spread irregularly across the surface. The various sizes are represented rather comprehensively, however, so that a continuous scale leads from the front to the back.

Gradients create depth because they give unequal things a chance to look equal. If the gradients in Figure 205 are completely successful, we see squares of equal size lined up at equal intervals. Furthermore, by creating depth the gradients transform the oblique slope of the row into a more stable arrangement on a horizontal plane. Thus there is a great gain in visual simplicity.

The steepness of the gradient determines the range of perceived depth: if we construct two equally long rows of squares, the one in which the size difference between the first and last squares is the greater will produce the deeper vista. As we shall see, steep gradients were preferred by Baroque artists such as Piranesi. Optically, they can be obtained in photography and film with the help of short-focus lenses.

Whenever size changes at a constant rate, the observer sees a correspondingly steady increase in depth. Thus, Figure 207a can be seen as a straight-line fence. However, when the rate of the gradient changes, the rate of increasing distance changes accordingly. In Figure 207b the gradient flattens out and results perceptually in a curved fence (even though in these figures the neglect of all other gradients, such as the thickness of the bars, the intervals between them, and the orientation in space, militates against the depth effect).

Similarly, as James J. Gibson has shown, a sudden change in rate will

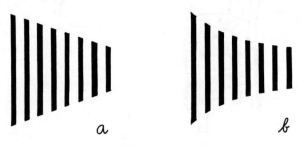

a

b

Figure 207

create an edge between two surfaces of different inclination, and a gap in the continuum of the gradient will create a hiatus or leap in the depth dimension. Some painters and photographers prefer a fairly dense continuum of space, leading without interruption from the front to the back. They thereby obtain a steady recession in an obliquely oriented composition. Others, with a greater stake in frontality, employ large leaps—for example, between foreground and background—thereby retaining the simple duality of figure and ground. In traditional portraits, such as Leonardo's *Mona Lisa*, the eye must jump from the frontal figure directly to the distant landscape.

We noted that gradients support constancy of size. If there are gaps in the gradient, constancy tends to break down since it does not come about by itself but must be created by visual factors. The figures in a distant landscape do not look the same size as the person portrayed in the foreground; and when we peer down from a tower or airplane things are by no means their natural size. "A little cloud out of the sea, like a man's hand," says the Bible.

What has been shown for size gradients holds true for other perceptual factors as well, e.g. for motion gradients. Just as the spatial intervals between the squares or telegraph poles diminish, so the speed of an object in an animated film must diminish if the object is to be seen as moving away at a constant speed. A motion gradient also adds to the depth effect in a landscape as we observe it from a car. Buildings and trees in the foreground race past us much faster than distant ones, and the difference in apparent speed correlates with our distance from what we see.

Aerial perspective relies on gradients of brightness, saturation, sharpness, texture, and to some extent of hue. In nature, the phenomenon is due to the increasing body of air through which objects are seen. However, aerial perspective is effective in painting not mainly because we know that it indicates distant expanses in nature. On the contrary, those vistas in nature are so deep because of the perceptual gradients they produce. Photographers know that the focus scale from blur to sharp image shapes the volume of an object convincingly even though the zoom lenses of our eyes have prepared us for no such experience. In portraits, for example, the relief of the head may be heightened when the eyes of the sitter are in focus but his ears and the tip of his nose are slightly blurred.

Not all gradients create depth. In the paintings of Rembrandt one can see that a scale of light, leading from the brightness near the source to complete darkness will not produce its usual strong depth effect when it extends like a halo in all directions around a center. In such a case the frontal pattern is not seen as the projection of a simpler one in depth. The same is true, for example, for the gradient of obliqueness. In one of René Magritte's trick paintings, "Euclidean Promenades," the oblique outlines of an avenue are placed next to a conic steeple of the same shape, and whereas the avenue recedes in depth the steeple does not.

Size gradients such as that of Figure 205 lead eventually to a point of convergence, which our pattern would reach if the squares and the intervals between them became smaller and smaller. This point of convergence stands for infinity in pictorial space. It is the vanishing point of central perspective and lies mostly on the horizon. In fact, our scale of squares is a narrow sector of a pictorial world constructed according to the principle of central perspective.

Toward a Convergence of Space

Isometric perspective, which we discussed earlier, is one of the great systems for unifying three-dimensional pictorial space. It accommodates the entire matter of the picture in systems of parallel lines, which enter at one side, run diagonally through the picture, and leave it again on the other side. This conveys the sense of a world that does not confront us at a stable location but moves past us like a train. Almost always the picture is asymmetrically oriented toward one side and seems destined to extend endlessly in both directions. It has no center but presents a segment of a ribbon-like sequence. As such, it is particularly well-suited to the Japanese hand scrolls, which in fact run endlessly in a horizontal panorama and could not accommodate the image of a centered world.

There is something curiously paradoxical about the world presented in isometric perspective, which moves away into depth because of its obliqueness but at the same time remains at an unchanging distance because size stays constant throughout. Although tilted, this world never seems to really leave the frontal plane of the picture—a property that recommends it for a style basically committed to the pictorial surface. But it is too confining for an urge toward the unbound infinity of space.

Furthermore, in a picture constructed isometrically everything is seen from the same side. This is an asset when the represented world conforms within itself to such parallelism, as does, for example, the orderly arrangement of the Japanese living quarters into which the Genji painters let us peep from above. But it is an obstacle for an artist in whose world things occupy three-dimensional space in various directions and therefore call for different viewpoints.

Figure 208, reproducing the main contours of a silver relief done in Germany around A.D. 1000, shows a world in which the unity of isometric paral-

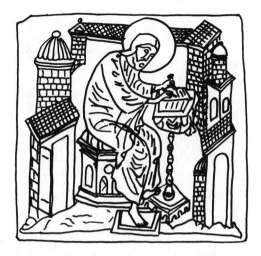

Figure 208

lelism has been abandoned. The profile figure of the evangelist Matthew is displayed in the frontal plane, but it is surrounded by elements of furniture and architecture, each of which has its own system of perspective presentation. There are frontal towers, variously tilted roofs, footstool, seat, and lectern jabbing at one another at different angles. Each element is spatially unified within itself—most of them are organized isometrically—but the unity of the total space has been abandoned. If the effect is nevertheless not chaotic, it is because contrasting elements are delicately balanced. This cannot but remind us of cubist compositions; however, the deliberate enjoyment of clash, contradiction, and mutual interference, which the art of the early twentieth century cultivated, did not exist in the centuries preceding the Renaissance. Instead, what we are faced with in examples such as Figure 208 is the struggle that ensues when a simpler principle of spatial unity has been outgrown and the search for a new one at a level of higher complexity is still in progress.

It is fascinating to observe the groping for spatial convergence in European paintings of the fourteenth and fifteenth centuries. In a transition from isometric perspective, the convergence of a ceiling or floor is represented first by symmetrical arrangements of parallel edges meeting awkwardly along a central vertical (Figure 209). An early reference to this principle is contained in Euclid's *Optics*; the procedure was known to Renaissance artists from the Pompeian murals of antiquity and is described, for example, in Cennino Cennini's treatise on the techniques of painting: "And put in the buildings

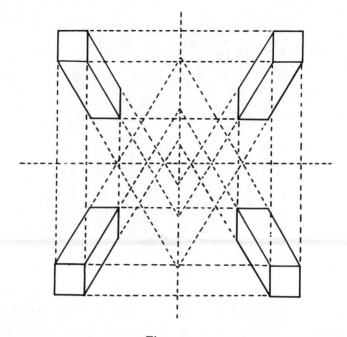

Figure 209

by this uniform system: that the moldings which you make at the top of the building should slant downward from the edge next to the roof; the molding in the middle of the building, halfway up the face, must be quite level and even; the molding at the base of the building underneath must slant upward, in the opposite sense to the upper molding, which slants downward." Later this system differentiates into a fan-shaped family of edges, which converges in a vanishing point more or less exactly, depending on whether they are constructed with a ruler or drawn freehand intuitively. The gradual change in direction among the edges unifies the plane of the floor or ceiling spatially. However, a separate vanishing point is often employed for each orthogonal surface, mainly in order to avoid the excessive foreshortening demanded by a common focus.

This intuitive search for spatial unity, supported by locally applied systems of construction, found its final geometrical codification in the principle of central perspective, which was formulated for the first time in the history of mankind in Italy by artists and architects such as Alberti, Brunelleschi, and Piero della Francesca.

The Two Roots of Central Perspective

It is significant for the visual characteristics of central perspective that it was discovered at only one time and place in man's entire history. The more elementary procedures for representing pictorial space, the two-dimensional "Egyptian" method as well as isometric perspective, were and are discovered independently all over the world at early levels of visual conception. Central perspective, however, is so violent and intricate a deformation of the normal shape of things that it came about only as the final result of prolonged exploration and in response to very particular cultural needs. Paradoxically, central perspective is at the same time by far the most realistic way of rendering optical space, and therefore should be expected to be not an esoteric refinement reserved to the happy few, but the method suggested most naturally to everyone by the evidence of visual experience.

This paradoxical nature of central perspective manifests itself in the two radically different roots from which it springs historically. On the one hand it is, as I have mentioned, the final solution to a long struggle for a new integration of pictorial space. In this respect, the search for the principle of convergence is a strictly intrapictorial matter, recommending itself to the artist by its elegant simplicity. It is a geometrical construct, involving elaborate rules on how to represent stereometric solids of various shapes and spatial locations.

In principle, this mathematical game of how to unify, by means of the straightedge, the subject matter of an entire picture in a simply and logically organized whole required no look at reality, no validation by the visual properties of the actual physical world. In fact, of course, no such independence existed. Central perspective came about as one aspect of the search for objectively correct descriptions of physical nature—a search that sprang during the Renaissance from a new interest in the wonders of the sensory world, and led to the great voyages of exploration as well as to the development of experimental research and the scientific standards of exactitude and truth. This trend of the European mind generated the desire to find an objective basis for the depiction of visual objects, a method independent of the idiosyncrasies of the draftsman's eye and hand.

The striving for mechanically correct reproduction received its theoretical basis from the notion of the visual pyramid adopted by Alberti in his treatise on painting of the year 1435. The optical relation between the eye of the observer and the object at which he looks can be represented by a system of straight lines issuing from each point of the object's frontal surface and meeting in the eye. The result is a kind of pyramid or cone, whose apex is at the point of the eye. If this pyramid of light rays is intersected by a pane of glass perpendicular to the line of sight, the image on the glass will be a projection of the object, so that by tracing on the glass the outlines of the object as seen from the point of observation, the viewer can record an exact duplicate of his image.

If this procedure is applied to a geometrically simple environment, such as the interior of a church, the resulting image will conform roughly to the rules of central perspective. It is obtained, however, without the help of any geometrical construct, just as the photographic camera by applying a similar method to the same subject will produce a picture in which all orthogonals of cornices, arches, floor and ceiling converge precisely in a vanishing point, located perhaps at the altar. However, this method of mechanical projection is by no means limited to geometrical solids. It will deliver the outlines of any object whatever, and therefore can be used, for example, to obtain a correct projection of intricate foreshortenings in the human figure.

Figure 210 shows the mechanism put into practice by Albrecht Dürer in his treatise on measurement. The draftsman staring through a peephole in order to guarantee an unchanging point of observation traces the outlines of his sitter on the vertical plate. In this primitive fashion the device has found little use, but it became popular as an application of the camera obscura. The pinhole camera was invented, it seems, by Leonardo da Vinci, and was supplied later with a lens and a mirror construction by which a painter could view his subject on a horizontal ground glass. There is good evidence that this device was used by painters such as Vermeer and in more recent times by others. The crowning achievement of this technological development was, of course, photography, which records the image with no manual help whatever.

In its more primitive form, the method of tracing faithful images on a transparent surface would have been certainly within the range of any reasonably advanced civilization. If nevertheless we have no other evidence of this kind than, say, the tracing of the outlines of human hands in the paintings of Australian aborigines and other early artists, the reason is surely that there was no demand for such mechanical exactness.

The discovery of central perspective bespoke a dangerous development in Western thought. It marked a scientifically oriented preference for mechanical reproduction and geometrical constructs in place of creative imagery. William Ivins has pointed out that, by no mere coincidence, central perspective was discovered only a few years after the first woodcuts had been printed in Europe. The woodcut established for the European mind the al-

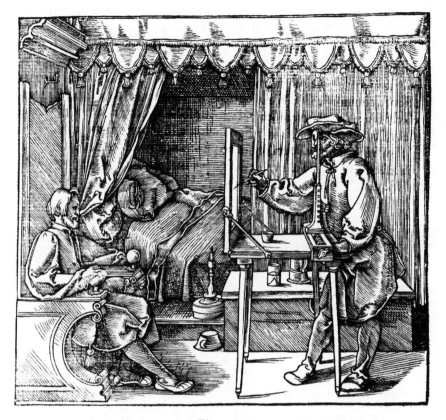

Figure 210

most completely new principle of mechanical reproduction. It is to the credit of Western artists and their public that despite the lure of mechanical reproduction, imagery has survived as a creation of the human spirit. Even in the age of photography it was imagination that engaged the service of the machine, not the machine that expelled imagination. Nevertheless, the lure of mechanical faithfulness has ever since the Renaissance tempted European art, especially in the mediocre standard output for mass consumption. The old notion of "illusion" as an artistic ideal became a menace to popular taste with the beginnings of the industrial revolution.

Not a Faithful Projection

Although the rules of central perspective produce pictures that closely resemble the mechanical projections yielded by the lenses of eyes and cameras, there are significant differences. Even in this more realistic mode of spatial representation, the rule prevails that no feature of the visual image will be deformed unless the task of representing depth requires it. In the earliest and simplest applications of one-point perspective, objects are placed frontally whenever possible. Only the orthogonals submit to convergence and meet in a single vanishing point (Figure 211). The other two spatial dimensions are accommodated in the frontal plane and remain undeformed. At a higher level of differentiation, two-point perspective defines the cubic object through the intersection of two families of converging edges (Figure 212). But even in this more refined system, all verticals remain undifferentiated parallels to the picture frame. In photographs of tall buildings we see the vertical edges deviate from parallelism in ways that can be codified approximately by introducing a third vanishing point, toward which they all converge.

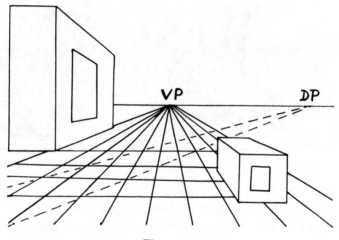

Figure 211

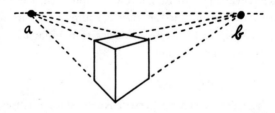

Figure 212

But even three vanishing points are only a geometrical simplification of the fact that all shapes get smaller in all directions with increasing distance from the eye. Consider a large frontal rectangle, perhaps the façade of a building. Such frontal shapes are represented in pictures as undeformed; we are shown a regular rectangle. However, since all areas of the surface, with increasing distance from the viewpoint of the observer's eyes, should become smaller, this should express itself, for example, in convex contours. This convexity is in fact observed in photographs taken at a sufficiently wide angle. It is not used by the draftsman because such a deformation is not translatable into recession, and therefore would be read by the eye as a distortion of the frontal object.

The geometrical construct of central perspective approximates the projection that would be received by the eye at one particular station point. Therefore, in order to see the picture "correctly," the viewer would have to assume the corresponding position of standing opposite the vanishing point with his eyes at the level of the horizon. He would also have to be at the proper relative distance, which in the example of Figure 211 would be equal to the distance between VP and the distance point DP. In fact, when the viewer assumes this position (which is possible if the drawing is sufficiently enlarged), he will find the depth effect most convincing and the shape of objects least distorted. In practice, however, we wander unconcernedly back and forth in front of, say, a Venetian cityscape by Guardi or Canaletto, and we change the viewing distance at will. The constancy of shape helps us somewhat to compensate for the lateral distortion, and the perspective construction is one of the invariants that survive the change of proportions.

Insistence on the "correct" viewing position can actually interfere with the perception of a painting. If the painter has placed the vanishing point outside of the picture, even the rigorist is not likely to take his stand to the side of the picture and fixate the wall. But when the perspective focus is inside the frame although placed laterally (Figure 217), he may be tempted to face that focus orthogonally. However, in doing so he will completely miss the picture, which is composed for a viewer standing in front of its center. The balance will be destroyed; the perspective focus, intended as a lateral dynamic accent, will assume the function of the center, and the depth effect will become so strong as to dig a crater into the spatial relief.

Pyramidal Space

The notion of perceptual constancy has led many theorists to assume that when looking around in the physical world, we see things at their real size and their real distance. This is not necessarily so. Although within a considerable range of distance observers can, under favorable conditions, see the size and shape of things correctly, this does not mean that when they actually compare objects close by with objects far away they perceive physically equal things as equal. This confusing situation is of some importance for our purposes.

The depth effect depends, we recall, on the relation between the structure of the two-dimensional projection and the structure available in the third dimension. If the frontal pattern has much simplicity it will influence the percept in the direction of flatness. Assume that Figures 213a and b were the outlines of a stage seen from two different seats on the main floor. The stage will look flatter for the person seeing a from a center seat because its projection is symmetrical and therefore tends to prevail, whereas the view from the left (b) is asymmetrical in the projection but can be straightened out into symmetry by a three-dimensional version. Similarly, as we look into a traditional church from the entrance we see a symmetrical pattern, which tends to reduce the depth effect.

Moreover, experiments have shown that the viewer's mental attitude can strongly influence the degree of the depth effect he sees. He can be asked to concentrate on the situation "as it really is" as distinguished from the way it looks, or inversely to pull the scene into the frontal plane as though it were a flat picture. His attitude will emphasize certain spatial features and play down others. An art student, trained in perspective drawing, has an easier time seeing rows of buildings projectively than the "man in the street"; the psychologist Robert Thouless has found that students from India, less familiar with perspective representation, saw tilted objects more nearly in their "real" shape and size than British students.

Now distance and size are strictly correlated. By staring at a black spot one can create a white afterimage, which then can be projected upon various

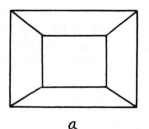 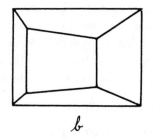

Figure 213

places in the room. One will notice that when the white spot is seen on a nearby piece of furniture it will look small, whereas on the more distant ceiling it will look large (Emmert's law). This will also happen when one projects the afterimage on close or distant areas of a painting that displays a convincing depth effect. We conclude that size and distance define each other. When two shapes are of objectively equal size, one of them will look larger if it is seen as located farther away; and two shapes of objectively unequal size will be perceived as located at correspondingly different distances if they are seen as equally large.

Convergence never straightens out entirely. When we look into the canyon of a city street we see parallel rows of buildings extending into depth, but we also see convergence. The buildings close to us look larger than the ones farther away on the distance gradient, but they also look the same size. Or we stand before a Renaissance painting: the figures in the foreground look larger than the ones in the background, but we also see them as alike. This confusing contradiction is not due to the difference between seeing one thing and knowing another. No, it is a genuine visual paradox: those objects look different and alike at the same time.

The situation is puzzling and paradoxical only as long as we apply the standards of Euclidean space. We are accustomed to thinking of the world as an infinitely large cube whose space is homogeneous, in the sense that things and the relations between them do not change when their location changes. But now imagine one side of the cube shrinking to the size of a point. The result will be an infinitely large pyramid. (It should be understood that I am not talking about an interior of pyramidal shape contained in the usual "cubic" world of our reasoning, but of a world which is itself pyramidal.) Such a world would be non-Euclidean. All the usual geometric concepts would hold, but they would apply to startlingly different phenomena. Parallels issuing from the side that had shrunk to a point would diverge in all directions while remaining parallels at the same time. Objects of very different size would be equal nevertheless, if their distances from the peak were proportional to their sizes. An object moving toward the peak would shrink without becoming smaller and slow down while maintaining a constant speed. If an object changed its spatial orientation it would change its shape but remain the same shape nevertheless.

All these crazy contradictions are resolved when we realize that size, shape, and speed are perceived in relation to the spatial framework in which they appear. In Euclidean space lines of equal size are seen as equal (Figure 214a); in pyramidal space the components of a gradient of size are seen as equal (b). The rules governing this anisotropic space are less simple than those

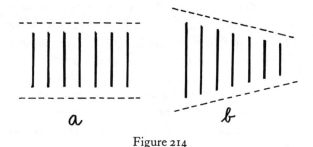

Figure 214

of Euclidean space, but they are nevertheless simple and consistent enough that, for example, a computer can produce a picture in central perspective of any set of geometric solids as seen from any point of observation by imposing upon the data a fairly simple principle of convergence.

The human sense of sight is presented with such a pyramidal space by virtue of the fact that in perception, convergent projections straighten out only partially. We see depth, but we see convergence at the same time. And the perceptual phenomena occurring in that convergent world are processed by the nervous system, in relation to the spatial framework, with the efficiency of a computer. James J. Gibson has pertinently remarked: "Scale, not size, is actually what remains constant in perception." And the nature of the scale is determined by the spatial framework.

There are what might be called "Newtonian oases" in perceptual space. Within a frontal plane, space is approximately Euclidean; and up to a few yards from the observer, shape and size are actually seen as unchangeable. It is from these areas that our visual reasoning obtains confirmation when, at an elementary level of spatial differentiation, it conceives of size, shape, and speed as independent of location. But even in the more clearly pyramidal world, the relations to the framework are perceived so directly that it is all but impossible for the naive observer to "see in perspective"; because seeing in perspective means perceiving the inhomogeneous world as a distorted homogeneous one, in which the effect of depth appears as the same kind of crookedness that we observe when a twisted thing is seen in a frontal plane.

Perhaps the perceptual influence of the spatial framework on visual objects is more easily understood if we consider the convergent space of central perspective as one of the "optical illusions," which, as Edwin Rausch has shown, are deformations caused by inhomogeneous spatial systems. Even in the flat plane it is almost impossible to see the two vertical lines in Figure 215 as equal. In this version of the so-called Ponzo illusion, the two lines look unequal

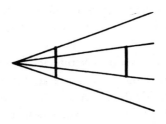

Figure 215

because we remain outside the deformation created by the spatial system in the drawing, whereas in a successful example of central perspective we enter the spatial system sufficiently to see such shapes as equal and unequal at the same time.

So far I have described the dynamics of central perspective one-sidedly, as an effect of the spatial framework upon particular visual objects. But, of course, the framework is nothing but a constellation of such objects, and what we are really dealing with is the interaction among visual things. The determining influence can be exerted by a single object. This is seen most convincingly when an isolated shape creates its own spatial surroundings. If the trapezoid of Figure 216 is shown on an empty surface, it may be perceived as a bird's-eye view of a rectangle flat on the ground. In that case the shape of the rectangle establishes the surrounding space by spontaneous induction as bounded by an horizon; and it is to the credit of the simplicity principle that among the infinity of such spatial settings available, the one most simply related to the figure is automatically perceived in the empty surroundings. In principle we could also see an irregular trapezium in a spatial system defined

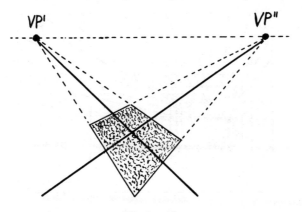

Figure 216

by vanishing points at different locations, or a rectangle tilted upward with vanishing points located above the horizon, etc. These versions would be less simple.

When the spatial frameworks of setting and object contradict each other, an interesting battle can be observed. There are three possible solutions: (1) the setting imposes itself and the object complies by assuming a deformation; (2) the object asserts itself and the spatial context becomes distorted; (3) neither contestant yields and the image splits apart into independent spatial systems. In the Ames room (Figure 203) the setting tends to win out over the size of the figures. Some more complex examples will be discussed at the end of this chapter.

Among the dynamic effects of pyramidal space is that of compression. Because the deformations of the receding shapes are only partially compensated, all objects appear compressed in the third dimension. This experience is particularly strong because the compression is seen not only as an accomplished fact but as developing gradually. At the periphery, as Figure 217 shows, distances are large, and decrease in size occurs at a slow speed. As the eye moves toward the center, neighboring lines approach one another faster and faster, until an almost intolerable degree of compression is reached. This effect is exploited in those periods and by those artists who favor a high pitch of excitement. In the baroque style even architectural vistas are subjected to this dramatic procedure. In Piranesi's etchings the long façades of the Roman streets are sucked into the focus of space with a breathtaking crescendo. Among modern artists, Van Gogh favored strong convergence; and an example by Henry Moore (Figure 218) shows how the objectively static theme of two

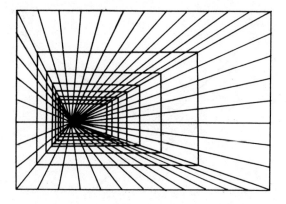

Figure 217

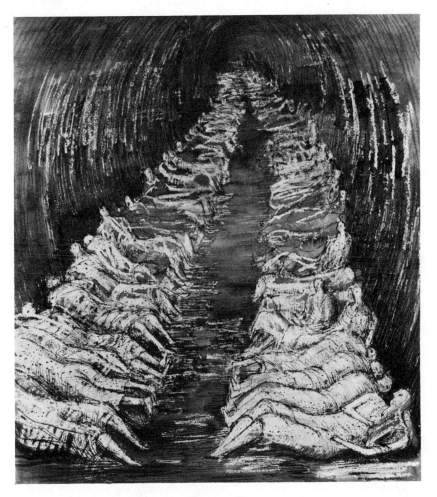

Figure 218
Henry Moore. *Tube Shelter Perspective*. Watercolor, 1941. Tate Gallery, London.

rows of sleepers in an underground tube acquires through perspective contraction the dramatic impact appropriate to the representation of an air-raid shelter. Other artists avoided the effect of receding lines. Cézanne used them rarely, and when they did occur in his work he often downplayed their effect by modifying them in the direction of the horizontal or vertical.

Among film directors Orson Welles is known for the dramatic use of short-focus lenses in his early films. Lenses do not modify perspective, but a lens of strong curvature will embrace a wider angle of space from a short distance. This produces steep gradients between foreground and background, resulting in a baroque tension as characters shrink and expand rapidly when moving away from or toward the camera.

The Symbolism of A Focused World

The early, two-dimensional method of spatial representation, found in the art of children and in Egyptian painting, makes the picture face the viewer like a flat wall, generously exposing all its content to his exploration but at the same time excluding him. It is a self-contained, closed world. Isometric perspective expands pictorial space into the third dimension, but this space, too, is self-contained. Its strong lateral movement takes place in a realm beyond the frontal plane.

With central perspective, the relation to the viewer changes. Its principal structural lines are a system of beams that issue from a focus within the picture space and deny the existence of the frontal plane as they rush forward and break through it. Although it takes strong optical devices to give a viewer the actual illusion of being enveloped by this expanding funnel of space, even an ordinary painting done in central perspective will establish a rather direct connection between the events in the picture space and the viewer. Instead of facing the viewer perpendicularly or obliquely, the funnel of central perspective opens like a flower toward the observer, approaching him directly and, when desired, symmetrically, by making the picture's central axis coincide with the viewer's line of sight.

This explicit acknowledgment of the viewer is at the same time a violent imposition upon the world represented in the picture. The perspective distortions are not caused by forces inherent in the represented world itself. They are the visual expression of the fact that this world is being sighted. And the construct of geometrical optics determines and prescribes the viewer's station point.

To this extent we can agree with the commonly accepted interpretation of central perspective as a manifestation of Renaissance individualism. The image presents a world as seen from the viewpoint of an individual observer, and in doing so raises the pictorial conception of space to a new level of differentiation. However, we have observed that in practice the viewer is quite independent of the prescribed station point. Within considerable limits he can freely move sideways and back and forth. And what he sees is—in partial contradiction of what I have just said—a world that contains within and by itself, i.e., quite independently of the viewer, a convergence toward a center.

The vanishing point is not only the reflection of the location from which the ideal viewer is looking at the picture; it is also and mainly the apex of the pyramidal world portrayed in the picture. "Perspective employs in distances two opposite pyramids," wrote Leonardo da Vinci, "one of which has its apex in the eye and its base as far away as the horizon. The other has the base towards the eye and the apex on the horizon."

Symbolically, such a centered world suits a hierarchical conception of human existence. It would hardly fit the Taoist or Zen philosophies of the East, which express themselves in the centerless continuum of the Chinese and Japanese landscapes shaped by isometric perspective.

In the West, quite apart from perspective, the altarpieces of medieval art create a religious hierarchy by the arrangement of their subject matter. The principal figure is large and central, surrounded by smaller secondary figures. Convergent perspective can be used for the same purpose. In Leonardo's *Last Supper* (Figure 219) the figure of Christ is placed in the center of the composition, which is at the same time the vanishing point. The frontally oriented table and back wall support the majestic stability of the principal figure, whereas the side walls and ceiling swing outward in a gesture of revelation. All the shapes and edges of the room emanate like a bundle of rays from the center; and conversely the entire setting points in unison toward the center. The depth effect is reduced and the solemnity of the scene is increased by the symmetry of the total composition.

Erwin Panofsky cites the architect Palladio as saying that the vanishing point should be placed in the center in order to give the picture *maestà e grandezza*. As the stylistic outlook changes, so does the use of perspective. Figure 217 indicates schematically the effect of an eccentric focus. Tension is created by the distance of the vanishing point from the center of the picture. The asymmetry of the pattern produces a much stronger depth effect. Instead of the world represented by Leonardo, in which the law of the whole har-

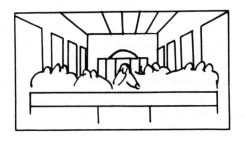

Figure 219

monically determines everything down to the smallest detail, we now see a tilted spatial system presented in the frontal framework of the picture. The pictorial and philosophical task is that of showing a world in which a life center with needs, demands, and values of its own challenges the law of the whole and in turn is challenged by it.

How can these contrasting ways of existence be balanced in an organized whole? Figure 217 shows how the perspective system itself provides for some such balance, in that the strong compression on the left goes with a smaller area whereas the large space on the right goes with less tension. It suggests a kind of formula by which the product of tension and area remains constant throughout the picture.

The theme of a composition based on such an eccentric pattern can be said to be the search for a more complex law that permits contradictory ways of existence to get along with each other. The price of unity and harmony has been raised. Dramatic conflict has been introduced into the image of reality. Such a conception could suit neither the philosophy of a Taoist nor the doctrines of the medieval Church. It did suit a period in the history of Western thought in which man took his stand against God and nature, and the individual began to assert his rights against authorities of any kind. The exciting discord that we usually consider a principal theme of modern art is sounded here at an early date.

To the two centers of the formal pattern—the center of the canvas and the focal point of the perspective—the content of the picture can add a third. In one of Tintoretto's representations of the Last Supper (Figure 220), painted some sixty years after Leonardo's, the focus of the room, as established by the lines of the table, the floor, and the ceiling, lies in the upper right corner. But the center of the story is the figure of Christ (encircled). The eccentricity of space indicates that the law of the world has lost its absolute validity. It is presented as one mode of existence among many other, equally possible ones. Its particular "slant" is revealed to the eye, and the action that takes place in this framework claims its own center and standards in defiance of the ways of the whole. Individual action and governing authority have become antagonistic partners enjoying equal rights. In fact, here the figure of Christ holds the center of the frame, as far as the horizontal plane is concerned, so that by deviating from the demands of the surrounding world the individual approaches a position of absolute validity—a turnabout that reflects the spirit of the new age. Other variations of this interplay among the three centers can be studied in other compositions of Tintoretto and his contemporaries.

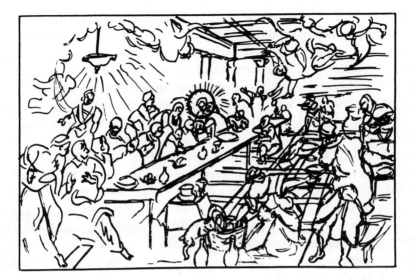

Figure 220

Centrality and Infinity

Central perspective involves a significant paradox. On the one hand it shows a centralized world. The focus of this world is an actual point on the canvas, on which the observer can put his finger. In the complete projection of two-dimensional space this center lies in the frontal plane. With increasing depth, the center withdraws into the distance, and in totally straightened-out space of 100 percent constancy it would lie in the infinite.

In an actual pictorial composition, therefore, the perceptual status of the focal point is ambiguous. The tangible center of the spatial framework at which the draftsman aims with his ruler is at the same time the vanishing point, which by definition lies in the infinite, where the parallels meet. Neither two-dimensional nor isometric perspective had explicitly faced the problem of the boundaries of space. They implied that space continues forever in its tangible concreteness. With the introduction of central perspective the artist includes a statement on the nature of infinity for the first time. It is hardly a coincidence that this happened in the same century in which Nicolas Cusanus and Giordano Bruno raised the problem for modern philosophy.

Centrality and infinity had been contradictory ideas since antiquity. A centralized world of Aristotelian conception called for a finite system of concentric shells. The infinite world of the atomists Democritus and Epicurus, on the other hand, excluded the possibility of a center; their follower Lucretius wrote: "All around us in every direction and on both sides and above and below through the universe there is no limit, even as I have shown; the fact itself cries aloud, and the nature of the unfathomable deep elucidates it." The notion that not only God is infinite, as the philosophers of the Middle Ages had maintained, but that the world is infinite as well is a conception of the Renaissance age. Cusanus attempted to reconcile centrality and infinity by describing God and world as infinite spheres, whose boundaries and centers were everywhere and nowhere. In central perspective the precarious relation between the two spatial conceptions is fully visible. Artists tend to hide the conflict by seeking to avoid spelling out the vanishing point. Its location is implied by the converging directions of the orthogonal lines and shapes, but their actual meeting place is usually kept under a cloud. Only in the ceiling paintings and landscapes of the baroque do we receive the image of a frankly open world that goes on forever.

Finally, it should be observed that central perspective portrays space as a flow oriented toward a specified end. It thereby transforms the timeless simultaneity of traditional, undeformed space into a happening in time—that is, a directed sequence of events. The world of being is redefined as a process of happening. In this way also, central perspective foreshadows and initiates a fundamental development in the Western conception of nature and man.

Playing With the Rules

Central perspective continues to interest the artist in three respects. It offers a strikingly realistic image of physical space; it supplies a rich and refined compositional pattern; and the conception of a converging world imparts its own characteristic expression.

As far as the compositional pattern is concerned, it will be sufficient to point out that the two-dimensional space of early art presented essentially a framework of verticals and horizontals located parallel to the frontal plane with a minimum of tension (Figure 221a). Isometric perspective overlays these fundamental coordinates with one or two sets of parallels, oriented obliquely toward the coordinates. This produces a wealth of new relations and angles and also introduces depth through obliqueness (Figure 221b). Central perspective, finally, overlays the frontal verticals and horizontals with a system of converging beams, which create a focal center and provide a complete range of angles (Figure 221c).

The realistic effect of central perspective was foremost in the minds of the

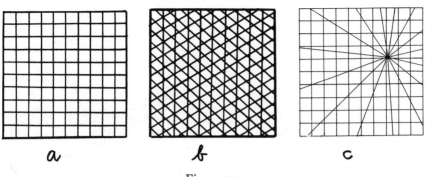

Figure 221

artists who worked out its system in the fifteenth century. Note, however, that from the beginning artists were willing to deviate from the rules because they led to unsightly distortions and unwelcome coercion of subject matter and expression when applied mechanically. The various parts of an architectural setting in a painting are not always made to conform to the same vanishing point. More technically, the psychologist Zajac has suggested that convergence above eye level acts more strongly than convergence below eye level and that therefore the former should be reduced, the latter increased.

Modifications of this kind are applied intuitively in order to make the picture fit the intended expression or look more natural. In our own century, the surrealists have manipulated the spatial framework to heighten the sense of the uncanny. Giorgio de Chirico, in particular, did this by smuggling perspective contradictions into his architectural landscapes. Figure 222 is taken from a de Chirico painting, *The Lassitude of the Infinite*. The mysterious, dreamlike quality of what at first glance looks like a straight realistic composition is obtained essentially by deviating from perspective rules. The setting as a whole is drawn in focused perspective, whereas the statue rests on an isometric cube. Owing to this conflict between two incompatible spatial systems, the statue looks like an apparition, projected onto the ground rather than materially resting on it. At the same time the pedestal of the statue, with its simpler, more compelling structure, tends to make the convergences appear as actual distortions, rather than as projections of receding parallels. The setting has little strength to resist such an attack, because it is full of internal contradictions. The edges of the piazza meet far above the horizon in A. Thus either the world comes abruptly to an end and the empty universe begins beyond the small railway train and tower in the background, or, if the horizon is accepted as the frame of reference, the piazza which ought to converge

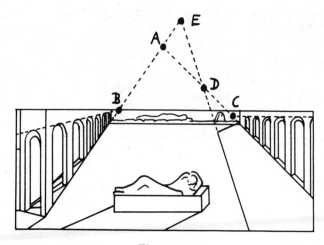

Figure 222

there, appears as immensely stretched sideways—a magic expanse, created where none could be and therefore all the emptier. In consequence the two colonnades seem to have been moved apart by the flat abyss. Or, if the eye accepts the shape of the piazza, the colonnades, which converge at points on or slightly below the upper margin of the picture (B, C), shrink paradoxically. Viewed in isolation from the rest of the setting, these colonnades look quite normal, except for the frontal arch at the extreme left, which strangely adapts its height to the flight of the receding façade. Finally, the shadow of the right colonnade produces two more vanishing points (D, E) incompatible with the others. Thus, a number of inherent inconsistencies create a world that looks tangible but unreal, and changes shape depending upon where we look and which element we accept as the basis for judging the rest.

The same dreamlike unreality pervades another of de Chirico's paintings, *Melancholy and Mystery of a Street* (Figure 223). At first glance the scene looks solid enough, and yet we feel that the unconcerned girl with the hoop is endangered by a world about to crack along invisible seams or to drift apart in incoherent pieces. Again a roughly isometric solid, the wagon, denounces the convergences of the buildings as actual distortions. Furthermore, the perspectives of the two colonnades negate each other. If the one to the left, which defines the horizon as lying high up, is taken as the basis of the spatial organization, the one to the right pierces the ground. Under the opposite condition the horizon lies invisibly somewhere below the center of the picture, and

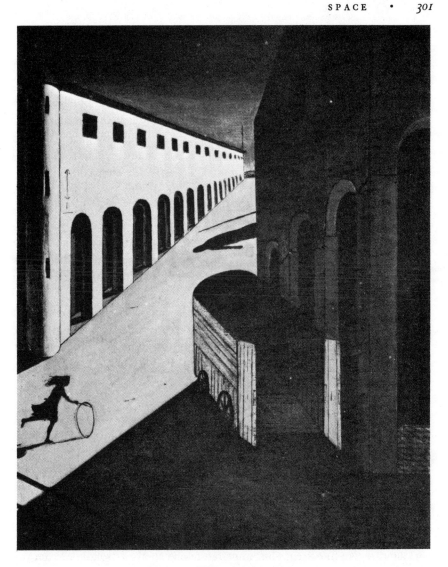

Figure 223
Giorgio de Chirico. *Melancholy and Mystery of a Street*, 1914. Coll. Stanley R. Resor.

the rising street with the bright colonnade is only a treacherous mirage guiding the child to a plunge into nothingness.

In order to make their illusions convincing, surrealists like de Chirico fitted their disparate spatial systems into a seamless, trustworthy-looking realistic whole. The cubists used a different procedure for a different purpose. They attempted to portray the modern world as a precarious interplay of independent units, each coherent and lawful in itself, but unrelated to the spatial coordinates governing its neighbors. I mentioned the cubists earlier, in comparison with the transitional stages between central and isometric perspectives (Figure 208), and I pointed out that the resulting visual clashes, contradictions, and mutual interferences were deliberately sought by artists such as Braque and Picasso. What they wanted to show was not a chaotic accumulation of objects, comparable to a mountain slope strewn with boulders, since this would be an instance of disorder in a perfectly coherent spatial setting. They were after a much more fundamental disorder, namely, the incompatibility inherent in total space itself. Each of the small units that together constitute a cubist still life or figure obeys its own spatial framework. Often these units are simple isometric rectangles. However, their spatial interrelation is deliberately irrational. They are not to be seen as parts of a continuous whole but as small, self-contained individualities, blindly crossing one another.

In order to show that these superpositions do not occur in coherent space, the cubists used the device of making the units render one another transparent or fade out into the neutral ground of the painting. The psychological effect becomes evident if we remember that the same means are used in motion pictures to represent discontinuity of space. If the scene shifts from the living room to the hotel lobby, the room fades out into spacelessness—that is, for a moment pictorial space gives way to the physical surface of the screen, after which the opposite process introduces the new space of the lobby. Or, in a lap dissolve, both scenes appear for a moment as overlaying each other, thereby indicating their spatial independence to the eye. But whereas in the conventional film story, fade and dissolve represent only leaps within homogeneous and orderly space, experimental films and cubist paintings use them as part of their attempts to obtain an integration of discordant orders.

Being forced into spatial simultaneity, the individual units cannot replace one another like film scenes but must refute one another's solidity. From the point of view of any one of them, the others are unreal. Only a delicate balancing of the innumerable forces meeting one another at innumerable angles can provide a semblance of unity. Perhaps this is the only kind of order available to modern man in his social relations and in dealing with the contradictory powers of his mind.

VI   LIGHT

If we had wished to begin with the first causes of visual perception, a discussion of light should have preceded all others, for without light the eyes can
observe no shape, no color, no space or movement. But light is more than
just the physical cause of what we see. Even psychologically it remains one of
the most fundamental and powerful of human experiences, an apparition
understandably worshiped, celebrated, and importuned in religious ceremo-
nies. To man as to all diurnal animals, it is the prerequisite for most activities.
It is the visual counterpart of that other animating power, heat. It interprets to
the eyes the life cycle of the hours and the seasons.

Yet, since man's attention is directed mostly toward objects and their
actions, the debt owed to light is not widely acknowledged. We deal visually
with human beings, buildings, or trees, not with the medium generating their
images. Accordingly even artists have been much more concerned with the
creatures of light than with light itself. Under special cultural conditions light
enters the scene of art as an active agent, and only our own time can be said to
have generated artistic experiments dealing with nothing but the play of
disembodied light.

The Experience of Light

Physicists tell us that we live on borrowed light. The light that brightens
the sky is sent through a dark universe to a dark earth from the sun over a
distance of ninety-three million miles. Very little in the physicist's description
accords with our perception. To the eye, the sky is luminous by its own power
and the sun is nothing but the sky's brightest attribute, affixed to it and perhaps generated by it. According to the Book of Genesis, the creation of light
produced the first day, whereas the sun, the moon, and the stars were added
only on the third. In Piaget's interviews with children, a seven-year-old as-

serted that it is the sky that provides light. "The sun is not like the light. Light illuminates everything, but the sun only where it is." And another child explained: "Sometimes when the sun gets up in the morning, he sees that the weather is bad, so he goes to where it's good."

Since the sun appears as nothing but a shiny object, light must reach the sky from somewhere else. S. R. Driver, in his comment on Genesis, says: "It seems thus that, according to the Hebrew conception, light, though gathered up and concentrated in the heavenly bodies, is not confined to them; day arises, not solely from the sun, but because the matter of light issues forth from its place and spreads over the earth, at night it withdraws, and darkness comes forth from its place, each in a hidden, mysterious way." This is more clearly expressed in the Lord's question to Job: "Where is the way were light dwelleth? And as for darkness, where is the place thereof, that thou shouldst take it to the bound thereof, and that thou shouldst know the paths to the house thereof?"

Instead of being an effect exerted by a few sources upon all other objects, "day" here is a bright thing which arrives from the beyond and moves over the vault of the sky. In the same way the brightness of objects on earth is seen basically as a property of their own rather than as a result of reflection. Apart from special conditions to be discussed below, the luminosity of a house, a tree, or a book on the table does not appear to the eye as a gift from a distant source. At most, the light of the day or of a lamp will seem to call forth the brightness of things, as a match ignites a pile of wood. Things are less bright than the sun and the sky, but not different in principle. They are weaker luminaries.

It follows that darkness is seen either as the extinction of the object's inherent brightness or as the effect of dark objects hiding bright ones. Night is not the negative result of withdrawn light, but the positive arrival of a dark cloak that replaces or covers the day. Night, according to children, consists of black clouds, which move close together so that none of the white can shine through. Some artists, such as Rembrandt or Goya, at least part of the time show the world as an inherently dark place, brightened here and there by light. They happen to endorse the findings of the physicists. But the prevailing view throughout the world seems to have been and to be that light, although originally born from primordial darkness, is an inherent virtue of the sky, the earth, and the objects that populate them, and that their brightness is periodically hidden or extinguished by darkness.

To assert that these are children's and primitives' misconceptions eradicated by modern science would be to close our eyes to universal visual experiences, which are reflected in artistic presentations. Knowledge has made us stop talking like children, ancient chroniclers, or Polynesian islanders. Our image of the world, however, is all but unchanged, because it is dictated by compelling perceptual conditions that prevail everywhere and always. Even so, we have trained ourselves to rely on knowledge rather than our sense of sight to such an extent that it takes accounts by the naive and the artists to make us realize what we see.

Relative Brightness

Another discrepancy between physical and perceptual facts is uncovered when we attempt to answer the question: How bright are things? It has often been observed that a handkerchief at midnight looks white, like a handkerchief at noon, although it may send less light to the eyes than a piece of charcoal under the mid-day sun. Here again, as in the case of the perception of size or shape, we cannot account for the facts by talking about the "constancy" of brightness, certainly not in the simple sense of asserting that objects are seen "as bright as they really are." The brightness we see depends, in a complex manner, on the distribution of light in the total situation, on the optical and physiological processes in the observer's eyes and nervous system, and on an object's physical capacity to absorb and reflect the light it receives.

This physical capacity is called luminance or reflectance. It is a constant property of any surface. Depending on the strength of the illumination, an object will reflect more or less light, but its luminance, i.e., the percentage of the light it throws back, remains the same. A piece of black velvet, which absorbs much of the light it receives, may under strong illumination send out as much light as a dimly lit piece of white silk, which reflects most of the energy.

Perceptually, there is no direct way of distinguishing between reflecting power and illumination, since the eye receives only the resulting intensity of light but no information about the proportion in which the two components contribute to this result. If a dark disk, suspended in a dimly lit room, is hit by a light in such a way that the disk is illuminated but not its environment, the disk will appear brightly colored or luminous. Brightness or luminosity will appear as properties of the object itself. The observer cannot distinguish between the brightness of the object and that of the illumination. Indeed, under such conditions he sees no illumination at all, though he may know that the light source is in action and may even see it. If, however, the room is made brighter, the disk appears correspondingly darker. In other words, the observed brightness of the object depends upon the distribution of brightness values in the total visual field.

Whether or not a handkerchief looks white is determined not by the absolute amount of light it sends to the eye, but by its place in the scale of brightness values provided by the total setting. Leon Battista Alberti said: "Ivory and silver are white, which, when placed near swan's down, seem pale. For this reason things seem very bright in painting when there is a good proportion of white and black as there is from lighted to shadowy in the objects themselves; thus all things are known by comparison."

The phenomenon of glow illustrates the relativity of brightness values. Glow lies somewhere between the bright sources of light (sun, fire, lamps) and the subdued luminosity of everyday objects. A glowing object is seen as a source sending out light energy of its own. This view, however, may not match the physical condition. Mere reflected light may produce the perception of glow. To do so the object must display a brightness well above that which corresponds to its expected place in the scale established by the rest of the field. Its absolute brightness may be quite low, as we know from Rembrandt's famous glowing gold tones, which shine through the dust of three centuries. In a blacked-out street a piece of newspaper glows like a light. If glow were not a relational effect, realistic painting would have never been able convincingly to represent the sky, candlelight, fire and even lightning, the sun, and the moon.

We can tell the difference between a dark place and a brightly lit one even when no direct comparison is available. But within certain limits we transpose the brightness level of a whole setting in such a way that the difference is not perceived. We may get so accustomed to the dimness of the light in a room that after a while we notice it no more than we do a constant odor. We can also immerse ourselves in an old painting or a television program to such an extent that we are surprised to find how dark the canvas or the image on the tube actually is. To some extent such transposition is due to adaptive mechanisms in the nervous system. The pupils of the eyes enlarge automatically when brightness decreases, thus admitting a greater amount of light. The receptor organs of the retina also adapt their sensitivity to the intensity of the stimulus.

The relative brightness of objects is perceived most reliably when the whole setting is subjected to equal illumination. Under such conditions, the nervous system can treat the illumination level as a constant and credit each object simply with the brightness it exhibits on the total scale leading from the darkest to the brightest object in the setting. Remarkably enough, however, the mechanism works quite well even when the lighting is not homogeneous but ranges, for example, from intense brightness near the light source to dark shadow. If I compare a white envelope on the window sill with one lying in the back of the room, I do not have to rely on knowledge or intellectual calculation to realize that they are both the same white. I see it directly and spontaneously because I see each envelope in relation to the brightness gradient of the whole setting.

This perceptual accomplishment corresponds directly to what we observed about the perception of size in three-dimensional space. Brightness at even illumination can be compared to a spatial situation in which all objects are at equal distance from the observer. A brightness gradient, on the other hand, corresponds to pyramidal space, where the size of any object has to be determined in relation to its position within that space. However, in the case of brightness as well as of size the nervous system can accomplish its remarkable computations only if the perceived unevenness of the total setting is both simple enough in itself and clearly distinguishable from the condition of the objects. Regular gradients are simple enough to be generated by a computer. The computer can impose upon the drawing of a cylinder the gradual crescendo and decrescendo of brightness that imitates the distribution of light and shade and thereby gives the cylinder its three-dimensional roundness.

When objects are of physically identical luminance, as in the example of the white envelopes, their brightness is most easily discriminated from that of the gradient. But if we cunningly painted a black-to-white gradient on a long strip of paper and viewed it in a setting pervaded by a light gradient of similar steepness, the painted gradient would either strengthen or neutralize the gradient of the lighting, depending on how it were placed. This sort of trick is used by stage designers to convey the illusion of lighting or to counteract the effect of light. The same device is operative in both man-made and natural camouflage. "In innumerable animals, belonging to groups as diverse as caterpillars and cats, mackerel and mice, lizards and larks, countershading forms the basis of their coloration. Such animals are colored darkest above, lightest beneath, with graded tones on the flanks. . . . Viewed under diffused lighting from the sky such animals seem to lack solidity." When in a room the walls containing windows are painted a shade lighter than those struck by daylight, the one-sided effect of illumination is partly compensated and the brightness of the room looks more even—which may be soothing or upsetting to the observer, depending on whether he tends to ignore or to consider the world outside the windows.

Another parallel to depth perception relates to the degree of constancy.

Even when the pattern of the illumination is clearly seen, constancy does not eliminate the effect of illumination. We can report with assurance that the two envelopes are both white, but we observe that they look different just the same. In the Rembrandt painting reproduced in Figure 224 we see Potiphar

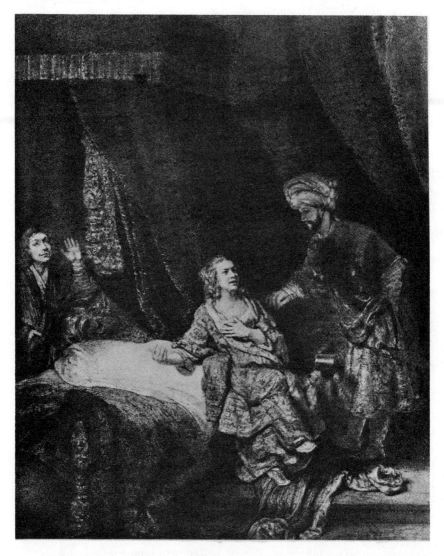

Figure 224
Rembrandt. *Joseph and Potiphar*, 1655. National Gallery, Washington, D.C.

as darker than his wife. This is essential to the function of light in the compo-sition. To this end, however, it is just as necessary that we see the effect as deriving from the lighting, not from a difference in complexion between husband and wife.

Illumination

The term "illumination" is not self-explanatory. At first thought it might seem as though illumination must be involved whenever we see anything, because unless light falls on an object it remains invisible. This, however, is physicists' reasoning. The psychologist and the artist can speak of illumina-tion only if and when the word serves to name a phenomenon that is directly discerned by the eyes. Is there such a thing, and under what conditions is it observed?

An evenly lighted field shows no sign of receiving its brightness from somewhere else. Its luminosity, as I said earlier, appears as a property inherent in the thing itself. The same is true for a uniformly lighted room. It even seems justifiable to say that a stage viewed from a darkened theater does not neces-sarily give the impression of being illuminated. When the light is evenly dis-tributed, the stage may appear as a very bright world, a large luminary. But illumination is something else.

I look at the small wooden barrel on the shelf. Its cylindrical surface dis-plays a rich scale of brightness and color values. Next to the left contour there is a dark brown, almost a black. As my glance moves across the surface, the color gets lighter and more clearly brown, until it begins to become paler and paler, approaching a climax at which whiteness has all but replaced brown. Beyond the climax the color reverts back to brown.

But this description is correct only as long as I examine the surface inch by inch, or better, if I scan it through a small hole in a piece of paper. When I look at the barrel more freely and naturally, the result is quite different. Now the whole object looks uniformly brown. On the one side it is overlaid with a film of darkness, which thins out and disappears while an ever thicker layer of brightness begins to replace it. Over most of its surface the barrel shows a double value of brightness and color, one belonging to the object itself and another, as it were, draped over it—a transparency effect. This happens even though the eye receives one unitary stimulation from each point of the object. Perceptually, the unity is split up into the two layers. Here is a phenomenon that requires a name. The bottom layer will be called the object brightness and object color of the barrel. The top layer is the illumination.

Just as in central perspective a system of convergence is imposed upon a setting of shapes, *illumination is the perceivable imposition of a light gradient upon the object brightness and object colors in the setting*. The superposition observed on the surface of illuminated things is, as I have said, a transparency effect. Such transparency can be obtained in painting by actual glazes and superposition. Around 1500, artists often used sheets of colored paper for their drawings as a ground of medium brightness, to which they added highlights by applying white ink, shadows by black hatching. Painters often started with a monochromatic underpainting, which laid out the shadows and was then covered with transparent glazes of local color. This separation of illumination and object color reflected the perceptual split observed by the painter as he looked at things in the physical world; it also manifested a practical, object-oriented attitude, intent on distinguishing properties of the objects themselves from transitory effects momentarily imposed upon them.

Quite a different attitude is expressed by painters of the nineteenth century who represented the sum of local brightness, local color, and the brightness and color of the illumination through a single shade of pigment. This technique not only confirmed the purely visual sensation as the finaly reality; it also asserted philosophically that the being of things is not untouchably permanent. Accidentals are seen as participating in the essence of things just as much as their invariant properties. This pictorial procedure also defined the individual as being partly the creature of its environment, subject to influences that cannot simply be shed like veils.

As in other instances of transparency, the illumination effect is brought about by the tendency toward simplest structure. When illumination is perceived as a superposition, the illuminated object is able to maintain a constant brightness and color, while shading and highlights are attributed to a light gradient, which has a simple structure of its own. It should be noted that there is no obvious answer to the question how the object's brightness–color value is determined. Thinking back to the example of the wooden barrel grazed by light, we realize that what the eyes actually receive is a gamut of shades. Is one of them designated as the "true" color of the object, perhaps because it is the most saturated, the least contaminated by grayness? Delacroix assumed the existence of such a true tone (*le ton vrai de l'objet*) and noted that it is found next to the "luminous point," i.e. the highlight. But perhaps no such tone is actually present in the percept, and object brightness and object color are instead medium values, which serve as common denominators of the various shades.

Light Creates Space

All gradients have the power to create depth, and gradients of brightness are among the most efficient. This is true for spatial settings, such as interiors and landscapes, but also for single objects. In an experiment by Gehrcke and Lau, a wooden, whitewashed cone, whose base had a diameter of about five inches was viewed from a distance of thirteen yards. The cone was placed with its vertex toward the observer, whose line of sight coincided with the main axis of the cone. When the cone was lighted evenly from all sides the observer saw no cone, simply a flat white disk. The cone became visible when the light fell from only one side. Evidently a three-dimensional view could provide no structural simplification as long as the lighting was even. When lateral illumination was used, however, it introduced a gradient of shading, which resulted in a strong three-dimensional effect revealing the shape of the cone.

The increase in relief produced by lateral lighting is well known. Goethe says of the sun that it receives an immaculate view of the world "because it never saw the shadow," and the amateur photographer obtains flat pictures when he mounts the flash bulb on his camera. When the moon is full, its mountains and depressions appear as mere spots, but they stand out in bold relief as soon as the light strikes the crescent laterally.

Overwhelming is the testimony of the scanning electron microscope, which has introduced the world of the infinitely small into our common visual experience by providing strong illumination effects. The flat sections supplied by the light microscope or the transmission electron microscope have their own beauty and informative value, but they can hardly be experienced as belonging to the same world as the animals and plants known to the naked eye. Under the scanning microscope, the tiny cones and rods of the retina look like the withered trunks of a petrified forest, and the red cells of human blood look like a field of densely grown fungi or a junkyard of discarded tires. By giving these small objects the tangible volume of things as we know them, the scanning microscope has extended the continuum of visual experience to the limits of the organic and inorganic worlds.

Curved surfaces are obtained by accelerating brightness gradients, which correspond to the fact that the curvature of an object is almost flat where the line of sight strikes it at a right angle but increases ever more rapidly from the center toward the boundary (Figure 225). By varying the steepness of the gradient, one can control the shape of the curvature perceived. A gradient

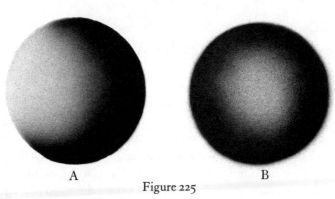

A   B

Figure 225

changing at a constant rate produces the effect of an inclined plane by reflecting the physical fact that the angle of inclination is constant throughout the surface.

In Figure 225, the gradient of *a* tends to create more compelling perceptual volume than that of *b* because in *b* the shading is as symmetrical as the spherical shape itself. Not much structural gain is obtained by perceiving such a symmetrical pattern as three-dimensional. Nor, in this case, does the object convey a strong impression of being lit by an outer light source. In 225*a*, by contrast, the gradient introduces an asymmetry, which can be detached from the object when the pattern is seen as a sphere struck obliquely by a light.

As we look at an object by itself, it is not always clear whether any brightness differences it shows in itself are due to illumination or to actual physical differences between white, black, and gray paint. This was nicely demonstrated long ago by Ernst Mach. When we look at Figure 226, we probably see a white and a dark wing regardless of whether we see a flat pattern or a folded one, and the central edge as in front or in back. If one then takes an actual piece of folded white cardboard and places it on the table, with its central edge toward the viewer and the light falling from the right, the percept will correspond to the physical facts: one sees a white card, shaded on one side by being turned away from the light source. Constancy of brightness is at work. However, if one closes one eye and forces the object to reverse so that it looks something like an open book with the central edge forming a distant groove, the situation changes radically. Now the left wing looks darkly colored, all the more dark because the light should strike it directly, and the right wing is white, all the more bright because it should be in the shadow. Thus illumination effects are strongly influenced by the light distribution perceived in the total spatial setting.

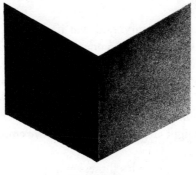

Figure 226

In whole settings as well as in single objects, steady gradients of brightness, like steady gradients of size, make for a continuous increase or decrease in depth. Brightness leaps help to produce distance leaps. The so-called *repoussoirs*, large objects in the foreground intended to make the background look farther away, are reinforced in painting, in photography and film, and on the stage if there is a strong brightness difference between foreground and background.

Since brightness of illumination means that a given surface is turned toward the light source whereas darkness means that it is turned away, the distribution of brightness helps to define the orientation of objects in space. At the same time it shows how various parts of a complex object are related to one another. Areas of similar spatial orientation are correlated visually by their similar brightness. The closer they come to meeting the incident light perpendicularly, the brighter they appear. We know that units of similar brightness are grouped together in perception. Thus a grouping by similarity of brightness indirectly produces a grouping by similarity of spatial orientation. Parallel surfaces are knitted together by the eye at whatever place in the relief they may occur, and this network of relations is a powerful means of creating spatial order and unity. Whereas a fly walking across an object would experience nothing but a bewildering irregular sequence of ups and downs, the surveying eye organizes the whole by correlating all areas of like spatial orientation.

A judicious distribution of light serves to give unity and order not only to the shape of single objects, but equally to that of a whole setting. The totality of the objects appearing within the frame of a painting or on a stage can be treated as one or several large objects, of which all the smaller elements are parts. The strong lateral light used by painters such as Caravaggio simplifies and coordinates the spatial organization of the picture. Roger de Piles, a French writer of the seventeenth century, said that if objects are arranged in such a way that all the lights are together on one side and their darkness on the other, this collection of lights and shades will keep the eye from wandering. "Titian called it the *bunch of grapes* because the grapes, being separated, would have each its light and shade equally, and thus dividing the sight into many rays, would cause confusion; but when collected into one bunch, and becoming thus but one mass of light and one of shade, the eye embraces them as a single object."

The neat analogy between brightness and spatial orientation is interfered with by cast shadows, because they may darken an area that would be bright otherwise, and by reflections that light up dark places. Differences in local brightness will also interact with the lighting scheme. In sculpture, dirt spots on the marble or irregularities of brightness in the grain of the wood will often distort shape by being subject to misinterpretation as effects of shading.

We are again up against the problem that arises from the eye's inability to distinguish directly between reflecting power and strength of illumination. Roger de Piles writes in a discussion of *claro-obscuro*: "*Claro* implies not only anything exposed to a direct light, but also all such colors as are luminous in their natures; and *obscuro*, not only all the shadows directly caused by the incidence and privation of light, but likewise all the colors which are naturally brown, such as, even when they are exposed to light, maintain an obscurity, and are capable of grouping with the shades of other objects."

In order to avoid the confusion between brightness produced by illumination and brightness due to the coloring of the object itself, the spatial distribution of light in the setting must be understandable to the eyes of the viewer. This is most easily achieved when no more than one light source is used. But often in photography or on the stage several light sources are combined in order to avoid excessively dark shadows.

Such dark shadows, it may be mentioned in passing, will destroy shape not only by hiding relevant portions of the object but also by cutting across the continuity of the curvature with sharp boundary lines between brightness and darkness. In recent years museums and art galleries have taken to murdering sculpture by illuminating it with focused spotlights to create a dramatic effect. Experiments have shown that attached shadows maintain their character of a transparent film only when their borders are blurred gradients. Hering observed: "A small shadow, thrown upon the surface of one's writing paper, appears as a casual spot of blurred gray superimposed upon the white paper. Under normal circumstances the white paper is seen *through* the shadow. There is no suggestion that it forms in any way a part of the genuine color of the paper. If, now, a heavy black line is drawn around the shadow so as to coincide exactly with its outline, a striking change may be observed to take place. The shadow ceases to appear as a shadow and becomes a dark gray spot on the surface of the paper, no longer a casual spot superimposed upon the paper but an actual part of the color of the paper." The focused spotlight creates the same sharp contours as Hering's black lines and therefore slashes the continuity of the sculptural surface mercilessly and produces a senseless arrangement of white and black shapes. Daylight, on the other hand, makes sculpture so beautifully visible because its diffuseness supplements the direct incidence of the sunlight and creates mellow gradients.

For lighting in art galleries or film studios or on the stage to avoid harsh one-sidedness, it must combine light sources in an organized whole. Several lights may add up to an even illumination, or each of them may create a clearly self-contained gradient of brightness values. The overall result can convey visual order. But the light sources may also interfere with one another by partly increasing or reversing the others' effects. This will make the shape of objects as well as their spatial interrelations incomprehensible. If several light sources are to cooperate, the photographer endeavours to organize them in a hierarchy, giving one of them the leading part of the "motivating source" and clearly weaker supporting roles to the others.

Shadows

Shadows may be either attached or cast. Attached shadows lie directly on the objects by whose shape, spatial orientation, and distance from the light source they are created. Cast shadows are thrown from one object onto another, or from one part onto another of the same object. Physically both kinds of shadow are of the same nature; they come about in those places of the setting where light is scarce. Perceptually they are quite different. The attached shadow is an integral part of the object, so much so that in practical experience it is generally not noted but simply serves to define volume. A cast shadow, on the other hand, is an imposition by one object upon another, an interference with the recipient's integrity.

By means of a cast shadow one house reaches across the street to streak its opposite number, and a mountain may darken the villages in the valley with an image of its own shape. Thus cast shadows equip objects with the uncanny power of sending out darkness. But this symbolism becomes artistically active only when the perceptual situation is made comprehensible to the eye. There are two things the eye must understand. First, the shadow does not belong to the object on which it is seen; and second, it does belong to another object, which it does not cover. Often the situation is understood intellectually but not visually. Figure 227 indicates the outlines of the two main figures of Rembrandt's *Night Watch*. On the uniform of the lieutenant we see the shadow of a hand. We can understand that it is cast by the gesticulating hand of the captain, but to the eyes the relation is not obvious. The shadow hand has no meaningful connection to the object on which it appears. It may look like an apparition from nowhere, because it acquires meaning only when related to the captain's hand. That hand is some distance away; it is not directly connected to the shadow, and, because of its foreshortening, is quite different in shape. Only if (1) the beholder has a clear awareness, conveyed to him by the picture as a whole, of the direction from which the light is falling, and (2) the projection of the hand evokes its objective three-dimensional shape, can the hand and its shadow be truly correlated by the eyes. Of course Figure 227 is unfair to Rembrandt in singling out two figures and showing one shadow in isolation from the impressive display of light of which it is a part. Nevertheless, shadow effects of this kind strain the capacity for visual comprehension to its limit.

Cast shadows have to be used with caution. In the simplest cases they are directly connected to the object from which they derive. The shadow of a man meets his feet on the ground; and when the ground is even and the rays of the sun fall at an angle of about forty-five degrees, the shadow will produce an undistorted image of its master. This duplication of a living or dead thing

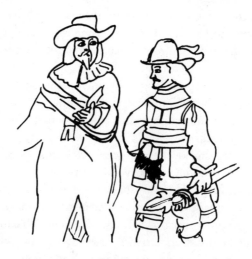

Figure 227

by an object that is tied to it and imitates its motions and at the same time is curiously transparent and immaterial has always attracted attention. Even under optimal perceptual conditions, shadows are not spontaneously understood as an effect of lighting. It is reported that certain tribesmen of western Africa avoid walking across an open square or clearing at noontime because they are afraid of "losing their shadow," that is, of seeing themselves without one. Their knowledge that shadows are short at noon does not imply understanding of the physical situation. When asked why they are not equally afraid when the darkness of the evening makes shadows invisible, they may reply that there is no such danger in darkness, because "at night all shadows repose in the shadow of the great god and gain new power." After the nightly "refill" they appear strong and big in the morning—that is, daylight feeds on the shadow rather than creating it.

Human thinking, perceptual as well as intellectual, seeks the causes of happenings as close to the place of their effects as possible. Throughout the world the shadow is considered an outgrowth of the object that casts it. Here again we find that darkness does not appear as absence of light but as a positive substance in its own right. The second, filmy self of the person is identical with or related to his soul or vital power. To step on a person's shadow is a serious offense, and a man can be murdered by having his shadow pierced with a knife. At a funeral, care must be taken to avoid having a living person's shadow caught by the lid of the coffin and thus buried with the corpse.

Such beliefs must not be ignored as superstitions but accepted as indications of what the human eye spontaneously perceives. The sinister appearance of the ghostly darker self in the movies, on the stage, or in surrealist painting keeps exercising its visual spell even on people who have studied optics in school; and Carl Gustav Jung uses the term "shadow" for "the inferior and less commendable part of a person."

As to the soberer properties of cast shadows, we note that, like attached shadows, they define space. A shadow cast across a surface defines it as plane and horizontal or perhaps as crooked and sloping; thereby it indirectly creates space around the object by which it is cast. It operates like an additional object creating a ground by lying on it. In Figure 228 the rectangle a lies flat on a frontal plane or at least creates no articulate space around itself. In b there is a clearer detachment from the ground, partly because of the contrast created by the black bar and partly because the obliqueness of the small edge suggests depth. But on the whole, b shows much less three-dimensionality than c or d, for the reason that the rectangular pattern formed by the bar and its shadow is simple and stable and can hardly be further simplified by more depth. In c

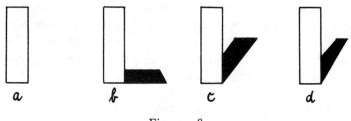

Figure 228

the three-dimensional version eliminates an oblique angle and allows the black bar to be seen as a complete rectangle. In *d* the shadow converges—an additional distortion, which makes straightening-out by depth even more compelling. In other words, the solid and its shadow function as one object, to which the rules for the spatial appearance of objects apply. Figure 229 shows how effectively shadows create space by defining the difference between vertical and horizontal and by contributing to the size gradients of convergent perspective.

A word about the convergence of shadows. Since the sun is so far away that within a narrow range of space its rays are practically parallel, its light produces an isometric shadow projection; that is, lines that are parallel in the object are also parallel in the shadow. But like any perceived thing a shadow is subject to perspective distortion, and therefore will be seen as converging from its base of contact with the object when it lies behind the object and as diverging when it lies in front of it. In addition, a near source of light, such as a lamp or a fire, will produce a pyramidal family of rays and consequently shadows of divergent physical shape. This objective divergence will be either increased, or compensated by perspective, depending upon the position of the shadow in relation to the observer.

Figure 230 shows that illumination adds the effects of another pyramidal system to those resulting from the convergence of shape. Just as the shape of the cube is deformed because its physically parallel edges meet in a vanishing point, so the shape of its cast shadow is deformed by converging toward another focusing point, created by the location of the light source. Illumination also distorts the homogeneous local brightness of the cube by darkening parts of its surface with attached shadows. In both perspective and illumination the structure of the distorting system is simple enough in itself to be distinguished by the eye from the constant properties of the object. The result is a two-fold visual subdivision. Both the shape and the local brightness of the object are

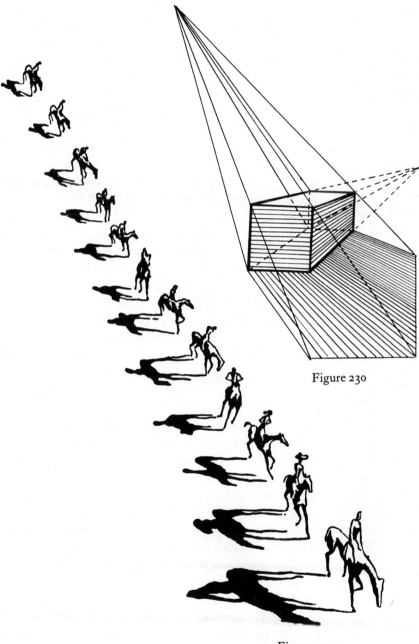

Figure 230

Figure 229

distinguished by the eyes from modifications imposed by spatial orientation and illumination.

Not only do the brightness patterns of shading get entangled with the brightness and darkness values of the object itself, but they also interfere with the clarity of the object's local colors and their interrelations. When painters began to create volume and space by means of illumination effects, this technique of chiaroscuro was soon found to disturb color composition. As long as shadows were conceived as applications of monochromatic darkness, they inevitably muddied and obscured the colors and thereby not only tampered unattractively with the saturation of the colors, but also dulled their identity. A blue coat shaded with black no longer looked truly blue and lost the simple homogeneity of its local color; an arm or leg underlaid with dark paint neither looked the color of skin nor presented a good, clear hue of pink.

It is quite possible that Leonardo da Vinci, whom Heinrich Wölfflin has called the father of chiaroscuro, was unable to complete some of his paintings because the desire to produce strong spatial relief by shading coincided in time with a new sensitivity to color organization. The unification of the two competing systems of pictorial form came gradually. Shadow was redefined as a modification of hue—a development that led from Titian by way of Rubens and Delacroix to Cézanne. "Light does not exist for the painter," wrote Cézanne to Emile Bonnard. In our own century, the color style of the Fauves often eliminated the problem by omitting all shading and by composing with saturated hues.

Painting without Lighting

Although the painter who uses effects of illumination is very much aware of their power, the influence of light and shadow is experienced in everyday life mostly in very practical ways. The seeking or avoidance of light is common at all levels of the animal world, and in the same way man seeks the light when he wants to see or be seen and avoids it otherwise. For these practical purposes, however, light is merely a means of dealing with objects. Light and shadow are observed, but hardly consciously for their own sake. They define the shape and spatial position of things and are consumed in this service. The naive observer is unlikely to mention them when asked to give a carefully detailed description of what he sees; he assumes that he is being asked about objects and their adherent characteristics.

Ernst Mach reports: "In my earliest youth the shadows and lights on pictures appeared to me as spots void of meaning. When I began to draw I regarded shading as a mere custom of artists. I once drew the portrait of our pastor, a friend of the family, and shaded, from no necessity, but simply from having seen something similar in other pictures, the whole half of his face black. I was subjected for this to a severe criticism on the part of my mother, and my deeply offended artist's pride is probably the reason that these facts remained so strongly impressed upon my memory." Early art everywhere represents objects by their outlines, local brightness and local color, and some cultures have retained this practice even at high levels of refinement. In the art work of young children, brightness values serve mostly to mark differences. Dark hair may be set off against a bright face. Light sources, such as the sun or a lamp, are often shown as sending out rays, but no indication is given that it is these rays which make objects visible. The same is true for early Egyptian painting. On Greek vases figures are detached from the background by strong contrast, but these differences appear as the result of object brightness or darkness, not of illumination. Literary sources indicate that in the course of the centuries Greek painters learned the use of shadows, and the results of these discoveries can be seen in the Hellenistic wall pictures or the Egyptian mummy portraits around the second and first centuries B.C. Here the chiaroscuro was handled with a virtuosity not rediscovered until the late Renaissance.

As the need to convey the roundness of solids arises, shading is introduced, later complemented by heightening. In physical space these effects are produced by illumination. But the use of shading does not necessarily originate from the observation of nature, and certainly is not always used in accordance with the rules of illumination. Rather, we can assume that after working for a while with the perceptually simpler means of line contour and homogeneously colored surfaces, the painter will discover the spatial virtues of unevenly distributed brightness. The perceptual effect of gradients becomes apparent to the eyes. Dark shading will make the surface recede toward the contours. Highlights will make it protrude. These variations are used to create roundness or hollowness; they do not necessarily imply a relation to a light source. Often the distribution of "shadows" follows different principles. Shading may issue from the contour all around the pattern, and give way gradually to lighter values toward the center. In the symmetrical compositions of medieval painters the figures at the left often have their highlights on the left side, those on the right on the right side; or in the laterally foreshortened faces the larger half may always appear bright, the narrower dark. Thus, in adapting itself to the requirements of composition and shape, brightness is often distributed in a way that would be termed incorrect if judged by the laws of illumination.

The same is true when brightness differences are used to detach overlapping objects from each other. When a depth interval between objects of nearly identical brightness is to be shown, shading is often introduced. As Figure 231 indicates, the brightness contrast obtained in this manner serves to enhance the overlapping, and there is no need to justify the result as an effect of illumination. In fact, Henry Schaefer-Simmern has pointed out that a genuine pictorial conception of illumination can develop only after the formal properties of shading have been mastered. Following a lead by Britsch, he gives examples from Eastern paintings and European tapestries in which the principle of Figure 231 is applied to overlapping scales of rocks, buildings, and trees. To speak here simply of "shadows" is to overlook the main pictorial function of the device.

Such an interpretation of shading and contrast becomes particularly compelling when we find that even after the art of rendering illumination realistically has been acquired, some painters will use brightness values in a way that is not derived from the rules, and at time even contradicts them. James M. Carpenter has pointed out that Cézanne separated planes in space "by a gradual lightening or darkening of the further plane where the two overlap." Using an example similar to that of Figure 232, he showed that Titian had the same technique. Particularly striking are the darkening of the buildings next to the sky and the brightening of the castle-like structure in the back, which is thereby set off against the roofs. Carpenter also demonstrates that Cézanne sometimes darkened the ground behind a light figure and rounded a cheek in a portrait by applying a gradient of darkness, which is an "abstract" use of the perceptual device rather than the rendition of an effect of lighting; illustrations from Filippino Lippi and Rembrandt are given to prove that here, too,

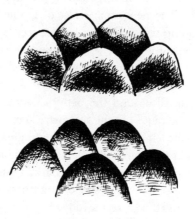

Figure 231

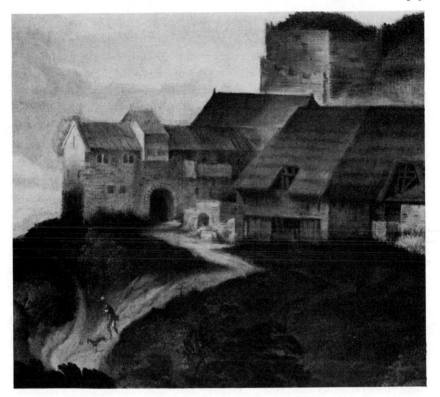

Figure 232
Titian. *Noli Me Tangere* (detail), 1511. National Gallery, London.

Cézanne was following a tradition. Somewhat later the cubists, as I mentioned earlier, used brightness gradients to show the mutual spatial independence of overlapping shapes.

Goethe once drew his friend Eckermann's attention to an inconsistency of the lighting in an engraving after Rubens. Most objects in the landscape were seen as illumined from in front and therefore as turning their brightest side toward the observer. In particular, the bright light falling on a group of laborers in the foreground was set off effectively against a dark foil. This contrast was achieved, however, by means of a large shadow, which fell from a group of trees toward the observer, in contradiction to the other light effects in the picture. "The double light," comments Goethe, "is indeed forced and, you might say, against nature. But if it is against nature, I will say at the same time that it is higher than nature."

The Symbolism of Light

During the early Renaissance, light was still used essentially as a means of modeling volume. The world is bright, objects are inherently luminous, and shadows are applied to convey roundness. A different conception is observable in the *Last Supper* of Leonardo da Vinci. Here the light falls as an active power from a given direction into a dark room, applying strokes of brightness to each figure, to the table top, and to the walls. The effect is pitched to the highest key in paintings by Caravaggio or Latour, who prepare the eyes for the electric spotlights of the twentieth century. This sharply focused light animates space with directed motion. It sometimes fractures the unity of bodies by tracing the boundary lines of darkness across the surfaces. It stimulates the sense of sight by playfully disfiguring familiar shape and excites it by violent contrast. A comparison with Hollywood movies is not entirely out of place, because in the one case as in the other, the impact of the dazzling rays, the dance of shadows, and the secret of darkness give tonic thrills to the nerves.

The symbolism of light, which finds such moving pictorial expression in the work of Rembrandt, probably goes as far back as the history of man. I mentioned earlier that in perception darkness does not appear as the mere absence of light, but as an active counterprinciple. The dualism of the two antagonistic powers is found in the mythology and philosophy of many cultures—for example, China and Persia. Day and night become the visual image of the conflict between good and evil. The Bible identifies God, Christ, truth, virtue, and salvation with light, and godlessness, sin, and the Devil with darkness. The influential philosophy of Neoplatonism, based entirely on the metaphor of light, found its visual expression in the use of illumination by daylight and candles in the churches of the Middle Ages.

The religious symbolism of light was, of course, familiar to the painters of the Middle Ages. However, the gold grounds, halos, and geometric star patterns—symbolic representations of the divine light—appeared to the eye not as effects of lighting, but as shiny attributes; on the other hand, the correctly observed light effects of the fifteenth and sixteenth centuries were essentially the products of curiosity, research, and sensory refinement. Rembrandt personifies the final confluence of the two sources. Divine light is no longer an ornament but the realistic experience of radiant energy, and the sensuous spectacle of highlights and shadows is transformed into a revelation.

Rembrandt's pictures typically present a narrow, dark scene, into which the beam of light carries the animating message of a beyond, unknown and invisible in itself but perceivable through its powerful reflection. As the light falls from above, life on earth is no longer in the center of the world but at its dark bottom. The eyes are made to understand that the human habitat is nothing but a valley of shadows, humbly dependent upon the true existence on the heights.

When the source of light is located inside the picture, the meaning changes. Now the life-giving energy establishes the center and the range of a narrow world. Nothing exists beyond the corners to which the rays reach. There is a *Holy Family* by Rembrandt in which the light seems to originate in the brilliantly lighted book from which Mary is reading, because the candle itself is hidden. The light of the Bible reveals the sleeping child in the cradle, and the listening Joseph is dwarfed by his own towering shadow, which is cast on the wall behind and above him. In another painting by Rembrandt, the light, again hidden, brightens the body of Christ, which is being taken down from the cross. The ceremony is performed in a dark world. But as the light falls from below, it heightens the limp body and imparts the majesty of life to the image of death. Thus the light source within the picture tells the story of the New Testament—that is, the story of the divine light transferred to the earth and ennobling it by its presence.

In Rembrandt's paintings, the objects receive light passively as the impact of an outer force, but at the same time they become light sources themselves, actively radiating energy. Having become enlightened, they hand on the message. The hiding of the candle is a means of eliminating the passive aspect of what is happening—the illuminated object becomes the primary source. In this way Rembrandt enables a book or a face to send out light without violating the requirements of a realistic style of painting. By this pictorial device he copes with the central mystery of the Gospel story, the light that has become matter.

How does Rembrandt obtain his glowing luminosity? I have already mentioned some of the perceptual conditions. An object appears luminous not simply by virtue of its absolute brightness, but by surpassing the average brightness established for its location by the total field. Thus the uncanny glow of rather dark objects comes about when they are placed in an even darker environment. Furthermore, luminosity results when brightness is not perceived as an effect of illumination. To this end, shadows must be eliminated or kept to a minimum. And the strongest light must appear within the confines of the object. Rembrandt frequently places a bright object in a dark field, keeps it almost free of shadow, and partially lights the objects around it. Thus in his *Wedding of Samson* Delilah is enthroned as a pyramid of light in front of a dark curtain, and the reflection of her splendor is seen on the table and the people around her. Similarly, in a *Toilet of Bathshebah* the body of the woman is singled out by a strong light, whereas the environment, including the two maids who minister to her, remains in the dark.

Glow is also associated with a lack of surface texture. Objects appear opaque and solid by means of texture, which establishes the frontal surface. A glowing object does not stop the glance by such an outer shell. Its limits are not clearly defined for the eyes. In David Katz's terms, it has "film color" rather than "surface color." Light seems to originate within the object at an indefinite distance from the observer. Rembrandt enhances luminosity by giving little detail to the areas of highest brightness. The indefiniteness of the outer surface endows his glowing objects with a transfigured, immaterial quality.

In a more didactic sense, illumination tends to guide attention selectively, in accordance with the desired meaning. An object can be singled out without having to be large or colorful or situated in the center. Similarly, secondary features of the scene can be subdued at will. All this without "surgical interventions," which would alter the inventory of the scene itself. Light can be made to fall on, or be withheld from, any object A given arrangement of dancers on the stage can be interpreted to the audience in different ways depending upon the scheme of lighting. Rembrandt uses this means of interpretation constantly without being much concerned about a realistic justification of the effect. In the aforementioned *Descent from the Cross* brilliant light falls on the fainting Mary, whereas the bystanders next to her remain relatively dark. Or we see Samson's hands brightly lighted as they explain a riddle to the wedding guests, while his face is kept in the dark because its contribution is secondary. In his representation of the Potiphar story Rembrandt translates the accusing words of the woman into visual language by throwing the strongest light on the bed (Figure 224).

In styles of painting that do not conceive of illumination, the expressive and symbolic character of brightness and darkness is rendered through properties adherent to the objects themselves. Death may appear as a figure clothed in black, or the whiteness of the lily may depict innocence. When illumination is represented, light and shadow tend to assume the task of producing these moods. An instructive example can be found in Dürer's engraving *Melencolia*. Traditionally the melancholic was given a black face, because it was assumed that a darkening of the blood—the word "melancholy" means literally "black bile"—was responsible for a depressed state of mind. Dürer places his melancholy woman with her back against the light so that her face is in the shadow. In this way the darkness of her face is at least partially justified by the absence of light.

For the realistic painter this method has the advantage of giving an object the degree of brightness that suits his purpose without interfering with its "objective" appearance. He can make a white thing dark without suggesting that it is dark in itself. The procedure is used constantly in Goya's etchings. In the movies also, back lighting serves to give a figure the sinister quality of darkness. The uncanny sensation obtained in this manner occurs in part because the dark figure is not visible positively as a solid material body with observable surface texture, but only negatively as an obstacle to light, neither round nor tangible. It is as though a shadow were moving in space like a person.

When darkness is so deep that it provides a foil of black nothingness, the beholder receives the compelling impression of things emerging from a state of non-being and likely to return to it. Instead of presenting a static world with a constant inventory, the artist shows life as a process of appearing and disappearing. The whole is only partly present, and so are most objects. One part of a figure may be visible while the rest is hidden in darkness. In the film *The Third Man* the mysterious protagonist stands unseen in a doorway. Only the tips of his shoes reflect a street light, and a cat discovers the invisible stranger and sniffs at what the audience cannot see. The frightening existence of things that are beyond the reach of our senses and yet exercise their power on us is represented by means of darkness.

Pictorial objects vanish not only into darkness but also into whiteness. In Far Eastern landscapes, most brilliantly in the "spattered ink" or *haboku* technique of the Japanese painter Sesshu, we see mountains emerge from a base hidden in fog. It would be quite misleading to say that in such instances "imagination completes" what the painter omitted. On the contrary, the meaning of the presentation depends precisely on the spectacle of objects emerging from nothingness to develop more and more articulate shape as they rise toward the peak. The heaviness of the mountain base is paradoxically replaced by the ethereal lightness of the white silk or paper, which acts as figure rather than ground but looks immaterial nevertheless. Thus the most gigantic formations on earth are made into apparitions.

Finally, two modern reinterpretations of illumination in painting should be mentioned. The impressionists played down the difference between light and shadow and blurred the contours of objects. They also replaced the variety of realistic textures with the uniform surface quality of small brushstrokes, which made the material differences between stone walls, trees, water, and sky vanish into uniformity. All these devices tend to replace the illumination of solid objects with a world of insubstantial luminosity. The effect is particularly strong in pointillism, the extreme form of the impressionist style. Here the pictorial unit is not the represented object. The picture consists of self-contained dots, each of which possesses only one brightness and color value. This even more thoroughly excludes the concept of an external, governing light source. Instead, each dot is a light source of its own. The picture is like a panel of radiant bulbs, each one equally strong and independent of the others.

In a very different way, painters like Georges Braque went beyond illumination, not by creating a universe of light, but by translating the darkness of shadows back into a property of the object. Figure 233a shows schematically an image of antagonism, in which black and white share as equal partners. We cannot tell whether we are seeing a black bottle hit by strong light from the right or a white bottle partly in the shade. Instead we see a dematerialized, flat object, independent of any outside source, maintaining its precarious unity against the powerful contrast of the two extreme brightness values. The ancient interplay of the powers of light and darkness is made to seize the single object, in which the conflict between oneness and duality creates a high level of dramatic tension, the clash of two opposites in an unconsummated union.

Light and shadow are no longer applied to the objects but constitute them. In the tracing after Braque's *Painter and Model* (Figure 233b), the dark self of the woman is thin, bounded by many concavities, actively presenting the profile of her face and stretching forth her arm. The bright woman is large, rounded by convexities, poised in a more static frontal position, and hiding her arm. In the man the dark self is dominant; his bright self is nothing but a broadening of the subordinate back contour. Both figures are tense, in themselves as well as in their relation to each other, with the antagonism of contrasting forces, which reflects a modern interpretation of the human community and the human mind.

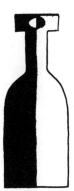

Figure 233*a*

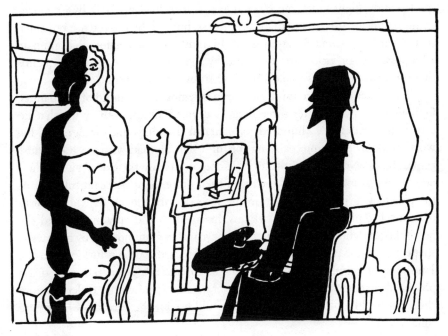

Figure 233*b*

VII   COLOR

If it is true that cats and dogs do not see colors, what is it they are missing? Of one thing we can be certain: the absence of color will deprive them of a most efficient dimension of discrimination. A ball rolling across a lawn can be spotted and caught much more surely if it is identified not only by its movement, shape, texture, and perhaps brightness, but also by the intense red color that sets it apart from the green grass. In addition, it is possible that animals who possess color vision are impressed by the powerfully enlivening quality that for us distinguishes a colorful world from a monochromic one.

This latter difference must have been foremost in the mind of the painter Odilon Redon when, after three decades devoted almost entirely to what he called "his blacks," i.e., hundreds of charcoal drawings and lithographs, his work suddenly burst into paintings of full color. He had written: "One must respect black. Nothing prostitutes it. It does not please the eye or awaken another sense. It is the agent of the mind even more than the beautiful color of the palette or prism." But when in the 1890's he abandoned the chilly purity of monochromatic light and darkness, he must have deeply appreciated the possibility of defining, say, the figure of a cyclopean giant not just by a fantastic shape, but by the particular color quality of an earthy brown lurking above a landscape of purple rocks; or the chance to create a green figure of death propelled through a world of burning orange—so profoundly different from the sober health of the spring colors he could use for the portrait of his young son.

From Light to Color

No one will ever be sure that his neighbor sees a particular color exactly the same way he himself does. We can only compare color relations, and even that raises problems. One can ask subjects to group colors that belong together or to match a certain nuance with an identical sample. Such procedures can avoid any reference to color names, but we cannot assume that different persons of similar background, let alone members of different cultures, have the same standards for what they consider "alike" or "the same" or "different." Within these limits, however, it is safe to state that color perception is the same for people of different ages, different backgrounds, or different cultures. Except for individual pathology, such as color blindness, we all have the same kind of retina, the same nervous system.

It is true, however, that when observers are asked to point out certain colors in the spectrum the results vary somewhat. This is so because the spectrum is a sliding scale, a continuum of gradations, and also because people mean different sensations by different color names.

Color names are somewhat indeterminate because the conceptualization of colors themselves is problematic. To be sure, the world of color is not simply an assortment of innumerable hues; it is clearly structured on the basis of the three fundamental primaries and their combinations. However, it takes a particular mental attitude to organize one's world of color according to these purely perceptual characteristics. Instead, a person's world is a world of objects, whose given perceptual properties matter in varying degrees. A particular culture may distinguish the colors of plants from those of the soil or water, but have no use for any other subdivision of hues—a perceptual classification that will be reflected in the vocabulary. An agricultural tribe may possess many words to describe subtle differences in the colors of cattle, but none to distinguish blue from green. In our own environment, certain occupations call for refined color distinctions and a correspondingly sophisticated vocabulary. Others call for none at all.

For our present purpose the most interesting difference in the conceptualizing of color relates to cultural development. Recent studies have suggested that the basic color names, relatively few in number, are common to all languages, but also that they cover different ranges of hues and that not all languages possess all these names. Anthropological research by Brent Berlin and Paul Kay indicates that color names do not occur in arbitrary selection. The most elementary nomenclature distinguishes only between darkness and lightness, and all colors are classified according to this simple dichotomy. When a language contains a third color name, it is always red. This new category absorbs the reds and oranges and most yellows, pinks, and purples, including violet. The remainder is divided between darkness and lightness (black and white).

If these data, gathered from twenty languages, are reliable, they tell us that the law of differentiation, which we applied to the development of form conception, holds also for color. At the earliest level only the simplest distinctions are made, and with each advance in differentiation the broader categories are limited to more specific ranges. Just as the rightangular relation of shapes stands at first for all angles but is confined later to the particular angle as one among others, so darkness and brightness at first embrace the whole realm of colors but eventually designate only the blacks, whites, and grays.

Shape is differentiated gradually, from the simplest structure to increasingly complex patterns. This seems to be true for color only in the quantitative sense. It is certainly simpler to divide the world of colors into only two categories than to employ six or eight. But no such rationale is evident in the sequence of colors discovered by Berlin and Kay. Why should red always be the first to modify the dark-light dichotomy? Is it the most conspicuous or the most practically relevant hue? Why should the next addition always be green or yellow? The languages of the six-color level were found to have names for dark, bright, red, green, yellow, and blue. Further differentiation completes the set of basic colors with brown, purple, pink, orange, gray.

The findings of Berlin and Kay support the observations of earlier writers, who discovered on the basis of such literature as the poems of Homer and of anthropological reports, that some civilizations seemed to lack certain color names. Red was well represented, but there was a deficiency of greens and blues. Some of those early explorers even suggested that in biological evolution, the human retina was responsive at first only to the long-wave colors and extended its range gradually—an untenable theory. We realize now that while the physiological mechanism of sight enables every unimpaired human being to distinguish thousands of nuances, the perceptual categories by which we grasp and conceptualize the sensory world develop from the simple to the complex.

Shape and Color

Strictly speaking, all visual appearance owes its existence to brightness and color. The boundaries determining the shape of objects derive from the eyes' capacity to distinguish between areas of different brightness and color. This is true even for the lines that define shape in drawings; they are visible only when the ink differs in color from the paper. Nevertheless, we can speak of shape and color as separate phenomena. A green disk on a yellow ground is just as circular as a red disk on a blue ground, and a black triangle is as black as a black square.

Since shape and color can be distinguished from each other, they can also be compared as perceptual media. If we look, first of all, at their power of discrimination, we acknowledge that shape lets us distinguish an almost infinite number of different individual objects. This is especially true for the thousands of human faces we can identify with considerable certainty on the basis of minute differences in shape. By objective measurement we can identify the fingerprints of one specific person among millions of others. But if we tried to construct an alphabet of twenty-six colors rather than shapes, we would find the system unusable. The number of colors we can recognize reliably and with ease hardly exceeds six, namely the three primaries plus the secondaries connecting them, even though the standard color systems contain several hundreds of hues. We are quite sensitive in distinguishing subtly different shades from one another, but when it comes to identifying a particular color by memory or at some spatial distance from another, our power of discrimination is severely limited.

This is so mainly because differences in degree are much harder to keep in mind than differences in kind. The four dimensions of color we can distinguish with confidence are redness, blueness, yellowness, and the gray scale. Even the secondaries can generate confusion because of their kinship to the primaries, for example, between a green and a blue or yellow; and by the time we try to tell a purple from a violet, only immediate juxtaposition allows assurance. This is evident in the color keying used for maps, charts, and other tools of orientation. On the other hand, when added to distinctions of shape, even a few crudely applied color dimensions will greatly enrich visual discrimination. An audience looking at a black-and-white film is often at a loss to identify the strange food the actors have on their plates. In signals, flags, uniforms, color extends the range of communicable differences.

By itself, shape is a better means of identification than color not only because it offers many more kinds of qualitative difference, but also because the distinctive characteristics of shape are much more resistant to environmental variations. Although the so-called constancy of shape is by no means as foolproof as is often thought, we have noted that people are remarkably capable of recognizing an object even though the angle from which they perceive it may present quite a different projection of it. We identify a human figure from almost every point of observation. What is more, shape is almost entirely unaffected by changes of brightness or color in the environment, whereas the local color of objects is most vulnerable in this respect.

Constancy of color does exist to some extent, not only for human beings but also for animals endowed with color vision. In a famous experiment by Katz and Révész, chickens were trained to peck only white grains of rice and to reject them when they were stained various colors. Presented with white grains that were illuminated by a strong blue light, the birds pecked without hesitation. Color constancy is aided by the physiological fact that the retina adapts to the given illumination. Just as sensitivity to light decreases automatically when the eyes are looking at a very bright field, so the different kinds of color receptors adapt their responses selectively when one particular color dominates the visual field. Confronted with a green light, the eyes decrease their response to greenness.

This compensation amounts to a leveling, which reduces the effect of colored lighting on the local color of objects. By the same token, however, we also perceive the color of the lighting itself incorrectly. An adaptation effect, described by Kurt Koffka and also by Harry Helson, makes us perceive the dominant color as "normal," that is, as more nearly colorless, and all the colors in the field as transposed in relation to this norm level. Adapted to red illumination, we see a gray surface in fact as gray, but only as long as its brightness equals the brightness prevailing in the field. If the gray surface is brighter, it is seen as red; if it is darker, it is seen as green.

In this connection I must also refer to the effect of light intensity on color. Under strong illumination the reds look particularly bright because the cones of the retina do most of the work and are most responsive to the longer wavelengths. Dim light will bring the greens and blues to the fore but also make them appear more whitish because now the retinal rods, which are more responsive to light of shorter wavelength, share in the work, although they do not contribute to the perception of hue. (This phenomenon is named after Johannes E. Purkinje, who first described it.)

For all these reasons, an artist's colors are very much at the mercy of the prevailing illumination, whereas his shapes are little affected by it. Wolfgang Schöne has pointed out that the color scheme of medieval murals is entirely altered when the original windows are replaced with modern colorless glass. The church windows of the early Middle Ages had a greenish or yellowish tinge and were translucent but not transparent. Needless to say, the stained glass of later centuries influenced illumination spectacularly, and not only mural painting but also book illustrations were adapted to the prevailing light conditions.

When a painting by Monet or Van Gogh done at strong daylight is seen under the color of tungsten lamps, we cannot pretend to perceive the hues intended by the artist; and as the colors change, so does their expression and organization. Artists of our time who assert that their pictures, produced under electric light, can be viewed in daylight without loss imply that color qualities and color relations matter to their work only in the crudest, most general sense.

We conclude that for practical purposes shapes are a more reliable means of identification and orientation than color, unless color discrimination is limited to the fundamental primaries. When a person is called upon to choose between shape relations and color relations, his behavior will be influenced by a variety of factors. In an experimental setup used by several investigators, children were presented, for example, with a blue square and a red circle. They were asked whether a red square was more like the square or like the circle. Under such conditions, children up to three years of age chose more often on the basis of shape, whereas those between three and six selected by color. Children over six were disturbed by the ambiguity of the task, but more often opted for shape as their criterion. In reviewing the evidence, Heinz Werner suggested that the reaction of the youngest children is determined by motor behavior and thus by the "graspable" qualities of the objects. Once the visual characteristics have become dominant, the majority of preschool children are directed by the strong perceptual appeal of the colors. But as culture begins to train the children in practical skills, which rely on shape much more heavily than on color, they turn increasingly to shape as the decisive means of identification.

More recent work by Giovanni Vicario has shown that the outcome of such experiments depends partly on which shapes are used. For example, when a child has to choose between a triangle and a circle rather than between a square and a circle, attributions on the basis of shape rather than color will increase. Apparently it is easier to neglect the difference between square and circle than that between triangle and circle.

Choices between color and shape can also be studied in the inkblot test. Some of the Rorschach cards give the observer an opportunity to base his description of what he sees on color at the expense of shape, or vice versa. One person may identify a pattern by its contour, even though the color contradicts the interpretation; another may describe two symmetrically placed blue rectangles as "the sky" or "forget-me-nots," thus neglecting shape in favor of color. Rorschach and his followers, whose observations were originally made on mental patients, assert that this difference in reaction is related to one in personality. Rorschach found that a cheerful mood makes for color responses, whereas depressed people more often react to shape. Color dominance indicated an openness to external stimuli. Such people are said to be sensitive, easily influenced, unstable, disorganized, given to emotional outbursts. A preference for shape reactions in patients goes with an introverted disposition, strong control over impulses, a pedantic, unemotional attitude.

Rorschach offered no theoretical explanation for the relationship he posited between perceptual behavior and personality. Ernest Schachtel, however, has suggested that the experience of color resembles that of affect or emotion. In both cases we tend to be passive receivers of stimulation. An emotion is not the product of the actively organizing mind. It merely presupposes a kind of openness, which, for example, a depressed person may not have. Emotion strikes us as color does. Shape, by contrast, seems to require a more active response. We scan the object, establish its structural skeleton, relate the parts to the whole. Similarly, the controlling mind acts upon impulses, applies principles, coordinates a variety of experiences, and decides on a course of action. Broadly speaking, in color vision action issues from the object and affects the person; but for the perception of shape the organizing mind goes out to the object.

A literal application of this theory might lead to the conclusion that color produces an essentially emotional experience, whereas shape corresponds to intellectual control. Such a formulation seems too narrow, particularly with reference to art. It is probably true that receptivity and immediacy of experience are more typical for color responses, whereas active control characterizes the perception of shape. But a picture can be painted or understood only by actively organizing the totality of color values; on the other hand, we passively surrender in the contemplation of expressive shape. Instead of speaking of color responses and shape responses, we may more appropriately distinguish between a receptive attitude to visual stimuli, which is encouraged by color but applies also to shape, and a more active attitude, which is prevalent in the perception of shape but applies also to color composition. More generally, it is probably the expressive qualities (primarily of color, but also of shape) that spontaneously affect the passively receiving mind, whereas the tectonic structure of pattern (characteristic of shape, but found also in color) engages the actively organizing mind.

It is tempting to explore these correlations between perceptual behavior and personality structure in the arts. The first attitude might be called a romantic one; the second, classicist. In painting, we might think, for example, of the approach of Delacroix, who not only bases his compositions on striking color schemes but also stresses the expressive qualities of shape, as against Jacques Louis David, who conceives mainly in terms of shape, employed for the relatively static definition of objects, and subdues and schematizes color.

Matisse has said: "If drawing is of the spirit and color of the senses, you must draw first, to cultivate the spirit and to be able to lead color into spiritual paths." He is voicing a tradition which holds that shape is more important and more dignified than color. Poussin said: "The colors in painting are, as it were, blandishments to lure the eyes, as the beauty of the verses in poetry is a lure for the ears." A Germanic version of this view can be found in the writings of Kant: "In painting, sculpture, and indeed in all the visual arts, in architecture, horticulture, to the extent to which they are fine arts, design is essential, for design serves as the foundation of taste only by the pleasures deriving from shape, not by the entertainment of sensation. The colors, which illuminate the pattern of outlines, belong to the stimulation. They may animate the sensation of the object but cannot make it worthy of contemplation and beautiful. Rather they are often greatly constrained by the requirements of beautiful shape and, even where stimulation is admitted, ennobled only by shape."

Given such views, it is not surprising that we find shape identified with the traditional virtues of the male sex, color with the temptations of the female. According to Charles Blanc, "the union of design and color is necessary to beget painting just as is the union of man and woman to beget mankind, but design must maintain its preponderance over color. Otherwise painting speeds to its ruin: it will fall through color just as mankind fell through Eve."

How Colors Come About

There is no need here to describe in detail the principles of optics and neurophysiology by which color perception has been explained in the past and is explained today. However, some general features, helpful in clarifying the overall character of the color phenomenon, are easily overlooked as the student of the arts tries to pick his way through the technicalities of atomic particles and wavelengths, cones and rods, lights and pigments. Moreover, certain key concepts have commonly been presented in a misleading manner.

The names of three of the early pioneers of color theory can stand for the three principal components of the process to be explained. Newton described colors as due to properties of the rays that compose light sources; Goethe proclaimed the contribution of the physical media and surfaces encountered by the light as it travels from its source to the eyes of the viewer; and Schopenhauer foresaw in a fanciful though uncannily prophetic theory the function of retinal responses in the eyes.

"As the rays of light differ in degrees of refrangibility," wrote Newton in his report of 1672 to the Royal Society, "so they also differ in their disposition to exhibit this or that particular color. Colors are not qualifications of light, derived from refractions, or reflections of natural bodies (as it is generally believed) but original and connate properties, which in divers rays are divers. Some rays are disposed to exhibit a red color and no other; some a yellow and no other, some a green and no other, and so the rest. Nor are there only rays proper and particular to the more eminent colors but even to all their intermediate gradations."

This meant that what Newton recognized to be primary for the purposes of the physicist was not the undivided and essentially colorless light source, acknowledged by direct experience, but the many inherently different kinds of rays, which he characterized and teased apart by means of their different degrees of refrangibility. Color was not what came about in vision when the original white light was deformed or mutilated by contingent circumstances. It was a sensation corresponding to a constituent attribute of any kind of light. It was hidden from sight only because different kinds of light were thrown together and thereby neutralized one another's particular character.

To assert that the "white" daylight was composed of the colors of the rainbow was against all visual evidence, and therefore Newton's theories encountered opposition. A century after Newton, the poet Goethe, accustomed to putting his trust in the direct testimony of the senses, rose in defense of the purity of sunlight. To him this was a distinctly moral issue. He also could not free himself of the Aristotelian prejudice that since all colors were darker than light, they could not be contained in it. I have mentioned before that to the naive observer darkness is not the absence of light but a substantial, physically real opponent. Goethe referred with approval to the Jesuit father Athanasius Kircher, who in the seventeenth century had described color as *lumen opacatum*, i.e. shaded light; and he adopted the Aristotelian notion that colors originate from the interaction of light and darkness. Colors, he said, are the "deeds and afflictions of light," and the afflictions were what took place when the virginal purity of light was subjected to somewhat opaque and hazy media and to partial absorption by reflecting surfaces.

There is an endearing poetic truth to Goethe's optic fantasies, and nobody has spoken more eloquently than he of the vicissitudes suffered by light as it wends its way through the world of physical impediments, penetrating and bouncing back and changing its nature in the process. But it was the young philosopher Schopenhauer who, having devoted himself to color theory at Goethe's suggestion, went beyond the master by speculating about the decisive role of the retina in the creation of color experience. Pleading the importance of the subjective, by which alone the objective exists, Schopenhauer proposed that the sensation of white comes about when the retina responds with full action, whereas black results from the absence of action. And pointing to the complementary colors produced by afterimages, he proposed that pairs of complementary colors come about by qualitative bipartitions of retinal function. Thus red and green, being of equal intensity, divided retinal activity into equal halves, whereas yellow and violet were produced by a ratio of three to one and orange and blue in the ratio of two to one. This led to the following scale:

Black	*Violet*	*Blue*	*Green*	*Red*	*Orange*	*Yellow*	*White*
0	¼	⅓	½	½	⅔	¾	I

Schopenhauer was unable to offer even the germ of a physiological theory. He admitted that "for the time being these ratios cannot be proved but must put up with being called hypothetical." But his scale of quantitative differences is of interest to us even now, and his basic conception of complementary pairs in retinal functioning strikingly anticipates the color theory of Ewald Hering. Hering proposed that "the visual system embodied three qualitatively distinct processes, and that each of these physiological processes is capable of two opponent modes of reaction. By analogy with plant metabolism, he described the opponent modes of response as catabolism and anabolism, respectively" (Hurvich and Jameson).

In his treatise on the theory of the light sense, Hering stated: "All rays of the visible spectrum have a dissimilating effect on the black-white substance, but the different rays to a different degree. But only certain rays have a dissimilating effect on the blue-yellow or the green-red substance, certain others have an assimilating effect, and certain rays none at all." In the opinion of color specialists, Hering's opponent-process theory is needed to complement the triple-receptor theory of Thomas Young, to which I shall refer in a moment, in order to account for the facts observed in color vision.

The Generative Primaries

For our present purpose we must be concerned with two principles underlying the optics, physiology, and psychology of the various color theories, namely the primary colors and complementarity. A great deal of confusion has been perpetuated by the term "primaries," which has been applied to two totally different concepts. One must draw a clear-cut distinction between *generative primaries* and *fundamental primaries*. By generative primaries I shall mean the colors needed to produce a large range of colors physically or physiologically; whereas fundamental primaries are the basic pure colors on which the sense of sight builds the organization of color patterns perceptually.

Generative primaries refer to the processes by which colors come about; funda-
mental primaries are the elements of what we see once colors appear in the
visual field. The latter will be discussed when I deal with color composition in
visual art; only the former are at issue now.

All systems of color theory and all practical procedures for the generation
of colors are based on the principle that a small number of hues is sufficient to
produce by combination a full or sufficiently large number of them. Neither
man nor nature could afford to use a mechanism that would provide a special
kind of receptor or generator for each color shade. There is nothing inviolable
about either the number or the nature of generative primaries. As I have mentioned, the Hering theory of color vision calls for sensitivity to six basic colors:
black and white, blue and yellow, green and red. Helmholtz, in endorsing the
trichromatic theory of Thomas Young, warned against the popular conviction
that the basic pure colors, red, yellow, and blue, were the ones naturally best
suited for the job. He pointed out, for example, that green could not be obtained by combining a pure blue and a pure yellow light. In fact, Young had
concluded from his experiments with colored lights, which he combined by
projecting them on a screen, that white light could be composed of "a mixture
of red, green, and violet only, in the proportion of about two parts red, four
green, and one violet."

These same three colors, red, green, and violet, were proposed by Young
and later by Helmholtz as being the most likely generative primaries for color
vision. Neither scientist could attempt to prove anatomically that this was so.
Only in the 1960's, experiments established that "color vision in vertebrates is
mediated by three light-sensitive pigments segregated in three different kinds
of receptor cells in the retina, and that one of these pigments is primarily responsible for sensing blue light, one for sensing green, and one for red" (Mac-
Nichol). Note here that color names such as "blue" or "violet" mean little
unless we know exactly which shade of color they refer to. Only by measuring
the corresponding spectral wavelengths can one get objective descriptions. The
experiments indicate that the three kinds of color receptor are most sensitive
to light of about 447 millimicrons (blue-violet), 540 (green), and 577 (yellow).
Each of these numerical values represents the peak of a sensitivity curve that
covers a fairly wide range of the spectrum and overlaps with the other two.
Thus the curve peaking in the yellow extends far enough into the red region
of the spectrum to let the corresponding type of receptor cell sense red as
well. The exact wavelengths obtained vary somewhat from experimenter to
experimenter.

These particular three generative primaries have proved their worth in biological evolution. In principle, however, any three colors will serve, according to James Clerk Maxwell, as long as no one of them can be matched by a mixture of the other two. Two primaries will suffice if a crude result is sufficient; more primaries will produce a more subtly faithful image. It is a matter of balancing economy against quality.

Addition and Subtraction

Which colors will best generate the whole range depends also on whether colors are combined by addition or by subtraction. Here again, misinformation is rampant. Particularly misleading is the statement that lights mix additively whereas pigments mix subtractively. Actually one can combine lights additively by superimposing them on a projection screen; but the colored light filters one may use to obtain them act subtractively upon the light passing through them. Similarly, two or three colored filters arranged in sequence subtract from the light. On the other hand, the particles of the pigments mixed by the painter or the color spots used in color printing are partly juxtaposed and partly superposed in so intricate a combination of addition and subtraction that the result is difficult to predict.

In *additive* combination, the eye receives the sum of the light energies that gather in one place, e.g., on a projection screen. Therefore the result is brighter than each of its components. Under ideal conditions a suitable combination of components produces white or light gray. For example, an additive combination of blue and yellow elements will do so. If one arranges segments of different color and brightness on a rotating disk, they will combine in proportion to the size of the surface they cover on the disk. The colors received by the sense of sight are the result of an additive process because the three kinds of color receptors, placed side by side in the central area of the retinal surface, pool the stimuli they receive. Thus, light stimulating all three kinds of receptor in the proper ratio will cause the sensation of white.

Subtraction produces color sensations by what is left over after absorption. Stained-glass windows are colored filters, which diminish the light passing through them from the outside. The local colors of objects result from the light they reflect after their surfaces have swallowed their share of the illumination; a red surface swallows everything but the wavelengths corresponding to red. The three generative primaries best suited for subtractive filters are a greenish blue (cyan), a yellow, and a magenta, any two of which combine by subtraction to blue, red, and green, respectively. Thus the colors that finally make the picture are more or less the same as the generative primaries of the additive process.

Additive color combination comes about according to a few simple rules, which depend entirely on the kind of stimulus produced in the eye by the participating colors. The result of subtraction, on the other hand, depends not just on how the colors look, but on their spectral constitution. As Manfred Richter has pointed out, if two colors that look alike are made up of different spectral components, they may yield different results when combined subtractively with the same third color. And whereas the outcome of addition corresponds to the sum of the spectra of the individual lights, that of subtraction derives from the product of the transmissivities for the filters involved. In view of this fact, George Biernson has suggested that the subtractive color combination might more aptly be called "multiplicative."

Generative Complementaries

If the reader is still with me, I would like now to point out that because the addition and subtraction of colors are such different processes, they involve different conditions for complementarity. When this difference is overlooked, one easily makes faulty assumptions or is confounded by apparent contradictions between statements that actually are referring to different facts. In a noteworthy article on the technique of the impressionists, J. Carson Webster has scored the widespread but mistaken belief that these painters obtained the effect of bright green by placing dabs of blue and yellow side by side and letting them fuse in the eye of the viewer. Webster finds that the impressionists did no such thing, for the good reason that the juxtaposition of blue and yellow would produce the additive effect of white or gray. Only by mixing blue and yellow pigments will one obtain green.

We distinguished between generative and fundamental primaries. The same distinction must now be applied to complementary colors. *Generative complementaries* are colors that in combination produce a monochromatic white or gray. *Fundamental complementaries* are colors that, in the judgment of the eye, require and complete each other. To confuse these two notions is to invite unnecessary trouble. Thus a diagrammatic color circle derived from the results of the optical superposition of lights will designate yellow and blue as a complementary pair by presenting them in diametrical opposition. This will arouse protest from the painters, who will assert that in their color system the pairing of yellow and blue produces a partial and incomplete effect; for the painter, yellow is complementary to a violet or purple, and blue to orange. There is no contradiction here. The two parties are talking about different things.

Generative complementaries can be verified by various methods. Offhand one would not necessarily expect that the colors that add up to white or gray in the combination of lights are the same that do so when colored surfaces are rotated on a wheel. However, as far as one can tell from the published results, the different additive methods all yield the same results. Woodworth and Schlosberg give the following complementary pairs:

red and blue green	yellow green and violet
orange and green blue	green and purple.
yellow and blue	

The results seem to agree also with the complementary pairs obtained by physiological mechanisms operating in the nervous system. This is true for simultaneous contrast, by which, for example, a small piece of gray paper placed on a green ground looks purple, and for afterimages, which according to Helmholtz yield the following complementary pairs:

red and blue green
yellow and blue
green and pink red.

Minor differences may be obscured by the fact that color names point only approximately to the exact hues observed in experiments.

It is remarkable that the results for generative complementaries should be in such consistent agreement since in at least one obvious respect they fail to correspond to the system of fundamental complementaries on which artists have insisted for good reasons. As I mentioned before, in that system the colors blue and yellow are by no means acceptable as complementaries, because red, the third fundamental primary, is missing from the combination. Apparently we are dealing here with a principle of visual relations which does not simply reflect the basic physiological opposites, manifest in the contrast phenomena, and which is not even disturbed by them.

For simplicity's sake I have spoken mostly of complementary pairs. But of course any number of colors, if suitably chosen, can combine to produce a monochromatic effect. The triplets operating in color vision, color printing, color television, are complementaries: any two of the three colors are complementary to the third. And Newton's principal discovery amounts to saying that every hue of the spectrum is complementary to all the rest of them together. Finally, it must be noted that complementarity holds not only for hue but also for brightness. A black square will produce a white one as its afterimage; and a light green will be contrasted by a dark red.

A Capricious Medium

Remarkably little has been written about color as a means of pictorial organization. There are descriptions of the palette used by particular painters; there are critical judgments praising or condemning an artist's use of color. But on the whole, one can only agree that, in the words of the art historian Allen Pattillo, "a large part of what has been written about painting, it is fair to say, has been written almost as if paintings were works in black and white." In some university art departments, black-and-white slides are preferred, either because colors "distract attention" from the shapes or, more sensibly, because the reproductions cannot be trusted.

Anyone working with color slides knows that no two slides of the same object look alike and that the differences are often far from subtle. Even under optimal conditions, the projection of transparencies on the screen transforms the subdued surface colors of paintings into rhapsodies of luminous jewelry, and the change in size also influences appearance as well as composition. The color reproductions in art books and magazines vary from excellent to miserable. Most of the time the viewer cannot judge how much of a truth or a lie he is being told.

Apart from false testimony, the originals themselves let us down. Most masterpieces of painting can be seen only through layers of darkened varnish, which has absorbed the dirt of the ages. We can have a more reliable view of fishes swimming in the muddy green water of an aquarium than we can of the Mona Lisa. No one has seen the Titians and Rembrandts for centuries, and the cleaning and restoring of paintings lead to notoriously unreliable results. Moreover, pigments are known to change chemically. By the time one has seen aggressive blues play havoc with the compositions of a Bellini or Raphael, or has seen a Harunobu print or Cézanne watercolor bleached beyond recognition by sunlight, one realizes that our knowledge of the pictures we possess is based to a considerable extent on hearsay and imagination.

I mentioned how thoroughly color is modified by illumination. Such modifications are not mere transpositions: light of a given color will affect different colors in a picture differently. Even more fundamental is the constant perceptual interaction among colors by contrast or assimilation. Place a triangle next to a rectangle, and you will find that they remain what they are, although the shapes influence each other somewhat. But a blue color placed next to a strong red veers toward the green, and two paintings hanging side by side on a wall may profoundly modify each other's colors.

A green hue that looked conservatively restrained in the sample booklet at the paint shop will overwhelm you when it covers the walls. The color trees and cones designed by Munsell and Ostwald as systematic presentations of colors according to hue, brightness, and saturation serve admirably to make us understand the complex interaction of the three dimensions; but a color seen in the context of its neighbors will change when placed in a different environment.

In no reliable sense can we speak of a color "as it really is"; it is always determined by its context. A white background is by no means a zero background but has strong idiosyncrasies of its own. Wolfgang Schöne has pointed out that in European paintings of the sixteenth to eighteenth centuries, the light is more important than the color and that therefore they are badly served by being displayed on white or very bright walls. Such mistreatment occurs, he says, at museums such as the Louvre, the Uffizi, the National Gallery in London, and the Hamburg Kunsthalle under the influence of modern painting, which stresses color rather than light—an effect enhanced by light-colored walls.

To all these uncertainties we must add the problems of perceptual and verbal identification. When observers are presented with a continuum of the rainbow colors, e.g. with a light spectrum, they do not agree on where the principal colors appear at their purest. This is true even for the fundamental primaries, especially for pure red, which may be located by observers anywhere between 660 and 760 millimicrons. Accordingly, any color name refers to a range of possible hues, so that verbal communication in the absence of direct perception is quite imprecise. Newton, for example, used "violet" and "purple" interchangeably—not a negligible matter since according to modern usage, violet is contained in the spectrum of light but purple is not. In our own time Hilaire Hiler has compiled a chart of color names which indicates, for example, that the color corresponding to the wavelength of 600 millimicrons is described by various authors as orange chrome, golden poppy, spectrum orange, bittersweet orange, oriental red, Saturn red, cadmium red orange, or red orange.

It will be evident why the discussion of color problems is fraught with obstacles and why so little useful discussion therefore takes place. However, these facts should not be taken to mean that what we see when we look at a painting is elusive, accidental, or arbitrary. On the contrary, in any successfully organized composition, the hue, place, and size of every color area as well as its brightness and saturation are established in such a way that all the colors together stabilize one another in a balanced whole. Ambiguities resulting from relations between parts compensate one another in the total context, and the complete work, when adequately perused, represents an objectively defined statement.

Individual colors resist abstractive generalization. They are tied to their particular place and time. But within any given order they behave lawfully and obey structural rules, which we sense intuitively, but about which we so far know much too little.

The Quest for Harmony

How are colors related to one another? Most theorists have dealt with this question as though it meant: Which colors go together harmoniously? They have tried to determine the assortments of colors in which all items blend readily and pleasantly. Their prescriptions were derived from the attempts to classify all color values in a standardized, objective system. The earliest of these systems were two-dimensional, depicting the sequence and some interrelations of hues by a circle or polygon. Later, when it was realized that color is determined by at least three dimensions—hue, brightness, and saturation—three-dimensional models were introduced. J. H. Lambert's color pyramid dates back to 1772. The painter Philipp Otto Runge published in 1810 an illustrated description of a spherical model, of which he wrote: "It will be impossible to think of any nuance produced by a mixture of the five elements (blue, yellow, red, white, and black) and not contained in this framework; nor can the whole system be represented by any other correct and complete figure. And since each nuance is given its correct relation to all the pure elements as well as to all mixtures, this sphere must be considered a universal chart, enabling anybody to orient himself as to the overall context of all colors." Later the psychologist Wilhelm Wundt also proposed a color sphere, as well as the kind of double cone developed after him by Ostwald. The color tree devised by the painter Albert Munsell in 1915 is also spherical in principle. A particularly attractive design of the overall system was done by Paul Klee for his students at the Bauhaus. He called it "Canon of Color Totality."

Although differing in shape, the various models of color classification are all based on the same principle. The central vertical axis presents the scale of achromatic brightness values from the lightest white at the top to the darkest black at the bottom. The equator, or the polygonal contour corresponding to it, contains the scale of hues at a medium brightness level. Each horizontal section through the solid presents all available degrees of saturation for all the hues at a given brightness level. The closer to the outer border of the section, the more saturated the color; the closer to the central axis, the greater its admixture with a gray of the same brightness.

Double pyramids, double cones, and spherical color solids, all agree in having their maximum girth at medium height and tapering off toward the poles. These idealizations neglect the fact that different hues reach their highest intensity of saturation at different brightness levels; thus yellow is purest at a relatively high level of brightness, purple blue at a lower one.

The cone and the pyramid on the one hand and the sphere on the other imply different theories of the rate at which the range of saturation changes with changing brightness. Again, the difference between the roundness of cone and sphere and the angularity of the pyramid distinguishes between theories that present the sequence of hues as a continuously gliding scale and others that emphasize three or four elementary colors as cornerstones of the system. Finally, there is a difference between regularly shaped color models, which provide space for all colors considered possible in principle, and irregularly shaped ones—like, for example, the Munsell color tree—which accommodate only the colors obtainable with the pigments at our disposal today.

These systems are supposed to serve two purposes: to allow an objective identification of any color, and to indicate which colors harmonize with one another. I am concerned here with the second function. Ostwald proceeded on the basic assumption that "two or more colors in order to harmonize must be equal with regard to essential elements." Uncertain whether brightness could be considered an essential element, he based his rules of harmony on identity either of hue or of saturation. This implied that all hues were consonant as long as they were equal in saturation. Even so, Ostwald believed certain hues fitted each other particularly well, notably those that faced each other in the color circle and represented a pair of complementaries. Any regular tripartition of the circle was also expected to yield an especially harmonious combination, because such triads too were complementary; that is, they added up to gray when mixed at equal parts. We note here the underlying assumption that colors which *generate* an achromatic color by their combination will also be *perceived* as fundamental complementaries.

Munsell, too, based his theory of harmony on the principle of common elements. Any horizontal circle around the axis of his color model represented a set of harmonious colors because it contained all the hues of equal brightness and saturation. Any vertical line defined harmony as the set of all colors differing only in brightness. And since every horizontal radius groups all the shades of saturation for a hue of given brightness, these gradients, too, were considered harmonious. However, Munsell went further, suggesting that "the center of the sphere is the natural balancing point for all colors," so that any straight line through the center would connect harmonizing colors. This meant that two complementary hues could be combined in such a way that the greater brightness of the one would be compensated by the lower brightness of the other. Munsell also admitted colors lying on a spherical surface "in a straight line," meaning presumably on a great circle.

Now harmony is indeed necessary, in the broad sense that all the colors of a composition must fit together in a unified whole if they are to be relatable to one another. It may also be true that all the colors used in a successful painting or by a good painter keep within certain limits, which exclude some hues, brightness values, or saturation levels. Since we now possess fairly reliable standards of objective identification, it would be valuable to measure the palette of specific works of art and specific artists. One such attempt has been made by Egbert Jacobson. What is much less probable is that the colors used by artists will in many cases be found to fit any such simple rules as those suggested by the systems of color harmony.

For one thing, the interrelation of colors is strongly modified by other pictorial factors. Both Ostwald and Munsell recognized the influence of size and suggested that large surfaces should have subdued colors whereas highly saturated colors should be used only in small patches. But it seems that even this one additional factor would so complicate the proposed rules of harmony as to render them practically useless—and there are many other relevant factors, which cannot be controlled by quantitative measurement as comfortably as size. The influential teacher Adolf Hölzel suggested at the beginning of the century that "a painting attains harmony only when all its colors, introduced in the proper artistic variety and arrangement, add up to white." If an approximation of this condition were tested experimentally by means of a color wheel, the results could be expected not to confirm the theory.

There are, however, more fundamental objections to the principle on which the rules of color harmony are based. This principle conceives of a color composition as a whole in which everything fits with everything else. All local relations between neighbors show the same pleasant conformity. Obviously this is the most primitive kind of harmony, suitable at best for the color schemes of nurseries and baby clothing. The art historian Max J. Friedländer has spoken of the "cheapest kind of harmony" in painting, obtained by the exaggerated warmth and darkness of colors as they are seen through layers of varnish. A color composition based on nothing but such a common denominator could describe only a world of absolute peace, devoid of action, static in mood. It would represent that state of deadly serenity at which, to borrow the physicist's language, entropy approaches an absolute maximum.

A glance at music may drive the argument home. If musical harmony

were concerned only with the rules determining which sounds go well together, it would be limited to a kind of aesthetic etiquette for dinner entertainment. Instead of telling the musician by which means he can express what, it
would teach him only how to be unobtrusive. Actually, this aspect of musical
harmony has proved to be of no permanent validity because it is dependent on
the taste of the period. Effects forbidden in the past are welcome today. Sometimes such rules are outmoded even as they are uttered. This has happened to
certain norms of color harmony as well. For example, Wilhelm Ostwald, com-
menting in 1919 on a rule which held that saturated colors should be presented
only in small bits, asserted that large-sized surfaces of pure vermilion, as found
in Pompeii, are crude, "and all the blindly superstitious belief in the artistic
superiority of the 'ancient' has been unable to keep attempts at the repetition of
such atrocities alive." In reading this today, we may recall a painting by
Matisse in which six thousand square inches of canvas are covered almost
completely and quite satisfactorily with a strong red, and we note that the
painting was done in 1911.

But—to return to music—the rules of suitable form are hardly concerned
with such matters. Arnold Schönberg says in his *Theory of Harmony*: "The
subject matter of the doctrine of musical composition is usually divided into
three areas: harmony, counterpoint, and the theory of form. Harmony is the
doctrine of the chords and their possible connections with regard to their
tectonic, melodic, and rhythmic values and relative weight. Counterpoint is
the doctrine of the movement of voices with regard to motivic combination.
. . . The theory of form deals with the disposition for the construction and
development of musical thoughts." In other words, musical theory is not concerned with which sounds go nicely together, but with the problem of giving
adequate shape to an intended content. The need for everything to add up to
a unified whole is only one aspect of this problem, and it is not satisfied in
music by drawing the composition from an assortment of elements that blend
smoothly in any combination.

To state that all the colors contained in a pictorial composition are part
of a simple sequence derived from a color system would mean no more—
and probably much less—than to say that all the tones of a certain piece of
music fit together because they belong to the same key. Even if the statement
were correct, still next to nothing would have been said about the structure of
the work. We would not know what the component parts were, or how these
parts were related to one another. Nothing would be known about the particular arrangement of the elements in space and time; and yet it is true that
the same assortment of tones will make a comprehensible melody in one

sequence and a chaos of sounds when shuffled at random, just as the same group of colors will produce a senseless jumble in one arrangement and an organized whole in another. Furthermore, it goes without saying that separations are as essential to composition as connections. When there are no segregated parts there is nothing to connect, and the result is an amorphous mash. It is useful to remember that the musical scale can serve as the composer's "palette" precisely because its tones do not all fit together in easy consonance but also provide discords of various degrees. The traditional theory of color harmony deals only with obtaining connections and avoiding separations, and is therefore at best incomplete.

The Elements of the Scale

How much do we know about the syntax of color—that is, about the perceptual properties that make organized patterns of color possible? First of all, what are the elementary units of color composition, and how many of them are there? The raw material comes in continuously gliding scales. The scale of hues is best known from the spectrum of sunlight. Brightness and saturation also produce scales, which lead from the lowest to the highest degrees of these properties. The maximum number of shades of gray the average observer can distinguish on the scale between black and white is, according to some sources, about 200. It is worth noticing that the number of hues distinguishable in a spectrum of pure colors between the two extremes of violet and purplish red is apparently somewhat smaller, about 160.

In music the number of tones used is considerably smaller than the number of pitch levels distinguishable by the human ear. Hence the familiar assertion that the musical medium is limited to a number of standardized elements, whereas the painter ranges freely through the entire continuum of colors: in the language of Nelson Goodman, that music has a disjoint notation whereas painting is syntactically dense. In a purely mechanical sense it is true, of course, that a painter can work with continuous gradations of color shades. However, if instead of scanning the surface with a colorimeter we consider the picture as it is actually perceived, we find that no visual organization is readable unless it is based on a limited number of perceptual values, which constitute the skeleton of the structure into which the finer gradations are fitted. The subtler mixtures appear as secondary inflections or variations of this fundamental scale, or they form a variety of chords in which the common elements remain discernible. Thus the color of a tablecloth may modulate in nuances composed of dozens of hues without relinquishing its basic whiteness, or a triad of green, violet, and yellow may combine in any number of proportions and yet remain visible in every spot of the picture as the underlying key.

The same kind of gradation is, of course, found in music if one listens to actual performance and does not confuse the music one hears with its notation. Especially in the practice of singers and string players, in the freely elaborating improvisations and harmonizing of jazz bands, in primitive and folk music, deviating intonation, slides, and glissandi are quite common and quite proper.

If we examine the raw material of color gradations, for example, in a spectrum, we observe that even though the sequence leads seamlessly from one hue to the next, certain colors are distinguished by their purity. By *purity* I intend two qualities, which need to be kept distinct: (1) an orange or a green looks pure when it is only itself, e.g., without an admixture that would make us speak of a reddish orange or a yellowish green; (2) a blue or yellow or red is pure because it is an irreducible element, i.e., it does not look like a mixture in the sense in which green looks like a combination of blue and yellow or purple like one of red and blue.

Such perceptual purity has nothing to do with physical or spectral purity. In the spectrum a single wavelength may produce a greenish blue that looks very much like a mixture, or a straight red may be obtained from the superposition of yellow and magenta filters. Nor does the distinction of the pure hues seem to be reflected in the wavelengths corresponding to them physically or in the way they are compounded by the additive cooperation of the retinal receptors.

The three indivisible, pure colors—blue, yellow, red—are the *fundamental primaries*. Whether green should be added as a fourth primary has been a matter of controversy, partly because the difference between fundamental and generative primaries was overlooked. For example, Hering presented a color circle, divided into four equal quadrants, in which blue and yellow opposed each other diametrically as a complementary pair. Although he warns against confusing "color as sensory quality and the materials to which the color seems to belong," he seems to have been influenced by the way colors are generated in additive combinations of lights, such as the opponent process of retinal receptors described in his own physiological theory. It may be true that a continuous scale of hues has a definite turning point in the pure green, whereas red may shift more smoothly in a continuous change of ratio through orange to yellow. If, on the other hand, a green is placed between a blue and a yellow, it behaves quite differently from a red in the same position. It will look intermediate between the two, whereas red will not. Perhaps green looks elementary under certain conditions and like a combination of yellow and blue under others.

Artists, from the English painter Moses Harris in the eighteenth century to Turner and Delacroix, Goethe, Van Gogh, and Albers, have been in agreement that the color system of the painter is based on the triad of red, blue, and yellow. "This really hurts!" said Paul Klee of the color circle based on four fundamentals.

Since the three fundamental primaries are indivisibly pure, they cannot be related to one another on the basis of a common denominator. Each of them completely excludes the other two. The only way in which they can be said to attract one another is by their roles as members of a complementary triad. This will be discussed shortly. Otherwise they can be related only through their brightness or saturation, not as hues.

However, a bridge can be established between any two of these fundamental primaries by means of mixtures. Orange will provide such a bridge between yellow and red. All mixtures of yellow and red can be ordered and compared according to their particular ratios of the two components. Green performs the same service for blue and yellow, and purple for red and blue.

The pure hues can never serve as such transitions. They are the poles. They stand isolated, or appear at the beginning or end of a sequence of color values; or they mark a climax at which the sequence turns in another direction. The red spots in Corot's landscapes are in contrast to, and in balance with, the colors surrounding them, but they are not connected with them by any path. Cézanne often indicates the highest point of a convexity—a cheek or an apple —by a pure red spot. Or he may put a pure blue in the depth of a hollow—for example, the corner of an eye. Unmixed hues also provide the composition with places of rest, with keynotes, serving as a stable frame of reference for mixtures. In Cézanne's late watercolors, which avoid unmixed hues, the anchorless violets, greens, and reddish yellows seem to move in a constant flux, with no rest anywhere except in the supreme balance of the picture as a whole.

The secondaries and other mixtures of the primaries derive their character from being perceived as hybrids. They have a vibrating duality, straining toward the stronger of their two poles or trying, by a constant dynamic interplay, to maintain the balance between their two parent hues. In a pictorial composition based on the secondary triad of orange, purple, and green, there is unceasing interaction among the three. Each color has a primary in common with each of the other two, so that each of them is pulled in two different directions. For example, the orange is pulled toward the yellow in the green and toward the red in the purple. Because of this common element, each pairing overlaps the other, and they can be said to slide into each other. At the same time, however, both neighbors of orange contain the third fundamental, namely blue, from which orange is excluded but toward which it strives for complementary completion (Figure 234). Hence the highly dynamic pattern of attractions and repulsions in such a scheme.

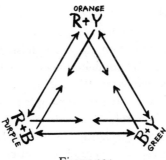

Figure 234

When the pure primaries act as subordinate elements in a composition based on the three secondaries, they function like the basic triad of the musical scale: they supply the framework for the various combinations and also increase tension by spelling out the foundation from which the mixtures deviate. When, on the contrary, the three primaries constitute the dominant theme, a classicist stability is obtained, as favored for instance by Poussin. In this case, the secondaries in a subordinate position help to enliven the static chord of the theme.

Syntax of Combinations

More specifically, I will refer again to the difference between mixtures that keep the two fundamentals in balance and those in which one of the fundamentals dominates. If for the sake of simplicity we exclude the additional hues resulting from combinations with black or white—such as the shades of brown—we obtain a system of nine principal mixtures:

BLUE	violet	blue + red	purple	RED
RED	yellow red	orange	red yellow	YELLOW
YELLOW	green yellow	green	green blue	BLUE

These mixtures can serve as stages of transition between the fundamentals. Compared with the first and third columns of mixtures, the balanced mixtures in the center column are fairly stable and self-contained, in spite of the interrelations mentioned above. The other six mixtures, in which one fundamental dominates the other, have the dynamic properties of "leading tones," that is, they appear as deviations from the dominant fundamental and exhibit a tension toward the purity of that fundamental. Just as in the key of C the B presses toward becoming C, so in the red-yellow scale a red yellow presses toward yellow, and a yellow red towards red.

We have observed that mixtures connect because of their common elements but may repel each other at the same time. Here we must consider the role of the constituents in each mixture. Compare the juxtaposition of a reddish yellow and a reddish blue with that of a reddish yellow and a bluish red. The first pair will be found to combine smoothly, whereas the second often seems to produce mutual repulsion. What is the difference? Both contain a common element—red. But in the first pair the red holds the same structural position in both colors; it is subordinate. In the second pair the structural positions are reversed; red is subordinate in one color, dominant in the other. Apparently this structural contradiction often produces a conflict or clash and therefore mutual repulsion, whereas in the first pair the correspondence of structural similarity lets the red establish a bridge between yellow and blue.

The two pairs of colors exemplify two types of mixture. The first type may be named "*Similarity of the Subordinate*" (Figure 235), the second, "*Structural Contradiction in One Common Element*" (Figure 236). It will be seen that in Figure 235, every pair lies equidistant from—that is, in symmetrical relation to—the poles determining the color of the subordinates. The two dominants of each pair are also equidistant from their poles. In Figure 236 there is no such simple structure. Each pair of mixtures is placed asymmetrically in relation to the three poles. The color shared by the two mixtures of each pair lies close to its pole for one mixture (dominant) and distant from it for the other (subordinate).

Let us carry this speculation a little further. What happens when we pair mixtures by "*Similarity of the Dominant*" (Figure 237)? For example, we place a yellow red in relation to a blue red. Here again each pair is placed symmetrically in relation to one pole, but this time the two mixtures lie close to that pole, that is, they share the dominant. The difference from the type illustrated in Figure 235 is that whereas similarity of the subordinate produces two essentially different colors related by the same admixture, similarity of the dominant produces two essentially identical colors distinguished by different admixtures. One color is torn into two different scales, for example, red into the red-yellow scale and the red-blue scale. The effect seems to be jarring and to produce some mutual repulsion.

"*Structural Inversion*" (Figure 238) takes place when the two elements exchange positions, that is, when the color that serves as subordinate in one mixture is the dominant of the other and vice versa. For instance, we combine a red blue and a blue red. At first glance one might expect that the double contradiction will lead here to a doubly strong repulsion. It should be observed, however, that in structural contradiction for one common element (Figure 236) the two mixtures always lie in two different scales, whereas here they lie in the same. Moreover, there is an element of symmetry in the exchange of structural places. Experiments may show that this leads to a harmonious relationship.

What about the juxtaposition of a pure fundamental with a leading tone that contains it? There are two possibilities. The fundamental may appear as the dominant in the mixture, for example, when one combines yellow and blue yellow (Figure 239). Or the fundamental may appear as the subordinate, for example, when yellow is combined with a yellow blue (Figure 240). In both circumstances the two colors to be combined lie on the same scale. Furthermore, in the first they are essentially alike. One hue dominates the pair. But when two such colors are coordinated, some disturbance arises from the fact that one of them is a pure fundamental whereas the other has an admixture of another color. They are asymmetrical. In the second pair there is even greater cause for a clash. The pure fundamental reappears as the subordinate in the mixture, which produces structural contradiction in addition to asymmetry. Here again, systematic experiments are needed to tell us how viewers react. Other combinations, such as those involving the three balanced mixtures (orange, green, and purple), should also be tested.

The effect of clash or mutual repulsion is not "bad," forbidden. On the contrary, it is a precious tool for the artist who wishes to make an articulate statement in color. It can help him detach the foreground from the background or the leaves of a tree from its trunk and branches, or keep the eye from traveling a compositionally undesirable road. However, the discord must fit the overall structure of the work as established by the other perceptual factors and the subject matter. If a discord occurs where a connection is required, or if the juxtaposition seems arbitrary, the result is confusion.

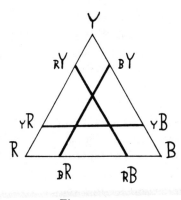

Figure 235

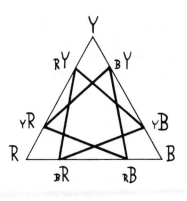

Figure 236

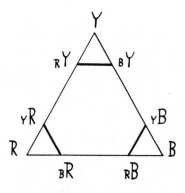

Figure 237

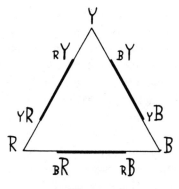

Figure 238

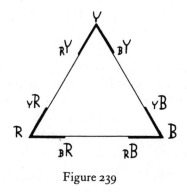

Figure 239

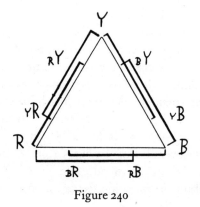

Figure 240

The Fundamental Complementaries

In most writings on our subject, complementary colors are defined by their capacity to generate an achromatic gray or white. Combined additively or subtractively, certain pairs or groups of colors will produce this effect optically, chemically, or physiologically. It is quite likely that these mechanisms have a bearing on the purely perceptual affinities I am about to discuss. After all, we assume that whatever is observed in experience must have its counterpart somewhere in the nervous system. Particularly since nothing in our conscious awareness accounts for the curious effect of mutual completion that we experience when certain colors are placed next to each other, this phenomenon is bound to be of physiological origin. As I have already pointed out, however, there are striking differences between the complementary pairs obtained, for example, through afterimages and those established by painters through their visual experience. There is, then, no simple relation between generative and fundamental complementaries, and in talking about the latter we do best to ignore the former.

It is merely by sensitive inspection that we notice the effect of mutual completion when certain pairs or triplets or larger groups of hues are presented. Any number of such combinations produce the same effect, but all of them can be ultimately reduced to one, namely the triplet of red, yellow, and blue.

These three fundamental primaries behave like the three legs of a stool. All three are needed to create complete support and balance. When only two of them are given they demand the third. The tension aroused by incompleteness of the triplet subsides as soon as the gap is filled. This encourages us even now to generalize and to conclude that there is something incomplete about any particular color whatever. Such incompleteness can be said to upset the equilibrium of the visual field as soon as a color appears by itself. The unique character of that color, its coldness or warmth, obtrusiveness or remoteness, affects us one-sidedly and points by its mere presence to the existence of a counterpart, which could re-establish balance in our visual experience.

Among all the groups of colors producing completeness the three fundamental primaries are unique. They are the only set of complementaries in which all constituents are pure hues and therefore totally exclude the other two. There is nothing yellow in the pure blue, nothing blue in the pure red, and so forth. At the same time the three colors require one another. This particular structural combination of mutual exclusion and attraction is the basis of all color organization—much as the particular structure of the diatonic scale is the basis of traditional Western music.

We see this color structure evolve from its base when we find that at the next higher level of organization, it groups each two primaries against the third (Figure 241). This produces a symmetrical system of three intertwining pairs of complementaries. Each pair consists of a pure hue and the balanced mixture of the other two: blue and orange, yellow and purple (or violet—whichever word one prefers for describing a balanced red-blue), blue and orange. This amounts to a two-level hierarchy, consisting of the three primary pure hues and three secondary balanced mixtures. Goethe describes the inter-relation of these six hues in his *Theory of Color*: "Single colors affect us, as it were, pathologically, carrying us away to particular sentiments. Vividly striving or softly longing, we feel elevated toward nobility or lowered toward the ordinary. However, the need for totality inherent in our organ guides us beyond this limitation. It sets itself free by producing the opposites of the particulars forced upon it and thus brings about a satisfying completeness."

(handwritten margin note: red + green)

This is the painter's system of the three basic complementary pairs, perhaps most clearly visualized in the triangular pattern that Delacroix drew in one of his sketchbooks (Figure 242). Whatever its physiological basis in the nervous system, the system recommends itself to the artist by the simplicity of its visual logic. Descartes observed that a person blind from birth could not arrive by any train of reasoning at perceiving colors in his mind; "but if a man has indeed once perceived the primary colors, though he has never seen the intermediate or mixed tints, it is possible for him to construct the images of those which he has not seen from their likeness to the others, by a sort of deduction."

When we listen to artists describing their use of complementaries, we notice that there are two apparently quite contradictory applications. On the

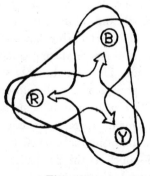

Figure 241

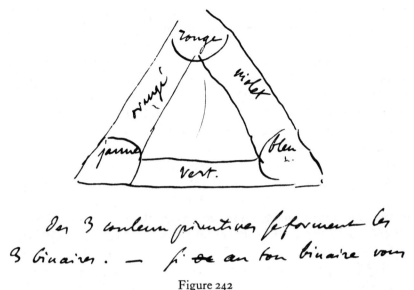

Figure 242
Eugène Delacroix. From a sketchbook of his journey to Morocco, 1832.

one hand, complementary pairs depict the peaceful unity of opposites. Thus Van Gogh thought of expressing the moods of the four seasons through four pairs: red and green (the apple blossoms and young corn of spring), blue and orange (the summer sky and the golden bronze of the ripe grain), yellow and violet (the autumn leaves), and the black and white of winter. He also wrote in 1888 that the affection of two lovers could be depicted by "the marriage of two complementary colors, their mixture, their mutual completion, and the mysterious vibration of the affined tones."

But the same Van Gogh said that in his *Night Café* he tried to express the terrible passion of men by means of red and green. He was probably influenced by Delacroix, who frequently used the contrast of red and green as a symbol of violence and terror. In fact, Van Gogh describes Delacroix's *Christ on Lake Genezareth* as follows: "Christ with his halo of pale lemon yellow, asleep, luminous in a setting of dramatic violet, somber blue, and blood-red, formed by the group of frightened disciples, on the terrifying emerald sea, which rises, rises all the way up to the frame."

The contradiction between two such different applications of the same device will seem less puzzling if we remember that the completion attained by complementarity involves not only maximum contrast but also mutual neutralization. Contrast is most evident when large areas of the colors are pitted against each other. When the same colors are combined in many small doses, as for example in the brushstrokes of divisionist paintings, or when viewed from a distance, they combine by addition to a silvery gray.

The variety of vital forces, displayed in many gentle steps, produces richness rather than contrast. Instead of being divided in large opposing camps, the colors show their total range in each area of the picture. The resulting overall grayness is loaded with life but serene. Kurt Badt has written: "In the late works of the great masters every particularity of feeling is extinguished by a unity of all opposites. Such pictures have neither grace nor grandeur nor splendor. They possess everything but are beyond any limitation. In these late works the details dissolve, the melodies dissipate, and even the accomplishments of middle life, namely clarity, richness, beauty of color, disappear. There remains an ultimate simplicity of effect and countereffect, of the spiritual and the material, of surface and space, of color and line. Nothing is any longer by itself, nothing predominant."

The antagonistic relationship of complementary pairs is beautifully expressed in Denise Levertov's poem *A Vision*, in which two angels, one with red wings, the other with green, are "poised on the brink of dispute" because they sense the threat of revealing each other's incompleteness. The conflict is solved when each angel gazing

> on the angelic wings of the other,
> the intelligence proper to great angels flew into their wings,
> the intelligence called *intellectual love*, which,
> understanding the perfections of scarlet,
>
> leapt up among blues and green strongshafted,
> and among amber down illumined the sapphire bloom,
>
> so that each angel was iridescent with the strange newly-seen
> hues he watched, and their discovering pause
> and the speech their silent interchange of perfection was
>
> never became a shrinking to opposites,
>
> and they remained free in the heavenly chasm,
> remained angels, but dreaming angels,
> each imbued with the mysteries of the other.

Since the eye spontaneously seeks out and links complementary colors, they are often used to establish connections within a painting between areas that lie at some distance from one another. However, a strong complementary duo or triad tends to be so self-contained and self-sufficient that it not only helps to hold a picture together but also poses a compositional problem. Like perfect circular shape, which does not fit easily into a context and therefore is often given a central or frankly isolated position, the complementary pattern subordinates itself only with difficulty to a larger color scheme. It functions best as a relatively independent subwhole, or as a central core or theme around which further color values are arranged.

Finally, the completion attainable by means of complementary pairs has served the colorists among the painters to make the three-dimensional volume of objects, such as fruits or human bodies, more salient. I have pointed out that the awkward competition between the local colors of objects on the one hand and the lights and shadows introduced by chiaroscuro on the other was resolved in Western painting by the introduction of colored shadows. This technique, in the work of Rubens or Delacroix, not only serves to create a unitary medium of representation that renders local coloration and the brightness values of illumination by the same device; it also shapes the roundness of a pictorial object in a particularly compelling way. Monochromatic shading is certainly effective in expressing volume by scales of gray. But the gray scale cannot mark the antagonistic poles of light and darkness by two strongly contrasting colors, as the colorist does when he opposes a pink in the illuminated area of a thigh or apple with a green in the shadow, or when yellow light goes with violet darkness. Also, the completeness of the complementary pair of colors confirms the boundaries of the object, whereas the gray scale is, as it were, boundless: there could be a brighter white and a darker shadow than those used for gradation in the object, and therefore the modeling by shading gives less finality to the volume.

Although it takes complementary colors to produce maximum contrast, there are other confrontations, such as blue and yellow, which also present mutually exclusive hues. There is no yellow in pure blue, no blue in pure yellow, and therefore the two colors articulate their difference neatly, even harshly. However, there is no real polarity in such opposition because it takes place within a limited sector of the color system. Both colors possess the same partial expression: a metallic coldness perhaps in blue and yellow, or a sweetish warmth in red and blue. I suggested earlier that there is something one-sided about any particular color. A similarly one-sided mood pervades a picture based on a palette that excludes one of the primaries. The absence of blue in the late works of Rembrandt presents the human experience through a particular temperament.

Interaction of Color

I referred earlier to the perplexing instability of colors. They are the most impressive demonstration of the fact that the same part in two different wholes is not the same thing. The same color in two different contexts is not the same color. John Ruskin warned the painter: "Every hue throughout your work is altered by every touch that you add in other places; so that what was warm a minute ago, becomes cold when you have put a hotter color in another place, and what was in harmony when you left it, becomes discordant as you set other colors beside it." Because of this extreme instability and reciprocal dependence, it is not surprising that psychological experiments in which random series of isolated colors or pairs of colors were presented to observers led to chaotic results. It is significant, however, that Johannes von Allesch, whose investigation brought out this ambiguity most clearly, remarks that the pregnancy or variability of any color is reduced when it is put in a context. We must emphasize here once more that the order of a pictorial composition stabilizes the character of each color, making it as unequivocal as is necessary for the artistic statement to be valid.

This means that the identity of a color does not reside in the color itself but is established by relation. We are aware of this mutual transfiguration, which makes every color dependent on the support of all the others, just as the stones of an arch hold one another in place. But whereas the stones counterbalance one another's weight physically, the web of interacting colors is created only by the eye, and this subjectivity—quite different from the sturdy objectivity of shapes—gives them the quality of apparitions. Kandinsky wrote in his *Reminiscences*: "I saw that there was nothing magical about any large surface by itself and that any such surface revealed at once its derivation from the palette; but through another surface, opposed to it, this surface acquired indeed a magic power, so that its origin on the palette seemed unbelievable at first impression."

The most prominent among the phenomena of interaction is, of course, *color contrast*. The principle received its classical formulation by Michel Eugène Chevreul, the French chemist and director of the Gobelin tapestry works. He described simultaneous contrast as follows: "If one views at the same time two areas of different brightness but of the same hue, or of the same brightness but of different hue, in juxtaposition, i.e., bordering on each other, the eye will observe (provided the areas are not too large) modifications that bear in the first case on the intensity of the color and in the second on the optical composition of the two juxtaposed colors."

Since the effect of color contrast operates in the direction of physiological complementarity, it serves to heighten it where it already exists, e.g., in the relation between blue and yellow, or to modify colors in the direction of such complementarity if they are reasonably close to it. Von Allesch experimented with a greenish yellow and a reddish yellow whose admixtures were so slight that when inspected separately both colors looked like pure yellows. Brought together they tended to emphasize their distinctness, looking clearly greenish and reddish and presumably producing the kind of clash already discussed as the effect of "Similarity of the Dominant." But if a third yellow of intermediate hue was placed between the two, the contrast diminished and the total arrangement showed a more unified yellow. Such effects of assimilation are also observed when, for example, one strongly red patch in a painting brings out subtly red components in the colors around it.

Much attention has been paid to color contrast. It has been superbly demonstrated in Josef Albers's *Interaction of Color*. The countereffect, namely *assimilation*, is rather neglected, although the antagonism of the two perceptual mechanisms makes it imperative that the one should not be considered without the other. Since perceptual patterns tend toward the most clear-cut organization available, a configuration of colors will strive either toward contrast or toward assimilation, depending on which is closer to the given stimulus information. We also can apply the concepts of *sharpening* and *leveling*, which served us to describe modifications of shapes.

Assimilation is closely related to the additive combination of colors. When the hues bordering on each other are sufficiently similar or when the areas carrying the hues are sufficiently small, the colors will approach each other rather than emphasize contrast. Jameson and Hurvich have proposed a physiological theory that accounts for at least some aspects of the phenomenon. They remind us that the microscopically small receptors in the retina do not act singly but as constituents of receptive fields, each of which combines the action of a large number of receptors and reports as a unit to a single ganglion cell. Within each field, the receptors respond antagonistically: in the central area the response to the intensity and color of light is positive, in the surrounding receptors it is negative. When these receptor fields are relatively small they discriminate sharply between stimulus areas of reasonably large size and emphasize the contrast between them.

When the stimulus areas are small, e.g., when they form a fine-grained dot pattern, as would reach the eye from a divisionist painting, there will be no resolution and the result will be a true additive mixture. When the units are somewhat larger, however, assimilation (sometimes called the Bezold

Spreading Effect) may result, owing to the fact that the receptor fields vary in size. Some are more than six times the size of others. In consequence, the narrower fields will be discriminating enough to tell the difference between areas of different colors, whereas the broader ones will encompass the different areas and thus reduce the brightness and color difference between them through additive interaction.

Relations between hues cannot be described adequately without reference to saturation and brightness. Experiments have shown that the distinctness of color depends more upon brightness than upon hue. Susanne Liebmann found that when, for example, a red figure is put on a green background of exactly equal brightness, the boundaries become fluid, soft, colloidal. The figure-ground distinction vanishes, objects look incorporeal, and differences of distance are hard to distinguish; shape tends to melt, the points of stars disappear, triangles look rounded, rows of dots merge. Therefore it is not surprising that painters usually reinforce differing hues by differing brightness. When they do entrust distinction between neighboring areas to hue alone, they rely mostly on what I have called clash or mutual repulsion. For example, there may be a blue-green background bordering on a reddish-blue coat of approximately identical brightness and saturation. This would seem to confirm the view that the most effective distinction between hues is brought about by clash.

Matisse and El Greco

A brief analysis of the color schemes in two paintings may serve to illustrate some of our syntactic principles. One example is taken from Matisse's painting *Luxury* (Figure 243), which shows three women in a landscape. Two of the figures are in the near foreground, the third is farther back. A slight overlap connects the frontal figures and also defines their spatial relation. The third is smaller; but in order to play down the difference in depth, overlapping is eschewed for this figure. Their identical coloring also tends to place all three women in the same plane. The environment is divided into three main areas: the orange foreground with the white drapery, the green water in the center, and the background with its slightly violet sky, white cloud, and two mountains, one bluish red, the other orange. There is, then, a kind of color symmetry between top and bottom. The white garment in the nearest foreground corresponds to the white cloud in the farthest background; the orange appears in both areas, and so does the yellow of the nude bodies. The approximate center of this symmetry is indicated by the bouquet of flowers. We cannot help feeling that the small woman is expending all her surprising energy and

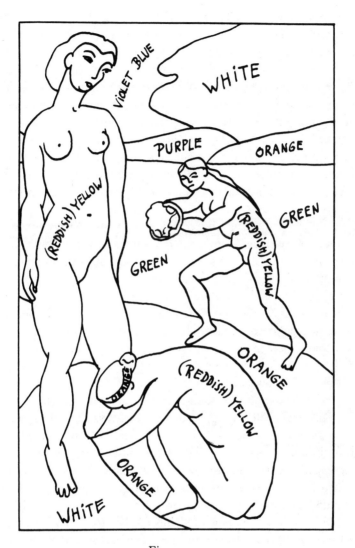

Figure 243

concentration in holding the pivot of the picture in her hands. The bouquet is small, but it attracts attention because its shape has the simplicity of a circle, outlined in a pure dark blue that is unique in the painting. The bouquet parallels the navel of the tall figure, thus making it clear that the center of that figure helps to establish the symmetry axis of the total composition.

The symmetry serves to counteract the depth of the landscape created by the superpositions of shape. The two whites, at the extremes of the total range of space, tend to lie in the same plane and thereby to compress the three-dimensional expanse. The orange areas do the same. The three yellow figures overlap the entire landscape and lie in front of it. But they are brought back into the spatial context by the distribution of the brightness values. The two white areas, being the brightest spots in the picture, protrude most strongly—that is, they move the somewhat darker human figures back to a place inside the distance scale, enclosing them between the brightest and darkest tones.

Except for the whites and the small spots of black and blue, there are no pure primaries in the picture. The yellow of the bodies is warmed by a reddish tinge. Yellow, established as the dominant color of the composition by the three figures, is also contained in the orange and the green, but is probably absent from the sky and the bluish-red mountain. Thus in the upper left corner the common color element is limited to red, which, however, is weak in the sky and quiet faint in the figure. Essentially the colors in that area are distinct to the point of being mutually exclusive.

Just as yellow is excluded from the upper corner of the background landscape, so blue, most clearly expressed in the sky and contained in the bluish-red mountain and the green water, is absent from the lower part of the picture. The two colors meet in balanced proportion in the central green. The only clash of hues seems to occur between the yellow red of the mountain and the blue red next to it (Similarity of the Dominant). Is this conflict justified by its function in the total composition or is it an unresolved problem?

The only example of an approximately exclusive distinction occurs, as I said before, between the sky and the yellow face and shoulders. Here is also the greatest depth interval. The figures are most intimately connected with the landscape at the bottom of the picture, where yellow and, to a slight extent, red are shared. The hair of the kneeling figure even picks up the orange. In the middle ground there is greater distinction. The bodies and the water contain yellow as one common fundamental, but the reddish admixture of the skin and the blue contained in the green emphasize mutual exclusion. The black hair of the small figure and the colors of the bouquet add to the feeling of detachment. The crescendo of separation reaches its climax in the upper left corner. The spatial leap between the head and shoulders and the sky is compensated, however, by an approximate complementarity between the reddish yellow of the human skin and the violet blue of the sky. The colors produce strong cleavage and at the same time bridge the gap by the harmony of their mutual completion.

As a second example I have chosen El Greco's *The Virgin with Santa*

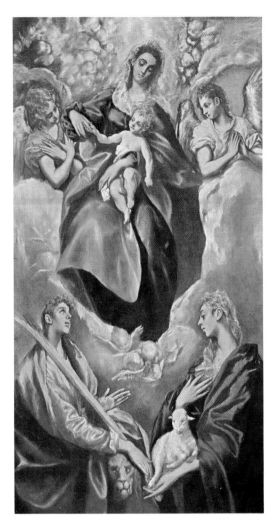

Plate II. El Greco. *The Virgin with Sta. Inés and
Sta. Tecla*, 1597–99. National Gallery,
Washington, D.C.

Inés and Santa Tecla (Plate 2). The basic skeleton of the composition is symmetrical. The Virgin, flanked by two angels, holds the center in the upper half of the picture; the two saints face each other in the lower half. The basic symmetry of the shapes is enlivened, however, by deviations, of which the following are relevant here. The attitudes of the Virgin and the child create a slanted axis. The tilt from the upper right toward the lower left links the figure in the clouds more directly to the saint on the left. This connection is stressed further by the closer contact of the coat of the Virgin with the head of the woman at the left, who looks upward and makes an outgoing gesture with her hand. In contrast, the woman on the right is farther from the central figure, her eyes are downcast as though she were wrapped in thought, and her hand points toward herself.

The color scheme of the picture echoes the compositional motif. The self-contained oval shape of the Virgin is subdivided into four main sections, which produce a kind of central symmetry around the Christ child. The two parts of the blue coat oppose each other, and so do those of her red dress. The blue and the red are clearly distinct from each other, but also connected by a suggestion of what I have called structural inversion, since the red is somewhat bluish and the blue somewhat reddish. The color range of the Virgin is kept within the areas of red and blue and therefore requires completion. The missing yellow is supplied by the hair of the child. The child has the role of a keystone, not only because of his central location, but also because he holds the color that is needed to create the triad of primaries.

The yellow hair of the four child angels at Mary's feet is related by similarity to the yellow coat and hair of the saint at the left, the palm branch, and the lion. The blue of the Virgin's coat is picked up by the blue sleeve. The blue and red of the upper figure add up to a purple; the blue and yellow of the lower are the components of a green; and purple and green approach complementarity. Hence the easy union between the central figure and the woman at the left. Compare this with the clash between the orange coat of the woman at the right and the purple scheme of the Virgin. The red, dominant in both areas, is torn into the conflicting scales of red-blue and red-yellow, and the barrier created by this clash prevents the eye from gliding across the interval between the two figures.

In the original painting, there is enough of a golden tinge in the shadows of the yellow coat at the left to prevent a true clash between it and the orange red of the coat at the right. The eye can connect the two colors by structural inversion, just as the contact of the two frontal hands, the parallelism of the other two hands, the symmetrical shape of the two-woman group, and the peaceable-kingdom theme of lion and lamb all strengthen the horizontal tie.

In sum, we find that in the lower half of El Greco's painting, shape and color combine in representing two united aspects of the religious attitude, inspiration and contemplation, receiving and meditating, dependence upon grace and freedom of will. The overall symmetry of the work makes the contrast of the two-fold human attitude fit into the greater harmony of godhead and man, dominance on high and submission on earth.

Reactions to Color

Nobody denies that colors carry strong expression, but nobody knows how such expression comes about. To be sure, expression is widely believed to be based on association. Red is said to be exciting because it reminds us of fire, blood, and revolution. Green calls up the refreshing thought of nature, and blue is cooling like water. But the theory of association is no more illuminating here than it is in other areas. The effect of color is much too direct and spontaneous to be only the product of an interpretation attached to the percept by learning.

On the other hand, we have not even a hypothesis to offer about the kind of physiological process that might account for the influence of color. Strong brightness, high saturation, and the hues of long-wave vibration produce excitement. A bright, pure red is more active than a subdued, grayish blue. But we have no information on what intense light energy does to the nervous system or why the wavelength of vibrations should matter. Some experiments have demonstrated a bodily response to color. Féré found that muscular power and blood circulation are increased by colored light "in the sequence from blue (least), through green, yellow, orange, and red." This accords with psychological observations on the effects of these colors, but there is no telling whether we are dealing here with a secondary consequence of the perceptual experience or a more direct nervous influence of light energy on motor behavior and blood circulation.

The same is true for observations by Kurt Goldstein, who found in his neurological practice, for example, that a patient with a cerebellar disease suffered disruption of her sense of balance, became dizzy, and was in danger of falling when she wore a red dress—symptoms that disappeared when she wore green. Goldstein investigated the phenomenon by experiments that deserve to be followed up. He asked patients with similar brain defects to look at a sheet of colored paper while holding their arms stretched out in front. The arms were hidden from view by a horizontal board. When the patient looked at a yellow paper his arms, controlled by the defective brain center, would deviate about 55 centimeters from the midline. The deviation was 50 centimeters for red, 45 centimeters for white, 42 centimeters for blue, 40 centimeters for green. When he closed his eyes the deviation was 70 centimeters. Goldstein concluded that the colors corresponding to long wavelengths go with an expansive reaction, whereas the short wavelengths make for constriction. "The whole organism . . . through different colors is swung toward the outer world or withdrawn from it and concentrated toward the center of the organism."

This physical reaction is paralleled by Kandinsky's remarks on the appearance of colors. He asserted that a yellow circle will reveal "a spreading movement outwards from the center which almost markedly approaches the spectator"; a blue circle "develops a concentric movement (like a snail hiding in its shell) and moves away from the spectator."

Warm and Cold

Hardly any attempt has been made to group the various colors in terms of their general expressive qualities. The distinction between warm and cold colors is fairly common. Artists use these terms, and references to them are found in books on the theory of color. But sketchy remarks based on subjective impressions do not get us very far. Von Allesch's experimental observations on this point seem to have led to inconclusive results, so far as can be judged from his brief references to the subject. Under these conditions it may be permissible for me to put forward a suggestion of my own. It has not been tested systematically and may turn out to be quite wrong; but at least it is something to shoot at.

The pure fundamental primaries can hardly be called either warm or cold. Is a pure red clearly more warm than a pure blue of equal saturation? Is a pure yellow cold or warm? But temperature quality seems to be more meaningful when applied to the admixture of a color. A bluish yellow or red tends to look cold, and so does a yellowish red or blue. On the contrary, a reddish yellow or blue seems warm. My suggestion is that not the main color but the color toward which it deviates may determine the effect. This would lead to the perhaps unexpected result that a reddish blue looks warm whereas a bluish red looks cold. Johannes Itten has designated the complementary pair of red orange and blue green as the temperature poles. This would support our observation that an admixture of red will warm the color whereas a tinge of blue will chill it. Mixtures of two evenly balanced colors should not show the effect clearly, although a blend of yellow and blue might be closest to coldness. Balanced combinations of red and blue or red and yellow might tend to be neutral or ambiguous.

Naturally, the instability of colors will influence their temperature. As a color changes its hue in response to the hues of its neighbors, its temperature may change as well. Brightness and saturation may also have a bearing on the phenomenon. In Albers's color circle the realms of cold and warm coincide roughly with those of dark and bright, and Itten associates cold with shady, warm with sunny.

If my approach is viable it may apply more generally to the expressive qualities of colors. Perhaps it is not so much the dominant hue but its "afflictions" that give a color its character. We noted that the pure fundamental primaries lack the dynamic qualities of mixtures; they may also be more neutral in expression, whereas a color producing a dynamic tension effect by leaning toward another color may be more expressive. Reddishness, yellowishness, bluishness, by drawing another color away from its own fundamental character, may produce the tension without which no expression is possible. Here, then, are suggestions that invite verification by experiment.

Finally, let us puzzle for a moment over the habit of using temperature sensations to describe colors. What is the common denominator? We are hardly reminded of a hot bath or summer heat when we perceive the dark red of a rose. Rather the color brings about a reaction also provoked by heat stimulation, and the words "warm" and "cold" are used to describe colors simply because the expressive quality in question is strongest and biologically most vital in the realm of temperature.

We are describing a quality emanating from the object as well as our reaction to that quality. The experience need not be perceptual. We also speak of a cold person, a warm reception, a heated debate. A cold person makes us withdraw. We feel like defending ourselves against an unwholesome power— we close up and shut the gates. We are ill at ease, inhibited in venting our thoughts and impulses. A warm person is one who makes us open up. We are attracted, willing to expose freely whatever we have to give. Our reactions to physical chill or warmth are obviously similar. In the same way, warm colors seem to invite us whereas cold ones keep us at a distance. Warm colors are outgoing, cold ones draw back. For the purposes of the artist, of course, both are welcome. They express different properties of reality calling for different responses.

If we wanted to discuss the expression of colors beyond what has been said so far, we would have to report on the character attributed to particular colors by various artists, writers, civilizations. In the earlier version of this book I gave samples of such attributions. It is an entertaining subject, and the observations of Goethe or Kandinsky on the character of red or yellow are attractively poetical. But no sufficiently good purpose seems to be served by such anecdotes. For one thing, these characterizations are so heavily overlaid with personal or cultural factors that they cannot claim much general validity. When Kandinsky taught in his Bauhaus seminar that the color yellow was akin to the shape of a triangle, blue to a circle, and red to a square, was he voicing more than a personal impression? And when yellow symbolized imperial splendor in China but indicated shame and contempt in the European Middle Ages, can we be sure that, as Goethe assumes, the Chinese referred to a golden yellow, whereas the color of the prostitutes and the persecuted Jews had a mean, greenish tinge?

If it is our task to search the perceived object for the formal factors that determine what the eyes see, we may claim to have examined the factors of color structure at least sketchily. But just as in the chapter on the expression of shape I shall refrain from lengthy speculation on the state of mind that takes to certain shapes, I propose not to rehearse here the facts of color preference. In the case of shape, we can analyze formal characteristics with considerable precision. The analogies between what shapes look like and what they express can therefore be explored with some confidence. We would accordingly be on relatively firm ground if we asked, as art historians have done, why Raphael's shapes differ from those of Dürer. But when it comes to color, can we do better than reflect vaguely on why Picasso preferred blue in the early years of our century or let Van Gogh tell us what he meant by yellow?

Quantitative studies on the color preferences of various populations have been numerous, partly because passing fashions are of interest to market researchers, partly because reactions to unanalyzed stimuli are easier for the experimenter to handle than studies requiring structural analysis. It is also true that the notion of "aesthetic pleasure," considered important in the traditional philosophy of art, has been impressed upon psychologists by philosophers. It was thought relevant to find out who was pleased by which colors. The results have been singularly unrewarding. Nothing of general validity emerged. Besides, preference has little bearing on art. "What a miserable fate for a painter who adores blondes," said Picasso to Christian Zervos, "to have to stop himself from putting them into a picture because they don't go with the basket of fruit!"

VIII MOVEMENT

Motion is the strongest visual appeal to attention. A dog or cat may be resting peacefully, unimpressed by all the lights and shapes that make up the immobile setting around him; but as soon as anything stirs, his eyes will turn to the spot and follow the course of the motion. Young kittens seem completely at the mercy of any moving thing, as though their eyes were tied to it. Human beings are similarly attracted by movement; I need only mention the effectiveness of mobile advertising, whether it be flashing neon signs or television commercials, or the much greater popular appeal of performances in motion, as compared to immobile photography, painting, sculpture, or architecture.

It is understandable that a strong and automatic response to motion should have developed in animal and man. Motion implies a change in the conditions of the environment, and change may require reaction. It may mean the approach of danger, the appearance of a friend or of desirable prey. And since the sense of vision has developed as an instrument of survival, it is keyed to its task.

Happenings and Time

We distinguish between things and happenings, immobility and mobility, time and timelessness, being and becoming. These distinctions are crucial to all visual art, but their meaning is far from obvious. We call the airport a thing, but the arrival of a plane a happening. Happenings are almost always activities of things. Pure, unattached action is rare; but it exists. Wertheimer found in his experiments with stroboscopic motion that what his observers perceived under certain conditions was not an object moving from one position to another, but rather "pure movement," taking place between two objects and unrelated to either. When we distinguish the flight patterns of a distant swallow from that of an airplane, the object is reduced to a shapeless dot and we can be said to be seeing pure movement—an experience similar to that of hearing a musical sound move along the rises and falls of a melody.

Mostly we are in the presence of objects, which appear to us as stable entities, and actions performed by them. The gestures of a speaker are actions, but the speaker himself is perceived as a persistent thing, whatever biologists and physicists may say to the contrary. Even a cloud is experienced not as an event, but as an object in transformation; and the same is true for examples in which change does not depend on movement—a lobster turning red, a potato getting tender.

Physically all things and events are located in time. Nowadays, when sculpture is attacked by air pollution, we notice with dismay that even marble or bronze moves on a lifeline of its own, which distinguishes its state of being today from that of yesterday. Psychologically, however, a statue is outside time. I do not perceive it as busy persisting the way the pedestrians and cars are busy moving past it. At any given moment the pedestrian is in a particular phase of his walk across the square. For the statue no such comparison of its states at different moments occurs; it does not "remain the same" or "stand still." Similarly, the figures depicted on the Grecian urn of John Keats are not stopped in their tracks. This is so because in each of these examples the setting as a whole—the city, the room, the vase—is perceived as being outside the time dimension. Within the setting certain changes or actions may occur. How do we describe those? Do we experience them as occurring in time?

The distinction between immobile and mobile things is clear enough. But is it identical with the distinction between timelessness and time? Is it really the experience of time's passing that distinguishes the performance of a dancer from the presence of a painting? When the dancer leaps across the stage, is it an aspect of our experience, let alone the most significant aspect, that time passes during that leap? Does she arrive out of the future and jump through the present into the past? And exactly which part of her performance belongs to the present? The most recent second of it, or perhaps a fraction of that second? And if the whole leap belongs in the present, at what point of the performance before the leap does the past stop?

The questions turn out to be absurd. Of course, we perceive the dancer's action as a sequence of phases. The performance contains an arrow, as the painting does not. But the performance cannot really be said to occur in time. Let us compare the following two events in an adventure film. From a helicopter the detective observes the gangster's car speeding along the highway. Will it turn into the side road or continue straight ahead? This episode, like the dancer's leap, is experienced as an event in space, not in time—except for our own feeling of suspense, which is not a part of the situation observed. All its relevant aspects are spatial. But now we see the rescuer racing toward the victim's cottage. Will he arrive "in time" to prevent the villainous deed? Here the time element is of the essence. Two independent spatial systems, the approach of the rescuer and the events in the cottage, are related solely by their placement in time, which will or will not lead to the desired coincidence.

When we watch a man exploring a cave, his progress is experienced as a happening in space. New aspects of the cave reveal themselves in succession. Such an event, in which a physical setting provides the framework, is not really different in principle from others in which no such framework exists. In a spirited discussion the argument also moves along a path, with one thought leading to the next in a logical sequence. Do we perceive the step-like progress of the argument as occurring in time, any more than the exploration of the cave? Not unless "time is running out" and the outcome of the discussion is anxiously awaited.

Our puzzling discovery has serious consequences for the apprehension of artistic performances. Evidently, in order to create or to understand the structure of a film or a symphony, one has to grasp it as a whole, exactly as one would the composition of a painting. It must be apprehended as a sequence, but this sequence cannot be temporal in the sense that one phase disappears as the next occupies our consciousness. The whole work must be simultaneously present in the mind if we are to understand its development, its coherence, the interrelations among its parts. We are tempted to call the object of this synopsis a spatial structure. In any case, it requires simultaneity and therefore is hardly temporal.

In a letter of 1789, attributed to Mozart but probably not written by him in this form, the phenomenon of musical simultaneity is admirably described. When a theme has caught the composer's attention, "it becomes larger and larger, and I spread it out more and more widely and clearly, and the thing really gets to be almost completed in my head, even if it is long, so that thereafter I survey it in my mind at one glance, like a beautiful picture or handsome person. And I hear it in my imagination not in sequence, as it will have to unfold afterward, but, at it were, right away all together (*wie gleich alles zusammen*)."

Something very similar is required for true understanding of a symphony, a film, or a dance. At any particular moment we may not know what will come next, but we must not dismiss from our consciousness what we have heard or seen before. The work grows step by step into a whole, and as we accompany its progress we must constantly hark back to what has disappeared from direct perception by ear or eye, but survives in memory. The past as such is never available to the mind. The percepts and feelings, not only of yesterday but of a second ago, are gone. They survive only to the extent that within us they have left remnants, i.e. memory traces. Whatever the nature of these traces in the brain, they certainly persist in spatial simultaneity, influence one another, and are modified by new arrivals. The introductory measures of a dance are no longer the same once we have seen the rest of the composition. What happens while the performance is in progress is not simply the addition of new beads to the chain. Everything that came before is constantly modified by what comes later.

Thus every newly arriving percept finds its place in the spatial structure of memory. In the brain every trace has an address, but no date. The structure of a performance derives from the interaction of the traces it leaves within us.

We realize now that what distinguishes the perception of happenings from that of objects is not that the former involves the experience of passing time, but that during a happening we witness an organized sequence in which phases follow one another in a meaningful one-dimensional order. When the event is disorganized or incomprehensible, the sequence breaks down into a mere succession. It loses its main characteristic; and even the succession lasts only as long as its elements are being squeezed through the gorge of immediate presence. The performance becomes kaleidoscopic: there is constant change but no progression, and there is no reason to remember past phases of the spectacle, except perhaps to admire its variety. No time bond connects these momentary phases, because time by itself can create succession, but not order. On the contrary, any experience of time presupposes some kind of order.

Simultaneity and Sequence

We are trying to describe the difference between two kinds of media. In one of them the sequence in which the parts of a composition are apprehended is prescribed by the work itself, whereas in the other it is immaterial. I remember a discussion between two students, a painter and a musician. The painter said: "I cannot understand how you can keep the parts of a piece of music together since they are never given to you at the same time!" The musician assured him that this was not much of a difficulty, but, he said, "what I don't understand is how you find your way in a painting, not knowing where to start and where to end, nor where to turn next at any point!"

The difference between the two kinds of media does not coincide with that between mobility and immobility. There are pictures that must be read in a prescribed sequence, e.g., from left to right like writing. Comic strips are of this kind, and so were certain narrative paintings, popular in the fifteenth century, in which one saw, from left to right, how Eve was created from the rib of Adam, how she presented him with the apple, how they were reprimanded by God and finally thrown out of paradise by the angel.

Conversely, there are mobile works that are not sequential. A dance composition is likely to unfold logically from its beginning to its end, but a waltz in the ballroom is not. Similarly, certain kinds of music, intended to establish a particular mood, are stationary, without a beginning, end, or development. The movements of a sculptural mobile have no progression. They reveal the varieties of spatial relation within a set of jointed elements. The order and coordination of the displacements at the various levels are left to chance, and the surprises of the unprescribed configurations are what we enjoy.

When sequence is confused with mobility, misinterpretations result. For example, it has been asserted that painting and sculpture are as much "time art" as music and the drama because the viewer must move with his eyes all over the surface of the work and therefore perceives its parts in succession. Actually, the order of a picture exists only in space, in simultaneity. The picture contains one or several dominant themes to which all the rest is subordinated. This hierarchy is valid and comprehensible only when all the relations it involves are grasped as being coexistent. The observer scans the various areas of the picture in succession because neither the eye nor the mind is capable of taking in everything simultaneously, but the order in which the exploration occurs does not matter. The path of the glance need not adhere to the vectorial directions created by the composition. A compositional "arrow" leading from left to right may be perceived correctly even if the eye moves in the opposite direction, or indeed crosses the tract in an arbitrary zigzag. Barriers erected in the picture by contours or color conflict do not stop the eye. On the contrary, they are noticed and experienced while they are traversed. I have already mentioned the many recent studies of eye movements. They show, not surprisingly, that the viewer spends most of his fixations on the items of prime interest. But the order of the fixations is largely accidental and irrelevant.

In a play or musical composition, by contrast, sequence is of the essence. To change the order of events means to change, and probably destroy, the work. It is imposed upon the viewer and listener and must be obeyed. In a dance there are one or several dominant themes, just as in a painting; but the order of their appearance is linked to definite phases of the total development, and different meanings adhere to different locations in the perceptual sequence. A theme may be presented at the very beginning and then demonstrated and

explored by a number of changes or variations. Or it may be subjected to en-
counters with other themes and deploy its nature through the resulting attractions or repulsions, victories or defeats. But the theme, perhaps embodied
in the principal dancer, may also make a late appearance, after a slow buildup
that leads through a crescendo to the climax. This different order in time
produces a completely different structure.

Even the objective movement of a piece of sculpture differs in principle
from the change of aspects we experience in walking around it; otherwise
sculptors would not bother, as some do, to mount their works on motorized
turntables. In such cases, the pace and direction of the rotation are prescribed
properties of the sculptural display itself. Moreover, we shall find that it makes
all the difference for perception and expression whether one sees a thing in
motion or walks past, around, or across it.

When a work based on linear succession narrates a story, it actually
contains two sequences, that of the events to be portrayed and the path of disclosure. In a simple fairy tale the two coincide. The account duplicates the
order of the events. In more complex works the journey that the author prescribes for the spectator or reader may differ considerably from the objective
sequence of the plot. For example, in *Hamlet* the inherent sequence leads from
the murder of the king through the wedding of his queen and brother to
Hamlet's discovery of the crime, and so to the end. The path of disclosure
starts somewhere in the middle of that sequence, and moves first backward
and then forward. It proceeds from the periphery of the problem toward its
center, introducing first the watchmen, then Hamlet's friend, then the mysterious ghost. Thus, while unfolding the dramatic conflict, the play also deals with
man's ways of discovering the facts of life—a secondary plot, of which the
spectator is the protagonist. And just as a traveler's route toward an unknown
city will influence the notion of it he receives, so the path of disclosure will
encourage a particular response to the subject of a work by giving precedence
to certain of its aspects and withholding others. Shakespeare's indirect approach to the Hamlet story stresses the effects of the crime before presenting
the crime itself, and sets the initial accents of night, disturbance of the peace,
mystery, and suspense.

We must take a further step and realize that in the last analysis even a
work based on sequence presents not only an event but, through the event, a
state of being. To use the formula offered by Lessing in his *Laocoon*: whereas
narrative painting or sculpture presents action by means of objects, the drama-
tist or novelist uses action to present states of affairs. ("Things that exist next
to one another or whose parts do so, are called objects. Therefore objects with

their visible properties are the true content of painting. Things that follow one another or whose parts do so are called actions. Therefore actions are the true content of literature.")

The Hamlet drama reveals an underlying configuration of antagonistic forces, love and hatred, loyalty and treachery, order and crime. The pattern could be represented in a diagram that would contain no reference to the sequence of the story. This pattern is gradually uncovered by the play, explored in its various relations, tested by the introduction of crucial situations. A man's biography, which describes his life from his birth to the grave, must add up to the presentation of a character, a state of being and behaving in its constant interplay with the polarity of life and death. And just as the young Michelangelo's *Pietà* in St. Peter's shows a mother holding her child and at the same time a man leaving his mother behind, so does the story of the Gospel, like every great narrative, contain its end in its beginning and its beginning in its end.

Together, the sequential and the nonsequential media interpret existence in its twofold aspect of permanence and change. This complementarity expresses itself in a reciprocal relation between space and force. The forces represented in a painting are defined primarily by space. The direction, shape, size, and location of the shapes that carry these forces determine where they apply, where they go, how strong they are. The expanse of space and its structural features—for example, its center—serve as a frame of reference for the characterization of forces. Conversely, the space of a theater or dance stage is defined by the motor forces that populate it. Expanse becomes real when the dancer runs across it; distance is created by actors withdrawing from each other; and the particular quality of central location is brought to light when embodied forces strive for it, rest at it, rule from it. In short, the interaction of space and force is interpreted with different emphasis.

When Do We See Motion?

Under what conditions do we perceive movement? A caterpillar crawls across the street. Why do we see it in motion and the street at rest rather than seeing the entire landscape, including ourselves, displaced in the opposite direction, with the caterpillar alone remaining at the same spot? The phenomenon is not explained simply by learning or knowledge because against our better knowledge we see the sun move across the sky and the moon through the clouds. Dante notes that when a person looks up to one of Bologna's leaning towers from "beneath its leaning" while a cloud moves in the opposite direction, the tower seems to topple over. Sitting in a rocking chair, we find ourselves in motion and the room standing still. But when an experiment makes the whole room revolve, like a rolling barrel, and the observer's chair stand perfectly still, the sensation that the chair is turning is so compelling that the observer will fall unless he is tied down. This happens even though the observer's kinesthetic sensations indicate the true state of affairs.

We can clarify at least a few elements of this complicated situation by noting that the visual experience of movement can be due to three factors: physical movement, optical movement, perceptual movement. To these we must add the kinesthetic factors, which can produce the sensation of motion all by themselves under certain conditions, e.g., by vertigo.

I see the caterpillar in motion because it is actually crawling; this is motion perception based on physical movement. But, as our examples show, physical movement does not necessarily correspond to what happens in the eyes or in perception. We can speak of *optical* motion when the projections of objects or of the entire visual field are displaced on the retina. Such optical displacement occurs when the observer's eyes do not follow the movements of the perceived objects. But physical motion may be recorded as optical standstill, e.g., when my eyes are locked on the caterpillar while it crawls across the street or when I see the cabin of the airplane surround me in perfect stillness even though both the plane and I are moving. On the other hand, the projection of my immobile workroom sweeps across the retinas optically as soon as I move my eyes or my head or get up from my chair. If someone could observe what goes on in my eyes while I examine the various parts of a painting on the wall, he would find that each time I change the fixation of my glance, the entire picture moves on the retinas in the opposite direction. And yet, most of the time such faulty optical information is not reflected in perceptual experience. I see the insect crawl although my eyes are locked onto it, and the painting remains unmoved even though my eyes scan it.

The most powerful factor compensating for such misleading input is kinesthetic perception. Any movement by eyes, head, or body is reported to the sensory motor center of the brain, and in fact the mere impulse to move is a brain event. The feedback from these motor processes influences visual perception. The information that I am moving my head induces the sense of sight to attribute the motion to the head visually as well, and to perceive the environment as immobile. In a film, however, the setting photographed by the traveling camera is seen as moving across the screen, mostly because the viewer receives the kinesthetic information that his body is at rest. Only in extreme cases, e.g., when enough of the entire environment is seen as moving, will the visual input overrule the kinesthetic.

In addition, there are specifically *visual* factors at work within the perceptual field that determine how the sense of sight handles motor ambiguities. Karl Duncker has pointed out that in the visual field, objects are seen in a hierarchic relation of dependence. The mosquito is attached to the elephant, not the elephant to the mosquito. The dancer is a part of the stage setting, not the stage setting the outer rim of the dancer. In other words, quite apart from motion, the spontaneous organization of the visual field assigns to certain objects the role of framework, on which others are seen to depend. The field represents a complex hierarchy of such dependences. The room serves as framework for the table, the table for the fruit bowl, the fruit bowl for the apples. Duncker's rule indicates that in motor displacement, the framework tends to be perceived as immobile and the dependent object as moving. When no dependence exists, the two systems may both be seen to move symmetrically, approaching or withdrawing from each other.

Duncker, and later Erika Oppenheimer, established some of the factors that produce dependence. Enclosedness is one of them. The "figure" tends to move, the "ground" to stand still. Variability is another. If one object changes in shape and size and the other remains constant—for example, a line "growing out of" a square—the variable object assumes the motion. The observer sees the line stretching away from the square, rather than the square withdrawing from an immobile line. Size difference is effective in the case of contiguous objects: when two objects lie close to each other, either laterally or in superposition, the smaller object will assume the motion. Intensity also plays a role. Since the dimmer object is seen as dependent on the brighter, the dimmer one moves when displacement occurs and the brighter one remains still.

The observer himself acts as a frame of reference. When he stands on a bridge and looks at the moving water, his perception will be "correct"; but when he fixates the bridge, he and the bridge may be seen as moving along the river. Duncker explains this phenomenon by pointing out that the object fixated assumes the character of the "figure," whereas the nonfixated part of the field tends to become ground. Since as a rule the "figure" does the moving, fixation makes for motion.

In any particular instance, the interaction of the various factors will determine the final perceptual effect. Physical motion of the object contributes only to the extent that it produces optical motion on the retina. The experiment by Metelli mentioned earlier (Figure 46) showed that the rotating section of the disk is not seen to be moving because optically there is a successive uncovering of segments but no displacement of the disk as a whole. Under such conditions perception reports immobility.

On the stage the actors are usually seen in motion against the foil of an immobile setting. This happens because the setting is large and enclosing and, in addition, anchored to the even larger environment of the theater in which the spectator is seated. It serves as frame of reference for the actors. Consequently the stage presents a concept of life that invests most of the physical and mental activity in man as opposed to the world of things, which serves mainly as the base and target of such action and in fact, as I mentioned earlier, is defined by the motor forces populating it. A different concept can be conveyed by the film. The picture taken by a camera that travels along a street does not produce the same experience we have when we walk in the street ourselves. Then the street surrounds us as a large environment, and our muscular experiences tell us that we are in motion. The street on the screen is a relatively small, framed part of a larger setting, in which the spectator finds himself at rest. Therefore the street is seen as moving. It appears to be actively encountering the spectator as well as the characters in the film, and assumes the role of an actor among actors. Life appears as an exchange of forces between man and the world of things, and things often play the more energetic part.

This is so also because the film represents with ease such natural motion as that of street traffic or the ebb and flow of the ocean, which is hardly possible on the stage. In a film like Robert Flaherty's *Man of Aran* the natural motion of the waves is reinforced by the cinematographic motion imposed on the scene by the moving camera. The film gives the world of things an opportunity to manifest its inherent powers and to act with or against man. In addition, things on the screen can be made to appear and disappear at will, which is also perceived as a kind of motion and which permits any object, large or small, to enter and leave the scene like an actor. For example, a dance film may be organized in such a way that the dancers do not monopolize movement. Instead, they interact with the setting and with other objects, the movement being created by camera motion and editing. This has been attempted in experimental films, e.g. by Maya Deren, and also in the choreographed scenes of some film "musicals." In such a visual composition, the part of the dancer is no more independent or complete than that of an instrument in an orchestra. The screen image as a whole presents a complex interplay of moving spaces, settings, objects, and human figures, whose motions come across only as integrated elements of the whole. Some television shows, intended simply to record what happens objectively on the stage, are not only dull but distorted to the point of being incomprehensible because the performance being shown was composed for the stage, not for the screen.

As long as the dominant framework stands still, any immobile object is perceived as being "outside time," just as the framework itself is. A moving framework, however, imparts action to the whole setting and the objects it contains, and it can translate timelessness into active resistance to motion. Just as a rock in the middle of a rushing stream exhibits stubborn opposition to motion, so a person standing still in a surrounding stream of walking or running people will not be perceived as outside the dimension of motion, but will appear, in terms of motion, as arrested, petrified, resistant. The same phenomenon is observed when stills are inserted into a film sequence. They look frozen, stopped in their tracks. Or a dancer stopping for a moment during a run looks arrested rather than at rest. The musician is familiar with the difference between dead and live intervals of silence. The pause between two movements of a symphony is not pervaded by movement, because it is excluded from the context. But when the structure of a piece is interrupted by silence, the heartbeat of the music seems to have stopped and the immobility of what should be motion creates suspense.

Direction

The more specific aspects of movement, such as direction and speed, are also perceived according to the conditions prevailing in the visual field. I mentioned that under certain conditions the objective direction of motion is reversed in perception. Although physically clouds may be moving east, we may see the moon speeding west instead. A movie shot taken through the rear window of the gangster's car may show his pursuer's car moving backward even though it is actually going forward, but more slowly than the car it is chasing.

On a dark screen in a dark room, Erika Oppenheimer projected two luminous lines in the position shown in Figure 244. Objectively the vertical moved to the right and the horizontal moved upward, so that after a while they assumed the positions indicated by the dotted lines. The observers, how-

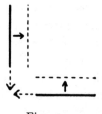

Figure 244

ever, saw the vertical line move downward and the horizontal move to the left (dotted arrows). Apparently it is structurally simpler for a line under these conditions to be perceived as moving in the direction of its own extension rather than at a right angle to it.

The relation of perceived direction to the context in which the movement occurs has also been demonstrated in studies on the rotation of wheels. The hub of a wheel will of course move along a path parallel to that of the whole wheel. Any other point of the wheel will be subjected to two motions: the translatory path and the rotation around the hub. The combination of the two motions will result physically in a wavy path, as indicated in Figure 245. This is in fact what is seen when the wheel moves in a dark room and nothing of it is visible but one luminous point somewhere off center. If, however, the hub can be seen, the whole motion pattern will subdivide into two structurally simpler ones: the wheel spins around itself and travels along its path at the same time. This shows that the rule of simplicity governs not only the subdivision of shape, but that of motion as well.

If the rule of simplicity did not operate, audiences would receive weird experiences from many dance movements. When the dancer turns somersaults, his body is seen as moving across the floor and at the same time rotating around its center. Any but the simplest movement is a combination of subsystems, which function independently and add up to a whole. When the arms are moved up and down while the body runs forward, the two themes must be, and are, distinguishable. The partial movements, however, do not seem to be strictly independent all the time. Figure 246 shows in a schematic way what happens physically when a bow is combined with a run. It would seem that something of the resulting curve comes through in perception. The structural principles that determine segregation and fusion could be studied fruitfully by comparing film shots of dance movements with others obtained from the same movements executed in the dark with only one point of the body marked by an attached flashlight—a technique first developed by the French physiologist Jules-Etienne Marey. The path traversed physically by any part of the body can be traced approximately in stroboscopic photography.

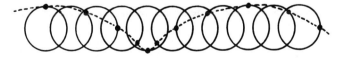

Figure 245

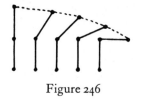

Figure 246

The Revelations of Speed

Motion, like any other kind of change, is perceivable only within a limited range of speed. The sun and the moon travel so slowly that they seem to stand still; a flash of lightning is so fast that its entire course appears simultaneously as a line. A glance at our watch tells us that the lower limit of perceivable speed is somewhere between that of the minute hand, whose movement remains unnoticed, and the second hand, which is visibly on the march. On Mark Twain's watch, which raced through whole seasons in one day after it had been treated by the watch-repair man, the motion of the hands must have been blurred like that of the blades of an electric fan. We cannot see a child grow up or a man grow old; but if we meet an acquaintance after a lapse of time, we can in a split second see him grow tall or shrivel in a kind of stroboscopic motion between a memory trace and the percept of the present moment.

Evidently the speed of change to which our sense organs respond has been keyed during evolution to that of the kind of event whose observation is vital to us. It is biologically essential that we see people and animals move from one place to another; we do not need to see the grass grow.

Does a turtle, which leads a slow life, see things move at greater speed than we do? The traffic of a big city does look faster after we have been in the country a while. Music and dance also establish adaptation levels for speed; a movement sounds or looks fast when it appears in a slow context, and vice versa. Some experiments suggest that the rate of the body's chemical processes may influence the perception of time. Thus Piéron asked people to press a Morse key three times a second as nearly as they could estimate this unit of time. When he slightly raised the body temperature of the observers diathermically, they pressed the key faster, thus indicating that the speed of subjective time had increased. Lecomte du Noüy, in citing these and other experiments, speculates that the slowing down of the "chemical clock" during a person's lifetime may account for the well-known fact that as one grows older, the years seem to fly faster. It seems doubtful, however, that chemical rather than psychological factors are responsible for this phenomenon.

The motion picture has broadened not only our knowledge but also our experience of life, by enabling us to see motion that is otherwise too fast or too slow for our perception. If the rate of shooting is lower than that of projection, for example, if only one frame is shot every hour, the action on the screen speeds up, and we can actually see what otherwise we could only reconstruct intellectually. If, however, the film moves through the camera at high speed, the audience can see a drop of milk bounce back from a surface in the shape of a beautiful white crown, or a bullet slowly break up a wooden panel.

The acceleration of natural motion, in particular, has impressed our eyes with a unity of the organic world of which we had at best only theoretical knowledge. The possibility of seeing a plant grow and die within one minute accomplished more than merely making the process surveyable. The single-frame camera has revealed that all organic behavior is distinguished by the expressive and meaningful gestures we formerly considered a privilege of man and animal. The activity of a climbing plant does not appear merely as a displacement in space. We see the vine searching around, fumbling, reaching, and finally taking hold of a suitable support with exactly the kind of motion indicative of anxiety, desire, and happy fulfillment. Sprouts, covered by a glass plate, remove the obstacle by action that does not resemble the mechanical labor of machines. There is a desperate struggle—a visible effort, a proud and victorious escape from oppression to freedom. Organic processes exhibit these "human" traits even at the microscopic level. Sherrington quotes a physiologist's description of a film showing a cell mass making bone. "Teamwork by the cell masses. Chalky spicules of bone-in-the-making shot across the screen, as if laborers were raising scaffold-poles. The scene suggested purposive behavior by individual cells, and still more by colonies of cells arranged as tissues and organs."

Even where the particular appeal of organic movement is lacking, the transformation of long-term changes into visible motion brings the forces of nature to life and thus impresses their impact on the mind. We know that the sun changes its place in the sky; but when a film, in condensing a day to a minute, shows the play of rapidly moving shadows interpret the plastic relief of architectural shape, we are made to think of light as a happening that assumes its place among the other productive motions of daily life.

When the film camera was still cranked by hand, the cameraman was accustomed to increasing his speed somewhat when he photographed rapid action. This slowed down the movements on the screen so that they could be perceived more comfortably. Conversely, a slow scene shot with a slightly reduced cranking movement condensed the action on the screen and thereby made the overall structure of the visible changes more compelling. However, the change of speed not only served to adapt visual movement to the range of human perception, but also changed the expressive qualities of an action. When street scenes were photographed at subnormal speed for the early slapstick comedies, cars did not simply move faster. They dashed around in an aggressive panic—a mood hardly suggested by their normal behavior. Conversely, high-speed shots make the movements of a sportsman or dancer not only slower, but wooly and soft.

In addition to the expressive qualities of the moving object, those of the invisible medium are affected. The slowed-down football player seems to be moving through water—that is, through a denser medium, which puts up resistance to motion and cushions the effect of gravity. Even to the naked eye a school of fast-moving fish makes the water look as thin as air, whereas a lazy goldfish seems to move through oil. This phenomenon is the result of an ambiguity of visual dynamics. The high speed of an object may be perceived as being caused by great motor power in the object, weak resistance of the medium, or both. Slowness is seen as weakness of effort on the part of the object, great resistance of the medium, or both.

This effect of *movimento frenato* has been investigated by Gian Franco Minguzzi, who had a black disk travel across a field, half of which was white, the other gray. As the disk reached the gray area, its velocity was abruptly slowed to about one-seventh its previous rate. Most observers saw the disk braked by the stronger friction encountered in the gray zone, which appeared "more viscous, dense, gelatinous." Interestingly enough, when Minguzzi reversed the situation by making the disk start out slowly in the gray area and increase its speed abruptly upon entering the white area, the effect was quite different. Only one out of ten subjects attributed the increase in speed to reduced friction in the white area. Four subjects saw no relation between the change of speed and the change of background brightness; and five reported positively that the disk "started to run." Speeding up was more compellingly attributed to the initiative of the object than slowing down.

Visual speed also depends on the size of the object. Large objects seem to move more slowly than small ones. A smaller surrounding field makes for faster motion. J. F. Brown had rows of figures move through rectangular frames. When the size of the frame as well as that of the figures was doubled, velocity seemed reduced by one half. In order to appear equal, velocities had to be in exact proportion to the size dimensions. This leads us to expect that on a narrow stage, dancers will seem to move faster, and that the larger the human figures or other objects on the movie screen, the slower their movement will seem, if their images move across the observer's retina at an objectively identical speed.

Stroboscopic Movement

All motion perception is basically stroboscopic. When a bird flies through my field of vision, its physical displacement is continuous. What I see of the flight, however, derives from a sequence of recordings by the individual receptors or "receptive fields," in the retina. As the bird arrives from the left, the receptors on the retinas' right side will be activated first, the ones to the left, last. The nervous system creates the sensation of continuous movement by integrating the sequence of these momentary stimulations, none of which records anything but a static change. H. L. Teuber reports that with certain brain injuries a moving motorcycle is seen as a string of overlapping cycles, each standing still. Whether the integration occurs at the retinal or the cortical level, the basic fact is that the experience of mobility derives from a sequence of immobile inputs.

Therefore, when the physical event is itself discontinuous, we have a difference in magnitude, but not in principle. The most obvious example is the motion picture. With exposure to a minimum of about twenty frames per second, we can see continuous motion. The same is true for the luminous panels of advertising signboards, on which the flashing on and off of light bulbs produces the moving images of letters, geometrical shapes, or human figures, even though objectively nothing moves.

The pioneering experiments on stroboscopic movement were done by Max Wertheimer. He investigated the perceptual effects induced by the successive flashing of two luminous objects, e.g. two lines, in the dark—a phenomenon familiar to us from the signal lights of airplanes and from traffic lights. When the two stimuli are close together in space or flash at a very short time interval, they look simultaneous. When the space or time distances are large, one sees two separate objects appearing one after the other. But when conditions are favorable, one sees a single object move from the first position to the second. For example, a vertical line is seen as tipping over and coming to rest in a horizontal position. In such cases, therefore, observers see motion even though physically there is a mere succession of immobile stimuli. This presupposes that the two stimuli produced an integrated process of sweeping displacement somewhere in the brain. Wertheimer concluded that in such cases the two stimulations, occurring close together in time and space, cause a kind of physiological short circuit, which makes the excitation flow from the first spot to the second. The psychological counterpart of this hypothetical brain process is the perceived movement.

Wertheimer's experiments were suggested by a children's toy invented and first described in 1834 by W. G. Horner. A series of pictures representing successive phases of the movement of some object, for example a jumping horse, were inserted in a tambour and viewed in succession through slots while the cylinder rotated. This device, called a Daedaleum by its inventor, and others of the same kind eventually led to the motion picture. The fusion of images in any of these devices is often attributed merely to the tendency of retinal stimulations to persist for a moment after their occurrence and thereby to blend with later stimulations in a coherent flow. However, film-makers know that under suitable conditions, even one-frame cutting may be experienced as a sequence of discrete, although not clearly distinguishable images. As Wertheimer's experiments show, we are dealing here not so much with fusion as with the creation of coherent shape in the time dimension. The rules of structural organization apply.

Why do the stimuli created by two luminous shapes in the dark blend into a unitary flow of excitation? We notice, first of all, that the phenomenon occurs only when the two shapes lie fairly close together, and we remember that similarity of location produces a visual link between neighbors. Second, the two stimuli are alone in an empty field. They play a similar part in the whole. And since similarity was found to relate elements in space, we are led to suspect that it does so also in time.

Consider a flying ball. The ball's successive positions in the visual field are represented in Figure 247 as though they were photographed on the frames of a film. If in this way we eliminate the time dimension, we clearly realize that the object describes a simply shaped path; and we tentatively conclude that the principle of consistent shape, which groups the elements of motionless patterns, may also be instrumental in preserving the identity of the moving object in time.

Experiments by Albert Michotte on the "tunnel effect" have shown that perceptual identity may also be preserved when the path of the movement is interrupted, e.g., when a moving object drops from sight while passing through a tunnel or behind a wall. Under favorable space and time conditions the observer sees the identical object pursue a unitary, though temporarily concealed, path—an experience quite different from simply knowing or assuming that the object emerging from behind the obstacle has remained the same.

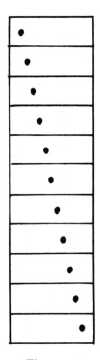

Figure 247

The other familiar principles of grouping also play their parts. An object in motion is the more likely to preserve its identity the less it changes in size, shape, brightness, color, or speed. Identity is threatened if a moving object changes direction—for example, if the ball of Figure 247 suddenly turns backward. As usual, in any particular instance these factors will either reinforce or counteract one another, and the result will depend on their relative strength. If a hunted hare suddenly doubles back on his path, the change in direction may not prevent us from seeing him still as the same animal. If at the moment of turning he changes into a turkey, identity may break down and we may see a second animal taking off from the spot where the first disappeared. But if the transformation of shape and color takes place without a change in course, the consistency of path and speed may be strong enough to make us see one and the same animal transforming itself during the chase.

The interaction of shape and motion has been investigated by W. Metzger, who wished to find out what happens when two or more moving objects cross each other's path (Figure 248a). At the meeting point, each object can be seen either as sharply changing its direction and turning back or as continuing its

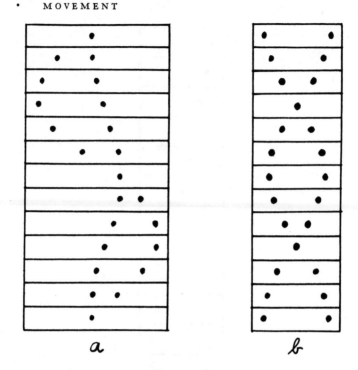

Figure 248

course consistently by crossing over to the other side. It was found that the latter version generally prevailed—a result that accords with the principle of grouping by consistent shape. Among other things, the experiments showed that when the objects move in a strictly symmetrical manner (Figure 248*b*), the result is less clear-cut. In that case many observers see the objects back up at the point of encounter and remain in their own wing of the field. This indicates that in movement, just as in motionless patterns, symmetry creates a subdivision along its axis, which tends to discourage crossings even where local consistencies of the path favor it.

Wertheimer's experiments had shown that under favorable structural conditions, objects appearing at successive moments in time at different locations will be perceived as two states of one identical object. His basic setup involved only two stimuli. What happens when the number of stimuli is increased and a more complex configuration offers a choice among several possible connections? Figures 249–251 give three examples from a study of this problem by Josef Ternus. Suppose three luminous spots in the position indicated by the upper row of Figure 249*a* are replaced by those of the lower

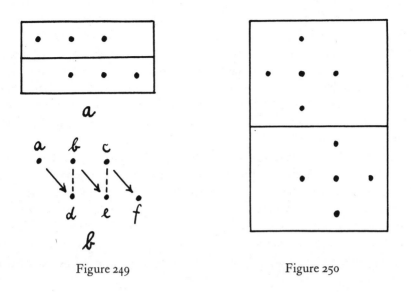

Figure 249   Figure 250

row, appearing at the same level in space. Since the locations coincide for two of the dots, we might expect that b and c (Figure 249b) will be identified with d and e—that is, remain immobile—while a will be replaced by f or perhaps leap to the position f. Instead, all three dots move in the manner indicated by the oblique arrows: a becomes d, b becomes e, c becomes f. Or rather, the entire triplet moves to the right. In other words, the pattern moves to the structurally analogous position in the second configuration. Each point identifies with its structural counterpart. This is the simplest change available within the total organization of the field.

For the same reason the entire cross in the initial phase of Figure 250 moves to the position of the cross in the second phase, even though again two

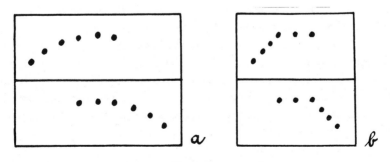

Figure 251

of the dots could remain in place were their behavior not affected by the demands of the whole pattern. A useful comparison is afforded by Figure 251. The six dots of *a* form a strongly unified arc. Consequently the whole arc is seen as moving to the right on a curved track. In *b* the angular break produces a subdivision that leaves the two triplets somewhat independent of each other. Under these conditions the horizontal triplet is free to adopt the comfortable solution of staying put while the left triplet leaps across to become its own counterpart on the right side.

Stroboscopic movement in vision has a direct parallel in the sequence of tones in music, as Victor Zuckerkandl has pointed out. The progression of a melody is made up of tones, each of which dwells without motion at one level of pitch; there is no physical equivalent to the upward and downward steps of movement we hear as one tone replaces another. In fact, musical notation, which reports each tone to the eye as a separate entity, belies the psychological fact that what we hear is actually only *one* tone moving up and down along the profile of the melody.

Some Problems of Film Editing

Visual identity is not problematic as long as an object remains in the same place and does not alter its appearance—for example, when the film camera, without changing its location, takes a shot of a building. Similarly an actor walking across the screen will be seen as persisting in his identity when he moves along a simple path (Figure 247) and does not change his shape or size noticeably. Trouble starts when visual conditions suggest identity where none is intended, or vice versa.

The film editor, like the comic strip artist, faces two problems in stringing together scenes referring to different points in time and space. He must preserve identity across the leaps, and he must make sure that different items are seen as different. The spectator knows only what he sees. Rapid succession suggests unity, and therefore strong means are needed to make a break apparent. Stroboscopic movement ignores the physical origin of the visual material. If a policeman in the stationhouse appears on the left side of the screen, and immediately afterward a lady of a similar general shape and stance appears in her living room on the same side of the screen, the policeman may be seen as changing into the lady. When their positions are not quite the same but other conditions are sufficiently similar, the policeman will perform a stroboscopic jump and change into the lady. This phenomenon can be used for magic tricks, as George Méliès did early in the century. Continuity of perceptual factors will bridge the space-time gap. In one of Maya Deren's experimental films, a dancer's leap starts in one setting and is completed in another. The two phases of the leap integrate so perfectly that one unified motion is seen in spite of the change in setting. Usually, however, it is desirable that no such cross-connection between shots should be seen.

The opposite problem is just as great. If a scene is composed of shots taken at different camera angles, the same objects, characters, and settings will look different; and it is necessary to make the audience see that the front-face figure at the left in the first shot is identical with the figure shown from the back at the right in the second shot. Similarly, if the first shot presents a corner of a room with a window and a piano, it must be apparent that the corner with the door and the table in the next shot belongs to the same place. A perceptual connection must be established, which, however, must not be so intimate as to produce stroboscopic jumps.

Here, as in so many other areas, the rules of thumb developed by practicing artists should be subjected to systematic experimentation by psychologists. The results would benefit both parties. In the meantime a few examples may serve. No stroboscopic short circuit is likely to occur as long as objects appear at sufficient distance from each other on the screen. If their location is identical or similar, only a considerable change of appearance will prevent fusion. A mere change of size, obtained when the object is photographed at two different distances from the camera, is insufficient: the object will be seen magically to shrink or expand. A turn of the head of, say, thirty degrees is likely to produce motion; but a cut from front face to profile involves such a strong change of what I have called the "structural skeleton" that the transition may be a little safer.

If a man walks across the screen from left to right and in the next shot from right to left, the movement will be visually discontinuous. Therefore other means of identification must come into play to ensure a correct reading. Strong differences in lighting may also disrupt identity. A seagull is white when lit frontally, black when taken against the light. The similarity of the flight pattern may suffice to make us see the same bird, although the sudden change in mood remains.

A final example illustrating the problems of location may be taken from an article by Rudy Bretz. If a sports match is covered by two television cameras located on opposite sides of the arena, a cut from one camera to the other will naturally invert the picture. The boxer on the left will suddenly be on the right, and vice versa. The obstacle is best overcome by having the cut occur during a pronounced action, which defines the roles of the antagonists so clearly that correct identification is preserved despite the paradoxical location and movement.

Visible Motor Forces

Geometrically, locomotion can be defined as a mere change of location, but for the naive observer, just as for the physicist, displacements are dynamic. The behavior of forces is always the more important part of the story. Artistically it is these forces that give an event visual expression and endow it with life. However, such forces are not visible in and by themselves; they are embodied only in the actions of the objects we see. The conditions that produce these effects require exploration.

Frequently, when watched from some distance, the motion of automobiles or airplanes has a "dead" quality. The vehicles show no sign of being possessed by forces. Magically and incomprehensibly propelled, they exhibit pure, uninspiring locomotion—the exception that confirms the rule. In comparison, horses galloping on distant fields or swallows cruising through the air are visibly active, and, in all fairness, so are cars in automobile races and slapstick comedies, or fighter planes in dogfights.

When it comes to human behavior, the expressive qualities of motion are entangled with what we know about its meaning. Perhaps the spectator is moved by Orpheus's gesture of wringing his hands only because he has known people to do the same when they were in despair and because the story has told him that Orpheus has lost Eurydice. It is therefore most desirable to observe expressive movement devoid of attached meaning. Good material can be found in nonmimetic ("abstract") animation films. Systematic experimentation has been initiated by Albert Michotte, whose work will be described here in some detail. In what follows I have selected the material and rephrased the theory somewhat to fit our particular purpose.

Michotte, limited by a primitive technique, worked with very simple patterns, mostly with squares moving along straight lines. Some of the experiments illustrate the problem of identity. As I mentioned, the unifying power of a consistent motion is such that the moving object is seen as remaining the same even when its shape changes abruptly. In one of Michotte's experiments —which puts my earlier example of the hare and the turkey to the test—a small, black square appears on the left side of a white field and moves horizontally toward the center. At a given moment it disappears and is replaced by a red square of the same size, which appears next to it and immediately moves on in the same direction and at the same speed. In this case the observers see one object, which in the course of a unitary movement changes in color.

A different effect results from the following demonstration (Figure 252). The black square A, again at the left, starts moving horizontally and stops directly above or beneath the red square B, which has been present but immobile. At the moment of A's arrival, B begins to move in the same direction. In this experiment, observers see two objects performing two movements, which are all but independent of each other. The same is true for the setup of Figure 253, in which B moves at right angles to A.

Between the extremes of undivided, unitary movement on the one hand and somewhat or completely independent movements on the other, various kinds of interaction, which are perceived as causal relations, can occur between the visual objects. Michotte's basic experiment on perceptual causality is the following. The red square (B) is in the center of the field; the black one (A) is some distance from it, to the left. At a given moment, A begins to move toward B. When the two touch, A stops and B starts moving. The observers see A give B a push that makes it move. In other words, the occurrence appears to involve cause and effect.

Of course no physical causality is there. The two squares are drawn or projected on a screen. Why, then, do observers see a causal process? According to Hume's well-known view, the percept itself contains nothing but a neutral succession of events. Accustomed to the fact that one kind of happening is followed by another, the mind assumes the connection to be necessary and expects it to be made every time. The quality of cause and effect is thus added secondarily to the percept by an association formed over a lifetime.

In opposition to this view, Michotte demonstrates that causality is as much an aspect of the percept itself as the shape, color, and movement of the objects. Whether and to what extent causality is seen depends exclusively upon the perceptual conditions. Strong causality results even in situations where practical experience must call it absurd—for example, when a wooden ball is seen

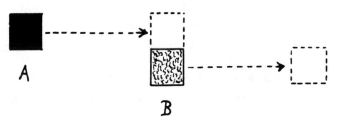

Figure 252

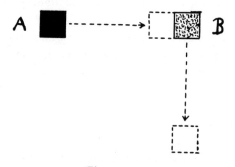

Figure 253

giving a push to a luminous disk projected on a screen. Causality may also be observed when a familiar situation is turned into its opposite, as in the following experiment. The red square B is moving fairly rapidly toward the right. A, moving even faster, catches up with B. At the moment of their contact, B suddenly slows down considerably and continues its course at the reduced speed. Under these paradoxical conditions, perceived causality is particularly compelling.

The kind of causal relation observed in these demonstrations consists in the visible transmission of energy from one object to another. At contact, the force animating the prime mover is seen leaping across to the secondary object, thereby setting it in motion. This type of causality comes about when the objects are sufficiently distinguished from each other to appear as not identical, and when at the same time the sequence of their activities is sufficiently integrated to appear as one unitary process. A slight interval of rest at the moment of contact will break the continuity of the movement and eliminate the experience of causality.

When the unity of the movement is diminished but sufficient, other forms of causality result. If, for example, at the moment when A reaches its immobile partner, B starts to move at a velocity considerably greater than that previously seen in A, B's motor energy no longer seems acquired from A. B starts to move under its own power. There is still causality, but it is limited to A's "giving the starting signal" to B. Michotte's observers describe this release effect in various ways. "A's arrival is the occasion for B's departure." "A throws an electric switch, which makes B go." "B is frightened by A's arrival and escapes." This last description is an example of the humorous effect often produced by the release phenomenon. Michotte explains it by the disproportion between the small antecedent and the big consequence. When, on the other hand, the sequence of speeds is reversed, i.e., when A moves faster than B, the active pushing effect is strong. B is perceived as acquiring some of A's energy.

When an object enters the field at a constant velocity, this is seen as the action of some kind of energy, but in a fairly neutral, inexpressive way. There is no way of telling whether the object moves under its own steam or is being pushed or pulled. A different effect is obtained when, as in Michotte's basic experiment, A is at rest for a moment before it begins to move toward B. With no other source of energy in sight, A is then seen as "taking off," that is, as generating its own motor energy. Hence the expression of inherent initiative conveyed by A. We could imagine that A might also be seen as being attracted magnetically by B. This, however, does not happen, evidently because B is not explicitly characterized as an object equipped with the kind of energy that would attract others.

The essential result of the experiments is that all properties of the objects must be "implicitly defined" by what can be seen. The objects convey no properties but the ones revealed perceptually by their behavior. A square at rest will not seem a center of attraction just because an observer, for some reason, assumes it to be such. This rule holds good even for situations in which knowledge supplements what is directly perceived. When a pretty girl is seen to attract an admirer, the scene will "work" only if the expressive traits of behavior and shape in both actors convey the dynamics of attracting and being attracted.

Michotte's technique can also be used to show that the dynamic effect depends not only on the local conditions at the moment of contact, but on the broader context of the total episode. In one of his experiments, B is seen to set itself in motion. It moves back and forth horizontally and repeats this action several times. Then A takes off, meeting B at the moment when B has returned to its point of departure for a last trip. Unless the observers focus on the meeting point, they see no pushing under these conditions, even though the last phase of the performance duplicates the basic experiment, described earlier. By its oscillations B has defined itself as moving under its own power, and its last trip to the right appears simply as a continuation of this autonomous movement, even though A has now made contact.

This experiment can be said to translate into action one of Wertheimer's demonstrations (Figure 254). When the eye moves along the zigzag line upward from the bottom, the line is seen as continuing its own path beyond the meeting point even though there is a straight-line continuation in one of the sides of the octagon. Both experiments show that the inner consistency of two elements will be prevented from making them fuse if the structure of the whole pattern separates the elements from each other.

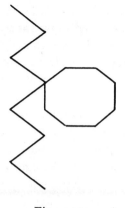

Figure 254

A Scale of Complexity

An object is perceived as generating its own motor power when after a period of immobility it suddenly takes off without any visible outside cause. This effect is greatly heightened when the change from immobility to motion does not occur for the whole object simultaneously but a part of it starts the motion and imparts it to the rest. In that case, the action is seen as generated by an internal change. Michotte used a horizontal bar of the proportions 2:1, located at the field's left (Figure 255). The bar starts getting longer at its right end until it has reached about four times its original length. As the right end stops, a contraction begins at the left end and continues until the bar has become as short as it was originally. Now the left end stops, the whole performance starts

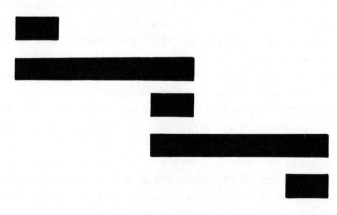

Figure 255

all over again and is repeated three or four times, which carries the bar to the right side of the field. Figure 255 shows the main stages for two full phases.

The effect is very strong. The observers exclaim: "It is a caterpillar! It moves by itself!" A notable feature is the internal elasticity exhibited by the bar. The entire body participates in the change imposed upon it by the displacement of one of its ends. There is no rigid distinction between the immobile and the moving parts. The body begins to stretch at one end, and the extension gradually involves more and more of it. The same happens in the contraction. This purely perceptual inner flexibility produces a strikingly organic quality.

A very different effect is obtained by the following modification (Figure 256). The experiment starts as before with the 2:1 rectangle at the left side of the field; but instead of getting longer the rectangle now splits up into two squares, the left one remaining immobile, the right one moving forward to the place occupied by the front end of the caterpillar in the preceding experiment. B stops there, only to be followed by A, until the two join and again form a rectangle of the original size. Now the whole action is repeated. Although the motions of the two squares equal those of the caterpillar's head and tail, the effect on the observer is quite different. A is seen as running after B and pushing it forward. The two squares are rigid, and the whole process looks mechanical rather than organic.

These experiments raise the question: Are there precise perceptual criteria for the distinction between organic and inorganic behavior? Offhand we might assume that such a distinction will depend simply upon whether an observed motion reminds us more of machines or of animals. This explanation, however, would neglect the most relevant aspect of the phenomenon.

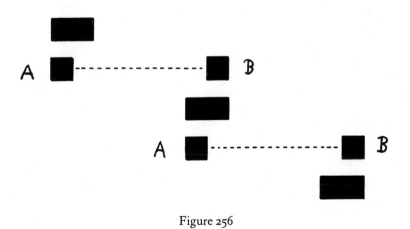

Figure 256

It is well known that the distinction between inorganic and organic things comes fairly late. At early stages of development primitives as well as children, guided by what they see, do not distinguish in principle between dead things and living ones. Stones are believed by some primitives to be male or female, to have offspring and to grow. They live forever, whereas animals and humans die. To the artist also the distinction is artificial. The painter sees no difference in principle between the sweep of a coastline and the undulation of a snake. Ordinary perception suggests no split in nature; it rather indicates various degrees of liveliness. Spring water looks more alive than a flower.

What is observed here is not just a difference in the amount or speed of motion. There is also a scale that leads from simpler to more complex behavior. And here it must be realized that the distinction between things that have consciousness, feelings, desires, intentions, and others that do not is equally alien to a world view based on spontaneous perception. There is a difference in degree between the rain that falls without much consideration of what it is hitting and a crocodile going after his prey. But this is not a difference between having or not having a mind or soul. It concerns the extent to which behavior seems directed by external goals as well as the complexity of the observable reactions. A Westerner living in the twentieth century is supposed to make a fundamental distinction between a man walking along a hotel corridor in search of his room number and a wooden cart, steered by a pair of photo-electric cells, that will set itself in motion and run after any bright light. But even the Westerner is strongly impressed by the "human" qualities of the phototropic robot.

There are good reasons for the comparison. The behavior of both the hotel guest and the wooden cart is distinguished by a visible striving toward specific aims, which is quite different from what we observe when the pendulum of a clock moves to and fro or when a bored museum guard strolls through the rooms assigned to his care. It might well be maintained that the difference between high-level and low-level performance is more essential than the fact that the hotel guest and the guard are supposed to have consciousness whereas the robot and the pendulum are not.

In his interviews with children, Jean Piaget studied their criteria for considering something alive and endowed with consciousness. At the lowest age level anything involved in some action is considered alive and conscious, whether it moves or not. At the second stage, movement makes the difference. A bicycle has consciousness, a table has not. At the third level, the child bases its distinction on whether the object generates its own movement or is moved from the outside. Older children consider only animals both alive and in possession of consciousness, although they may count plants among the living creatures.

It will be seen that the modern scientist's way of separating the inanimate from the animate and the mindless from the mindful, does not hold for spontaneous perception. To repeat, it does not hold for the artist either. To a film director, a thunderstorm can be more alive than the passengers sitting impassively on the benches of a streetcar. A dance is not a means of conveying to us the feelings or intentions of the person represented by the dancer. What we experience is much more direct. When we see agitation or calm, escape or pursuit, we watch the behavior of forces whose perception does not require a distinction between a physical outside and a mental inside.

What counts is the level of complexity in the observed behavior. If we attempt informally to sketch some of the pertinent criteria, we find the following. In agreement with the opinions of children, there is first the difference between what moves and what does not move. Second, flexible movement, which involves internal change, is at a higher level of complexity than the mere displacement of rigid objects or parts of objects. Third, an object that mobilizes its own power and determines its own course is higher than one that is moved and steered—that is, passively submits to being pushed, pulled, repelled, attracted—by an external agent. Fourth, among the "active" objects there is a distinction between those that move merely on an internal impulse and others whose behavior is influenced by external centers of reference. Within this latter group there is lower-level behavior, which requires direct contact by the outer agent (e.g., object B's "taking off" when touched by A), and higher-level behavior, which involves response to the object of reference across some distance in space (e.g., A is seen as moving "toward" B, or B escapes while A is approaching).

The level of the fourth group does not presuppose that the objects "have awareness." All we are implying is that the behavior pattern of the observed forces is more complex when it involves an interplay between the object and its environment. Such interplay may occur even though the forces are purely physical, as in the phototropic robot; on the other hand, the obtuse "blindness" of the lower level may be found in a sophisticated dreamer, who pursues his path without regard for events around him.

When an object moves along a complex path at varying speed it seems to be controlled by correspondingly complex forces. Compare, for example, the difference between A's moving toward B in a straight line and at constant speed with the following hypothetical situations. A slows down while approaching and suddenly "leaps at" B, with a sharp increase in speed. Or A

slows down, stops, proceeds again, stops again, and suddenly turns around and withdraws very quickly. Or *A* starts out in the "wrong" direction, moves slowly along the zigzag path indicated in Figure 257, and after the last turn quickly joins *B*. Presumably these demonstrations would give the impression of sneaking up, hesitating and escaping, and searching. Their dynamics is more complex than that of the straight movement at constant speed, because we observe the effect of an interplay of force and counterforce, of contradictory forces taking over at different times, of changes in course because of what is found or not found at a given place, and so on.

These expressive qualities appear not only in the behavior of visible objects, but also in the indirectly perceived movements of the film camera. As long as these movements are relatively simple—for example, when the camera travels forward or backward in a straight line and at constant speed, or when it rotates on the tripod for a horizontal or vertical panorama shot—they appear as fairly neutral displacements. The spectator's attention is concentrated on the new aspects of the setting uncovered by the camera. But the path of the camera can describe curves of a higher order. Its motions can become quite irregular, particularly when it is controlled by hand. Its speed can vary. It can search and hesitate, explore, turn its attention suddenly to some event or object, leap at its prey. Such complex motions are not neutral. They portray an invisible self, which assumes the active role of a character in the plot. The strivings and reactions of this character are conveyed by a pattern of forces, which becomes manifest in the motor behavior of the camera.

It should be noted here that these camera motions fulfill their function only when they convey expressive impulses and responses rather than merely the mechanical effect of physical action. Just as pictures of sexual intercourse tend to look ludicrous rather than passionate when they reduce man to a toiling machine, so the rhythmical rocking of pictures taken by a walking cameraman produces more nausea than meaning.

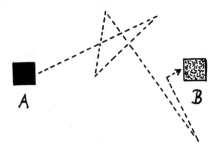

Figure 257

At an even more complex level, we may observe "feedback" effects of what happened before upon what happens after. For example, while A approaches, B suddenly runs toward A and pushes it back. A approaches again; but while B starts for a new attack, A withdraws "in time." A short film in which a large triangle, a small triangle, and a circle act out a story was prepared by Fritz Heider and Marianne Simmel for experimental purposes. It was found that the observers spontaneously endowed the geometric figures, on the basis of their motions, with "human" properties. For example, the larger triangle was described by 97 percent of the observers as: "Aggressive, warlike, belligerent, pugnacious, quarrelsome, troublesome, mean, angry, bad-tempered, temperamental, irritable, quick to take offense, bully, villain, taking advantage of his size, picking on smaller people, dominating, power-loving, possessive." The surprisingly strong expression of geometrical figures in movement has been demonstrated in the more elaborate "abstract" films of Oskar Fischinger, Norman MacLaren, Walt Disney, and others.

The more complex the pattern of forces that manifests itself in motor behavior, the more "human" the performance looks. But we cannot indicate a particular level of complexity at which behavior begins to look human, animate, conscious. Human behavior is often strikingly mechanical. In fact, Henri Bergson maintained in his book on laughter that what impresses us as comical is the discovery of mechanical aspects in human behavior. Moreover, within the same organic or inorganic mechanism, motor behavior may vary widely in its complexity and subtlety. Among the organs of the human body the hand has the most refined motor behavior to be encountered anywhere in nature, whereas a knee can accomplish little more than the ball-and-socket joint of a machine.

These considerations hold also for shape. Some artists—for example, the cubists—have given the human figure the angularity of inorganic objects, whereas Van Gogh represented trees and even hills and clouds by means of flexible, humanizing curves. In the work of Picasso or Henry Moore we find the whole range of complexity, from rigid cubes to subtly inflected curves of high order.

The Body as Instrument

A dancer has a body of flesh and blood, whose physical weight is controlled by physical forces. He has sensory experiences of what happens inside and outside his body, and also feelings, wishes, goals. As an artistic instrument, however, the dancer consists—at least for his audience—of nothing but what can be seen of him. His properties and actions, like those of Michotte's squares, are implicitly defined by how he looks and what he does. One hundred and sixty pounds of weight on the scales will not exist if to the eye he has the winged lightness of a dragonfly. His yearnings are limited to what appears in posture and gesture.

This does not mean that the human figure is the same as an abstract pattern. Figure 258*a* shows an attempt by the painter Kandinsky to translate a photograph of the dancer Palucca, roughly like Figure 258*b*, into a line pattern. It will be seen that the design retains, perhaps even intensifies, certain properties of the dancing body—its symmetry, its squat proportion, the radiation of limbs from a massive base. But it lacks other characteristics, some of which spring from our knowledge of the human body. The photograph of the dancer derives strong dynamic properties from our perceiving the pose as a deviation from a normal or key position. The legs are not just a flat circular curve; they are stretched apart. The arms are not just directed upward; they are raised. The head is more than one of three dots; it is the seat of the sense organs and the mind—that is, the center of incoming and outgoing forces. And the whole figure is seen as propelled off the ground rather than reposing on a neutral piece of drawing paper.

Thus some of the known properties and functions of the body are an inseparable part of its visible character. This poses a peculiar problem for the

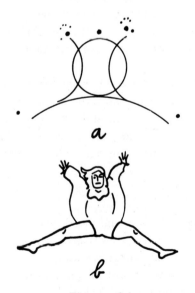

Figure 258

dancer. The center of the nervous system, which receives all information and directs all action, is located not in the visible center of the body, but in the head, a relatively small and detached appendage. Only in a limited way can activity be shown as issuing from this appendage—for example, by facial expression, or by making the head turn toward an object of interest or nod or shake. But even these motions are difficult to coordinate with the rest of the body. In daily life the head alone performs a good deal of action while the body rests, an essentially unconcerned base. The same is true for the hands. The dancer can frankly exclude the body, as in Hindu dances, which can be performed even when the dancer is seated; they consist of stories told by the hands while the head and face supply a responsive accompaniment. But if the whole body is to be involved, action must issue from its visible and motor centers in the torso rather than from the center of the nervous system. If man were constructed like a starfish, there would be no trouble. But the peculiar discrepancy of the human build moves the appropriate center of the dancer's action away from the visible locus of the mind.

It is true that since antiquity the sections of the body have been identified with the principal functions of the organism. The French dance teacher François Delsarte maintained that the human body as an instrument of expression is "divided into three zones: the head and neck being the mental zone; the torso, the spiritual-emotional zone; the abdomen and hips, the physical zone. The arms and legs are our contact with the outer world—but the arms, being attached to the torso, take on a predominantly spiritual-emotional quality; the legs, being attached to the heavy lower trunk, take on a predominantly physical quality. Each part of the body subdivides again into the same three zones; in the arm, for instance, the heavy upper arm, physical; the forearm, spiritual-emotional; the hand, mental. In the leg: thigh, physical; foreleg, spiritual-emotional; foot, mental." This description blends what we know about the mental and physical functions and their location in the body with the spontaneous symbolism of the body as a visual image.

Isadora Duncan reasoned as a dancer when she asserted that the solar plexus was the bodily habitation of the soul because the visual and motor center of dance movement is the torso. But her statement hides the fact that when movement issues from the torso, human activity is represented as directed by the vegetative functions rather than by the cognitive capacities of the mind. The torso-centered dance shows man primarily as a child of nature, not as a carrier of the spirit. Many a young dancer's difficulties involve a conscious or unconscious resistance to shifting from the safe control of reason to an "immodest" acknowledgment of instinct. It would be tempting to follow up the parallel with sculpture, where the compositional theme is frequently developed from the center of the body and sometimes limited to a headless and limbless torso.

Just as in other forms of art, all movement in dancing and acting must be subordinated to a dominant theme. In daily life the body accomplishes motor coordination with little difficulty, once the initial stages of training are overcome. When a child first learns to walk, each step is innervated deliberately and separately. The same lack of integration can be observed whenever a new motor skill is being acquired. For the purposes of dancing and acting, all motor behavior must be learned afresh until it becomes spontaneous again at a higher level of form and control.

When one feels self-conscious, the smooth submission to the dominant theme of a motion is disturbed by the sudden conscious control of secondary centers of action. In an essay on the puppet theater the poet Heinrich von Kleist recommended to the dancer the example of the marionette, which in his opinion has the negative advantage of never being affected. "For affectation, as you know, appears when the soul (*vis motrix*) finds itself at a point other than that of the center of gravity of the movement. Since the puppeteer, when he holds this wire, has no other point in his power but this one, all other limbs are what they should be, dead; they are only pendula and just follow the law of gravitation; an excellent quality, which we seek in vain with most of our dancers. . . . Look at young F. when, as Paris, he stands among the three goddesses and hands the apple to Venus; his soul—it is awful to look at—is seated in his elbow. Such mistakes . . . are unavoidable since we have eaten of the tree of knowledge. But Paradise is bolted, and the cherub is behind us; we must make the voyage around the world and see whether, perhaps, it is open again somewhere at the back." To be sure, Kleist simplified the condition of grace. No model of perfection is produced at the lowest level of integration when dead limbs drag behind the motion of a central point. Even the puppeteer is faced with the delicate task of organizing the various centers of motion in accordance with their functions in the whole.

The Kinesthetic Body Image

In dancing and acting, the artist, his tool, and his work are fused into one physical thing: the human body. One curious consequence is that the performance is essentially created in one medium while it appears to the audience in another. The spectator receives a strictly visual work of art. The dancer uses a mirror occasionally; he also has at times a more or less vague visual image of his own performance; and of course as a member of a group or as a choreographer, he sees the work of other dancers. But as far as his own body is concerned, he creates mainly in the medium of the kinesthetic sensations in his muscles, tendons, and joints. This fact is worth noting, if only because some aestheticians have maintained that only the higher senses of vision and hearing yield artistic media.

All kinesthetic shape is dynamic. Michotte has observed that "movement seems to be essential to the phenomenal existence of the body, and posture is probably experienced only as the terminal phase of motion." Merleau-Ponty points out that "my body appears to me as posture"; and that, in contrast to visually observed objects, it does not have a spatiality of position but one of situation. "When I stand in front of my desk and lean on it with both hands, the accent is all on my hands, while my entire body trails behind them like the tail of a comet. Not that I am unaware of the locations of my shoulders or hips, but they are only implied in that of my hands, and my entire posture is, as it were, readable through the hands' leaning on the desk."

The dancer builds his work from the feelings of tension and relaxation, the sense of balance, which distinguishes the proud stability of the vertical from the risky adventures of thrusting and falling. The dynamic nature of kinesthetic experience is the key to the surprising correspondence between what the dancer creates by his muscular sensations and the image of his body seen by the audience. The dynamic quality is the common element uniting the two different media. When the dancer lifts his arm, he primarily experiences the tension of raising. A similar tension is visually conveyed to the spectator through the image of the dancer's arm.

When dancers and actors coordinate the kinesthetic with the visual medium, learning how much to give is a major problem. The performer's initial uncertainty in this matter may be partly the result of the fact that, as Michotte has pointed out, our dynamic body image has poorly defined limits. It is a "kinesthetic amoeba"; it has no contour. Michotte explains that this is true because the body is the one and only content of the kinesthetic field. There is nothing beyond and around it, no "ground" from which it could detach itself as the figure. Thus we can judge the size and strength of our motions in relation to one another, but we have little concept of their impact as a visual image in the surrounding field. The dancer must learn how large or fast a gesture should be in order to achieve the desired effect.

Of course the proper dimensions depend also on the function of the movement pattern in the whole performance and on the size of the image received by the spectator. The movement of the dancer can be more extensive than that of the actor, whose visual behavior is subservient to speech. For the same reason gestures had to be toned down when the sound film added dialogue to the picture. Stage acting requires larger movement than screen acting, and the slight raising of an eyebrow in a close-up will equal an intensive gesture of surprise in a long shot. To meet these requirements the dancer and the actor have to develop appropriate kinesthetic scales of size and speed.

Finally, it is essential for the performance of the dancer and the actor that visual dynamics be clearly distinguished from mere locomotion. I noted earlier that movement looks dead when it gives the impression of mere displacement. Of course, physically all motion is caused by some kind of force. But what counts for artistic performance is the dynamics conveyed to the audience visually; for dynamics alone is responsible for expression and meaning.

The difference between mere displacement of body and limbs and the visual expression obtained through dynamic action is clearly spelled out in Rudolf von Laban's system of dance analysis. In the earlier version of this system, a movement was defined simply by the attributes of physical vectors, namely, by Path (its direction in space), Weight (its point of application), and Duration (its speed). This purely metric description left out the most important property of human motor behavior: the nature of the impulse or effort, called *Antrieb* by Laban. The shape of the movement in space had to be related to the impulse giving rise to it, because only the proper impulse could create the proper movement. Irmgard Bartenieff, in explaining this Effort-Shape Analysis, has pointed, for instance, to the following difference. A purely gestural displacement of a part of the body is generated by a narrow local impulse, as distinguished from a postural action, which spreads from the center through the entire body, visibly affecting all parts and reaching its final manifestation in the particular gesture of pointing, pushing, or stretching. Laban's earlier system might describe these two examples of behavior in identical terms, whereas his later categories emphasize the crucial difference.

The three variables of the later system are qualitative: *Space* refers to the path of the movement, which may be straight and direct or flexible and indirect; *Force* indicates the difference between vigorous strength and delicate weightlessness; *Time* distinguishes between slow lingering and a sudden start. In conceiving of his or her activities in these terms the student learns, not by imitating bodily positions from the outside but by understanding the impulses that produce the desired effect. What the dancer or actor wishes to obtain is not like the sign language of a semaphore transmitting its coded message to the intellect of the recipient by gesticulation. It is rather a pattern of visual forces, whose impact is immediately felt. This example leads us to the subject of the final chapters of this book: the dynamics of directed tension and the expression inherent in it.

IX DYNAMICS

In trying to discover what makes a visual object or event look the way it looks, we have so far been safely directed by what I have called the principle of simplicity. This principle, a basic guideline of gestalt psychology, holds that any visual pattern will tend toward the simplest configuration available to the sense of sight under the given circumstances. It has explained to us why certain shapes or colors fuse into units or come apart, why some things look flat while others have volume and depth; it has enabled us to understand the rationale of completeness and incompleteness, whole and part, solidity and transparency, motion and standstill. If one basic principle elucidates so many different phenomena, we owe it gratitude. However, at this point it is necessary to acknowledge that the tendency toward simplicity alone cannot do justice to what we see; it leads to one-sided descriptions unless it is counterbalanced by a second, equally influential principle.

Simplicity Is Not Enough

If simplicity were the one overriding goal of art, evenly stained canvases or perfect cubes would be the most desirable art objects. In recent years, artists have in fact provided us with such examples of "minimal art." Historically, they were needed to soothe the eyes of a generation that had gotten lost in complexity and disorder, but they also served to prove that once it has fulfilled its therapeutic function, so bland a diet does not satisfy.

The lesson has been most useful, if only because a tradition of classicist aesthetics had taught us to describe and evaluate artistic form in terms of harmony and equilibrium alone—that "noble simplicity and quiet grandeur" which Johann Joachim Winckelmann had proclaimed in the eighteenth century as the ideal of ancient Greek art and the abiding standard for the present. We have begun to realize that the description of any visual object, be it Greek or minimal or otherwise, remains fatally incomplete if it limits itself to pointing out that everything fits nicely together. The analysis of balance and unity, though indispensable, avoids the question without which any visual statement remains incomprehensible: What is it that is being balanced and unified? This question cannot be answered by reference to subject matter alone. It refers first of all to the form we see.

In the physical world, the simplicity principle rules unopposed only in closed systems. When no new energy can enter, the forces constituting the system rearrange themselves until equilibrium is reached and no further change is possible. This final state demonstrates itself visually by exhibiting the simplest shape available under the circumstances. Thus, water poured into a system of communicating upright pipes will come to reach the same level in each pipe. The organism, however, is by no means a closed system. Physically, it counteracts the running-down of usable energy within itself by constantly drawing resources of heat, oxygen, water, sugar and salt, and other nutrients from its environment. Psychologically, too, the living creature replenishes its fuel for action by absorbing information through the senses and processing and transforming it internally. Brain and mind envisage change and crave it; they strive for growth, invite challenge and adventure. Man prefers life to death, activity to inactivity. Laziness, far from being a natural impulse, generally is caused by infirmity, fear, protest, or some other disturbance. At the same time, the tendency toward simplicity is constantly at work. It creates the most harmonious and unified organization available for the given constellation of forces, thereby ensuring the best possible functioning both within the mind and body and in their relation to the social and physical environment.

We envisage the human mind as an interplay of tension-heightening and tension-reducing strivings. The tendency toward tension-reduction cannot run its course unopposed, except in the final disintegration of death. It is checked by what I have called elsewhere the anabolic or constructive tendency, the creation of a structural theme. This structural theme constitutes what the mind is about, what it is after. The same is true for all of the mind's particular functions and works. Not even the most elementary act of seeing could materialize if the brain were ruled only by the simplicity tendency. The result would be a homogeneous field, in which every particular input would dissolve like salt crystals in water. Instead, as the eye is directed toward an object, the optical projection of that object imposes itself upon the field of vision as a constraint, a structural theme. If this stimulus pattern offers some leeway, the forces inherent in the visual field will organize or even modify it to give it as much simplicity as attainable. Here again, an interplay between tension-heightening and tension-reducing tendencies is at work. The result of this highly dynamic process is the visual object as we see it.

The same twofold dynamics is reflected in every work of visual design. There is a structural theme, suggested perhaps by the subject matter, but constituted first of all by a configuration of perceived forces. This theme is given the simplest form compatible with the character of the statement. Depending on the message and style of the work, tension may be low and the order simple, as, for example, in a row of frontal figures in a Byzantine mosaic or the stillness of a Greek profile; or tension may be high and the order complex, as in the jagged profiles of Daumier's burghers or the swinging, contorted, violently foreshortened figures of a Tiepolo. One could try to assign every particular style of art its place on a scale leading from a minimum to a maximum of visual tension. In elementary perceptual situations, we saw these varying ratios of tension-reduction and tension-heightening at work when we discussed the phenomena of visual leveling and sharpening.

Dynamics and Its Traditional Interpretations

It turns out that every visual object is an eminently dynamic affair. This fact, fundamental to all perception, is easily overlooked when we adhere to the common practice of describing sensory phenomena by purely metric properties. What is an equilateral triangle? A combination of three straight lines of equal length, meeting one another at angles of sixty degrees. What are reds and oranges meeting on a canvas? Wavelengths of 700 and 610 millimicrons. And a movement? It is defined by its speed and direction. Although useful for practical and scientific purposes, such metric descriptions overlook the primary quality of all perception, the aggressive outward pointing of the triangle, the dissonant clash of the hues, the onrush of the movement.

These dynamic properties, inherent in everything our eyes perceive, are so fundamental that we can say: *Visual perception consists in the experiencing of visual forces.* This is true even in the most practical sense. A rock that blocks my way is not primarily defined by the dimensions of its shape, size, and color, but as a brusque interruption of the forward flow, the dynamic experience of the road leading me on. Any observer not hopelessly spoiled by the practice of static measurements, which dominates our civilization, will confirm Henri Bergson's observation: "C'est que la forme est pour nous le dessin d'un mouvement."

Poetic vision focuses on the dynamics of perception as the carrier of expression. For example, Howard Nemerov writes:

The painter's eye attends to birth and death
Together, seeing a single energy
Momently manifest in every form,
As in the tree the growing of the tree
Exploding from the seed not more nor less
Than from the void condensing down and in,
Summoning sun and rain.

Similarly loaded with dynamic words is any adequate description of works of art. Nikolaus Pevsner discusses the purpose of the Gothic style in architecture: "This purpose was to enliven inert masses of masonry, to quicken spatial motion, to reduce a building to a seeming system of innervated lines of action." The language is metaphoric. It describes the visual forces as though they were mechanical forces acting upon physical matter. Yet no more appropriate terminology is available to describe what we see when we look at a Gothic building. And only by pointing to the dynamics can one make it clear that a building is more than an agglomeration of variously shaped stones.

It is natural enough that the term "movement" or "motion" has been used consistently to describe visual dynamics. T. S. Eliot says of a Chinese jar that it "moves perpetually in its stillness." Artists attribute great importance to this quality. A painted figure that lacks it is, according to Leonardo da Vinci, "doubly dead, since it is dead because it is a figment and dead again when it shows movement neither of the mind nor of the body."

Since, however, to speak of movement is obviously metaphorical when one refers to painting, sculpture, architecture, or photography, where nothing moves physically, what precisely is the nature of the visual phenomenon thus described? The one theory prevalent among philosophers and psychologists avoids the challenge by asserting that in such cases the observer is under the illusion that actual locomotion is taking place, or, more subtly but less clearly, that the image feels as though it were in motion—perhaps because the viewer generates within his own body appropriate kinesthetic reactions. This latter theory can be found, for example, in Hermann Rorschach's discussion of movement responses to his inkblots.

The assumption underlying the theory is that the image, issuing as it does from an immobile physical object, cannot itself possess dynamic properties, and that these properties therefore must be added to the percept from some other resource of the viewer. This resource is supposedly the viewer's past acquaintance with things in actual locomotion. Looking at the bronze figure of a dancer, the observer remembers what a dancer in motion looks like. This knowledge fools him into seeing motion where there is none, or at least into endowing the immobile object with a vague mobility.

It is a pedestrian theory, which conflicts with the facts in several ways. Snapshot photography proves every day that although some action pictures show a dancer or football player in vivid motion, others have the human figure awkwardly arrested in mid-air as though struck by sudden paralysis. In a good picture or sculpture, bodies swing freely. In bad ones, they may be stiff and rigid. These differences occur even though good and bad photographs, paintings, or statues have equal chances of being associated by the observer with past experiences. In bad ones, we understand that motion is represented; but not only do we not see it, we find it painfully absent.

This objection can be met by another, more refined version of the same theory, which might maintain that the association is based not on the objects as such (running man, waterfall), but on the shapes, directions, brightness values, with which objects are represented. From everyday experience certain perceptual properties are known to be associated with motion and with objects that move. For example, movement through water leaves a wedge-shaped trace. Fish, boats, arrows, birds, airplanes, motorcars have convergent, pointed shapes. Similarly, an oblique position on the part of objects suggests potential or actual motion because it deviates from the positions of rest, i.e., from hanging perpendicularly or lying on the ground horizontally. Again, blur or scales of shading are observed in fast-moving wheels, cars, flags, arms, legs. Therefore, according to this version of the traditional theory, it can be assumed that any visual image that presents objects by means of such perceptual qualities as wedge shape, oblique direction, shaded or blurred surface, will give the impression of movement; whereas the same objects will look stiff in pictures that do not fulfill the perceptual conditions.

The perceptual properties enumerated by this version of the empiricist theory tend in fact to produce visual dynamics. Moreover, by using formal criteria rather than referring to subject matter, the theory avoids limiting the effect to images of mobile objects. It can explain why pictures of trees or mountains may look strongly dynamic and why this may also be true for wholly "abstract" shapes in art or architecture.

Both versions of the theory, however, derive visual dynamics from the experience of locomotion and assume that the quality perceived in the image is a full or partial re-enactment of such actual locomotion. This assumption is incorrect. Paradoxically enough, when immobile shapes come closest to giving the impression of actual displacement in space, they do not look dynamic but, on the contrary, painfully paralyzed. In imperfectly balanced compositions, for example, the various shapes do not stabilize one another's locations, but look as though they wanted to move to more suitable places. This tendency, far from making the work appear more dynamic, turns "movement" into inhibition. Shapes look frozen, arrested in arbitrary positions. The dimension of time, which does not belong in the immobile arts, has been introduced, and it creates a false interpretation.

In El Greco's *St. Jerome* (Figure 259) the slight movement of the beard to the right counterbalances the location of the hands and the book at the left.

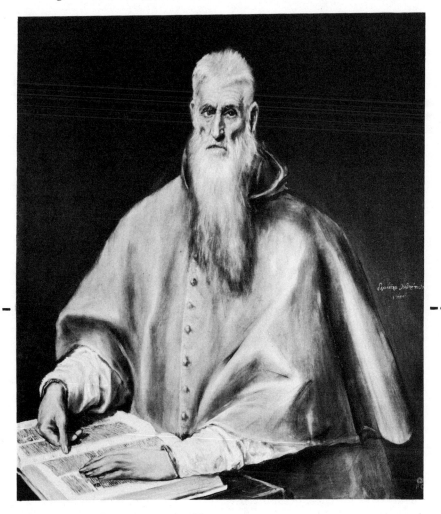

Figure 259
El Greco. *St. Jerome*. 1594–1600. Frick Coll., New York.

If the section below the dotted line is covered, balance is destroyed. The beard now looks as though it were being blown sideways by an electric fan and wanted to return to a vertical state of rest. Does this tendency make it appear more dynamic? On the contrary, whereas the beard flows freely in the complete picture, it is awkwardly kept from motion in the incomplete composition. The quality that painters and sculptors call the "movement" of immobile form does not appear unless any indication that the object might actually change or move is carefully checked.

A Diagram of Forces

If we want to do justice to visual dynamics, we had better speak of "movement" as little as possible. Wassily Kandinsky, analyzing the properties of point, line, surface, declared: "I replace the almost universally accepted concept 'movement' with 'tension.' The prevalent concept is imprecise and therefore leads to incorrect approaches, which in turn cause further terminological misunderstandings. Tension is the force inherent in the element; as such it is only one component of active movement. To this must be added direction."

Directed tension, then, is what we are talking about when we discuss visual dynamics. It is a property inherent in shapes, colors, and locomotion, not something added to the percept by the imagination of an observer who relies on his memories. The conditions creating dynamics have to be sought in the visual object itself.

Considering that dynamics is the very essence of perceptual experience and so readily acknowledged by poets, artists, and critics, it is remarkable that so little attention has been paid to it by theorists and experimentalists. Even so perceptive an observer as the philosopher Hans Jonas asserts that "no force-experience, no character of impulse and transitive causality, enters into the nature of the image." Such blindness to a conspicuous fact is probably due to what psychologists call the "stimulus error," namely the assumption that if a property cannot be found in the physical stimulus object, it cannot exist in the perceptual image either.

Let us approach the phenomenon step by step. Natural objects often possess strong visual dynamics because their shapes are the traces of the physical forces that created the objects. Motion, expansion, contraction, the processes of growth—they all can manifest themselves as dynamic shapes. The highly dynamic curve of an ocean wave is the result of the upward thrust of the water bent by the counterpull of gravity. The traces of waves on the wet sand of a beach owe their sweeping contours to the motion of the water; and in the expansive convexities of clouds and the rising and breaking outlines of mountains, we directly perceive the nature of the mechanical forces that generated them.

The winding, twisting swelling shapes of tree trunks, branches, leaves, and flowers retain and repeat the motions of growth. The biologist Paul Weiss points out that "what we perceive as static form is but the product, transitory or lasting, of formative processes"; and the work of D'Arcy Thompson is based on the fact that the form of an object is "a diagram of forces." Max Burchartz uses the following illustration. "Snails in building their shells offer an example of rhythmical construction. The shells are made from excretions of liquid chalk paste, which is shaped by rhythmical motions of the body and then crystallizes. Snails' shells are fixated expressive movements of the first order." Thus nature is alive to our eyes partly because its shapes are fossils of the events that gave rise to them. The past history is not merely inferred intellectually from clues, but directly experienced as forces and tensions present and active in visible shape.

Works of art are seldom produced physically by the forces we perceive in their shapes. The spiral twist of a baroque figure was not created by the same sort of twisting of physical materials that is responsible for the spiraling of a rope or a ram's horns. No spiraling forces shaped or inhabit the marble. The work of art is created by external forces applied by the artist's arms and body, and the chisel strokes of the sculptor have rarely any formal affinity to the shape of the statue.

These motor acts, however, leave their imprint by what we may call their graphological qualities. The motions of the hand can be sensed in the traces of the pen on paper in writing. Here the standardized shapes of letters are re-created by motor activity, and the graphologist is accustomed to weighing the contribution of motion against the effect of the intention to copy the model pattern visually. When the motor factor is strong, it tilts the letter obliquely in the direction of the movement—that is, mostly toward the right—to cut corners, slur angles, omit detail. The line shows an unbroken overall flow, which often reduces the intended patterns to illegibility. In this way the graphologist indirectly gauges the strength of temperament and vital impulses in their relation to the controlling will, which tends to guide activity in accordance with the prescribed task. Handwriting is a live diagram of psychophysical forces.

In some works of the visual arts also, we can evaluate the relative strength of the two factors. Drawings that Picasso executed by moving a flashlight in a dark room were recorded photographically. The swinging curves clearly showed dominance of the motor factor over visual organization, and thus differed from what is seen in most of Picasso's drawings on paper. Quick sketches are similarly distinguished from careful elaboration, and the style of any individual artist or period reveals a characteristic state of mind in the extent to which the motor factor is given free play. When during and after the Renaissance there developed a tendency to consider and appreciate the work of art as a product of individual creation, the plainly visible brush stroke became a legitimate element of artistic form, and the imprints of the sculptor's fingers were preserved, somewhat paradoxically, even in the bronze casts of clay figures. Drawings, formerly mere preparatory stages of the workshop process, were now collected as works of art in their own right. The dynamics of the act of creation had become a valued addition to whatever action was contained in the created shapes themselves.

Graphologically significant differences can be discovered between the uninhibited, spontaneous strokes of a Velázquez or Frans Hals, the violently twisted ones of Van Gogh, the carefully but lightly applied layers of touches in the paintings of the impressionists or Cézanne. There is something painfully mechanical about the uniform stipples of the pointillists; and the careful leveling of any personal trace in the texture and line of Mondrian, Vasarely, or other hard-edge painters goes with the absence of curves in their patterns and the remoteness from the subject matter of life and nature in their themes.

Artists know that the dynamic traits of the physical motor act leave reflections in their work and show up as dynamic qualities of corresponding character. Not only do artists practice relaxed wrist and arm motion, which will translate itself into fluent, life-giving line, but many will even attempt to put their body in a kinesthetic state appropriate to the nature of the subject to be represented. Bowie discusses the principle of "living movement" (*Sei Do*) in Japanese painting: "A distinguishing feature in Japanese painting is the strength of the brushstroke, technically called *fude no chikara* or *fude no ikioi*. When representing an object suggesting strength, such, for instance, as rocky cliffs, the beak or talons of a bird, the tiger's claws, or the limbs and branches of a tree, the moment the brush is applied the sentiment of strength must be invoked and felt throughout the artist's system and imparted through his arm and hand to the brush, and so transmitted into the object painted." The dead quality of many printed reproductions and plaster casts is due partly to the fact that the strokes, touches, lines, and edges have been produced not, as is true in the originals, by forces active along the trails of movement, but by the perpendicular pressure of the printing press or the shapeless liquid of the plaster.

At the end of the preceding chapter, I pointed out that dancers and actors also must make a special effort to endow their movements with the appropriate visual dynamics; and it is known that some film-makers practice the techniques of karate and Chinese gymnastics for the purpose of guiding the hand-held camera with the kind of smooth and concentrated motion that will come across on the screen.

Experiments on Directed Tension

By no means are all the dynamic qualities in works of art created by corresponding physical forces. Michelangelo carefully smoothed the volumes of his figures, thereby eliminating the marks of his chisel, which are still visible in some of his unfinished works; and no physical expansion from the inside of the marble accounts for the swelling muscles of his Moses.

But even if all visual dynamics were due to the direct manifestation of physical forces, this would not account for the perceptual effect of the final product on the mind of the observer. This effect is not due to the observer's knowledge of its cause. Rather, we must look for the visible properties of the percept that are responsible for the phenomenon.

In the present state of research, the physiological counterpart of perceptual dynamics cannot be traced directly in the nervous system. However, there is tangible evidence that the visual field is pervaded by active forces. When the size or shape of patterns we see differs from that of the projection on the retina, dynamic processes in the nervous system must be at work to modify the stimulus input. So-called optical illusions are the most conspicuous demonstrations of the more universal fact that, to adopt the language of Edwin Rausch, in perception the *phenogram* often does not duplicate the *ontogram*. What we see is not identical with what is imprinted upon the eye.

Earlier, in discussing balance, we noted that visual space is anisotropic; e.g., the same line looks longer in the vertical direction, shorter in the horizontal. Similar distortions of what is objectively given are brought about by certain patterns within the visual field. Rausch cites the well-known Müller-Lyer illusion (Figure 260). In the ontogram of this figure, the two horizontal

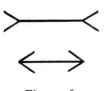

Figure 260

lines are of equal length; in the phenogram, which we see, they are unequal. Dynamically, the arrowheads in the upper figure can be said to compress the pattern, whereas the ones in the lower figure expand it. This creates tension, to which the horizontal bars yield: "To the degree that the figure gives in to the tendency toward undoing the tension (*Entzerrungstendenz*), the effect manifests itself in the shortening or lengthening of the principal line." The perceptual "gain" of the modification is a reduction of visual tension.

The Poggendorf illusion (Figure 261*a*) is cited by Rausch as another example of the same mechanism. Any obliquely oriented shape creates tension, which produces a striving toward orthogonality. To the extent that the two oblique lines give in to this tendency by making the angle with the verticals somewhat more like one of 90 degrees (Figure 261*b* shows an exaggeration of the effect), they run parallel rather than looking like two sections of the same line. Again the deviation from the ontogram accomplishes a diminution of tension.

A slightly more complex situation is illustrated by the Hering illusion (Figure 262*a*). An objectively straight line crossing a sunburst of radii bends toward the center. In this case the centric, expanding pattern creates an inhomogeneous field, in which objective straightness is no longer as devoid of tension as it would be in a homogeneous field (*b*). Its equivalent in the centric field would be a circular line (Figure 262*c*) because all sections of such a line would be in the same relation to the field and to its center. The straight line in *a*, on the other hand, changes angle, size, and distance from the center in each of its sections. To the extent that the line gives in to the tendency toward tension-reduction we see it curving, although the stimulus quality of straightness is too strong to yield to a complete transformation of *a* into *c*.

Similar effects can be obtained, as the experiments of Köhler and Wallach on the so-called figural aftereffect have shown, when a part of such a pattern is fixated by itself and the remainder looked at afterward.

Still another set of experiments illustrates the directional tendency in-

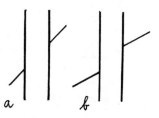

Figure 261

herent in certain simple shapes. Werner and Wapner found that when, in a
dark room, they placed a luminescent square before an observer in such a way
that the median plane coincided objectively with the left or right edge (Figure
263*a*), the observer tended to displace the median plane toward the center of
the figure, thereby reducing the tension created by the asymmetrical placement of the square. If a triangle (20 cm. high and 20 cm. wide) was then
substituted for the square, the apparent sagittal plane was again displaced
toward the center of the figure, but the displacement toward the left was 6.4
cm. for Figure 263*b* and only 3.8 cm. for Figure 263*c*. This result seems to demonstrate that inherent in the triangle was a lateral push, which demanded a
stronger compensation when it pointed to the right than in the opposite case.

These experiments bring to mind certain earlier findings in the studies on
locomotion by Oppenheimer and Brown, mentioned in the foregoing chapter.
Straight lines or rectangles were seen to move faster through the field when
they were oriented with the direction of the movement than they did when at
right angles to it. It was also found that visual objects preferred to move with
the direction of their main axis, their second choice being the direction per-

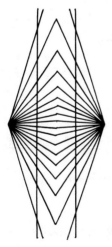

Figure 262*a*

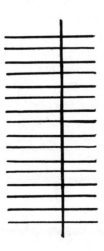

Figure 262*b*

Figure 262*c*

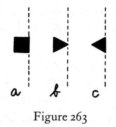

Figure 263

pendicular to that of the main axis. These results suggest that perceived locomotion is intensified when it conforms to the directed tensions within the
object. J. F. Brown also observed that disks seemed to move much faster upward than they did laterally.

In the experiments cited thus far, the effect of visual dynamics was evi-
denced indirectly but measurably by changes of shape, orientation, or location
in the phenogram. Such changes must be common in works of art or design
as well, but they cannot generally be pinned down with precision in the more
complex patterns created by the artist. Instead, directed tension is observed as
an intrinsic property of every visual object. Here I shall refer once more to
the work of Rausch, who used line figures of rectangles, tilted parallelograms,
and rhombs to ask his subjects: "What kind of change in these figures would
seem arbitrary or forced? Which other changes might seem natural, compatible, appropriate, or even potentially inherent in the figure?"

As in the experiments referred to earlier, a tendency to undo distortion
and thereby to reduce tension was noted in the reactions of the subjects. It
seemed natural to them to turn parallelograms such as Figure 264a to an upright position or to compress rhombs (b) along their more extended axis to
make them into squares. Many subjects seemed to feel that in making these
changes they merely restored the figures to their original shape. They saw the
parallelogram as a tilted rectangle, the rhomb as an expanded square. On the
other hand, the observers were quite reluctant to propose changes for regular

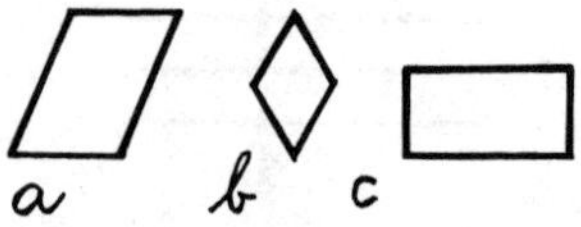

Figure 264

squares or rectangles. "They are all right the way they are," was the typical reaction.

Immobile Motion

Directed tension is as genuine a property of visual objects as size, shape, and color. The nervous system of the observer generates it at the same time that it produces the experience of size, shape, and color from the stimulus input. There is nothing arbitrary or willful in these dynamic components of percepts, although they can be ambiguous. They are strictly determined by the nature of the visual pattern, even in the range of their ambiguities.

Perhaps the difference between visual dynamics and the perception of locomotion will be clarified by a few examples of the way motion is represented in immobile media. The most simple-minded suggestion on how this feat can be accomplished is to assume that the artist picks a momentary phase from the process of movement—a single frame, as it were from the filmstrip depicting the sequence in the time dimension. This view is neatly expressed in a statement made by Alexander Archipenko when he attempted in 1928 to launch a kind of kinetic painting: "Static painting must, in order to interpret movements, resort to symbols and conventions. It did not advance further than the fixation of a single 'moment' in the series of moments that constitute a movement; and all the other 'moments' situated hitherto and beyond the fixed movement are left to the imagination and to the fantasy of the spectator." I have already noted that snapshots, authentic though they are, often fail badly to convey a sense of action. No imagination or fantasy will supply what is missing.

Furthermore, sometimes the most effective representation does not correspond to any phase of the depicted event. An amusing illustration has been offered by Salomon Reinach, who observes that "of the four attitudes in which European art had represented the galloping horse during the various periods of its history, only one was confirmed by photographic snapshots, and this one, used by the Attic artists of the fifth century B.C., had been almost completely abandoned by Roman art and remained unknown to medieval and modern art up to the discovery of the Parthenon frieze." The three others turned out to be entirely "wrong." The conventional attitude of the galloping horse with outstretched legs, as seen in Géricault's *Derby at Epsom* (Figure 265) was used in Mycenaean, Persian, and Chinese art, and reappeared in Europe in the British color prints of the late eighteenth century, possibly under Chinese influence.

When photography gave the lie to this ancient pattern, painters main-

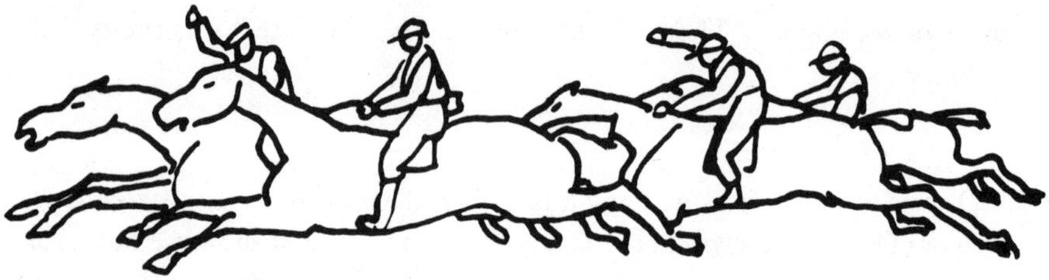

Figure 265

tained with good reason that the snapshots were wrong and the artists right; for only the maximum spread of the legs translates the intensity of the physical motion into pictorial dynamics, although no running horse can ever assume that position except during a leap. Even in the twentieth century we find, for example in the work of Kandinsky, galloping animals which, unabashed by the revelations of photography, continue to exhibit the full stretch of their legs.

Action pictures portray motion precisely to the degree displayed by the figure. In one of Muybridge's serial photographs, a sequence showing a blacksmith at work, the full impact of the blow appears only in those pictures in which the hammer is lifted high. In-between phases are not seen as transitional stages of the smashing blow, but as a more or less quiet lifting of the hammer, the intensity depending upon the angle represented. In snapshots of a man walking, the step will look small or large depending upon the given angle between the legs. Myron's discus-thrower and Bernini's David show the deflection of the arm at the extreme of intensity.

The most important fact to remember, however, is that in a successful work of photography, painting, or sculpture, the artist synthesizes the represented action as a whole in a way that translates the temporal sequence into a timeless pose. Consequently, the immobile image is not momentary, but outside the dimension of time. It can combine different phases of an event in the same image without committing an absurdity. Wölfflin has pointed out that, quite legitimately, Donatello's David "still" holds the rock in his hand, although Goliath's head "already" lies at the feet of the victor. And when the same sculptor's Judith raises her sword, she is not about to decapitate Holofernes, who is already dead, but is making a gesture of defiance and triumph independent of momentary motion.

The Dynamics of Obliqueness

Oblique orientation is probably the most elementary and effective means of obtaining directed tension. Obliqueness is perceived spontaneously as a dynamic straining toward or away from the basic spatial framework of the vertical and horizontal. With the mastery of oblique orientation the child as well as the primitive artist acquires the main device for distinguishing action from rest—for example, a walking figure from a standing one. Auguste Rodin states that in order to indicate movement in his busts, he often gave them "a certain slant, a certain obliquity, a certain expressive direction, which would emphasize the meaning of the physiognomy."

A most dramatic demonstration of what obliqueness does for the artist occurred when in the mid-1920s Theo Van Doesburg, a leader of the *De Stijl* group in Holland, overrode Piet Mondrian's stern doctrine, which held that vertical and horizontal shapes were the only ones admissible in painting. Van Doesburg asserted that the modern spirit felt a need to express a sharp contrast to the rightangular framework prevalent in architecture as well as in the forest and the landscape. In the drawing reproduced in Figure 266, he demonstrated how this contrast was to be expressed through the oblique direction.

The windmills in Dutch landscapes stand still if their arms are painted in a vertical-horizontal position (Figure 267). The arms show a little more dy-

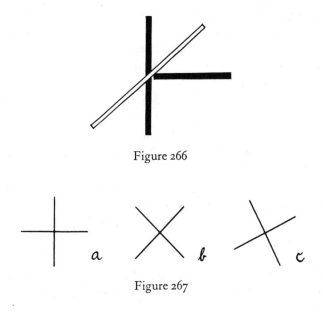

Figure 266

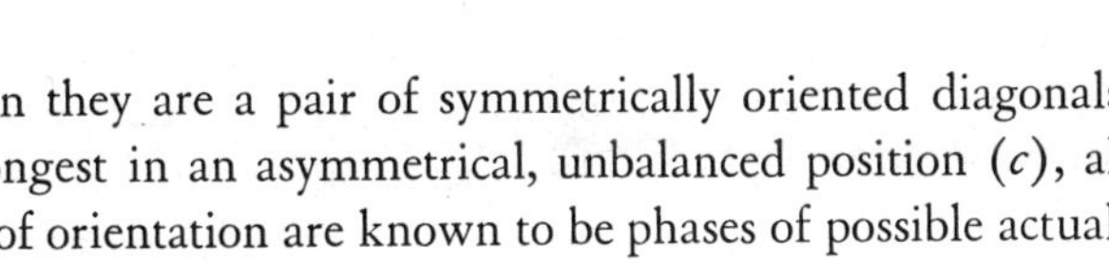

Figure 267

namics when they are a pair of symmetrically oriented diagonals (*b*). The effect is strongest in an asymmetrical, unbalanced position (*c*), although all three kinds of orientation are known to be phases of possible actual motion or rest. Sometimes the effect of obliquity is reinforced by the spectator's knowledge of the object's norm position, from which the perceived position deviates. A Y-shaped pattern shows more tension when it represents a man with raised arms than when it stands for a tree; for the branches are seen in a "normal" position, while the arms are known to be momentarily raised. (Compare here my remarks on Kandinsky's drawing after the photograph of a dancer.) In the latter case the perceived position is in a relation of tension not only to the framework directly inherent in the picture but also to the memory trace of the object's normal attitude (arms hanging at rest).

The tension created by obliqueness is a principal impulse toward depth perception. Under certain conditions the tension can be diminished by an escape into the third dimension, which straightens out the obliqueness to some degree. We have observed how converging rails approach parallelism when we see them in depth. However, this release of tension is only partial, and therefore some of the perspective compression persists. This explains why the pictorial depth obtained by an oblique orientation of shapes always retains some of its dynamic character—a quality particularly congenial to the baroque style. Wölfflin describes how, during the transition from Renaissance to baroque painting, oblique views become more and more dominant. At first only single figures and objects are shown in diagonal position. "Finally, the axis of the entire picture, architectonic space and group composition, is directed obliquely toward the observer." The result may be studied, for example, in Tintoretto's work (cf. Figure 220).

The wedge shape, noticed in the convergence of rails or the edges of a street, makes for active dynamics even when no such depth effect is involved. A characteristic remark on the dynamic quality of such wedge shapes is contained in a treatise by Lomazzo, a painter and writer of the sixteenth century. Speaking about the proportions of the human figure in paintings, he said: "For the greatest grace and life that a picture can have is that it express motion, which the painters call the spirit of a picture. Now there is no form so fit to express this motion as that of the flame of fire, which according to Aristotle and the other philosophers is the element most active among all others because the form of the flame is more apt for motion. It has a cone or sharp point with which it seems to divide the air so that it may ascend to its proper sphere." Lomazzo concludes that a human figure having this shape will be most beautiful.

A flame, though pointed, does not generally present itself, either in nature or in pictures, as a wedge shape in the strict geometrical sense. It curves and twists, and these complications of the basic shape add greatly to its visual

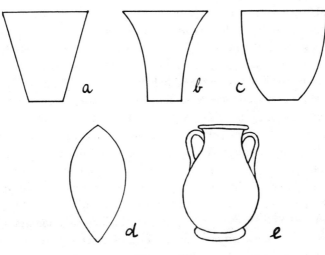

Figure 268

dynamics. As long as the sides of a wedge are straight, we see a gradient of breadth that decreases at a constant rate; and there is no change of direction. Figure 268a illustrates the rigidity of a crescendo or decrescendo proceeding along straight edges. The dynamics is increased if the rate of the gradient varies. When we watch Figure 268b rising from the ground we experience a quickening of expansion as the profile of the vase bends outward. Conversely, Figure 268c shows a gradual slowing down, ending in standstill at the rim. In both examples the dynamics is livelier, more flexible; and the more complex formula makes for a more "organic" appearance (cf. Chapter VIII). The movement is even freer when, in leaves or vases (d, e), the orientation turns, from expansion to contraction or vice versa. (By covering the drawings with

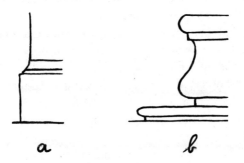

Figure 269

a piece of paper and then slowly uncovering them vertically, one can nicely observe the full effect of the swelling and converging.)

Baroque architecture used the dynamics of curved shapes to increase tension. Figures 269*a* and *b*, taken from Wölfflin, compare the profile of a typical foot from a building of the early Renaissance with one by Michelangelo. The festoons of fruit and leaves, so popular with baroque architects, combine the curve of the crescent with a swelling of breadth, and the oblique spiral volutes add a growing expansion to the step-like enlargement of the façade.

Finally, examples should be mentioned in which obliqueness is not limited to particular shapes, but applies to the total field of the image. We saw that in isometric perspective, a grid of tilted parallel edges underlies the composition and thereby imparts a sense of overall action to what is often an otherwise peaceful scene. Similar dynamic effects are obtained by photographers when they tilt the camera or change the angle of the original negative in order to add an element of heightened life or excitement. The cubists and expressionists gave violent action to their subjects by building Eiffel Towers, churches, trees, or human figures out of piles of oblique units.

Tension in Deformation

By now it will be evident that all tension derives from deformation. Whether we are dealing with a bent steel blade, a sheet of rubber, a funhouse mirror, an expanding bubble, or the rising emotion of a heated argument, there is always a forceful deviation from a state of lower tension in the direction of tension increase. The effect comes about only when the base of departure remains implicitly present, just as the dynamics inherent in the varying pitches of a diatonic melody is perceived only when we hear the notes as rising above the zero base (tonic) or as straining away from it downward. In Rausch's examples (Figure 264) the parallelogram acquires its dynamics by being seen as pulling away from a rectangular base, and the rhomb appears as a deformation of a more squarish figure.

Architectural proportions furnish us with simple examples. As the Renaissance develops into the baroque, preference shifts from circular forms to oval ones, from the square to the rectangle, thus creating "tension in the proportions." This can be observed particularly in the ground plans of rooms, courtyards, churches. In a circular area the visual forces radiate symmetrically in all directions, whereas in the oval or rectangle there is directed tension along the greater axis.

Wölfflin points out that when the square yields to the rectangle, the favorite proportions of the rectangle are rarely those of the golden section, whose character is relatively harmonious and stable. The baroque prefers the slimmer or squatter proportions. They contain more tension; they appear as compressed or drawn-out versions of more simply proportioned oblongs. Moreover, the characteristic swing of the façade invests the entire building with tension. "The façade is somewhat curved inward at the ends while its center exhibits a vivid forward movement, directed toward the observer." This forward and backward movement is so strong because it seems to derive from a lateral compression of the building. In resisting this compression, the façade dramatizes for the eye the symmetrical outward pushes from the center of the building toward its flanks.

Not only the shape of objects, but also that of the intervals between them, is dynamic. The empty space that separates objects or parts of objects from one another in sculpture, painting, and architecture is compressed by the objects, and compresses them in turn. According to rules that are entirely unexplored, this dynamics depends not only upon the size, shape, and proportion of the intervals themselves, but also upon those of the neighboring objects. Given a set of windows of a particular dimension and shape, the wall spaces between them will look too large and therefore oppressive, too small and therefore squeezed, or just right. The same phenomenon can be studied in the mats of framed pictures, the white margins of the printed page, or, under much more complex conditions, in the relations between figure and ground in pictorial compositions. In baroque architecture, says Wölfflin, "the quickening of the pulse is clearly indicated in the changed proportions of the arches and the intervals between pilasters. The intervals keep getting narrower, the arches slimmer, the speed of succession increases."

When the artist represents familiar shapes he can rely on the norm image the viewer harbors within himself. By deviating from this norm image one can create tension. Wilhelm Lehmbruck's late figure sculptures and the oval faces in Modigliani's portraits owe their tense slimness not only to the proportions of the visual pattern as such, but also to their deviations from the familiar shapes of the human body. In order to read such shapes correctly, the viewer must obey the rules of the game, spelled out by the total image or indeed by the style of the period. A caricature distorts everything and thereby notifies the viewer that he is not seeing cripples, in the manner of Velásquez's dwarfs, but more normally proportioned persons subjected to interpretative exaggeration. At the same time, however, caricaturists often vary the proportions of their characters, portraying one man as skinny, the other as plump, which tells us that they aim at the particular traits of individuals. This differs from the message delivered when a single property, e.g., elongation in the work of

El Greco, is imposed upon the image as a whole. In such a case a statement on the human condition quite in general is being conveyed. In the Gothic style, the asthenic character of elongated shapes expresses itself in the proportions of architecture and statuary alike.

When such dynamic variations pervade all manifestations of a given style, they tend to vanish from the consciousness of the population immersed in that style even though they constantly reflect and confirm a way of life. In our own civilization, the grotesquely elongated women of fashion designs look normal to us, not simply because we are used to them, but because their slender bodies conform to an image of the desirable woman deeply rooted in modern man. There are, however, limits beyond which the frame of reference will not stretch. It is probable that for many a beholder the flagpole-shaped figures of the sculptor Giacometti or the obese nudes of Gaston Lachaise are not fully relatable to the human body; these figures appear as creatures of their own kind, whose visual dynamics is perceived only in part with reference to the human norm and otherwise in accordance with their own inherent shape and proportion, as happens when we look at a giraffe or a pig.

The directed tensions in visual shapes are displayed most directly when the total expanse of the shapes is made visible. However, Henry Moore has warned that "only to make relief shapes on the surface of the block is to forgo the full power of expression of sculpture." What Moore has in mind was spelled out more explicitly before him by Auguste Rodin, who tells that one of his teachers admonished him never to view shapes in extension but always in depth: "Never consider a surface as anything but the extremity of a volume, as its more or less broad point, directed toward you." It takes more than an intellectual inference, however, to make the observer see the volumes of a sculpture as pushing outward from a center inside the block. The visible part of the volume must be defined by the artist in such a way that its continuation in depth is seen as an integral part of the shape.

When the incompleteness of a well-structured pattern is displayed to the eye, a tension toward closure is created. Thus in Moslem architecture the horseshoe arch, which presents circular shape beyond the halfway mark, clearly contains forces in the direction of the completed circle (Figure 270). Incompleteness is frequently brought about by overlapping. As discussed earlier, the overlapped pattern tends to break free from the intruder by detaching itself from it in depth. Nevertheless the superposition remains visible, and it makes the interlocking units strive to pull apart. In the baroque style this device is used to reinforce the movement toward freedom by the pressure of imprisonment. In the library of San Lorenzo in Florence, Michelangelo buries the back

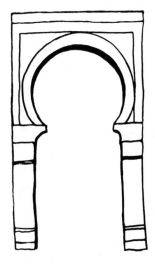

Figure 270

of the columns in the wall; and in some of his unfinished statues, notably in the so-called *Slaves*, the body remains partly embedded in the block of marble and thus exhibits an impressive struggle for completeness, for liberty.

Often architectural units are made to overlap one another in fugue-like scales, and painted or sculptured figures and ornaments reach beyond the limits assigned to them by the architectural skeleton of the building. Such devices are sought after or avoided by individual artists and cultural periods, depending on whether they welcome or reject the tension created in this way. The cubists obtained highly dynamic compositions by building up volumes from irregularly crowded units, which constantly interfere with one another's shape.

In Chapter VII I had occasion to refer to the dynamic aspects of color experiences, e.g., to the attraction between opposites, so characteristic of complementaries. Here I will only point out an analogy to what we observed just now about the dynamics generated by the deformation of shape. Tension is created, I noted, by the implicit presence of the norm base from which a shape deviates. Something similar can be seen in colors quite close to a simple hue, for example, a pure red afflicted with a subordinate admixture of blue. Johannes von Allesch, in his phenomenological study of color experiences, pointed out that color perception can be dynamic in a twofold sense: certain colors leave the viewer free to select one of the hues contained in it as the base, so that the impression received of the same color may differ for different observers; at the same time the color itself may exhibit a striving either toward or away from a pure hue to which it is related much as the leading tone in music is to the tonic. We found earlier that the pure fundamental primaries seem to lack tension. They are basic norms, such as circles or squares.

Dynamic Composition

The dynamics inherent in any particular shape, color, or movement can make its presence felt only if it fits the comprehensive dynamics of the total composition. To supply a single line, a single shape, with directed tension is, of course, much easier than to accomplish this for a complex pattern as a whole. Hence one can often observe visual elements that, although quite dynamic within themselves, undo one another and add up to a frustrating blockage. Similar conditions prevail in music. Victor Zuckerkandl, who has described musical dynamics most convincingly, writes: "An order in which every point reveals its position in the whole must be called a dynamic order. The dynamic qualities of tones can be understood only as manifestations of ordered forces. The notes of our tonal system are events in a field of forces, and the sounding of each tone expresses the precise constellation of forces existent at the point of the field in which the tone is located. The sounds of music are carriers of active forces. To hear music means to hear the effects of forces." Thus, the particular dynamic quality of each element is defined and sustained by the context. The elements stabilize one another.

The dynamics of a composition will be successful only when the "movement" of each detail fits logically in the movement of the whole. The work of art is organized around a dominant dynamic theme, from which movement radiates throughout the entire area. From the main arteries the movement flows into the capillaries of the smallest detail. The theme struck up at the higher level must be carried through at the lower level, and elements at the same level must go together. The eye perceives the finished pattern as a whole together with the interrelations of its parts, but the process of making a picture or statue requires each part to be made separately. For this reason the artist is tempted to concentrate on the part at hand in isolation from its context.

More clearly perhaps than in any other period of history, the shortcomings of the piecemeal approach showed up in the minor artists of the nineteenth century who concentrated on carefully copying models from nature. The lack of integration carries over even to their free inventions. Examples such as the picture by Hans Thoma reproduced in Figure 271 make us marvel how dynamics can be so completely absent even from subjects eminently suited to convey it. If we examine the figure of the angel more closely, we observe first

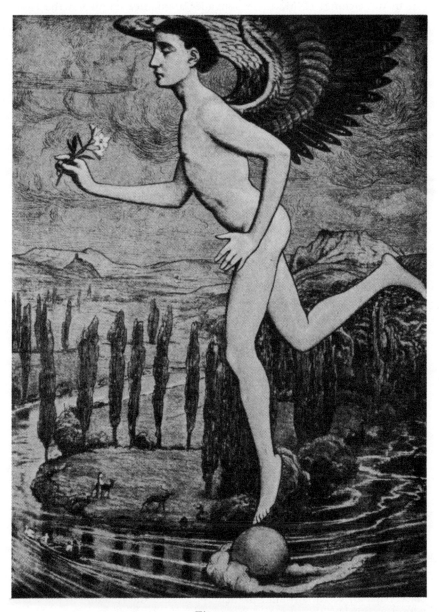

Figure 271
Hans Thoma. Illustration from *Quickborn*, 1898.

of all a number of rigid breaks in the hips, the elbows, and the knees. Angular breaks as such do not interfere with movement, as can be easily seen in Gothic art. In the etchings of Martin Schongauer angularity dominates the entire picture, the relations of the figures to one another, the posture of each figure, and every detail of fold or finger. In Thoma's drawing there is no such unified conception of form. The breaks in the joints stop the dynamics because they conflict with the soft flow of the outlines. Furthermore, the front line of the chest and the contour of the shoulder and upper left arm show a halfhearted wavering rather than a consistently swinging shape because they are constructed piece by piece. Their elements stop one another rather than being fitted to an overall flow of directed tension. If we consider the shape of the volumes, we find that most of them show complex, irregular relations among the contours. Once this high level of complexity is set, the simplicity of the horn-shaped lower arms produces inorganic stiffness. In the left leg the front and back contours do not add up to volumes of understandable form or movement, and the sudden simple parallelism between the cap and the back of the knee stops the intended rhythm of the entire leg. Examples of mechanically realistic and therefore visually incomprehensible shape interfering with integrated dynamics can also be found in the lines of the trees, mountains, and clouds.

Such instances of failure make it clear why artists consider directed tension so fundamental. If "movement" is absent, the work is dead; none of the other virtues it may possess will make it speak to the beholder. The dynamics of shape presupposes that the artist conceives of every object or part of an object as a happening rather than a static bit of matter, and that he thinks of the relations between objects not as geometric configurations but as mutual interaction. Sometimes this dynamic nature of vision is expressed in the way artists talk about their work; thus Matisse, discussing a series of self-portraits, points to "the way in which the nose is rooted in the face, the ear screwed into the skull, the lower jaw hung; the way in which the glasses are placed on the nose and ears; the tension of the gaze and its uniform density in all the drawings."

Stroboscopic Effects

Strong dynamic effects result from what may be called the immobile equivalent of stroboscopic motion. Stroboscopic motion occurs between visual objects that are essentially alike in their appearance and function in the whole field, but differ in some perceptual feature—for example, location, size, or shape. Under suitable conditions such constellations produce a dynamic effect

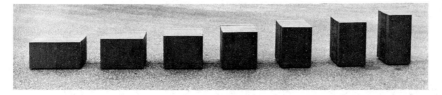

Figure 272

also in simultaneity, the most obvious example being stroboscopic photographs, which show the same object at a number of locations in the same picture or series of pictures The sequence of the locations forms a simply shaped, consistent path, and the internal changes of the object—for example, the change in posture of a leaping athlete—also occur gradually. Figure 272 shows a series of shapes, constructed by Franz Rudolf Knubel on the basis of a suggestion by Theodor Fischer. The central block is a cube; the others have the ratios of elementary musical intervals: 2/1, 3/2, 5/4, 1/1, 4/5, 2/3, 1/2. The similarity of shape and the gradualness of the changes in height and width induce the viewer to see a coherent event of transformation rather than a sequence of independent shapes. The event is compellingly dynamic: the object contracts and rises, thereby changing its character from solid repose on the ground to towering strength.

The visual action of such a sequence is particularly convincing when the elements overlap. The effect has been used by artists, notably the futurists, who tried to render motion through the multiplication of figures or parts of figures. Duchamp's *Nude Descending a Staircase* and Balla's many-legged dog are well-known examples. In a less obvious way other artists have used the same device throughout the ages. Brueghel's blind men have been cited earlier. Auguste Rodin, in his conversations with Paul Gsell, maintains that "movement is the transition from one position to another," and that therefore the artist, in order to express movement, often represents successive phases of an action in different parts of a figure.

In many pictures, different figures are arranged in such a way that they can also be perceived as the same figure in different positions. Thus the weeping angels in the sky of Giotto's *Lamentation* represent gestures of despair in such a way that the group as a whole looks like a highly dynamic composite picture of one activity (Figure 276). Riegl has pointed out that Michelangelo's figures of Night and Day, at the monument for Giuliano de' Medici in Florence, together create an effect of rotation. The eye combines them because of their symmetrical positions in the whole and because of their similar outlines. Yet

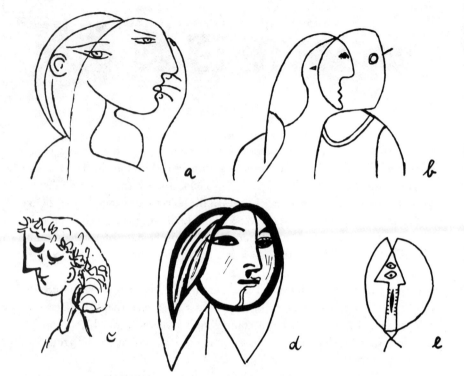

Figure 273

the two figures are inversions of each other. Night is seen from the front and seems to approach, whereas Day shows its back and seems to recede. Hence the rotation of the group.

A useful study of these "stroboscopic" phenomena could be based on the practice of some modern painters, particularly Picasso, of duplicating parts of figures or objects. Figure 273a shows a double profile head. The two heads are placed obliquely. They are clearly distinguished from each other, but at the same time they prevent each other from being complete, and together also form a unified perceptual whole. The intimate connection of the incompatible, along with the similarity and fugue-like parallelism of the two overlapping units, produces tension in the oblique direction established by the analogous features of the two heads, particularly the two eyes. This forward and upward thrust enhances the vigorous activity of the profile. It will also be noticed that the transition from the lower to the higher head involves an increase in articulation and directed action. The lower head has no profile line, and the pupil of its eye rests in a central position. A pulpy front develops into a sharply defined profile, and a dreamingly inactive eye into the intensely directed forward glance of the upper head. We experience a crescendo of increasing keenness, entirely in keeping with the subject of the painting.

The opposite procedure leads to a rather terrifying result in Figure 273*b*. In the painting from which this detail is taken, Picasso makes an articulate profile, equipped with an explicit eye, change into a flat mask, in which a glanceless circle represents the eye. Here intense life is seen as degenerating into a dead hull.

In Figure 273*c* the device is limited to a pair of eyes, which stand for the two eyes of the human face but at the same time are a duplication of one profile eye. Again this serves to strengthen the forward movement of the head—the expression of an active, exploring mind (Figure 273*c* is the head of a woman painter at work).

Picasso's figures demonstrate also that the dynamic effect of such displacements does not depend primarily upon what the observer knows about the "correct" spatial position of the elements involved, but rather upon the structure of the perceptual pattern. The combination of profile and front face, as it can be seen, for example, in the *Girl before a Mirror* (Figure 273*d*), makes for a fairly static substitution effect rather than movement as we switch from one version to the other. This happens even though the observer knows that in physical space either he himself or the perceived object would have to make a turn of ninety degrees in order to bring about the change. The two versions, however, are so smoothly integrated, and the pattern as a whole rests so stably on an essentially vertical-horizontal skeleton, that little tension results. Similarly, when two eyes in a profile face are placed horizontally rather than obliquely, there is hardly any movement. The same is true for vertically oriented eyes or mouths (*e*). Past experience would require a switch from the familiar horizontal, but the perceptual stability of the vertical excludes movement.

How Does Dynamics Come About?

If in every visual experience shape, color, and movement possess dynamic qualities, we must ask more explicitly: how does the dynamics get into the percept? I hope to have made it evident that we are not dealing simply with an observer's subjective and arbitrary additions to what he sees. The dynamics is an integral part of what an observer sees as long as his natural sensory responsiveness has not been repressed by an education geared to the static metrics of inch and foot, wavelength, and miles per hour. The dynamics is not a property of the physical world, but the stimulus patterns projected upon our retinas can be shown to determine the range of dynamic qualities inherent in the percept.

The stimulus material reaching our eyes acquires dynamics while it is being processed by the nervous system. How are we to understand this? Remember, first of all, that the perceptual raw material is not stamped mechanically upon a passive receptor surface, as inked typefaces imprint letters on paper. Perception reflects an invasion of the organism by external forces, which upset the balance of the nervous system. A hole is torn in a resistant tissue. A struggle must result as the invading forces try to maintain themselves against the physiological field forces, which endeavor to eliminate the intruder or at least to reduce it to the simplest possible pattern. The relative strength of the antagonistic forces determines the resulting percept.

At no time does stimulation congeal into a static arrangement. As long as light affects the brain centers of vision, the pushing and pulling keep going on, and the relative stability of the result is nothing but the balance of opposing forces. Is there any reason to assume that only the outcome of the struggle is reflected in visual experience? Why should the play of the physiological forces itself not also find its counterpart in perception? I suggest that it is these forces which we perceive as "directed tension" or "movement" in immobile patterns. In other words, *we are dealing with the psychological counterpart of the physiological processes that result in the organization of perceptual stimuli.* These dynamic aspects belong to any visual experience as intimately and directly as the static qualities of shape, size, or color. To the sensitive eye, even the simplest picture—a dark spot on a light ground—presents the spectacle of an object expanding from its center, pushing outward, and being checked by the counterforces of the environment. The fact that all visual presence is visual action brings about expression, thus making it possible to use percepts as an artistic medium.

Earlier I cited experiments indicating the tangible action of field forces in visual experience. I will mention here still another group of observations, which have a particularly close affinity to the directed tensions perceived in geometrical figures. The so-called gamma motion comes about when objects suddenly appear or disappear. A traffic light flashing on at night seems to expand from its center toward the outside in all directions. Similarly, its disappearance is seen as a centripetal shrinking toward the inside. Experiments have shown that this motion varies with the shape and orientation of the object. It occurs essentially along the axes of what I called the structural skele-

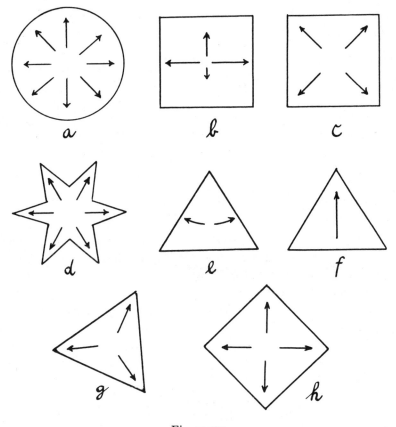

Figure 274

ton of the pattern or, to use Edwin B. Newman's language, along the lines of
force. It issues from a vaguely circular central spot and, in a disk-shaped object, radiates in all directions (Figure 274*a*). A square or rectangle unfolds in
the directions of its sides (*b*), but there is also motion toward the corners (*c*).
A star appears through the outward shooting of its corners (*d*). When an
equilateral triangle stands on one of its sides, the base remains quiet, whereas
the other two sides strike energetically outward and upward as though they
were hinged on the apex (*e*). The same figure will come about by a violent
upward thrust of the apex from the base if the exposure time is very short (*f*).
When the square or triangle stands on edge, the corners push outward more or
less symmetrically (*g*, *h*). There is, however, a tendency of the motion to be
strongest in the horizontal directions, and in the vertical there is more upward

than downward push. This is demonstrated in the square (*b*). The lateral motion is most pronounced, the upward one weaker, the downward one almost absent.

The gamma motion permits us to observe the perceptual forces at work in the creation of patterns. And perhaps we may assume that it also furnishes a kind of anatomy of the forces or tensions characterizing patterns when they are at rest. Up to now the procedure seems to have been applied experimentally only to a very few, elementary patterns. It would be in the interest of psychologists and artists alike if these studies were continued with more complex shapes and configurations.

Examples from Art

Directed tension is so universal a property of perception that it goes far beyond the visual portrayal of objects engaged in locomotion. In a painted landscape no difference in principle exists between the movement perceived in the sinuous contour of a coastline and in the shape of the waves. The swinging contour of a beret in a Rembrandt portrait can be just as dynamic as the skirt of a dancer drawn by Toulouse-Lautrec, even though the beret is known to be motionless and the skirt known to be moving.

In fact, the meaning of a work may be conveyed through a complete reversal of the dynamics suggested by physical action. In Piero della Francesca's

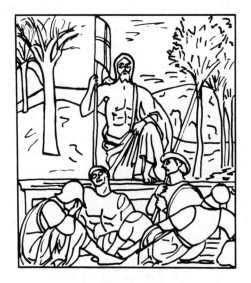

Figure 275

Resurrection (Figure 275) the figure of the rising Christ is given a minimum of pictorial movement. He is located in the center of the picture, and his position is frontal and symmetrical. The posture of his body, the flag he holds in his hand, the tomb from which he emerges—all conform to a vertical-horizontal framework. The resurrection is not interpreted literally as a transition from death to life. Christ is given a permanent existence, which contains the aspects of both death and life, represented in the bare trees to the left and those full of leaves to the right. These trees also lack all indication of transition. They are vertical, like the figure of Christ, which they flank symmetrically. Perceptually as well as symbolically they appear as his attributes The motif of rising is indicated only as a secondary theme in the folds of the robe, whose convergence forms a wedge pointing to the right—the direction of life.

Forceful pictorial movement is reserved to the four Roman soldiers, who are physically at rest. Many perceptual devices are used to obtain the dynamic effect. The main axes of the bodies run obliquely. The heads and arms offer varying phases of posture, almost adding up to the picture of one man tossing in uneasy sleep. The figures strongly interfere with one another by overlapping; together they form a triangle, whose left side bulges outward, is burst like a bubble by the tread of Christ's foot, and peaks obliquely in the head of the man with the spear. Evidently, Piero's picture sets the unrest of temporal material life in opposition to the monumental serenity of Christ, who, as the top of the pyramid, rules between life and death.

The dynamic configuration of a picture and its relation to its content will now be examined in more detail for a particular example. In one of Giotto's frescoes in Padua, the subject of the *Lamentation* (Figure 276) is interpreted by the painter as a story of death and resurrection, which in formal terms calls for an interplay between the horizontal and the vertical. The horizontal of death is indicated but left behind by the body of Christ, which has been lifted and thus endowed with the dynamic quality of oblique position. The arms, in turn, are made to deviate obliquely from the body—a further element of animation. This motif of revival is taken up and developed into one of the two dominant themes of movement by the diagonal ridge of the hill. Just broad enough for a man to walk upward, it leads through the entire picture, from the horizontal of death to the verticals of the two upright men, the vertical edge of the picture frame, and the tree. The tree takes over where the diagonal of the hill is about to end and turns the oblique climbing into straight rising. The intense vertical of the tree trunk is gently dispersed in all directions by the branches. As the movement rises, it dematerializes, spreads throughout space, becomes universal, and gradually disappears from sight.

But, owing to the ambiguity of direction in all movement, the diagonal of the hill also points downward, indicating the great fall that has occurred. This descending arrow is directed significantly from right to left. The viewer follows it only reluctantly because it runs against the direction of the glance. A man who was upright like the two standing men has been felled. There is "stroboscopic movement" between the two standing male figures and the dead body on the ground. The ninety-degree turn of the fall is just being completed by the dead body. The descent toward death occurs from the right to the left, and is superseded by the rising movement toward resurrection from left to right.

The angels are spread irregularly about the sky like a swarm of birds stirred up in panic. The motion of despair enacted by them is not given in gradual stages, but in its extreme phases; thus, in shifting from the central angel to

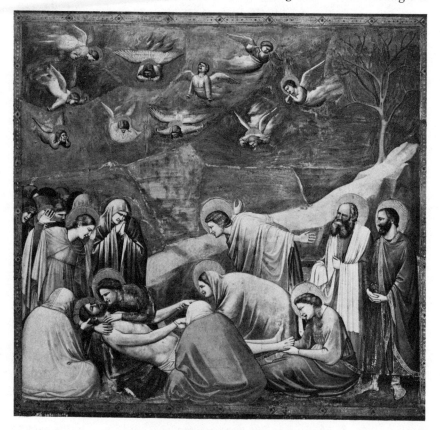

Figure 276
Giotto. *Lamentation*. Fresco from the Arena Chapel, Padua, 1303–5.

his neighbors and back, we see the body convulsively flapping up and down.

Similarly in the group of humans to the left, the standing woman with the clasped hands is placed next to one with outstretched arms—again a leap from one extreme to the other. With equal abruptness the outburst is hushed by the two motionless and faceless women squatting on the ground. But from this nadir, at which distress has paralyzed action and left the mind blank, feeling rises again; and the face, distorted by grief, reappears in the seated woman to the right. Yet the posture is still passive. It serves as a base for the forward thrust of the next woman. The arms, no longer reposing in the lap, now reach out to hold the hands of Christ. And finally, in another violent contrast of movement, the arms are spread apart desperately in the figure of John rising above and behind the crouching woman.

Consider the second dominant theme of movement—the expressive curve formed by the row of mourners. It starts on the left with the praying woman, moves backward to her neighbor; then, by a tensely stretched interval, it arrives at its extreme and turning point in the hooded woman crouching in the corner. The curve is "taken aback" and brought to a standstill by the fall of Christ. Broken by the figure of the dead man, but resumed in the second hooded woman, it now swings upward in a release of emotion to the standing figure with the outstretched arms. It reminds me of the curve of the melodic line in the recitative that tells of Peter's weeping in Bach's *Passion According to St. Matthew* (Figure 277).

But next to the climax of emotion stands the concluding vertical. We see the two men watching in quiet contemplation. Beyond the temporal tragedy they indicate the positive aspect of the sacrifice, the stability of the doctrine to be carried on, and—in their visible relation to the tree of resurrection above their heads—the immortality of the spirit.

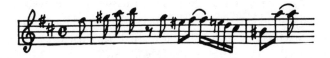

Figure 277

X   EXPRESSION

If the preceding chapters have done their work properly, not very much should remain to be said about visual expression. From the beginning it was evident that one could not do justice to what we see by describing it only with the measurements of size, shape, wavelength, or speed. The dynamic qualities of shapes, colors, and events have proved to be an inseparable aspect of all visual experience. In acknowledging the direct and universal presence of such dynamics we not only made our description of natural and man-made things more complete, we also gained access to what now remains to be discussed explicitly as "expression." As long as one talks about the mere measurements or practical earmarks of visual objects, it is possible to ignore their direct expression. One notes: this is a hexagon, a digit, a chair, a pileated woodpecker, a Byzantine ivory. But as soon as we open our eyes to the dynamic qualities conveyed by any such thing, inevitably we see them as carrying expressive meaning.

This can be observed, for example, when a writer chooses to limit himself strictly to the dynamic features of something he is describing. In his little essay "The Theory of Gaits," Balzac reports on a passerby: "He walked with his hands crossed behind his back, the shoulders effaced and intense, the shoulder blades close together; he looked like a roasted baby partridge on a piece of toast. He seemed to move forward only with his neck, and his whole body received its impulse from the chest." Vaguely but unavoidably, one senses the kind of character expressed in these movements. The same is true for pictorial shapes. In many of the examples referred to in earlier chapters of this book, expressive characteristics came to the fore explicitly or by implication, as soon as we focused on the dynamics of the image.

All perceptual qualities have generality. We see redness, roundness, small-ness, remoteness, swiftness, embodied in individual examples, but conveying a *kind* of experience, rather than a uniquely particular one. This is equally true for dynamics. We see compactness, striving, twisting, expanding, yielding —generalities again, but in this case not limited to what the eye sees. Dynamic qualities are structural; they are experienced in sound, in touch, in muscular sensations, as well as in vision. What is more, they also describe the nature and behavior of the human mind, and they do so quite compellingly. The aggressiveness of lightning comes with the swift zigzag of its descent, and sneakiness comes with the locomotions of a snake whenever these motions are seen as more than geometrically definable curves. Colors serve to symbolize human temperaments, as they have done in many cultures, only when these colors are perceived as dynamic. And the dynamic differences between Romanesque and Gothic architecture translate themselves automatically into states of mind characterizing the corresponding cultural periods.

Thus, *we define expression as modes of organic or inorganic behavior displayed in the dynamic appearance of perceptual objects or events.* The structural properties of these modes are not limited to what is grasped by the external senses; they are conspicuously active in the behavior of the human mind, and they are used metaphorically to characterize an infinity of non-sensory phenomena: low morale or the high cost of living, the spiraling of prices, the lucidity of argument, the compactness of resistance.

Traditional Theories

It is necessary to distinguish the particular way I am using the term "expression" for perceptual and aesthetic purposes from both narrower and broader meanings ascribed to it in common usage. In the narrower sense, expression is said to exist only where there is a mind to be expressed. The face and the gestures of a human being express what is going on inside, and the same may be acknowledged for the bodily behavior of animals. But rocks, waterfalls, and thunderclouds are supposed to carry expression only in a figurative sense, by mere analogy to human behavior.

For our purposes, this limitation to living creatures is unacceptable. The concept becomes at once too narrow and too broad because it goes beyond perceptual qualities. Information about a person's mind can be gathered not only from his face and gestures, but also from the way he talks, dresses, and keeps his room, not to mention the opinions he holds or the way he reacts to events. Much of this information can be interpreted only by intellectual inference, as, for example, when a man's way of spending his money tells me that he is generous or stingy.

Facial and gestural expression plays an important role in the visual media of art, film, and the theater, and although it represents a special case, I shall discuss it first. When humans deal with humans, animals with animals, or when a cat and his owner try to get along with each other, they constantly read their partner's external behavior and control their own. This seems a remarkable achievement once we realize that the eyes of the person or of the cat see nothing but a relief of muscles and bones covered with skin and subjected to various displacements, contractions, and expansions. What can such purely physical patterns have in common with states of mind, which offer no perceivable shape? What makes us see pleasure in a smiling face?

Physiognomics as a method of direct cognition has been earnestly sustained and strongly attacked since antiquity, when Aristotle wrote a treatise on the subject. We read of an edict under the first Queen Elizabeth, which decreed that "all persons fayning to have knowledge of Phisiognomic or like Fantasticall Ymaginacions" were liable to "be stripped naked from the middle upwards and openly whipped until his body be bloudye." The art of telling people's character from the form of their faces, especially the profile, flourished in the eighteenth century. The traditional explanation of how this was to be accomplished can be gathered from a playful review of Johann Kaspar Lavater's *Physiognomic Fragments for the Advancement of the Knowledge and Love of Our Fellow Man*, written by the poet Matthias Claudius around 1775. "Physiognomics is a science of faces. Faces are *concreta* for they are related *generaliter* to natural reality and *specialiter* are firmly attached to people. Therefore the question arises whether the famous trick of the 'abstractio' and the 'methodus analytica' should not be applied here, in the sense of watching out whether the letter *i*, whenever it appears, is furnished with a dot and whether the dot is never found on top of another letter; in which case we should be sure that the dot and the letter are twin brothers, so that when we run into Castor we can expect Pollux not be to be far away. For an example we posit that there be one hundred gentlemen, all of whom are very quick on their feet, and they had given sample and proof of this, and all of these hundred gentlemen had a wart on their noses. I am not saying that gentlemen with a wart on their noses are cowards but am merely assuming it for the sake of the example.... Now *ponamus* there comes to my house a fellow who calls me a wretched scribbler and spits me into the face. Suppose I am reluctant to get into a fist fight and also cannot tell what the outcome would be, and I am standing there and considering the issue. At that moment I discover a wart on his nose, and now I cannot refrain myself any longer. I go after him courageously and, without any doubt, get away unbeaten. This procedure would represent, as it were, the royal road in this field. The progress might be slow but just as safe as that on other royal roads."

In a more serious vein, the theory was stated early in the eighteenth century by the philosopher Berkeley. In his essay on vision he speaks about the way an observer reads shame or anger in a man's looks. "Those passions are themselves invisible: they are nevertheless let in by the eye along with colors and alterations of countenance, which are the immediate object of vision, and which signify them for no other reason than barely because they have been observed to accompany them: without which experience, we should no more have taken blushing for a sign of shame for gladness." Charles Darwin, in his book on the expression of emotions, devoted a few pages to the same problem. He believed that external manifestations and their psychical counterparts are connected by the observer on the basis either of an inborn instinct or of learning. "Moreover, when a child cries or laughs, he knows in a general manner what he is doing and what he feels; so that a very small exertion of reason would tell him what crying or laughing meant in others. But the question is, do our children acquire their knowledge of expression solely by experience through the power of association and reason? As most of the movements of expression must have been gradually acquired, afterwards becoming instinctive, there seems to be some degree of *a priori* probability that their recognition would likewise have become instinctive."

A more recent version of the traditional theory developed from a curious tendency on the part of some social scientists to assume that when people agree on some fact, it is probably based on an unfounded convention. According to this view, judgments of expression rely on "stereotypes," which individuals adopt ready-made from their social group. For example, they have been told that aquiline noses indicate courage and that protruding lips betray sensuality. The promoters of the theory generally imply that such judgments are wrong, as though information not drawn from a person's firsthand experience could never be trusted. Actually the danger lies not in the social origin of the information, but rather in the fact that people tend to acquire simply structured concepts on the basis of insufficient evidence, which may have been gathered firsthand or secondhand, and to preserve these concepts unchanged despite contrary experience. Although this may make for many one-sided or entirely wrong evaluations of individuals and groups of people, the existence of stereotypes does not explain the origin of physiognomic judgments. If these judgments stem from tradition, what is the tradition's source? Even though often misapplied, traditional interpretations of physique and behavior may still be based on sound observation. They may even be so hardy because they are so true.

Within the framework of associationist thinking, a step forward was made by Lipps, who pointed out that the perception of expression involves the activity of forces. His theory of "empathy" was designed to explain why we find expression even in inanimate objects, such as the columns of a temple. The reasoning went as follows. When I look at the columns I know from past experience the kind of mechanical pressure and counterpressure that occurs in them. Equally from past experience, I know how I should feel myself if I were in the place of the columns and if those physical forces acted upon and within my own body. I project my own kinesthetic feelings onto the columns. Furthermore, the pressures and pulls called up from the stores of memory by the sight tend also to provoke responses in other areas of the mind. "When I project my strivings and forces into nature I do so also as to the way my strivings and forces make me feel, that is, I project my pride, my courage, my stubbornness, my lightness, my playful assuredness, my tranquil complacence. Only thus my empathy with regard to nature becomes truly aesthetic empathy."

Common to all the varieties of traditional theorizing was the disavowal of any intrinsic kinship between perceived appearance and the expression it conveyed. How the two belonged together had to be learned, as a language is learned. The letters P A I N mean suffering in English and bread in French; nothing in the letters suggests the one rather than the other meaning. Similarly, one has to learn which expression goes with which state of mind because one could perhaps comprehend how the one was generated by the other, but one could not perceive expression as directly as one does colors and shapes.

Even according to empathy theory, the visual information served only to apprise the viewer of the situation, from which he had to draw his inferences. "The column is carrying a load"—this knowledge sufficed to endow the sight with all the feelings about load-bearing that the viewer could marshal from his own past experience. There was no explicit awareness of how much depended on the particular dynamic qualities of the percept. The art historian Max J. Friedländer has observed: "A bad column looks as though it had been drawn with the ruler. For a good architect, a column is an animated, suffering, victorious, supporting, and burdened being. The hardly measurable gentle swelling of the contour expresses strength, tension, pressure, and resistance." Depending on whether or not these dynamic qualities register with the viewer, he will or will not experience the architectural expression, regardless of how he interprets the statics of the building or what loads he himself has carried in former years.

I shall mention in passing that the theory of empathy has afflicted generations of aestheticians with a host of pseudoproblems. One asked: Are the feelings expressed in sights and sounds those of the artist who created them or those of the recipient? Does one have to be in a melancholy mood in order to produce, perform, or apprehend a melancholy composition? Can "emotions" be expressed in a Bach fugue or a painting by Mondrian? These and other similar questions become incomprehensible once one has understood that expression resides in perceptual qualities of the stimulus pattern.

Expression Embedded in Structure

William James was less certain that body and mind have nothing intrinsically in common. "I cannot help remarking that the disparity between motions and feelings, on which these authors lay so much stress, is somewhat less absolute than at first sight it seems. Not only temporal succession, but such attributes as intensity, volume, simplicity or complication, smooth or impeded change, rest or agitation, are habitually predicated of both physical facts and mental facts." Evidently James reasoned that although body and mind are different media—the one being material, the other not—they might still resemble each other in certain structural properties.

This point was insisted upon by gestalt psychologists. Max Wertheimer in particular asserted that the perception of expression is much too immediate and compelling to be explainable merely as a product of learning. When we watch a dancer, the sadness of happiness of the mood seems to be directly inherent in the movements themselves. Wertheimer concluded that this was true because formal factors in the dance reproduced identical factors in the mood. What he meant may be illustrated by reference to an experiment by Jane Binney. Members of a college dance group were asked individually to give improvisations of such subjects as sadness, strength, or night. The dancers' performances showed much agreement. For example, in the representation of sadness the movement was slow and confined to a narrow range. It was mostly curved in shape and showed little tension. The direction was indefinite, changing, wavering; and the body seemed to yield passively to the force of gravity rather than being propelled by its own initiative. It will be admitted that the psychical mood of sadness has a similar pattern. In a depressed person the mental processes are slow and rarely go beyond matters closely related to immediate experiences and momentary interests. All his thinking and striving displays softness and lack of energy. He shows little determination, and activity is often controlled by outside forces.

To be sure, there is a traditional way of representing sadness in a dance, and the performances of the students may have been influenced by it. What counts, however, is that the movements, whether spontaneously invented or copied from other dancers, exhibited a formal structure so strikingly similar to that of the intended mood. And since such visual qualities as speed, shape, or direction are immediately accessible, it seems legitimate to assume that they are the carriers of an expression directly comprehensible to the eye.

"Isomorphism," that is, the structural kinship between the stimulus pattern and the expression it conveys, can be shown most neatly in simple curves. If we compare a section of a circle with a section of a parabola, we find that the circular curve looks more rigid, the parabolic one more gentle. What is the cause of this difference? It derives from the geometric structure. The constant curvature of the circle obeys a single condition: it is the locus of all points equidistant from one center. A parabola satisfies two such conditions. It is the locus of all points that are equidistant from one point and one straight line. Because of this twofold dependence the curvature of the parabola varies; that of the circle is constant. The parabola may be called a compromise between two structural demands. Either condition yields to the other. In other words, the rigid hardness of the circular line and the gentle flexibility of the parabola can be derived from the inherent make-up of the two curves.

Now for an analogous example from architecture. In the outlines of the dome that Michelangelo designed for St. Peter's in Rome, we admire the synthesis of massive heaviness and free rising. This expressive effect is obtained in the following way. The two contours that make up the section of the outer cupola (Figure 278) are parts of circles, and thus possess the firmness of circular curves. But they are not parts of the same circle. They do not form a hemisphere. The right contour is described around the center a, the left around b. In a Gothic arch the crossing of the curves would be visible at the apex. Michelangelo hides it with the lantern. In consequence both contours appear as part of one and the same curve, which, however, does not have the rigidity of a hemisphere. It compromises between two different curvatures and thus appears flexible as a whole while preserving circular hardness in its components. The total contour of the dome appears as a deviation from a hemisphere, one that has been stretched upward. Hence the effect of vertical striving.

It will also be seen that at level A, the curvature of the cupola reaches the vertical. This would make it look quite static. Perhaps for this reason, the verticality is hidden by the drum between A and B. The cupola is seen as resting on B rather than on A. Consequently the contours meet the base at an oblique rather than a right angle. Instead of moving straight upward, the

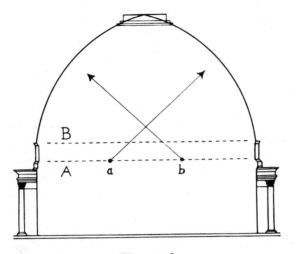

Figure 278

cupola tilts inward, which produces an oblique sagging, a heaviness. The delicate balancing of all these dynamic factors creates the complex and at the same time unified expression of the whole. "The symbolic image of weight," says Wölfflin, "is maintained, yet dominated by the expression of spiritual liberation." Michelangelo's dome thus embodies "the paradox of the baroque spirit in general."

We are beginning to see that perceptual expression does not necessarily relate to a mind "behind it." This is true even for responses to human behavior. Köhler has pointed out that people normally respond to external behavior in itself, rather than thinking of it explicitly as a mere reflection of mental attitudes. People perceive the slow, listless, "droopy" movements of one person as contrasted to the brisk, straight, vigorous movements of another, but do not necessarily go beyond the appearance to think of psychic weariness or alertness behind it. Weariness and alertness are contained in the physical behavior itself; they are not distinguished in any essential way from the weariness of slowly floating tar or the energetic ring of the telephone bell. It is true, of course, that during a crucial conversation one person may be greatly concerned with trying to read the other's thoughts and feelings through what can be seen in his face and gestures. "What is he up to? How is he taking it?" But in such circumstances one clearly goes beyond what is apparent in the perception of expression itself.

From here it takes only one small further step to acknowledge that visual expression resides in any articulately shaped object or event. A steep rock, a willow tree, the colors of a sunset, the cracks in a wall, a tumbling leaf, a flowing fountain, and in fact a mere line or color, or the dance of an abstract shape on the movie screen have as much expression as the human body, and may serve the artist equally well. In some ways they serve him even better, for the human body is a particularly complex pattern, not easily reduced to the simplicity of shape and motion that transmits compelling expression. In addition, it is overloaded with non-visual associations. Vincent Van Gogh once made two drawings, one called *Sorrow* and representing a nude girl sitting with her head buried in her arms, the other a sketch of bare trees with gnarled roots. In a letter to his brother Theo he explained that he tried to put the same sentiment in both, "clinging to the earth convulsively and passionately and yet being half torn up by the storm. I wanted to express something of the struggle for life, in that pale, thin woman's figure as well as in the black, gnarled, and knotty roots." Actually, the almost abstract shapes of the roots carry the message more successfully than the conventionally drawn figure. The human body is not the easiest, but the most difficult vehicle of visual expression.

If one thinks of expression as something reserved for human behavior, one can account for the expression perceived in nature only as the result of the "pathetic fallacy"—a notion apparently introduced by John Ruskin and intended to describe, say, the sadness of weeping willows as a figment of empathy, anthropomorphism, primitive animism. However, if expression is an inherent characteristic of perceptual patterns, its manifestations in the human figure are but a special case of a more general phenomenon. The comparison of an object's expression with a human state of mind is a secondary process. The willow is not "sad" because it looks like a sad person. Rather, because the shape, direction, and flexibility of the branches convey passive hanging, a comparison with the structurally similar state of mind and body that we call sadness imposes itself secondarily.

Once expression has been anthropomorphized, it is natural to use words derived from human states of mind to describe objects, processes, or the dynamics of music. Actually it would be instructive and appropriate to do the opposite, and describe human behavior and expression by the more general properties pertaining to nature as a whole. Goethe once remarked: "It is our conviction that the quest for adjectives to express diversities of character has by no means exhausted the possibilities. For instance, one may attempt to use metaphorically the differences pointed up in the physical theory of cohesion; there would be strong, firm, dense, elastic, flexible, agile, rigid, tough, fluid, and who knows what other characters." In following Goethe's advice, one would get a better sense of human expression as a special case of organic and inorganic behavior, instead of insisting on man as the center and standard of nature. With regard to such phenomena, science is still waiting for its Copernicus.

When we go by the perceived patterns of forces, some objects and events resemble each other; others do not. On the basis of their expressive appearance, our eye spontaneously creates a kind of Linnean classification of all existing things. This perceptual classification cuts across the order suggested by other kinds of categories. Particularly in our modern Western civilization we are accustomed to distinguishing between animate and inanimate things, human and nonhuman creatures, the mental and the physical. But in terms of expressive qualities, the character of a given person may resemble that of a particular tree more closely than that of another person. The state of affairs in a human society may be similar to the tension in the skies just before the outbreak of a thunderstorm. Poets use such analogies, and so do other unspoiled people.

So-called primitive languages give us an idea of the kind of world that derives from a classification based on perception. Instead of restricting itself to the verb "to walk," which rather abstractly refers to locomotion, the language of the African Ewe takes care to specify for every kind of walking the particular expressive qualities of the movement. There are expressions for "the gait of a little man whose limbs shake very much, to walk with a dragging step like a feeble person, the gait of a long-legged man who throws his legs forward, of a corpulent man who walks heavily, to walk in a dazed fashion without looking ahead, an energetic and firm step," and many others. These distinctions are made not as an aesthetic exercise, but because the expressive properties of the gait are believed to reveal important and useful information on the kind of man who is walking and his intent at the time.

Although such languages often surprise us by their wealth of subdivisions for which we see no need, they also reveal generalizations that to us may seem unimportant or absurd. For example, the language of the Klamath Indians has prefixes for words referring to objects of similar shape or movement. Such a prefix may describe "the outside of a round or spheroidal, cylindrical, discoid or bulbed object, or a ring; also voluminous; or again, an act accomplished with an object which bears such a form; or a circular or semi-circular or waving movement of the body, arms, hands, or other parts. Therefore this prefix is to be found connected with clouds, celestial bodies, rounded slopes on the earth's surface, fruits rounded or bulbed in shape, stones and dwellings (these last being usually circular in form). It is employed, too, for a crowd of animals, for enclosures, social gatherings (since an assembly usually adopts the form of a circle), and so forth."

Such a classification groups things together that to our way of thinking belong in very different categories and have little or nothing in common. At the same time, these features of primitive language remind us that the poetical habit of uniting practically disparate objects by metaphor is not a sophisticated invention of artists, but derives from and relies on the universal and spontaneous way of approaching the world of experience.

Georges Braque advises the artist to seek the common in the dissimilar. "Thus the poet can say: The swallow knifes the sky, and thereby makes a knife out of a swallow." It is the function of the metaphor to make the reader penetrate the conventional shell of the world of things by juxtaposing objects that have little in common but the underlying pattern. Such a device, however, works only if the reader of poetry is still alive, in his own daily experience, to the symbolic or metaphoric connotation of all appearance and activity. For example, hitting or breaking things normally evokes, if ever so slightly, the overtone of attack and destruction. There is a tinge of conquest and achievement to all rising—even to climbing a staircase. If the shades are pulled up in the morning and the room is flooded with light, more is experienced than a simple change of illumination.

One aspect of the wisdom that belongs to a genuine culture is the constant awareness of the symbolic meaning expressed in a concrete happening, the sensing of the universal in the particular. This gives significance and dignity to all daily pursuits and prepares the ground on which the arts can grow. At its pathological extreme such spontaneous symbolism manifests itself in what is known to the psychiatrist as the "organ speech" of psychosomatic and other neurotic symptoms. There are people who cannot swallow because there is something in their lives they "cannot swallow," or whom an unconscious sense of guilt compels to spend hours every day on washing and cleaning.

The Priority of Expression

Let me emphasize once more that in our particular civilization we have come to think of perception as the recording of shapes, distances, hues, motions. The awareness of these measurable characteristics is actually a fairly late accomplishment of the human mind. Even in twentieth-century Western man, it presupposes special conditions. It is the attitude of the scientist and the engineer, or of the salesman who estimates the size of a customer's waist, the shade of a lipstick, the weight of a suitcase. But when I sit in front of a fireplace and watch the flames, I do not normally register certain shades of red, various degrees of brightness, geometrically defined shapes moving at such and such a speed. I see the graceful play of aggressive tongues, flexible striving, lively color. The face of a person is more readily perceived and remembered as being alert, tense, and concentrated than it is as being triangularly shaped, having slanted eyebrows, straight lips, and so on. This priority of expression, although somewhat modified in adults by a scientifically oriented education, is striking in children and primitives, as has been shown by Werner and Köhler. The profile of a mountain is soft or threateningly harsh; a blanket thrown over a chair is twisted, sad, tired.

The priority of physiognomic properties should not come as a surprise. Our senses are not self-contained recording devices operating for their own sake. They have been developed by the organism as an aid in reacting to the environment, and the organism is primarily interested in the forces active around it—their place, strength, direction. Hostility and friendliness are attributes of forces. And the perceived impact of forces makes for what we call expression.

If expression is the primary content of vision in daily life, the same should be all the more true of the way the artist looks at the world. The expressive qualities are his means of communication. They capture his attention, they enable him to understand and interpret his experiences, and they determine the form patterns he creates. Therefore the training of art students should be expected to consist basically in sharpening their sense of these qualities, and in teaching them to look to expression as the guiding criterion for every stroke of the pencil, brush, or chisel. In fact many good art teachers do precisely this. But in other cases the student's spontaneous sensitivity to expression not only is not developed further, it is even impaired and suppressed. There is, for example, an old-fashioned but not extinct way of teaching students to draw from the model by asking them to establish the exact length and direction of contour lines, the relative position of points, the shape of masses. In other words, students are to concentrate on the geometric-technical qualities of what they see. In its modern version this method consists in urging the young artist to think of the model or of a freely invented design as a configuration of masses, planes, direction. Again interest is focused on geometric technical qualities.

Such teaching follows principles of description often employed in mathematics or physical science rather than those of spontaneous vision. There are, however, teachers who will proceed differently. With a model sitting on the floor in a hunched-up position, such a teacher will not begin by making the students notice that the whole figure can be inscribed in a triangle. Instead he will ask about the expression of the figure; he may be told that the person on the floor looks tense, tied together, full of potential energy. He will suggest, then, that the student try to render this quality. In doing so the student will watch proportions and directions, but not as static geometric properties, "correct" for correctness's sake. These formal features will be understood as means of making the primarily observed expression come across on paper, and the correctness and incorrectness of each stroke will be judged on the basis of whether or not it captures the dynamic "mood" of the subject.

Equally, in a lesson on design, it will be made clear that to the artist just as to any unspoiled human being, a circle is not a line of constant curvature whose points are all equidistant from a center, but first of all a compact, hard, stable thing. Once the student has understood that roundness is not identical with circularity, he may try for a design whose structural logic will be controlled by the primary concept of something to be expressed. An artificial concentration on mere shapes and colors as such will leave the student at a loss as to which pattern to select among innumerable and equally acceptable ones. An expressive theme will serve him as a natural guide to forms that fit his purpose.

It will be evident that what is advocated here is not so-called "self-expression." The method of self-expression plays down, or even annihilates, the theme to be represented. It recommends a passive, "projective" pouring-out of what is felt inside. On the contrary, the method discussed here requires active, disciplined concentration of all organizing powers upon the expression found in one's vision of the world.

It might be argued that an artist must practice the purely formal technique before he can hope to render expression successfully. But this notion reverses the natural order of the artistic process. In fact all good practicing is highly expressive. This first occurred to me many years ago when I watched the dancer Gret Palucca perform one of her most popular program pieces, which she called "Technical Improvisations." This number was nothing but the systematic exercise that the dancer practiced every day in her studio to loosen up the joints of her body. She would start out by doing turns of her head, then move her neck, then shrug her shoulders, ending up wriggling her toes. This purely technical practice succeeded with the audience because it was thoroughly expressive. Forcefully precise and rhythmical movements presented quite naturally the entire repertoire of human pantomime. They passed through all the moods from lazy happiness to impertinent satire.

In order to achieve technically precise movements, a capable dance teacher may ask students not to perform "geometrically" defined positions, but to strive for the muscular experience of uplift, or attack, or yielding, that will be created by correctly executed movements. Comparable methods are nowadays applied in physical therapy. For example, the patient is asked to concentrate not on the meaningless, purely formal exercise of flexing and stretching his arm, but on a game or piece of work that involves suitable motions of the limbs as means to a sensible end.

Symbolism in Art

All perceptual qualities have generality. I mentioned this earlier, and I intended the statement to mean that to some extent we see redness in every red spot or speed in every fast movement. The same is true for expression. When Picasso conveys to us in a painting the gentle ways in which a mother guides the first steps of her unsteadily walking child, we see gentleness as a general quality exemplified in a particular case. In this sense it is valid to say that Picasso's picture symbolizes gentleness. In fact, for our purpose, the terms expression and symbolization can be used interchangeably. The example also suggests that the task of expressing or symbolizing a universal content through a particular image is carried out not only by the formal pattern, but by the subject matter as well, if there is one.

Only with regard to subject matter can the term symbolism be used in a more restricted sense. When Rembrandt depicts Aristotle contemplating the bust of Homer, it makes sense to ask whether the artist intended to narrate a scene that has taken place or might have taken place in a world of history or fable, or whether the scene is meant as purely "symbolic." In the latter case the subject matter and its arrangement are designed to embody an idea, and they may indicate this purpose by the unlikelihood of their occurrence in any real or imagined world. A clear instance of such symbolism is the painting by Titian commonly referred to as "Sacred and Profane Love"; it will hardly be taken by anyone as a genre scene, in which a clothed and a nude woman sit together on a well. The same is true for the engraving of Dürer's in which a winged woman with a goblet in her hand stands on a sphere moving through the clouds.

The correct reading of such a picture depends heavily on conventions. These conventions tend to standardize the way a certain idea is to be depicted, so that, for example, in Christian art a lily is known to symbolize the virginity of Mary, lambs are disciples, and two deer drinking from a pond show the recreation of the faithful.

However, the more an artistic experience depends on knowledge, the less direct it is likely to be. Therefore symbolism in this sense is hardly relevant to the subject of the present book. Of minor interest also is "symbolism" in the sense of Freudian psychoanalysis. Freud's interpretation differs in a crucial way from what is considered here as the nature of art. He treats symbolism not as the relation between a concrete image and an abstract idea, but rather as a relation between equally concrete objects, e.g., between a dagger and the erect male genital. If after penetrating the work of a great artist we were left with nothing but references to organs and functions of the human body, we would rightly wonder what makes art such a universal and supposedly vital creation of the human mind.

A moment of reflection shows that sex, like any other particular subject matter, can never be the ultimate content of a valid artistic experience. It can only serve as formal material, employed by the artist to point to the ideas at which his work ultimately aims. This formal material is constituted by the entirety of the visual facts presented in the work. In this sense, we find symbolism even in works that, at first sight, seem to be little more than arrangements of fairly neutral objects. We need only glance at the bare outlines of the two still lifes sketched in Figure 279 to experience two different conceptions of reality. Cézanne's picture (*a*) is dominated by the stable framework of verticals and horizontals in the background, the table, and the axes of bottles and glass. This skeleton is strong enough to give support even to the sweeping folds of the fabric. A simple order is conveyed by the upright symmetry of each bottle and that of the glass. There is abundance in the swelling volumes and emphasis on roundness and softness even in the inorganic matter. Compare this image of prosperous peace with the catastrophic turmoil in Picasso's work (*b*). Here we find little stability. The vertical and horizontal orientations are avoided. The room is slanted, the right angles of the table, which is overturned, are either hidden by oblique position or distorted. The four legs do not run parallel. The bottle topples, the desperately sprawling corpse of the bird is about to fall off the table. The contours tend to be hard, sharp, and lifeless, even in the body of the chicken.

In great works of art the deepest significance is transmitted to the eye with powerful directness by the perceptual characteristics of the compositional pattern. The "story" of Michelangelo's *Creation of Man*, on the ceiling of the Sistine Chapel in Rome (Figure 280), is understood by every reader of the book of Genesis. But even the story is modified in a way that makes it more comprehensible and impressive to the eye. The Creator, instead of breathing a living soul into the body of clay—a motif not easily translatable into an expressive pattern—reaches out toward the arm of Adam as though an animating spark, leaping from fingertip to fingertip, were transmitted from the maker

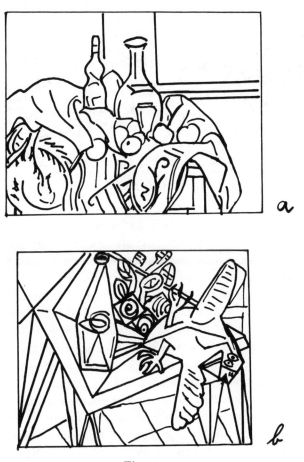

Figure 279

to the creature. The bridge of the arm visually connects two separate worlds: the self-contained compactness of the mantle that encloses God and is given forward motion by the diagonal of his body; and the incomplete, flat slice of the earth, whose passivity is expressed in the backward slant of its contour. There is passivity also in the concave curve over which the body of Adam is molded. It is lying on the ground and enabled partly to rise by the attractive power of the approaching creator. The desire and potential capacity to get up and walk are indicated as a subordinate theme in the left leg, which also serves as a support of Adam's arm, unable to maintain itself freely like the energy-charged arm of God.

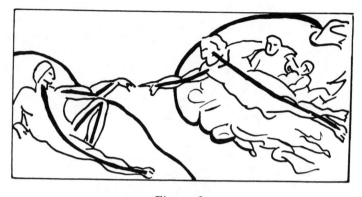

Figure 280

Our analysis shows that the ultimate theme of the image, the idea of creation, is conveyed by what strikes the eye first and continues to organize the composition as we examine its details. The structural skeleton reveals the dynamic theme of the story. And since the pattern of transmitted, life-giving energy is not simply recorded by the sense of vision but presumably arouses in the mind a corresponding configuration of forces, the observer's reaction is more than a mere taking cognizance of an external object. The forces that characterize the meaning of the story come alive in the observer and produce the kind of stirring participation that distinguishes artistic experience from the detached acceptance of information.

What matters most is that the image does not just elucidate the meaning of the individual story presented in the work. The dynamic theme revealed by the compositional pattern is not limited to the biblical episode at hand, but is valid for any number of situations that may occur in the psychical and physical world. Not only is the perceptual pattern a means of understanding the story of the creation of man, but the story becomes a means of illustrating a kind of event that is universal and therefore abstract and therefore in need of being clad with flesh and blood so that the eye may see it.

Consequently, the visual form of a work of art is neither arbitrary nor a mere play of shapes and colors. It is indispensable as a precise interpreter of the idea the work is meant to express. Similarly, the subject matter is neither arbitrary nor unimportant. It is exactly correlated with the formal pattern to supply a concrete embodiment of an abstract theme. The kind of connoisseur who looks only for the pattern does as little justice to the work as the kind of layman who looks only for the subject matter. When Whistler called the portrait of his mother *Arrangement in Gray and Black*, he treated his picture as one-sidedly as someone who sees nothing in it but a dignified lady sitting in a chair. Neither the formal pattern nor the subject matter is the final content of the work of art. Both are instruments of artistic form. They serve to give body to an invisible universal.

Viewed in this fashion, traditional representational art leads without a break to the nonmimetic, "abstract" art of our century. Anyone who has grasped the abstraction in representational art will see the continuity, even though art ceases to depict objects of nature. In its own way, nonmimetic art does what art has always done. Each successful work presents a skeleton of forces whose meaning can be read as directly as that inherent in Michelangelo's story of the first man. Such "abstract" art is not "pure form," because we have discovered that even the simplest line expresses visible meaning and is therefore symbolic. It does not offer intellectual abstractions, because there is nothing more concrete than color, shape, and motion. It does not limit itself to the inner life of man, or to the unconscious, because for art the distinctions between the outer and the inner world and the conscious and the unconscious mind are artificial. The human mind receives, shapes, and interprets its image of the outer world with all its conscious and unconscious powers, and the realm of the unconscious could never enter our experience without the reflection of perceivable things. There is no way of presenting the one without the other. But the nature of the outer and inner worlds can be reduced to a play of forces, and this "musical" approach is attempted by the misnamed abstract artists.

We do not know what the art of the future will look like. No one particular style is art's final climax. Every style is but one valid way of looking at the world, one view of the holy mountain, which offers a different image from every place but can be seen as the same everywhere.

NOTES

NOTES TO CHAPTER I. BALANCE

The Hidden Structure of a Square (pp. 10–16)

Preliminary testing of the "magnetic" effects described here was done by one of my students, Toni Cushing. See also Goude (163). (Numbers in parentheses refer to the Bibliography.)

The repulsion of the disk from the edge of the square brings to mind experiments by Köhler and Wallach (249) on the visual aftereffect. A line figure was fixated by observers for a few minutes, after which a new figure was introduced for inspection in order to test the influence of the previously fixated pattern. It was found that visual objects recede from areas previously occupied by other visual objects. The effect was weak when the objects were close together; it approached a climax at a certain distance, and it weakened again as distance increased further. A physiological explanation is offered by the authors.

Wertheimer (445), p. 79.

What Are Perceptual Forces? (pp. 16–18)

Compare Kepes (232), p. 29: "The actual visual elements are only the focal points of this field; they are the concentrated energy."

On the physiology of shape perception see, e.g., Lettvin (266) and Hubel (203).

Psychological and Physical Balance (pp. 19–20)

Ross (376), p. 23.

Why Balance? (pp. 20–23)

Compare Ross (376), p. 25: "In any unsymmetrical relation of positions (directions, distances, intervals), in which the balance-center is not clearly and sufficiently indicated, there is a suggestion of movement. The eye, not being held by any balance, readily follows this suggestion." See also Arnheim (18), p. 76.

Figs. 7–10 are adapted from Figs. 21, 24, 1, and 9 of Graves (165), by permission of the Psychological Corporation, New York.

Weight (pp. 23–26)

For the lever principle and other factors of balance see Langfeld (261), chs. 9 and 10, and the earlier literature cited there.

Puffer (356) on the vista effect.

On emphasis by isolation on the stage see Dean (91), p. 146.

Direction (pp. 26–29)

Toulouse-Lautrec's *At the Circus: The Tandem*, painted in 1899, is in the Knoedler Collection, New York.

For perceptual aftereffects found in experiments by James J. Gibson and others, see Köhler and Wallach (249), p. 269.

Patterns of Balance (p. 29)

A systematic study of compositional patterns has been made by Rudrauf (379). He distinguishes between *compositions diffuses*, in which units are evenly and homogeneously distributed with no center of radiation or accent (Bosch, Brueghel, Persian miniatures), and *compositions scandées*, which have spatial rhythm and a hierarchy of accents. He divides the latter into (1) axial compositions, organized around the pivot of a principal figure or group; (2) centered compositions, radiating from a point of gravitation; and (3) polarized compositions, made up of two opposing figures or groups, between which there is a dynamic relation.

Top and Bottom (pp. 30–33)

Interferences with the correct perception of verticality have been demonstrated by Witkin (456) and Wapner (433).

Langfeld (261), p. 223.

Greenough (167), p. 24.

One of my students, Charlotte Hannaford, presented subjects randomly with abstract paintings in their four spatial positions, asking them to find the orientation (A) intended by the artist. The following results were obtained from twenty observers:

	A	B	C	D
Bauer I	15	3	1	1
Bauer II	4	3	3	10
Bauer III	10	5	3	2
Mondrian	11	1	4	4
Kandinsky	10	2	8	0
	50	14	19	17

The overall result showed exactly 50 percent correct judgments. The result was negative for Bauer II (notice, however, the high agreement on one "wrong" judgment), weak for Kandinsky, and clearly positive for the other three. Mere probability would have made for only 25 percent correct judgments. The comments obtained from observers in such experiments are enlightening and deserve more study.

Kanizsa and Tampieri (223), p. 52, show letters and numbers in which upper and lower parts look "almost equal" in their upright position but quite different when viewed upside-down.

If one turns the picture of a reclining woman by 90°, one suddenly sees her as pressed violently in the direction of her support. Downward pressure, unobserved under normal conditions, becomes noticeable as lateral pressure.

Jackson Pollock painting on the floor: O'Connor (329), p. 40.

Right and Left (pp. 33–36)

On left-right discrimination see Corballis and Beale (85, 86) and Olson (332) p. 10; also the richly documented book by Fritsch (123), who quotes the Goethe statement.

Wölfflin published two papers on the right-left problem (466). Gaffron's first observations appear in a book on Rembrandt's etchings (127). An article of hers in English cites the earlier literature (126).

Nearness in photographs: Bartley (43).

During the controversy on whether Raphael intended the compositions for his tapestries as they are in the cartoons, or inverted as they appear in the tapestries,

A. P. Oppé pointed out that the left-right effect is all but reversed when a picture is approached and viewed obliquely from the right side. See Oppé (334) and White and Shearman (449).

Dean (91), p. 132.

Nothing decisive is known so far on the neurology of visual asymmetry. Cf. Gazzaniga (131) and Geschwind (136, 137).

On size discrimination and lateral movement see Van der Meer (424).

Eye movements: Buswell (71) and Yarbus (474).

Balance and the Human Mind (pp. 36–37)

Freud (118), p. 1.

On the relations of entropy to art see Arnheim (15).

Whyte (451).

The definition of motivation is quoted from Freeman (117), p. 239. Compare also Krech and Crutchfield (255), ch. 2, and Weber (434).

Regarding the organism and the law of entropy see Köhler (243), ch. 8.

Madame Cézanne in a Yellow Chair (pp. 37–41)

Ross (376), p. 26.

For the analysis of a similar portrait by Cézanne see Loran (279), plate 17.

NOTES TO CHAPTER II. SHAPE

Agnosia: Gelb and Goldstein on experiments with brain-injured patients in (134), pp. 324ff; also Gelb's more recent paper (133).

Vision as Active Exploration (pp. 42–43)

On collective mechanisms in perception see Lettvin (266).

Plato, *Timaeus*, ¶45; T. S. Eliot (103), p. 4.

Grasping the Essentials (pp. 43–44)

Köhler's chimpanzees (244), p. 320.

Recognizing of snapshots: Segall *et al.* (395), p. 32.

Perceptual Concepts (pp. 44–46)

On stimulus equivalence see Gellermann (135); also Hebb (177), pp. 12ff., who asserts that the grasping of perceptual features develops gradually.

Lashley quoted by Adrian (2) p. 85.

Perceptual concepts are discussed in more detail in Arnheim (18), pp. 27–50 and (16).

The Influence of the Past (pp. 48–51)

Kanizsa (224), p. 31.

Effect of verbal instruction: Carmichael (72).

Gottschaldt (162). Fig. 23 is not one of Gottschaldt's patterns. I found it sketched in pencil on the margin of Gottschaldt's paper by the late Max Wertheimer in his personal copy of the *Psychologische Forschung*.

Gombrich (158), p. 216. See also Bruner and Krech (67), pp. 15–31.

Seeing Shape (pp. 51–54)

Fig. 25 is reproduced from an engraving in Leon Battista Alberti, *Della Pittura e della Statua*, Milan, Società Tipografica De' Classici Italiani, 1804, p. 123.

Agnosia: Gelb and Goldstein in (134), p. 317.

Fig. 29 is after Berliner (49), p. 24.

Simplicity (pp. 55–63)

Simplicity and order are not the same thing, but certain observations on the nature of the one apply also to the other. Spinoza's remark on the subjectivity of order

(*Ethics*, appendix to Part I) is cited in a paper by Hartmann and Sickles on the theory of order (173). These authors, who seem to think of order mainly, or perhaps exclusively, as a characteristic of grouping—that is, as a relationship between discrete objects—assert that "order is the term applied to any subjective quality or sensation which is produced by, and dependent upon, the number of straight lines which can be drawn through three or more actual or supplied points or centers of the sensory field; it varies directly with the degree to which these lines tend to become parallel with each other and with the vertico-horizontal coordinate system natural to the organism." This definition, applicable also to simplicity, points correctly to the importance of the spatial frame of reference and of parallel orientation. But it describes the effect of parallelism in terms of a summation of elements and is inadequate also in considering only two specific factors. For example, circles, which contain no parallels, have a high degree of order. In a second paper Sickles (401) realizes that a circular arrangement of objects would possess order, but maintains that no such arrangement is ever perceived, because "the eyes never see curves save when these are objectively present—all subjective intervals being straight lines." This assertion is based on insufficient observation (see, e.g., our Fig. 28).

Alexander and Carey (4).

Hochberg *et al.* on simplicity (195 and 197).

Peter Blake, in a review of the book *The Road Is Yours* by R. M. Cleveland and S. T. Williamson, published in the *New York Times*, 1951.

Chaplin: Cocteau (79), p. 16.

Parsimony: Cohen and Nagel (80), pp. 212, 384.

Newton: *Mathematical Principles*, Book III, rule 1.

Badt on simplicity (36).

Ben Nicholson's relief is illustrated in *Circle* (297), plate 6.

Victory Boogie-Woogie, a painting by Piet Mondrian (312), p. 55. *Rebellion Tamed by Wise Government* is the title of a painting by Rubens, c. 1631.

Isomorphism: Koffka (250), pp. 56–68.

Simplification Demonstrated (pp. 63–66)

Lucretius: *De Rerum Natura*, Book IV, 353. Leonardo (291), vol. 2, p. 238.

A detailed survey of experiments on the reactions to subdued stimuli can be found in the first edition of Woodworth (469), ch. IV, "Memory for Form." Consult also Koffka (250), pp. 493–505. Considerable controversy has been aroused by experiments based on the effect of memory. The pioneering study by Wulf (472) was done under the guidance of Koffka. Among the more recent publications, that of Goldmeier (153) is particularly relevant. Hebb and Foord (178) interpreted their results as being contrary to gestalt predictions. The examples of reactions to Fig. 38, which is adapted from Wohlfahrt in Neue Psychologische Studien 1928/32, derives from demonstrations in my classes. Fig. 40a is based on Wulf, Fig. 40d on Allport (6). See also Arnheim (16), pp. 81–84.

Leveling and Sharpening (pp. 66–67)

On *Prägnanz* see Rausch (364), pp. 904ff. An example of the confusion created by *pregnance*: Woodworth and Schlosberg (470), p. 419.

On leveling and sharpening in the transmission of rumors see Allport and Postman (7), reprinted in Katz *et al.* (225), pp. 394–404.

A Whole Maintains Itself (pp. 67–69)

On the principles of Gestalt psychology see the books of Köhler (241) and Koffka (250), as well as the anthologies edited by Ellis (104) and Henle (188).

Torroja (421) p. 285.

The law of simplicity, as I prefer to call it, has often been called the law of the good gestalt or of *prägnanz*. The notion of "goodness" suggests subjective value judgment rather than objective fact. On *prägnanz* see p. 67 and the note relating to it.

Köhler's book on physical gestalten (246) has not been translated, but references to the subject abound in his later writings. The quotation is from (240), p. 242.

Ivo Kohler on experiments with goggles (253).

Hemianopia: Gelb (133) and Teuber (415), pp. 1614f.

Figs. 41 and 46 are taken from Metelli (303) by permission of the author.

Subdivision (pp. 69–73)

Fig. 42 is after Arnheim, in Whyte (452), p. 202.

On the golden section see Arnheim (18), pp. 102–119, and the literature cited there.

Why the Eyes Often Tell the Truth (pp. 73–74)

Wertheimer's example of the bridge on p. 336 of the German original (444). The drawing is mine.

Stein (407) p. 11. On camouflage in nature see Cott (87).

Compare Köhler (241), pp. 156–160. Wertheimer explains the correspondence between perceptual and physical organization as an evolutionary adaptation of the nervous system to the environment; p. 336 of the German original (444), omitted in the summary by Ellis (104).

Subdivision in the Arts (pp. 74–76)

Brancusi's stone sculpture of 1908 is in the Philadelphia Museum.

What Is a Part? (pp. 76–78)

Fig. 50 on p. 323 of Wertheimer's original paper (444).

Early formulations of the gestalt principle assumed the existence of an additional "gestalt quality." Cf. Ehrenfels (102), reprinted in Weinhandl (436), pp. 11–43; also Arnheim in Henle (188) pp. 90–96.

In a "gestalt" the structure of the whole is determined by the structure of the parts, and vice versa. For a list of definitions of "gestalt" see Katz (226), p. 91. For an introduction to the theory see Wertheimer (446), Köhler (241), and Koffka (250).

Picasso's sketches for Guernica: Arnheim (19).

Waddington's article on biological shape in Whyte (452), pp. 44–56. Waddington also criticizes modern sculpture from the anatomist's point of view.

Similarity and Difference (pp. 79–88)

Rules of grouping: Wertheimer (445), Musatti (321). On experiments with animals see Ellis (104), selections 18–21.

Dante: *Paradiso* III, 14.

Aristotle on similarity: *On Memory and Reminiscence*, 451b. See also Plato's *Phaedo*, 74.

Mosconi in the Rivista di Psicologia, 1965.

Figs. 52–56 are adapted from my paper in Whyte (452), p. 200.

The piecemeal character of the rules of grouping is often overlooked. Wertheimer himself was well aware of it. After introducing his rules he called them "a poor abstraction," thus giving his paper a dramatic turning point. He described the law of similarity as "a special case of the law of good gestalt," and asserted that visual patterns should not be treated in terms of "distances and relations between pieces."

Fig. 59 is traced from a reproduction in Duncan (98), p. 54. The painting dates from 1908.

Big Dipper: reproduced by permission of Prof. Weiss from (437).

Walter Piston (353), p. 20. Other principles found in visual organization could also be beneficially applied to music.

Examples from Art (pp. 88–92)

Brueghel's *Parable of the Blind Men*, painted in 1568, is in the Naples Museum. The biblical reference is to Matthew 15:14.

Grünewald's altar, finished c. 1515, is in the Museum of Colmar. Gombrich (156), p. 259.

Five versions of El Greco's *Expulsion from the Temple* are known. I am referring to the one in the Frick Collection, New York.

Van Gogh's *Bedroom*, painted in Arles in 1888, is in the Chicago Art Institute.

The Structural Skeleton (pp. 92–95)

Delacroix (93), I, Etudes Esthétiques, p. 69.

Eye movements: Yarbus (474) and Buswell (71).

Fig. 72 is derived from a procedure suggested by Wertheimer on p. 318 of the original paper (444).

Wittgenstein (458), part II, sect XI.

NOTES TO CHAPTER III. FORM

Ben Shahn (398), p. 61.

Wittgenstein (458), p. 235.

Goethe, *Dichtung und Wahrheit*, Book 11.

Illusionistic doctrine: cf. Arnheim (14), p. 125.

Pliny on Zeuxis: Panofsky (339), p. 99.

Orientation in Space (pp. 98–103)

Gellermann (135).

Tilted square: e.g., Piaget (348). The influence of orientation on the shape of the square was first pointed out in 1896 by Mach (293), p. 106.

Kopfermann (254), p. 352.

Picasso's still life *The Red Tablecloth*, painted in 1924, is reproduced as plate 187 by Barr (42).

Witkin (457).

For two early studies on children's responses to orientation see Stern (408) and Rice (370); more recently Ghent (139).

Projections (pp. 103–106)

Wölfflin, in a paper on the reproduction and interpretation of works of art (464), pp. 66–76, complains about the distorting effect of photographs that show pieces of sculpture from inappropriate viewpoints. In a photograph such distortion occurs more easily than in direct perception because it presents an isolated aspect under conditions of greatly reduced three-dimensionality. When the shape of a statue is rather complex, an obliquely taken picture may produce a "pseudo-front"—that is, the impression that the observer is facing the front view of the statue. Hence the distortion.

Projective geometry deals with a similar problem by determining the structural "invariants," which remain untouched by distortion through projection. See Courant and Robbins (88), pp. 165ff.

Bower on constancy in infants (60).

Depth perception in infants: Gibson (140).

Which Aspect is Best? (pp. 106–111)

Galton (129), p. 68.

Eidetic images: Haber (170).

Hogarth's *Analysis of Beauty*, Introd.

Computer graphics: Sutherland (411).

Chesterton in "The Eye of Apollo," one of his Father Brown stories. On Giacometti see Lord (280), p. 14.

Kerschensteiner (236), pp. 229–230.

The Egyptian Method (pp. 112–116)

Mach (292).

Schäfer (386), p. 254, fig. 199; elevations of the sphinx, p. 202.

Oskar Schlemmer's *Tischgesellschaft*, painted in 1923, is in the Ströher Collection, Darmstadt.

Foreshortening (pp. 116–120)

If we think of the sections of the foreshortened bodies, we realize more easily how a partially given simple shape tends toward its completion.

Fig. 88 is drawn after a detail from an Attic amphora of the early sixth century, in the possession of the Metropolitan Museum of Art in New York (illustrated in *Greek Painting* [166], p. 8). The compelling power of structurally simple patterns is demonstrated by the fact that such monsters can be produced in a period when the sense of the visually significant was otherwise so strict that even mild foreshortenings, e.g., of heads or feet, were avoided. The symmetry of the front view is so inviting that its inadequacy is overlooked. It also affords a simple solution to the problem of representing a set of four horses (cf. p. 125). Rathe (360), p. 37, mentions similar cases in Far Eastern art as examples of the impact ("Durchschlagskraft") of such projections.

Delacroix, *Journal* (94), vol. 3, p. 13, entry of Jan. 13, 1857.

Fig. 90 is enlarged from Fernand Léger's film *Ballet Mécanique* (1924). I am indebted for the photograph to Guido Aristarco, editor of *Cinema Nuovo*.

Andrea Mantegna's foreshortened figure of Christ is in the Brera, Milan.

Figs. 91*a* and *b* are sketched after pp. 9 and 36 of Cooper (84).

The Barlach quotation is translated from a letter of June, 1889 (41), p. 17.

Overlapping (pp. 120–123)

The Picasso examples of Fig. 92 are sketched from Cooper (84), pp. 13 and 14.

Apologies are due Rockwell Kent, a detail of whose woodcut *The Lovers* gave me the idea for Fig. 93.

Michelangelo's *Last Judgment* in the Sistine Chapel of the Vatican was painted in 1536–1541.

Low-cut dresses that end in a horizontal line slice the shoulders from the rest of the body, whereas the oblique V-shaped cut deviates from the axes of the body strongly enough not to interfere with its unity.

What Good Does Overlapping Do? (pp. 123–127)

Fig. 98 is taken from an Egyptian relief at Abydos (c. 1300 B.C.) representing King Sethos I and the goddess Isis.

Rubens' *Shepherd Embracing a Young Woman* of 1636–1638 is in the Munich Pinakothek.

For further examples of how superposition is used to convey meaning in films see Arnheim (20) pp. 47ff.

Alschuler and Hattwick (8), vol. 2, p. 129.

The picture of St. Ursula from a calendar manuscript in Stuttgart is reproduced by Gombrich (156), p. 129.

The parallel noted in the development of music and the visual arts refers mainly to the sequence of comparable steps, not to coincidence in history. It may be mentioned, however, that although in Western culture visual overlapping precedes musical harmony by thousands of years, the arrangement of pictures in horizontal rows gives way to an integrated organization of the depth. dimension only in the Renaissance. See Bunim (69) and White (448).

Interplay of Plane and Depth (pp. 127–130)

The group in Fig. 102 is a detail from a scroll painted by a Sung emperor Hui Tsung (1082–1135). The scroll is a copy of a work done in the Tang period.

My presentation of the relation between perspective projection and visual conception has profited greatly from conversations with Henry Schaefer-Simmern.

Competing Aspects (pp. 130–133)

Fig. 104 is taken from Boas (54), pp. 224–225.

Morin-Jean (315), pp. 86, 87, 138, 139, 152.

Fig. 105a is taken from a drawing by a five-and-a-half-year old child, 105b from Picasso's *Still Life with an Enamel Saucepan*, painted in 1945 (Musée d'Art Moderne, Paris).

On interpretations of the cubist procedure see, e.g., Paul Laporte's article (262).

Picasso's head of a bull is sketched from his *Mise à Mort* of 1934.

Realism and Reality (pp. 134–136)

Wölfflin (468), p. 63. Fig. 107 gives the outlines of the figure of Abias from the lunettes of the Sistine Chapel.

What Looks Lifelike? (pp. 136–139)

Boccaccio on Giotto in the fifth story on the sixth day of the *Decamerone*.

Adaptation level: Helson (184).

On holography see, e.g., Pennington (344).

Picasso on lifelikeness, cf. Ashton (33) p. 67; on originality, Couturier (89).

Form as Invention (pp. 139–144)

Giacometti: Selz (396), p. 17.

Hochberg and Brooks (196) on picture perception of infants.

Rudrauf on Annunciations (379).

Levels of Abstraction (pp. 144–152)

Parts of the following discussion are adapted from Arnheim (28). A pertinent analysis can be found in Worringer's book on abstraction and empathy (471). See also Blanshard (53).

Worringer (471), p. 68, quoting Von den Steinen without specifying the reference.

I am not concerned here with the special problem of realism in paleolithic or bushman art. Although the animal pictures of the Altamira type have the earmarks of a late, mature style, as Meyer Schapiro pointed out many years ago (390), the question remains whether highly realistic pictures are ever produced at a primitive level of development by a kind of spontaneous "photographic" recording of momentary visual impressions—that is, whether under special conditions the visual conception of the object may be overruled by the impact of a specific percept. At present I know of no evidence to support this assertion.

On primitive thinking consult Lévy-Bruhl (269) and Radin (358).

A survey of the literature on "artistic behavior in the abnormal" has been published by Anastasi and Foley (10). Many examples can be found in the *American Journal of Art Therapy*, formerly the *Bulletin of Art Therapy*. Nijinsky's drawings are reproduced in his diary (327). A good characterization of the schizoid temperament is given in ch. 10 of Kretschmer's book on physique and character (257). Alfred Bader (35) has published a monograph on Friedrich Schröder-Sonnenstern.

Coomaraswamy (82), pp. 85–99, has pointed out that traditionally an ornament or decoration is an integral part of the work of art and not "millinery," as it is considered today. Etymologically the Latin "ornate" means primarily to "fit out, furnish, provide with necessaries," and even in the sixteenth century one reads of the "tackling or ornaments of a ship." Similarly, asserts Coomaraswamy, "décor" is related to "decorous" or "decent," meaning "suitable to a character or time, place, and occasion" and to "decorum," that is, "what is befitting."

Hodler's painting *Silvaplanersee* of 1907 is in the Kunsthaus, Zurich.

Hogarth (199) chs. III and VII.

For the observation that symmetry is frequent in the staging of comedies, I am indebted to my student Toni Cushing.

Bergson in his book on laughter (47).

Tua res agitur: "This concerns you." Horace, *Epistles*, I, 18, 84.

La Source (pp. 152–156)

Muther (322), vol. III, p. 163.

Visual Information (pp. 156–161)

Leonardo da Vinci's *Notebooks* (291), vol. I, p. 105.

The subway map is reproduced by permission of London Transport.

Notebooks (291), vol. I, p. 107.

NOTES TO CHAPTER IV. GROWTH

The main ideas presented in the first section of this chapter were developed earlier in a paper of mine on perceptual abstraction and art (28).

The literature on comparisons between children's art and primitive art is summarized by Anastasi and Foley (10), vol. II, pp. 48–65. In particular see Levinstein (268), Eng (105), Britsch (64), and Löwenfeld (284).

The Intellectualistic Theory (pp. 164–167)

Compare Herbert Read's remarks on the "'conceptual fallacy" (365), p. 134. Read discusses many of the most important among the books and papers that had been written on the subject of the present chapter until then.

Luquet (287) asserts that the child's drawings go through three main stages: incapacity for synthesis, intellectual realism, and visual realism. See also Goodenough (159).

Gesell (138) and Bower (59).

They Draw What They See (pp. 167–169)

On perceiving and performing in children see Olson and Pagliuso (333). The symposium consists of papers by Maccoby, McNeill, Olson, Staats, and Arnheim.

Representational Concepts (pp. 169–171)

The Matisse anecdote is reported by Gertrude Stein (407), p. 17.

Olson on diagonals (332). Quotation from Arnheim in Olson, p. 206.

We often read that children endlessly repeat "stereotyped schemas" they have worked out. The adult tends to pay more attention to the basic patterns that keep reappearing in the drawings than to the variations obtained with these patterns. It is true that children will cling to a formal discovery and experiment with its capacities until its virtues are exhausted and something new is needed. This, however, is good practice, fortunately not limited to children. The question whether or not the drawings and paintings of children are "art" may be safely left to the philosophers.

Little of Gustaf Britsch's teaching is available in his own words. The book *Theorie der Kunst* (64), published in 1926 under his name with his student Egon Kornmann indicated as editor, was actually written by Kornmann after Britsch's death. He relied on oral communication and on Britsch's notes and papers, some of which are quoted verbatim in the last part of the book. The main ideas are summarized in English in the introduction to (388) by Britsch's disciple, Henry Schaefer-Simmern, who applied and developed them. Frequent conversations with Professor Schaefer-Simmern have been of the greatest value to me in writing the present chapter.

Drawing as Motion (pp. 171–174)

On the paintings of apes see Morris (316); also Köhler (244) p. 96.

The basic texts on graphology, still untranslated, are by Klages (237) and Pulver (357).

Goodnow (161). For an example of a disconnected drawing by a weak-sighted child see Löwenfeld (284), p. 155, fig. 3. Occasionally such drawings occur also in normal children, but they are not frequent enough to represent a typical phase ("incapacity for synthesis"), as Luquet has maintained (287). Luquet arrived at his conclusion by including in this category the so-called "tadpole" drawings. He relied here on the common erroneous view that in these drawings arms are attached to the head or the legs. Compare also Piaget (350), p. 65.

Baudelaire in his report on the Salon of 1859. The passage is repeated in his "L'oeuvre et la vie d'Eugène Delacroix" of 1863. See (44), pp. 1043 and 1121. The translation is mine.

The Primordial Circle (pp. 174–179)

The example of the horses was sometimes used by Max Wertheimer in his lectures.

Cott (87) on animal camouflage.

Charlotte Rice (370) p. 133. Also Goodenough (159) and Spears (403), who lists recent literature on shape preference in infants.

Piaget and Inhelder (350).

Jonas (211) contains his two essays on sight and image-making.

Experiments in which children are asked to copy geometrical figures have shown that between the ages of three and four they often employ, e.g., two concentric circles to represent a triangle inscribed in a circle. Piaget (350), p. 75, and Bender (46) chs. 2 and 4.

Fig. 122*k* is drawn after Werner (440) p. 122; *a* and *g* are originals; the other examples are copied from originals.

The Law of Differentiation (pp. 179–182)

On biological differentiation see Arnheim (15), p. 40.

Piaget (349), p. 12.

Gombrich (157), ch. XI.

On marked and unmarked concepts see Lyons (289), p. 79.

Goodenough (159) and more recently Harris (172).

Vertical and Horizontal (pp. 182–187)

Kellogg (230).

Delacroix's remark is quoted after (92), p. 8, where it is dated 1843.

Kerschensteiner's statement (236), p. 17, is substantially—but not entirely—correct, since the very first two samples he reproduces show a linear trunk, misinterpreted by him as "one leg, to which feet are attached." However, even in these samples, heads, fingers, and feet are given as outline figures, which keep the whole pattern, as it were, visually afloat.

Wölfflin (464), p. 79.

On the copying of figures in intelligence tests see Terman and Merrill (413), pp. 92, 98, 219, 230. Also Piaget (350), ch. 2: the drawing of geometrical figures.

Hubel and Wiesel (203) on feature analyzers in the cat's brain.

Attneave (34); Mondrian (312).

Obliqueness (pp. 187–190)

Olson's monograph on children's conception of the diagonal (332). See also *The Structurist*, 1969, #9, a special issue on the oblique in art.

The office furniture of Fig. 130 is manufactured by the Oxford Pendaflex Corporation in Garden City, N.Y., as "The Cluster 120 Work Station."

The Fusion of Parts (pp. 191–194)

For an early drawing of a person sitting on a chair see Eng (105), p. 69.

Five-year-old children who have become aware of the perspective effect but are not yet able to tackle the deformation of shape will sometimes draw a tilted disk as a smaller but perfectly round circle rather than as an ellipse. Piaget (350), p. 214.

Size (pp. 195–197)

Löwenfeld (284), pp. 25–31, and (282), fig. 26, p. 167. For distances between objects see pp. 41, 47, 49, 77, 127, in Löwenfeld (284), who is inclined to explain the long arms as an expression of the muscular feeling of stretching experienced in such situations. There seems to be no need for resorting to a specific kinesthetic factor when a universal visual factor provides a full explanation.

The Misnamed Tadpoles (pp. 97–199)

A characteristic in-between position on the interpretation of the *têtards* is assumed by Luquet (287). He realizes that the omission of the trunk may be only apparent, but attributes it to lack of importance for the child.

Fig. 139 is traced from Kerschensteiner (236), table 82.

Translation into Two Dimensions (pp. 199–203)

Abbott on Flatland (1). The Australian bark painting of the kangaroo is in the National Museum of Victoria in Melbourne.

Clark (76).

Educational Consequences (pp. 203–208)

Cocteau (78), p. 19.

On Arnold Schönberg as a teacher see Wellesz (439), pp. 49ff.

On the forerunners of central perspective see White (448) and Bunim (69).

Quotation from Arnheim (16), pp. 306–7.

Herbert Read (365), plate 18b.

Sticks and Slabs (pp. 209–215)

A curious solution of the head-face problem may be seen in the small Sumerian bronzes that show divinities with four faces symmetrically arranged around the head. Examples are in the Oriental Institute, Chicago. Illustrated in *Master Bronzes* (299), plates 1 and 2. On the flatness of early faces in the work of beginners see, e.g., Schaefer-Simmern (388), pp. 98–99.

Examples of early sculpture on plates 83, 86, 404–409, in Bossert's book on ancient Crete (58).

Lange's law of frontality (260).

The fusion of units in sculpture may be compared with the analogous development in drawings described earlier in the section "The Fusion of Parts."

The Cube and the Round (pp. 215–217)

Löwy (285).

Fig. 150 is drawn after plate viii of Perrot and Chipiez (345), vol. II, p. 130.

For the quote from Lomazzo see Holt (200), p. 260.

NOTES TO CHAPTER V. SPACE

Line and Contour (pp. 219–223)

Hogarth in the Introduction to his *Analysis of Beauty* (199).

Moholy-Nagy (311).

Experiments on density in figure-ground situations by Gelb and Granit are discussed in Koffka (250), p. 187.

Kennedy on discontinuity (231).

The soap-film experiments are described by Courant and Robbins (88), pp. 386ff. It would be mistaken to assume that in physics simplest possible shape and shortest connection always go together. For example, the solution of Plateau's problem for the edges of a cube does not lead to a cube. Similarly, the shortest connections between three or four points do not necessarily form triangles or quadrilaterals. See Fig. 281, taken from Courant and Robbins (88), pp. 355 and 361.

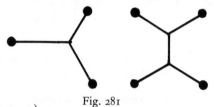

Fig. 281

Contour Rivalry (pp. 223–227)

Fig. 156 is after Hempstead (187).

For the copying of geometric figures see Piaget (350), pp. 72ff. The experiment by Rupp (381).

Rubin's goblet with the two faces in (377). Picasso's *La Vie*, painted in 1903, is in the Cleveland Museum.

Figure and Ground (pp. 227–233)

A thorough analysis of the figure-ground phenomenon in Koffka (250), ch. 5. Perception of the stellar sky: Munitz (318), p. 236.

On the Canadian flag see Gardner (130). Attneave on multistability (34).

Prominence of the lower area: Rubin (377), p. 83. The evidence on the spatial distance and density of color is discussed by Argelander (12), pp. 106–109. See also the figure-ground experiment of Goldhamer (152), who tentatively suggests that the brighter surface is likely to be the ground.

On the effect of symmetry see Bahnsen (39), discussed by Koffka (250), p. 195.

Figure-ground effect of motion: Gibson (146).

Stereoscopy: Julesz (212).

Application to Painting (pp. 234–239)

Luria's experiment is cited by Olson (332), p. 88. Fig. 157 is from Rupp (381), p. 277.

Weiss (437), pp. 806, 807.

Frames and Windows (pp. 239–241)

The framing of modern paintings is discussed by Kahnweiler (216), p. 86.

Concavity in Sculpture (pp. 241–245)

The section on concavity in sculpture is based on Arnheim (26), reprinted in (18). A useful series of photographs illustrating five stages of sculpture (1. blocklike; 2. modeled or scooped out; 3. perforated; 4. suspended; 5. mobile) can be found in Moholy-Nagy (311).

Gibson (143), p. 183, notes the underestimation of interspaces and the overestimation of solids.

For a psychoanalytic interpretation of Moore's "holes" see Wight (454).

Henry Moore's *Family Group* exists in a small version done in 1946 as well as a life-sized one of 1949. Bronze casts of both are in the Museum of Modern Art, New York.

On the internal spaces of architecture see Arnheim (21). St. Ivo's chapel in the courtyard of the Sapienza in Rome was built by Borromini c. 1650. The photograph by Ernest Nash is reproduced here with his permission.

Why Do We See Depth? (pp. 245–248)

Gestalt psychology of depth perception: Kopfermann (254) and Koffka (252).

Depth by Overlapping (pp. 248–253)

Compare Aristotle's remarkable passage on the mutilation of shape in *Metaphysics*, Book 5, ch. 27.

Gibson on occlusion (146); also Dinnerstein (96).

Helmholtz on *Perception of Depth* in (181), part III, ¶30, pp. 281, 282. Quoted by Ratoosh (361), whose mathematical formulation asserts that "continuity of the first derivative of the object's contour at the points of intersection is the sole determiner of relative distance."

Gibson (143), p. 142.

The film director Josef von Sternberg once told me that to him space was most visible when crowded with objects. For the eyes of others an empty expanse may perform the same service.

Klee's gouache, dated 1939 and owned by Douglas Cooper, is illustrated in (83), plate 26.

Philostratus: *Imagines*, Book I, 4. For the interpretation of the term *analogy* I am indebted to Prof. Wolfgang M. Zucker.

Mary Cassatt's painting of 1893 is in the Chester Dale Collection, New York.

Kopfermann (254), pp. 344–349.

Transparency (pp. 253–258)

For the examples of polyphonic and harmonic music, I am indebted to Jan Meyerowitz.

Fig. 184 is taken from a publicity folder of Cinema 16, New York.

Oyama (337, 338) and Morinaga (314).

Kanizsa (222) comments on transparency by induction.

Giedion on transparency (148), p. 50.

Deformations Create Space (258–261)

Bazin on perspective (45), p. 12.

On perception of deformations see Rausch (363).

Giacometti: Lord (280), p. 22.

Holbein's *Ambassadors* of 1533 is in the National Gallery, London. On anamorphic images see Gombrich (157), p. 252.

John Locke: *An Essay Concerning Human Understanding*, Book 2, ch. 29, sect. 8.

Boxes in Three Dimensions (pp. 261–269)

Koffka (252), p. 166, formulates: "When simple symmetry is achievable in two dimensions, we shall see a plane figure; if it requires three dimensions, then we shall see a solid."

Inverted perspective: Arnheim (14).

For the reference to the Vitruvius illustration I am indebted to Arthur Wheelock.

A monograph on children's drawings of houses by Kerr (235).

Figure 195a is taken from a Spanish altarpiece of 1396 at the Chicago Art Institute.

The Window, a 1919 gouache by Picasso, is in the collection Alice Paalen, Mexico. Fig. 196 is a tracing of a detail.

An isometric view of Walter Gropius's office at the Bauhaus was executed in 1922 by Herbert Bayer. A flat symmetry is obtained by the use of the same angle for both directions. For one of Van Doesburg's "axiomatic drawings" see, e.g., *The Structurist*, 1969, #9, p. 18 (57).

Help From Physical Space (pp. 269–271)
> Wittgenstein (458), p. 248.
> Visual cliff: Gibson (140).
> A survey of depth-determined factors in space perception is given by Woodworth and Schlosberg (470), ch. 16.

Simple Rather Than Truthful (pp. 271–275)
> On Borromini consult Hempel (186).
> Vitruvius (428), Book 3, ch. 3. Plato's *Sophist*, ¶236. Vasari, *On Sculpture*, ch. 1, ¶36.
> Ames demonstrations: Lawrence (264) and Blake and Ramsay (51), pp. 99–103.

Gradients Create Depth (pp. 275–280)
> Gibson on gradients (143).
> Van Gogh's chairs are from his *Bedroom*, painted in Arles in 1888. The painting is in the Art Institute, Chicago. So is Seurat's *Afternoon on the Grande Jatte* of 1886. The Bible on "a little cloud": I Kings, ch. 18:44.
> In his work for the Army Air Forces (141) Gibson showed that the point of the environment toward which an airplane or car is directed becomes the center of a centrifugal expansion imparted to the entire surroundings. The world seems to fly apart. In looking backward, we find that the point from which the vehicle is moving away marks the center of a constriction or centripetal movement.
> Magritte's painting "Euclidean Promenades" is in the Minneapolis Institute of Art.

Toward a Convergence of Space (pp. 280–282)
> The scroll paintings for the *Tale of Genji* are of the twelfth century. The surviving fragments are in the Tokugawa Collection and the Goto Museum in Tokyo.
> The silver relief of St. Matthew is in the museum of Aachen cathedral.
> On the development of central perspective consult White (448), Bunim (69), Kern (233, 234), and Panofsky (340). The quotation from Cennini is in ch. 87 of his *Il Libro dell'Arte o Trattato della Pittura*, written before 1437.

The Two Roots of Central Perspective (pp. 283–285)
> The first treatise on central perspective, *Della Pittura Libri Tre*, was written by Leon Battista Alberti in 1435.
> Dürer's treatise *Underweysung der Messung* was first published in Nuremberg in 1525.
> On Vermeer and the camera obscura see Seymour (397) and Fink (112).
> Ivins (206), p. 9.

Pyramidal Space (pp. 287–294)
> Thouless (418).
> Afterimages and depth: on Emmert's law see Woodworth (470), p. 486, and Koffka (250), ch. 6.
> Gibson (143), p. 181.
> Optical illusions: Rausch (362).
> Cézanne's perspective: Novotny (328).
> On perspective in film see Spottiswoode (406) pp. 40–43, and Arnheim (20), pp. 11, 58.

The Symbolism of a Focused World (pp. 294–296)
> Leonardo in (291), vol. 2, p. 376.
> Panofsky (340), p. 161.
> Tintoretto's *Last Supper*, c. 1560, is in the church of San Giorgio Maggiore in Venice.

Centrality and Infinity (pp. 297–298)
> Lucretius: *De Rerum Natura*, Book 2: 1048.

On infinity see, e.g., Weizsäcker (438) pp. 118ff. Spengler (404) pp. 175ff., discusses the presence of the infinite in definitions of the finite as characteristic of modern European thinking.

Playing With the Rules (pp. 298–302)
 Zajac on perspective (477).
 Giorgio de Chirico's *Lassitude of the Infinite*, painted in 1912, is in the Collection Pierre Matisse, New York.

NOTES TO CHAPTER VI. LIGHT

The Experience of Light (pp. 303–305)
 Piaget (351), chs. 8 and 9.
 Driver (97), p. 6. Job 38: 19–20.
Relative Brightness (pp. 305–309)
 On the relativity of brightness see Wallach (430) and MacLeod (294). The Alberti quotation is from his treatise on painting. See also Helson on adaptation level (183, 184).
 On the three-dimensional effect of brightness gradients see Turhan (422) and Gibson (143), pp. 94ff. For "obliterative shading," see Cott (87), p. 124.
Illumination (pp. 309–310)
 On light and illumination in the history of painting see the fundamental treatise by Schöne (392).
 Delacroix on the true color (94), Jan. 13, 1857.
Light Creates Space (pp. 311–315)
 Gehrke and Lau (132).
 Goethe, *Faust*, Part II, Act 3.
 On the use of lighting in film see Arnheim (20), pp. 65ff.
 Scanning microscope: Everhart (107) and Gilmore (150).
 Mach's lecture, "Why Man Has Two Eyes?" in (292) and (293), ch. 10, sect. 6.
 Roger de Piles quoted after Holt (200), pp. 412–413.
 Quotation from Hering by MacLeod (294), pp. 11–12, who later investigated the "penumbra" effect systematically (295).
Shadows (pp. 315–320)
 On the spatial effect of shadows: Lauenstein (263).
 Rembrandt's *Night Watch*, painted in 1642, is in the Rijksmuseum in Amsterdam. A detailed analysis of the use of light in this picture is in Fromentin (124), chs. 21 and 22.
 On the primitive view of shadows consult Lévy-Bruhl (269), pp. 54–56, and (270), pp. 136ff.
 Jung (213), p. 173.
 Fig. 229 is taken from an advertisement for *Eleven Came Back*, a novel by Mabel Seeley (New York: Doubleday, 1943).
 Cézanne's letter to Bernard of Dec. 23, 1904.
Painting Without Lighting (pp. 320–323)
 Mach (292).
 Bunim (69), p. 27, notes that Apollodorus, a painter of the fifth century B.C., was famous for his effects of light and shade. The evidence is of course indirect since no works of the early Greek painters have survived.
 Britsch (64), pp. 34–35, and Schaefer-Simmern (388), pp. 22–25.
 A striking example is provided by the dark cloud behind the face in Piero di Cosimo's portrait of Simonetta in Chantilly.

Carpenter (73). Fig. 232 is a detail from Titian's *Noli Me Tangere* in the National Gallery, London.

Goethe's conversations with Eckermann, Apr. 18, 1827. The description of the picture matches best, though not perfectly, with Rubens's *Return from the Labor in the Fields*, painted c. 1640, in the Palazzo Pitti in Florence. Perhaps the engraving was made after this landscape. See also Lindsay's and Huppé's observation that in Brueghel's *Le Monde Renversé* (Netherlandish Proverbs) of the Berlin Museum the buildings and human figures are illuminated from the front although the sun is visible at the far distance above the horizon (276).

The Symbolism of Light (pp. 324–329)

Wölfflin (467).

See the article on "Light and Darkness" in Hastings (174), vol. 8.

Rembrandt's *Holy Family*, painted c. 1644, is in the Lennox Collection in Scotland. *The Descent from the Cross* of 1634 is in Hermitage, Leningrad.

The Wedding of Samson of 1638 belongs to the Dresden Gallery. *The Toilet of Bathshebah* of 1643 is in the Metropolitan Museum of Art, New York.

Katz (227), pp. 7ff., on the appearance of colors. The relation between luminosity and surface quality is discussed by Wallach (430).

Interpretations of Dürer's *Melencolia* are given by Panofsky and Saxl (341) and by Wölfflin (465), pp. 96–105.

Wölfflin (467), ch. 1.

The Third Man is a British film, directed by Carol Reed in 1949.

Georges Braque's *Painter and Model* of 1939 is in the collection of Walter P. Chrysler, Jr.

On the "antagonism of contrasting forces" cf. Freud's doctrine of the ego and the id or the dialectic process in Marxism.

NOTES TO CHAPTER VII. COLOR

Color perception in animals: Ash (32).

Odilon Redon: Rewald (369).

From Light to Color (pp. 330–332)

On anthropological aspects of color vision see Segall (395), pp. 37–48, and Berlin (48).

Law of differentiation is discussed in Ch. IV.

Shape and Color (pp. 332–337)

Color constancy: Katz and Révész (229) and Wallach (431).

Helson (185) and Koffka (250), p. 254.

Experiments with children: Werner (440), pp. 234–237, and Vicario (427).

Rorschach (375) and Schachtel (384).

Kretschmer (257), ch. 13 ("Experimentelle Typenpsychologie"), pp. 190–191, refers to experiments that show cyclothymes to be more sensitive to color, schizothymes to shape. The former group comprises people whose temperament is represented in its pathological extreme by manic-depressives. The chapter, added to Kretschmer's book in the seventh edition, is not included in the English translation. However, the translation does contain Kretschmer's reference to the way the two types express themselves in the visual arts (257), pp. 239–241.

Matisse (300), p. 15.

Poussin quoted from Holt (200), p. 369.

Kant, *Critique of Judgment,* part I, sect. I, Book I, ¶14.

Charles Blanc (52), p. 23.

How Colors Come About (pp. 337–339)

Newton: *Philos. Transactions of the Royal Society* #80, 1672, p. 131.

Goethe (151). Schopenhauer: *Ueber das Sehen und die Farben,* 1815. Helmholtz on Goethe's theory of color (182), also Deane Judd's introduction to (151). For a visualization of Schopenhauer's quantification of hues see the section on "quantity contrast" in Itten (205), who mistakenly attributes the principle to Goethe.

On Hering see (190) and the introduction therein by Jameson and Hurvich. Teevan and Birney (412) have edited a good reader on the historical theories of color.

The Generative Primaries (pp. 339–341)

Helmholtz on trichromatic theory: Teevan and Birney (412), p. 10; also Young in (412), p. 7.

Color receptors in the retina: MacNichol (296).

Maxwell's principle: Rushton (382).

The Generative Complementaries (pp. 342–343)

Webster on impressionism (435).

Woodworth and Schlosberg (470), p. 391.

Helmholtz on afterimages (181), vol. 2, pp. 240, 267.

On the theory of complementary colors see Parsons (342), pp. 38ff., Woodworth (469), pp. 552–553. Boring (56), pp. 141–145.

A Capricious Medium (pp. 344–346)

Pattillo, *Art Bulletin,* Sept. 1954, vol. 36.

Schöne (392), p. 109.

Newton's color names: Biernson (50). Hiler (193), p. 211.

The Quest for Harmony (pp. 346–350)

Runge (380).

Klee's "canon of color totality" in (238).

Jacobson (207).

The history of color diagrams is described by Boring (56), pp. 145–154. Characteristic attempts at color classification are described by Wilhelm Ostwald in his introduction to the theory of color and by Munsell in his work on color notation (319).

Ostwald, *Einführung in die Farbenlehre,* pp. 137, 146–148. Munsell (319).

The influence of subject matter on color is discussed by Kandinsky (220), pp. 82–85.

Hölzel (198), p. 124.

Friedländer (122) in the section on picture restoring.

Schönberg (391), p. 8. Retranslated from the German original.

Matisse's *The Studio* of 1911 is in the Museum of Modern Art, New York.

The Elements of the Scale (pp. 350–353)

Chandler (74), pp. 69–70, maintains that an average of 214 gradations of gray can be discriminated. Freeman (117), p. 380, speaks of 700 such gradations.

Goodman (160), pp. 133ff.

Hering (190), plate I.

On the controversy about the nature of green consult Boring (56), p. 131.

Turner's color system was based on Moses Harris's *Natural System of Colors,* published in 1766. See Gowing (164), p. 23.

Syntax of Combinations (pp. 353–356)

I am indebted to Meyer Schapiro for suggesting that I illustrate my discussion of color pairs with triangular diagrams.

The Fundamental Complementaries (pp. 357–361)

Goethe in his *Theory of Colors* (Der Farbenlehre didaktischer Teil), part 6, sect. 812. Translation mine.

Delacroix's sketchbook is in the Museum of Chantilly and reproduced by Guiffrey (169).

Descartes: *Rules for the Direction of the Mind*, rule 14.

Van Gogh on the colors of the seasons cited after Badt (37), pp. 125, 124. The description of Delacroix's painting is in a letter to Emile Bernard of 1888.

In experiments by H. and S. Kreitler (256), p. 36, 83% of the colors called "tension-laden" were found to be complementary pairs. Cf. also the discussion on their p. 374.

Badt on late works of masters (36), p. 13.

Denise Levertov's lines are quoted from *The Sorrow Dance*, p. 73, by permission of New Directions.

McCandless (290), p. 56, talking about stage lighting says: "By using warm and cool colors on opposite sides and varying the intensity between the two, it is possible to retain a considerable amount of the plastic quality." Carpenter (73), p. 180, maintains that there is no such thing as modeling without gradation of brightness, "and Cézanne rarely tries to model form just with changes of hue." He concludes that modeling with change of color alone does not work. Compare, however, Delacroix in his *Journals* (July 10, 1847). Speaking of the head of Magdalen in the *Christ in the Tomb* (Boston Museum), he says that "it was sufficient to color the whole shaded area with warm, reflected tones, and although the bright and shaded areas are almost of the same brightness value, the cold tones of the one and the warm ones of the other are sufficient to set the accents in the whole."

Interaction of Color (pp. 362–364)

Ruskin (383), p. 138. Von Allesch (5), p. 46.

Kandinsky (221), p. 17. Translation mine. See also Herbert (189), p. 28.

Chevreul on contrast (75).

Albers (3).

Sharpening and leveling: Wulf (472).

Assimilation: Jameson and Hurvich (209).

Liebmann (273), pp. 308 ff.

Matisse and El Greco (pp. 364–368)

Matisse's *Le Luxe II* (1907 or 1908), is in the Copenhagen Statens Museum for Kunst. A sketchier version, *Le Luxe I*, is at the Musée National d'Art Moderne in Paris. Given the considerable inaccuracies of color reproductions, the reader should not be surprised to find discrepancies between the descriptions given here and his own impressions of a work. In the present case, a color print may reproduce the foreground and the hill to the right as a rusty brown rather than orange; the left hill may appear violet rather than purple.

Reactions to Color (pp. 368–369)

Féré (110), pp. 43–47, as quoted by Schachtel (384), p. 403.

Goldstein (154). Vol. 1942 of "Occupational Therapy and Rehabilitation" contains several other articles on color therapy.

Kandinsky (220), pp. 61–62.

Warm and Cold (pp. 369–371)

Von Allesch (5), pp. 234–235.

Itten (205). Albers (3), sect. 21.

On expressive qualities shared by different sensory media see Hornbostel (201).

On the expressiveness of color see Kreitler (256), pp. 67ff. Also Chandler (74), ch. 6. Goethe's classical treatment of the subject appears in the sixth section of his

Theory of Colors (151). Kandinsky on the "language of form and color" (220), pp. 63–72.

Color preferences: Kreitler (256), p. 64. Chandler (74), pp. 70ff., characteristically opens his discussion of the subject with the remark, "The first efforts in the experimental aesthetics of color were naturally directed to the problem of the pleasantness and unpleasantness of color." Such an approach is "natural" only when a hedonistic theory of art is taken for granted.

Picasso after Ashton (33), p. 35.

NOTES TO CHAPTER VIII. MOVEMENT

On eye movements: Thomas (416).

Retinal receptors for movement: Lettvin (266).

Happenings and Time (pp. 372–375)

Wertheimer (443) p. 63.

My discussion of time is influenced by Merleau-Ponty's treatment of the subject (302), pp. 469ff.

On the spatialization of time in memory see Koffka (250), p. 446. For the psychological concept of the past as an aspect of the present see Lewin (272). Compare also Freud's assertion in his *Interpretation of Dreams* that the dream translates temporal relations into spatial ones.

For the text of the letter attributed to Mozart see, e.g., Storck (409), letter no. 179. Translation mine.

Simultaneity and Sequence (pp. 375–378)

Persons who maintain that motion and time are just as inherent in painting and sculpture as they are in the dance or film, because the eyes and the legs of the spectators move, may find their thinking clarified by Gregory's remark (168), pp. 25–26, that time is involved in applied geometry "in the first degree only, i.e., in the purely qualitative sense that to observe, to test, to measure, to advance, to retreat, to rotate a line about a point, a plane about a line, etc., all take time, and change of some kind is involved. The important thing is, however, that the amount of time taken is of no consequence, [whereas] with rotating and revolving bodies, swinging pendulums, wave motion generally, and changing currents in electric circuits, the rate of motion is an additional quantity to be determined." That is, in the latter cases, motion is an integral part of the phenomenon itself.

On eye movements: Buswell (71), Yarbus (474), Thomas (416).

For examples of "exposition" in film and literature see Arnheim (16), p. 248.

Lessing, *Laocoon*, sect. 16.

Michelangelo's early *Pietà* of 1498–1500 is in St. Peter's, Rome. Firestone (113) points out that the motif of the sleeping Christ child was intended and understood during the Renaissance as a prefiguration of the death of Christ.

When Do We See Motion? (pp. 378–382)

Dante, *Inferno*, canto 31, verses 136–138.

On the perception of motion: Gibson (145).

Kinesthetic feedback: Teuber (415), p. 198.

Duncker (100), p. 170. Oppenheimer (335).

Metelli (303).

Direction (pp. 382–383)

On the rotation of wheels see Rubin (378) and Duncker (100), pp. 168–169.

The Revelations of Speed (pp. 384–387)

Piéron cited by Lecomte du Noüy (265), ch. 9, pp. 145–177.

Spottiswoode (406), pp. 120–122, on synthesizing space and time.

In T. H. White's *The Sword in the Stone* the young son of King Arthur is introduced by his tutor, the owl Archimedes, to the goddess Athene, who, divinely independent of human time perception, shows him the moving life of the trees and the geological ages (450), pp. 244–251.

Dru Drury quoted by Sherrington (400), p. 120. On accelerated motion see also Arnheim (20).

Pirandello (352) describes the work of a cameraman in the days of the silent film. Minguzzi (309).

Brown (65, 66) discussed by Koffka (250), pp. 288ff.

Stroboscopic Movement (pp. 387–392)

Teuber (415), p. 191.

Stroboscopic movement: Boring (56), pp. 588–602.

Wertheimer (443). Horner's Daedaleum (202).

Michotte's tunnel effect (308), part 2.

Fig. 248 adapted from Metzger (305), p. 12. To produce the effect of movement, the reader may cut a narrow horizontal slot in a piece of white cardboard and make the drawing slide vertically underneath it.

Figs. 249–251 are adapted from Ternus (414), pp. 150 and 159.

Zuckerkandl on progression in music (478), ch. 4.

Some Problems of Film Editing (pp. 392–394)

On editing: Reisz (367).

Maya Deren's film *Pas de Deux* (*Choreographies for Camera*) was made in 1945. Bretz (63).

Visible Motor Forces (pp. 394–397)

Michotte on perception of causality (307). He distinguishes the pushing effect (*effet lancement*) from the release effect (*effet déclenchement*).

Fig. 254 after Wertheimer's drawing (444), p. 323 of the German original. Not included in the English summary by Ellis (445).

A Scale of Complexity (pp. 398–403)

Primitive perception of life: Lévy-Bruhl (270), Introduction. Also Piaget (351), part 2; and Köhler (240), pp. 376–397, also reprinted in Henle (188), pp. 203–221.

Heider and Simmel (179).

Focillon's essay on the human hand (116).

The Body as Instrument (pp. 403–406)

Psychology of the dance: Arnheim (18), pp. 261–265.

Fig. 258 is adapted from Kandinsky (219).

Hindu dance: La Meri (259).

Description of Delsarte's system after Shawn (399), p. 14.

Kleist (239). Translation revised.

The Kinesthetic Body Image (pp. 406–409)

Merleau-Ponty (302), p. 116.

Michotte (307), p. 196.

The writings of Irmgard Bartenieff on the Laban method are available through the Dance Notation Bureau, New York.

NOTES TO CHAPTER IX. DYNAMICS

Simplicity Is Not Enough (pp. 410–412)

For a more explicit treatment of the interplay between the reduction and the heightening of tension see my essay on entropy and art (15). Also Köhler (243) ch. 8.

Dynamics and Its Traditional Interpretations (pp. 412–416)

Bergson (47), p. 21.

The quotation from Howard Nemerov's "The Painter Dreaming in the Scholar's House," in (324), is used by permission of the author.

Pevsner (346), p. 90.

Eliot (103), p. 7.

Leonardo, quoted by Justi (215), vol. 3, p. 480.

Rorschach on M-responses in (375). See also Arnheim (27), pp. 74–101, and Schachtel (385).

A Diagram of Forces (pp. 416–419)

Kandinsky (219), p. 51.

Jonas (211), p. 147.

Weiss (437), Thompson (417).

Burchartz (70), p. 156.

On graphology see Klages (237) and Pulver (357); in English: Klara G. Roman (374).

Bowie (61), pp. 35, 77–79, quoted by Langfeld (261), p. 129.

Experiments on Directed Tension (pp. 419–423)

Rausch (362) and (363).

Köhler and Wallach (249).

Werner and Wapner (442); Oppenheimer (335); Brown (66).

Immobile Motion (pp. 423–424)

Archipenko (11).

Reinach (366). Rodin (373), p. 77, justifies the outstretched legs of the galloping horse in a way differing from mine. Ogden (330) pp. 213–215, reproduces the Géricault painting of 1824 (in the Louvre, Paris), and compares it with a more "correct" but grotesquely motionless drawing of a running horse.

Muybridge (323).

Wölfflin (462), pp. 72–76.

The Dynamics of Obliqueness (pp. 424–428)

A special issue of *The Structurist* devoted to the oblique in art was edited by Bornstein (57).

Rodin (373), pp. 66.

Fig. 266 is from a statement by Van Doesburg on "contra-composition," published in *De Stijl*, 1926.

Wölfflin (467), ch. 2.

The Lomazzo quotation is adapted from the translation in Holt (200), p. 261.

Figs. 269a and b after Wölfflin (460), p. 47; a is from the Cancelleria, b from the Palazzo Farnese, both in Rome.

Tension in Deformation (pp. 428–432)

Rausch (363).

Henry Moore in "The Sculptor's Aims."

Rodin (373), p. 46.

Von Allesch (5).

Dynamic Composition (pp. 432–434)

Zuckerkandl (479), p. 39. Translation mine.

Von Allesch (5).

Hans Thoma's picture is reproduced from *Quickborn*, vol. 1, Oct. 15, 1898.

Matisse (300), p. 33.

Stroboscopic Effects (pp. 434–437)

Fig. 272, reproduced by courtesy of Rudolf Knubel, is based on Fischer (114), p. 78.

Rodin (373), ch. 4. It would seem, however, that in the examples from sculpture cited by Rodin, "movement" is obtained not so much because the figure represents different phases of a time sequence as because there is a gradual change of visual dynamics—for example, in the *Age of Iron*—from the relaxed posture of the legs to the high charge of tension in the chest, the neck, and the arms.

Riegl (372), p. 33.

Figs. 273*a–e* are tracings from works by Picasso reproduced as numbers 249, 209, 268, 246, 216, by Barr (42).

How Does Dynamics Come About? (pp. 437–440)

Cf. Arnheim (18), p. 62.

Newman (325) and Lindemann (275) investigated gamma motion.

Examples from Art (pp. 440–443)

Piero della Francesca's *Resurrection* of c. 1450 is in the town hall of Borgo San Sepolcro.

Bach, *St. Matthew Passion*, no. 46, recitative.

NOTES TO CHAPTER X. EXPRESSION

Balzac on expression of gait (40), p. 166.

A more theoretical treatment of the psychology of expression is given in Arnheim (24).

Traditional Theories (pp. 445–449)

Article on "physiognomics" in Encyclopedia Britannica, 11th edition, vol. 21, p. 550.

Quotation translated from Claudius (77), vol. 1, p. 177.

Berkeley, *An Essay Towards a New Theory of Vision*, ¶65.

Darwin (90).

The quotation by Lipps is translated from (278), p. 359. Compare also his (277) and Langfeld's presentation of empathy (261), pp. 113ff. Lipps's rather complex theoretical position is discussed in Arnheim (24), pp. 159–160, and (17).

Friedländer on columns (122), p. 155.

Aesthetic theories of expression are discussed by Osborne (336), chs. 4 and 5.

Expression Embedded in Structure (pp. 449–454)

James (208), ch. 6, p. 147. He is referring to a somewhat different subject—the relations between the nervous system and psychical experience—but his reasoning applies to the problem of expression as well.

On the gestalt psychology of expression see Wertheimer (446), pp. 94–96, Köhler (241), pp. 216–247, Koffka (250), pp. 654–661, Arnheim (24), and Asch (31), chs. 5–7.

Jane Binney, a student of mine, performed the experiment at Sarah Lawrence College in 1946. It is discussed in more detail in (24).

In terms of projective geometry the parabola as a conic section is intermediate between the horizontal section of the cone, i.e. the circle, and the vertical section, i.e. the straight-edged triangle.

Wölfflin on St. Peter's cupola (460), p. 306. Note, however, that after Michelangelo, the mannerist architect Giacomo della Porta modified the external contour and the lantern somewhat, in the direction of more weightlessness; cf. Frey (121), p. 66.

Fig. 278 is derived from Wölfflin (460), p. 297. I have corrected a mechanical error in Wölfflin's drawing, which resulted in the centers of the circles being placed slightly too high.

Van Gogh's letter is dated May 8, 1882.

Ruskin on "pathetic fallacy" in *Modern Painters*, vol. 3, ch. 12.

Goethe remarks on character description in an essay on Newton, contained in his *Theory of Color*.

On physiognomic perception cf. Werner (440), pp. 67–82, and Köhler (245).

The examples from primitive languages after Lévy-Bruhl (269).

Braque (62). On metaphors see Arnheim (29).

Schizophrenics seem to revert to a primitive kind of logic. E. von Domarus, in his study on the relations between normal and schizophrenic thinking, formulates the following principle: "Whereas the normal person accepts identity only upon the basis of identical subjects, the paleologician accepts identity based upon identical predicates." See Arieti (13).

Symbolism in Art (pp. 457–461)

On Freudian symbolism in art cf. Arnheim (18), pp. 215–221.

Fig. 279: Cézanne's still life of c. 1890 is in the National Gallery in Washington. Picasso's *Still Life with Fowl* of 1942 is reproduced in Boeck (55), p. 81.

BIBLIOGRAPHY

1 Abbott, Edwin A. Flatland. A romance of many dimensions by A. Square. New York, 1952.
2 Adrian, E. D. The physical background of perception. Oxford, 1947.
3 Albers, Josef. Interaction of color. New Haven, Conn., 1963.
4 Alexander, Christopher and Susan Carey. Subsymmetries. Perception and Psychophysics 1968, vol. 4, pp. 73–77.
5 Allesch, G. J. von. Die aesthetische Erscheinungsweise der Farben. Psychol. Forschung 1925, vol. 6, pp. 1–91, 215–281.
6 Allport, Gordon W. Change and decay in the visual memory image. Brit. Journal Psych. 1930, vol. 21, pp. 133–148.
7 —— and Leo J. Postman. The basic psychology of rumor. Transact. New York Acad. Sciences 1945, Series II, pp. 61–81.
8 Alschuler, Rose H. and La Berta Weiss Hattwick. Painting and personality. Chicago, 1947.
9 Ames, Adalbert, Jr., C. A. Proctor, and Blanche Ames. Vision and the technique of art. Proc. Amer. Acad. Arts and Sciences 1923, vol. 58, #1.
10 Anastasi, Anne and John P. Foley, Jr. A survey of the literature on artistic behavior in the abnormal. I. Journal General Psych., 1941, vol. 25, pp. 111–142; II. Annals New York Acad. Science 1941, vol. 42, pp. 1–112; III. Psychol. Monogr. 1940, vol. 52, #6; IV. Journal General Psych. 1941, vol. 25, pp. 187–237.
11 Archipenko, Alexander. Archipentura—a new development in painting. Catalogue. New York: Anderson Gall., 1928.
12 Argelander, Annelies. Das Farbenhören und der synaesthetische Faktor der Wahrnehmung. Jena, 1927.
13 Arieti, Silvano. Special logic of schizophrenic and other autistic thought. Psychiatry 1948, vol. 11, pp. 325–338.
14 Arnheim, Rudolf. Inverted perspective in art: display and expression. Leonardo, Spring 1972, vol. 5, pp. 125–135.
15 ——. Entropy and art: an essay on order and disorder. Berkeley and Los Angeles, 1971.
16 ——. Visual Thinking. Berkeley and Los Angeles, 1969.
17 ——. Abstraction and empathy in retrospect. Confinia Psychiatrica 1967, vol. 10, pp. 1–15.
18 ——. Toward a psychology of art. Berkeley and Los Angeles, 1966.

19 ——. Picasso's Guernica. Berkeley and Los Angeles, 1962. (Re-issued in 1973 as: The genesis of a painting.)

20 ——. Film as art. Berkeley and Los Angeles, 1957.

21 —— et al. Inside and outside in architecture. Journal Aesth. Art Critic. 1966, vol. 25, pp. 3–15.

22 ——. The priority of expression. Journal Aesth. Art Crit. 1949, vol. 8, pp. 106–109.

23 ——. Concerning the dance. *In* Arnheim (18) pp. 261–265.

24 ——. The gestalt theory of expression. *In* Arnheim (18) pp. 51–73.

25 ——. Gestalt psychology and artistic form. *In* Whyte (452) pp. 196–208.

26 ——. The holes of Henry Moore. *In* Arnheim (18) pp. 245–255.

27 ——. Perceptual and aesthetic aspects of the movement response. *In* Arnheim (18) pp. 74–89.

28 ——. Perceptual abstraction and art. *In* Arnheim (18) pp. 27–50.

29 ——. Psychological notes on the poetical process. *In* Arnheim et al. Poets at Work. New York, 1948.

30 —— and Abraham Klein. Perceptual analysis of a Rorschach card. *In* Arnheim (18) pp. 90–101.

31 Asch, Solomon E. Social psychology. New York, 1952.

32 Ash, Philip. Sensory capacities of infrahuman mammals. Psych. Bull. 1951, vol. 48.

33 Ashton, Dore, ed. Picasso on art. New York, 1972.

34 Attneave, Fred. Multistability in perception. Scient. Amer., Dec. 1971, vol. 225, pp. 63–72.

35 Bader, Alfred. Geisteskranker oder Künstler? Bern, 1972.

36 Badt, Kurt. Einfachheit in der Malerei. *In* Badt. Kunsttheoretische Versuche. Cologne, 1968.

37 ——. Die Farbenlehre Van Goghs. Cologne, 1961.

38 ——. Eugène Delacroix' drawings. Oxford, 1946.

39 Bahnsen, Poul. Eine Untersuchung über Symmetrie und Asymmetrie bei visuellen Wahrnehmungen. Zeitschr. Psych. 1928, vol. 108, pp. 129–154.

40 Balzac, Honoré de. Traité de la vie élégante, suivi de la théorie de la démarche. Paris, 1922.

41 Barlach, Ernst. Aus seinen Briefen. Munich, 1949.

42 Barr, Alfred H., ed. Picasso—40 years of his art. New York, 1939.

43 Bartley, S. Howard and H. J. Adair. Comparisons of phenomenal distance in photographs of various sizes. Journal Psych. 1959, vol. 47, pp. 289–295.

44 Baudelaire, Charles. Oeuvres complètes. Paris, 1961.

45 Bazin, André. What is cinema? Berkeley and Los Angeles, 1967.

46 Bender, Lauretta. A visual motor gestalt test and its clinical use. New York, 1938.

47 Bergson, Henri. Le rire. Paris, 1940. (Engl.: Laughter, Gloucester, Mass., n.d.)

48 Berlin, Brent and Paul Kay. Basic color terms: their universality and evolution. Berkeley and Los Angeles, 1969.

49 Berliner, Anna. Lectures on visual psychology. Chicago, 1948.

50 Biernson, George. Why did Newton see indigo in the spectrum? Amer. Journal Physics 1972, vol. 40, pp. 526–533.

51 Blake, Robert R. and Glenn V. Ramsay, eds. Perception, an approach to personality. New York, 1951.

52 Blanc, Charles. Grammaire des arts du dessin. Paris, 1870.

53 Blanshard, Frances Bradshaw. Retreat from likeness in the theory of painting. New York, 1945.

54 Boas, Franz. Primitive art. Cambridge, Mass., 1927.

55 Boeck, Wilhelm and Jaime Sabartés. Picasso. New York, 1961.

56 Boring, Edwin G. Sensation and perception in the history of experimental psychology. New York, 1942.

57 Bornstein, Eli, ed. The oblique in art. Special issue of The Structurist 1969, #9.

58 Bossert, Helmuth Theodor. The art of ancient Crete. London, 1937.

59 Bower, T. G. R. The object in the world of the infant. Scient. Amer., Oct. 1971, vol. 225, pp. 30–38.

60 ———. The visual world of infants. Scient. Amer., Dec. 1966, vol. 215, pp. 80–92.

61 Bowie, Henry P. On the laws of Japanese painting. New York, 1911.

62 Braque, Georges. Notebook 1917–1947. New York, n.d.

63 Bretz, Rudy. Television cutting technique. Journal Soc. Motion Pict. Engineers 1950, vol. 54, pp. 247–267.

64 Britsch, Gustaf. Theorie der bildenden Kunst. Munich, 1926.

65 Brown. J. F. Ueber gesehene Geschwindigkeiten. Psychol. Forschung 1928, vol. 10, pp. 84–101.

66 ———. The visual perception of velocity. Psychol. Forschung 1931, vol. 14, pp. 199–232.

67 Bruner, Jerome S. and David Krech, eds. Perception and personality. Durham, N.C., 1950.

68 Brunswik, Egon. The psychology of objective relations. In Marx (298) pp. 386–391.

69 Bunim, Miriam Schild. Space in medieval painting and the forerunners of perspective. New York, 1940.

70 Burchartz, Max Albrecht. Gleichnis der Harmonie. Munich, 1949.

71 Buswell, G. Th. How people look at pictures. Chicago, 1935.

72 Carmichael, Leonard, H. P. Hogan, and A. A. Walter. An experimental study of the effect of language on the reproduction of visually perceived form. Journal Exper. Psych. 1932, vol. 15, pp. 73–86.

73 Carpenter, James M. Cézanne and tradition. Art Bull. 1951, vol. 33, pp. 174–186.

74 Chandler, Albert R. Beauty and human nature. New York, 1934.

75 Chevreul, Michel Eugène. De la loi du contraste simultané, etc. Paris, 1899. (Engl.: Principle of harmony and contrasts of color. New York, 1967.)

76 Clark, Arthur B. The child's attitude towards perspective problems. Studies in Education 1897, vol. 1.

77 Claudius, Matthias. Sämtliche Werke des Wandsbecker Boten. Dresden, 1938.

78 Cocteau, Jean. Le rappel à l'ordre. Paris, 1918.

79 ———. La difficuté d'être. Monaco. 1957. (Engl.: Difficulty of being. New York. 1967.)

80 Cohen, Morris R. and Ernest Nagel. An introduction to logic and scientific method. New York, 1934.

81 Coomaraswamy, Ananda K. Why exhibit works of art? London, 1943. (Amer. ed.: Christian and oriental philosophy of art. New York, 1957.)

82 ———. Figures of speech or figures of thought? London, 1946.

83 Cooper, Douglas. Paul Klee. Harmondsworth, 1949.

84 ———. Pablo Picasso: Les Déjeuners. New York, 1963.

85 Corballis, Michael C. and Ivan L. Beale. On telling left from right. Scient. Amer., March 1971, vol. 224, pp. 96–104.

86 ———. Bilateral symmetry and behavior. Psych. Review 1970, vol. 77, pp. 451–464.

87 Cott, Hugh B. Animal form in relation to appearance. In Whyte (452) pp. 121–156.

88 Courant, Richard and Herbert Robbins. What is mathematics? New York, 1951.

89 Couturier, Marie-Alain. Se garder libre. Paris. 1962.

90 Darwin, Charles. The expression of emotions in man and animal. Westport, Conn., 1955.

91 Dean, Alexander. Fundamentals of play directing. New York, 1946.
92 Delacroix, Eugène. Mein Tagebuch. Berlin, 1918.
93 ———. Oeuvres littéraires. Paris, 1923.
94 ———. Journal. Paris, 1950. (Engl.: The journal of E. D., New York, 1937.)
95 Dennis, Wayne, ed. Readings in general psychology. New York, 1950.
96 Dinnerstein, Dorothy and Michael Wertheimer. Some determinants of phenomenal overlapping. Amer. Journal Psych. 1957, vol. 70, pp. 21–37.
97 Driver, S. R. The book of Genesis. London, 1926.
98 Duncan, David Douglas. Picasso's Picassos. New York, n.d.
99 Duncker, Karl. Ueber induzierte Bewegung. Psychol. Forschung 1929, vol. 12, pp. 180–259.
100 ———. Induced motion. In Ellis (104) pp. 161–172.
101 Duthuit, Georges. The fauvist painters. New York, 1950.
102 Ehrenfels, Christian von. Ueber Gestaltqualitäten. In Weinhandl (436) pp. 11–43.
103 Eliot, T. S. Four quartets. New York, 1943.
104 Ellis, Willis D., ed. A source book of gestalt psychology. New York, 1939.
105 Eng, Helga. The psychology of children's drawings. New York, 1931.
106 Evans, C. R. and A. D. J. Robertson, eds. Brain physiology and psychology. Berkeley and Los Angeles, 1966.
107 Everhart, Thomas E. and Thomas L. Hayes. The scanning electron microscope. Scient. Amer., Jan. 1972, vol. 226, pp. 55–69.
108 Farnham-Diggory, Sylvia, ed. Information processing in children. New York, 1972.
109 Fenollosa, Ernest Francisco. The Chinese written characters as a medium for poetry. London, 1936.
110 Féré, Charles. Sensation et mouvement. Paris, 1900.
111 Fiedler, Konrad. Vom Wesen der Kunst. Munich, 1942.
112 Fink, Daniel A. Vermeer's use of the camera obscura. Art Bull. 1971, vol. 53, pp. 493–505.
113 Firestone, G. The sleeping Christ child in Italian Renaissance representations of the Madonna. Marsyas 1942, vol. 2, pp. 43–62.
114 Fischer, Theodor. Vorträge über Proportionen. Berlin, 1955.
115 Fleming, William. The element of motion in Baroque art and music. Journal Aesth. Art Crit. 1946, vol. 5, pp. 121–128.
116 Focillon, Henri. Vie des formes. Paris, 1939. (Engl.: Life of forms in art. New York, n.d.)
117 Freeman, Ellis. Principles of general psychology. New York, 1939.
118 Freud, Sigmund. Beyond the pleasure principle. New York, 1970.
119 ———. Leonardo da Vinci. New York, 1932.
120 ———. The relation of the poet to daydreaming. In Freud, Collected Papers, vol. 4. London, 1949.
121 Frey, Dagobert. Grundlegung zu einer vergleichenden Kunstwissenschaft. Darmstadt, 1970.
122 Friedländer, Max J. Von Kunst und Kennerschaft. Berlin, 1957. (Engl.: On art and connoisseurship. Los Angeles, n.d.)
123 Fritsch, Vilma. Links und rechts in Wissenschaft und Leben. Stuttgart, 1964. (Engl.: Left and right in science and life. London, 1968.)
124 Fromentin, Eugène. Les maîtres d'autrefois. Vienna, n.d. (Engl.: The masters of past time. New York, 1948.)
125 Fuchs, Wilhelm. On transparency. In Ellis (104) pp. 89–103.

126 Gaffron, Mercedes. Right and left in pictures. Art Quarterly 1950. vol. 13, pp. 312–313.

127 ———. Die Radierungen Rembrandts. Mainz, 1950.

128 Gallatin, A. E., ed. Of art. New York, 1945.

129 Galton, Francis. Inquiries into human faculty. New York, 1908.

130 Gardner, Martin. Of optical illusions, etc. Scient. Amer., May 1970, vol. 222, pp. 124–127.

131 Gazzaniga, Michael S. The split brain in man. Scient. Amer., Aug. 1967, vol. 217, pp. 24–29.

132 Gehrcke, E. and E. Lau. Ueber Erscheinungen beim Sehen kontinuierlicher Helligkeitsverteilungen. Zeitschr. Sinnesphysiol. 1922, vol. 53, pp. 174–178.

133 Gelb, Adhemar. Zur medizinischen Psychologie und philosophischen Anthropologie. Acta Psychol. 1937, vol. 3, pp. 193–271.

134 Gelb, Adhemar and Kurt Goldstein. Analysis of a case of figural blindness. *In* Ellis (104) pp. 315–325.

135 Gellermann, Louis W. Form discrimination in chimpanzees and two-year-old children. Psychol. Seminary and Journal Genet. Psych. 1933, vol. 42, pp. 2–27.

136 Geschwind, Norman. Language and the brain. Scient. Amer., April 1972, vol. 226, pp. 76–83.

137 Geschwind, Norman. The organization of language and the brain. Science 1970, vol. 170, pp. 940–944.

138 Gesell, Arnold. Infant vision. Scient. Amer., Feb. 1950, vol. 182, pp. 20–22.

139 Ghent, Lila. Recognition by children of realistic figures, etc. Canad. Journal Psych. 1960, vol. 14, pp. 249–256.

140 Gibson, Eleanor J. and Richard D. Walk. The "visual cliff." Scient. Amer., April 1960, vol. 202, pp. 64–71.

141 Gibson, James J. Motion picture testing and research. Report #7. U. S. Army Airforces Aviation Psych. Program. Washington, D.C., 1947.

142 ———. Adaptation, aftereffect, and contrast, etc. Journal Exper. Psych. 1933, vol. 16, pp. 1–31.

143 ———. The perception of the visual world. Boston, 1950.

144 ———. What is a form? Psychol. Review 1951, vol. 58, pp. 403–412.

145 ———. What gives rise to the perception of motion? Psychol. Review 1968, vol. 75, pp. 335–346.

146 ——— et al. The change from visible to invisible. Perception and Psychophysics 1969, vol. 5, pp. 113–116.

147 ——— and Doris Robinson. Orientation in visual perception. Psychol. Monogr. 1935, vol. 46, #6, pp. 39–47.

148 Giedion, Siegfried. The eternal present, vol. I: The beginnings of art. New York, 1962.

149 Gilinsky, Alberta S. Perceived size and distance in visual space. Psychol. Review 1951, vol. 58, pp. 460–482.

150 Gilmore, C. P. The scanning electron microscope. New York, 1972.

151 Goethe, Johann Wolfgang von. Zur Farbenlehre. (Engl.: Theory of colors. Cambridge, Mass., 1970.)

152 Goldhamer, H. The influence of area, position, and brightness in visual perception of a reversible configuration. Amer. Journal of Psych. 1934, vol. 46, pp. 189–206.

153 Goldmeier, Erich. Progressive changes in memory traces. Amer. Journal Psych. 1941, vol. 54, pp. 490–503.

154 Goldstein, Kurt. Some experimental observations concerning the influence of colors

on the function of the organism. Occup. Therapy and Rehabil. 1942, vol. 21, pp. 147–151.

155 Golomb, Claire. Evolution of the human figure in a three-dimensional medium. Developm. Psych. 1972, vol. 6, pp. 385–391.

156 Gombrich, E. H. The story of art. New York, 1950.

157 ——. Art and illusion. New York, 1960.

158 ——. Meditations on a hobby horse. *In* Whyte (452) pp. 209–222.

159 Goodenough, Florence L. Measurement of intelligence by drawings. Yonkers, N.Y., 1926.

160 Goodman, Nelson. Languages of art. Indianapolis, Ind., 1968.

161 Goodnow, Jacqueline J. Rules and repertoires, rituals and tricks of the trade, etc. *In* Farnham-Diggory (108).

162 Gottschaldt, Kurt. Gestalt factors and repetition. *In* Ellis (104) pp. 109–122.

163 Goude, Gunnar and Inga Hjortzberg. An experimental prövning, etc. University of Stockholm, 1967.

164 Gowing, Lawrence. Turner: imagination and reality. New York, 1966.

165 Graves, Maitland. Design judgment test. New York, 1946.

166 Greek painting. The Metropolitan Museum of Art. New York, 1944.

167 Greenough, Horatio. Form and function. Berkeley and Los Angeles, 1947.

168 Gregory, C. C. L. Shape and distance considered by an astronomer. *In* Whyte (452) p. 23–42.

169 Guiffrey, Jean, ed. Le voyage de Eugène Delacroix au Maroc. Paris, 1913.

170 Haber, R. N. Eidetic images. Scient. Amer., April 1969, vol. 220, pp. 36–44.

171 Hanawalt, Nelson Gilbert. Memory traces for figures in recall and recognition. Archives Psych. 1937, #26.

172 Harris, Dale. Children's drawings. New York, 1963.

173 Hartmann, George W. and William R. Sickles. The theory of order. Psychol. Review 1942, vol. 49, pp. 403–421.

174 Hastings, James, ed. Encyclopedia of religion and ethics. New York, 1916.

175 Hastorf, A. H. The influence of suggestion on the relationship between stimulus size and perceived distance. Journal Psych. 1950, vol. 29, pp. 195–217.

176 Hayter, Stanley William. The convention of line. Magazine of Art 1945, vol. 38, pp. 92–95.

177 Hebb. D. O. The organization of behavior. New York, 1949.

178 —— and Esme N. Foord. Errors of visual recognition and the nature of the trace. Journal Exper. Psych. 1945, pp. 335–348.

179 Heider, Fritz and Marianne Simmel. An experimental study of apparent behavior. Amer. Journal of Psych. 1944, vol. 57, pp. 243–259.

180 Helmholtz, Hermann von. Popular scientific lectures. New York, 1962.

181 ——. Handbuch der physiologischen Optik. Hamburg, 1910. (Engl.: Treatise on physiological optics. New York, 1962).

182 ——. On Goethe's scientific researches. *In* Helmholtz (180) pp. 1–21.

183 Helson, Harry. Adaptation-level as frame of reference for prediction, etc. Amer. Journal Psych. 1947, vol. 60. pp. 1–29.

184 ——. Adaptation-level theory. New York, 1964.

185 ——. Fundamental problems in color vision. Journal Exper. Psych. 1938, vol. 23, pp. 439–476.

186 Hempel, Eberhard. Francesco Borromini. Vienna, 1924.

187 Hempstead, L. The perception of visual form. Amer. Journal Psych. 1900, vol. 12, pp. 185–192.

188 Henle, Mary, ed. Documents of gestalt psychology. Berkeley and Los Angeles, 1961.

189 Herbert, Robert L. Modern artists on art. Englewood Cliffs, N.J. 1964.

190 Hering, Ewald. Outlines of a theory of the light sense. Cambridge, Mass., 1964.

191 Hertz, Mathilde. Figural perception in the jay bird. *In* Ellis (104) pp. 238–252.

192 Hildebrand, Adolf. Das Problem der Form in der bildenden Kunst. Baden-Baden, 1961. (Engl.: The problem of form. New York, 1907.)

193 Hiler, Hilaire. Some associative aspects of color. Journal Aesth. Art Crit. 1946, vol. 4, pp. 203–217.

194 Hochberg, Carol Barnes and Julian E. Hochberg. Familiar size and the perception of depth. Journal Psych. 1952, vol. 34, pp. 107–114.

195 Hochberg, Julian. The psychophysics of pictorial perception. Audio-Visual Commun. Review, Sept./Oct. 1962, vol. 10, pp. 22–54.

196 —— and Virginia Brooks. Pictorial recognition as an unlearned ability. Amer. Journal Psych. 1962, vol. 75, pp. 624–628.

197 —— and Edward McAlister. A quantitative approach to figural "goodness." Journal Exper. Psych. 1953, pp. 361–364.

198 Hölzel, Adolf. Ueber künstlerische Ausdrucksmittel. Kunst für Alle, Dec. 15, 1904.

199 Hogarth, William. The analysis of beauty. New York, 1955.

200 Holt, Elizabeth Gilmore, ed. Literary sources of art history. Princeton, N.J., 1947.

201 Hornbostel, Erich Maria von. The unity of the senses. *In* Ellis (104) pp. 210–216.

202 Horner, W. G. On the properties of the Daedaleum, a new instrument of optical illusion. London and Edinburgh Philos. Magazine and Journal of Science 1834, vol. 4, pp. 36–41.

203 Hubel, D. H. and T. N. Wiesel. Receptive fields of single neurones in the cat's striate cortex. *In* Evans and Robertson (106) pp. 129–150.

204 Hungerland, Helmut. Consistency as a criterion in art criticism. Journal Aesth. Art Crit. 1948, vol. 7, pp. 93–112.

205 Itten, Johannes. The art of color. New York, 1961.

206 Ivins, William M. On the rationalization of sight. Metropolitan Museum of Art Papers, #8. New York, 1938.

207 Jacobson, Egbert. Basic color. Chicago, 1948.

208 James, William. The principles of psychology. New York, 1950.

209 Jameson, Dorothea and Leo M. Hurvich. From contrast to assimilation: in art and in the eye. In press.

210 Janis, Harriet and Sidney. Picasso—the recent years, 1939–1946. Garden City, N.Y., 1946.

211 Jonas, Hans. The phenomenon of life. New York, 1966.

212 Julesz, Bela. Foundations of cyclopean perception. Chicago, 1971.

213 Jung, Carl Gustav. The integration of the personality. New York, 1939.

214 ——. Modern man in search of a soul. London, 1947.

215 Justi, Carl. Winckelmann und seine Zeitgenossen. Leipzig, 1923.

216 Kahnweiler, Daniel-Henry. Juan Gris, his life and work. New York, 1947.

217 ——. Klee. Paris, 1950.

218 Kainz, Friedrich. Gestaltgesetzlichkeit und Ornamententwicklung. Zeitschr. angew. Psych. 1927, vol. 28, pp. 267–327.

219 Kandinsky, Wassily. Punkt und Linie zur Fläche. Munich, 1926.

220 ——. Concerning the spiritual in art. New York, 1946.

221 ——. Rückblick. Baden-Baden, 1955. (Engl.: Reminiscences. In Herbert (189) pp. 19–44.)

222 Kanizsa, Gaetano. Condizioni ed effetti della trasparenza fenomenica. Rivista Psicol. 1955, vol. 49.

223 —— and Giorgio Tampieri. Nuove osservazioni sull'orientamento retinico ed ambientale. *In* Kanizsa (224) pp. 49–68.

224 —— and Giovanni Vicario, eds. Ricerche sperimentali sulla percezione. Trieste, 1968.

225 Katz, Daniel et al. Public opinion and propaganda. New York, 1954.

226 Katz, David. Gestalt psychology. New York, 1950.

227 ——. The world of color. London, 1935.

228 ——. Ein Beitrag zur Kenntnis der Kinderzeichnungen. Zeitschr. Psych. 1906, vol. 41, pp. 241–256.

229 —— and G. Révész. Experimentelle Studien zur vergleichenden Psychologie. Zeitschr. angew. Psych. 1921, vol. 18, pp. 307–320.

230 Kellogg, Rhoda. Analyzing children's art. Palo Alto, Calif., 1969.

231 Kennedy, John M. Icons and information. *In* Olson (331).

232 Kepes, Gyorgy. Language of vision. Chicago, 1944.

233 Kern, Guido Joseph. Die Anfänge der zentralperspektivischen Konstruktion in der italienischen Malerei des 14. Jahrhunderts. Mitt. Kunsthist. Inst. Florence 1912. vol. 2, pp. 39–65.

234 ——. Die Grundzüge der linearperspektivischen Darstellung, etc. Leipzig, 1904.

235 Kerr, Madeline. Children's drawings of houses. Brit. Journal Med. Psych. 1936, vol. 16, pp. 206ff.

236 Kerschensteiner, Georg. Die Entwicklung der zeichnerischen Begabung. Munich, 1905.

237 Klages, Ludwig. Handschrift und Charakter. Leipzig, 1923.

238 Klee, Paul. The thinking eye. New York.

239 Kleist, Heinrich von. Essay on the puppet theatre. Partisan Review, Jan.–Feb. 1947, pp. 67–72.

240 Köhler, Wolfgang. Selected papers. New York, 1971.

241 ——. Gestalt psychology. New York, 1947.

242 ——. Dynamics in psychology. New York, 1940.

243 ——. The place of value in a world of facts. New York, 1938.

244 ——. The mentality of apes. New York, 1931.

245 ——. Psychological remarks on some questions of anthropology. *In* Köhler (240) pp. 376–397.

246 ——. Die physischen Gestalten in Ruhe und im stationären Zustand. Braunschweig, 1920.

247 —— and David A. Emery. Figural aftereffects in the third dimension of visual space. Amer. Journal Psych. 1947, vol. 60, pp. 159–201.

248 —— and Richard Held. The cortical correlate of pattern vision. Science 1949, vol. 110, pp. 414–419.

249 —— and Hans Wallach. Figural aftereffects. Proc. Amer. Philos. Soc. 1944, vol. 88, #4, pp. 269–357.

250 Koffka, Kurt. Principles of gestalt psychology. New York, 1935.

251 ——. The growth of the mind. New York, 1924.

252 ——. Some problems of space perception. *In* Murchison (320) pp. 161–187.

253 Kohler, Ivo. Experiments with goggles. Scient. Amer., May 1962, vol. 206, pp. 63–72.

254 Kopfermann, Hertha. Psychologische Untersuchungen über die Wirkung zweidimensionaler Darstellungen, etc. Psychol. Forschung 1930, vol. 13, pp. 292–364.

255 Krech, David and Richard Crutchfield. Theory and problems of social psychology. New York, 1948.

256 Kreitler, Hans and Shulamith. Psychology of the arts. Durham, N.C., 1972.

257 Kretschmer, Ernst. Körperbau und Charakter. Berlin, 1936. (Engl.: Physique and character. New York, 1936.)

258 Kühn, Herbert. Die Kunst der Primitiven. Munich, 1923.

259 La Meri. The gesture language of the Hindu dance. New York, 1964.

260 Lange, Julius. Die Darstellung des Menschen in der älteren griechischen Kunst. Strasbourg, 1899.

261 Langfeld, Herbert Sidney. The aesthetic attitude. New York, 1920.

262 Laporte, Paul M. The space-time concept in the work of Picasso. Magazine of Art, Jan. 1948, pp. 26–32.

263 Lauenstein, Lotte. Ueber räumliche Wirkung von Licht und Schatten. Psychol. Forschung 1938, vol. 22, pp. 267–319.

264 Lawrence, Merle. Studies in human behavior. Princeton, N.J., 1949.

265 Lecomte du Noüy, Pierre. Biological time. New York, 1937.

266 Lettvin, J. Y. et al. What the frog's eye tells the frog's brain. In Evans and Robertson (106) pp. 95–122.

267 Levertov, Denise. The sorrow dance. New York, 1963.

268 Levinstein, Siegfried. Kinderzeichnungen bis zum vierzehnten Lebensjahr. Leipzig, 1905.

269 Lévy-Bruhl, Lucien. How natives think. New York, n.d.

270 ———. The "soul" of the primitive. Chicago, 1971.

271 Lewin, Kurt. Ueber die Umkehrung der Raumlage, etc. Psychol. Forschung 1923, vol. 3, pp. 210–261.

272 ———. Defining the "field at a given time." In Lewin, Field theory in social science, pp. 43–59. New York, 1951.

273 Liebmann, Susanne. Ueber das Verhalten farbiger Formen bei Helligkeitsgleichheit, etc. Psychol. Forschung 1927, vol. 9, pp. 300–353.

274 Liesegang, P. Zahlen und Quellen zur Geschichte der Projektionskunst, etc. Berlin, 1926.

275 Lindemann, Erich. Gamma movement. In Ellis (104) pp. 173–181.

276 Lindsay, Kenneth and Bernard Huppé. Meaning and method in Brueghel's painting. Journal Aesth. Art Crit., March 1956, vol. 14, pp. 376–386.

277 Lipps, Theodor. Aesthetische Einfühlung. Zeitschr. Psych. Physiol. Sinnesorgane 1900, vol. 22, pp. 415–450.

278 ———. Aesthetik. In Lipps et al., Systematische Philosophie, Berlin, 1907.

279 Loran, Erle. Cézanne's composition. Berkeley and Los Angeles, 1943.

280 Lord, James. A Giacometti portrait. New York, n.d.

281 Lorenz, K. Z. The role of gestalt perception in animal and human behavior. In Whyte (452) pp. 157–178.

282 Löwenfeld, Viktor. The nature of creative activity. New York, 1939.

283 ———. Tests for visual and haptic attitudes. Amer. Journal Psych. 1945, vol. 58, pp. 100–111.

284 ———. Creative and mental growth. New York, 1947.

285 Löwy, Emanuel. Die Naturwiedergabe in der älteren griechischen Kunst. Rome, 1900.

286 Luneburg, Rudolf K. Mathematical analysis of binocular vision. Princeton, N.J., 1947.

287 Luquet, Georges Henri. Les bonhommes têtards dans le dessin enfantin. Journal de Psych. 1920, vol. 27, pp. 684ff.

288 Luria, A. R. Speech and the regulation of normal and abnormal behavior. New York, 1961.

289 Lyons, John. Introduction to theoretical linguistics. Cambridge, Eng., 1968.

290 McCandless, Stanley. A method of lighting the stage. New York, 1939.

291 MacCurdy, Edward, ed. The notebooks of Leonardo da Vinci. New York, n.d.

292 Mach, Ernst. Popular scientific lectures. Chicago, 1910.

293 ———. Die Analyse der Empfindungen. Jena, 1911. (Engl.: Analysis of sensations. New York, 1959.)

294 MacLeod, Robert Brodie. An experimental investigation of brightness constancy. Archives Psych. 1932, #135.

295 ———. The effects of artificial penumbrae, etc. Miscellanea Psychologica, Albert Michotte. Louvain, 1947.

296 MacNichol, Edward F., Jr. Three-pigment color vision. Scient. Amer., Dec. 1964, vol. 211, pp. 48–56.

297 Martin, J. L., Ben Nicholson, and N. Gabo, eds. Circle. Intern. survey of constructive art. London, 1937.

298 Marx, Melvin H., ed. Psychological theory. New York, 1951.

299 Master bronzes. Albright Gallery, Buffalo, N.Y., 1973.

300 Matisse, Henri. Catalogue of Philadelphia Museum of Art, 1948.

301 May, Renato. Il linguaggio del film. Milan, 1947.

302 Merleau-Ponty, Maurice. Phénoménologie de la perception. Paris, 1945. (Engl.: Phenomenology of perception. New York, 1962.)

303 Metelli, Fabio. Zur Theorie der optischen Bewegungswahrnehmung. In Reports on the 24th Congress of the Deutsche Gesellschaft für Psych. Göttingen, 1965, pp. 85–91.

304 ———. Zur Analyse der phänomenalen Durchsichtigkeitserscheinungen. In Mühlher and Fischl (317) pp. 285–304.

305 Metzger, Wolfgang. Beobachtungen über phänomenale Identität. Psychol. Forschung 1934, vol. 19, pp. 1–60.

306 ———. ed. Handbuch der Psychologie. Göttingen, 1966.

307 Michotte, Albert. La perception de la causalité. Louvain, 1946.

308 ———. Causalité, permanence et réalité phénoménales. Louvain, 1962.

309 Minguzzi, Gian Franco. Sulla validità della distinzione fra percezione di nessi causali, etc. In Kanizsa and Vicario (224) pp. 161–196.

310 Mock, Elizabeth and J. M. Richards. An introduction to modern architecture. New York, 1947.

311 Moholy-Nagy, Laszlo. The new vision. New York, 1947.

312 Mondrian, Piet. Plastic art and pure plastic art. New York, 1945.

313 Morgan, Clifford T. Some structural factors in perception. In Blake and Ramsay (51) pp. 25–55.

314 Morinaga, Shiro et al. Dominance of main direction in apparent transparency. Japan. Psychol. Research 1962, vol. 4, pp. 113–118.

315 Morin-Jean. Le dessin des animaux en Grèce d'après les vases peints. Paris, 1911.

316 Morris, Desmond. The biology of art. London, 1962.

317 Mühlher, Robert and Johann Fischl, eds. Gestalt und Wirklichkeit. Berlin, 1967.

318 Munitz, Milton K. Theories of the universe. New York, 1957.

319 Munsell, Albert H. A grammar of color. New York, 1969.

320 Murchison, Carl, ed. Psychologies of 1930. Worcester, Mass., 1930.

321 Musatti, Cesare L. Forma e assimilazione. Archivio italiano di psicologia 1931, vol. 9, pp. 61–156.

322 Muther, Richard. Geschichte der Malerei. Berlin, 1912.

323 Muybridge, Eadweard. The human figure in motion. New York, 1955.

324 Nemerov, Howard. Gnomes and occasions. Chicago, 1973.

325 Newman, Edwin B. Versuche über das Gamma-Phänomen. Psychol. Forschung 1934, vol. 19, pp. 102–121.

326 Newton, Sir Isaac. Mathematical principles. Berkeley, Calif., 1934.

327 Nijinsky, Romola, ed. The diary of Vaslav Nijinsky. Berkeley and Los Angeles, 1968.

328 Novotny, Fritz. Cézanne und das Ende der wissenschaftlichen Perspektive. Vienna, 1938.

329 O'Connor, Francis V. Jackson Pollock. New York, 1967.

330 Ogden, Robert Morris. The psychology of art. New York, 1938.

331 Olson, David R., ed. Communication, media, and education. 73rd Yearbook of the Nat. Soc. for the Study of Education. Chicago. In press.

332 ——. Cognitive development. New York, 1970.

333 —— and Susan M. Pagliuso, eds. From perceiving to performing. Ontario Journal of Educational Research 1968, vol. 10, #3.

334 Oppé, A. Paul. Right and left in Raphael's cartoons. Journal Warburg and Courtauld Inst. 1944, vol. 1, pp. 82–94.

335 Oppenheimer, Erika. Optische Versuche über Ruhe und Bewegung. Psychol. Forschung 1935, vol. 20, pp. 2–46.

336 Osborne, Harold. The art of appreciation. London, 1970.

337 Oyama, Tadasu. Figure-ground dominance, etc. Journal Exper. Psych. 1950, vol. 60, pp. 299–305.

338 Oyama, Tadasu and Jun-Ichi Nakahara. The effects of lightness, hue, and area upon apparent transparency. Japan. Journal Psych. 1960, vol. 31, pp. 35–48.

339 Panofsky, Erich. Idea. Studien Bibl. Warburg. Leipzig, 1924. (Engl.: Idea. Columbia, S.C., 1968.)

340 ——. Die Perspektive als "symbolische Form." Vorträge Bibl. Warburg 1924–1925, pp. 258–330. Leipzig, 1927.

341 Panofsky, Erwin and Fritz Saxl. Melencolia I. Studien Bibl. Warburg. Leipzig, 1923.

342 Parsons, John Herbert. An introduction to the study of colour vision. Cambridge, Eng., 1924.

343 Pelt, John Vedenburgh van. The essentials of composition as applied to art. New York, 1913.

344 Pennington, Keith S. Advances in holography. Scient. Amer., Feb. 1968, vol. 218, pp. 40–48.

345 Perrot, Georges and Charles Chipiez. A history of art in Chaldaea and Assyria. London, 1884.

346 Pevsner, Nikolaus. An outline of European architecture. Baltimore, 1943.

347 Philostratus. Imagines. Loeb Class. Libr. #256. Cambridge, Mass., n.d.

348 Piaget, Jean. Genetic epistemology. Columbia Forum, Fall 1969, vol. 12, pp. 4–11.

349 ——. Six psychological studies. New York, 1968.

350 —— and Bärbel Inhelder. La représentation de l'espace chez l'enfant. Paris, 1948. (Engl.: The child's conception of space. New York, 1967.)

351 ——. La représentation du monde chez l'enfant. Paris, 1926. (Engl.: The child's conception of the world. New York, 1929.)

352 Pirandello, Luigi. Quaderni di Serafino Gubbio, operatore. Florence, 1925.

353 Piston, Walter. Harmony. New York, 1941.

354 Pratt, Carroll C. The role of past experience in visual perception. Journal Psych. 1950, vol. 30, pp. 85–107.

355 Pressey, Sidney L. The influence of color upon mental and motor efficiency. Amer. Journal Psych. 1921, vol. 32, pp. 326–356.

356 Puffer, Ethel D. Studies in symmetry. Psychol. Monogr. 1903, vol. 4, pp. 467–539.

357 Pulver, Max. Symbolik der Handschrift. Zurich, 1931.

358 Radin, Max. Music and medicine among primitive peoples. *In* Schullian and Schoen (393) pp. 3–24.

359 Rapaport, David and Roy Schaefer. Manual of diagnostic psychological testing. Publ. Josiah Macy, Jr. Foundation. New York, 1946.

360 Rathe, Kurt. Die Ausdrucksfunktion extrem verkürzter Figuren. London, 1938.

361 Ratoosh, P. On interposition as a cue for the perception of distance. Proc. Nat. Acad. Sciences, 1949, vol. 35, #5, pp. 257–259.

362 Rausch, Edwin. Struktur und Metrik figural-optischer Wahrnehmung. Frankfurt a.M., 1952.

363 ———. Zur Phänomenologie figural-optischer Dynamik. Psychol. Forschung 1950, vol. 23, pp. 185–222.

364 ———. Das Eigenschaftsproblem in der Gestalttheorie der Wahrnehmung. *In* Metzger (306) vol. 1, pp. 866–953.

365 Read, Herbert. Education through art. New York, 1945.

366 Reinach, Salomon. La représentation du galop dans l'art ancien et moderne. Revue Archéologique 1900–1901, vol. 36, pp. 217–251, 441–450; vol. 37, pp. 244–259; vol. 38, pp. 27–45, 224–244; vol. 39, pp. 1–11.

367 Reisz, Karel. The technique of film editing. London, 1953.

368 Reitman, Francis. Psychotic art. New York, 1951.

369 Rewald, John. Odilon Redon. *In* Redon, Moreau, Bresdin. Museum of Modern Art. New York, 1961.

370 Rice, Charlotte. The orientation of plane figures as a factor in their perception by children. Child Devel. 1930, vol. 1, pp. 111–143.

371 Richter, Manfred. Grundriss der Farbenlehre der Gegenwart. Dresden, 1940.

372 Riegl, Alois. Barockkunst in Rom. Vienna, 1923.

373 Rodin, Auguste. L'art. Paris, 1951. (Engl.: On art and artists. New York, n.d.)

374 Roman, Klara G. Handwriting, a key to personality. New York, 1952.

375 Rorschach, Hermann. Psychodiagnostics. New York, 1942.

376 Ross, Denman W. A theory of pure design. New York, 1933.

377 Rubin, Edgar. Visuell wahrgenommene Figuren. Copenhagen, 1921.

378 ———. Visuell wahrgenommene wirkliche Bewegungen. Zeitschr. Psychologie 1927, vol. 103, pp. 384–392.

379 Rudrauf, Lucien. L'annonciation. Etude d'un thème plastique et de ses variations en peinture et en sculpture. Paris, 1943. (Engl. summary in Journal Aesth. Art Crit. 1949, vol. 7, pp. 325–354.)

380 Runge, Philipp Otto. Farbenkugel. Hamburg, 1810.

381 Rupp, Hans. Ueber optische Analyse. Psychol. Forschung 1923, vol. 4, pp. 262–300.

382 Rushton, W. A. H. Visual pigments in man. Scient. Amer., Nov. 1962, vol. 207, pp. 120–132.

383 Ruskin, John. The elements of drawing in three letters to beginners. New York, 1889.

384 Schachtel, Ernest G. On color and affect. Psychiatry 1943, vol. 6, pp. 393–409.

385 ——. Projection and its relation to character attitudes, etc. Psychiatry 1950, vol. 13, pp. 69–100.

386 Schäfer, Heinrich. Von ägyptischer Kunst, besonders der Zeichenkunst. Leipzig, 1922.

387 Schäfer, Heinrich. Grundlagen der ägyptischen Rundbildnerei, etc. Leipzig, 1923.

388 Schaefer-Simmern, Henry. The unfolding of artistic activity. Berkeley and Los Angeles, 1948.

389 Schapiro, Meyer. On a painting of Van Gogh. View, Fall 1946, pp. 9–14.

390 ——. Rendering of nature in early Greek art. The Arts 1925, vol. 8, pp. 170–172.

391 Schönberg, Arnold. Harmonielehre. Leipzig, 1911. (Engl.: Theory of harmony. New York, 1948.)

392 Schöne, Wolfgang. Ueber das Licht in der Malerei. Berlin, 1954.

393 Schullian, Dorothy M. and Max Schoen. Music and medicine. New York, 1948.

394 Senden, M. von. Raum- und Gestaltauffassung bei operierten Blindgeborenen, etc. Leipzig, 1932.

395 Segall, Marshall H. et al. The influence of culture on visual perception. Indianapolis, Ind., 1966.

396 Selz, Peter. Alberto Giacometti. New York, 1965.

397 Seymour, Charles, Jr. Dark chamber and light-filled room: Vermeer and the camera obscura. Art Bull. 1964, vol. 46, pp. 323–332.

398 Shahn, Ben. The shape of content. Cambridge, Mass., 1957.

399 Shawn, Ted. Fundamentals of a dance education. New York, 1937.

400 Sherrington, Charles. Man on his nature. New York, 1941.

401 Sickles, William R. Psycho-geometry of order. Psychol. Review 1944, vol. 51, pp. 189–199.

402 Skira, Albert, ed. History of modern painting from Picasso to Surrealism. Geneva, 1950.

403 Spears, William C. Assessment of visual preference and discrimination in the four-month-old infant. Journal Compar. Physiol. Psych. 1964, vol. 57, pp. 381–386.

404 Spengler, Oswald. The decline of the West. New York, 1932.

405 Spitz, René A. The smiling response. Genetic Psych. Monogr. 1946, vol. 34, pp. 57–125.

406 Spottiswoode, Raymond. Film and its technique. Berkeley and Los Angeles, 1951.

407 Stein, Gertrude. Picasso. London, 1939.

408 Stern, William. Ueber verlagerte Raumformen. Zeitschr. ang. Psych. 1909, vol. 2, pp. 498–526.

409 Storck, Karl, ed. Mozarts Briefe. Elberfeld, n.d.

410 Stratton, George M. Vision without inversion of the retinal image. Psychol. Review 1896, vol. 4, pp. 342–351, 466–471. Reprinted in Dennis (95) pp. 24–40.

411 Sutherland, Ivan E. Computer displays. Scient. Amer., June 1970, vol. 222, pp. 57–81.

412 Teevan, Richard C. and Robert C. Birney, eds. Color vision. Princeton, N.J., 1961.

413 Terman, Lewis M. and Maud A. Merrill. Measuring intelligence. Boston, 1937.

414 Ternus, Josef. The problem of phenomenal identity. In Ellis (104) pp. 149–160.

415 Teuber, Hans-Lukas. Perception. In J. Field et al. Handbook of Physiology, Section I, Neurophysiology, vol. 3, chapter 65, pp. 1595–1668. Washington, D.C., 1960.

416 Thomas, E. Llewellyn. Movements of the eye. Scient. Amer., Aug. 1968, vol. 219, pp. 88–95.

417 Thompson, D'Arcy. On growth and form. Cambridge, Eng., 1969.

418 Thouless, Robert H. Phenomenal regression to the real object. Brit. Journal of Psych. 1931, vol. 21, pp. 339–359.

419 ——. A racial difference in perception. Journal Soc. Psych. 1933, vol. 4, pp. 330–339.

420 Tinbergen, Niko. The study of instinct. Oxford, 1951.
421 Torroja, Eduardo. Philosophy of structures. Berkeley and Los Angeles, 1967.
422 Turhan, Müntaz. Ueber räumliche Wirkungen von Helligkeitsgefällen. Psychol. Forschung 1937, vol. 21, pp. 1–49.
423 Valéry, Paul. Variété V. Paris, 1945.
424 Van der Meer, Hendrika Christina. Die Links-Rechts-Polarisation des phänomenalen Raumes. Groningen, 1958.
425 Vasari, Giorgio. Vasari on technique. London, 1907.
426 Venturi, Lionello. Il gusto dei primitivi. Bologna, 1926.
427 Vicario, Giovanni. Il metodo dello smistamento nello studio della preferenza forma-colore. *In* Kanizsa (224) pp. 241–296.
428 Vitruvius Pollio. The ten books of architecture. New York, 1960.
429 Waddington, C. H. The character of biological form. *In* Whyte (452) pp. 43–52.
430 Wallach, Hans. Brightness constancy and the nature of achromatic colors. *In* Henle (188) pp. 109–125.
431 —— and Alice Galloway. The constancy of colored objects in colored illumination. Journal Exper. Psych. 1946, vol. 36, pp. 119–126.
432 —— and D. N. O'Connell. The kinetic depth effect. In Henle (188) pp. 126–145.
433 Wapner, S. et al. Experiments on sensory-tonic field theory of perception. Journal Exper. Psych. 1951, vol. 42, pp. 341–345.
434 Weber, Christian O. Homeostasis and servo-mechanisms for what? Psychol. Review 1949, vol. 56, pp. 234–239.
435 Webster, J. Carson. The technique of impressionism. College Art Journal, Nov. 1944, vol. 4, pp. 3–22.
436 Weinhandl, Ferdinand, ed. Gestalthaftes Sehen. Darmstadt, 1960.
437 Weiss, Paul A. One plus one does not equal two. In G. C. Quarton, ed., The Neurosciences. New York, 1967.
438 Weizsäcker, Carl Friedrich von. Zum Weltbild der Physik. Stuttgart, 1949.
439 Wellesz, Egon. Arnold Schönberg. Leipzig, 1921.
440 Werner, Heinz. Comparative psychology of mental development. Chicago, 1948.
441 —— and Bernard Kaplan. The developmental approach to cognition. Amer. Anthropologist 1956, vol. 58, pp. 866–880.
442 —— and Seymour Wapner. Studies in physiognomic perception, I. Journal Psych. 1954, vol. 38, pp. 51–65.
443 Wertheimer, Max. Experimentelle Studien über das Sehen von Bewegung. Zeitschr. Psych. 1912, vol. 61, pp. 161–265. (Also in Wertheimer, Drei Abhandlungen zur Gestalttheorie, Erlangen, 1925.)
444 ——. Untersuchungen zur Lehre von der Gestalt II. Psychol. Forschung 1923, vol. 4, pp. 301–350.
445 ——. Laws of organization in perceptual forms. *In* Ellis (104) pp. 71–88.
446 ——. Gestalt theory. Social Research 1944, vol. 11, pp. 78–99.
447 Wertheimer, Michael. Hebb and Senden on the role of learning in perception. Amer. Journal Psych. 1951, vol. 64, pp. 133–137.
448 White, John. The birth and rebirth of pictorial space. New York, 1972.
449 —— and John Shearman. Raphael's tapestries and their cartoons. Art Bull. 1958, vol. 40, pp. 193–222, 299–324.
450 White, T. H. The sword in the stone. New York, 1939.
451 Whyte, Lancelot Law. The unitary principle in physics and biology. New York, 1949.
452 ——, ed. Aspects of form. Bloomington, Ind., 1961.

453 Wiener, Norbert. The human use of human beings. Boston, 1950.
454 Wight, Frederick S. Henry Moore: the reclining figure. Journal Aesth. Art Crit. 1947, vol. 6, pp. 95–105.
455 Wilhelm, Richard. The secret of the golden flower. With commentary by C. G. Jung. New York, 1938.
456 Witkin, H. A. et al. Psychological differentiation. New York, 1962.
457 Witkin, H. A. The nature and importance of individual differences in perception. *In* Bruner and Krech (67) pp. 145–170.
458 Wittgenstein, Ludwig. Philosophische Untersuchungen. Frankfurt a.M., 1967. (Engl.: Philosophical investigations. New York, 1968.)
459 Wittkower, Rudolf. Architectural principles in the age of humanism. New York, 1965.
460 Wölfflin, Heinrich. Renaissance und Barock. Munich, 1888. (Engl.: Renaissance and Baroque. Ithaca, N.Y., 1967.)
461 ——. Gedanken zur Kunstgeschichte. Basel, 1941.
462 ——. Kleine Schriften. Basel, 1946.
463 ——. Prolegomena zu einer Psychologie der Architektur. *In* Wölfflin (462) pp. 13–47.
464 ——. Ueber Abbildungen und Deutungen. *In* Wölfflin (461) pp. 66–82.
465 ——. Zur Interpretation von Dürers "Melancholie." *In* Wölfflin (461) pp. 96–105.
466 ——. Ueber das Rechts und Links im Bilde. *In* Wölfflin (461) pp. 82–96.
467 ——. Principles of art history. New York, 1950.
468 ——. Classic art. London, 1952.
469 Woodworth, Robert S. Experimental psychology. New York, 1939.
470 —— and Harold Schlosberg. Experimental psychology. New York, 1954.
471 Worringer, Wilhelm. Abstraktion und Einfühlung. Munich, 1911. (Engl.: Abstraction and empathy. New York, 1963.)
472 Wulf, Friedrich. Tendencies in figural variation. *In* Ellis (104) pp. 136–160.
473 Wulff, Oscar. Die umgekehrte Perspektive und die Niedersicht. *In* Kunstwiss. Beiträge August Schmarsow gewidmet. Leipzig, 1907.
474 Yarbus, Alfred L. Eye movements and vision. New York, 1967.
475 Yeats, W. B. The collected poems. New York, 1951.
476 Yin, Robert K. Looking at upside-down faces. Journal Exper. Psych. 1969, vol. 81, pp. 141–145.
477 Zajac, J. L. Studies in perspective. Brit. Journal Psych. 1961, vol. 52, pp. 333–340.
478 Zuckerkandl, Victor. Vom musikalischen Denken. Zurich, 1964. (Engl.: The sense of music. Princeton, N.J., 1959.)
479 ——. Die Wirklichkeit der Musik. Zurich, 1963. (Engl.: Sound and symbol. New York, 1956.)

INDEX